SECOND EDITION
TRAIL ATLAS OF ·MICHIGAN·

Nature • Mountain Biking • Hiking
Cross Country Skiing

Dennis R. Hansen

Hansen Publishing Company — Okemos, Michigan

Second Printing — April 1998
First Printing — May 1997

TRAIL ATLAS OF MICHIGAN 2nd Edition — Nature, Mountain Biking, Hiking, Cross Country Skiing is published by Hansen Publishing Company, 1801 Birchwood Drive, Okemos, MI 48864.

Printed in the United States of America.

Library of Congress Catalog Card Number   97-93489
ISBN: 0-930098-06-4

With All My Love,
to my wife Barbara
and daughters Stephanie and Lisa,

without who's continued understanding and support for the last twenty years, this book would not have been possible.

CONTENTS

INTRODUCTION

Welcome to the **Second Edition** of the *Trail Atlas of Michigan*. You have in your hands the most comprehensive guide to Michigan hiking, cross country skiing, mountain biking and interpretive (nature and history) trails. This edition continues a series of guide books and numerous editions that began in 1977 with the publication of the 134 page *Michigan Cross Country Skiing Atlas*.

The information is the most complete and current available. It now includes over 600 trail systems from every corner of the state as well as a few in Canada and Wisconsin border areas. If individual trails were considered, the actual total number of trails would exceed 800.

Similar to the last edition, this atlas is not intended to be an in-depth review of each trail mile by mile. With the number of trails presented, that would be impossible. Therefore, I leave that up to you to explore. Rather, each trail entry contains at least one trail map (often more) and a snapshot description of the trail. However, based on years of feedback from readers, all important information is included that trail enthusiasts need. For those who need that individual map, brochure or just specific information, addresses and phone numbers are provided to make inquiry easy. Also included is a comprehensive list of travel and tourist organizations to assist you in your trip planning.

Since many of these trails are developed with volunteer help, a directory of trail advocacy and nature Conservancy organizations is provided at the end of the atlas. They all need continual volunteer support to promote and execute the missions of

their individual organizations. Many of the trails listed in this atlas would not exist without that critical volunteer effort. If you are not already a member, I encourage you to get evolved with one of those organizations or contact one of the National Forests or the Department of Natural Resources and volunteer your time.

With the continued rapid expansion of the Michigan rail-trail system, mountain bike trails and interpretive trails, in the future this information will become incomplete. I encourage you to contact the trail manager and local, state or federal land managers should critical information need confirmation.

I continue to welcome and encourage your comments, corrections, additions, questions and especially information about new trails. Please send them to me at the address found on the copyright page.

Dennis Hansen
Okemos
May 1997

1

HOW TO USE THIS ATLAS

LOCATING A TRAIL

The *Trail Atlas of Michigan* has adopted, with permission, the *Michigan Atlas and Gazetteer* grid system by DeLorme Mapping of Freeport, Maine. This location system will easily locate and identify the large number of trails that are in this trail atlas.

Although you do not need the *Michigan Atlas and Gazetteer* to find the trail of your choice, having a copy will make the task considerably easier. However, the *Trail Atlas of Michigan* will function very adequately if you have one of several Michigan map books organized by county rather than this grid system. Each entry also lists the county(ies) where the trail is located. Regardless of the type of map book you use, you should easily find any trail you desire.

By trail name...

For purposes of simplicity, trails are listed in alphabetical order in the Master Index. For trails that go by several names, the master index also lists multiple entries to aid in locating the specific trail of interest.

By grid or map location...

To find a specific trail or several trails in a specific area of the state, the *Trail Atlas of Michigan* is organized by uniform size geographic areas called grids. These grids are designated by consecutive numbers from 18 through 119 beginning in the southwest corner of the lower peninsula and ending in the north end of the Keweenaw Peninsula in the upper peninsula. The grid number is also the page number in the *Michigan Atlas and Gazetteer*. In the *Trail Atlas of Michigan*, the grid number is found in the top right corner of each trail data page.

For trails that cover more than one grid map, the lowest grid map number is used to determine where the trail is located in the atlas. Therefore, if the name of the trail is not available or if it desired to find all trails in a specific grid, it may be necessary to search adjoining grid number maps in all four directions to insure that all trails are included. For trails such as the North Country Trail, Shore to Shore Trail, larger trail systems and many of the rail-trails, this kind of search will most likely be necessary.

ABOUT THE TRAIL INFORMATION

Trail Location

The *Michigan Atlas and Gazetteer* location is a series of numbers and letters that designates the exact location(s) where the trail can be found in the *Michigan Atlas and Gazetteer* map book. For trails that span more than a single page (grid), the additional page entries are separated by a comma. Each entry begins with a page number. The page number is followed by letter(s) which are horizontal axis locators found on the right or left edge of the page. The letter(s) are then followed by numerals which are the vertical axis locators found only on the top of each page.

For example: a typical entry could read "56A6." This entry means that the trail is found on page 56. On page 56, the trail is located within the "A" horizontal axis and "6" on the vertical axis. Multiple axis references such as "ABC," "234" or "2-7" indicates the trail extends over a greater length.

Trail Type

Trail type is represented in both text form and as an icon at the top of each entry.

The purpose of an **interpretive** trail is to allow the user to experience the natural environment of the surrounding landscape. In some cases, trail side information may not be provided. Information when provided may be about the flora, fauna, or history of the area. Often no distinction is made because many interpretive trails mix historical and natural information. In addition, the historical content could be either natural and/or human. Overall, the information provided may vary greatly in quality, content and quantity.

A **walking/hiking** trail may be used separately or in combination with other designations. Walking is included since the shorter trails might not be considered a "hike" by some individuals.

A **mountain biking** trail refers to the specific type of trail most commonly associated with the activity, namely loose surfaced trails, single track, 2 track, or gravel roads. Paved trails will not list mountain biking as a trail type if only a paved trail exists. Only trail systems that have at least an additional natural surface trail such as Maybury State Park will list mountain biking. Since mountain biking is a very rapidly evolving recreation, each entry should be confirmed by the managing organization to verify that the specific trail is of sufficient length and that mountain biking is currently permitted.

A **cross country** skiing trail includes both groomed and ungroomed trails. Many manmade and weather factors contribute to the current condition of the trail. Therefore, the author suggests that a call ahead may be appropriate to reduce disappointment.

Handicapper Accessibility

The handicapper symbol is added near the top right corner of the page to easily identify trails that offer some type of accommodation for handicappers. The type and amount of accommodation is not listed, but usually consists of at least one paved trail segment. Often more facilities are provided. If handicapper accommodation is important to you, the author suggests you contact the trail manager/owner for current information.

Terminology

To save space, frequently used terms or names are abbreviated as follows:

DNR — Michigan Department of Natural Resources
HNF — Hiawatha National Forest
HMNF — Huron Manistee National Forest
ONF — Ottawa National Forest
SFCG — state forest campground
NFCG — national forest campground
FH — forest highway — usually paved and a major road in a
      national forest (national forest designation)
NCT or NCNST — North Country National Scenic Trail
NCTA — North Country Trail Association

Legend

The following is a legend of some of the typical graphic symbols that are found on the maps or in the text. Even though the maps do not all have identical symbols, the symbols used are easily identified, and should be easily understood.

 cross country skiing trail

 walking/hiking trail

 mountain bike trail

 interpretive trail

 trail with some type of accommodation for handicappers

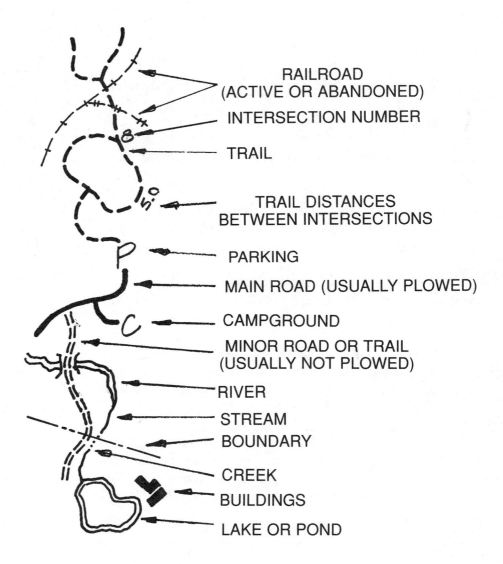

RAILROAD
(ACTIVE OR ABANDONED)

INTERSECTION NUMBER

TRAIL

TRAIL DISTANCES
BETWEEN INTERSECTIONS

PARKING

MAIN ROAD (USUALLY PLOWED)

CAMPGROUND

MINOR ROAD OR TRAIL
(USUALLY NOT PLOWED)

RIVER

STREAM

BOUNDARY

CREEK

BUILDINGS

LAKE OR POND

4

Michigan Atlas &
Gazetteer Index Map

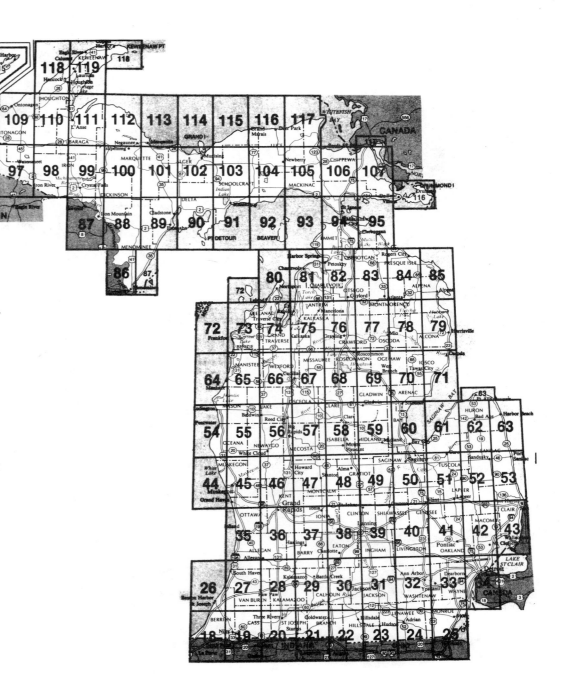

Use this map to identify trails in any specific location in the state, by following these simple instructions:

First, locate the portion of the state where the trail(s) you desire to investigate

Second, identify the grid number(s) that covers that part of the state

Third, turn to the portion of the Atlas where the trail information is presented

Fourth, turn to the specific pages where the grid number(s) is/are found in the top right corner of each page that corresponds to the grid number(s) on the map.

Cook Energy Information Center
PO Box 115
Bridgeman, MI 49106

800-548-2555

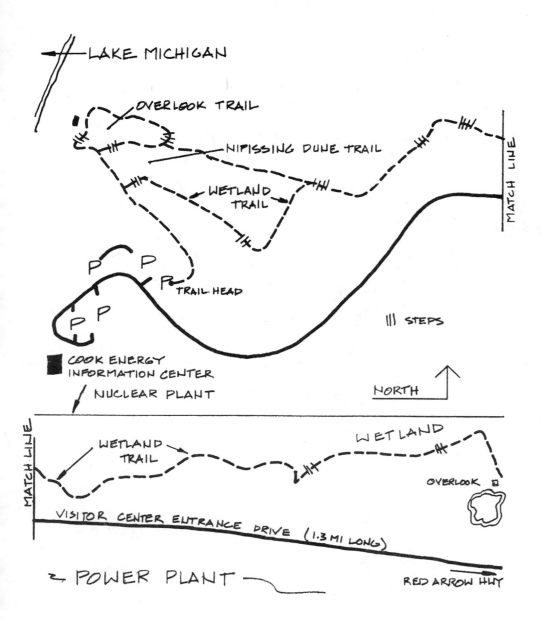

Michigan Atlas & Gazetteer Location: 18A2

County Location: Berrien

Directions To Trailhead:
Off I-94 at exit 16, just south of Bridgeman. Then 3.5 miles north on Red Arrow Highway.

Trail Type: Hiking/Walking, Interpretive
Trail Distance: 2.5 mi   Loops: 3   Shortest: .5 mi   Longest: 1 mi
Trail Surface: Natural
Trail Use Fee: None
Method Of Ski Trail Grooming: NA
Skiing Ability Suggested: NA
Hiking Trail Difficulty: Moderate to difficult with many steps
Mountain Biking Ability Suggested: NA
Terrain: Steep 40%, Hilly 30%, Moderate 20%, Flat 10%
Camping: Public and private campgrounds nearby

Owned by Indiana - Michigan Power Company
Site of a nuclear power plant.
There are three trails in the system. The Nipissing Dune Trail, the Overlook Trail and the Wetland Trail. The Overrlook trail covers the Lake Michigan shoreline and the primary dune area. The Nipissing Dune Trail covers the secondary dune area. A third trail called the Wetland Trail passes through a wetland along the trail.
The trail is very steep with many irregular steps and loose sand.

NIPISSING DUNE TRAILS

Tabor Hill Vineyard
185 Mt Tabor Rd.
Buchanan, MI 49107

616-422-2787
800-283-3363

Michigan Atlas & Gazetteer Location: 18A3

County Location: Berrien

Directions To Trailhead:
7 miles east of Bridgeman and 6 miles west of Berrien Springs, just south of Snow Rd on Mt Tabor Rd.
Take exit 16 from I-94, then Lake St. east and follow signs.

Trail Type: Cross Country Skiing
Trail Distance: 11mi   Loops: MAny   Shortest: Longest:
Trail Surface: Natural
Trail Use Fee: None
Method Of Ski Trail Grooming: None
Skiing Ability Suggested: Novice to intermediate
Hiking Trail Difficulty: NA
Mountain Biking Ability Suggested: NA
Terrain: Steep 5%, Hilly 45%, Moderate 25%, Flat 25%
Camping: None

Privately operated vineyard with trails.
Warming shelter, wine tasting and tours and snack bar.
Panoramic views of Lake Michigan dunes

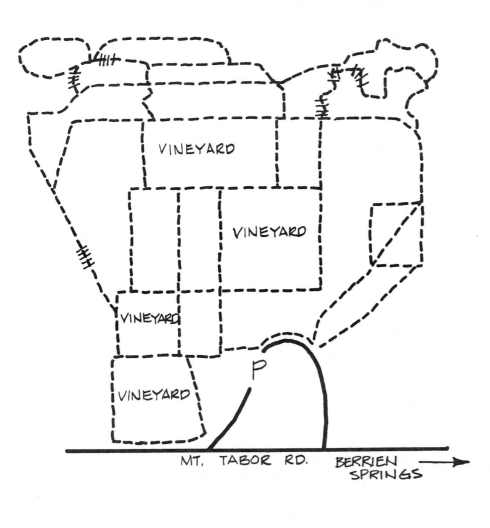

NO SCALE

TABOR HILL VINEYARD

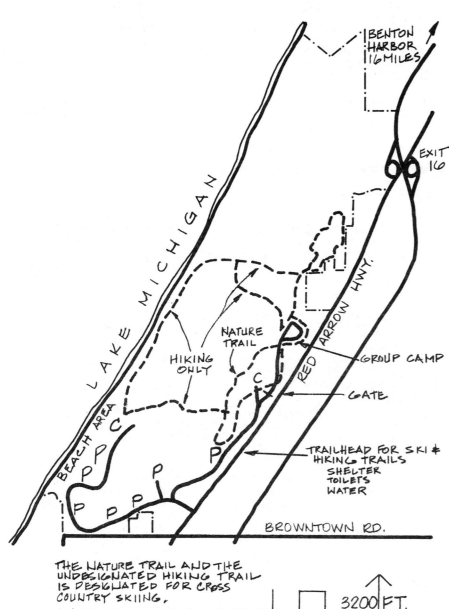

THE NATURE TRAIL AND THE
UNDESIGNATED HIKING TRAIL
IS DESIGNATED FOR CROSS
COUNTRY SKIING.

ALL TRAILS AVAILABLE FOR HIKING

BENTON
HARBOR
16 MILES

EXIT
16

LAKE MICHIGAN

BEACH AREA

NATURE
TRAIL

HIKING
ONLY

RED ARROW HWY.

GROUP CAMP

GATE

TRAILHEAD FOR SKI &
HIKING TRAILS
SHELTER
TOILETS
WATER

BROWNTOWN RD.

3200 FT.

WARREN DUNES STATE PARK

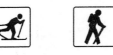

Warren Dunes State Park

Warren Dunes State Park
Red Arrow Hwy
Sawyer, MI 49125

616-426-4013

DNR Parks and Recreation Division

517-373-1270

Michigan Atlas & Gazetteer Location: 18A2

County Location: Berrien

Directions To Trailhead:
On Lake Michigan about 16 miles south of Benton Harbor.
Off I-94 between exits 12 and 16 on Red Arrow Hwy.

Trail Type: Hiking/Walking, Cross Country Skiing, Interpretive
Trail Distance: 6.75 mi   Loops: Many   Shortest: .25 mi Longest: 4.5 mi
Trail Surface: Natural
Trail Use Fee: None, but vehicle permit is required
Method Of Ski Trail Grooming: None
Skiing Ability Suggested: Novice to intermediate
Hiking Trail Difficulty: Easy to Moderate
Mountain Biking Ability Suggested: NA
Terrain: Steep 0%, Hilly 0%, Moderate 20%, Flat 80%
Camping: Available on site

Maintained by the DNR Parks and Recreaton Division
Terrain above is for trails, except where noted below.
Trail length listed above is the total length for all trails.
Ski trail - 2.75 miles
Hiking trail -3 miles Terrain: Steep 15%, Hilly 15%, Moderate 45%, Flat 25%
Nature trail is 1 mile long.
Trailhead is at parking lot located between the campground and the main
entrance.

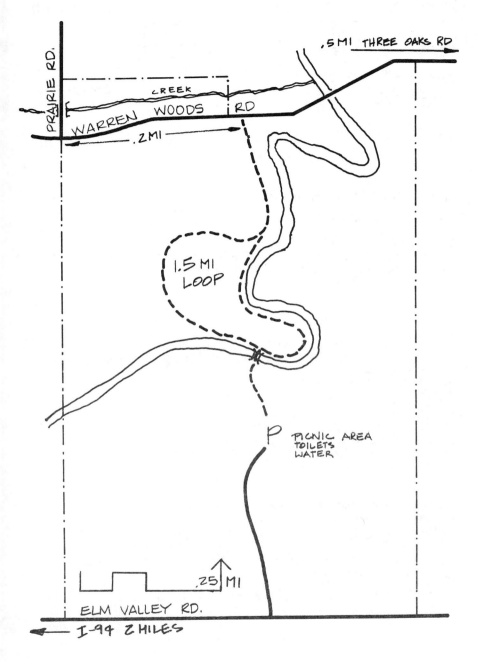

.5 MI THREE OAKS RD
PRAIRIE RD.
CREEK
WARREN WOODS RD
.2 MI
1.5 MI LOOP
PICNIC AREA
TOILETS
WATER
P
.25 MI
ELM VALLEY RD.
I-94 2 MILES

WARREN WOODS
NATURAL AREA

Warren Dunes State Park
Red Arrow Hwy
Sawyer, MI 49125

616-426-4013

DNR Parks and Recreation Division

517-373-1270

Michigan Atlas & Gazetteer Location: 18B2

County Location: Berrien

Directions To Trailhead:
3 miles from Lake Michigan and 5 miles from Indiana state line Exit I-94 at Union Pier Rd., then west 2.5 miles on Elm Valley Rd. to the park, which is on the north side of the road.
Warren Woods State Park is about 7 miles north of Warren Dunes State Park

Trail Type: Hiking/Walking, Cross Country Skiing, Interpretive
Trail Distance: 1.5 mi   Loops: 1   Shortest: NA   Longest: 1.5 mi
Trail Surface: Natural
Trail Use Fee: None, but vehicle permit required
Method Of Ski Trail Grooming: None
Skiing Ability Suggested: Novice
Hiking Trail Difficulty: Easy
Mountain Biking Ability Suggested: NA
Terrain: Steep 0%, Hilly 0%, Moderate 40%, Flat 60%
Camping: Camping at Warren Dunes State Park to the north

Maintained by the DNR Parks and Recreation Division
Mostly undeveloped park except for the trails and picnic area.
A primeval 200 acre forest preserve of virgin hardwoods.

Michigan Nature Association
7981 Beard Rd, Box 102
Avoca, MI 48006

810-324-2626

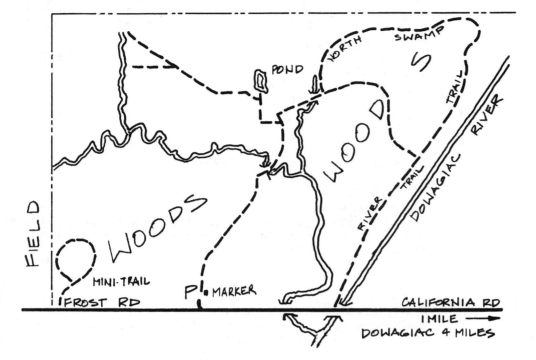

Michigan Atlas & Gazetteer Location: 19A5

County Location: Cass

Directions To Trailhead:
Take M62 west of Dowagiac about 2 miles to California Rd, then south on California Rd for 1 mile to Frost Rd.. Then west on Frost Rd for 1 mile to sanctuary entrance.

Trail Type: Hiking/Walking, Interpretive
Trail Distance: 2.5 mi   Loops: 3   Shortest: .25 mi Longest: 2 mi
Trail Surface: Natural
Trail Use Fee: None
Method Of Ski Trail Grooming: NA
Skiing Ability Suggested: NA
Hiking Trail Difficulty: Easy to moderate
Mountain Biking Ability Suggested: NA
Terrain: Steep 0%, Hilly 0%, Moderate 20%, Flat 80%
Camping: None

Owned by the Michigan Nature Association.
A truely unique property.
Considered the largest moist virgin soil woodland in Michigan. Other than occasional lumber harvesting, this property has never been tilled.
In the spring, this sanctuary is filled with an abundance of wildflowers.
The most outstanding is the Blue -eyed Mary flower.
Almost 400 plants have been catalogued.
An area not to be missed for those interested in Michigan"s flora.

DOWAGIAC WOODS
NATURE SANCTUARY

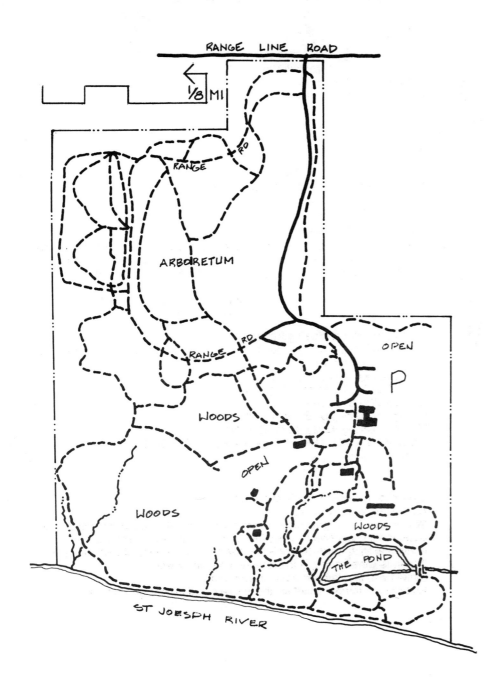

Fernwood Botanic Garden
13988 Range Line Rd
Niles, MI 49120

616-695-6491

Michigan Atlas & Gazetteer Location: 19B4

County Location: Berrien

Directions To Trailhead:
From US 12, take US 31 3.6 miles north to Walton Rd (end of limited access),
then 1.6 miles southwest to Range Line Rd, then north 1.7 miles to entrance on
the west side of the road.

Trail Type: Hiking/Walking, Interpretive
Trail Distance: 4 mi   Loops: Many   Shortest: .5 mi   Longest: 1 mi
Trail Surface: Paved, gravel and natural
Trail Use Fee: Yes, memberships available
Method Of Ski Trail Grooming: NA
Skiing Ability Suggested: NA
Hiking Trail Difficulty: Easy
Mountain Biking Ability Suggested: NA
Terrain: Steep 15%, Hilly 25%, Moderate 20%, Flat 40%
Camping: None

A non-profit botanical garden.
Visitor Center, Fern House, Nature Center Building, Art Studio, Boydston Winter
House, Summer House, Pottery Studio, Gazebo, Herb Garden Terrace Garden,
Tea Room and many gardens and collections.
100 acres and over 125' of elevation change along the bank of the St. Joseph
River.
Many facilities and programs are available.
Extensive and varied collections.
Call or write for their brochure.

FERNWOOD

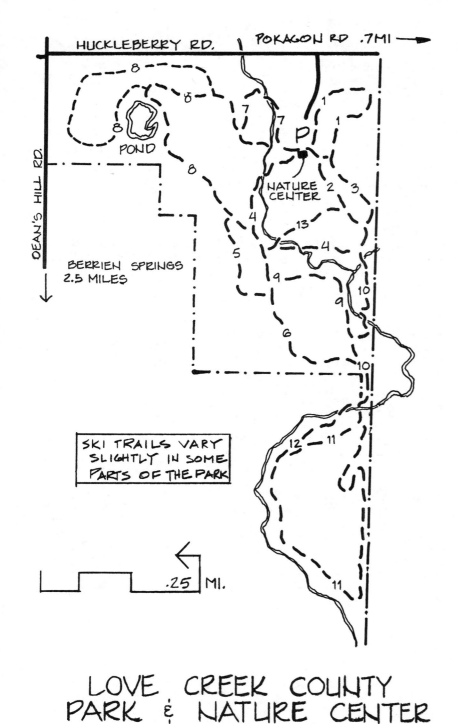

HUCKLEBERRY RD.

POKAGON RD .7 MI →

DEAN'S HILL RD.

8
8
8
7
7
7
P
1
1
1
POND
NATURE CENTER
2
3
4
13
4
5
9
9
10
6
9
10
12 — 11
11

BERRIEN SPRINGS
2.5 MILES

SKI TRAILS VARY
SLIGHTLY IN SOME
PARTS OF THE PARK

.25 MI.

LOVE CREEK COUNTY PARK & NATURE CENTER

Love Creek County Park & Nature Center
9228 Huckleberry Rd.
Berrien Springs, MI 49102

616-471-2617

Berrien County Parks and Recreation Department
Berrien County Courthouse
St Joesph, MI 49085

616-983-7111
ext 435

Michigan Atlas & Gazetteer Location: 19A4

County Location: Berrien

Directions To Trailhead:
From Berrien Springs, take US31 south about .5 mile to Deans Hill Rd.,turn left,
then turn immediately right on Pokagon Rd. for 1.7 miles to Huckleberry Rd.,
then north .9 mile to the park entrance on the left.

Trail Type: Hiking/Walking, Cross Country Skiing, Interpretive
Trail Distance: 6 mi   Loops: Many   Shortest: Longest:
Trail Surface: Natural
Trail Use Fee: Yes for skiing
Method Of Ski Trail Grooming: Track set
Skiing Ability Suggested: Intermediate to advanced
Hiking Trail Difficulty: Easy to moderate
Mountain Biking Ability Suggested: NA
Terrain: Steep 5%, Hilly 25%, Moderate 60%, Flat 10%
Camping: None

Operated by the Berrien County Parks and Recreation Department.
Separate classic and skating cross country ski trails.
Rentals and ski instruction available.
Lake effect snow provides excellent conditions throughout season.
Additional trails available for hiking during the rest of the year.
Separate winter hiking and snowshoeing trails are provided.
Some trails are different for summer hiking.
Spectacular spring woodland wildflower show in late April & early May.
Call or write for their brochure.

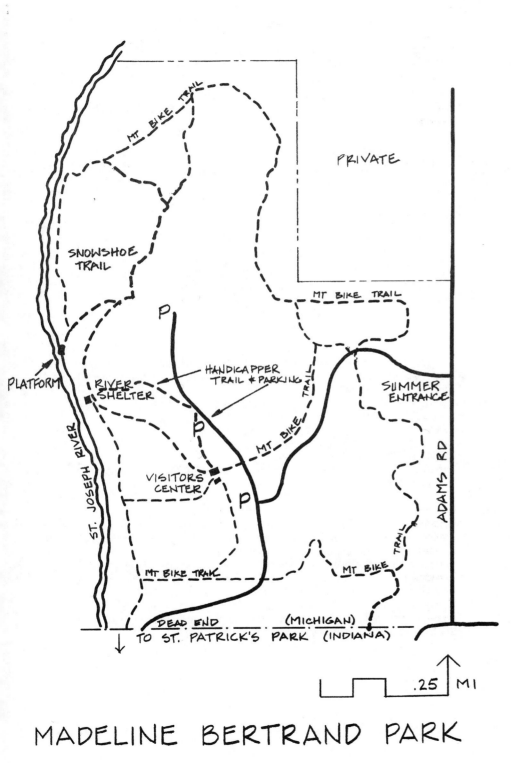

MADELINE BERTRAND PARK

Madeline Bertrand County Park
3038 Adams Rd.
Niles, MI 49120

616-683-8280

Berrien County Parks and Recreation Department
Berrien County Courthouse
St. Joseph, MI 49085

616-983-7111
ext. 435

Michigan Atlas & Gazetteer Location: 19BC45

County Location: Berrien

Directions To Trailhead:
4 miles south of Niles on the St. Joseph River at the Michigan/Indiana state line.
Take US 33 south from Niles to Stateline Rd., then west to Adams Rd., then
north to the park entrance

Trail Type: Hiking/Walking, Cross Country Skiing, Mountain Biking, Interpretive
Trail Distance: 3.5 mi   Loops: 2   Shortest: .2 mi   Longest: 1 mi
Trail Surface: Natural
Trail Use Fee: Yes, vehicle and trail fee on weekends
Method Of Ski Trail Grooming: Track set
Skiing Ability Suggested: Novice
Hiking Trail Difficulty: Easy
Mountain Biking Ability Suggested: NA
Terrain: Steep 0%, Hilly 0%, Moderate 2%, Flat 98%
Camping: None

Maintained by the Berrien County Parks and Recreation Department
Park closed Monday and Tuesday. Park is adjoining the St. Patrick's County
Park in Indiana, with connecting trails for added skiing and hiking trail distance.
Heated visitor center. Picnicing/resting area in Bertrand Lodge. The lodge is
dominated by a large stone fireplace. Trails wind through a stately evergreen
forest. Torch-lighted skiing is available on most weekends. Snowshoe rental
available. Ski rentals are available at adjoining St. Patrick's Park. Separate
snowshoe trails provided. Scheduled naturalist activities throughout the year.
Facilities available for rent and/or private torch-light skiing.
Mountain biking permitted on all trails. Trails are marked one way.

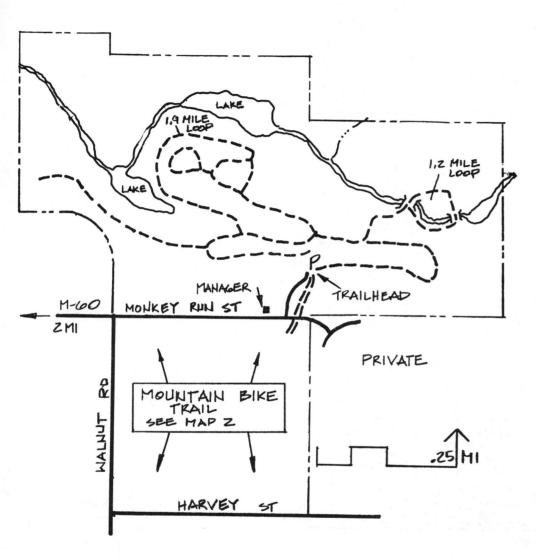

Cass County Parks Department
340 N. O'Keefe St.
Cassopolis, MI 49031

616-445-8611

Dr T.K. Lawless Park
15122 Monkey Run St.
Vandalia, MI 49095

616-476-2730

Michigan Atlas & Gazetteer Location: 20A1

County Location: Cass

Directions To Trailhead:
Between Cassopolis and Three Rivers off of M60. 12 miles east of Cassopolis
and about 3 miles southeast of Vandalia. Take Lewis Lake St. south off of M60
about 1 mile, then east on Monkey Run Street to the park entrance .

Trail Type: Hiking/Walking, Cross Country Skiing, Mountain Biking, Interpretive
Trail Distance: 15+ mi   Loops: 9   Shortest: .3 mi   Longest: 10 mi
Trail Surface: Natural
Trail Use Fee: None, but vehicle entry fee required
Method Of Ski Trail Grooming: Track set
Skiing Ability Suggested: Novice to advanced
Hiking Trail Difficulty: Easy to difficult
Mountain Biking Ability Suggested: NA
Terrain: Steep 25%, Hilly 25%, Moderate 25%, Flat 25%
Camping: Group camping only.

Operated by the Cass County Parks Department.
Tubing hill, warming shelter with fireplace, ice fishing and picnic area with grills
and restrooms is available in addition to the trails.
In addition to the 5 miles of hiking trails, an outstanding 10 mile mountain biking
trail was added in 1995. It is totally separate from the other trails in the park. A
very popular trail for SW Michigan and northern Indiana riders. The trail is
closed during some hunting seasons and during wet conditions. It is best to call
ahead so you will not be disappointed. It is definately worth the effort to plan a
trip to experience this trail.

MAP 1

DR. T. K. LAWLESS COUNTY PARK

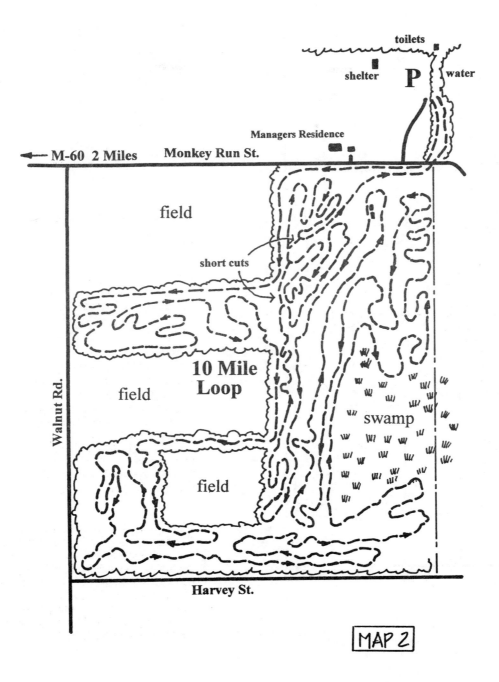

toilets

shelter **P** **water**

Managers Residence

← **M-60 2 Miles** **Monkey Run St.**

field

short cuts

10 Mile Loop

field

field

Walnut Rd.

swamp

Harvey St.

MAP 2

Dr. T.K. Lawless County Park

14.1

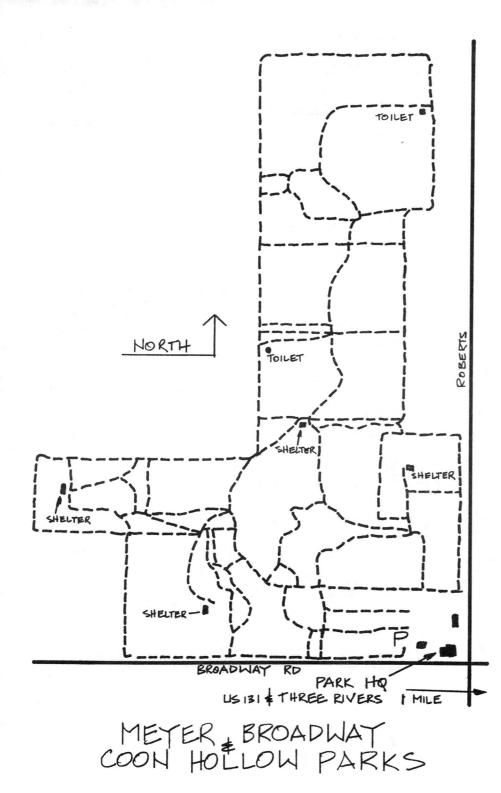

NORTH

TOILET

TOILET

ROBERTS

SHELTER

SHELTER

SHELTER

SHELTER

P

BROADWAY RD

PARK HQ

US 131 & THREE RIVERS   1 MILE

MEYER & BROADWAY COON & HOLLOW PARKS

St. Joseph County Parks
PO Box 427   616-467-5519
Centreville, MI 49032

Michigan Atlas & Gazetteer Location: 20A2

County Location: St. Joseph

Directions To Trailhead:
About 3 miles southwest of Three Rivers. Take US 131 south of Three Rivers to Broadway Rd, then west on Broadway about 1 mile to the park entrance at the corner of Roberts Rd.

Trail Type: Hiking/Walking, Cross Country Skiing, Interpretive
Trail Distance: 4+ mi   Loops: Many   Shortest: Longest:
Trail Surface: Natural
Trail Use Fee: None, but donations accepted
Method Of Ski Trail Grooming: Not known
Skiing Ability Suggested: Novice to advanced
Hiking Trail Difficulty: Easy to moderate
Mountain Biking Ability Suggested: NA
Terrain: Steep 5%, Hilly 15%, Moderate 60%, Flat 25%
Camping: None

Owned by the St Joesph Co Parks
Complete county park with all facilities including 4 tubing hills

Hillsdale Parks and Recreation Department
43 McCollum St
Hillsdale, MI 49242

518-437-3579

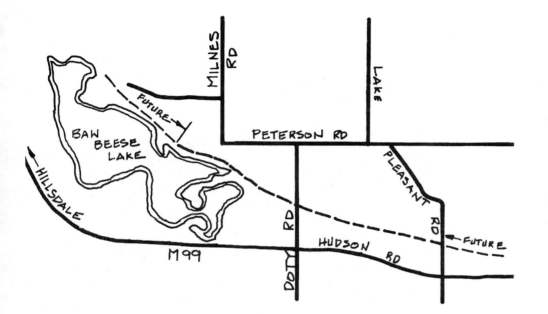

Michigan Atlas & Gazetteer Location: 22A34

County Location: HIllsdale

Directions To Trailhead:
Trail begins on the northeast side of Baw Beese Lake and ends at Lake Pleasant Rd. just north of Hudson Rd (M99) southeast of Hillsdale. Trail crosses Doty Rd about .3 mile north of M99. East trailhead - Follow Water Works Ave on the north side of Baw Beese Lake past several parks to Sandy Beach park. The trailhead is .3 mile east at bollards in corridor.

Trail Type: Hiking/Walking, Cross Country Skiing,
Trail Distance: 2 mi   Loops: NA   Shortest: NA   Longest: NA
Trail Surface: Paved
Trail Use Fee: None
Method Of Ski Trail Grooming: NA
Skiing Ability Suggested: Novice
Hiking Trail Difficulty: Easy
Mountain Biking Ability Suggested: NA
Terrain: Steep 0%, Hilly 0%, Moderate 0%, Flat 100%
Camping: None

Owned by City of Hillsdale.
When completed the trail will be 6 miles long. Extensions will be in both directions into Hillsdale and eastward.
Part of the North Country Trail.

BAW BEESE TRAIL

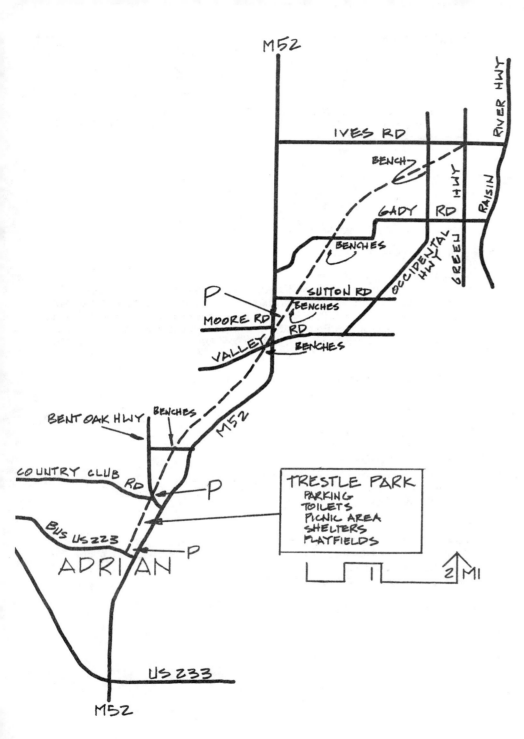

Director of Community Service, City of Adrian
100 E. Church
Adrian, MI 49221

517-263-2161

Michigan Atlas & Gazetteer Location: 24A1

County Location: Lenawee

Directions To Trailhead:
South trailhead - Parking lot for the Country Market/Arbor Drugs off Maumee Rd west of downtown
No parking at north trailhead.

Trail Type: Hiking/Walking, Cross Country Skiing
Trail Distance: 7 mi   Loops: NA   Shortest: NA   Longest: NA
Trail Surface: Paved
Trail Use Fee: None
Method Of Ski Trail Grooming: None
Skiing Ability Suggested: Novice
Hiking Trail Difficulty: Easy
Mountain Biking Ability Suggested: NA
Terrain: 100% Flat
Camping: None

Owned by the City of Adrian
According to the Roger Storm, former Director, Michigan Chapter of the Rails-to-Trails Conservancy "Trestle Park puts this trail in a league all its own. Of all the facilities developed thus far along a rail-trail, this could well be the finest. The City of Adrian truly did themselves proud. Trying to describe Trestle Park is almost a disservice. You have to see it to really get a feel for what has been created here....Oh yes, the trail is nice too."
Benches provided along the trail.

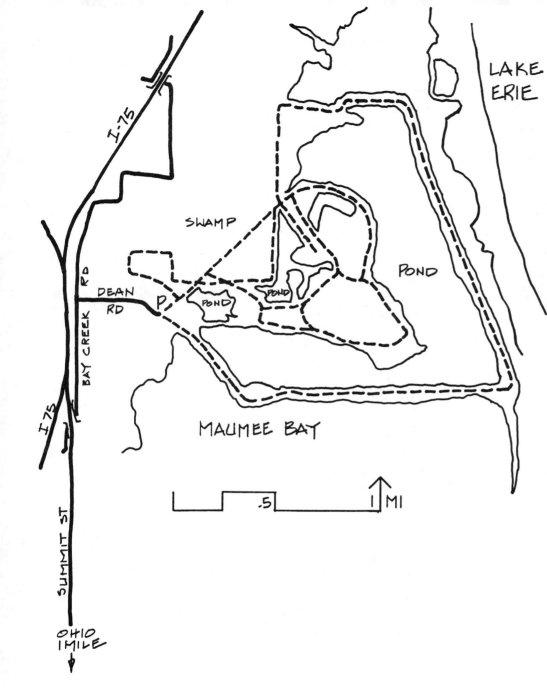

The Nature Conservancy, Michigan Chapter
2840 East Grand River, Suite 5
East Lansing, MI 48823

517-332-1741

Michigan Atlas & Gazetteer Location: 25B6

County Location: Monroe

Directions To Trailhead:
Take I-75 south to exit 2. Exit on Summit Rd and pass over I-75 to Brewer's Boat Livery(at the intersection with Sterns Rd). Make a U-turn at Sterns Rd and head north .2 mile to Bay Creek Rd, which is the first road to the right. Follow Bay Creek Rd .8 mile north to Dean Rd. Turn right onto Dean Rd and travel 1 mile to the Erie Shooting Club cottages. Park here. Follow the dikes that traverse the preserve .

Trail Type: Interpretive
Trail Distance: 5+ mi   Loops: Shortest: Longest:
Trail Surface: Gravel and natural
Trail Use Fee: None
Method Of Ski Trail Grooming: NA
Skiing Ability Suggested: NA
Hiking Trail Difficulty: Easy
Mountain Biking Ability Suggested: NA
Terrain: Steep 0%, Hilly 0%, Moderate 0%, Flat 100%
Camping: None

Owned by the Nature Conservancy
Follow dikes. No marked trails.
Closed in October and November.
Don't block roads or private property at trailhead

ERIE MARSH PRESERVE

Sterling State Park
2800 State Park Rd., Rte 5
Monroe, MI 48161

313-289-2715

DNR Parks and Recreation Division

517-373-1270

Michigan Atlas & Gazetteer Location: 25A6

County Location: Monroe

Directions To Trailhead:
East of Monroe on Lake Erie Take Dixie Hwy east from the I75 exit about 1 mile to park entrance

Trail Type: Hiking/Walking
Trail Distance: 2.6 mi   Loops: 1   Shortest: Longest: 2.6 mi
Trail Surface: Natural
Trail Use Fee: None, but vehicle permit required
Method Of Ski Trail Grooming: NA
Skiing Ability Suggested: NA
Hiking Trail Difficulty: Easy
Mountain Biking Ability Suggested: NA
Terrain: Flat
Camping: Campgound in park

Maintained by the DNR Parks and Recreation Division
Trail along backwater marsh of Lake Erie, and includes a small open air shelter and several displays with an observation tower to overlook the marsh area. Swimming available at beach area.

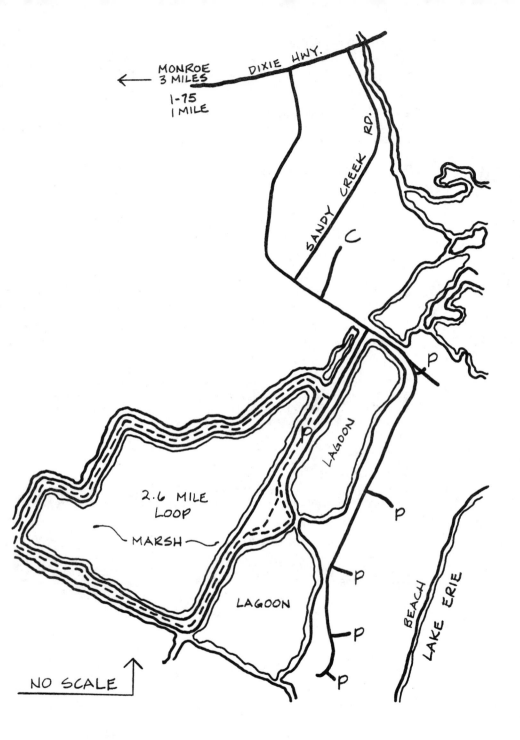

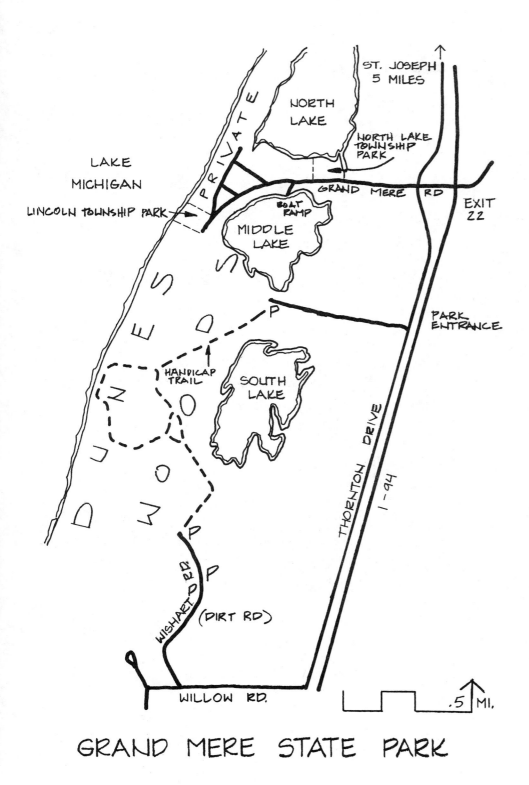

Warren Dunes State Park
12032 Red Arrow Highway
Sawyer, MI 49125

616-426-4013

DNR Parks and Recreation Division

517-373-1270

Michigan Atlas & Gazetteer Location: 26D2

County Location: Berrien

Directions To Trailhead:
5 miles south of St Joesph on I-94 at exit 22 (Grand Mere Rd), then west 100 feet to Thornton Drive, then south 1/2 mile to the park entrance. Grand Mere Rd ends at a township park on Lake Michigan.

Trail Type: Hiking/Walking, Cross Country Skiing, Interpretive
Trail Distance: 3.5 mi   Loops: Several   Shortest: Longest:
Trail Surface: Paved and natural
Trail Use Fee: None, but vehicle entry permit required
Method Of Ski Trail Grooming: None
Skiing Ability Suggested: None
Hiking Trail Difficulty: Easy to moderate
Mountain Biking Ability Suggested: NA
Terrain: Steep 0%, Hilly 0%, Moderate 0%, Flat 100%
Camping: Campground available at Warren Dunes SP, 10 miles south of this park

Maintained by the DNR Parks and Recreation Division
Trails in Lake Michigan dune area. Great for bird watching around the lakes. The park has a 1/2 mile paved handicapper accessible nature trail with accessible restrooms.
Many other unmarked trails throughout the dunes.

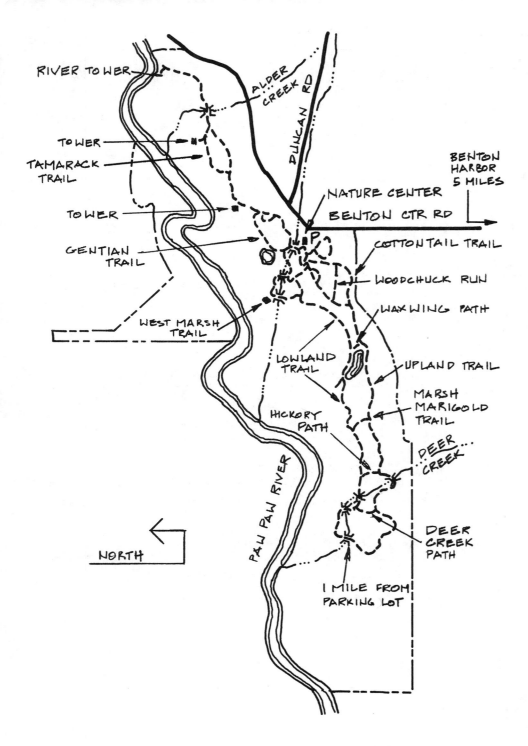

Sarett Nature Center

Sarett Nature Center
2300 Benton Center Rd
Benton Harbor, MI 49022

616-972-4832

Michigan Atlas & Gazetteer Location: 26C34

County Location: Berrien

Directions To Trailhead:
From I-94, take exit 35, then exit 1(Red Arrow Hwy), then left onto Red Arrow
Drive .6, turn right(north) onto Benton Center Rd. for .75 mile to the center

Trail Type: Hiking/Walking, Cross Country Skiing, Interpretive
Trail Distance: 5+ mi   Loops: 3   Shortest: .25 mi Longest: 3 mi
Trail Surface: Natural
Trail Use Fee: No, but donations accepted
Method Of Ski Trail Grooming: None
Skiing Ability Suggested: Novice
Hiking Trail Difficulty: Easy
Mountain Biking Ability Suggested: NA
Terrain: Steep 0%, Hilly 5%, Moderate 20%, Flat 75%
Camping: None

Owned by the Michigan Audubon Society
Trails have boardwalks, towers, elevated platforms and benches throughout the
350 acre preserve.
A detailed trail guide is available.

SARETT NATURE CENTER

Map labels: RIVER TOWER, ALDER CREEK, DUNCAN RD, TOWER, TAMARACK TRAIL, TOWER, GENTIAN TRAIL, NATURE CENTER, BENTON CTR RD, BENTON HARBOR 5 MILES, COTTONTAIL TRAIL, WOODCHUCK RUN, WAXWING PATH, WEST MARSH TRAIL, LOWLAND TRAIL, UPLAND TRAIL, MARSH MARIGOLD TRAIL, HICKORY PATH, DEER CREEK, DEER CREEK PATH, PAW PAW RIVER, NORTH, 1 MILE FROM PARKING LOT

Fred Russ Forest Park

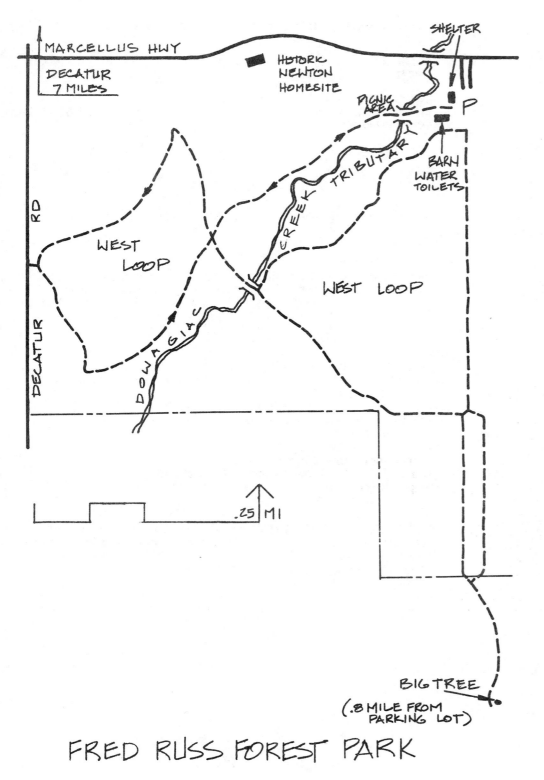

Cass County Parks Department
340 N. Okeefe St
Cassopolis, MI 49031

616-445-8611

Michigan Atlas & Gazetteer Location: 27D7

County Location: Cass

Directions To Trailhead:
.5 mile east of the intersection of Marcellus Hwy and Decatur Rd

Trail Type: Hiking/Walking, Cross Country Skiing, Interpretive
Trail Distance: 2 mi   Loops: 2   Shortest: 1 mi   Longest: 1.5 mi
Trail Surface: Natural
Trail Use Fee: Donations
Method Of Ski Trail Grooming: Not known
Skiing Ability Suggested: Novice
Hiking Trail Difficulty: Easy
Mountain Biking Ability Suggested: NA
Terrain: Steep 0%, Hilly 0%, Moderate 0%, Flat 100%
Camping: None

Managed by the Cass County Parks Department
Class A trout stream goes through the property.
Also called Newton Woods
Picnic area, shelter, and playground provide in the park.

FRED RUSS FOREST PARK

Van Buren State Park
23960 Ruggles Rd., PO Box 122-B   616-637-2788
South Haven, MI 49090

DNR Parks Division and Recreation

       517-373-1270

Michigan Atlas & Gazetteer Location: 27A567,28B123

County Location: VanBuren & Kalamazoo

Directions To Trailhead:
Between Kalamazoo and South Haven
East trailhead -Just west of US131 on 10th St between G & H Avenues
West trailhead-In South Haven on the south side of the Black River, west of the Blue Star Hwy at the corner of Bailey St and Wells St.

Trail Type: Hiking/Walking, Cross Country Skiing, Mountain Biking
Trail Distance: 34.1 mi   Loops: NA   Shortest: NA   Longest: NA
Trail Surface: Crushed limestone
Trail Use Fee: Yes, daily, family and annual passes are available
Method Of Ski Trail Grooming: None
Skiing Ability Suggested: Novice
Hiking Trail Difficulty: Easy
Mountain Biking Ability Suggested: Novice
Terrain: Steep 0%, Hilly 0%, Moderate 0%, Flat 100%
Camping: Some campgrounds along or near the trail

Maintained by the DNR Parks and Recreation Division and the Friends of the Kal-Haven Trail, a nonprofit organization. New members welcome.
A very popular rail trail. The first rail trail in Michigan.
The trail passes through farm land, wooded areas and over rivers.
Equestrian use is limited to a parallel and separate trail from 68th St to 51st St. Both ends and along the trail are toilets and each end has a picnic area and drinking water available. Communities along the trail provide various services for trail users.
Write or call for more information and a brochure

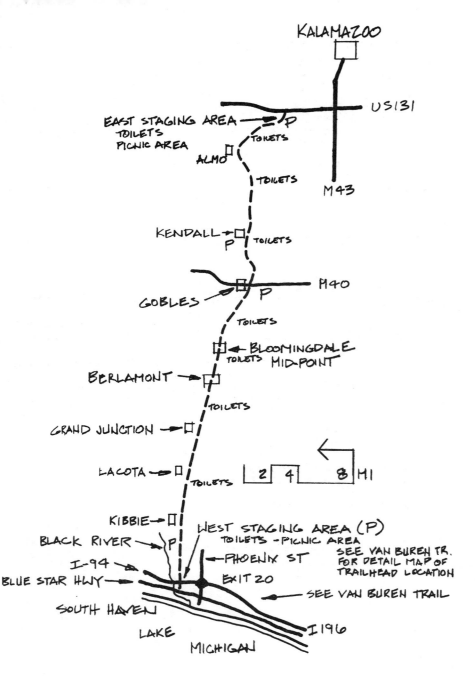

KAL-HAVEN TRAIL
SESQUICENTENNIAL STATE PARK

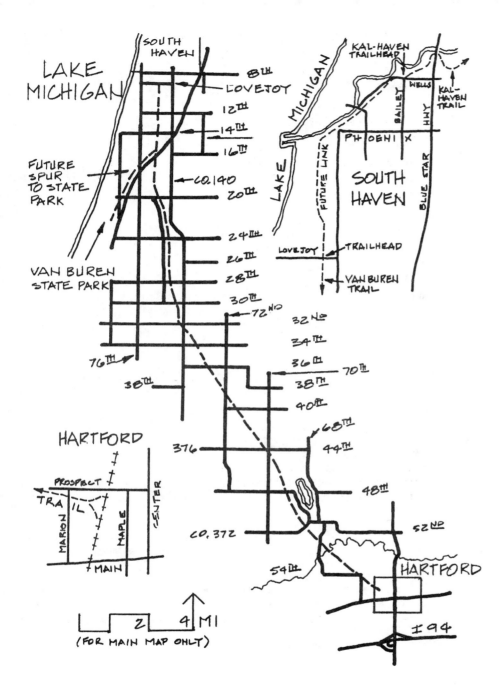

Van Buren State Park
23960 Ruggles Rd, Box 122B
South Haven, MI 49090

616-637-2788

DNR Parks and Recreation Division

517-322-1300
517-373-1270

Michigan Atlas & Gazetteer Location: 27AB45

County Location: Van Buren

Directions To Trailhead:
North trailhead - Lovejoy Rd, .5 mile west of Bus I-196, just south of South Haven
Future connection north along railroad corridor to Kal-Haven Trail trailhead at the corner of Wells St and Bailey St on the south side of the Black River and just west of the Blue Star Hwy.
South trailhead - Hartford, northwest corner of town at Prospect St. and Marion St., just west of the north-south   railroad track
Trail Type: Hiking/Walking, Cross Country Skiing, Mountain Biking
Trail Distance: 14.3 mi   Loops: NA   Shortest: NA   Longest: NA
Trail Surface: Ballast and natural
Trail Use Fee: Yes,
Method Of Ski Trail Grooming: None
Skiing Ability Suggested: Novice
Hiking Trail Difficulty: Easy
Mountain Biking Ability Suggested: Novice
Terrain: 100% Flat
Camping: Van Buren State Park

Managed by the DNR Parks and Recreation Division
Currently under development but useable for hiking and mountain biking

VAN BUREN TRAIL STATE PARK

Kalamazoo Nature Center
7000 N. Westnedge Ave
Kalamazoo, MI 49004

616-381-1574

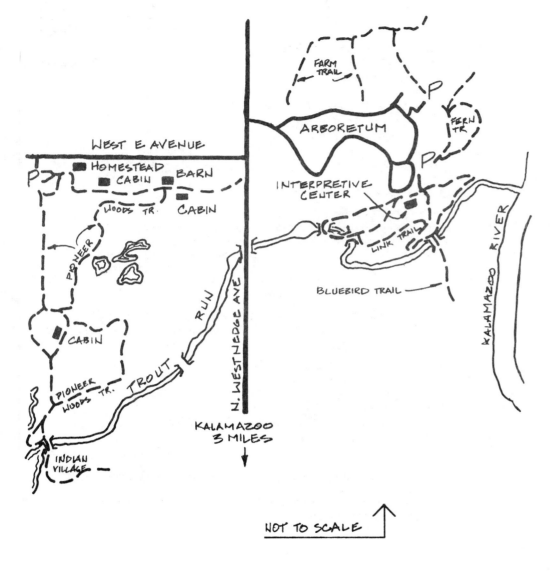

Michigan Atlas & Gazetteer Location: 28B3

County Location: Kalamazoo

Directions To Trailhead:
At US131 and D Ave. go east on D Ave about 3 miles to Westnedge Ave., then south on Westnedge Ave one mile. Entrance is on the left.

Trail Type: Hiking/Walking, Cross Country Skiing, Interpretive
Trail Distance: 10 mi   Loops: Many   Shortest: Longest:
Trail Surface: Natural
Trail Use Fee: No, but addmission fee is requried.
Method Of Ski Trail Grooming: None
Skiing Ability Suggested: Novice
Hiking Trail Difficulty: Easy to moderate
Mountain Biking Ability Suggested: NA
Terrain: Steep 0%, Hilly 10%, Moderate 80%, Flat 10%
Camping: None

Maintained by The Nature Center,a non-profit, scientific, environmental education and land-conservancy institution originally founded to save the property from development..
Cooper's Glen, site of the Nature Center, was named for James Fenimore Cooper, a frequent visitor to this area in the 1840's.
Trails, interpretive center, barnyard, farm, arboretum, botanic garden, Delano Homestead and a gift shop are part of the nature center.
Cross country skiing permitted only on the property west of Westnedge.
A brochure is available

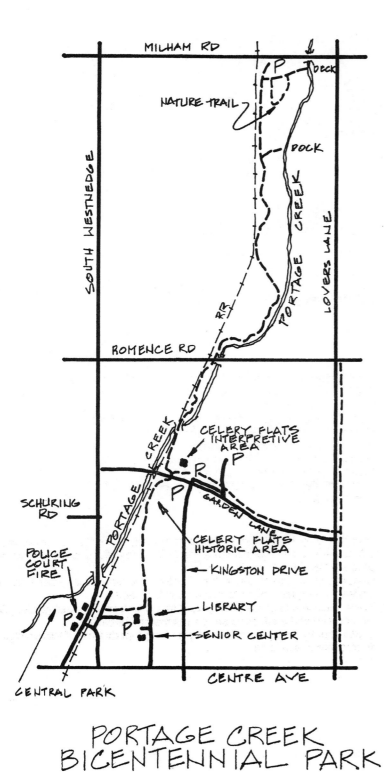

PORTAGE CREEK
BICENTENNIAL PARK

City of Portage, Parks and Recreation Department
7900 S. Westnedge   616-329-4522
Portage, MI 49002

Michigan Atlas & Gazetteer Location: 28C3

County Location: Kalamazoo

Directions To Trailhead:
I-94 to exit 76A(S. Westnedge), then take Westnedge about .5 mile to Milham Rd., then left for about .5 mile to the park entrance.

Trail Type: Hiking/Walking, Cross Country Skiing, Interpretive
Trail Distance: 2.25 mi   Loops: NA   Shortest: NA   Longest: NA
Trail Surface: Paved
Trail Use Fee: None
Method Of Ski Trail Grooming: None
Skiing Ability Suggested: Novice
Hiking Trail Difficulty: Easy
Mountain Biking Ability Suggested: NA
Terrain: Steep 0%, Hilly 0%, Moderate 20%, Flat 80%
Camping: None

Maintained by the City of Portage, Parks and Recreation Department
100 acre linear park.
The Celery Flats Interpretive and Historical Area is along this trail.
Call or write for the brochure.

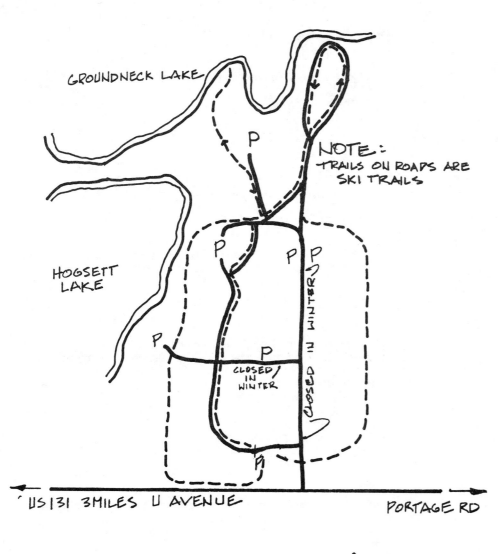

GROUNDNECK LAKE

P

NOTE:
TRAILS ON ROADS ARE
SKI TRAILS

HOGSETT
LAKE

P

P P P

CLOSED IN WINTER

P

P

CLOSED
IN
WINTER

P

← US131 3MILES   U AVENUE   PORTAGE RD →

.5 MI

PRAIRIE VIEW PARK

Kalamazoo County Parks and Recreation Department
2900 Lake St.   616-383-8778
Kalamazoo, MI 49001

Michigan Atlas & Gazetteer Location: 28C3

County Location: Kalamazoo

Directions To Trailhead:
South of Kalamazoo about 9 miles on US131, then east on U Ave 3 miles to the park entrance

Trail Type: Hiking/Walking, Cross Country Skiing
Trail Distance: 5 km   Loops: Several   Shortest: Longest:
Trail Surface: Natural
Trail Use Fee: None, but vehicle entry fee required
Method Of Ski Trail Grooming: Track set
Skiing Ability Suggested: Novice
Hiking Trail Difficulty: Easy
Mountain Biking Ability Suggested: NA
Terrain: Steep 0%, Hilly 0%, Moderate 5%, Flat 95%
Camping: None

Operated by the Kalamazoo County Parks Department
Ski trails use some vehicle roads that are closed during the winter.
Sledding hill, warming shelter, beach, concessions, picnic shelters and play fields.
Park is about 210 acres

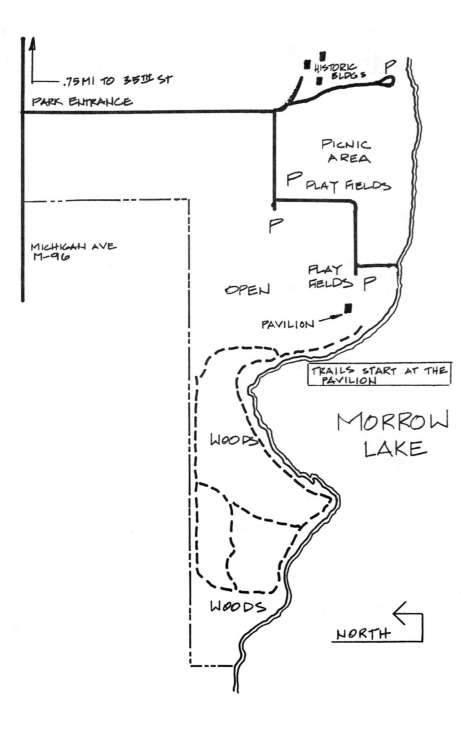

.75 MI TO 35TH ST
PARK ENTRANCE

HISTORIC BLDGS

P

PICNIC AREA

P PLAY FIELDS

P

MICHIGAN AVE M-96

OPEN

PLAY FIELDS

P

PAVILION

TRAILS START AT THE PAVILION

MORROW LAKE

WOODS

WOODS

NORTH

RIVER OAKS COUNTY PARK

River Oaks County Park

Kalamazoo County Parks and Recreation Department.
2900 Lake St
Kalamazoo, MI 49001

616-383-8778

Michigan Atlas & Gazetteer Location: 28B34

County Location: Kalamazoo

Directions To Trailhead:
North on 35th St from I-94 to M96, then west .75 mile to park

Trail Type: Hiking/Walking, Cross Country Skiing
Trail Distance: 2 mi   Loops: Several   Shortest: Longest:
Trail Surface: Natural
Trail Use Fee: None, but entry fee required
Method Of Ski Trail Grooming: None
Skiing Ability Suggested: Novice
Hiking Trail Difficulty: Easy
Mountain Biking Ability Suggested: NA
Terrain: 100%Flat
Camping: None

Maintained by the Kalamazoo County Parks and Recreation Department
Park is along the north shore of Morrow Lake.

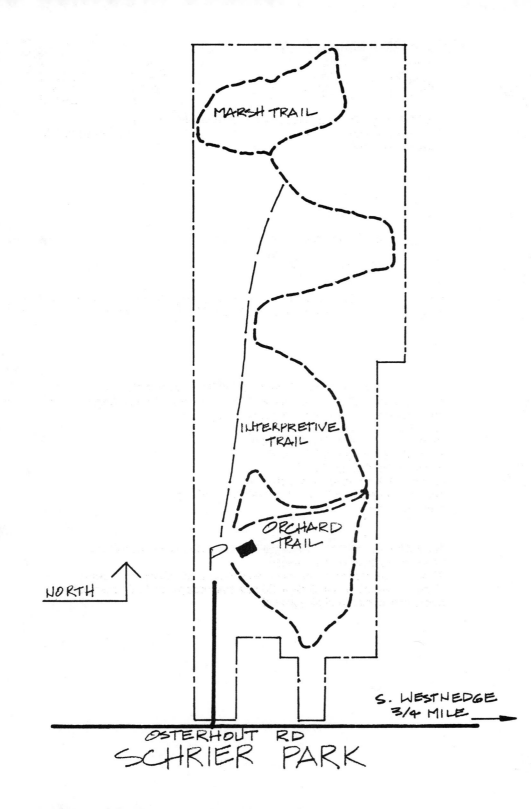

Schrier Park

City of Portage, Parks and Recreation Department
7900 S. Westnedge
Portage, MI 49002

616-329-4522

Michigan Atlas & Gazetteer Location: 28C3

County Location: Kalamazoo

Directions To Trailhead:
I-94 to exit 76A(S. Westnedge), then south on Westnedge about 5 miles to
Osterhout Rd., then right about 3/4 mile to Schrier Park

Trail Type: Hiking/Walking, Cross Country Skiing, Interpretive
Trail Distance: 1.5 mi   Loops: 3   Shortest: .25 mi Longest: .75 mi
Trail Surface: Natural and paved
Trail Use Fee: None
Method Of Ski Trail Grooming: None
Skiing Ability Suggested: Novice
Hiking Trail Difficulty: Easy
Mountain Biking Ability Suggested: NA
Terrain: Steep 0%, Hilly 0%, Moderate 30%, Flat 70%
Camping: None

Maintained by the City of Portage, Parks and Recreation Department
Park with playground, pavilion and picnic area
50 acre park.
Handicapper facilities include restrooms, .25 mile paved trail, paviliion and
playground

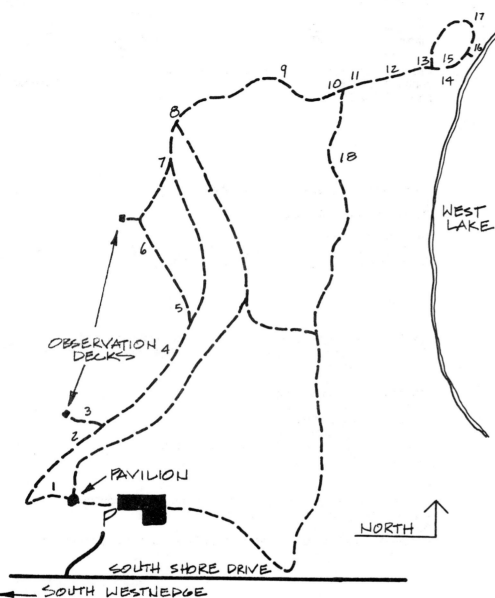

West Lake Nature Preserve

City of Portage, Parks and Recreation Department
7900 S. Westnedge
Portage, MI 49002

616-329-4522

Michigan Atlas & Gazetteer Location: 28C3

County Location: Kalamazoo

Directions To Trailhead:
I-94 to exit 76-A(S. Westnedge), then south on Westnedge about 4 miles to South Shore Drive, then left about 100 yards to the park entrance.

Trail Type: Hiking/Walking, Cross Country Skiing, Interpretive
Trail Distance: 1.5 mi   Loops: 2   Shortest: .25 mi   Longest: 1 mi
Trail Surface: Bark, natural, boardwalk and paved
Trail Use Fee: None
Method Of Ski Trail Grooming: None
Skiing Ability Suggested: Novice
Hiking Trail Difficulty: Easy
Mountain Biking Ability Suggested: NA
Terrain: Steep 0%, Hilly 0%, Moderate 20%, Flat 80%
Camping: None

Maintained by the City of Portage, Parks and Recreation Department
Three interpretive trails available.
80 acres preserve with extensive wetland area and observation decks
Handicapper faclities include a .25 mile handicapper trail with overlook, restrooms, shelter and playground.

WEST LAKE NATURE PRESERVE

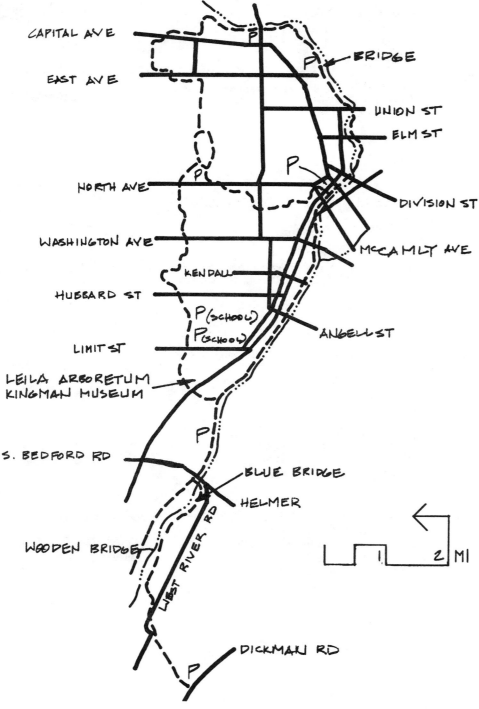

City of Battle Creek, Parks and Recreation Department
124 E. Michigan Ave
Battle Creek, Mi 49017

616-966-3431

Michigan Atlas & Gazetteer Location: 29B56

County Location: Calhoun

Directions To Trailhead:
In downtown Battle Creek and west to Dickman Rd

Trail Type: Hiking/Walking, Cross Country Skiing, Interpretive
Trail Distance: 17 mi   Loops: 3   Shortest: 2 mi   Longest: 8 mi
Trail Surface: Paved
Trail Use Fee: None
Method Of Ski Trail Grooming: None
Skiing Ability Suggested: Novice
Hiking Trail Difficulty: Easy
Mountain Biking Ability Suggested: NA
Terrain: Steep 5%, Hilly 5%, Moderate 40%, Flat 50%
Camping: None

Owned by Battle Creek
Excellent looped city trail system.
Restaurants and shops along the trail.
During the winter holiday season, a light show is presented along the trail.
Great trail for roller blading and other hard surfaced trail activities.

BATTLE CREEK LINEAR PARK

Binder Park Inc.

Binder Park Inc.
123 E. Michigan Ave.
Battle Creek, MI 49017

616-966-3431

Michigan Atlas & Gazetteer Location: 29C6

County Location: Calhoun

Directions To Trailhead:
South of I94 on M66, then east on B Drive South. about 1.75 miles to
intersection. Enter to the left.

Trail Type: Hiking/Walking, Cross Country Skiing
Trail Distance: 7 mi   Loops: 6   Shortest: .25 mi Longest: 3 mi
Trail Surface: Natural
Trail Use Fee: Yes
Method Of Ski Trail Grooming: Packed with snowmobile
Skiing Ability Suggested: Novice to advanced
Hiking Trail Difficulty: Easy to moderate
Mountain Biking Ability Suggested: NA
Terrain: Steep 10%, Hilly 40%, Moderate 25%, Flat 25%
Camping: None

Operated by Binder Park Inc., a non-profit corporation.
Rentals, snack bar, instruction and sledding area is available.
Additional 1 mile long cross country skiing loop is on adjacent golf course
accessable from Binder Park.
Picnic area and playground available in the summer.

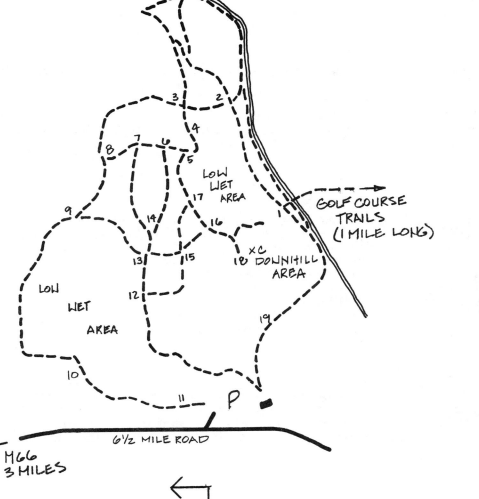

CREEK

3   2

4

7   6

8

5

LOW
WET
AREA

17

GOLF COURSE
TRAILS
(1 MILE LONG)

9

14

16

XC
DOWNHILL
AREA

13   15   18

12

LOW

WET

AREA

19

10

11   P

6½ MILE ROAD

M66
3 MILES

NO SCALE

BINDER PARK

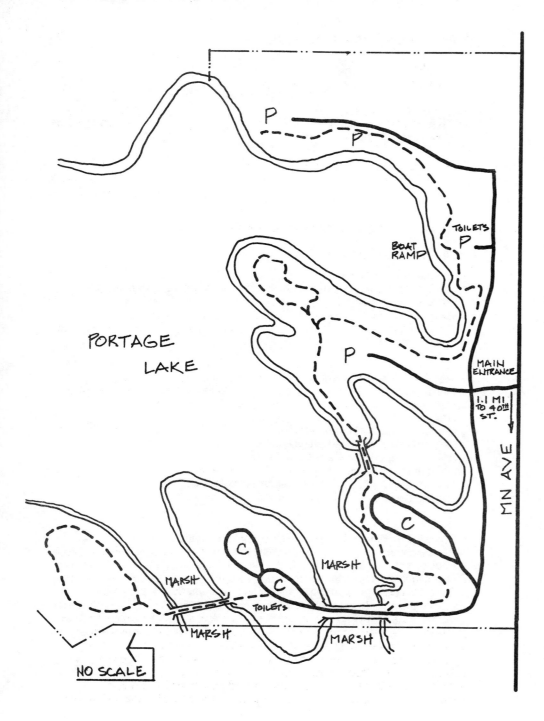

Kalamazoo County Parks and Recreation Department
2900 Lake St.   616-383-8778
Kalamazoo, MI 49001

Michigan Atlas & Gazetteer Location: 29B5

County Location: Kalamazoo

Directions To Trailhead:
Between Battle Creek and Kalamazoo, just south of I64. Exit I64 at 35th Street
for about 1.5 miles to MN Ave. Then turn   left (east) to the park entrance which
will be on the left about 4 miles, just past 42nd Street..

Trail Type: Hiking/Walking, Cross Country Skiing
Trail Distance: 4.5 mi   Loops: 2   Shortest: Longest:
Trail Surface: Natural
Trail Use Fee: None but vehicle entry fee required
Method Of Ski Trail Grooming: None
Skiing Ability Suggested: Novice
Hiking Trail Difficulty: Easy
Mountain Biking Ability Suggested: NA
Terrain: Flat to slightly rolling
Camping: Summer camping with both rustic and improved sites available

Maintained by the Kalamazoo County Parks and Recreation Department.
This is complete recreation area with swimming, boat rentals, camping picnic
grounds with shelters, ice fishing, ice skating, boat ramp and access to three
lakes. The park contains about 275 acres.

COLDBROOK COUNTY PARK

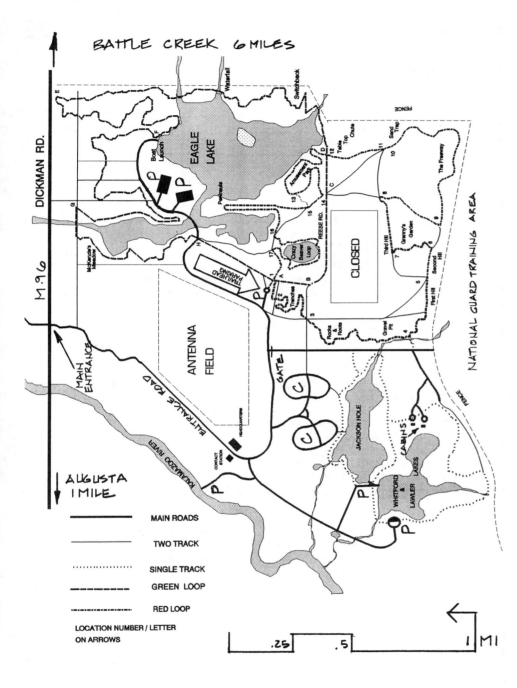

BATTLE CREEK 6 MILES

DICKMAN RD.

M 96

AUGUSTA 1 MILE

EAGLE LAKE

Boat Launch

McKenzie's Meadow

Waterfall

Switchback

FENCE

NATIONAL GUARD TRAINING AREA

ANTENNA FIELD

CLOSED

Crazy Basswood Loop

REESE RD.

Arrowhead Pass

Peninsula

Table Top

Table Chute

Sand Trap

The Freeway

Granny's Garden

Third Hill

Second Hill

First Hill

Rocks & Roots

Trenches

Gravel Pit

GATE

MAIN ENTRANCE

BUTRALKE ROAD

KALAMAZOO RIVER

CONTACT STATION

HEADQUARTERS

JACKSON HOLE

CABINS

WHITFORD & LAWLER LAKES

TRAILHEAD PARKING

MAIN ROADS

TWO TRACK

SINGLE TRACK

GREEN LOOP

RED LOOP

LOCATION NUMBER / LETTER ON ARROWS

.25   .5   1 MI

FORT CUSTER STATE RECREATION AREA

Fort Custer Recreation Area

Fort Custer Recreation Area
5163 W. Fort Custer Drive
Augusta, MI 49012

616-731-4200

DNR Parks and Recreation Division

517-373-1270
517-322-1300

Michigan Atlas & Gazetteer Location: 29B5

County Location: Kalamazoo

Directions To Trailhead:
About 5 miles west of Battle Creek and .25 mile east of Augusta on M 96 (Dickman Rd.)
Trailhead - At Whitford and Lawler Lakes picnic area
Trailhead - Main multi-use trailhead parking lot just east of the campground off the main park road

Trail Type: Hiking/Walking, Cross Country Skiing, Mountain Biking, Interpretive
Trail Distance: 20+ mi   Loops: Many   Shortest: .75 mi Longest: 8+ mi
Trail Surface: Paved(some rough), gravel and natural
Trail Use Fee: None, but vehicle entry fee required
Method Of Ski Trail Grooming: None
Skiing Ability Suggested: Novice for limited trails
Hiking Trail Difficulty: Easy for limited trails
Mountain Biking Ability Suggested: Novice to advanced
Terrain: Steep 5%, Hilly 15%, Moderate 35%, Flat 45%
Camping: Campground available in the recreation area

Maintained by the DNR Parks and Recreation Division
Many old military reservation road, old trails, new trails and DNR trails available for use.
Horse back riding is permitted in the area but infrequently used in recent years.
The best hiking and skiing trails are around Jackson and Whitford/Lawler Lakes.
Recently the members of the Michigan Mountain Biking Association have been expanding the trail system with additional excellent technical single track trails.
All trails in the park are open to mountain biking. In addition there are many old military roads availble for the less experienced mountain bikers
Jackson Lake loop is 2 miles, Whitford Lake loop is 3 miles, Green loop is 7 miles and the Red loop(most difficult) is 8 miles long.
A campground located along the lake and on part of the trail system
Rental cabins are available. They are also located on part of the trail system.

Eaton County Parks and Recreation Area
3808 Grand Ledge Hwy
Grand Ledge , MI 48837

517-627-7351

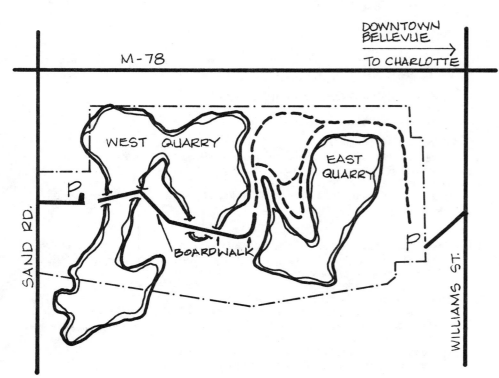

DOWNTOWN
BELLEVUE →
TO CHARLOTTE

M-78

SAND RD.

P

WEST QUARRY

EAST QUARRY

BOARDWALK

P

WILLIAMS ST.

NO SCALE

Michigan Atlas & Gazetteer Location: 29A7

County Location: Eaton

Directions To Trailhead:
I-96 to exit 98A (27/I69 south) towards Charlotte. Travel 23 miles to exit 48(Bellevue exit M78 west). Turn right on west M78 to park

Trail Type: Hiking/Walking, Cross Country Skiing, Interpretive
Trail Distance: 1.5 mi   Loops: 2   Shortest: .3 mi   Longest: .5 mi
Trail Surface: Natural
Trail Use Fee: None
Method Of Ski Trail Grooming: Track set
Skiing Ability Suggested: Novice
Hiking Trail Difficulty: Easy
Mountain Biking Ability Suggested: NA
Terrain: Steep 0%, Hilly 0%, Moderate 2%, Flat 98%
Camping: Campground available in Olivet

Operated by the Eaton County Parks and Recreation Department
Picnic area availible.
Naturalist programs available with reservations.
Fishing and ice skating available.

KEEHNE ENVIRONMENTAL AREA

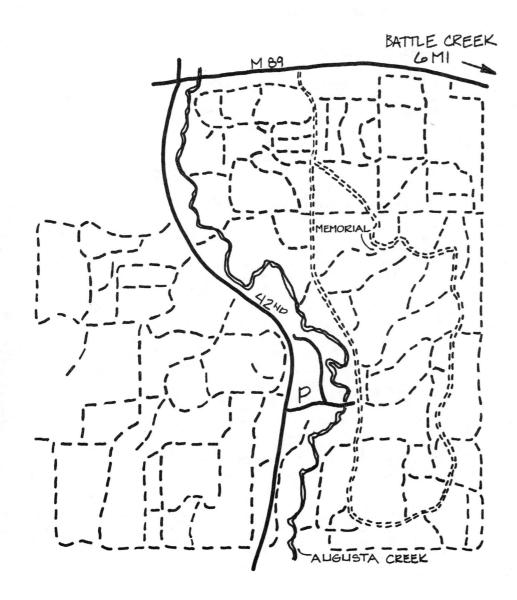

BATTLE CREEK 6 MI →

M 89

MEMORIAL

42ND

P

AUGUSTA CREEK

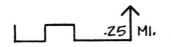

.25 MI.

KELLOGG FOREST

Kellogg Forest
42nd Street
Augusta , MI 49012

616-731-4597

Michigan Atlas & Gazetteer Location: 29B5

County Location: Kalamazoo

Directions To Trailhead:
9 miles west of Battle Creek on M89 at 42nd St.
Parking lot on 42nd St. about .5 mile south of M89.

Trail Type: Hiking/Walking, Interpretive
Trail Distance: 40 mi   Loops: Many   Shortest: Longest: 2.25 mi
Trail Surface: Gravel and natural
Trail Use Fee: None
Method Of Ski Trail Grooming: None
Skiing Ability Suggested: Novice to intermediate
Hiking Trail Difficulty: Easy
Mountain Biking Ability Suggested: NA
Terrain: Steep 0%, Hilly 15%, Moderate 60%, Flat 25%
Camping: None

Operated by Michigan State University as a forestry research station
Trails used for skiing and hiking are lanes developed for research purposes.
Off trail skiing is not permitted.
Some snowmobiles in the general area but they usually do not use the lanes
that are used for hiking and skiing
Open 8am to 5pm everyday except holidays

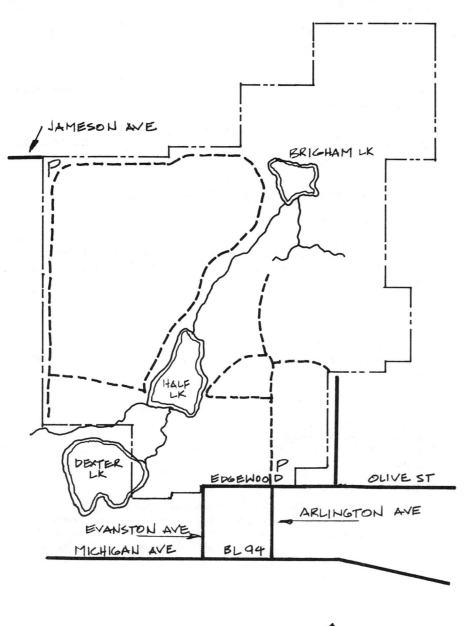

JAMESON AVE

BRIGHAM LK

HALF LK

DEXTER LK

EDGEWOOD

OLIVE ST

ARLINGTON AVE

EVANSTON AVE

MICHIGAN AVE

BL 94

NORTH

HARVEY N. OTT
BIOLOGICAL PRESERVE

Calhoun County Road Commission and Park Trustees
13300 15 Mile Rd
Marshall, MI 49068

616-781-9841
800-781-5512

Michigan Atlas & Gazetteer Location: 29B67

County Location: Calhoun

Directions To Trailhead:
 Just east of Battle Creek, off Business loop I 94 between Wattles Rd and
Raymond Rd.

Trail Type: Hiking/Walking, Cross Country Skiing, Interpretive
Trail Distance: 2.2 mi   Loops: 2   Shortest: .8 mi   Longest: 1.2 mi
Trail Surface: Natural
Trail Use Fee: None
Method Of Ski Trail Grooming: None
Skiing Ability Suggested: Novice to intermediate
Hiking Trail Difficulty: Moderate
Mountain Biking Ability Suggested: NA
Terrain: Steep 15%, Hilly 70%, Moderate 10%, Flat 5%
Camping: None

Owned by the Calhoun County Road Commission and Parks Trustees
Undeveloped 300+ acres with the exception of the trails.
Original acreage purchased in 1911 by two local school teachers to be used as a
nature preserve. Later owners included Harvey Kellogg, Battle Creek
College(now closed), Albion College with generous support of Harvey Ott.

Scotts Mill Park
8507 S. 35th St
Scotts, MI 49088

616-626-9738

Kalamazoo County Parks an Recreation Department
2900 Lake St
Kalamazoo, MI 49001

616-383-8778

Michigan Atlas & Gazetteer Location: 29C4

County Location: Kalamazoo

Directions To Trailhead:
I-94 to exit 85, south on 35th St to MN Ave, then west on MN Ave to 34th St.,
then south on 34th St. to Q Ave, then east on Q Ave to 35th St, then south on
35th St to the park.

Trail Type: Interpretive
Trail Distance: 1 mi   Loops: 1   Shortest: NA   Longest: 1 mi
Trail Surface: Natural
Trail Use Fee: Yes, varies
Method Of Ski Trail Grooming: NA
Skiing Ability Suggested: NA
Hiking Trail Difficulty: NA
Mountain Biking Ability Suggested: NA
Terrain: 100%Flat
Camping: None

Maintained by the Kalamazoo County Parks and Recreation Department
1870 working Grist Mill powered water wheel
Fishing docks pedal and row boats and picnic area, ball field, play equipment

NO MAP

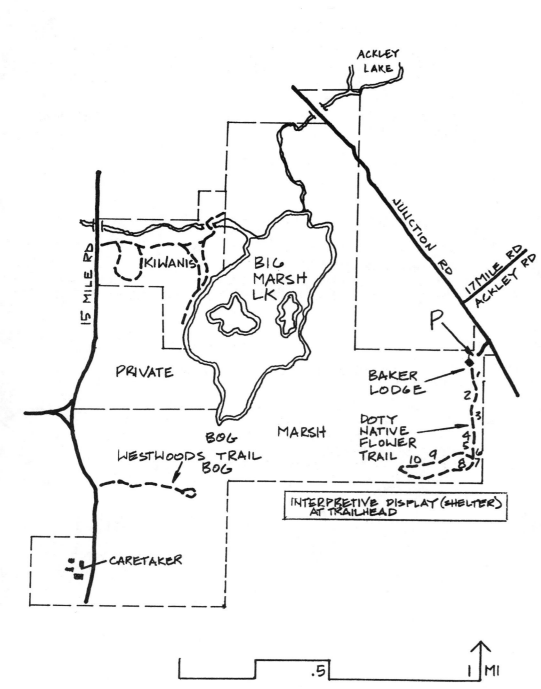

Michigan Audubon Society
21145 15 Mile Rd
Bellevue, MI 49021

616-763-3090

Michigan Atlas & Gazetteer Location: 30A1

County Location: Calhoun

Directions To Trailhead:
North on I-69 from I-94 to the first exit(N Drive North), then west to 16 Mile Rd,
then take 16 Mile Rd which changes name to Junction Rd, then north 3.4 miles
to the sanctuary on the left.
South on I-69 to exit 48, west (right) Hwy 78 at off ramp, .9 miles to Babcock Rd,
south to stop sign, right on Base Line Rd, then turns south on and changes
name to 16 Mile Rd, left at Junction Rd 1.2 miles to the sanctuary which is on
the right (somewhat hidden sign) side of the road.
Trail Type: Hiking/Walking, Interpretive
Trail Distance: 1.25 mi   Loops: 2   Shortest: .25 mi Longest: 1 mi
Trail Surface: Paved and natural
Trail Use Fee: None
Method Of Ski Trail Grooming: NA
Skiing Ability Suggested: NA
Hiking Trail Difficulty: Easy
Mountain Biking Ability Suggested: NA
Terrain: Steep 0%, Hilly 0%, Moderate 50%, Flat 50%
Camping: None

Owned by the Michigan Audubon Society.
The main trail in the sanctuary is the Doty Native Flower Trail. This is a 10
station interpretive trail.
Lodge on site is available for rent.
Resident manager is present.
Call or write for brochures on the sanctuary and the trail.

BAKER SANCTUARY

City of Albion
112 W. Cass St
Albion, MI 49224

517-629-5535

NO MAP

Michigan Atlas & Gazetteer Location: 30BC23

County Location: Calhoun

Directions To Trailhead:
Exit I-94 at exit 121, then south on Eaton St. to first light, then turn right onto
Austin Ave to the first light, then left onto Albion St to Brownswwod Rd. and to
the Park

Trail Type: Hiking/Walking, Cross Country Skiing, Mountain Biking

Trail Surface: Wood chips
Trail Use Fee: None
Method Of Ski Trail Grooming: None
Skiing Ability Suggested: Novice
Hiking Trail Difficulty: Easy
Mountain Biking Ability Suggested: Novice
Terrain: 100% Flat
Camping: None

Owned by the City of Albion
Underdevelopment at this time (1994)

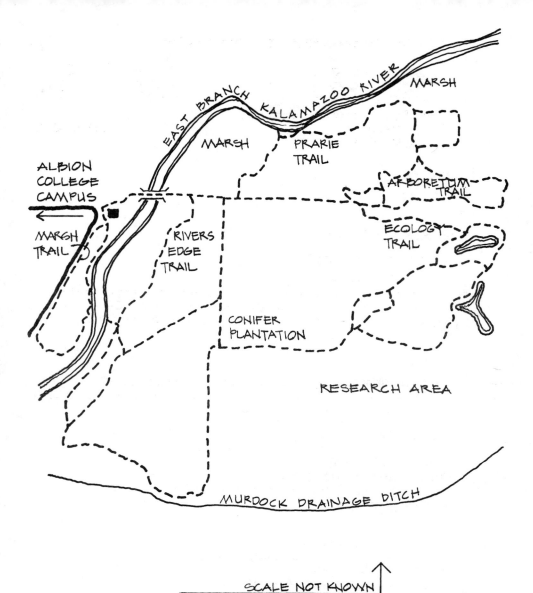

ALBION COLLEGE CAMPUS

EAST BRANCH KALAMAZOO RIVER

MARSH

MARSH

PRARIE TRAIL

ARBORETUM TRAIL

ECOLOGY TRAIL

MARSH TRAIL

RIVERS EDGE TRAIL

CONIFER PLANTATION

RESEARCH AREA

MURDOCK DRAINAGE DITCH

SCALE NOT KNOWN

Whitehouse Nature Center
Albion College
Albion, MI 49224

517-629-2030

Michigan Atlas & Gazetteer Location: 30C3

County Location: Calhoun

Directions To Trailhead:
Located 1/4 mile southeast of Albion College main campus, on the east branch of the Kalamazoo River at the end of the athletic field.

Trail Type: Hiking/Walking, Interpretive
Trail Distance: 5 mi   Loops: 5   Shortest: Longest:
Trail Surface: Natural
Trail Use Fee: None
Method Of Ski Trail Grooming: NA
Skiing Ability Suggested: NA
Hiking Trail Difficulty: Easy
Mountain Biking Ability Suggested: NA
Terrain:
Camping: None

Owned and maintained by Albion College
Established in 1972
Six self guiding nature/hiking trails are provided:
    Rivers Edge Trail - 1.3 miles
    Prairie Trail - 1.1 miles
    Ecology Trail - 2.4 miles (1.5 miles short loop)
    Marsh Trail - .5 mile
    Ewell A. Stowelll Arboretum Trail - 1 mile
    History Trail -
Brochure available

WHITEHOUSE NATURE CENTER

Dahlem Environmental Education Center
7117 S. Jackson Rd
Jackson, Mi 49201

517-782-3453

Michigan Atlas & Gazetteer Location: 31C5

County Location: Jackson

Directions To Trailhead:
I-94 to exit 142, then south on M127 to Monroe exit, then left on McDevitt to the 1st traffic light, then left(south) and follow signs to the Dahlem Center. Center is located just west of Jackson Community College on west side of Browns Lake Rd.

Trail Type: Hiking/Walking, Cross Country Skiing, Interpretive
Trail Distance: 5 mi   Loops: 8   Shortest: .4 mi   Longest: 2 mi
Trail Surface: Paved and natural
Trail Use Fee: Skiing for members only, otherwise free
Method Of Ski Trail Grooming: None
Skiing Ability Suggested: Novice and intermediate
Hiking Trail Difficulty: Easy
Mountain Biking Ability Suggested: NA
Terrain: Steep 0%, Hilly 0%, Moderate 75%, Flat 25%
Camping: None

Public non-profit environmental education center
Visitor Center building houses exhibits, offices and gift shop.
Many activities for the family.
Many special programs held seasonally.
Cross country skiing is limited to members and guests only.
Contact the center to become a member.

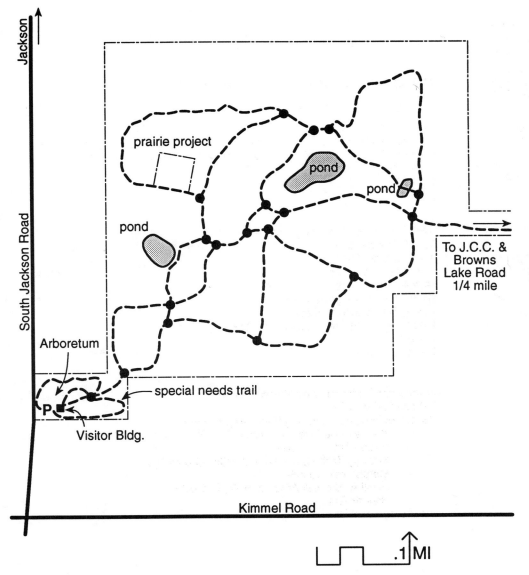

Dahlem Environmental Education Center

Pinckney Recreation Area
8555 Silver Lake Rd
Pinckney, MI 48169

313-426-4913
fax 426-1916

DNR Parks and Recreation Division

517-373-1270

Michigan Atlas & Gazetteer Location: 31A7, 32A12

County Location: Livingston, Ingham

Directions To Trailhead:
West trailhead - M52 in Stockbridge
Middle trailhead - Pinckney
East trailhead - Hamburg, just west of US23 via M36 (under development

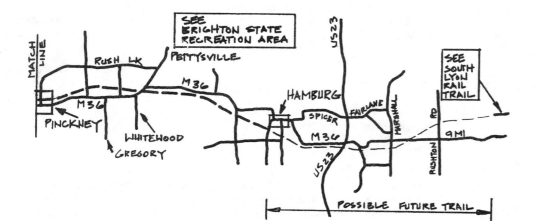

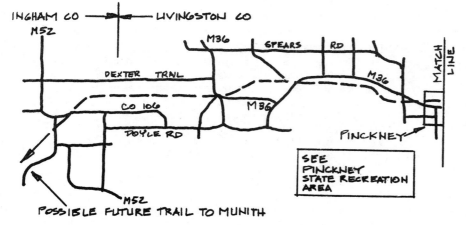

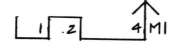

Trail Type: Hiking/Walking, Cross Country Skiing, Mountain Biking
Trail Distance: 21 mi   Loops: NA   Shortest: NA   Longest: NA
Trail Surface: Crushed stone
Trail Use Fee: None, but subject to change
Method Of Ski Trail Grooming: None
Skiing Ability Suggested: Novice
Hiking Trail Difficulty: Easy
Mountain Biking Ability Suggested: Novice
Terrain: 100% Flat
Camping: None along trail but nearby at adjacent recreation areas

Managed by the DNR Parks and Recreation Division
Opened in 1994.
Pinckney to Hamburg section is still in development.
Future plans are to expand east of Stockbridge and west to connect to the South Lyons Trail.
Many nearby trails in Waterloo, Brighton, Pinckney Recreation Areas; Huron Meadows Metropark, Independence Lake County Park and more.

LAKELANDS TRAIL STATE PARK

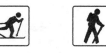

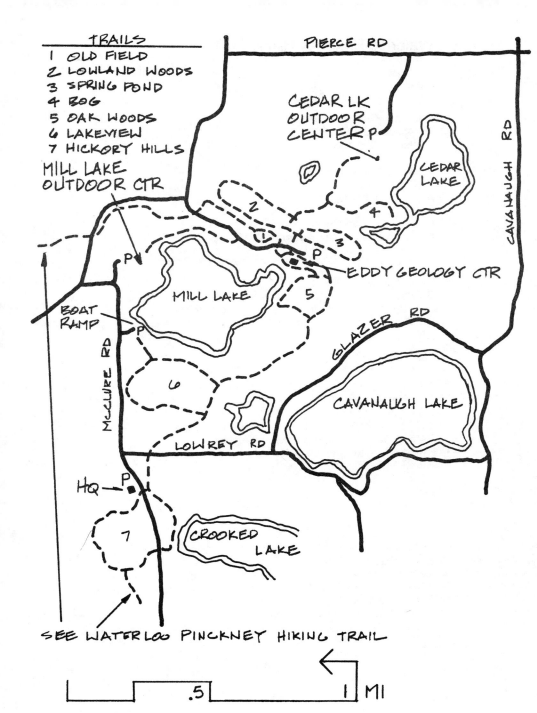

Waterloo Recreation Area
16345 McClure Rd, Rte 1
Chelsea, MI 48118

313-475-8307

DNR Parks and Recreation Division

517-373-1270

Michigan Atlas & Gazetteer Location: 31AB67,32AB1

County Location: Jackson & Washtenaw

Directions To Trailhead:
Adjacent to and NW of I94 and M52 and the city of Chelsea. Winter trailhead-From Chelsea east on Cavanaugh Lake Rd. to Pierce Rd., then north .5 mile to the Cedar Lake Outdoor Center. Summer trailhead-Mill Lake Outdoor Center or Eddy Geology Interpretive Center

Trail Type: Hiking/Walking, Cross Country Skiing, Interpretive
Trail Distance: 41 mi   Loops: Many   Shortest: .13 mi Longest: 23 mi
Trail Surface: Natural
Trail Use Fee: None, but vehicle entry fee required
Method Of Ski Trail Grooming: None
Skiing Ability Suggested: Novice to advanced
Hiking Trail Difficulty: Easy to difficult
Mountain Biking Ability Suggested: NA
Terrain: Steep 15%, Hilly 40%, Moderate 25%, Flat 20%
Camping: Two modern and two rustic campgrounds available

Maintained by the DNR Parks and Recreation Division.
Eddy Geology Center features many exhibits and a staff naturalist.
Eddy Geology Center is the trailhead for the trails listed on the map.
Warming shelter & snack bar open winter weekends at Cedar Lake Lodge.

TRAILS

1 OLD FIELD
2 LOWLAND WOODS
3 SPRING POND
4 BOG
5 OAK WOODS
6 LAKEVIEW
7 HICKORY HILLS

EDDY GEOLOGY CENTER HIKING TRAILS
WATERLOO RECREATION AREA

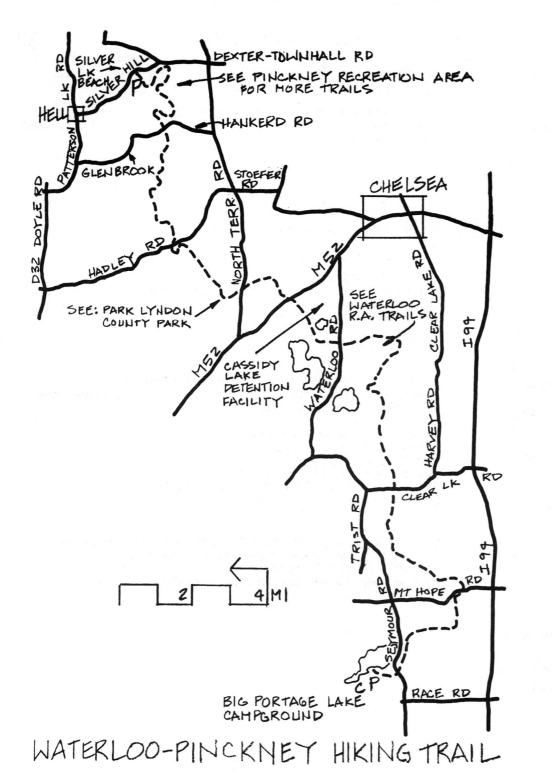

Waterloo Recreation Area
16345 McClure Rd, Rte 1
Chelsea, MI 48118

313-475-8307

Pinckney Recreation Area
8555 Silver Hill Rd., Rte 1
Pinckney, MI 48169

313-426-4913

Michigan Atlas & Gazetteer Location: 31B7,32AB12

County Location: Jackson, Washtenaw & Livingston

Directions To Trailhead:
Between Waterloo and Pinckney Recreation Areas, NW of Ann Arbor
East trailhead-Silver Lake Beach in Pinckney Recreation Area
West trailhead-Big Portage Lake Picnic Area in Waterloo Recreation Area
Other trailhead - Waterloo Recreation Area Headquarters

Trail Type: Hiking/Walking, Cross Country Skiing
Trail Distance: 25 mi   Loops: NA   Shortest: NA   Longest: NA
Trail Surface: Natural
Trail Use Fee: None, but vehicle entry fee required
Method Of Ski Trail Grooming: None
Skiing Ability Suggested: Advanced
Hiking Trail Difficulty: Moderate
Mountain Biking Ability Suggested: NA
Terrain: Steep 2%, Hilly 20%, Moderate 60%, Flat 18%
Camping: Campgrounds available at both recreation areas

Maintained by the DNR Parksand Recreation Division
This trail was not designed for skiing, but portions can be skied. Trail is
connected to the Waterloo Recreation Area ski trail at the Cedar Lake Outdoor
Center on Pierce Rd and the Potawatomi Trail system in the Pinckney
Recreation Area and Big Portage Lake Campground. Trail marking may not be
complete is some sections. Be prepared by taking   a compass along with you.
Call to confirm adequacy of trail markings. The trail section between McClure Rd
west of the Hq's and Katz Rd is used by horseback riders. The Pond Lily
Lookout has a spectacular view. Many side trails are not shown. See also
Waterloo Recreation Area and Pinckney Recreation Area for more trails.

WATERLOO-PINCKNEY HIKING TRAIL

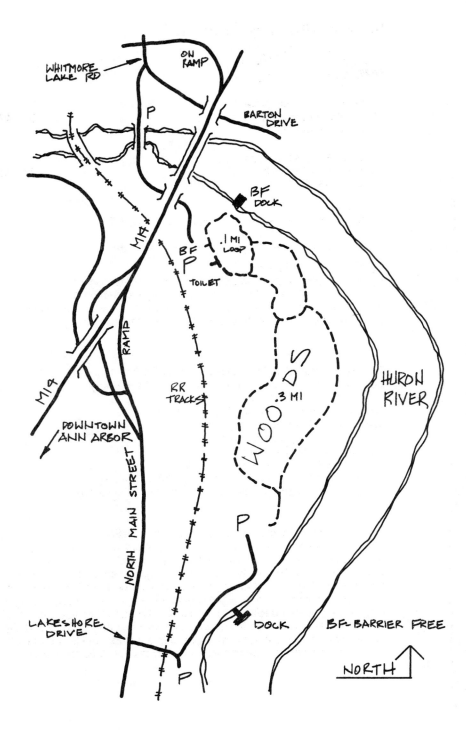

BANDEMER PARK

Bandemer Park and Nature Center

City of Ann Arbor, Department of Parks and Recreation
PO Box 8647
Ann Arbor, MI 48107

313-994-2780

Michigan Atlas & Gazetteer Location: 32B4

County Location: Washtenaw

Directions To Trailhead:
In Ann Arbor with entrances on Barton Drive at Whitmore Lake Rd and N. Main
St at Lakeshore Drive via M 14

Trail Type: Hiking/Walking, Cross Country Skiing, Interpretive
Trail Distance: .5 mi   Loops: 3   Shortest: .1 mi   Longest: .34 mi
Trail Surface: Natural, slag and asphalt
Trail Use Fee: None
Method Of Ski Trail Grooming: None
Skiing Ability Suggested: Novice
Hiking Trail Difficulty: Easy
Mountain Biking Ability Suggested: Novice
Terrain: Steep 0%, Hilly 0%, Moderate 25%, Flat 75%
Camping: None

Maintained by the City of Ann Arbor Department of Parks and Recreation
Handicapper parking, toilets and short asphalt trail is provided.
The park is along the Huron River.
Picnic area with a shelter, tables and grill is available

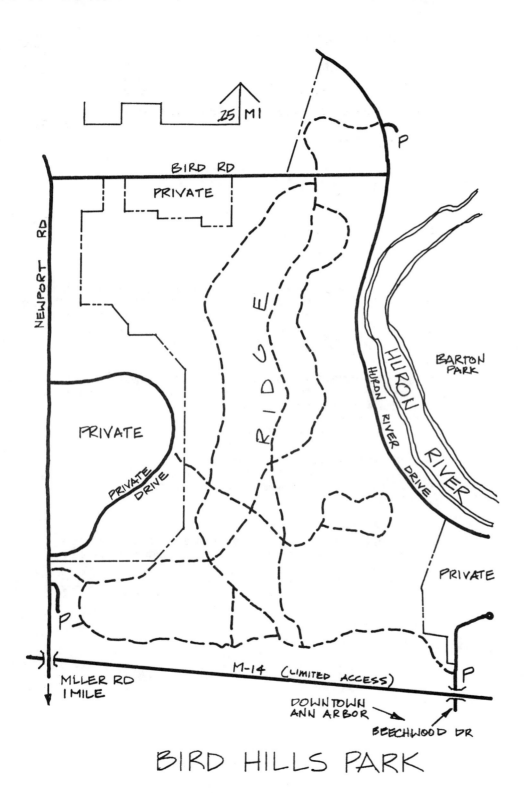

BIRD HILLS PARK

City of Ann Arbor, Department of Parks and Recreation
PO Box 8647
Ann Arbor, MI 48107

313-994-2780

Michigan Atlas & Gazetteer Location: 32B3

County Location: Washtenaw

Directions To Trailhead:
Bordering M 14 and the Huron River on the northwest side of town. Take M 14 to Maple Rd, south to Miller Rd, east to Newport. Parking on the east side of the road just past the freeway overpass.

Trail Type: Hiking/Walking, Cross Country Skiing, Interpretive
Trail Distance: 3+ mi   Loops: 5   Shortest: .5 mi   Longest: 1.5+ mi
Trail Surface: Natural
Trail Use Fee: None
Method Of Ski Trail Grooming: None
Skiing Ability Suggested: Intermediate to Advanced
Hiking Trail Difficulty: Moderate
Mountain Biking Ability Suggested: NA
Terrain: Steep 25%, Hilly 25%, Moderate 25%, Flat 25%
Camping: None

Maintained by the City of Ann Arbor Department Of Parks and Recreation
This nature area is undeveloped with the exception of the extensive trail system
Five access points with three parking areas is available
Brochure available

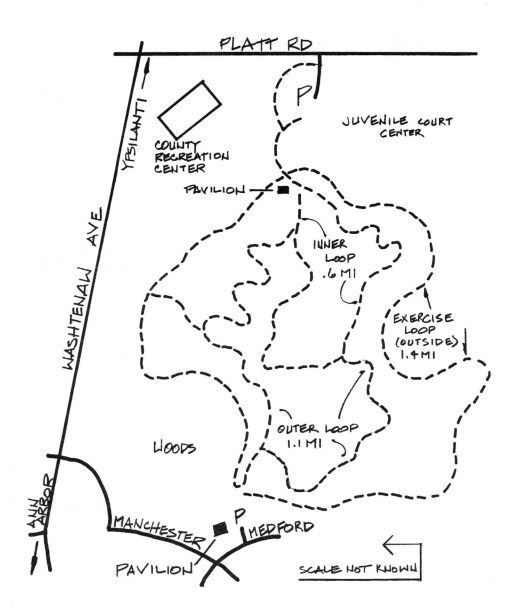

PLATT RD

YPSILANTI

WASHENAW AVE

COUNTY RECREATION CENTER

JUVENILE COURT CENTER

P

PAVILION

INNER LOOP .6 MI

EXERCISE LOOP (OUTSIDE) 1.4 MI

OUTER LOOP 1.1 MI

WOODS

ANN ARBOR

MANCHESTER

PAVILION

P MEDFORD

SCALE NOT KNOWN

County Farm Park

Washtenaw County Parks & Recreation Commission
PO Box 8645
Ann Arbor, MI 48107

313-971-6337

Michigan Atlas & Gazetteer Location: 32B4

County Location: Washtenaw

Directions To Trailhead:
Between Ann Arbor and Ypsilanti on Washtenaw Ave, just east of the Washtenaw and East Stadium Blvd intersection. WEST TRAILHEAD-Take Platt Rd. south from Washtenaw Ave to parking lot. EAST TRAILHEAD-Take Manchester south from Washenaw Ave past a water tower to the first intersection, then east(left) on Medford to parking lot.

Trail Type: Hiking/Walking, Cross Country Skiing, Interpretive
Trail Distance: 3.5 mi   Loops: 4   Shortest: .5 mi   Longest: 1.4 mi
Trail Surface: Natural and crushed limestone
Trail Use Fee: None
Method Of Ski Trail Grooming: None
Skiing Ability Suggested: Novice to intermediate
Hiking Trail Difficulty: Easy to moderate
Mountain Biking Ability Suggested: NA
Terrain: Steep 15%, Hilly 25%, Moderate 50%, Flat 10%
Camping: None

Maintained by the Washtenaw County Parks and Recreation Commission
Open and wooded landscape in the heart of the Ann Arbor metro area.
Shelter with restrooms, Par course along one trail.
The trail surface is crushed limestone
The 18 acre Britton Woods Nature Area is located in the northwest corner of the park. .
The Parcourse exercise trail is 1.4 miles long

COUNTY FARM PARK

Ann Arbor Parks and Recreation
POB 8647
Ann Arbor, MI 48107

313-994-2780

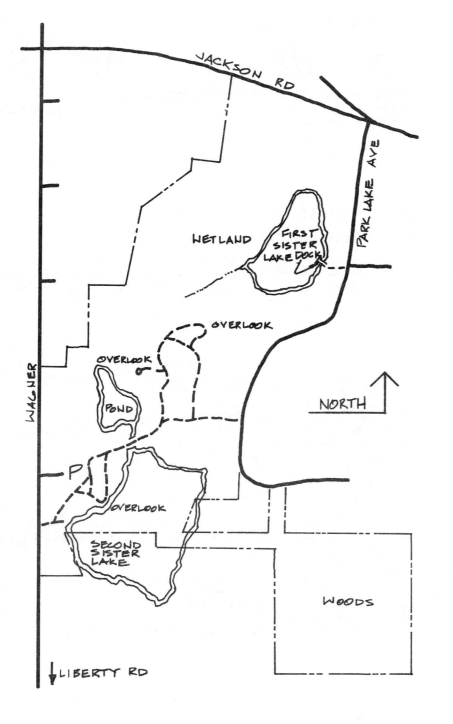

JACKSON RD

PARK LAKE AVE

WETLAND

FIRST SISTER LAKE DOCK

OVERLOOK

OVERLOOK

POND

WAGNER

NORTH

P

OVERLOOK

SECOND SISTER LAKE

WOODS

LIBERTY RD

DOLPH PARK NATURE AREA

Michigan Atlas & Gazetteer Location: 32B3

County Location: Washtenaw

Directions To Trailhead:
On the west side of Ann Arbor, northeast of Liberty Rd.(St.) and Wagner Rd. .1 mi north of Liberty Rd. on Wagner Rd to the parking lot on the east side of the road.

Trail Type: Hiking/Walking, Cross Country Skiing, Interpretive
Trail Distance: .5 mi   Loops: 2   Shortest: Short   Longest: .5 mi
Trail Surface: Natural
Trail Use Fee: None
Method Of Ski Trail Grooming: None
Skiing Ability Suggested: Intermediate
Hiking Trail Difficulty: Easy
Mountain Biking Ability Suggested: NA
Terrain: Steep 0%, Hilly 0%, Moderate 2%, Flat 98%
Camping: None

Maintained by the Ann Arbor Parks and Recreation
44 acre park with lakes, dock and overlooks.
Interpretive sign at the trailhead.
Brochure available.

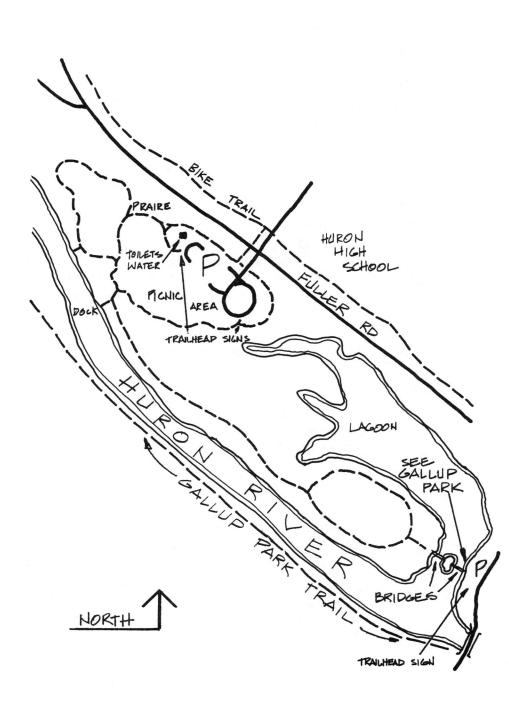

NORTH

FURSTENBERG PARK

City of Ann Arbor, Department of Parks and Recreation
PO Box 8647
Ann Arbor, MI 48107

313-994-2780

Michigan Atlas & Gazetteer Location: 32B4

County Location: Washtenaw

Directions To Trailhead:
From US23, take Geddes Rd exit westbound. At Huron Parkway, intersection go straight (Geddes Rd turns into Fuller Rd). Park is located on the south side of the road.

Trail Type: Hiking/Walking, Cross Country Skiing, Interpretive
Trail Distance: 2+ mi   Loops: Several   Shortest: .25 mi Longest: 1+ mi
Trail Surface: Paved, gravel and boardwalk
Trail Use Fee: None
Method Of Ski Trail Grooming: None
Skiing Ability Suggested: Novice
Hiking Trail Difficulty: Easy
Mountain Biking Ability Suggested: NA
Terrain: 100%Flat
Camping: None

Maintained by the City of Ann Arbor Department of Parks and Recreation
With trails recently expanded, this 48 acre park has become a wonderful place for nature study.
All trails are barrier free.
Picnic area, with restrooms and drinking fountain is provided.
Prairie garden and restoration area in the park.
Canoe landing, overlook and dock along the Huron River.
Connecting trail to Gallup Park.
Brochure is available describing 14 natural features in the park.

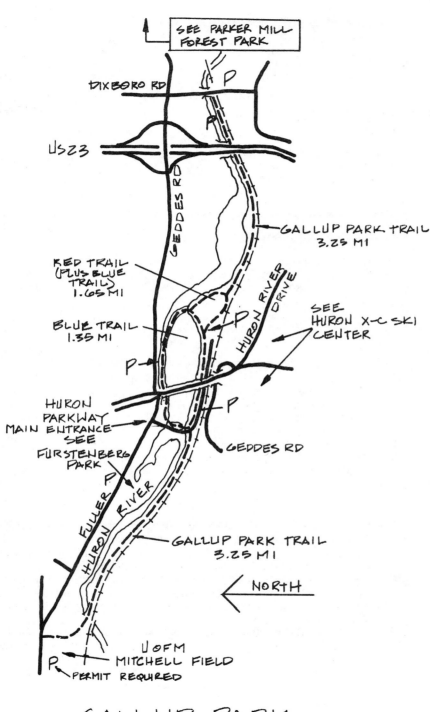

SEE PARKER MILL
FOREST PARK

DIXBORO RD

US23

GEDDES RD

GALLUP PARK TRAIL
3.25 MI

RED TRAIL
(PLUS BLUE
TRAIL)
1.65 MI

BLUE TRAIL
1.35 MI

HURON RIVER DRIVE

SEE
HURON X-C SKI
CENTER

HURON
PARKWAY
MAIN ENTRANCE
SEE
FURSTENBERG
PARK

GEDDES RD

FULLER RD

HURON RIVER

GALLUP PARK TRAIL
3.25 MI

NORTH

U OF M
MITCHELL FIELD
PERMIT REQUIRED

GALLUP PARK

Gallup Park

City of Ann Arbor, Department of Parks and Recreation
PO Box 8647
Ann Arbor, MI 48107

313-994-2780

Michigan Atlas & Gazetteer Location: 32B4

County Location: Washtenaw

Directions To Trailhead:
From US 23 take Geddes Rd exit westbound, then at Huron Parkway intersection go straight (Geddes Rd becomes Fuller Rd) take first left hand turn into park.

Trail Type: Hiking/Walking, Cross Country Skiing, Interpretive
Trail Distance: 5.28 mi   Loops: 2   Shortest: 1.35 mi Longest: 1.65 mi
Trail Surface: Paved and wood chips
Trail Use Fee: None
Method Of Ski Trail Grooming: None
Skiing Ability Suggested: Novice
Hiking Trail Difficulty: Easy
Mountain Biking Ability Suggested: NA
Terrain: 100% Flat
Camping: None

Maintained by the City of Ann Arbor, Parks and Recreation Department
In addition to the two loop trails mentioned above there are additional point to point trails. They are the Dixboro Mile - 1mi; Arboretum Mile - 1mi and the Mitchell Filed Link - .28 mi. In addition the Gallup Park Trail (which include the above three) is designated a National Recreation Trail that is 3.25 miles long. The park facilities include a bike, paddleboat and canoe rentals, picnic shelters, fishing pond for youth, ball fields, meeting bldg, boat launch, play grounds, and and interpretifve display.
See Huron Golf Course and Cross Country Ski center trails which adjoin this park to the south.
Trails connect to Furstenburg Park Nature Area to the west and Parker Mill Park to the east (see other listing).

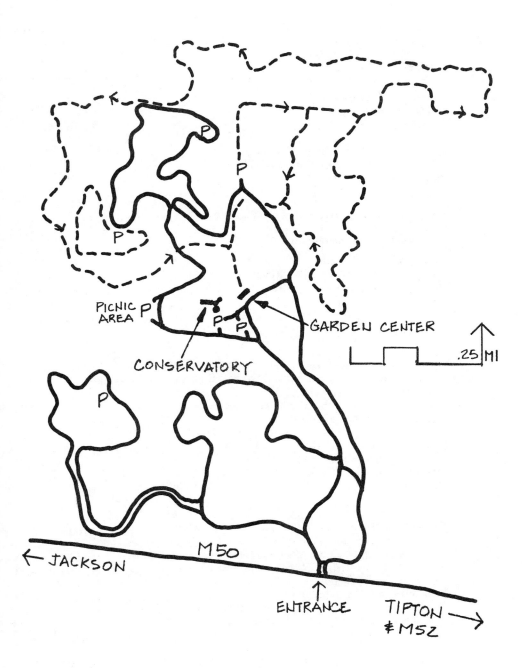

PICNIC AREA

P

CONSERVATORY

GARDEN CENTER

.25 MI

← JACKSON

M50

ENTRANCE

TIPTON → & M52

Director
Hidden Lake Gardens
Tipton, MI 49287

517-431-2060

Division Of Campus Park & Planning
412 Olds Hall, Michigan State University
East Lansing, MI 48824

517-355-9582

Michigan Atlas & Gazetteer Location: 32D1

County Location: Lenawee

Directions To Trailhead:
SE of Jackson on M50 west of Tipton

Trail Type: Hiking/Walking, Interpretive
Trail Distance: 5 mi   Loops: 4   Shortest: .2 mi   Longest: 3 mi
Trail Surface: Paved and natural
Trail Use Fee: None, but entry fee required
Method Of Ski Trail Grooming: NA
Skiing Ability Suggested: NA
Hiking Trail Difficulty: Easy to moderate
Mountain Biking Ability Suggested: NA
Terrain: Steep 0%, Hilly 80%, Moderate 10%, Flat 10%
Camping: None

Maintained by Michigan State University and administered by the Division of Campus Park & Planning.
This facility is a landscape arboretum. The gardens include 670 acres on which is a Plant Conservatory that contains a tropical dome, arid dome and greenhouse; a Visitor Center   with informative exhibits, auditorium, meeting rooms, library and gift shop; a picnic area; and over 6 miles of one way roads. The Gardens are set in the scenic Irish Hills which provides many scenic vistas along the many trails .
Open 365 days from 8AM to dusk during April through October and 8AM to 4PM weekdays and 9AM to 4:30 weekends and holidays during November to March.

HIDDEN LAKE GARDENS

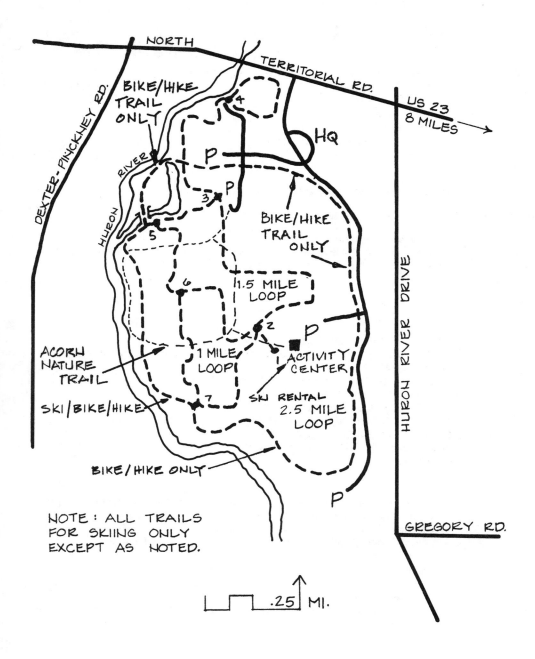

BIKE/HIKE TRAIL ONLY

NORTH

TERRITORIAL RD.

US 23
8 MILES

DEXTER-PINCKNEY RD.

HURON RIVER

HQ

4

P

P

3

5

BIKE/HIKE TRAIL ONLY

1.5 MILE LOOP

6

ACORN NATURE TRAIL

SKI/BIKE/HIKE

1 MILE LOOP

2

P

ACTIVITY CENTER

SKI RENTAL 2.5 MILE LOOP

7

HURON RIVER DRIVE

BIKE/HIKE ONLY

NOTE: ALL TRAILS FOR SKIING ONLY EXCEPT AS NOTED.

P

GREGORY RD.

.25 MI.

HUDSON MILLS METROPARK

Hudson-Mills Metropark
880 N. Territorial Rd.
Dexter, MI 48130

313-426-8211
800-47-PARKS

Huron-Clinton Metropolitan Authority
13000 High Ridge Drive, PO Box 2001
Brighton, MI 48116-8001

810-227-2757

Michigan Atlas & Gazetteer Location: 32B2

County Location: Washtenaw

Directions To Trailhead:
NW of Ann Arbor on the Huron River. On North Territorial Rd just west of Huron River Drive, 8 miles west of US23

Trail Type: Hiking/Walking, Cross Country Skiing, Interpretive
Trail Distance: 7.5 mi   Loops: Several   Shortest: .5 mi   Longest: 2.5 mi
Trail Surface: Paved and natural
Trail Use Fee: None, but vehicle entry fee required
Method Of Ski Trail Grooming: Track set
Skiing Ability Suggested: Novice to intermediate
Hiking Trail Difficulty: Easy
Mountain Biking Ability Suggested: NA
Terrain: Steep 0%, Hilly 0%, Moderate 30%, Flat 70%
Camping: Group campground only, reservations required

Operated by the Huron-Clinton Metropolitan Authority.
Ski rentals, snack bar, picnic grounds and bike rentals.
Separate skiing, bike/hike and nature trails.
Ski trail loops are 1, 1.5, 2.5 and 2.5 miles.
The bike/hike trail is paved.
Ice skating when weather permits.
Typical summer recreation facilities are available.
Call or write for their Metropark Guide, published each year.

City of Ann Arbor, Parks and Recreation Department
PO Box 8647   313-994-2780
Ann Arbor, MI 48107   313-971-6840

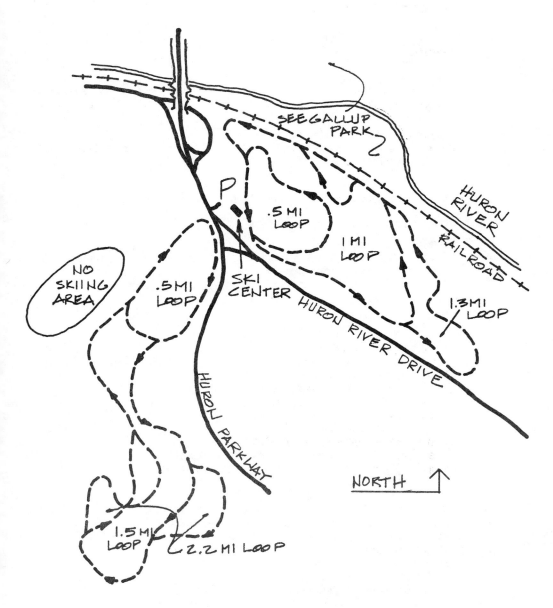

Michigan Atlas & Gazetteer Location: 32B4

County Location: Washtenaw

Directions To Trailhead:
Take US23 to Washtenaw Ave exit west, then right onto Huron Parkway, then
right onto Huron Drive, parking on left with overflow on right

Trail Type: Cross Country Skiing
Trail Distance: 2.2 mi   Loops: 6   Shortest: .5 mi   Longest: 2.2 mi
Trail Surface: Natural
Trail Use Fee: Yes, daily fee varies with day of the week
Method Of Ski Trail Grooming: Track set
Skiing Ability Suggested: Novice to intermediate
Hiking Trail Difficulty: NA
Mountain Biking Ability Suggested: NA
Terrain: Steep 1%, Hilly 10%, Moderate 19%, Flat 70%
Camping: None

Maintained by the City of Ann Arbor Parks and Recreation Department
135 acre golf course used for cross country skiing.
Trailhead and Ski Center at golf course club house.
Ski rental available at the Ski Center.

Huron Meadows Metropark
8765 Hammel Rd.
Brighton, MI 48130

810-227-2757
800-47-PARKS

Huron-Clinton Metropolitan Authority
13000 High Ridge Drive
Brighton, MI 48116-8001

810-227-2757

Michigan Atlas & Gazetteer Location: 32A3

County Location: Livingston

Directions To Trailhead:
South of Brighton on US23, exit Silver Lake Rd. west, then south on Whitmore Lake Rd. 500 ft to Winans Lake Rd., then west .5 mile to Rickett Rd., then north on Rickett Rd. 1 mile to Hammel Rd., then west to park entrance

Trail Type: Hiking/Walking, Cross Country Skiing
Trail Distance: 16+ mi   Loops: Many   Shortest: 1.5 mi Longest: 6.1
Trail Surface: Natural
Trail Use Fee: None, but vehicle entry fee required
Method Of Ski Trail Grooming: Track set
Skiing Ability Suggested: Novice to intermediate
Hiking Trail Difficulty: Easy
Mountain Biking Ability Suggested: NA
Terrain: Steep 0%, Hilly 25%, Moderate 50%, Flat 25%
Camping: None

Operated by the Huron-Clinton Metropolitan Authority.
Warming area, ski rentals and snack bar available.
Hiking and cross country ski trails overlap and are separate.
Mileage listed is total distance of both ski and hiking trails measured separately.
Some trails on the golf course.
Summer recreation includes golf course and picnic grounds.
Call or write for their Metropark Guide, published each year.

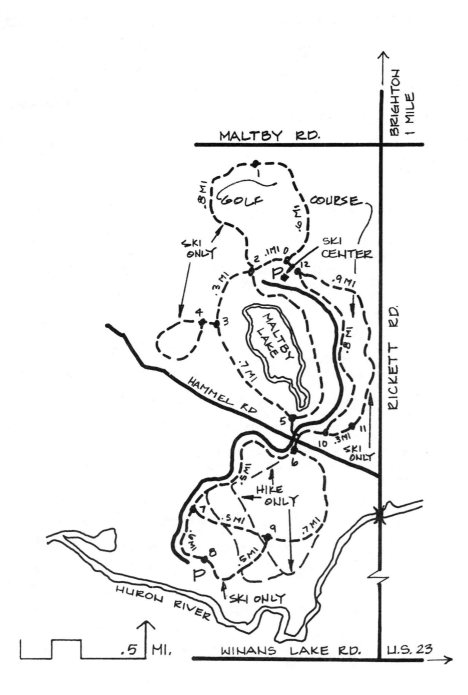

HURON MEADOWS METROPARK

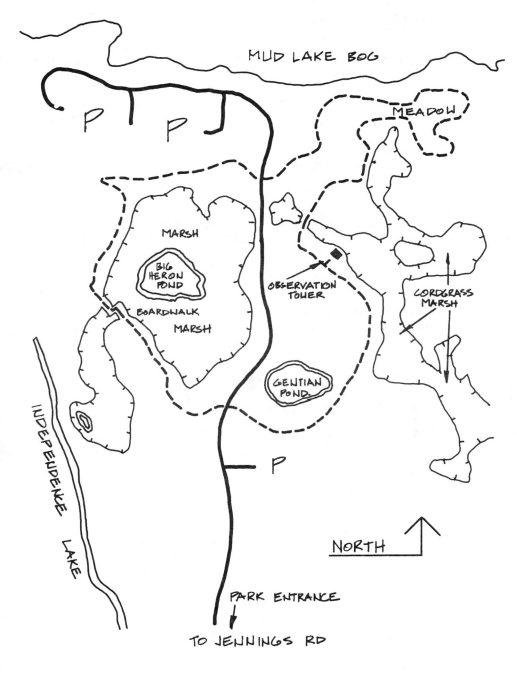

Independence Lake Park
3200 Jennings Rd.
Whitmore Lake, MI 48189

313-449-4437

Washtenaw County Parks and Recreation Commission
PO Box 8645
Ann Arbor, MI 48107

313-971-6337

Michigan Atlas & Gazetteer Location: 32A3

County Location: Washtenaw

Directions To Trailhead:
NW of Ann Arbor 2 miles west of US23 off Jennings Rd., 3 miles SW of Whitmore Lake

Trail Type: Hiking/Walking, Interpretive
Trail Distance: 1.3 mi   Loops: 1   Shortest: Longest: 1.3 mi
Trail Surface: Natural
Trail Use Fee: None, but an entrance fee is required
Method Of Ski Trail Grooming: None
Skiing Ability Suggested: Novice
Hiking Trail Difficulty: Easy to moderate
Mountain Biking Ability Suggested: NA
Terrain: Flat to rolling
Camping: None

Maintained by the Washtenaw County Parks and Recreation Commission
Restrooms available.
A nature area open only in the spring through fall seasons.
Pavilions available for rent.
Call ahead for park hours.

INDEPENDENCE LAKE PARK

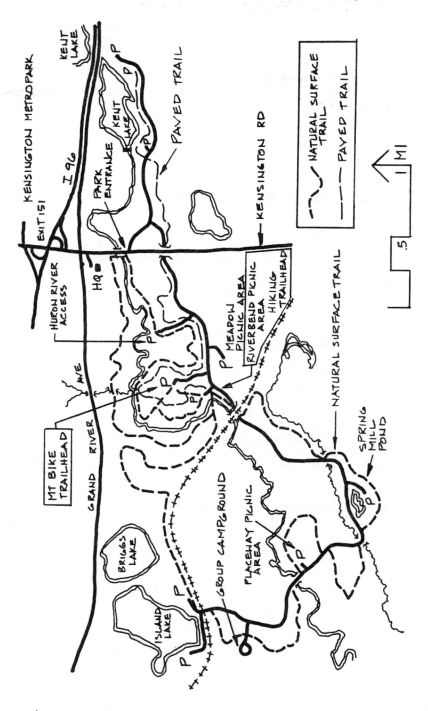

ISLAND LAKE RECREATION AREA

Island Lake Recreation Area
12950 East Grand River
Brighton , MI 48116

313-229-7067

DNR Parks and Recreation Division

517-373-1270

Michigan Atlas & Gazetteer Location: 32A4,40D4

County Location: Livingston

Directions To Trailhead:
West of Brighton on Grand River Ave to Kensington Rd., then south to the park entrance; or I-96 exit 151at Kensington Rd., then south to park entrance. Mountain bike trailhead is at a special designated trailhead between the Huron River access and Riverbend Picnic Area. Other trailheads at Riverbend and Placeway Picnic Areas.

Trail Type: Hiking/Walking, Cross Country Skiing, Mountain Biking
Trail Distance: 14 mi   Loops: 2   Shortest: 6 mi   Longest: 8 mi
Trail Surface: Natural
Trail Use Fee: None, but vehicle entry fee required
Method Of Ski Trail Grooming: None
Skiing Ability Suggested: Novice to intermediate
Hiking Trail Difficulty: Easy
Mountain Biking Ability Suggested: Novice to intermediate
Terrain: Steep 1%, Hilly 20%, Moderate 60%, Flat 19%
Camping: Rustic, semi modern and organized campgrounds avaiable

Maintained by the DNR Parks and Recreation Division
Picnic areas, swimming, group camping, canoe rental and rental cabins available.
The 7 miles of the Huron River within the park boundary is designated as "country scenic", under the Natural Rivers Act.
Adjacent to Kensington Metropark on the north.
The two main trail loops are popular mountain bike trails. Separate trailhead parking provided. Loops are one-way trails for mountain bikes which alternate periodically.
New paved accessible trail will be built (mileage not included above) in 1997.
Future plans call for it to be connected to the Kensington Metropark trail system.
Some snowmobile conflict on summer non-motorized trails.
Open to hunting - wear hunter orange during hunting season.

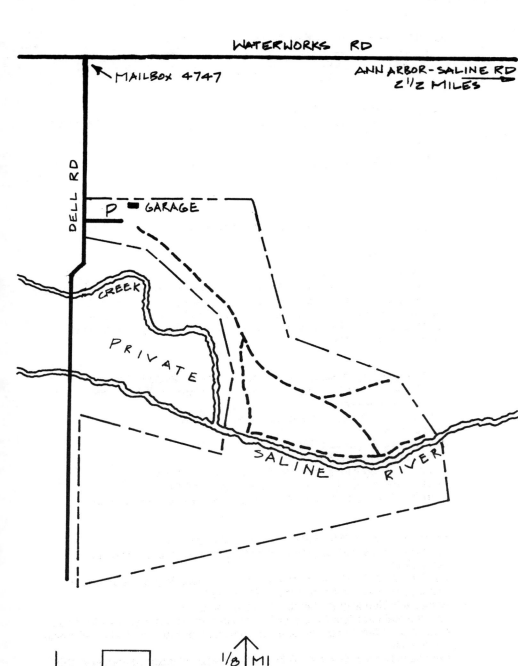

Michigan Nature Associaton
PO Box 102
Avoca, MI 48006

810-324-2626

Michigan Atlas & Gazetteer Location: 32C3

County Location: Washtenaw

Directions To Trailhead:
From Saline, take Ann Arbor -Saline Rd to the edge of town, then left (west) on
Saline Waterworks Rd. Go about 2 miles and turn left(south) on a long straight
drive marked with a mailbox 4747. Go about 500' south and take the fork to the
left. Park by the MNA storage building (garage).

Trail Type: Interpretive
Trail Distance: .5 mi   Loops: 1   Shortest: NA   Longest: .5 mi
Trail Surface: Natural
Trail Use Fee: None
Method Of Ski Trail Grooming: NA
Skiing Ability Suggested: NA
Hiking Trail Difficulty: Easy
Mountain Biking Ability Suggested: NA
Terrain: Steep 0%, Hilly 0%, Moderate 20%, Flat 80%
Camping: None

Maintained by the Michigan Nature Association
Mostly floodplain area of the Saline River for 750' on both sides of the river.

RODMAN MEMORIAL PLANT PRESERVE

Leslie Science Center
1831 Traver Rd.
Ann Arbor, MI 48105

313-662-7802

City of Ann Arbor, Department of Parks and Recreation
100 N. 5th Ave, POB 8647
Ann Arbor, MI 48107

313-994-2780

Michigan Atlas & Gazetteer Location: 32B4

County Location: Washtenaw

Directions To Trailhead:
In Ann Arbor next to the Leslie Golf Course on the northwest side of town.
From Plymouth Rd, northwest on Barton Dr. to Traver Rd, then northeast to the science center

Trail Type: Hiking/Walking, Interpretive
Trail Distance: 1.2 mi   Loops: 5   Shortest: .1 mi   Longest: .75 mi
Trail Surface: Natural
Trail Use Fee: None
Method Of Ski Trail Grooming: NA
Skiing Ability Suggested: NA
Hiking Trail Difficulty: Moderate plus
Mountain Biking Ability Suggested: NA
Terrain: Steep 0%, Hilly 30%, Moderate 65%, Flat 5%
Camping: None

Maintained by the City of Ann Arbor Department of Parks and Recreation
A nature center with emphasis on education of children. Many programs throughout the year. Operates an extensive summer camp program from mid-June through mid-August.
Trails not open to mountain biking or cross country skiing
Brochure and program materials available.

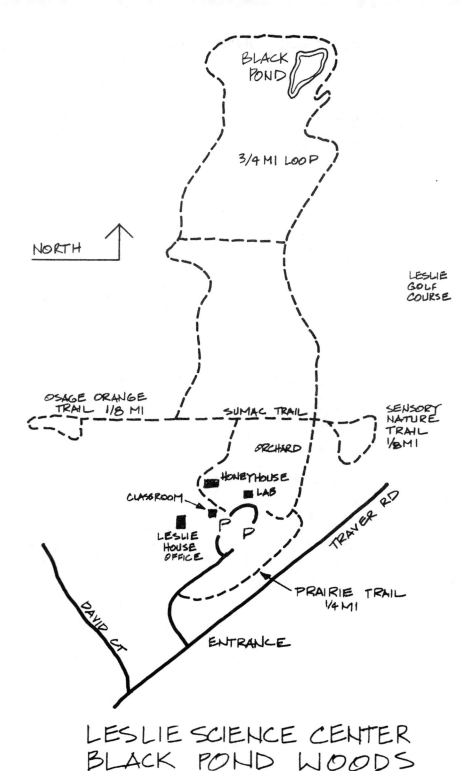

BLACK POND

3/4 MI LOOP

NORTH

LESLIE GOLF COURSE

OSAGE ORANGE TRAIL 1/8 MI

SUMAC TRAIL

SENSORY NATURE TRAIL 1/8 MI

ORCHARD

HONEYHOUSE
LAB

CLASSROOM

P P

LESLIE HOUSE OFFICE

TRAVER RD

PRAIRIE TRAIL 1/4 MI

DAVID CT

ENTRANCE

LESLIE SCIENCE CENTER BLACK POND WOODS

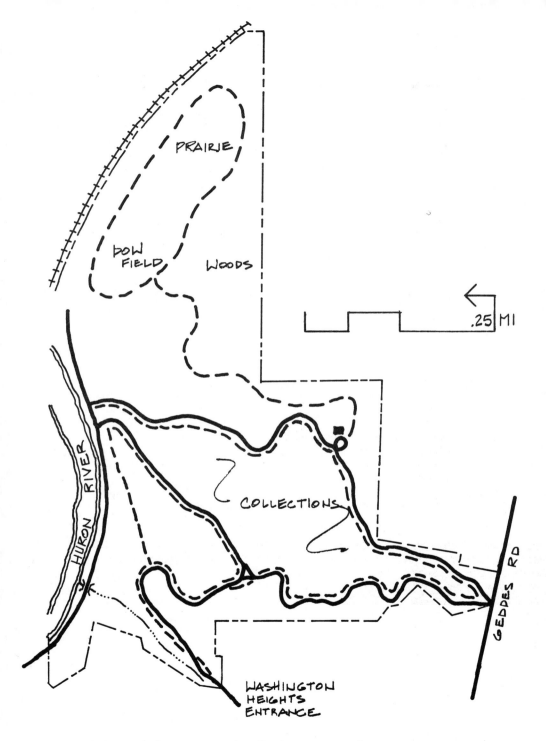

NICHOLS ARBORETUM

Nichols Arboretum

Nichols Arboretum
3012 D Dana, UM
Ann Arbor, MI 48109-1115

313-763-5823

Michigan Atlas & Gazetteer Location: 32B4

County Location: Washtenaw

Directions To Trailhead:
From I-94, take US23 north, then take Washtenaw Ave west , then right onto
Observatory St., then right onto East Medical Campus Drive to Hosipital lot M29.

Trail Type: Hiking/Walking, Cross Country Skiing, Interpretive
Trail Distance: 3.5 mi   Loops: 4   Shortest: .25 mi Longest: 2.5 mi
Trail Surface: Natural and gravel
Trail Use Fee: None
Method Of Ski Trail Grooming: None
Skiing Ability Suggested: Novice
Hiking Trail Difficulty: Easy to moderate
Mountain Biking Ability Suggested: NA
Terrain: Steep 20%, Hilly 25%, Moderate 30%, Flat 23%
Camping: None

Owned by the University of Michigan.
124 acres, 1/2 mile of the Huron River shoreline
Write for their brochure.

Washtenaw County Parks and Recreation Commission
PO Box 8645
Ann Arbor, MI 48107

313-971-6337

Michigan Atlas & Gazetteer Location: 32B3

County Location: Washtenaw

Directions To Trailhead:
Northwest of Ann Arbor on the Huron River on East Delhi Rd.
I-94 to Zeeb Rd, then north to Miller Rd, east on Miller to E. Delhi, then left on E. Delhi to trailhead on right side of the road.

Trail Type: Hiking/Walking, Interpretive
Trail Distance: 1.13 mi   Loops: NA   Shortest: NA   Longest: NA
Trail Surface: Natural
Trail Use Fee: None
Method Of Ski Trail Grooming: NA
Skiing Ability Suggested: NA
Hiking Trail Difficulty: Easy
Mountain Biking Ability Suggested: NA
Terrain: Steep 0%, Hilly 25%, Moderate 0%, Flat 75%
Camping: None

Maintained by Washtenaw County Parks and Recreation Commission
Point to point trail along the Huron River near the Delhi Metropark

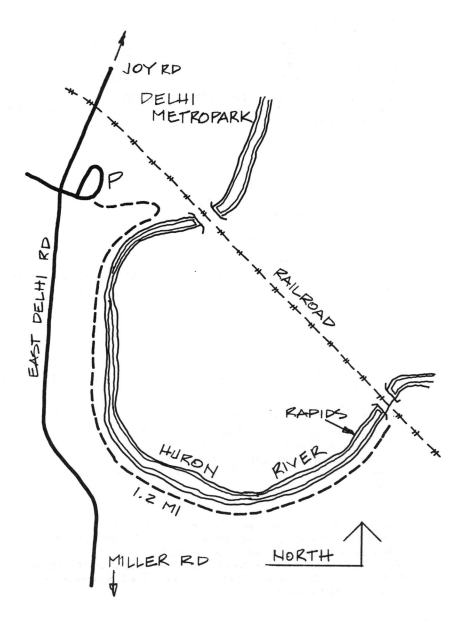

OSBORNE MILL PRESERVE
NATURE TRAIL

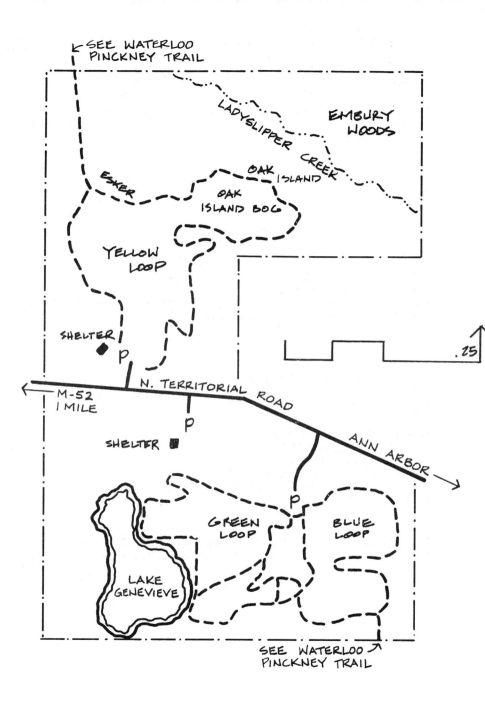

Washtenaw County Parks and Recreation Commission
PO Box 8645
Ann Arbor, MI 48107

313-971-6337

Michigan Atlas & Gazetteer Location: 32A1

County Location: Washtenaw

Directions To Trailhead:
5 miles north of Chelsea and northwest of Ann Arbor 1 mile east of M52 on
North Territorial Rd.

Trail Type: Hiking/Walking, Interpretive
Trail Distance: 2.75 mi   Loops: 3   Shortest: .75 mi Longest: 1.3 mi
Trail Surface: Natural
Trail Use Fee: None
Method Of Ski Trail Grooming: None
Skiing Ability Suggested: Intermediate to advanced
Hiking Trail Difficulty: Easy to moderate
Mountain Biking Ability Suggested: NA
Terrain: Steep 30%, Hilly 30%, Moderate 30%, Flat 10%
Camping: None

Maintained by the Washtenaw County Parks and Recreation Commission.
Restrooms, picnic grounds, restrooms, shelter and water available.
The 47 mile Waterloo-Pinckney Trail passes through this park.
Park Lyndon South contains the Embury Swamp Natural Area Preserve.
Naturalist available to lead walks for groups of 15 or more if advance
arrangements are made.

PARK LYNDON

TRAIL NOTES

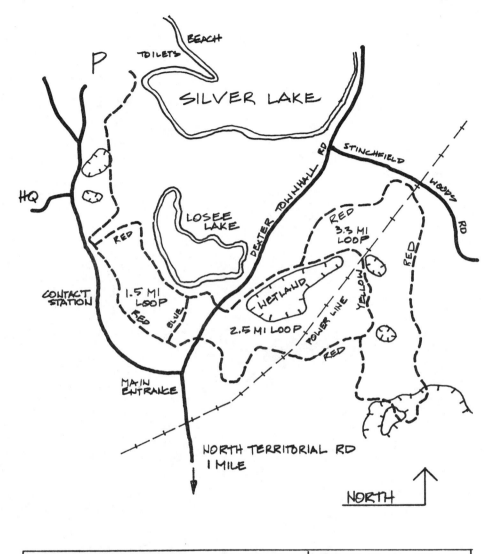

Pinckney Recreation Area
8555 Silver Hill Rd., Rte 1
Pinckney, MI 48169

313-426-4913

DNR Parks and Recreation Division

517-373-1270

Michigan Atlas & Gazetteer Location: 32A12

County Location: Livingston & Washtenaw

Directions To Trailhead:
15 miles NW of Ann Arbor at the Washtenaw/Livingston County line.
Trailhead - From US23 west on N. Territorial Rd. about 10 miles to Dexter-Townhall Rd., turn north for 1.2 miles to Silver Hill Rd., bear left to parking lot at Silver Lake Beach.

Trail Type: Hiking/Walking, Cross Country Skiing, Mountain Biking, Interpretive
Trail Distance: 30+ mi   Loops: 6   Shortest: 1.5   Longest: 17.5 mi
Trail Surface: Natural and geoweb
Trail Use Fee: None, but vehicle entry fee required
Method Of Ski Trail Grooming: None
Skiing Ability Suggested: Intermediate
Hiking Trail Difficulty: Easy to moderate
Mountain Biking Ability Suggested: Novice to advanced
Terrain: Steep 5%, Hilly 15%, Moderate 65%, Flat 15%
Camping: Campgrounds available in the recreation area

Maintained by the DNR Parks and Recreation Division
Complete 10,000 acre recreation area with camping, beaches, picnic areas and trails.
Mountain biking(one way travel) is permitted on the Potowawatomi, Silver Lake and Crooked Lake Trails.
Much of the trail maintenance on those trails is done by the Michigan Mountain Biking Association.
Camping is available throughout the year.
Mountain biking is not permitted on the Pinckney-Waterloo Hiking Trail west of the Potawatomi Trail or on the Losee Lake Hiking Trail.
The Potawatomi, is 17+ miles, Silver Lake is 2 miles, Crooked Lake is 3.5 miles and Losee Lake is 3.3 miles.

LOSEE LAKE HIKING TRAIL
PINCKNEY STATE RECREATION AREA

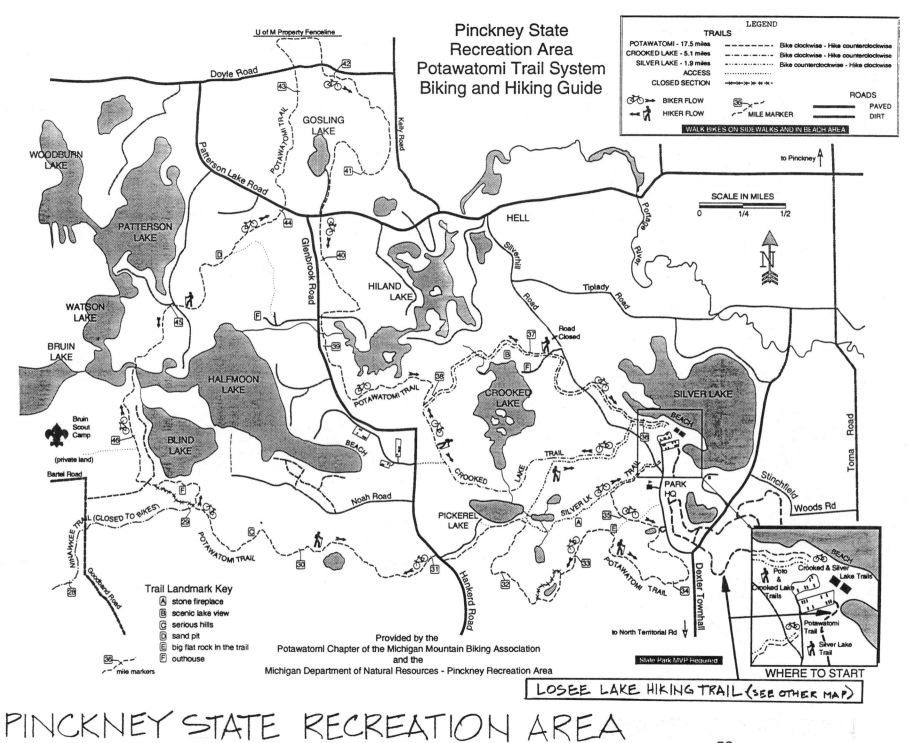

PINCKNEY STATE RECREATION AREA

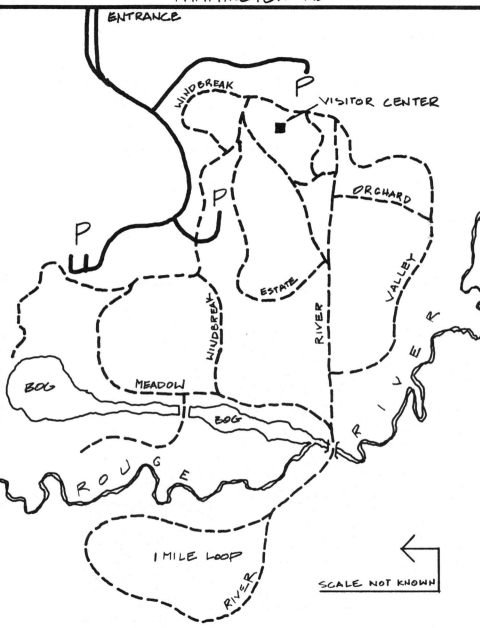

FARMINGTON RD

ENTRANCE

WINDBREAK

P

VISITOR CENTER

ORCHARD

P

P

ESTATE

WINDBREAK

RIVER

VALLEY

RIVER

BOG

MEADOW

BOG

ROUGE

RIVER

1 MILE LOOP

RIVER

SCALE NOT KNOWN

HERITAGE PARK

 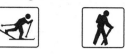

City of Farmington Hills
31555 11 Mile Rd.
Farmington Hills, MI 48018

810-473-9570

Michigan Atlas & Gazetteer Location: 33A6

County Location: Oakland

Directions To Trailhead:
Located on Farmington Rd between 10 and 11 Mile Rds in Farmington Hills

Trail Type: Hiking/Walking, Cross Country Skiing, Interpretive
Trail Distance: 3 mi   Loops: Many   Shortest: .5 mi   Longest: 1.5 mi
Trail Surface: Paved and natural
Trail Use Fee: None
Method Of Ski Trail Grooming: Track set
Skiing Ability Suggested: Novice to intermediate
Hiking Trail Difficulty: Easy
Mountain Biking Ability Suggested: NA
Terrain: Steep 0%, Hilly 0%, Moderate 50%, Flat 50%
Camping: None

Maintained by the City of Farmington Hills.
Year around 211 acre park with some paved trails.
Ski rental, warming area, sledding hill, hockey rink, and ice skating available.
Along the banks of the Rouge River.

Wayne County Divsion of Parks
33175 Ann Arbor Trail
Westland, MI 48170

313-261-1990

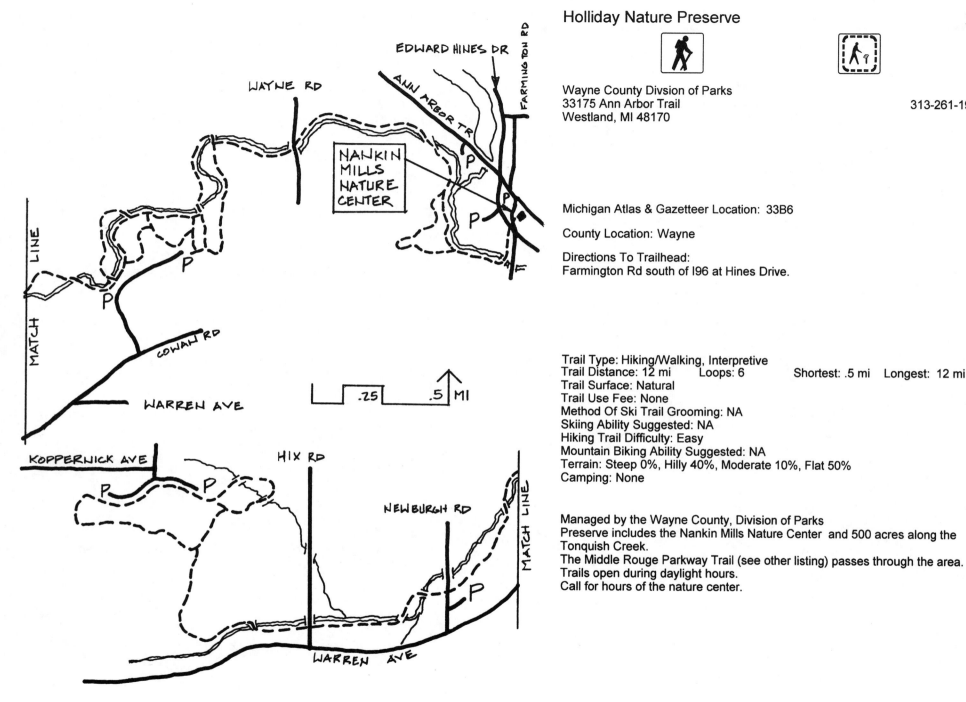

Michigan Atlas & Gazetteer Location: 33B6

County Location: Wayne

Directions To Trailhead:
Farmington Rd south of I96 at Hines Drive.

Trail Type: Hiking/Walking, Interpretive
Trail Distance: 12 mi   Loops: 6   Shortest: .5 mi   Longest: 12 mi
Trail Surface: Natural
Trail Use Fee: None
Method Of Ski Trail Grooming: NA
Skiing Ability Suggested: NA
Hiking Trail Difficulty: Easy
Mountain Biking Ability Suggested: NA
Terrain: Steep 0%, Hilly 40%, Moderate 10%, Flat 50%
Camping: None

Managed by the Wayne County, Division of Parks
Preserve includes the Nankin Mills Nature Center and 500 acres along the
Tonquish Creek.
The Middle Rouge Parkway Trail (see other listing) passes through the area.
Trails open during daylight hours.
Call for hours of the nature center.

HOLLIDAY NATURE PRESERVE

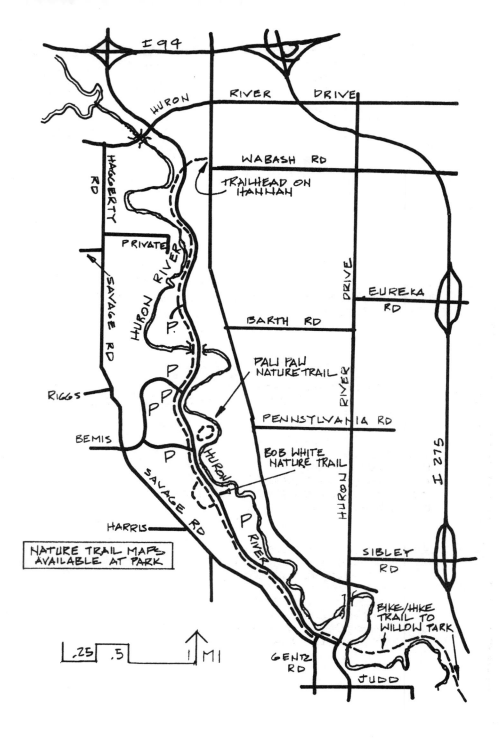

Huron Clinton Metropolitan Authority
13000 High Ridge Drive, PO Box 2001
Brighton, MI 48116

810-227-2757
800-47-PARKS

Michigan Atlas & Gazetteer Location: 33C6

County Location: Wayne

Directions To Trailhead:
Exit I-94 at Haggerty Rd exit south .5 mile to park entrance

Trail Type: Hiking/Walking, Cross Country Skiing, Interpretive
Trail Distance: 7+ mi   Loops: 2*   Shortest: NA*   Longest: NA*
Trail Surface: Paved and natural
Trail Use Fee: None, but vehicle entry fee required
Method Of Ski Trail Grooming: None
Skiing Ability Suggested: Novice
Hiking Trail Difficulty: Easy
Mountain Biking Ability Suggested: NA
Terrain: Steep 0%, Hilly 0%, Moderate 40%, Flat 60%
Camping: None

Operated by the Huron Clinton Metropolitan Authority
Pool, Par 3 golf, picnic areas and ball fields are available in this park.
* The main trail is bike-hike point to point trail.
There are also two loop nature trails in the park for short distances. The Bob White (18 station) and Paw Paw (16 station) Nature Trails.
Separate nature trail guides are available.
Call or write for their Metropark Guide, published each year.

LOWER HURON METROPARK

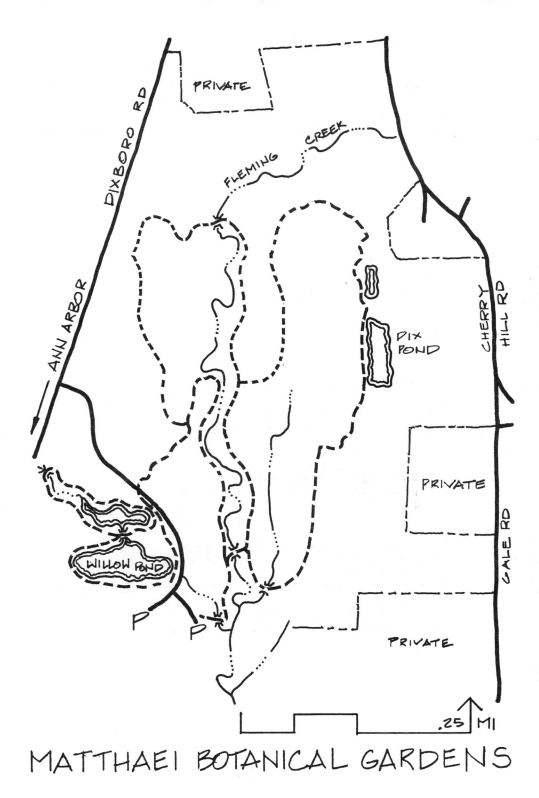

Matthaei Botanical Gardens
1800 N. Dixboro Rd
Ann Arbor, MI 48105

313-998-7061

Michigan Atlas & Gazetteer Location: 33B4

County Location: Washtenaw

Directions To Trailhead:
Exit US23 at the Plymounth Rd exit, then 1 mile east to Dixboro Rd, then south on Dixboro. Garden is .5 mile down
Dixboro/Plymouth Rd.

Trail Type: Hiking/Walking, Interpretive
Trail Distance: 3.6 mi   Loops: Several   Shortest: .6 mi   Longest: 1.8 mi
Trail Surface:
Trail Use Fee: None
Method Of Ski Trail Grooming: NA
Skiing Ability Suggested: NA
Hiking Trail Difficulty: Easy
Mountain Biking Ability Suggested: NA
Terrain: Steep 0%, Hilly 0%, Moderate 10%, Flat 90%
Camping: None

Owned by the University of Michigan
Including the trails, there is a conservatory , display gardens, shade garden, wildflower display and praire plantings
The four main trails are:
        Parker Brook Trail - .6 mile
        Musclewood Trail - .6 mile
        Fleming Creek Trail - 1.2 miles
        Dix Pond Trail - 1.8 miles

MATTHAEI BOTANICAL GARDENS

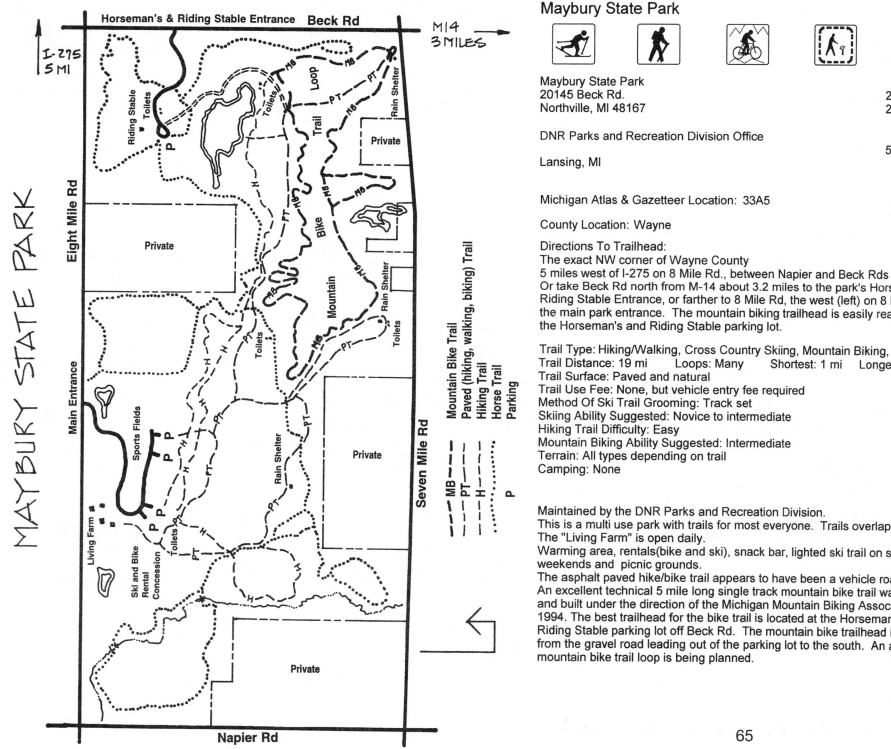

MAYBURY STATE PARK

Horseman's & Riding Stable Entrance Beck Rd

M14 3 MILES

I-275 5 MI

Eight Mile Rd

Main Entrance

Seven Mile Rd

Napier Rd

Riding Stable Toilets

Private

Private

Private

Private

Private

Sports Fields

Living Farm

Ski and Bike Rental Concession

Rain Shelter

Rain Shelter

Rain Shelter

Toilets

Toilets

Toilets

Toilets

Bike Mountain Trail Loop

MB — — — Mountain Bike Trail
PT — — — Paved (hiking, walking, biking) Trail
H — — — Hiking Trail
· · · · Horse Trail
P Parking

Maybury State Park

33

Maybury State Park
20145 Beck Rd.
Northville, MI 48167

248-349-8390
248-348-1190

DNR Parks and Recreation Division Office

Lansing, MI

517-373-1270

Michigan Atlas & Gazetteer Location: 33A5

County Location: Wayne

Directions To Trailhead:
The exact NW corner of Wayne County
5 miles west of I-275 on 8 Mile Rd., between Napier and Beck Rds
Or take Beck Rd north from M-14 about 3.2 miles to the park's Horseman's and Riding Stable Entrance, or farther to 8 Mile Rd, the west (left) on 8 Mile Rd to the main park entrance. The mountain biking trailhead is easily reached from the Horseman's and Riding Stable parking lot.

Trail Type: Hiking/Walking, Cross Country Skiing, Mountain Biking, Interpretive
Trail Distance: 19 mi   Loops: Many   Shortest: 1 mi   Longest: 8 mi
Trail Surface: Paved and natural
Trail Use Fee: None, but vehicle entry fee required
Method Of Ski Trail Grooming: Track set
Skiing Ability Suggested: Novice to intermediate
Hiking Trail Difficulty: Easy
Mountain Biking Ability Suggested: Intermediate
Terrain: All types depending on trail
Camping: None

Maintained by the DNR Parks and Recreation Division.
This is a multi use park with trails for most everyone. Trails overlap seasonally.
The "Living Farm" is open daily.
Warming area, rentals(bike and ski), snack bar, lighted ski trail on some weekends and picnic grounds.
The asphalt paved hike/bike trail appears to have been a vehicle road in the past
An excellent technical 5 mile long single track mountain bike trail was designed and built under the direction of the Michigan Mountain Biking Association in 1994. The best trailhead for the bike trail is located at the Horseman's and Riding Stable parking lot off Beck Rd. The mountain bike trailhead is accessed from the gravel road leading out of the parking lot to the south. An additional mountain bike trail loop is being planned.

Wayne County, Division of Parks
33175 Ann Arbor Trail
Westland, MI 48185

313-261-2034

Michigan Atlas & Gazetteer Location: 33AB67

County Location: Wayne

Directions To Trailhead:
From 7 Mile Rd in Northville to Ford Rd in Dearborn along the Rouge River and Edward Hines Drive

Trail Type: Hiking/Walking, Cross Country Skiing
Trail Distance: 17 mi   Loops: NA   Shortest: NA   Longest: NA
Trail Surface: Asphalt
Trail Use Fee: None
Method Of Ski Trail Grooming: None
Skiing Ability Suggested: Novice
Hiking Trail Difficulty: Easy
Mountain Biking Ability Suggested: NA
Terrain: Flat to slightly rolling
Camping: None

Maintained by the Wayne County, Division of Parks.
Currently under construction, to be completed in 1997.
Warren Valley Golf Course and Nankin Mills (see other listings) are along this trail.
Many recreation areas all along this trail.

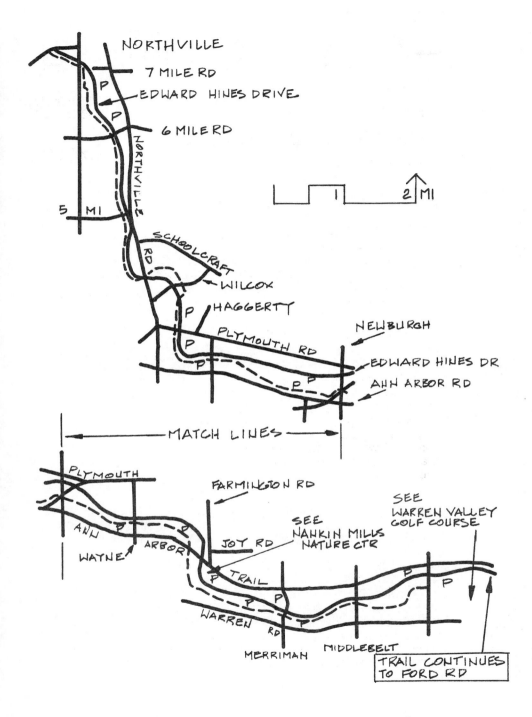

MIDDLE ROUGE PARKWAY

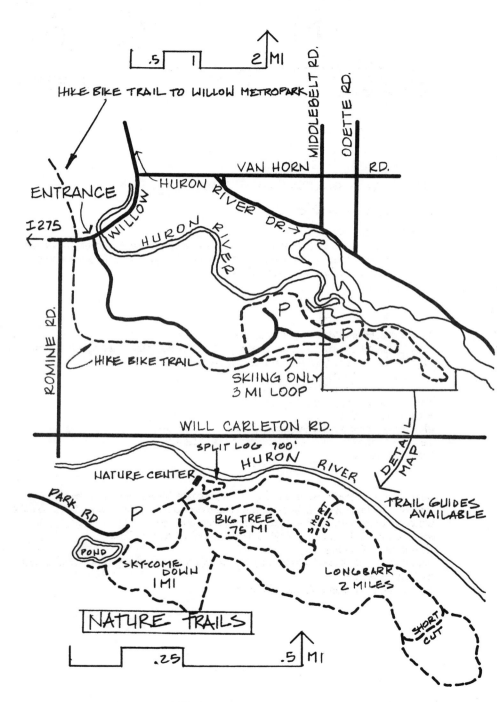

HIKE BIKE TRAIL TO WILLOW METROPARK

.5 | 1 | 2 MI

VAN HORN RD.

MIDDLEBELT RD.

ODETTE RD.

ENTRANCE

HURON RIVER DR. →

HURON RIVER

WILLOW

I 275

ROMINE RD.

HIKE BIKE TRAIL

SKIING ONLY
3 MI LOOP

WILL CARLETON RD.

DETAIL MAP

SPLIT LOG 700'

HURON RIVER

NATURE CENTER

PARK RD

P

POND

SKY-COME DOWN 1 MI

BIG TREE .75 MI

KNOLL .5 MI

LONGBARK 2 MILES

SHORT CUT

TRAIL GUIDES AVAILABLE

NATURE TRAILS

.25 | .5 MI

OAKWOODS METROPARK

Oakwoods Metropark

Oakwoods Metropark
PO Box 332
Flat Rock, MI 48134

313-697-9181
800-47-PARKS

Huron-Clinton Metropolitan Authority
13000 High Ridge Drive, PO Box 2001
Brighton, MI 48116-8001

810-227-2757

Michigan Atlas & Gazetteer Location: 33D7

County Location: Wayne

Directions To Trailhead:
From I-275 exit 11 at S. Huron, west to Bell Rd., south to Willow, east on Willow Rd .75 mile to the park (past the entrance to Willow Metropark)

Trail Type: Hiking/Walking, Cross Country Skiing, Interpretive
Trail Distance: 4 mi   Loops: 5   Shortest: .25 mi Longest: 3 mi
Trail Surface: Natural
Trail Use Fee: None, but vehicle entry fee required
Method Of Ski Trail Grooming: Track set
Skiing Ability Suggested: Novice
Hiking Trail Difficulty: Easy
Mountain Biking Ability Suggested: NA
Terrain: Steep 0%, Hilly 0%, Moderate 30%, Flat 70%
Camping: None

Operated by the Huron-Clinton Metropolitan Authority
Warming area, picnic grounds, nature center and nature study area available.
The nature center has 4 separate nature trails with separate trail guides available.
Hiking and nature trails are different then the ski trail.
The 700' long Splitlog trail is paved for handicappers.
Hike/Bike trail connects to Willow and Lower Huron Metroparks (see other listings).
Call or write for their Metropark Guide, published each year.

Wastenaw County Parks and Recreation Commission
PO Box 8645
Ann Arbor, MI 48107

313-971-6337

Michigan Atlas & Gazetteer Location: 33BC4

County Location: Washtenaw

Directions To Trailhead:
Between Ann Arbor and Ypsilanti along the Huron River and immediately east of
US 23. Parking lots available on Dixboro Rd at Gallup Park connector and on
Geddes Rd at the Fleming Creek Bridge

Trail Type: Hiking/Walking, Interpretive
Trail Distance: 2+ mi   Loops: many   Shortest: short   Longest: 1.1 mi
Trail Surface: Paved, wood, crushed stone & natural
Trail Use Fee: None
Method Of Ski Trail Grooming: None
Skiing Ability Suggested: Novice
Hiking Trail Difficulty: Easy
Mountain Biking Ability Suggested: NA
Terrain: Steep 0%, Hilly 0%, Moderate 0%, Flat 100%
Camping: None

Maintained by the Washtenaw County Parks and Recreation Commission
Intensively developed 45 acre park containing walking trails, nature trails, wildlife
blind, historic mills, visitior center, restrooms and more.
Includes the 1.1 mile long Hoyt G. Post Memorial Nature Trail.
Connects to Gallup Park.
Handicapper facilities include parking, restrooms, picnicking, boardwalk nature
trail and grist mill.
Additional improvements are planned.

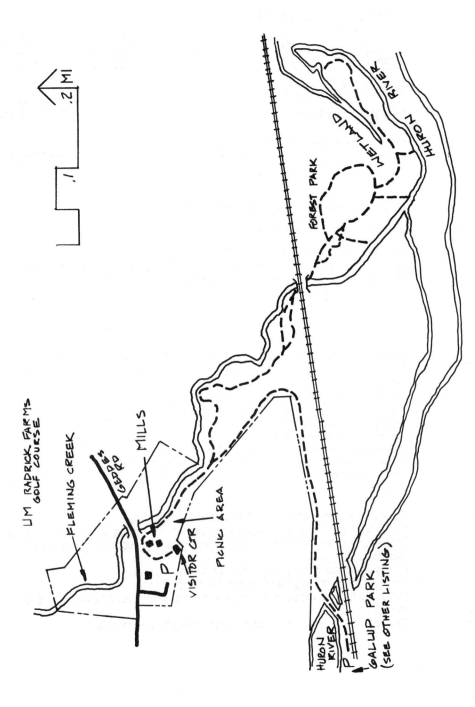

PARKER MILL PARK

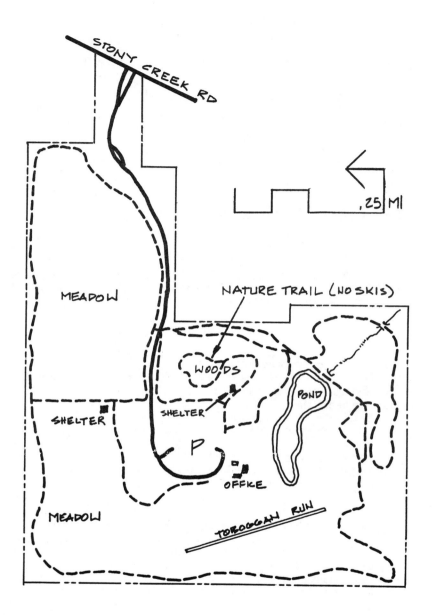

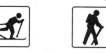

Rolling Hills County Park
7660 Stony Creek Rd.
Ypsilanti, MI 48197

313-484-3870

Washtenaw County Parks and Recrecation Commission
PO Box 8645
Ann Arbor, MI 48107

313-971-6337

Michigan Atlas & Gazetteer Location: 33C4

County Location: Washtenaw

Directions To Trailhead:
From I-94, use the Huron Street exit (183) and proceed south to Stony Creek Rd., then turn right and go 5 miles on Stony Creek Road. The park entrance is on the right side of the road. The entrance is .5 mile north of Bemis Road. Follow brown park directional signs.

Trail Type: Hiking/Walking, Cross Country Skiing, Interpretive
Trail Distance: 3 mi   Loops: Several   Shortest: .5 mi   Longest: 3 mi
Trail Surface: Gravel and natural
Trail Use Fee: None, but entrance fee required
Method Of Ski Trail Grooming: Track set
Skiing Ability Suggested: Novice to intermediate
Hiking Trail Difficulty: Easy
Mountain Biking Ability Suggested: NA
Terrain: Flat to rolling
Camping: None

Maintained by the Washtenaw County Parks and Recreation Commission
Ski rentals, tobboggan rentals, tobboggan run, lighted ski trails, ice skating, warming shelter, picnic area, water park, fishing pond, ball fields and much more make for a complete year-around recreational facility.
Skiing permitted on all trails except the nature trail (.5 mile)

ROLLING HILLS
COUNTY PARK

Washtenaw Audubon Society
1733 Jackson Ave
Ann Arbor, MI 48103

313-994-3569
313-994-6287

Michigan Atlas & Gazetteer Location: 33C4

County Location: Washtenaw

Directions To Trailhead:
Take US23 south from Ann Arbor to Willis Rd exit 31, then east about 1.25 miles, then continue east on Bolla Rd due east as Willis turns south, continue east .4 miles on Willis to the Preserve. Gate and sign designate the entrance.

Trail Type: Hiking/Walking, Cross Country Skiing, Interpretive
Trail Distance: 1 mi   Loops: Shortest: Longest:
Trail Surface: Natural
Trail Use Fee: None
Method Of Ski Trail Grooming: None
Skiing Ability Suggested: Novice
Hiking Trail Difficulty: Easy
Mountain Biking Ability Suggested: NA
Terrain: Steep 0%, Hilly 0%, Moderate 30%, Flat 70%
Camping: Camgground about 4 miles north.

Owned by the Washtenaw Audubon Society.
A 50 parcel that is full of plants and yes, birds.
Trails are not marked but are easy to locate.

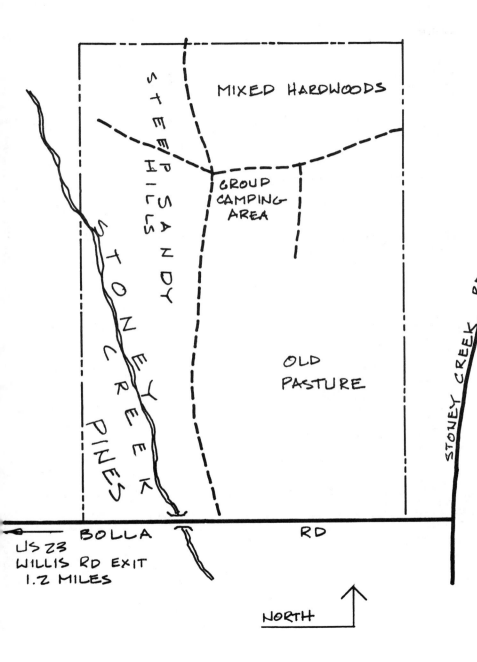

SEARLES AUDUBON NATURE PRESERVE

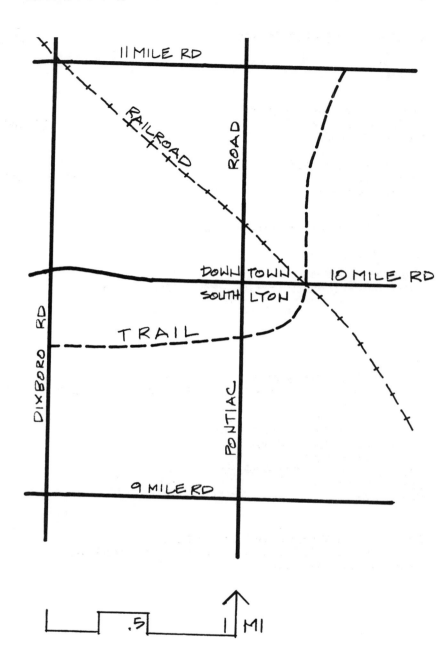

City of South Lyon
214 West Lake St.
South Lyon, MI 48178

810-437-1735

Michigan Atlas & Gazetteer Location: 33A4

County Location: Oakland

Directions To Trailhead:
In the City of South Lyon, from Dixboro on the southwest to 11 Mile Rd on the northeast

Trail Type: Hiking/Walking, Cross Country Skiing
Trail Distance: 2.7 mi   Loops: NA   Shortest: NA   Longest: NA
Trail Surface: Paved
Trail Use Fee: None
Method Of Ski Trail Grooming: None
Skiing Ability Suggested: Novice
Hiking Trail Difficulty: Easy
Mountain Biking Ability Suggested: NA
Terrain: 100%Flat
Camping: None

Owned by the City of South Lyon

SOUTH LYON RAILTRAIL

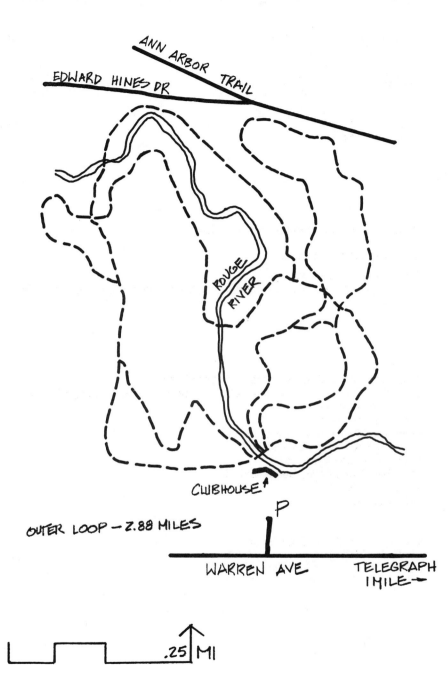

ANN ARBOR TRAIL

EDWARD HINES DR

ROUGE RIVER

CLUBHOUSE

P

OUTER LOOP — 2.88 MILES

WARREN AVE

TELEGRAPH
1 MILE →

.25 MI

WARREN VALLEY GOLF COURSE

Wayne County, Division of Parks
33175 Ann Arbor Trail
Westland, MI 48135

313-261-1990

Warren Valley Golf Course
26116 West Warren
Dearborn, MI 48127

313-561-1040

Michigan Atlas & Gazetteer Location: 33B7

County Location: Wayne

Directions To Trailhead:
In Dearborn Heights on Warren Rd. just east of Beech Daly Rd.

Trail Type: Cross Country Skiing
Trail Distance: 5 mi   Loops: Many   Shortest: Longest:
Trail Surface: Natural
Trail Use Fee: None
Method Of Ski Trail Grooming: Track set
Skiing Ability Suggested: Novice
Hiking Trail Difficulty: NA
Mountain Biking Ability Suggested: NA
Terrain: Flat to rolling
Camping: None

Operated by the Wayne County, Division of Parks
Warming area, rentals, lessons, restaurant, lounge and snack bar.
All trails are on a golf course.

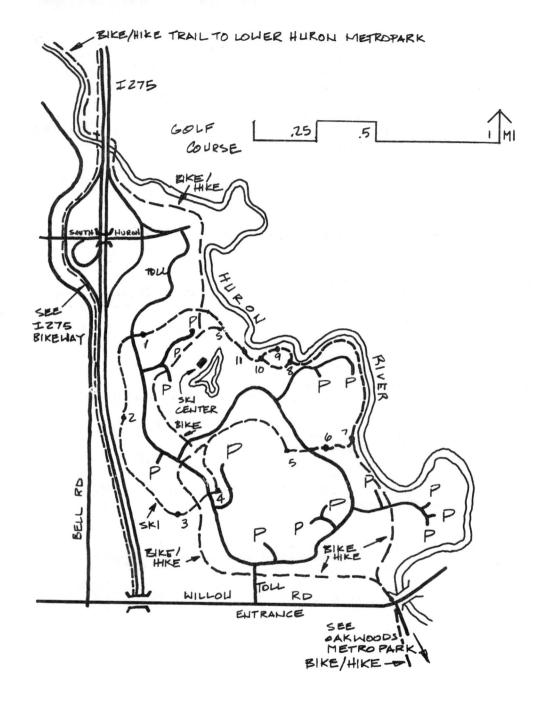

Willow Metropark
17845 Savage Rd.
Belleville, MI 48111

313-697-9181
800-47-PARKS

Huron-Clinton Metropolitan Authority
13000 High Ridge Drive, PO Box 2001
Brighton, MI 48116-8001

810-227-2757

Michigan Atlas & Gazetteer Location: 33D7

County Location: Wayne

Directions To Trailhead:
Off I-275 south of I-94 interchange at South Huron Rd exit.

Trail Type: Hiking/Walking, Cross Country Skiing
Trail Distance: 8.3* mi   Loops: 3*   Shortest: NA   Longest: 4.5* mi
Trail Surface: Natural
Trail Use Fee: None, but vehicle entry fee required.
Method Of Ski Trail Grooming: Track set when snow depth permits
Skiing Ability Suggested: Novice
Hiking Trail Difficulty: Easy
Mountain Biking Ability Suggested: NA
Terrain: Steep 0%, Hilly 10%, Moderate 35%, Flat 55%
Camping: None

Operated by the Huron-Clinton Metropolitan Authority.
Warming area, sledding hill, picnic grounds, ski rentals and snack bar.
Bike/hike trail connects Willow with Oakwoods and Lower Huron Metroparks.
(*) Trail lengths - Separate trails for winter and summer
    Hike/bike trail is about 4.5 miles long (two loops)
    Ski trail is about 3.8 miles long.
Call or write for their Metropark Guide, published each year.

WILLOW METROPARK

U of M, Natural Areas Department
4901 Evergreen
Dearborn, MI 48128

313-593-5338

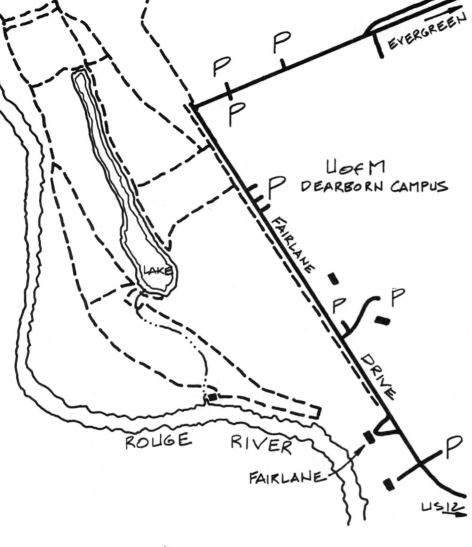

Michigan Atlas & Gazetteer Location: 34B1

County Location: Wayne

Directions To Trailhead:
Adjacent to Fairlane Manor in the University of Michigan - Dearborn Campus. Also near Fairlane Mall and Greenfield Village. North of Michigan Ave off Monteith Blvd via Evergreen Rd or Fairlane Drive.

Trail Type: Hiking/Walking, Interpretive
Trail Distance: 5 mi   Loops: Many   Shortest: .25 mi Longest: 2 mi
Trail Surface: Paved and natural
Trail Use Fee: None
Method Of Ski Trail Grooming: NA
Skiing Ability Suggested: NA
Hiking Trail Difficulty: Easy
Mountain Biking Ability Suggested: NA
Terrain: Steep 0%, Hilly 0%, Moderate 5%, Flat 95%
Camping: None

Owned by the University of Michigan - Dearborn Campus
This natural area is the grounds of the Henry Ford estate home on the Rouge River.
NO motor vehicles, bicycles, jogging, swimming, fishing, pets or picnicking.
Call or write for brochure.

UNIVERSITY of MICHIGAN
DEARBORN ENVIRONMENTAL STUDY AREA

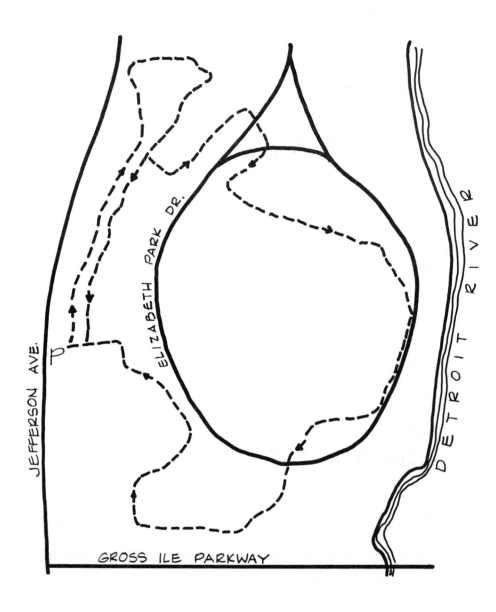

JEFFERSON AVE.

ELIZABETH PARK DR.

DETROIT RIVER

GROSS ILE PARKWAY

NO SCALE

ELIZABETH PARK

Elizabeth Park

Wayne County , Division of Parks
33175 Ann Arbor Trail
Westland, MI 48135

313-261-1990

Elizabeth Park
4250 Elizabeth Park Drive
Trenton, MI 48183

313-675-8037

Michigan Atlas & Gazetteer Location: 34C1

County Location: Wayne

Directions To Trailhead:
I-75 to eastbound West Rd., then 3.5 miles to southbound Jefferson, then to 3873 W. Jefferson.
Trailhead is at the first recreation building on the left side past Solcum St.

Trail Type: Hiking/Walking, Cross Country Skiing
Trail Distance: 2 mi   Loops: 1   Shortest: Longest:
Trail Surface: Natural
Trail Use Fee: None
Method Of Ski Trail Grooming: None
Skiing Ability Suggested: Novice
Hiking Trail Difficulty: Easy
Mountain Biking Ability Suggested: NA
Terrain: Steep 0%, Hilly 0%, Moderate 40%, Flat 60%
Camping: None

Operated by the Wayne County Department of Parks and Recreation
Scenic views of the Detroit River from along the trail.

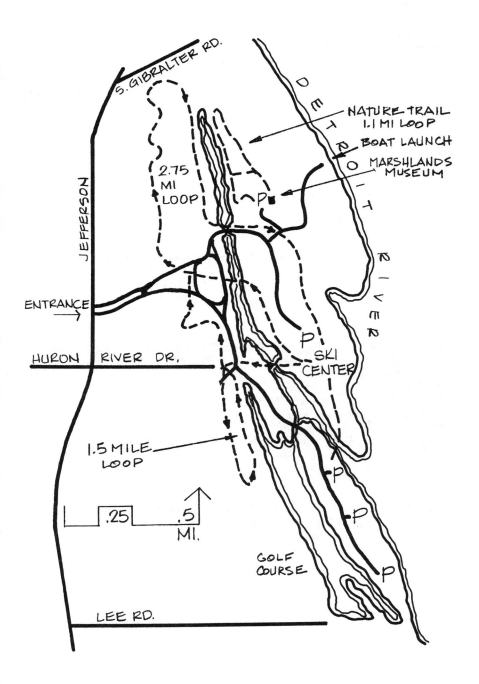

ENTRANCE →

HURON RIVER DR.

S. GIBRALTER RD.

JEFFERSON

DETROIT RIVER

NATURE TRAIL 1.1 MI LOOP

BOAT LAUNCH

MARSHLANDS MUSEUM

2.75 MI LOOP

P

SKI CENTER

1.5 MILE LOOP

P

P

P

P

.25   .5
MI.

GOLF COURSE

LEE RD.

LAKE ERIE METROPARK

Lake Erie Metropark
32481 West Jefferson, PO Box 120
Rockwood , MI 48173

313-379-5020
800-24-PARKS

Huron-Clinton Metropolitan Authority
13000 High Ridge Drive, PO Box 2001
Brighton, MI 48116-8001

810-227-2757

Michigan Atlas & Gazetteer Location: 34D1

County Location: Wayne

Directions To Trailhead:
South of Gibraltar on Jefferson Ave along the shore of Lake Erie. Just north of Huron River Drive east of Jefferson Ave

Trail Type: Cross Country Skiing, Interpretive
Trail Distance: 6 mi   Loops: 2   Shortest: 1.25 mi Longest: 2.75 mi
Trail Surface: Natural
Trail Use Fee: None, but vehicle entry fee required
Method Of Ski Trail Grooming: Track set
Skiing Ability Suggested: Novice
Hiking Trail Difficulty: NA
Mountain Biking Ability Suggested: NA
Terrain: Steep 0%, Hilly 0%, Moderate 20%, Flat 80%
Camping: None

Operated by the Huron-Clinton Metropolitan Authority.
Nature trail is 1.25 miles long
Marshlands Museum is connected to the nature trails.
Ski rentals and snack bar available.
Great Wave Pool, picnic area, golf course and a marina are in the park.
Call or write for the Metropark Guide, published each year.

Albert C. Keppel Forest Preserve

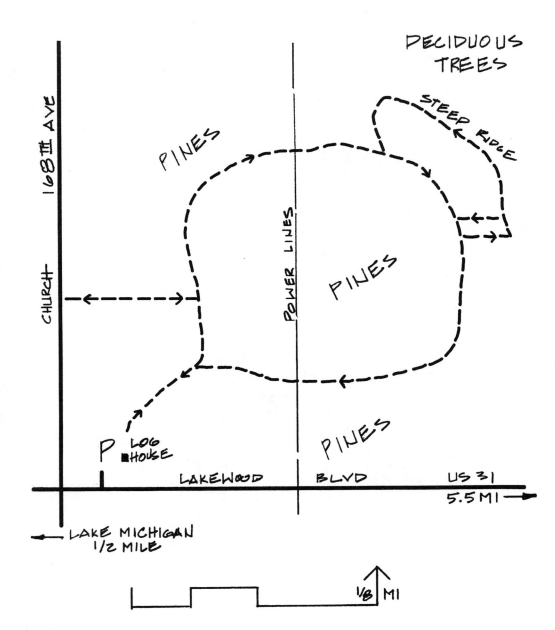

DECIDUOUS TREES

STEEP RIDGE

PINES

168TH AVE

CHURCH

POWER LINES

PINES

PINES

PINES

P LOG HOUSE

LAKEWOOD BLVD US 31

5.5 MI →

LAKE MICHIGAN 1/2 MILE

1/8 MI

Park Township
52 152nd Ave
Holland, MI 49424

616-399-4520

Michigan Atlas & Gazetteer Location: 35B5

County Location: Ottawa

Directions To Trailhead:
Northwest of Holland. From Holland go north to Lakewood Blvd, then west 4 miles to parking lot.

Trail Type: Hiking/Walking, Cross Country Skiing, Mountain Biking, Interpretive
Trail Distance: 1.5 mi   Loops: 2   Shortest: Longest:
Trail Surface: Natural
Trail Use Fee: None
Method Of Ski Trail Grooming: None
Skiing Ability Suggested: Novice
Hiking Trail Difficulty: Easy
Mountain Biking Ability Suggested: Novice
Terrain: Steep 0%, Hilly 0%, Moderate 10%, Flat 90%
Camping: Holland State Park nearby

Owned by Park Township
A small 40 acre park with limited trail opportunities.
No motorized vehicles permitted.

ALBERT C KEPPEL FOREST PRESERVE

TRAIL NOTES

Allegan State Game Area
4590 118th Ave
Allegan, MI 49010

616-673-2430
616-788-5055

DNR Wildlife Division

517-373-1263

Michigan Atlas & Gazetteer Location: 35D67

County Location: Allegan

Directions To Trailhead:
Headquarters is 7 miles west of Allegan on Monroe Rd. (118th Ave)

Trail Type: Hiking/Walking, Cross Country Skiing, Mountain Biking, Interpretive
Trail Distance: 30+ mi   Loops: Many   Shortest: 2.5 mi Longest: 14 mi
Trail Surface: Natural
Trail Use Fee: None
Method Of Ski Trail Grooming: None
Skiing Ability Suggested: Novice to intermediate
Hiking Trail Difficulty: Easy
Mountain Biking Ability Suggested: Novice to intermediate
Terrain: Steep 0%, Hilly 1%, Moderate 9%, Flat 90%
Camping: Campground available on the east side of Swan Creek Pond

Maintained by the DNR Wildlife Division.
Trail specifications are for the ski/mountain biking trail system.
Skiing not permitted until January 1st. Ski trails and hiking trails are not all identical.
The trails are well marked.
Cross country ski trailhead is located 1/10 mile north of 118th Ave. on 46th St.
Swan Creek Foot Trail is not suitable for skiing or mountain biking.
        Terrian:Hilly 5%, Moderate 15%, and Flat 80%.
        Trailhead: The parking area north of Swan Creek Pond and just west of the dam.
The Northwest Trail and the Cross Country Foot Trail are not open to mountain bikes.
Trail users are the guests of hunters. Wear bright clothing during the hunting season .

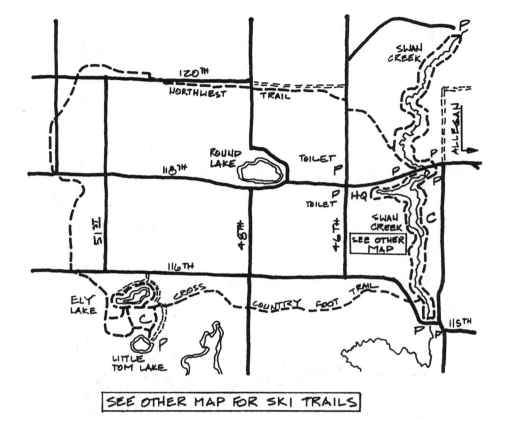

FOOT TRAILS
ALLEGAN STATE GAME AREA

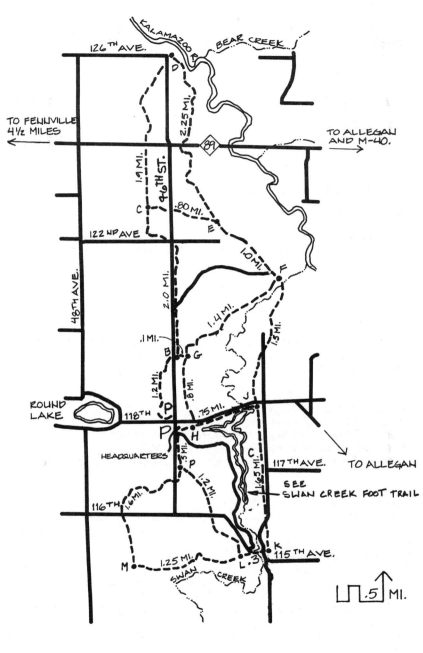

CROSS COUNTRY SKI TRAIL
ALLEGAN
STATE GAME AREA

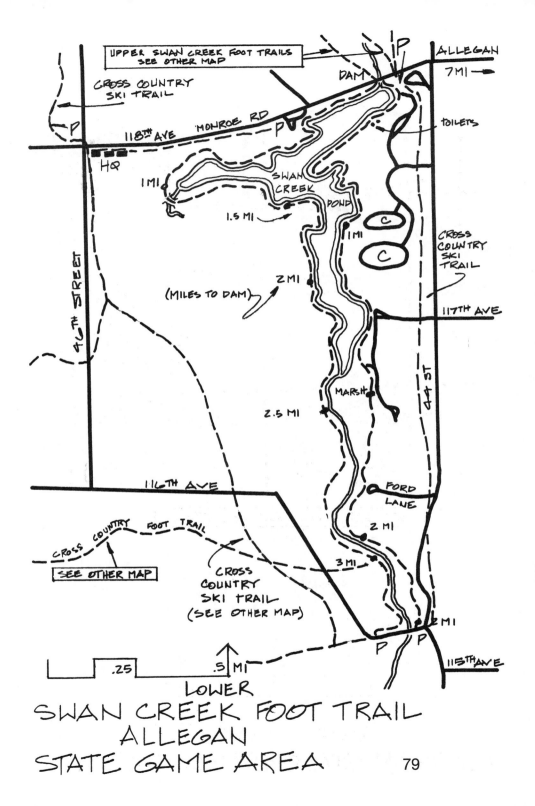

SWAN CREEK FOOT TRAIL
ALLEGAN
STATE GAME AREA

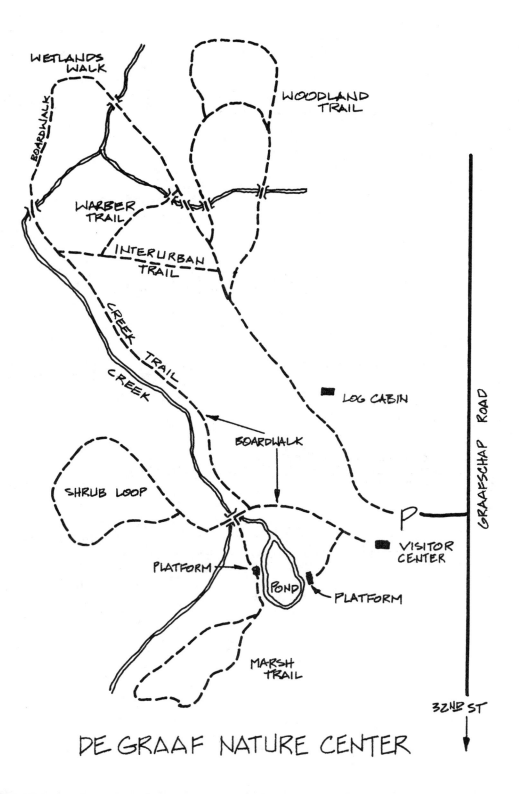

WETLANDS WALK

WOODLAND TRAIL

BOARDWALK

WARBER TRAIL

INTERURBAN TRAIL

CREEK TRAIL

CREEK

LOG CABIN

BOARDWALK

SHRUB LOOP

PLATFORM

POND

PLATFORM

MARSH TRAIL

GRAAFSCHAP ROAD

VISITOR CENTER

32ND ST

DE GRAAF NATURE CENTER

De Graaf Nature Center
600 Graafschap Rd
Holland, Mi 49423-4549

616-396-2739

City Of Holland, Cultural & Leisure Serivces Dept
150 West 8th St
Holland, MI 49423

616-392-9044

Michigan Atlas & Gazetteer Location: 35B5

County Location: Ottawa

Directions To Trailhead:
In Holland, from US31, take 32nd St west about 2.6 miles to Graafschap Rd.,
then north(right) to nature center about .2 mile on Graafschap Rd to the nature
center.
Or from US 31 take 16th St. west to the end, then continue on South Shore Dr.
about 3 miles to Graafschap Rd., then south to the nature center.

Trail Type: Hiking/Walking, Cross Country Skiing, Interpretive
Trail Distance: 1.5 mi   Loops: Several   Shortest: Longest:
Trail Surface: Paved and natural
Trail Use Fee: None
Method Of Ski Trail Grooming: Not known
Skiing Ability Suggested: Novice
Hiking Trail Difficulty: Easy
Mountain Biking Ability Suggested: NA
Terrain: Steep 0%, Hilly 0%, Moderate 15%, Flat %85%
Camping: None

Maintained by the City of Holland, Cultural and Leisure Services Department.
This small 15 acre nature center is located within the city limits.
A 26 station nature trail is provided and trail guide is available.
Nature center building at trailhead.
Many activities take place at the nature center.

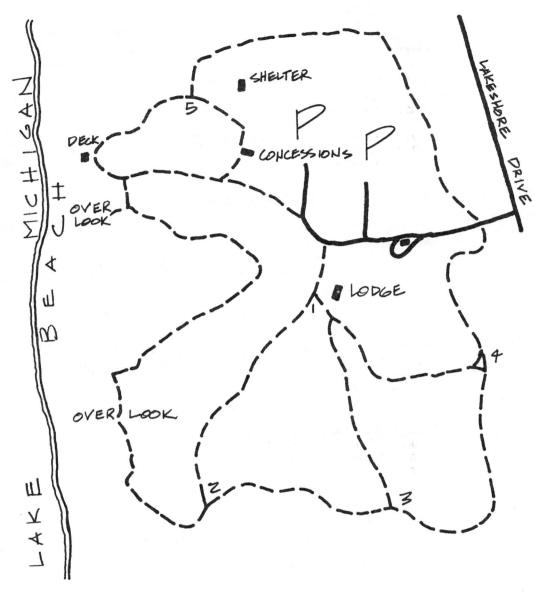

Kirk Park

Ottawa County Parks and Recreation Commission
414 Washington St   616-846-8117
Grand Haven, MI 49417

Michigan Atlas & Gazetteer Location: 35A5

County Location: Ottawa

Directions To Trailhead:
Take US31 south of Grand Haven for 8 miles to Stanton Rd, then west 2 miles
to Lakeshore Drive, then north .5 miles to the park entrance

Trail Type: Hiking/Walking, Cross Country Skiing
Trail Distance: 2 mi   Loops: 3   Shortest: .4 mi   Longest: 1 mi
Trail Surface: Natural
Trail Use Fee: None
Method Of Ski Trail Grooming: None
Skiing Ability Suggested: Intermediate t o advanced
Hiking Trail Difficulty: Moderate
Mountain Biking Ability Suggested: NA
Terrain: Steep 10%, Hilly 40%, Moderate 20%, Flat 30%
Camping: None

Owned by the Ottawa County Parks and Recreation Commission
This area is a sensitive primary dune area with overlooks and established trails.
Help preserve this enviornment by not leaving these trails.
Trails designed for hiking an cross country skiing only.

LITTLEJOHN LAKE COUNTY PARK

Map

113TH AVE

ALLEGAN 1 MILE →

EAST DRIVE

WEST DRIVE

WETLAND

.5 MILE TRAIL

PAVILION

P

STREAM

LITTLEJOHN LAKE

NORTH ↑

Allegan Country Parks and Recreation Commission
108 Chestnut Street
Allegan, MI 49010

616-673-0376

Michigan Atlas & Gazetteer Location: 35D7

County Location: Allegan

Directions To Trailhead:
Take M40 south from Allegan, then west on Thomas St, then south on Ely St, then just past 34th St is the park entrance. The trailhead is just south of the volleyball court

Trail Type: Hiking/Walking
Trail Distance: .5 mi   Loops: 1   Shortest: NA   Longest: .5 mi
Trail Surface: Natural
Trail Use Fee: None
Method Of Ski Trail Grooming: None
Skiing Ability Suggested: Novice
Hiking Trail Difficulty: Easy
Mountain Biking Ability Suggested: NA
Terrain: Not known
Camping: None

Maintained by the Allegan County Parks and Recreation Commission
Small county park just outside Allegan.

Pigeon Creek Park

Ottawa County Parks and Recreation Commission
414 Washington St.
Grand Haven, MI 49417

616-846-8117

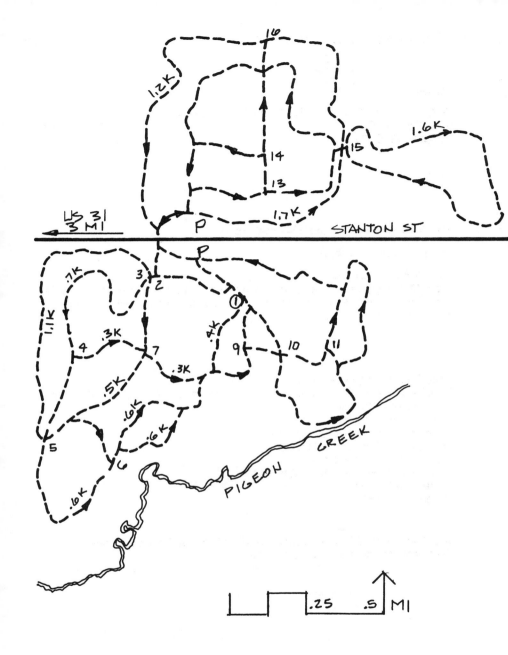

Michigan Atlas & Gazetteer Location: 35A6

County Location: Ottawa

Directions To Trailhead:
Take US31 south of Grand Haven 8 miles to Stanton Rd, then east 3 miles to the park.

Trail Type: Hiking/Walking, Cross Country Skiing, Mountain Biking
Trail Distance: 10+ mi   Loops: Many   Shortest: .5 mi   Longest: 8 mi
Trail Surface: Natural
Trail Use Fee: None
Method Of Ski Trail Grooming: None
Skiing Ability Suggested: Novice to intermediate
Hiking Trail Difficulty: Easy
Mountain Biking Ability Suggested: Novice to intermediate
Terrain: Steep 0%, Hilly 10%, Moderate 50%, Flat 40%
Camping: None

Managed by the Ottawa County Parks and Recreation Commission
A 430 acre park with a lodge and sledding hill.
The lodge is used for ski rentals and snack bar during the snow months. It is available for rent in the non snow months.
One mile lighted trail for skiing.
Skating lane is also available.
Popular trail for skiing and mountain biking.
Horseback riding is allowed in the park.

PIGEON CREEK PARK

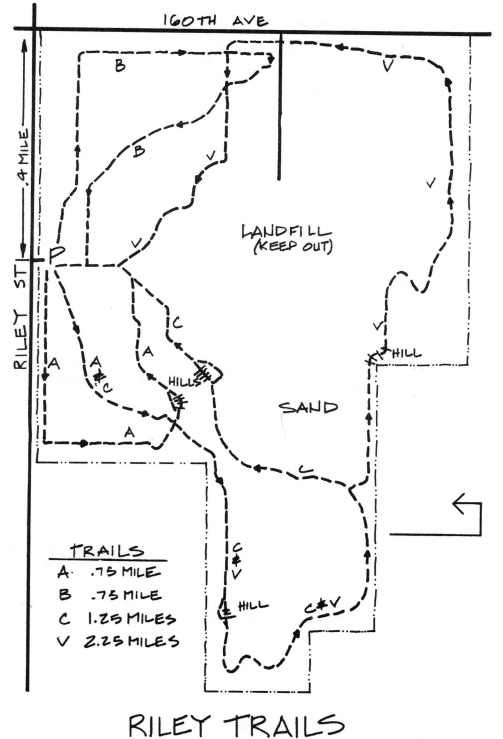

Park Township
52 152nd Ave
Holland, MI 49424

313-399-4520

Michigan Atlas & Gazetteer Location: 35B5

County Location: Ottawa

Directions To Trailhead:
Northwest of Holland about 1 mile from Lake Michigan.
4.7 miles west of US31 on Riley St.
Just west of 160th Ave.

Trail Type: Hiking/Walking, Cross Country Skiing, Mountain Biking
Trail Distance: 5+ mi   Loops: 4   Shortest: .75 mi Longest: 2.25 mi
Trail Surface: Natural
Trail Use Fee: None
Method Of Ski Trail Grooming: Not known
Skiing Ability Suggested: Novice
Hiking Trail Difficulty: Easy
Mountain Biking Ability Suggested: Novice to advanced
Terrain: Steep 0%, Hilly 10%, Moderate 25%, Flat 65%
Camping: None

Owned by Park Township, Ottawa County.
Multi use recreational area for hiking, mountain biking and cross country skiing.
Popular mountain biking area for local riders.
Wooded trails throughout.
Trail map is usually posted in the parking area at the trailhead.

RILEY TRAILS

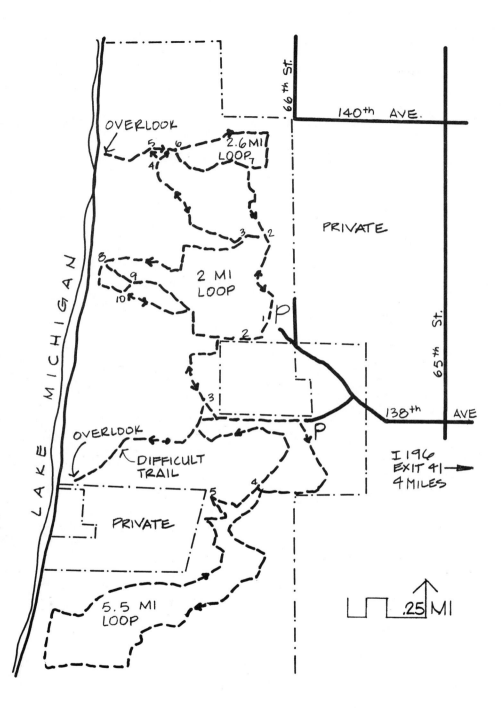

OVERLOOK

5
6
R
4

2.6 MI LOOP
7

PRIVATE

3   2

8

2 MI LOOP

9

10 R

P

1

2

3

OVERLOOK

DIFFICULT TRAIL

3

P

5

4

PRIVATE

5.5 MI LOOP

LAKE MICHIGAN

66th St.

140th AVE.

65th St.

138th AVE

I 196
EXIT 41 →
4 MILES

.25 MI

SAUGATUCK DUNES
STATE PARK

Van Buren State Park
23960 Ruggles Rd.   616-637-2788
South Haven , MI 49090

DNR Parks and Recreation Division

517-373-1270

Michigan Atlas & Gazetteer Location: 35C5

County Location: Allegan

Directions To Trailhead:
1 mile north of Saugatuck via north on A2 to 64th St., then north 1 mile to 138th St, then west 1 mile to the park entrance .

Trail Type: Hiking/Walking, Cross Country Skiing
Trail Distance: 13.5 mi   Loops: 7   Shortest: 2 mi   Longest: 5.5 mi
Trail Surface: Natural and granular surface
Trail Use Fee: None, but vehicle entry fee required
Method Of Ski Trail Grooming: Track set
Skiing Ability Suggested: Novice (limited) & advanced
Hiking Trail Difficulty: Moderate
Mountain Biking Ability Suggested: NA
Terrain: Steep 10%, Hilly 30%, Moderate 50%, Flat1 10%
Camping: None

Maintained by the DNR Parks and Recreation Division
Scenic view of Lake Michigan and the dunes.
Over 1000 acres of hardwoods, pine forests and sand dunes.
Sand dunes raise up to 180 feet above Lake Michigan.
Beach and picnic grounds are provided.

TRAIL NOTES

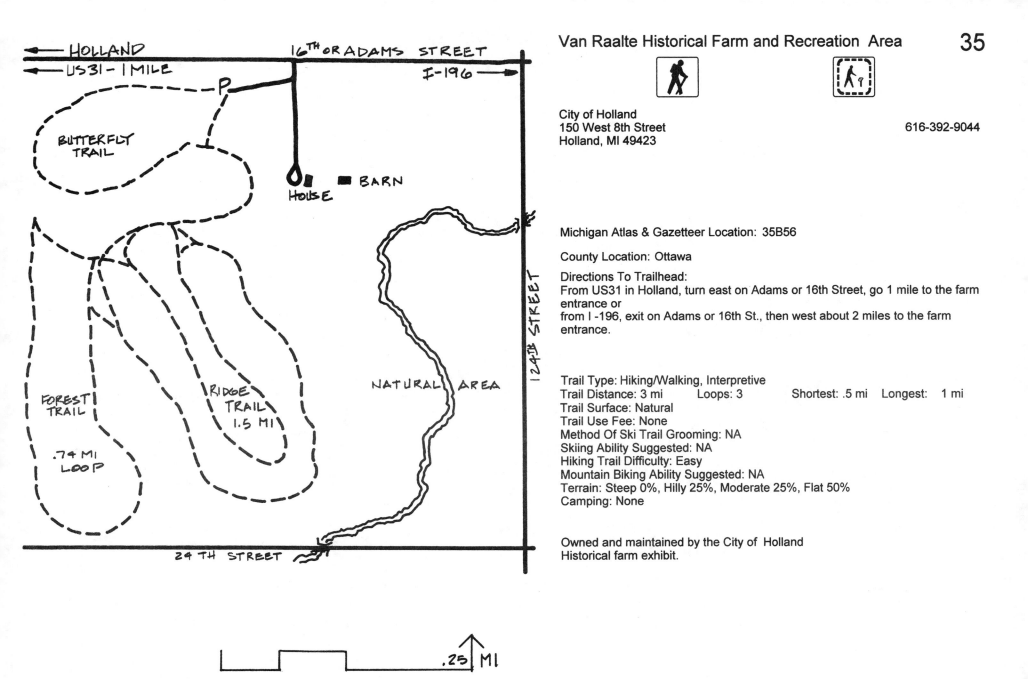

City of Holland
150 West 8th Street
Holland, MI 49423

616-392-9044

Michigan Atlas & Gazetteer Location: 35B56

County Location: Ottawa

Directions To Trailhead:
From US31 in Holland, turn east on Adams or 16th Street, go 1 mile to the farm entrance or
from I-196, exit on Adams or 16th St., then west about 2 miles to the farm entrance.

Trail Type: Hiking/Walking, Interpretive
Trail Distance: 3 mi   Loops: 3   Shortest: .5 mi   Longest: 1 mi
Trail Surface: Natural
Trail Use Fee: None
Method Of Ski Trail Grooming: NA
Skiing Ability Suggested: NA
Hiking Trail Difficulty: Easy
Mountain Biking Ability Suggested: NA
Terrain: Steep 0%, Hilly 25%, Moderate 25%, Flat 50%
Camping: None

Owned and maintained by the City of Holland
Historical farm exhibit.

VAN RAALTE
HISTORICAL FARM & RECREATION AREA

Grand Rapids Parks & Recreation Department
201 Market St SW
Grand Rapids, MI 49503

616-456-3216

Michigan Atlas & Gazetteer Location: 36A1

County Location: Ottawa

Directions To Trailhead:
6 miles west olf Grand Rapids on Lake Michigan Drive (M-45)

Trail Type: Hiking/Walking, Cross Country Skiing
Trail Distance: 3 mi   Loops: 3   Shortest: .9 mi   Longest: 2 mi
Trail Surface: Natural
Trail Use Fee: None
Method Of Ski Trail Grooming: Snowmobile packed after 2" snowfall
Skiing Ability Suggested: Novice to intermediate
Hiking Trail Difficulty: Easy
Mountain Biking Ability Suggested: NA
Terrain: Steep 0%, Hilly 10%, Moderate 30%, Flat 60%
Camping: None

Maintained by the Grand Rapids Parks and Recreation Department
Trail follows the Sand Creek.
Mature Beech-Maple forest.
Variety of wildflowers present. Please leave flowers for others to enjoy.

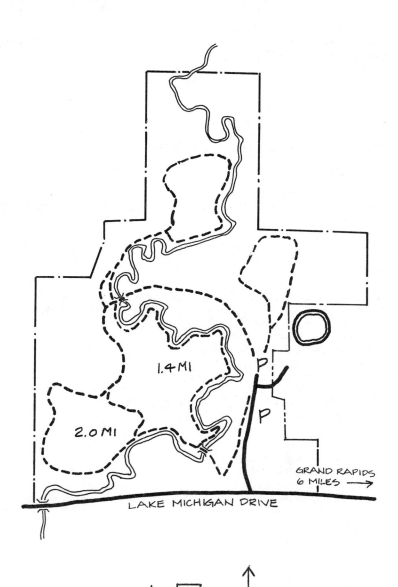

AMAN PARK

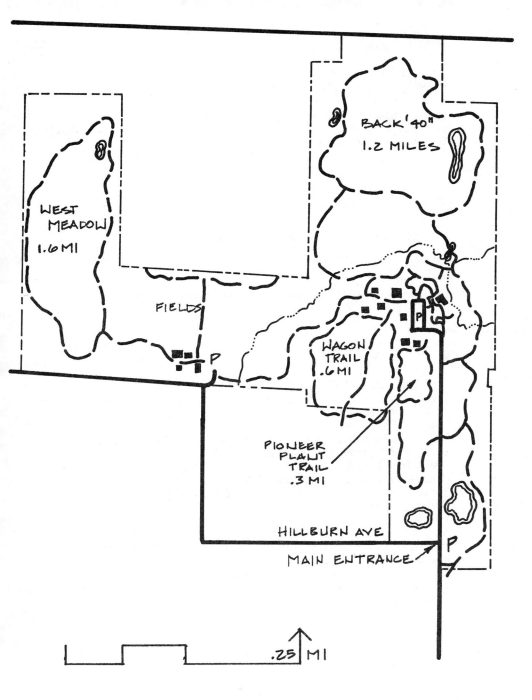

Public Museum of Grand Rapids
1715 Hillburn NW
Grand Rapids, MI 49504

616-453-6192

Michigan Atlas & Gazetteer Location: 36A2

County Location: Kent

Directions To Trailhead:
Exit 131 at Leonard St, then west 3 miles to Hillburn, then right to parking lot .5 miles ahead.

Trail Type: Hiking/Walking, Cross Country Skiing, Interpretive
Trail Distance: 4 mi   Loops: 9   Shortest: .1 mi   Longest: 1.6 mi
Trail Surface: Paved and natural
Trail Use Fee: None
Method Of Ski Trail Grooming: None
Skiing Ability Suggested: Novice
Hiking Trail Difficulty: Easy to moderate
Mountain Biking Ability Suggested: NA
Terrain: Steep 5%, Hilly 20%, Moderate 50%, Flat 25%
Camping: None

Owned by the Public Museum of Grand Rapids
Heritage settlement and farmstead are part of the complex
Trails cover a diverse habitat.
Visitor Center houses exhibits and the Wildlife Care Center.
Open daily except major holidays.
Trails are open from dawn to dusk.

BLANDFORD NATURE CENTER

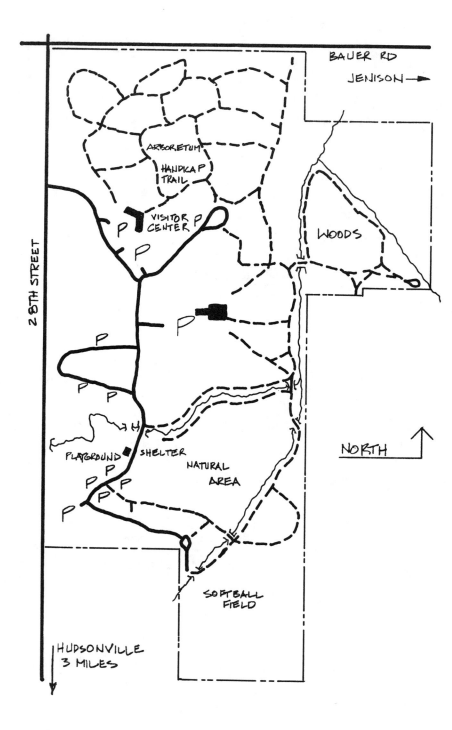

HAGER PARK

Ottawa County Parks and Recreation Department
414 Washington   616-846-8117
Grand Haven, MI 49417

Michigan Atlas & Gazetteer Location: 35A1

County Location: Ottawa

Directions To Trailhead:
Corner of 28th Ave and Bauer Rd in Jenison. 3 miles north of Hudsonville.

Trail Type: Hiking/Walking, Cross Country Skiing, Interpretive
Trail Distance: 2 mi   Loops: 5   Shortest: .25 mi Longest: 1 mi
Trail Surface: Natrual
Trail Use Fee: None
Method Of Ski Trail Grooming: None
Skiing Ability Suggested: Novice
Hiking Trail Difficulty: Easy
Mountain Biking Ability Suggested: NA
Terrain: 100% Flat
Camping: None

Maintained by the Ottawa County Parks and Recreation Commission.
Intensively developed park with many trails, an arboretum, visitors center, picnic
area, natural area with nature trails and playground.

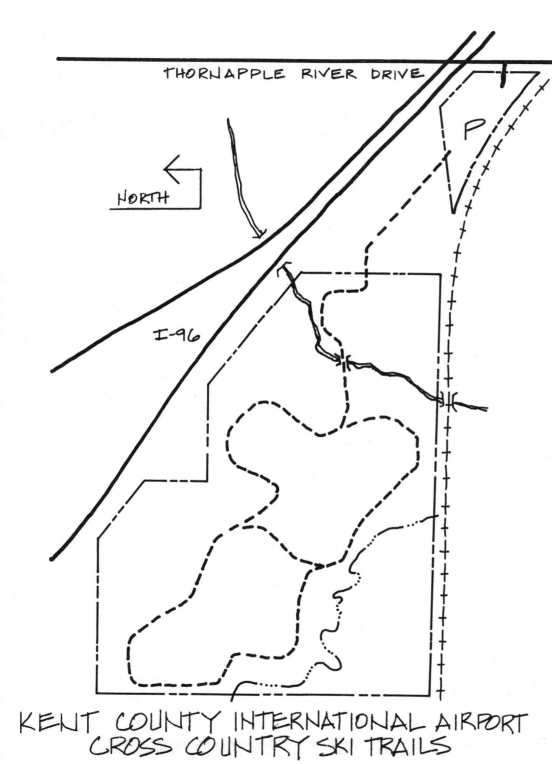

THORNAPPLE RIVER DRIVE

NORTH

I-96

P

KENT COUNTY INTERNATIONAL AIRPORT
CROSS COUNTRY SKI TRAILS

Kent County Parks Department
1500 Scribner Ave, NW
Grand Rapids, MI 49504

616-242-6948
616-774-3697

Michigan Atlas & Gazetteer Location: 36A3

County Location: Kent

Directions To Trailhead:
Thornapple Drive south of I-96

Trail Type: Cross Country Skiing
Trail Distance: 1.25 mi   Loops: 2   Shortest: .7 mi   Longest: 1.1 mi
Trail Surface: Natural
Trail Use Fee: None
Method Of Ski Trail Grooming: Track set
Skiing Ability Suggested: Novice
Hiking Trail Difficulty: Easy
Mountain Biking Ability Suggested: Novice
Terrain: Steep 0%, Hilly 0%, Moderate 10%, Flat 90%
Camping: None

Maintained by the Kent County Parks Department

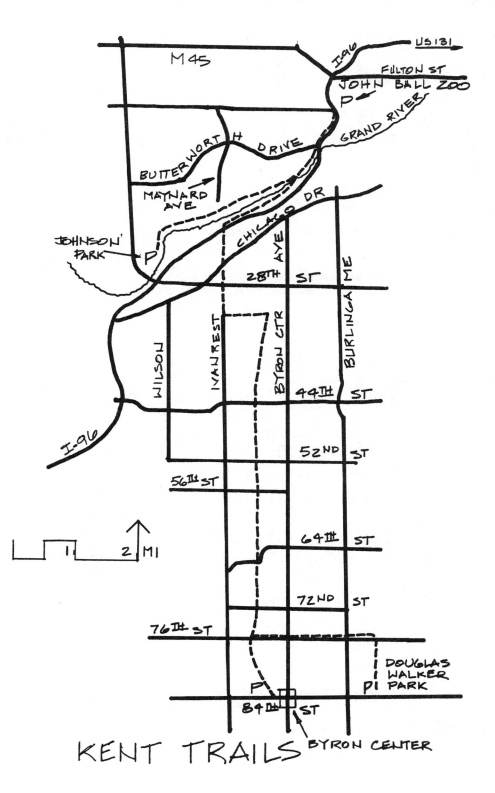

Kent Trails

Kent County Parks Department
1500 Scribner Ave, NW
Grand Rapids, MI 49504

616-242-6948
616-774-3697

Michigan Atlas & Gazetteer Location: 36AB12

County Location: Kent

Directions To Trailhead:
North trailhead - John Ball Park Zoo at Fulton St and I-96
South trailhead - Byron Center or Douglas Walker Park on 84th St

Trail Type: Hiking/Walking, Cross Country Skiing,
Trail Distance: 13 mi   Loops: NA   Shortest: NA   Longest: NA
Trail Surface: Paved
Trail Use Fee: None
Method Of Ski Trail Grooming: None
Skiing Ability Suggested: Novice
Hiking Trail Difficulty: Easy
Mountain Biking Ability Suggested: NA
Terrain: Steep 0%, Hilly 0%, Moderate 10%, Flat 90%
Camping: None

Maintained by the Kent County Parks Department
Part of the trail is rail-trail conversion
Some of the trail is on city sidewalks.

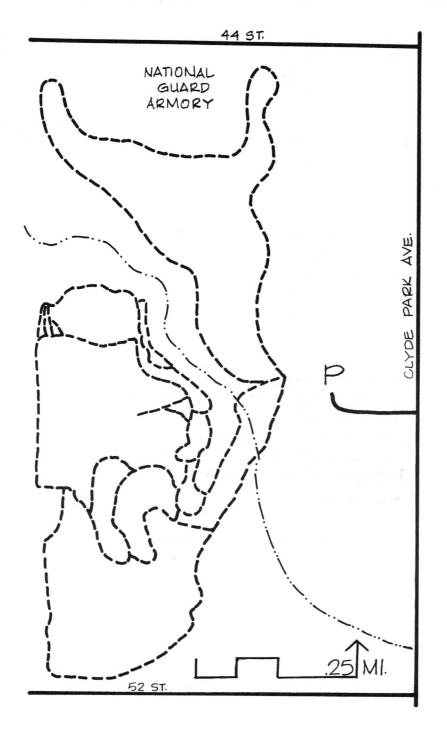

44 ST.

NATIONAL
GUARD
ARMORY

CLYDE PARK AVE.

P

.25 MI.

52 ST.

PALMER PARK

Kent County Park Department
1500 Scribner Ave. NW
Grand Rapids, MI 49504

616-774-3697
616-224-6948

Michigan Atlas & Gazetteer Location: 36AB2

County Location: Kent

Directions To Trailhead:
In Wyoming (Grand Rapids), at 52nd St and Clyde Park Ave.

Trail Type: Hiking/Walking, Cross Country Skiing
Trail Distance: 5 mi   Loops: Several   Shortest: Longest:
Trail Surface: Natural
Trail Use Fee: Fee for skiing only
Method Of Ski Trail Grooming: Track set occasionally
Skiing Ability Suggested: Novice
Hiking Trail Difficulty: Easy
Mountain Biking Ability Suggested: NA
Terrain: Flat to rolling
Camping: Camping not permitted

Maintained by the Kent County Park Commission
Warming building, rentals, snacks and lighted practice area available.
Trails on a golf course.

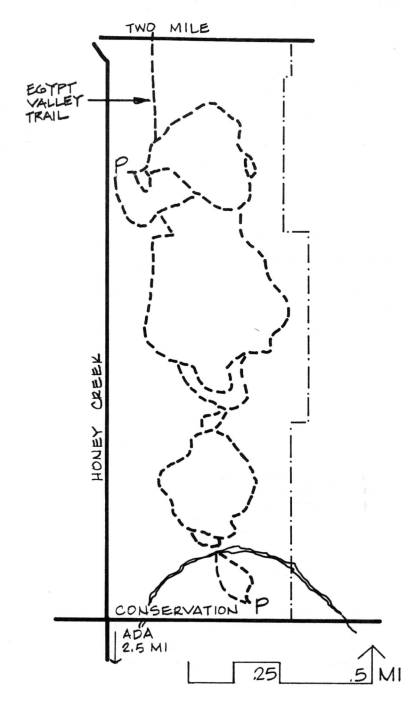

TWO MILE

EGYPT
VALLEY
TRAIL

P

HONEY CREEK

CONSERVATION   P

ADA
2.5 MI

.25   .5 MI

SEIDMAN PARK

Seidman Park

Kent County Park Commission
1500 Scribner Ave. NW
Grand Rapids, MI 49504-3299

616-774-6968
616-242-6948

Michigan Atlas & Gazetteer Location: 36A4

County Location: Kent

Directions To Trailhead:
Honey Creek Ave between 2 Mile Rd and Conservation Rd

Trail Type: Hiking/Walking, Cross Country Skiing
Trail Distance: 4.5 mi   Loops: 3   Shortest: Longest:
Trail Surface: Natural
Trail Use Fee: None
Method Of Ski Trail Grooming: None
Skiing Ability Suggested: Novice to intermediate
Hiking Trail Difficulty: Easy
Mountain Biking Ability Suggested: NA
Terrain: ?
Camping: None

Maintained by the Kent County Park Commission

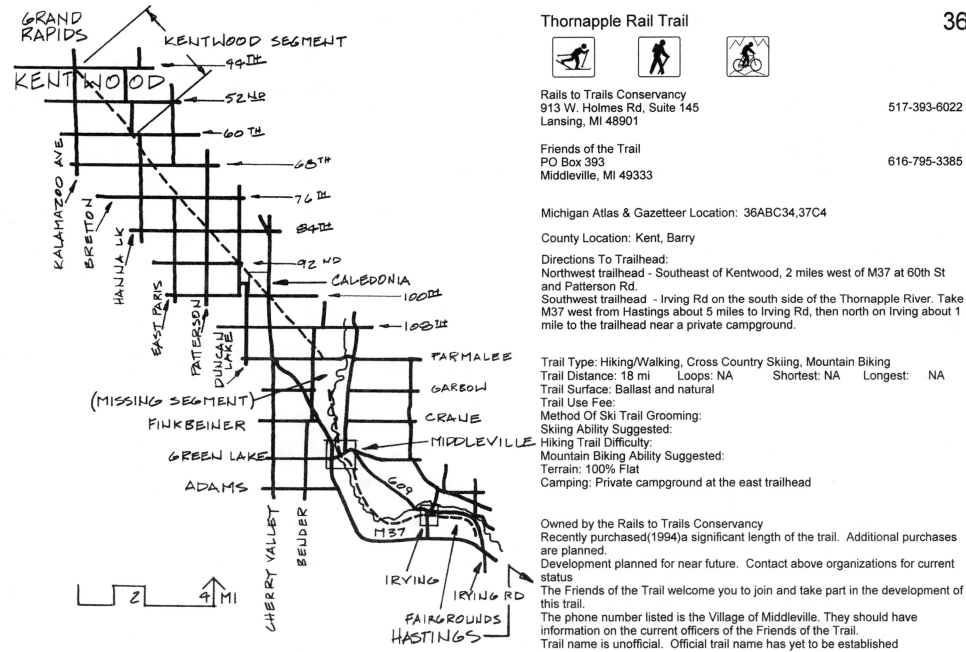

GRAND RAPIDS

KENTWOOD SEGMENT

KENTWOOD

44TH
52ND
60TH
68TH
76TH
84TH
92ND
100TH
108TH

KALAMAZOO AVE
BRETTON
HANNA LK
EAST PARIS
PATTERSON
DUNCAN LAKE

CALEDONIA

(MISSING SEGMENT)

FINKBEINER

GREEN LAKE

ADAMS

PARMALEE
GARBOW
CRANE
MIDDLEVILLE

CHERRY VALLEY
BENDER

M37

609

IRVING
IRVING RD

FAIRGROUNDS
HASTINGS

2   4 MI

Thornapple Rail Trail

Rails to Trails Conservancy
913 W. Holmes Rd, Suite 145
Lansing, MI 48901

517-393-6022

Friends of the Trail
PO Box 393
Middleville, MI 49333

616-795-3385

Michigan Atlas & Gazetteer Location: 36ABC34,37C4

County Location: Kent, Barry

Directions To Trailhead:
Northwest trailhead - Southeast of Kentwood, 2 miles west of M37 at 60th St and Patterson Rd.
Southwest trailhead - Irving Rd on the south side of the Thornapple River. Take M37 west from Hastings about 5 miles to Irving Rd, then north on Irving about 1 mile to the trailhead near a private campground.

Trail Type: Hiking/Walking, Cross Country Skiing, Mountain Biking
Trail Distance: 18 mi   Loops: NA   Shortest: NA   Longest: NA
Trail Surface: Ballast and natural
Trail Use Fee:
Method Of Ski Trail Grooming:
Skiing Ability Suggested:
Hiking Trail Difficulty:
Mountain Biking Ability Suggested:
Terrain: 100% Flat
Camping: Private campground at the east trailhead

Owned by the Rails to Trails Conservancy
Recently purchased(1994)a significant length of the trail. Additional purchases are planned.
Development planned for near future. Contact above organizations for current status
The Friends of the Trail welcome you to join and take part in the development of this trail.
The phone number listed is the Village of Middleville. They should have information on the current officers of the Friends of the Trail.
Trail name is unofficial. Official trail name has yet to be established

THORNAPPLE RAIL TRAIL

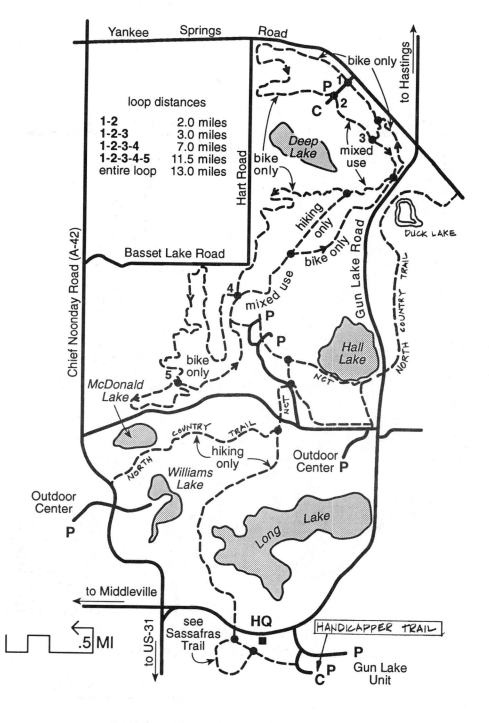

Yankee Springs Recreation Area

loop distances

1-2	2.0 miles
1-2-3	3.0 miles
1-2-3-4	7.0 miles
1-2-3-4-5	11.5 miles
entire loop	13.0 miles

Yankee Springs Recreation Area

Yankee Springs Recreation Area
2140 Gun Lake Rd.
Middleville, MI 49333

616-795-9081
517-322-1300

DNR Parks and Recreation Division

517-373-1270

Michigan Atlas & Gazetteer Location: 36BC34

County Location: Barry

Directions To Trailhead:
9 miles west of Hastings on Co Rd A42. Skiing trailhead - Long Lake Outdoor Center on Gun Lake Rd.
Hiking trailheads - Park Hdqs, Long Lake Outdoor Center, near Chief Noonday Outdoor Center and and Beach CG. Mountain biking trailhead - Deep Lake Campground Contact Station.

Trail Type: Hiking/Walking, Cross Country Skiing, Mountain Biking, Interpretive
Trail Distance: 20+ mi   Loops: Many   Shortest: .5 mi   Longest: 13 mi
Trail Surface: Natural
Trail Use Fee: None, but vehicle entry fee required
Method Of Ski Trail Grooming: Track set as needed
Skiing Ability Suggested: Novice to advanced
Hiking Trail Difficulty: Easy to moderate
Mountain Biking Ability Suggested: Intermediate to advanced
Terrain: Varies depending on trail system
Camping: Campgrounds in the recreation area

Maintained by the DNR Parks and Recreation Division.
Recreation area with many facilities. Call or write for information.
Separate maps of each trail type.
Hiking, mountain biking and cross-country ski trails are overlapping systems.
Hiking/walking: 11 mi.; 4 trails; 2 to 5 mile loops; S5%, H35%, M30%, F30%
X-C skiing: 7 mi; 6 loops; .5 to 5 mile loops; S5%, H35%, M50%; F10%
Mountain biking: 13 mi; 5 loops; 2 to 13 mile loops; S10%, H45%, M30%; F15%
Nature trail: 1/2 mile; 1 loop; F100%
Popular ski area due to reliable lake effect snow off Lake Michigan. Warming shelter at the Long Lake Outdoor Center. Open weekends and holidays.
Popular mountain bike trail (part of hiking trail). Part of trail developed by the Michigan Mountain Biking Association members.
Great swimming and boating on Gunn Lake and Deep Lake.
North Country Trail passes through this recreation area.

Yankee Springs Recreation Area

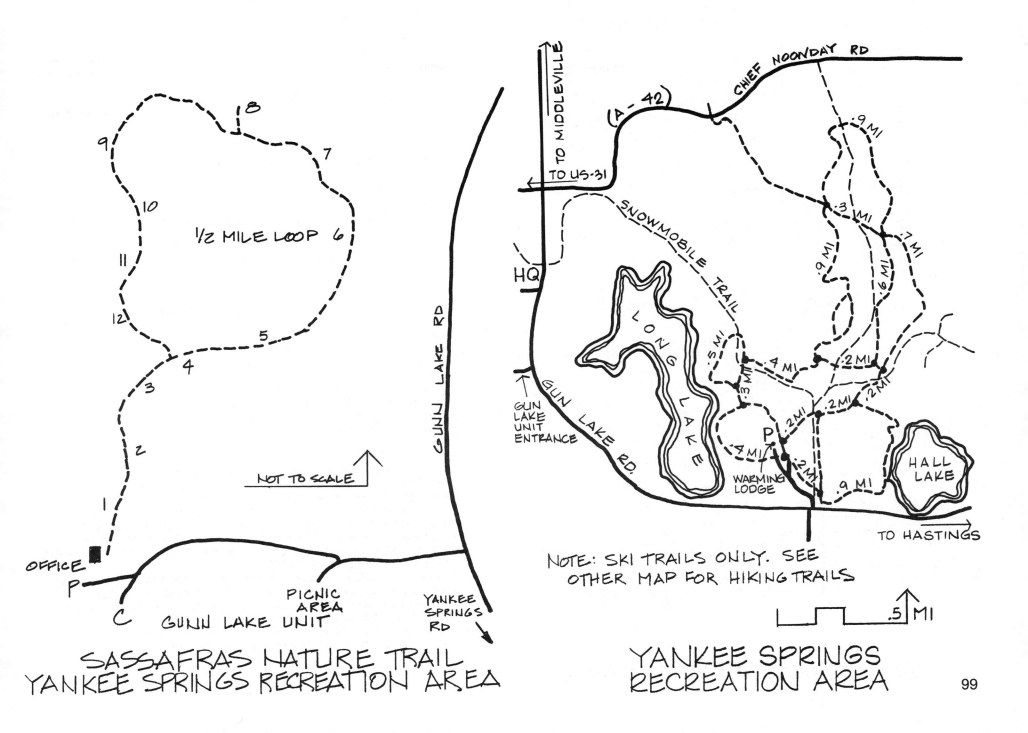

SASSAFRAS NATURE TRAIL
YANKEE SPRINGS RECREATION AREA

YANKEE SPRINGS
RECREATION AREA

99

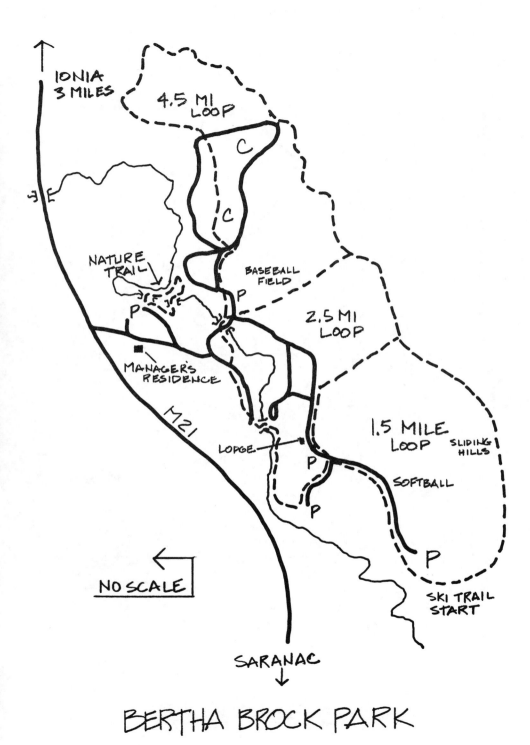

IONIA
3 MILES

4.5 MI LOOP

C
C

NATURE TRAIL

BASEBALL FIELD

P

P

2.5 MI LOOP

MANAGER'S RESIDENCE

M21

LODGE

1.5 MILE LOOP

SLIDING HILLS

P

SOFTBALL

P

P

P

NO SCALE

SKI TRAIL START

SARANAC

BERTHA BROCK PARK

Ionia County Parks Department
2311 W Bluewater Hwy, Rte 3
Ionia, MI 48846

616-527-0478

Michigan Atlas & Gazetteer Location: 37A6

County Location: Ionia

Directions To Trailhead:
3 miles west of Ionia on M21

Trail Type: Hiking/Walking, Cross Country Skiing, Interpretive
Trail Distance: 8.5 mi   Loops: 4   Shortest: 1.5 mi Longest: 4.5 mi
Trail Surface: Natural including gravel
Trail Use Fee: None
Method Of Ski Trail Grooming: None
Skiing Ability Suggested: Novice to intermediate
Hiking Trail Difficulty: Easy to moderate
Mountain Biking Ability Suggested: NA
Terrain: Flat to rolling
Camping: Rustic campground in the park

Operated by the Ionia County Parks Department.
Warming shelter, sledding and tubing hill on site.
Interpretive trail is not for skiing
Tennis courts, ball fields and playground provided on site.
Rustic lodge available for rent.

Charlton Park
2545 S. Charlton Park Rd
Hastings, MI 49058

616-945-3775

Michigan Atlas & Gazetteer Location: 37D6

County Location: Barry

Directions To Trailhead:
1/10 mile north of M79 between Nashville and Hastings on Charlton Park Rd.

Trail Type: Hiking/Walking, Cross Country Skiing, Mountain Biking, Interpretive
Trail Distance: 5 km   Loops: Several   Shortest: Longest:
Trail Surface: Natural
Trail Use Fee: Yes
Method Of Ski Trail Grooming: NA
Skiing Ability Suggested: Novice
Hiking Trail Difficulty: Easy
Mountain Biking Ability Suggested: Novice
Terrain: Steep 0%, Hilly 0%, Moderate 80%, Flat 20%
Camping: None

Owned by a non-profit organization
Historical village re-creation.
Special events held throughout the year.

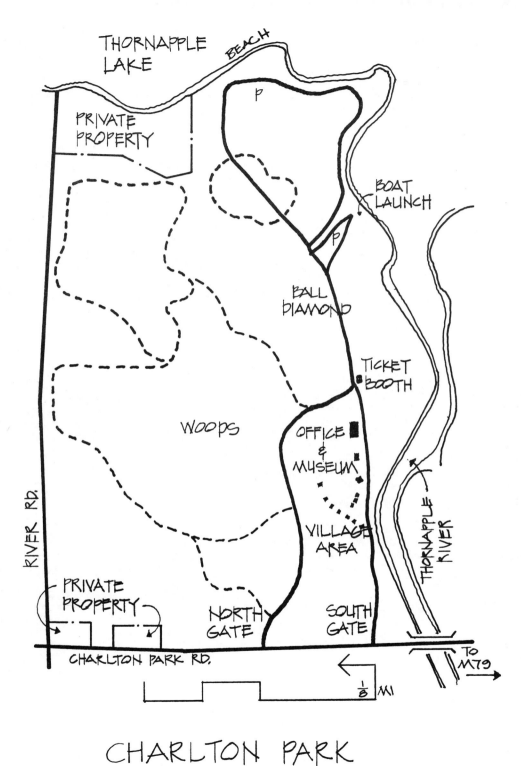

THORNAPPLE LAKE

BEACH

PRIVATE PROPERTY

P

BOAT LAUNCH

P

BALL DIAMOND

TICKET BOOTH

WOODS

OFFICE & MUSEUM

VILLAGE AREA

THORNAPPLE RIVER

RIVER RD.

PRIVATE PROPERTY

NORTH GATE

SOUTH GATE

CHARLTON PARK RD.

TO M79

1/8 MI

CHARLTON PARK

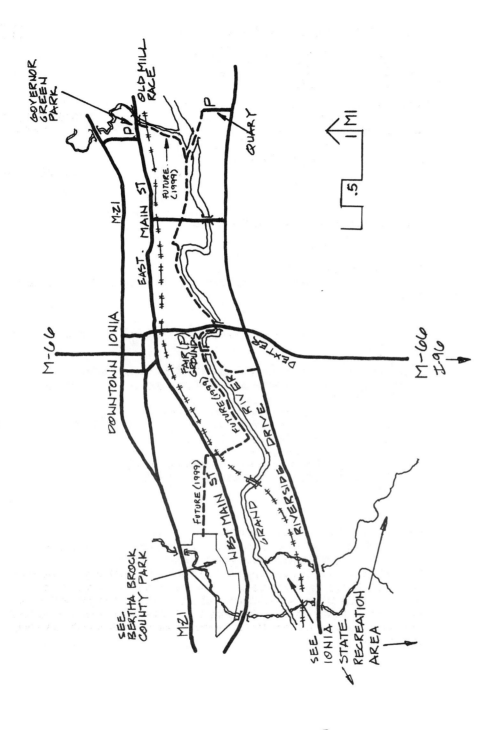

IONIA RIVER TRAIL

City of Ionia
114 N. Kidd St.
Ionia, MI 48864

616-527-4170

Michigan Atlas & Gazetteer Location: 37A67

County Location: Ionia

Directions To Trailhead:
In and around the community of Ionia

Trail Type: Hiking/Walking, Cross Country Skiing
Trail Distance: 8 mi   Loops: NA   Shortest: NA   Longest: NA
Trail Surface: Paved
Trail Use Fee: None
Method Of Ski Trail Grooming: None
Skiing Ability Suggested: Novice
Hiking Trail Difficulty: Easy
Mountain Biking Ability Suggested: NA
Terrain: Steep 0%, Hilly 0%, Moderate 90%, Flat 10%
Camping: Bertha Brock County Park and Ionia State Recreation Area

Maintained by the City of Ionia
Currently under development
Focal point is the 585' long trestle across the Grand Rvier with its wonderful view
of the river.
Future plans call for linkage with Bertha Brock Park and the Ionia State
Recreation Area. Both are listed separately.

Ionia State Recreation Area
2880 David Highway
Ionia, MI 48846

616-527-3750
517-322-1300

DNR Parks and Recreation Division

517-372-1270

Michigan Atlas & Gazetteer Location: 37A67

County Location: Ionia

Directions To Trailhead:
South from Ionia 5 miles on M66 to David Hwy, then west 3 miles to Recreation Area entrance.
Trailheads: Beechwood Picnic Area, Point Picnic Area and Riverside Picnic Area.
Mountain bike trailhead: On Riverside Drive, 3 miles west of Ionia on the south side of the Grand River.

Trail Type: Hiking/Walking, Cross Country Skiing, Mountain Biking
Trail Distance: 22+ mi   Loops: 8+   Shortest: .2 mi   Longest: 5.8 mi
Trail Surface: Natural
Trail Use Fee: None, but vehicle entry fee required
Method Of Ski Trail Grooming: None
Skiing Ability Suggested: Novice to advanced
Hiking Trail Difficulty: Easy to difficult
Mountain Biking Ability Suggested: Novice to intermediate
Terrain: Steep 2%, Hilly 15%, Moderate 45%, Flat 38%
Camping: Campground on site

Maintained by the DNR Parks and Recreation Division
Greatly varied terrain with woods, lakes, fields, streams, rivers and numerous scenic views. Separate equestrain trails are also in the park.
The Chief Cob-Moo-Sa mountain bike trail is along the north side of Riverside Drive off M 66 west of Ionia. Developed by the Michigan Mountain Biking Association, an access trail is also available from a parking lot inside the main part of the park.(see maps). Three loops of 2.5, 3.1 and 5.8 miles are provided. Additional loops are planned for the same area along the river to the east of the existing trail.

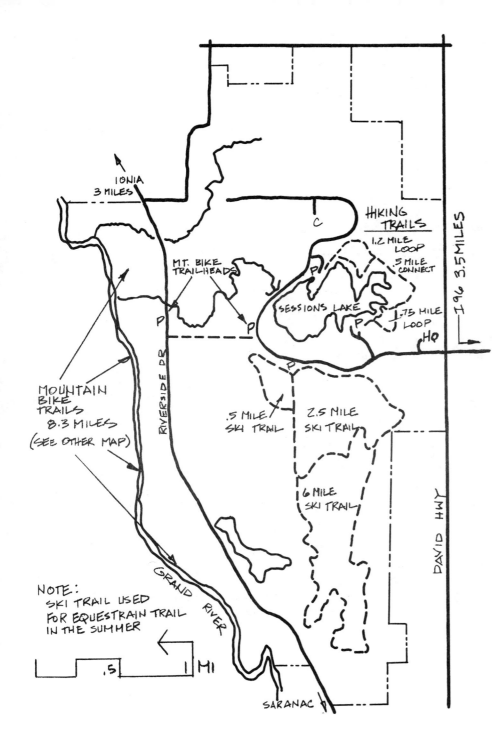

IONIA STATE RECREATION AREA

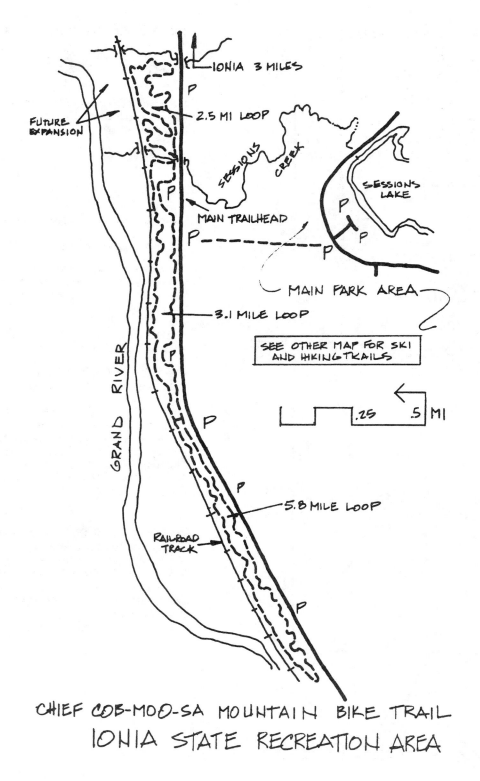

IONIA 3 MILES

FUTURE EXPANSION

2.5 MI LOOP

SESSIONS CREEK

SESSIONS LAKE

MAIN TRAILHEAD

MAIN PARK AREA

GRAND RIVER

3.1 MILE LOOP

SEE OTHER MAP FOR SKI AND HIKING TRAILS

.25   .5 MI

5.8 MILE LOOP

RAILROAD TRACK

CHIEF COB-MOO-SA MOUNTAIN BIKE TRAIL
IONIA STATE RECREATION AREA

102.1

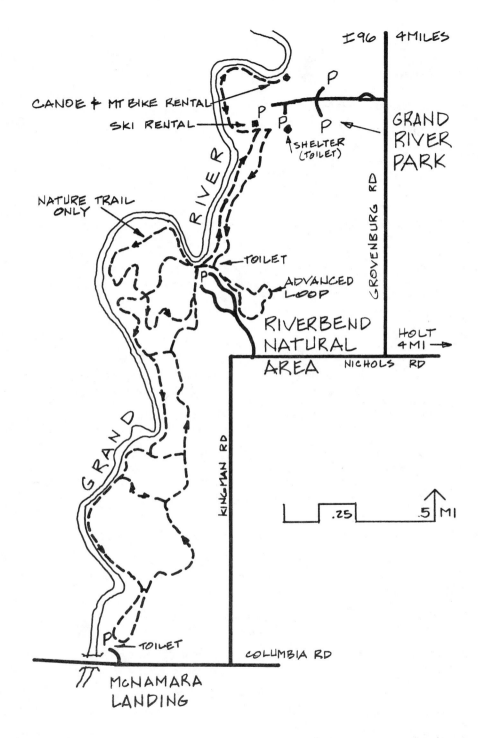

Ingham County Parks Department
630 1/2 North Cedar St., PO Box 178
Mason, MI 48854

517-676-2233

Michigan Atlas & Gazetteer Location: 38D4

County Location: Ingham

Directions To Trailhead:
SW of Lansing on Grovenburg Rd, just north of Nichols Rd. Use Logan St exit south off I-96, then turn left on Bishop Rd. east to Grovenburg Rd., then south to the park past Holt Rd..

Trail Type: Hiking/Walking, Cross Country Skiing, Mountain Biking
Trail Distance: 4.5 mi   Loops: 5   Shortest: .8 mi   Longest: 4.5 mi
Trail Surface: Natural
Trail Use Fee: None, but vehicle entry fee charged
Method Of Ski Trail Grooming: Track set as snow condition permits.
Skiing Ability Suggested: Novice to intermediate
Hiking Trail Difficulty: Easy to moderate
Mountain Biking Ability Suggested: Novice
Terrain: Steep 5%, Hilly 30%, Moderate 45%, Flat 20%
Camping: None

Operated by the Ingham County Parks Department.
Marked 4.5 mile mountain bike trail is provided.
Ski rentals, canoe rentals, snack bar, 700' iced toboggan run, ice skating, sledding, swimming, softball diamond and picnic grounds are provided seasonally.
Additional services are provided seasonally.

BURCHFIELD/GRAND RIVER PARK

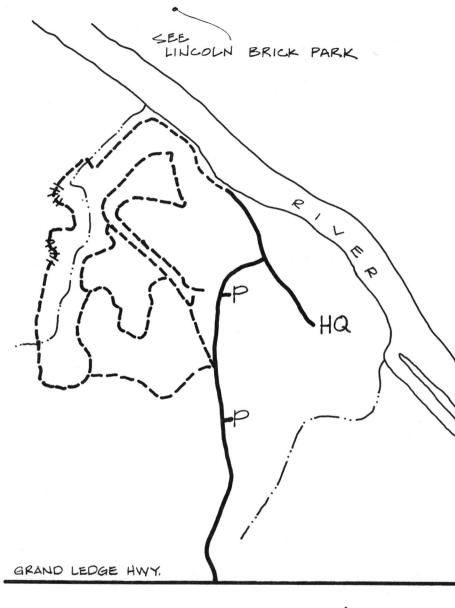

SEE LINCOLN BRICK PARK

R I V E R

P

HQ

P

GRAND LEDGE HWY.

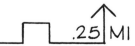
.25 MI

FITZGERALD PARK

Fitzgerald Park

Eaton County Parks and Recreation Department
3808 Grand Ledge Highway
Grand Ledge, MI 48837

517-627-7351

Michigan Atlas & Gazetteer Location: 38B2

County Location: Eaton

Directions To Trailhead:
I-96 to exit 93A (M-43 Saginaw Hwy West), then west on M-43 to Grand Ledge,
then east on Jefferson.St to park entrance.

Trail Type: Hiking/Walking, Cross Country Skiing, Interpretive
Trail Distance: 3 mi   Loops: 3   Shortest: .25 mi Longest: 1 mi
Trail Surface: Gravel and natural
Trail Use Fee: None but vehicle entry permit is required (in season)
Method Of Ski Trail Grooming: Track set when snow depth permits
Skiing Ability Suggested: Novice to advanced
Hiking Trail Difficulty: Easy to moderate
Mountain Biking Ability Suggested: NA
Terrain: Steep 0%, Hilly 2%, Moderate 80%, Flat 28%
Camping: None

Operated by the Eaton County Parks and Recreation Commission.
This park is famous for its sedimentary rock outcrops.
Popular location for local rock climbers.
Ski rentals available and warming shelter open on winter weekends.
Night skiing on selected winter weekends.
Naturalist programs provided free with advance arrangements.
Nature center and 1/2 mile self guided interpretive trail.
Picnic facilities, canoe rentals and game fields available.

Eaton County Parks & Recreation Department
3808 Grand Ledge Hwy
Grand Ledge, MI 48837

517-627-7351

Michigan Atlas & Gazetteer Location: 38C3

County Location: Eaton

Directions To Trailhead:
I-96 to exit 66, Potterville, M-100, then north on M-100 to Gresham Hwy, then west on Gresham Hwy to the park entrance.

Trail Type: Hiking/Walking, Cross Country Skiing, Interpretive
Trail Distance: 2 mi   Loops: 3   Shortest: .5 mi   Longest: 1 mi
Trail Surface: Natural
Trail Use Fee: None, but vehicle fee during summer months
Method Of Ski Trail Grooming: None
Skiing Ability Suggested: Novice
Hiking Trail Difficulty: Easy
Mountain Biking Ability Suggested: NA
Terrain: Steep 0%, Hilly 0%, Moderate 2%, Flat 98%
Camping: None

Operated by the Eaton County Parks and Recreation Commission.
Picnic facilities and concession stand available.
Trails around several ponds and through wooded areas.
Swimming, fishing, Ice fishing, ice skating available seasonally.

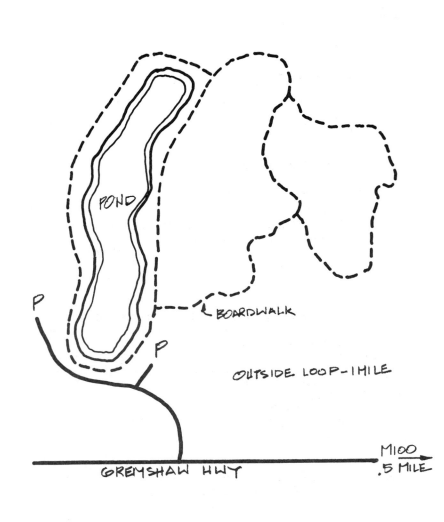

POND

BOARDWALK

OUTSIDE LOOP-1 MILE

M100
.5 MILE

GRENSHAW HWY

NO SCALE

FOX PARK

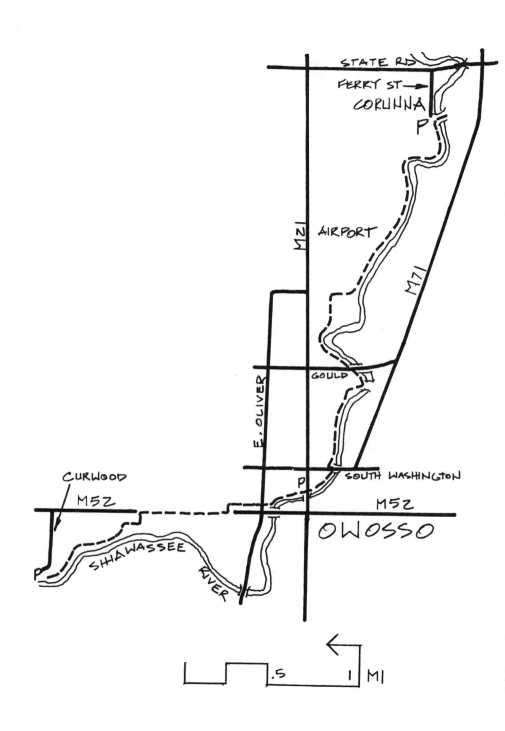

Owosso-Corunna Chamber of Commerce
215 N. Water St.
Owosso, MI 48867

517-723-5149

City of Owosso - Community Development
301 W. Main St.
Owosso, MI 48867

517-725-0540

Michigan Atlas & Gazetteer Location: 38A7

County Location: Shiawassee

Directions To Trailhead:
Located in Owosso and continues to Corunna.
Northwest trailhead is on Curwood St, west of M 52.
Southeast trailhead is on the river at the north end of Norton St, north of M 71 on the west side of Corunna.

Trail Type: Hiking/Walking, Cross Country Skiing, Interpretive
Trail Distance: 3.5 mi   Loops: None   Shortest: NA   Longest: NA
Trail Surface: Crushed limeston
Trail Use Fee: None
Method Of Ski Trail Grooming: None
Skiing Ability Suggested: Novice
Hiking Trail Difficulty: Easy
Mountain Biking Ability Suggested: NA
Terrain: Steep 0%, Hilly 0%, Moderate 0%, Flat 100%
Camping: None

Maintained by the Cities Owosso and Cornna

JAMES MINER WALKWAY

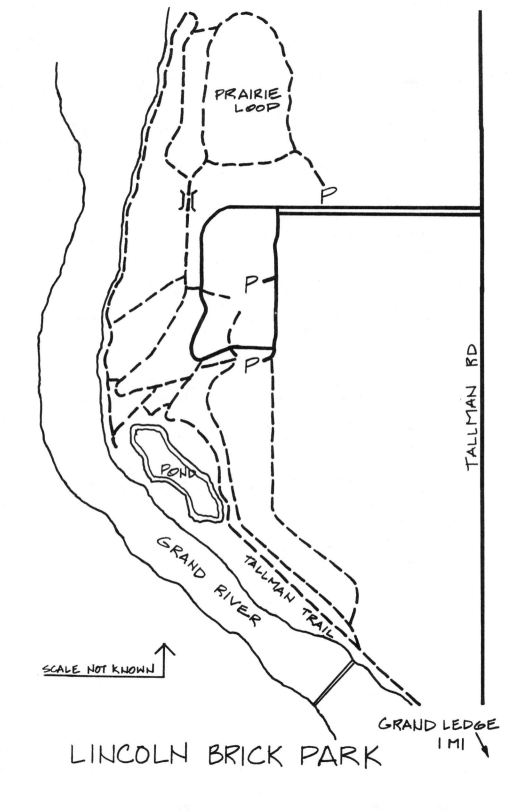

LINCOLN BRICK PARK

PRAIRIE LOOP

TALLMAN RD

POND

GRAND RIVER

TALLMAN TRAIL

SCALE NOT KNOWN

GRAND LEDGE 1 MI

Lincoln Brick Park

Eaton County Parks and Recreation Commission
3808 Grand Ledge Hwy   517-627-7351
Grand Ledge, MI 48837

Michigan Atlas & Gazetteer Location: 38B2

County Location: Eaton

Directions To Trailhead:
I-96 to Grand Ledge exit, M43 west to M100, then north to Main Street, then north to Tallman Rd, then west to park entrance.

Trail Type: Hiking/Walking, Cross Country Skiing
Trail Distance: 3 mi   Loops: 8   Shortest: .5 mi   Longest: 2 mi
Trail Surface: Natural
Trail Use Fee: None, but vehicle entry fee charged from April through October
Method Of Ski Trail Grooming: None
Skiing Ability Suggested: Novice to intermediate
Hiking Trail Difficulty: Easy to moderate
Mountain Biking Ability Suggested: NA
Terrain: Steep 0%, Hilly 25%, Moderate 40%, Flat 35%
Camping: None

Owned by the Eaton County Parks and Recreaton Commission
County park with picnic area, pavilions, playgrounds, fishing, archery, and much more
Ski trails marked with orange flags

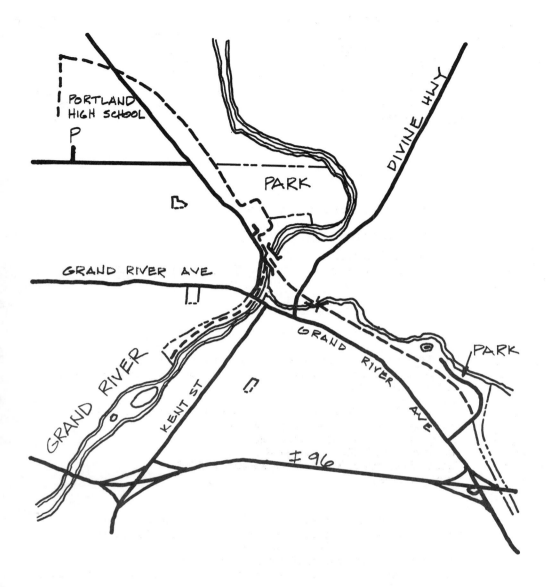

City of Portland
259 Kent St
Portland, MI 48875

517-647-7985

Michigan Atlas & Gazetteer Location: 38AB1

County Location: Ionia

Directions To Trailhead:
In downtown Portland along the Grand River.

Trail Type: Hiking/Walking, Cross Country Skiing, Interpretive
Trail Distance: 3.5 mi   Loops: NA   Shortest: NA   Longest: NA
Trail Surface: Paved
Trail Use Fee: None
Method Of Ski Trail Grooming: None
Skiing Ability Suggested: Novice
Hiking Trail Difficulty: Easy
Mountain Biking Ability Suggested: Paved
Terrain: 100%Flat
Camping: None

Owned by the City of Portland
The trail connects two city parks and has several bridges.

PORTLAND RIVERTRAIL PARK

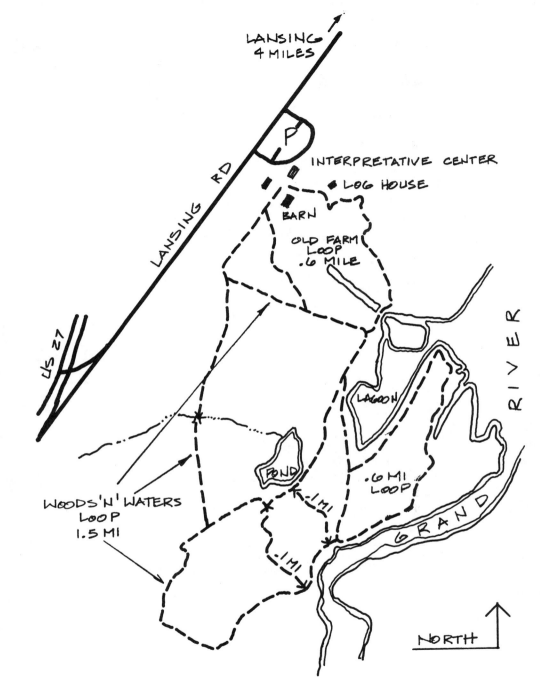

Woldumar Nature Center

Nature Way Association
5539 Lansing Rd.
Lansing, MI 48917

517-322-0030

Michigan Atlas & Gazetteer Location: 38C34

County Location: Eaton

Directions To Trailhead:
SW of Lansing on Lansing Rd off BR US27, just NE of I-96 exit 98B

Trail Type: Hiking/Walking, Cross Country Skiing, Interpretive
Trail Distance: 2.75 mi   Loops: 5   Shortest: .25 mi Longest: 1.5 mi
Trail Surface: Natural
Trail Use Fee: Yes
Method Of Ski Trail Grooming: Skied in by naturalist after each snowfall
Skiing Ability Suggested: Novice to advanced
Hiking Trail Difficulty: Easy to moderate
Mountain Biking Ability Suggested: NA
Terrain: Steep 5%, Hilly 15%, Moderate 70%, Flat 10%
Camping: None

A non-profit nature center with nature trails
Some hiking trails may not be suitable for skiing because of steps.
Area borders the Grand River for one mile.
Very scenic area with a wide selection of forest cover.
Warming shelter that serves snacks is open Tuesday - Friday from 9am to 5pm
and weekends from 1 to 5.
Very nice moderate sized trail system.
Write for brochure.

WOLDUMAR NATURE CENTER

East Lansing Pubic Works and Enviornmental Services
2000 Merritt Rd
East Lansing, MI 48823

517-337-9459

Michigan Atlas & Gazetteer Location: 39B5

County Location: Ingham

Directions To Trailhead:
From downtown East Lansing, take Abbott Rd north past Bus.I-69 and Lake Lansing Rd. Park entrance is on the right(west) side of the road.

Trail Type: Hiking/Walking, Cross Country Skiing, Interpretive
Trail Distance: 1.48 mi   Loops: 3   Shortest: .51 mi Longest: .89 mi
Trail Surface: Natural
Trail Use Fee: None
Method Of Ski Trail Grooming: Track set when snow depth permits
Skiing Ability Suggested: Novice
Hiking Trail Difficulty: Easy
Mountain Biking Ability Suggested: NA
Terrain: Flat
Camping: None

Maintained by the City of East Lansing
Handicapper parking available.
Natural area for wildlife observation

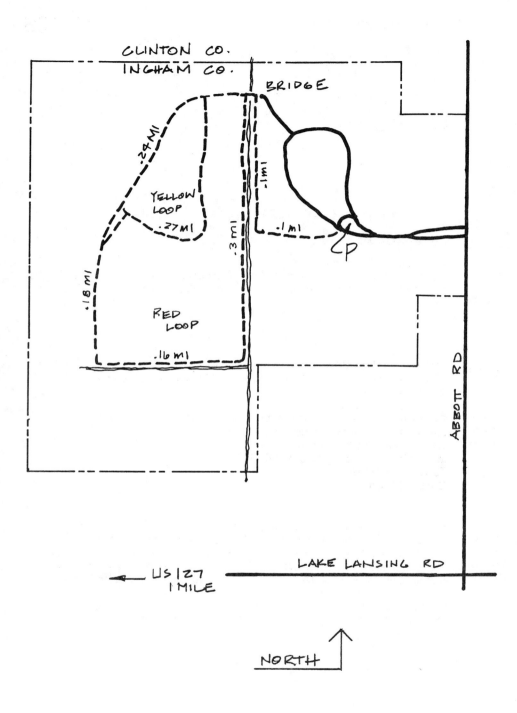

ABBOTT ROAD PARK

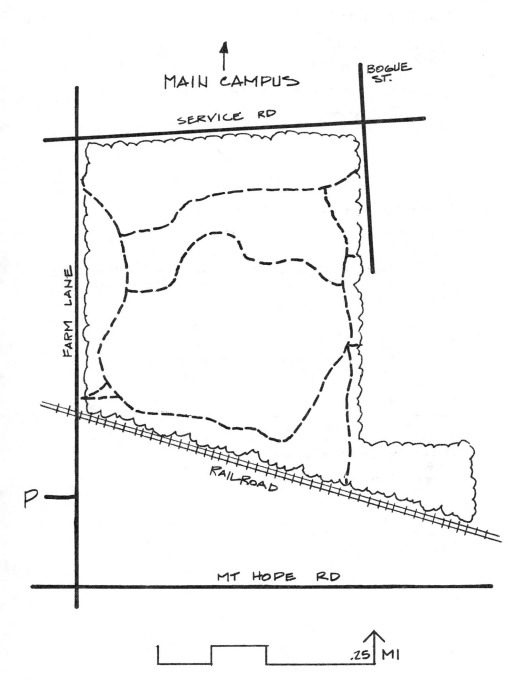

MAIN CAMPUS

BOGUE ST.

SERVICE RD

FARM LANE

RAILROAD

P

MT HOPE RD

.25 MI

BAKER WOODLOT

Secretary, Natural Areas Committee, M.S.U.
Div. of Campus Park and Planning, 412 Olds Hall   517-355-9582
East Lansing, MI 48824

Michigan Atlas & Gazetteer Location: 39C5

County Location: Ingham

Directions To Trailhead:
On the Michigan State University Campus. Bordered by Service Rd on the
north, Farm Lane on the west and Bogue St. on the east

Trail Type: Hiking/Walking, Interpretive
Trail Distance: 2.5+ mi   Loops: Several   Shortest: Longest:
Trail Surface: Natural
Trail Use Fee: None
Method Of Ski Trail Grooming: NA
Skiing Ability Suggested: Novice
Hiking Trail Difficulty: Easy
Mountain Biking Ability Suggested: NA
Terrain: 100% Flat
Camping: None

Owned by Michigan State University.
One of many natural areas managed for research and preservation.
Access to woodlot from one of several gates along Farm Lane and Bogue St.
This 78 acres woodlot is heavily used for research and recreational walking by
the campus community.

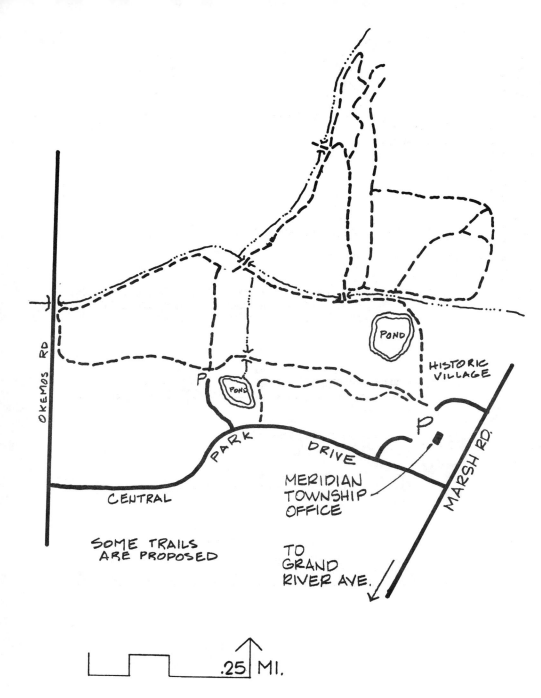

Meridian Township Park Commission
5151 Marsh Rd.
Okemos, MI 48864

517-349-1200

Michigan Atlas & Gazetteer Location: 39C5

County Location: Ingham

Directions To Trailhead:
From Grand River Ave (M-43) and Marsh Rd intersection, .25 mile north of
Grand River Ave on the west side of Marsh Rd., behind the township offices.
Immediately north of the Meridian Mall.

Trail Type: Hiking/Walking, Cross Country Skiing, Interpretive
Trail Distance: 5 mi   Loops: 6   Shortest: .75 mi Longest: 1.5 mi
Trail Surface: Natural
Trail Use Fee: None
Method Of Ski Trail Grooming: None
Skiing Ability Suggested: Novice
Hiking Trail Difficulty: Easy
Mountain Biking Ability Suggested: NA
Terrain: Steep 0%, Hilly 0%, Moderate 5%, Flat 95%
Camping: None

Maintained by the Meridian Township Park Commission
Trails start at the Meridian Historical Village located behind the township offices
and from a parking lot on the north side of Central Park Drive.
The park contains over 230 acres with ball fields picnic area, ponds and creeks.

SOME TRAILS ARE PROPOSED

.25 MI.

CENTRAL PARK

Meridian Township Park Commission
5151 Marsh Rd
Okemos, Mi 48864

517-349-1200

Michigan Atlas & Gazetteer Location: 39C5

County Location: Ingham

Directions To Trailhead:
From the intersection of Grand River Ave and Okemos Rd in Okemos, take Grand River (M43) east for 4.5 miles to Meridian Rd, turn right(south) on Meridian Rd to the park entrance which is on the west side.

Trail Type: Hiking/Walking, Cross Country Skiing, Interpretive
Trail Distance: 1.2 mi   Loops: 2   Shortest: .35 mi Longest: .85 mi
Trail Surface: Natural
Trail Use Fee: None
Method Of Ski Trail Grooming: None
Skiing Ability Suggested: Novice
Hiking Trail Difficulty: Easy
Mountain Biking Ability Suggested: NA
Terrain: Steep 0%, Hilly 25%, Moderate 55%, Flat 20%
Camping: None

Maintained by the Meridian Township Park Commission.
Property follows the Red Cedar River.
Beautiful river enviorment.
Connects with the Harris Center Park which connects to Legg Park.

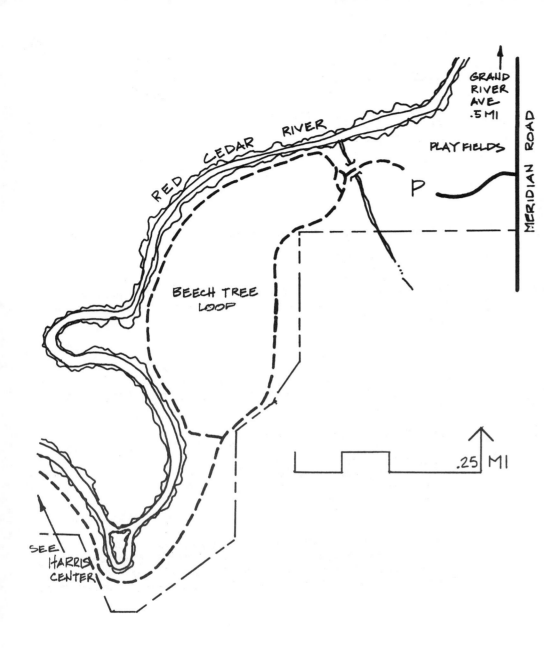

EAST GATE PARK

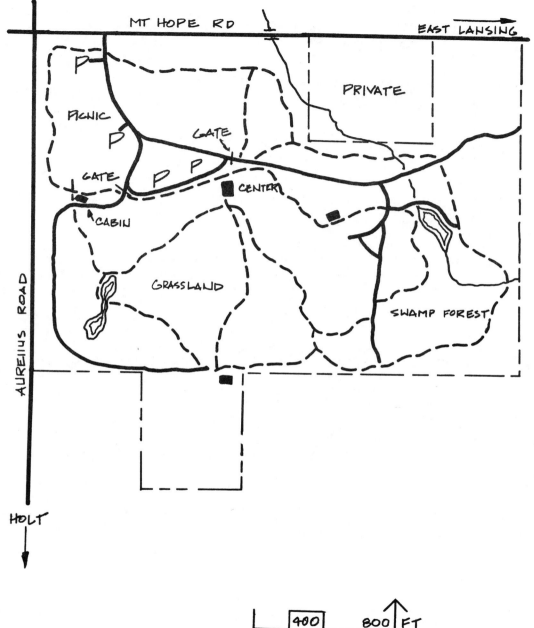

MT HOPE RD

EAST LANSING

PRIVATE

PICNIC

GATE

GATE

P P

CABIN

CENTER

GRASSLAND

SWAMP FOREST

AURELIUS ROAD

HOLT

| 400 | 800 | FT |

Fenner Arboretum
2020 E. Mt. Hope Rd
Lansing, MI 48910

517-483-4224

Lansing Park and Recreation Department

517-483-4277

Michigan Atlas & Gazetteer Location: 39C5

County Location: Ingham

Directions To Trailhead:
On the east side of Lansing at the corner of Aurelius Rd and Mt Hope Rd.
About 1.5 miles south of Michigan Ave.

Trail Type: Hiking/Walking, Interpretive
Trail Distance: 4.5 mi   Loops: 6+   Shortest: .5 mi   Longest: 1 mi
Trail Surface: Paved, gravel and natural
Trail Use Fee: None
Method Of Ski Trail Grooming: NA
Skiing Ability Suggested: NA
Hiking Trail Difficulty: Easy
Mountain Biking Ability Suggested: NA
Terrain: Steep 0%, Hilly 0%, Moderate 10%, Flat 90%
Camping: Group campground on site

Owned by the City of Lansing.
Features include a multi-purpose visitor center, pioneer cabin, picnic grounds,
ponds and bison exhibit.

FENNER ARBORETUM

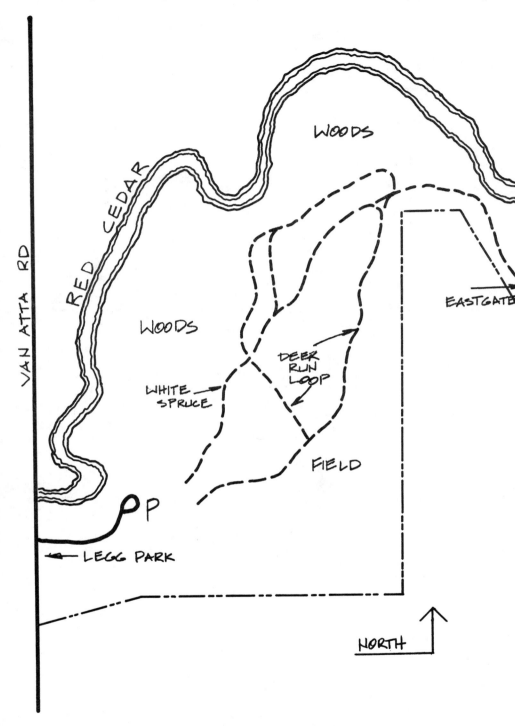

Harris Center

Meridian Township Parks Commission
5151 Marsh Rd
Okemos, MI 48864

517-349-1200

Michigan Atlas & Gazetteer Location: 39C5

County Location: Ingham

Directions To Trailhead:
Take Okemos Rd north to Jolly Rd, then east about 3.5 miles to Van Atta Rd, then north 1 mile to park.

Trail Type: Hiking/Walking, Cross Country Skiing, Interpretive
Trail Distance: 1.5 mi   Loops: 3   Shortest: .35 mi Longest: .65 mi
Trail Surface: Natural
Trail Use Fee: None
Method Of Ski Trail Grooming: None
Skiing Ability Suggested: Novice
Hiking Trail Difficulty: Easy
Mountain Biking Ability Suggested: NA
Terrain: Steep 0%, Hilly 0%, Moderate 10%, Flat 90%
Camping: None

Owned by the Charter Township of Meridian
Adjacent to East Gate and Legg Parks along the Red Cedar River.

HARRIS CENTER

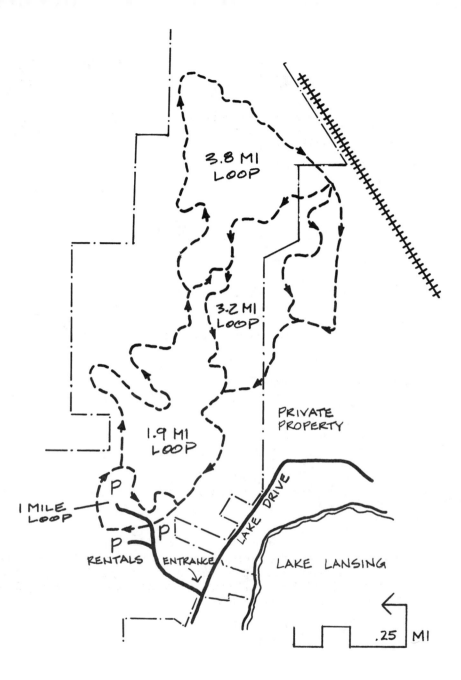

Ingham County Parks Department
PO Box 38
Mason, MI 48854

517-676-2233

Michigan Atlas & Gazetteer Location: 39B5

County Location: Ingham

Directions To Trailhead:
Northeast of Lansing on the north shore of Lake Lansing near Haslett. Take Saginaw Hwy to Haslett Rd., then left on Marsh Rd. about 1.5 miles to North Lake Drive (bear to the right), follow for about 1.5 miles, the park is on the left side of the road.

Trail Type: Hiking/Walking, Cross Country Skiing
Trail Distance: 4.5 mi   Loops: 3   Shortest: 1 mi   Longest: 3.8 mi
Trail Surface: Natural
Trail Use Fee: None
Method Of Ski Trail Grooming: Track set
Skiing Ability Suggested: Novice to intermediate
Hiking Trail Difficulty: Easy
Mountain Biking Ability Suggested: NA
Terrain: Flat to rolling
Camping: None

Operated by the Ingham County Parks Department
Ski rentals and warming building are available.
Picnic grounds and ball fields are available.
Mountain bikes are not permitted on the trails in this park.

LAKE LANSING PARK-NORTH

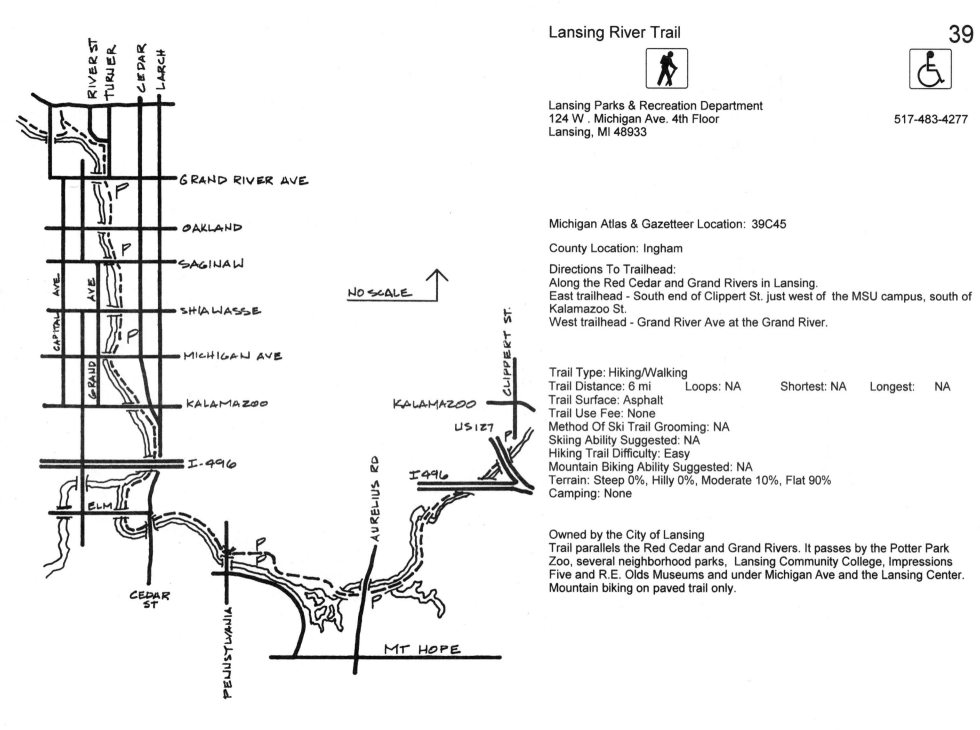

Lansing Parks & Recreation Department
124 W . Michigan Ave. 4th Floor
Lansing, MI 48933

517-483-4277

Michigan Atlas & Gazetteer Location: 39C45

County Location: Ingham

Directions To Trailhead:
Along the Red Cedar and Grand Rivers in Lansing.
East trailhead - South end of Clippert St. just west of the MSU campus, south of Kalamazoo St.
West trailhead - Grand River Ave at the Grand River.

Trail Type: Hiking/Walking
Trail Distance: 6 mi   Loops: NA   Shortest: NA   Longest: NA
Trail Surface: Asphalt
Trail Use Fee: None
Method Of Ski Trail Grooming: NA
Skiing Ability Suggested: NA
Hiking Trail Difficulty: Easy
Mountain Biking Ability Suggested: NA
Terrain: Steep 0%, Hilly 0%, Moderate 10%, Flat 90%
Camping: None

Owned by the City of Lansing
Trail parallels the Red Cedar and Grand Rivers. It passes by the Potter Park Zoo, several neighborhood parks, Lansing Community College, Impressions Five and R.E. Olds Museums and under Michigan Ave and the Lansing Center. Mountain biking on paved trail only.

LANSING RIVER TRAIL

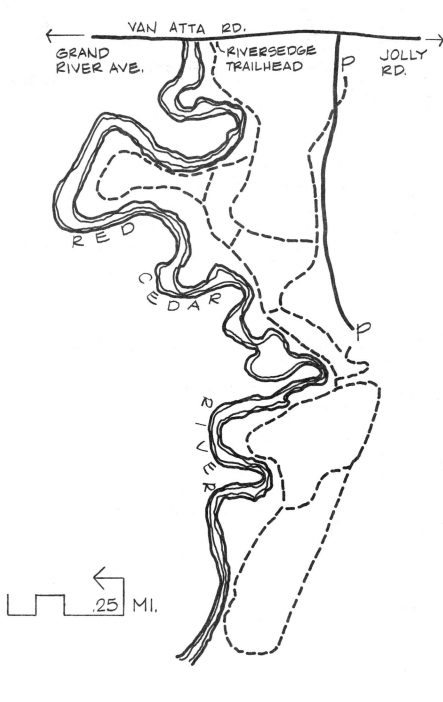

Legg Park

Meridian Township Park Commission
5151 Marsh Rd.
Okemos, MI 48864

517-349-1200

Michigan Atlas & Gazetteer Location: 39C5

County Location: Ingham

Directions To Trailhead:
East of Okemos on Grand River Ave to Van Atta Rd., then south 1 mile across the Red Cedar River to the park entrance on the right (west) side of the road. There is a trailhead on Van Atta Rd. at the Red Cedar River at the bridge but parking is very limited.

Trail Type: Hiking/Walking, Cross Country Skiing, Interpretive
Trail Distance: 2.25 mi   Loops: 3   Shortest: .5 mi   Longest: 1 mi
Trail Surface: Natural
Trail Use Fee: None
Method Of Ski Trail Grooming: None
Skiing Ability Suggested: Novice to intermediate
Hiking Trail Difficulty: Easy
Mountain Biking Ability Suggested: NA
Terrain: Flat with some rolling terrain
Camping: None

Maintained by Meridain Charter Township
Trail along the Red Cedar River.
The area is designated as a riverfront natural area.
Toilets provided at the trailhead.
Terrian has both floodpain and upland enviorments represented.

LEGG PARK

East Lansing Public Works and Enviornmental Services
2000 Merritt Rd   517-337-9459
East Lansing, MI

Michigan Atlas & Gazetteer Location: 39B5

County Location: Ingham

Directions To Trailhead:
On the north side of East Lansing from Whitehills subdivision to Abbott Road Park. Also through Henry Fine Park.

Trail Type: Hiking/Walking, Cross Country Skiing
Trail Distance: 2.7 mi   Loops: NA   Shortest: NA   Longest: 2.7 mi
Trail Surface: Paved and natural
Trail Use Fee: None
Method Of Ski Trail Grooming: Not known at this time
Skiing Ability Suggested: Novice
Hiking Trail Difficulty: Easy
Mountain Biking Ability Suggested: NA
Terrain: Steep 0%, Hilly 0%, Moderate 5%, Flat 95%
Camping: None

Maintained by the City of East Lansing
Proposed trail system to be under construction beginning in 1997

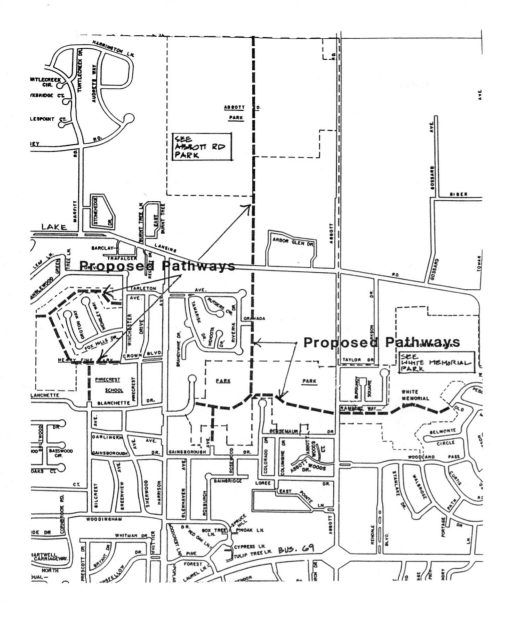

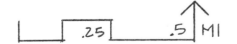

NORTHERN TIER PATHWAYS

City of East Lansing Public Works and Environmental Services
2000 Merritt Rd   517-337-9459
East Lansing, MI 48824

Michigan Atlas & Gazetteer Location: 39C5

County Location: Ingham

Directions To Trailhead:
In the city on Alton Rd

Trail Type: Cross Country Skiing
Trail Distance: 1.1 mi   Loops: 2   Shortest: .4   Longest: .7 mi
Trail Surface: Natural
Trail Use Fee: None
Method Of Ski Trail Grooming: Track set
Skiing Ability Suggested: Novice
Hiking Trail Difficulty: NA
Mountain Biking Ability Suggested: NA
Terrain: Steep 0%, Hilly 0%, Moderate 0%, Flat 100%
Camping: None

Maintained by the City of East Lansing Public Works and Enviornmental
Services
Park includes a shelter, ball fields and playgrounds.

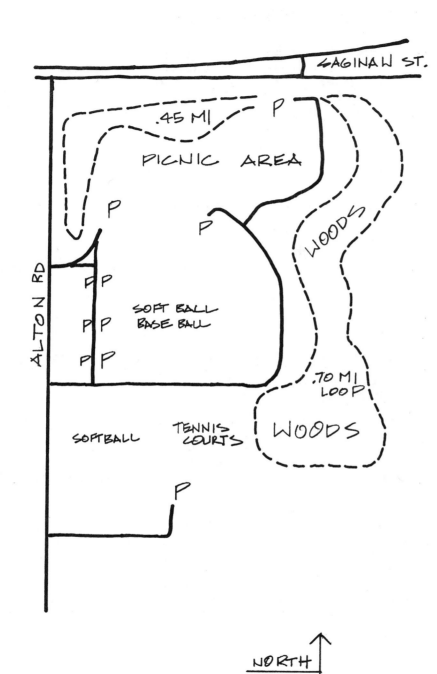

PATRIARCHE PARK

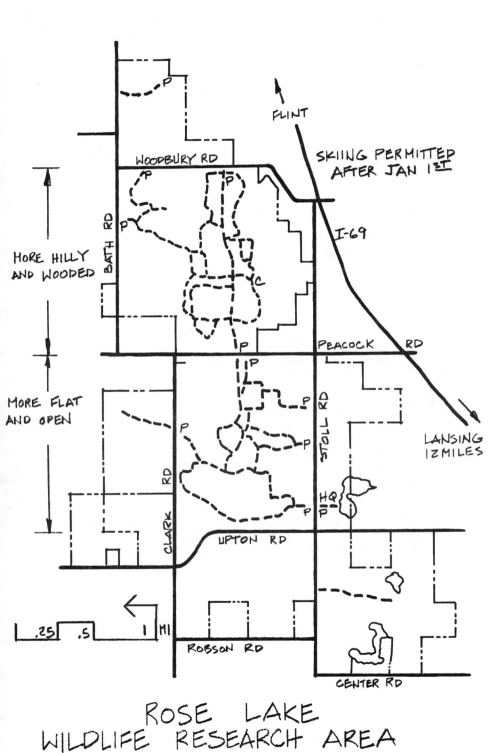

ROSE LAKE
WILDLIFE RESEARCH AREA

Rose Lake Wildlife Research Area
8562 East Stoll Rd.   517-373-9358
East Lansing, MI 48823

DNR Wildlife Division Office

517-373-1263

Michigan Atlas & Gazetteer Location: 39B56

County Location: Clinton

Directions To Trailhead:
12 miles NE of Lansing off I-69 From I-69 north on Upton, Peacock or Woodbury
Rds to parking areas.

Trail Type: Hiking/Walking, Cross Country Skiing, Mountain Biking
Trail Distance: 10+ mi   Loops: Many   Shortest: Longest:
Trail Surface: Natural
Trail Use Fee: None
Method Of Ski Trail Grooming: None
Skiing Ability Suggested: Novice to intermediate
Hiking Trail Difficulty: Easy to moderate
Mountain Biking Ability Suggested: Novice to intermediate
Terrain: Steep 5%, Hilly 10%, Moderate 30%, Flat 55%
Camping: Youth group campground available, with reservations only

Maintained by the DNR Wildlife Division.
Skiing not permitted until January 2nd.
Very popular area for Lansing area residents and MSU students.
The best terrain with the most wooded trails are between Woodbury and
Peacock Roads. This land was purchased with hunting licenses.
Please respect the rights of the hunters when in this area. Use of the area for
non hunting purposes is discouraged during the firearm hunting season.
If you must use the trails during the hunting season, it is strongly suggested that
hunter orange should be worn.

Secretary, Natural Areas Committee
Div. of Campus Park and Planning, 412 Olds Hall
MSU, East Lansing, MI 48824

517-355-9582

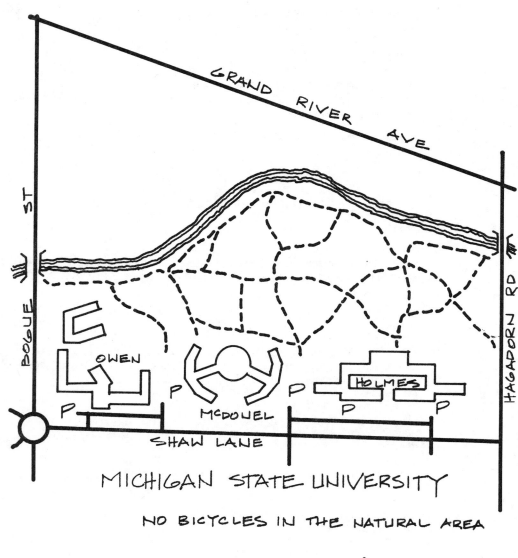

GRAND RIVER AVE

ST

BOGUE

HAGADORN RD

OWEN

P

McDOUEL

P

HOLMES

P

P

P

SHAW LANE

MICHIGAN STATE UNIVERSITY

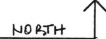

NO BICYCLES IN THE NATURAL AREA

NORTH

Michigan Atlas & Gazetteer Location: 39C5

County Location: Ingham

Directions To Trailhead:
On the Michigan State University campus. Bordered by the Red Cedar River on the north, Hagadorn Rd on the east , Bogue St on the west and just north of Shaw Lane on the south.

Trail Type: Hiking/Walking, Cross Country Skiing, Interpretive
Trail Distance: 11 mi   Loops: Many   Shortest: Longest:
Trail Surface: Natural
Trail Use Fee: None
Method Of Ski Trail Grooming: None
Skiing Ability Suggested: Novice
Hiking Trail Difficulty: Easy
Mountain Biking Ability Suggested: NA
Terrain: 100% Flat
Camping: None

Owned by Michigan State University
Managed as a research and natural area.
This 34 acres forest is heavily used by MSU students since several residence hall border the natural area on the south.
Bicycles area strictly prohibited in this area.

SANFORD NATURAL AREA

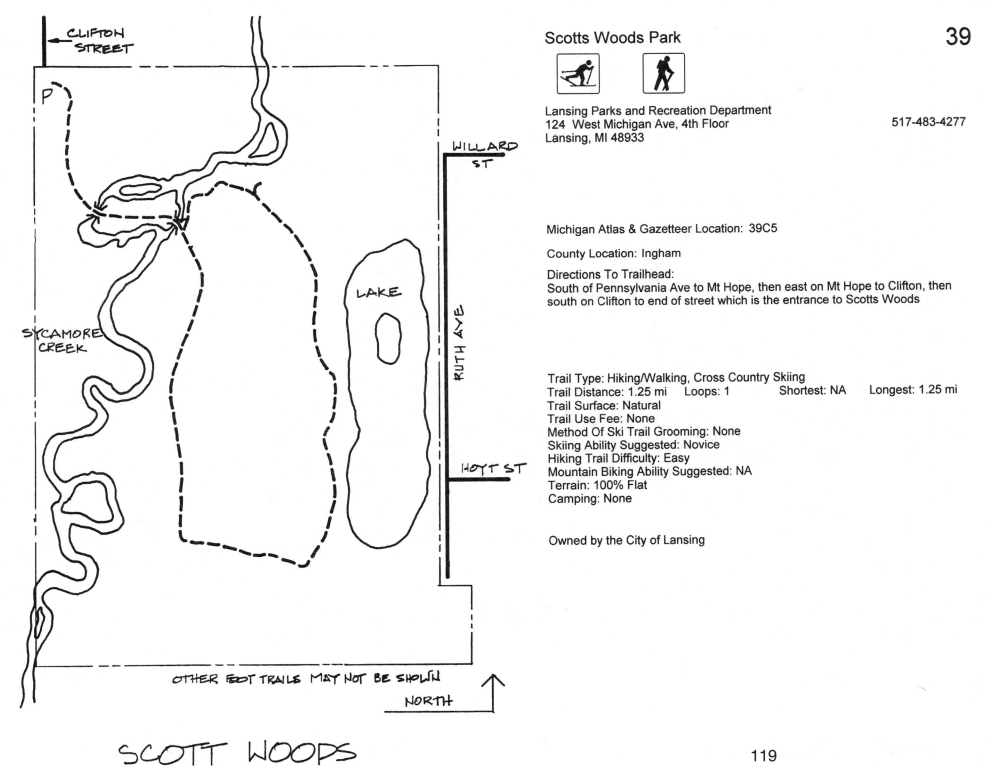

Scotts Woods Park

Lansing Parks and Recreation Department
124 West Michigan Ave, 4th Floor
Lansing, MI 48933

517-483-4277

Michigan Atlas & Gazetteer Location: 39C5

County Location: Ingham

Directions To Trailhead:
South of Pennsylvania Ave to Mt Hope, then east on Mt Hope to Clifton, then
south on Clifton to end of street which is the entrance to Scotts Woods

Trail Type: Hiking/Walking, Cross Country Skiing
Trail Distance: 1.25 mi   Loops: 1   Shortest: NA   Longest: 1.25 mi
Trail Surface: Natural
Trail Use Fee: None
Method Of Ski Trail Grooming: None
Skiing Ability Suggested: Novice
Hiking Trail Difficulty: Easy
Mountain Biking Ability Suggested: NA
Terrain: 100% Flat
Camping: None

Owned by the City of Lansing

CLIFTON STREET

WILLARD ST

RUTH AVE

LAKE

HOYT ST

SYCAMORE CREEK

P

OTHER FOOT TRAILS MAY NOT BE SHOWN

NORTH

SCOTT WOODS

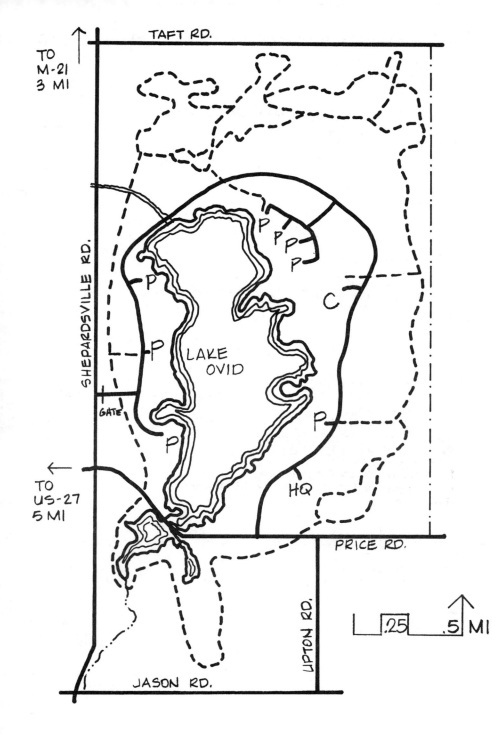

Sleepy Hollow State Park
7835 Price Rd.
Lainsburg, MI 48848

517-651-6217
616-527-3750

DNR Parks and Recreation Division

517-373-1270
517-322-1300

Michigan Atlas & Gazetteer Location: 39A5

County Location: Clinton

Directions To Trailhead:
15 miles NE of Lansing From US27 take Price Rd. east 6 miles to park entrance.

Trail Type: Hiking/Walking, Cross Country Skiing, Mountain Biking
Trail Distance: 15.75 mi   Loops: Several   Shortest: 1.7 mi Longest: 12.6 mi
Trail Surface: Natural
Trail Use Fee: None, but vehicle entry fee required
Method Of Ski Trail Grooming: Track set with sufficient snow depth
Skiing Ability Suggested: Novice to intermediate
Hiking Trail Difficulty: Easy to moderate
Mountain Biking Ability Suggested: Novice
Terrain: Steep 2%, Hilly 4%, Moderate 20%, Flat 74%
Camping: Modern campground in park

Maintained by the DNR Parks and Recreation Division
Park has campground, swimming and great fishing.
Cross country ski trail maps are available at the park office.
Cross country ski trail system is less extensive than the hiking trail system shown.

SLEEPY HOLLOW STATE PARK

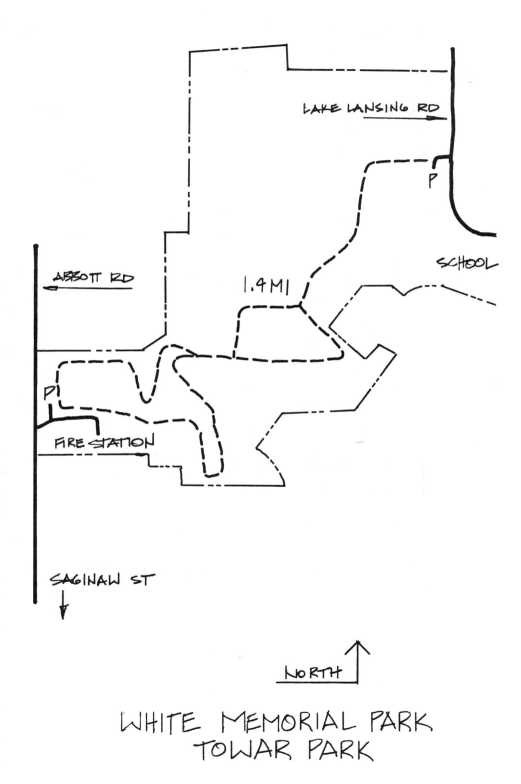

LAKE LANSING RD →

ABBOTT RD ←

1.4 MI

SCHOOL

P

FIRE STATION

SAGINAW ST ↓

NORTH ↑

WHITE MEMORIAL PARK
TOWAR PARK

East Lansing Public Works and Enviornmental Services
2000 Merritt Rd
East Lansing, MI 48823

517-337-9459

Michigan Atlas & Gazetteer Location: 39C5

County Location: Ingham

Directions To Trailhead:
Located on the north side of the city in the Whitehills subdivision

Trail Type: Cross Country Skiing
Trail Distance: 1.4 mi   Loops: 1   Shortest: NA   Longest: 1.4 mi
Trail Surface: Natural
Trail Use Fee: None
Method Of Ski Trail Grooming: Track set
Skiing Ability Suggested: Novice
Hiking Trail Difficulty: NA
Mountain Biking Ability Suggested: NA
Terrain: Steep 0%, Hilly 0%, Moderate 20%, Flat 80%
Camping: None

Maintained by the City of East Lansing Department of Public Works and
Enviornmental Services.
60 acre park with playgrounds
Handicapper facilities limited to the parking area

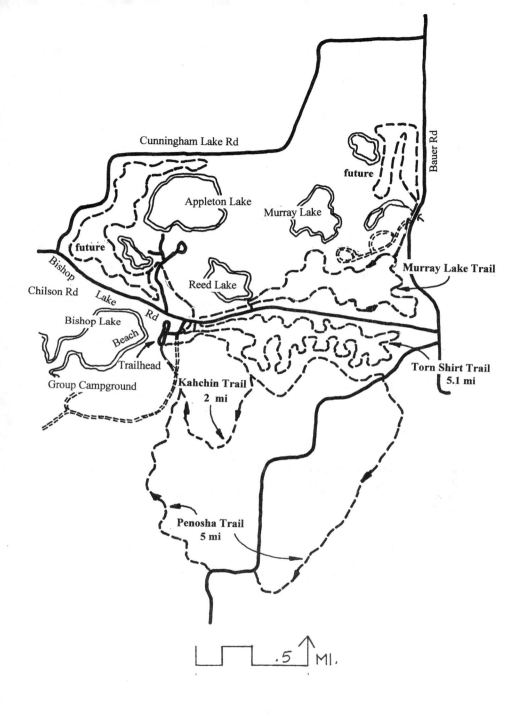

BRIGHTON RECREATION AREA

Brighton Recreation Area
6360 Chilson Rd., Rte 3
Howell , MI 48843

313-229-6566

DNR Parks and Recreation Division

517-373-1270

Michigan Atlas & Gazetteer Location: 40D3

County Location: Livingston

Directions To Trailhead:
West from Brighton on Brighton Rd. about 4 miles to Chilson Rd., then south 1.5 miles to Bishop Lake Rd., then east 1.5 miles to Bishop Lake picnic area. Trailhead is located at the south end of the east Bishiop Lake parking lot.

Trail Type: Hiking/Walking, Cross Country Skiing, Mountain Biking
Trail Distance: 16 mi   Loops: 4   Shortest: 2 mi   Longest: 5.1 mi
Trail Surface: Natural
Trail Use Fee: None, but vehicle entry fee required
Method Of Ski Trail Grooming: None
Skiing Ability Suggested: Novice to intermediate
Hiking Trail Difficulty: Easy to moderate
Mountain Biking Ability Suggested: Novice to advanced
Terrain: Steep 5%, Hilly 25%, Moderate 40%, Flat 30%
Camping: Campground available at Bishop Lake and Appleton Lake.

Maintained by the DNR Parks and Recreation Division
In 1997 two new trails were designed and built by the Michigan Mountain Biking Association. The Torn Shirt Trail (5.1mi) is rated intermediate to advanced and the Murray Lake Trail (3.5 mi but to be extended several more miles in 1998) is rated novice to intermediate. Both start at the new handicapper toilet at the Bishop Lake Beach parking lot. Another loop near Appleton Lake is also planned for the future. The two original multi-use loops, the Penosha and Kahchin Trails are rated novice for mountain biking. Since these are also open to hiking which were their original purpose, mountain bikers should follow the posted directional arrows. When the new mountain bike loops are completed, the Penosha and Kahchin Trails will be closed to mountain bike use. After a hike or ride try out the swimming beach to cool down on a hot summer day. For those who like to explore, there are additional unmarked trails in the recreation area.
This nearly 5,000 acre recreation area has numerous lakes for fishing.

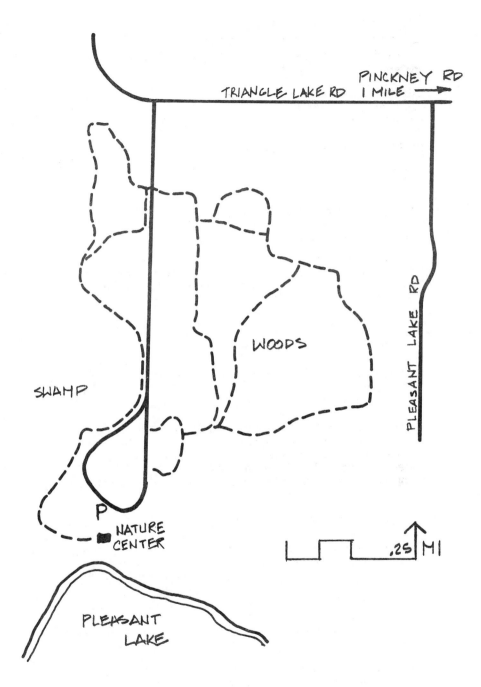

Howell Nature Center Attn. Dick Grant
1005 Triangle Rd.
Howell, MI 48843

517-546-0249

Michigan Atlas & Gazetteer Location: 40D2

County Location: Livingston

Directions To Trailhead:
South of Howell, 4.5 miles on Pinckney Rd., then west on Triangle Rd. for about
1.5 miles to the nature center entrance

Trail Type: Hiking/Walking, Cross Country Skiing, Interpretive
Trail Distance: 3 mi   Loops: 4   Shortest: .25 mi Longest: 2 mi
Trail Surface: Natural
Trail Use Fee: Yes
Method Of Ski Trail Grooming: None
Skiing Ability Suggested: Novice to intermediate
Hiking Trail Difficulty: Easy to moderate
Mountain Biking Ability Suggested: NA
Terrain: Steep 5%, Hilly 65%, Moderate 20%, Flat 10%
Camping: None

Operated by the Presbytery of Detroit.
Available to any organized group for day or overnight use.
Ski rentals and lodge available for groups with advance reservations.

HOWELL NATURE CENTER

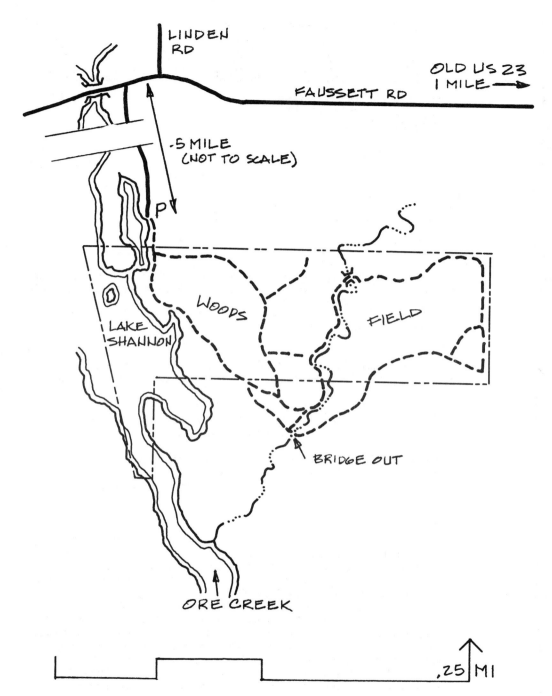

Michigan Nature Association
PO Box 102
Avoca, MI 48006

810-324-2626

Michigan Atlas & Gazetteer Location: 40C3

County Location: Livingston

Directions To Trailhead:
From US23/M59 , go north 3 miles on US23 to Clyde Rd.exit, then west and turn north on Old US23, then north 2 miles to Faussett Rd., then one mile west to the 2 track access road, which goes south. It is about 200 feet west of Linden Rd. Drive through unlocked plastic gate about .5 mile south to a mowed parking area. Follow 2 track to the sanctuary entrance gate.

Trail Type: Hiking/Walking, Interpretive
Trail Distance: .75 mi   Loops: 2   Shortest: .3 mi   Longest: .75 mi
Trail Surface: Natural
Trail Use Fee: None
Method Of Ski Trail Grooming: NA
Skiing Ability Suggested: NA
Hiking Trail Difficulty: Easy
Mountain Biking Ability Suggested: NA
Terrain: Steep 0%, Hilly 0%, Moderate 20%, Flat 80%
Camping: None

Maintained by the Michigan Nature Association
Small but full of interesting plants.
Many birds nest in the area.

SHANNON NATURE SANCTUARY

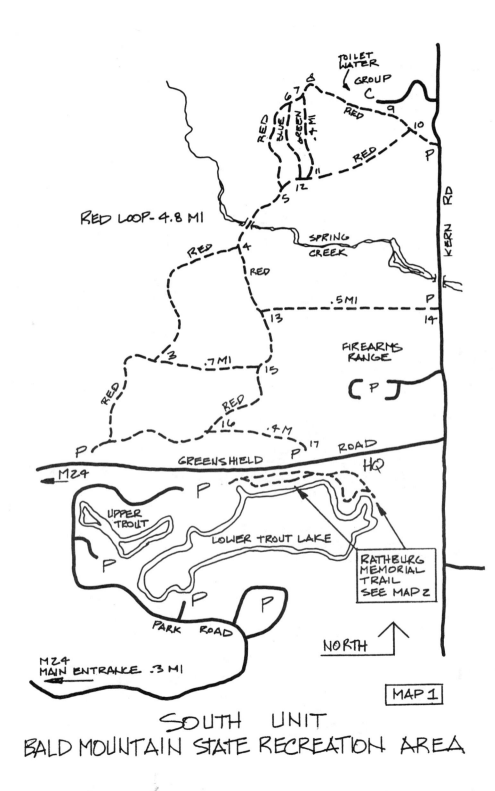

RED LOOP - 4.8 MI

SOUTH UNIT
BALD MOUNTAIN STATE RECREATION AREA

MAP 1

NORTH

Bald Mountain Recreation Area

Bald Mountain Recreation Area
1330 Greenshield Rd., Rte 1
Lake Orion, MI 48060

248-693-6767

DNR Parks and Recreation Division

517-373-1270

Michigan Atlas & Gazetteer Location: 41BC7,42B1

County Location: Oakland

Directions To Trailhead:
9 miles north of Rochester and 4 miles east of Lake Orion on West Romeo Rd.
Headquarters-Northbound M24 from I-75 3 miles to Greenshield Rd. Turn right
(east) and proceed for 1.5 miles to HQ.
Trailhead parking areas along Greenshield Rd, Stoney Creek Rd, Harmon Rd,
Miller Rd and Predmore Rd.

Trail Type: Hiking/Walking, Cross Country Skiing, Mountain Biking
Trail Distance: 16.6 mi   Loops: 6   Shortest: 1.5   Longest: 4.8 mi
Trail Surface: Natural
Trail Use Fee: None, but vehicle entry fee required.
Method Of Ski Trail Grooming: Skied-in trails only
Skiing Ability Suggested: Intermediate to advanced
Hiking Trail Difficulty: Easy to moderate
Mountain Biking Ability Suggested: Novice to intermediate
Terrain: Steep 5%, Hilly 40%, Moderate 50%, Flat 5%
Camping: Group campground only but rustic cabins may be rented

Maintained by the DNR Parks and Recreation Division.
Mostly wooded trails that are well signed and marked with some road crossings.
Scenic trails with vistas and many lakes make this trail system a pleasent
experience. Water pumps are located at the rustic cabins on Tamarack Lake
and the group campground on Kern Rd. Wildflowers are plentiful in the spring.
Sledding available on Stoney Creek Rd.
Mountain biking opportunities are excellent for cyclists of all skill levels, since the
terrain is not very demanding but is enjoyable for the more skilled riders. The
south unit can be very wet and slippery in the spring for mountain biking. Cross
country skiing is recommended only in the North Unit since snowmobiling is
allowed on the South Unit trails. Rathburg Memorial Trail along the north shore
of Lower Trout Lake is handicapper accessible (under construction in 1997).
Since hunting is permitted, wear bright clothing during the hunting season.

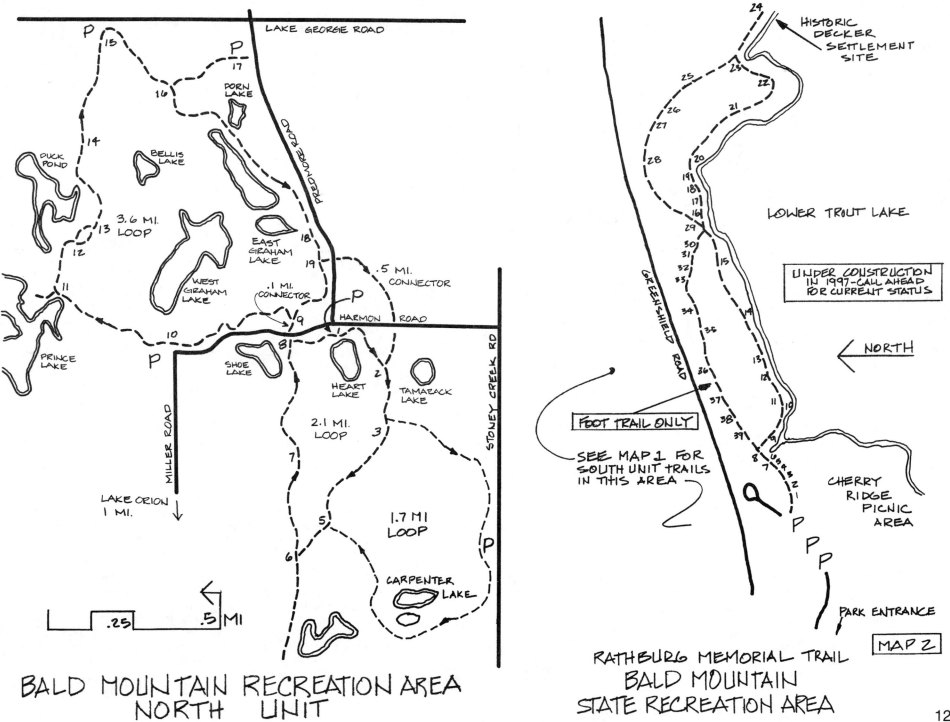

BALD MOUNTAIN RECREATION AREA
NORTH UNIT

RATHBURG MEMORIAL TRAIL
BALD MOUNTAIN
STATE RECREATION AREA

125

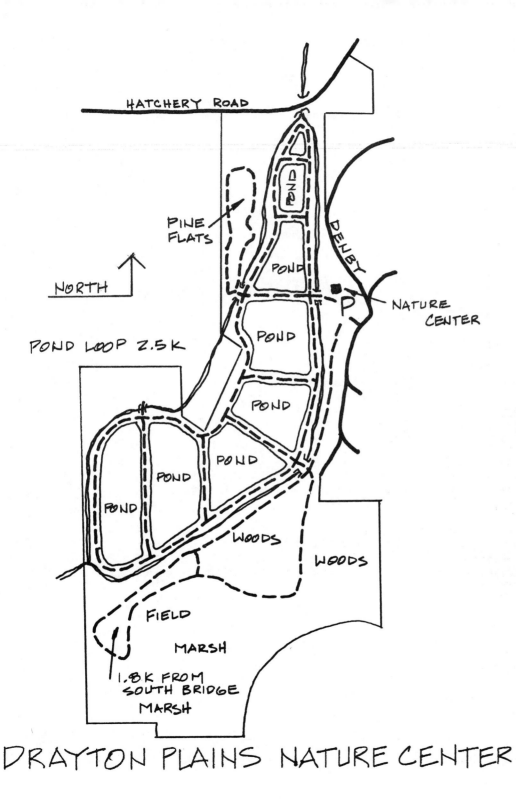

Drayton Plains Nature Center, Inc.
2125 Denby Drive
Waterford, MI 48329

810-674-2119

Michigan Atlas & Gazetteer Location: 41C67

County Location: Oakland

Directions To Trailhead:
North on US24 from Pontiac about 5 miles to Hatchery Rd., then west 3/4 mile,
then south on Edmore and follow signs to the center.

Trail Type: Hiking/Walking, Cross Country Skiing, Interpretive
Trail Distance: 6 km   Loops: Several   Shortest: .5 km   Longest: 2.5 km
Trail Surface: Natural and gravel
Trail Use Fee: Donations requsted
Method Of Ski Trail Grooming: None
Skiing Ability Suggested: Novice
Hiking Trail Difficulty: Easy
Mountain Biking Ability Suggested: NA
Terrain: Steep 0%, Hilly 0%, Moderate 40%, Flat 60%
Camping: None

A profit non profit nature center.
Formerally the second oldest fish hatchery (1903 to 1960) in Michigan.
Large (137 acres) nature center within an urban area.

DRAYTON PLAINS NATURE CENTER

Bloomfield Hills Public Schools
3325 Franklin Rd
Bloomfield Hills, MI 48302

810-339-3497

Michigan Atlas & Gazetteer Location: 41D7

County Location: Oakland

Directions To Trailhead:
On Franklin Rd Between Long Lake Rd and Square Lake Rd, .25 mile west of Telegraph Rd

Trail Type: Hiking/Walking, Interpretive
Trail Distance: 1.7 mi   Loops: 4   Shortest: .2 mi   Longest: .9 mi
Trail Surface: Natural
Trail Use Fee: None
Method Of Ski Trail Grooming: NA
Skiing Ability Suggested: NA
Hiking Trail Difficulty: Easy
Mountain Biking Ability Suggested: NA
Terrain: Steep 0%, Hilly 15%, Moderate 15%, Flat 70%
Camping: None

Owned by the Bloomfield Hills Public Schools
Trail guide available.
Open to the public with special event throughout the year.

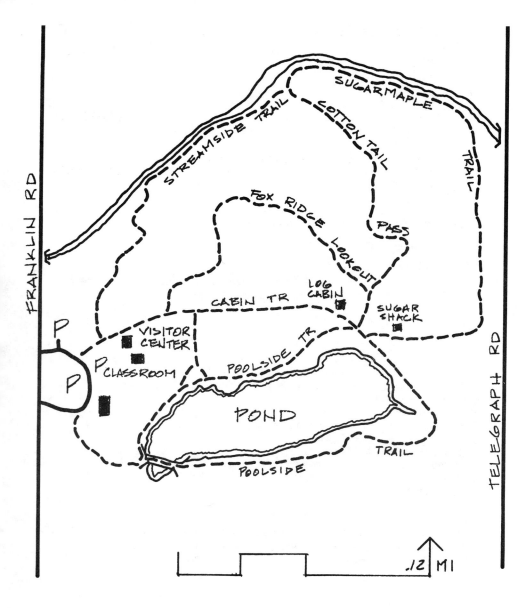

E.J. JOHNSON
NATURE CENTER

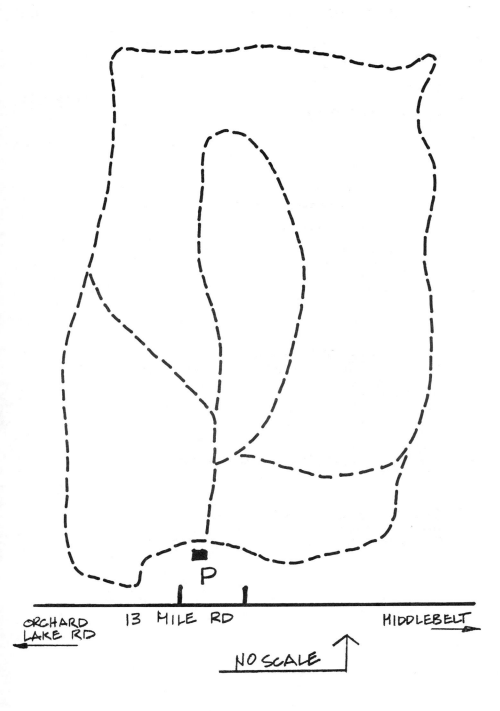

Glen Oaks County Park
30500 West 13 Mile Rd.   810-851-8356
Farmington Hills, MI 48018

Oakland County Parks & Recreation Commission
2800 Watkins Lake Rd.   810-858-0906
Pontiac, MI 48054-1697

Michigan Atlas & Gazetteer Location: 41D7

County Location: Oakland

Directions To Trailhead:
Between Orchard Lake and Middlebelt Rds on 13 Mile Rd.

Trail Type: Cross Country Skiing
Trail Distance: 5.7 km   Loops: 3   Shortest: Longest:
Trail Surface: Natural
Trail Use Fee: None
Method Of Ski Trail Grooming: Packed
Skiing Ability Suggested: Novice
Hiking Trail Difficulty: NA
Mountain Biking Ability Suggested: NA
Terrain: Steep 0%, Hilly 0%, Moderate 80%, Flat 20%
Camping: None

Operated by the Oakland County Parks and Recreation Commission.
Warming area, snack bar and ski rental available.
Trails on a golf course.

13 MILE RD

ORCHARD
LAKE RD

MIDDLEBELT

NO SCALE

GLEN OAKS GOLF COURSE

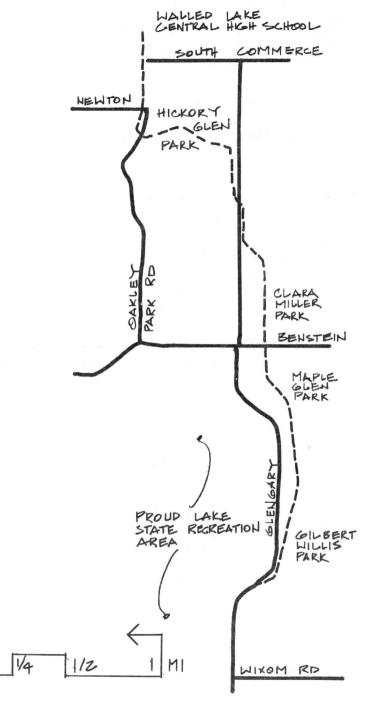

Charter Township of Commerce
2840 Fisher
Commerce, MI 48390

248-960-7050

Michigan Atlas & Gazetteer Location: 41D5

County Location: Oakland

Directions To Trailhead:
At the west end of Proud Lake State Park.
East end is 1/4 mi east of Wixom Rd.
Follows Oakley Park Rd and Glengary Rd.

Trail Type: Hiking/Walking, Cross Country Skiing
Trail Distance: 3.6 mi   Loops: NA   Shortest: NA   Longest: NA
Trail Surface: Paved
Trail Use Fee: None
Method Of Ski Trail Grooming: None
Skiing Ability Suggested: Novice
Hiking Trail Difficulty: Easy
Mountain Biking Ability Suggested: NA
Terrain: Steep 0%, Hilly 0%, Moderate 0%, Flat 100%
Camping: None

Maintained by the Charter Township of Commerce
Trail passes through Gilbert Park, Maple Glen Park, Clara Miller Park and Hickory Glen Park.
Future extensions are planned.
Call for current information.
Handicapper facilities are limited to Richardson Park.

GLENGARY NON-MOTORIZED PATH

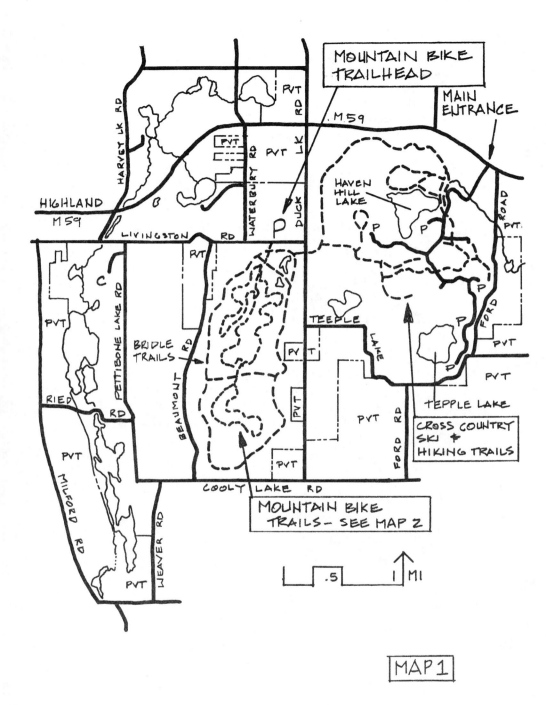

MOUNTAIN BIKE
TRAILHEAD

MAIN ENTRANCE

M.59

HAVEN HILL LAKE

HIGHLAND M59

LIVINGSTON RD

HARVEY LK RD

WATERBURY RD

PVT LK RD

PVT RD

PVT

DUCK LK

FORD ROAD

PVT

PVT

TEEPLE LAKE

BRIDLE TRAILS

PETTIBONE LAKE RD

BEAUMONT RD

RIED RD

PVT

PVT

MILFORD RD

WEAVER RD

COOLY LAKE RD

TEPPLE LAKE

CROSS COUNTRY SKI + HIKING TRAILS

FORD RD

PVT

PVT

PVT

PVT

MOUNTAIN BIKE
TRAILS - SEE MAP 2

.5   1 MI

MAP 1

Highland Recreation Area

Highland Recreation Area
5200 East Highland Rd.
White Lake, MI 48383

248-887-5135

DNR Parks and Recreation Division

517-373-1270

Michigan Atlas & Gazetteer Location: 41C5

County Location: Oakland

Directions To Trailhead:
Main park entrance: NE of Milford off M 59 1 mile east of Duck Lake Rd.
Mountain bike trailhead: From M 59 take Duck Lake Rd south about 1 mile to Livingston Rd, then west to the first parking lot. Trailhead is on the south side of Livingston Rd across from the parking lot at the large sign.

Trail Type: Hiking/Walking, Cross Country Skiing, Mountain Biking
Trail Distance: 16+ mi   Loops: Many   Shortest: 1 mi   Longest: 26 mi
Trail Surface: Natural
Trail Use Fee: None, but vehicle entry fee required
Method Of Ski Trail Grooming: Track set
Skiing Ability Suggested: Novice to intermediate
Hiking Trail Difficulty: Easy to moderate
Mountain Biking Ability Suggested: Intermediate to advanced
Terrain: Rolling to very hilly
Camping: Campground within the recreation area

Maintained by the DNR Parks and Recreation Division
Winter warming building, rentals and snack bar on weekends.
Trail uses may overlap seasonally.
Bridle trails are also in this recreation area but do not conflict with the skiing, hiking and bike trails.
The mountain bike trails developed by the Michigan Mountain Biking Association consist of 4 loops for intermediate and advanced riders only. This is not a trail for beginners!! Very challenging trails for the most advanced mountain bikers but an intermediate rider could handle the trails. A very popular trail for southern Michigan mountain bikers. See the separate trail map for the mountain bike trails. Hunting permitted in season throughout the mountain bike trail area.

HIGHLAND   RECREATION   AREA

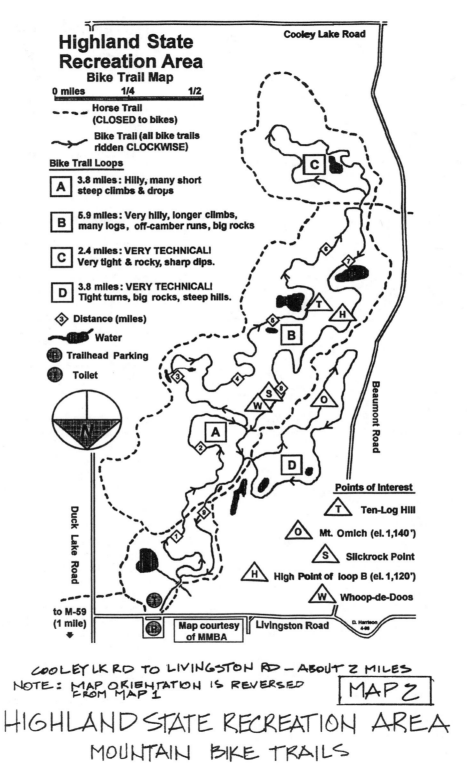

COOLEY LK RD TO LIVINGSTON RD — ABOUT 2 MILES

NOTE: MAP ORIENTATION IS REVERSED FROM MAP 1

MAP 2

HIGHLAND STATE RECREATION AREA

MOUNTAIN BIKE TRAILS

129.1

Holly Recreation Area
8100 Grange Hall Rd.   248-634-8811
Holly , MI 48442

DNR Parks and Recreation Division

517-373-1270

Michigan Atlas & Gazetteer Location: 41B56

County Location: Oakland

Directions To Trailhead:
Main Entrance:Exit I-75 at Grange Hall Rd. (east of Holly), then east 2.5 miles to
the recreation area entrance .
Mountain Bike Trail Entrance: Exit I-75 at Grange Hall Rd, then west to Hess
Rd.(first road to the north - may not be signed with either a road name or a DNR
sign), then north about a mile on Hess Rd to the trailhead.

Trail Type: Hiking/Walking, Cross Country Skiing, Mountain Biking, Interpretive
Trail Distance: 40+ mi   Loops: Many   Shortest: .8 mi   Longest: 15.5 mi
Trail Surface: Natural to wood decking
Trail Use Fee: None, but vehicle entry fee required
Method Of Ski Trail Grooming: None
Skiing Ability Suggested: Novice to advanced
Hiking Trail Difficulty: Easy to difficult
Mountain Biking Ability Suggested: Novice to advanced
Terrain: Steep 5%, Hilly 15%, Moderate 60%, Flat 20%
Camping: Campground available on site

Maintained by the DNR Parks and Recreation Division
Hiking, skiing, nature and mountain biking trails are provide throughout the park
Map 1 shows the entire recreation area with some hiking/skiing trails.
Map 2 shows detailed hiking/skiing trails in the McGinnis/Heron/Wildwood Lakes.
Map 3 shows the 23+ mile mountain bike trail complex.
Map 4 shows the West and North Loops for mountain biking.
The new East Loop for mountain biking is 15.5 miles long. It was constructed
late in 1997 and I would rate it as Advanced. A detailed trail map was not
available at printing time. The entrance to the East Loop is from the North Loop
trailhead. It travels generally clock wise (the outbound portion goes south along
the Interstate and the return portion, north along Hess Rd. All the mountain bike
trails were designed and built by the dedicated members of the Holly/Flint
Chapter of the Michigan Mountain Biking Association.
This information was revised in January 1998.

SEE MAPS ON NEXT 2 PAGES

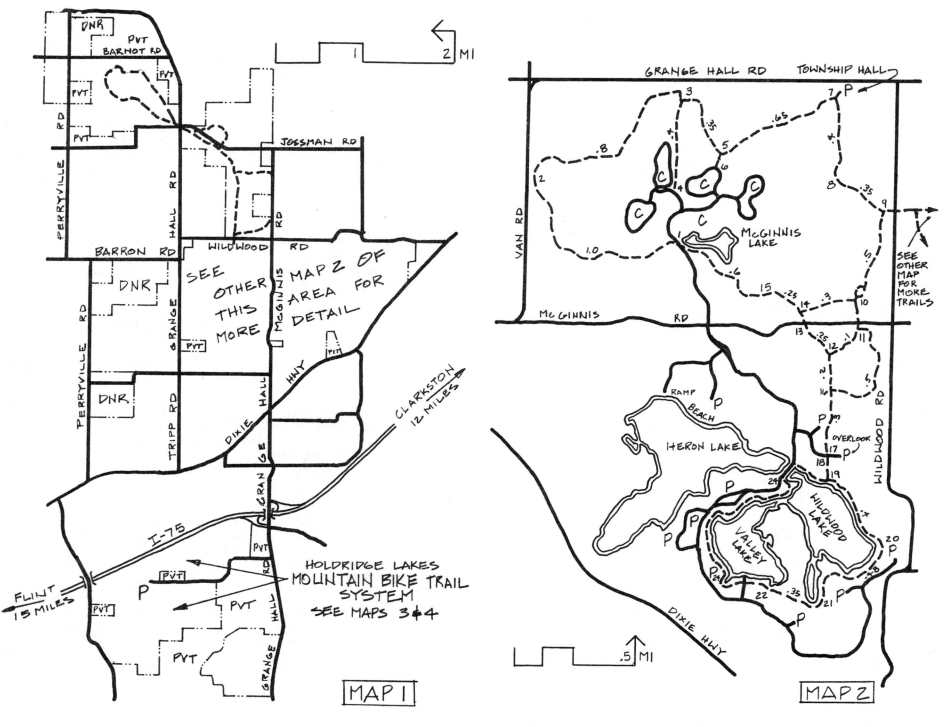

HOLLY RECREATION AREA

HOLLY RECREATION AREA

131

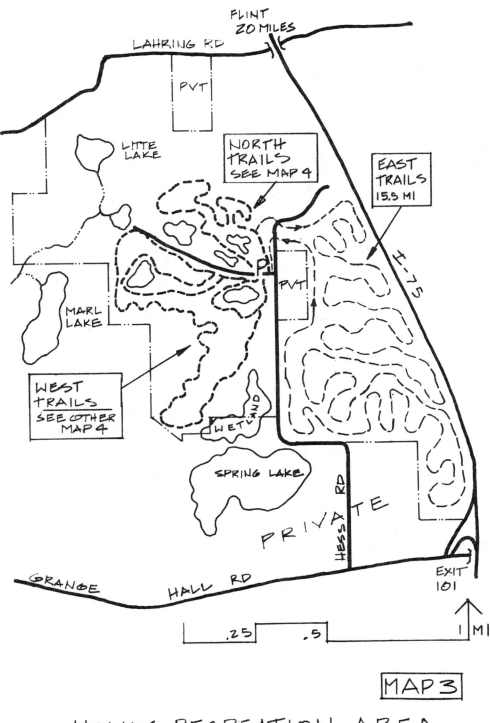

MAP 3

HOLLY RECREATION AREA
MOUNTAIN BIKE AREA

Labels on Map 3:

- FLINT 20 MILES
- LAHRING RD
- PVT
- LITTE LAKE
- NORTH TRAILS SEE MAP 4
- EAST TRAILS 15.5 MI
- I-75
- MARL LAKE
- PVT
- WEST TRAILS SEE OTHER MAP 4
- WETLND
- SPRING LAKE
- PRIVATE
- HESS RD
- GRANGE HALL RD
- EXIT 101
- .25   .5   1 MI

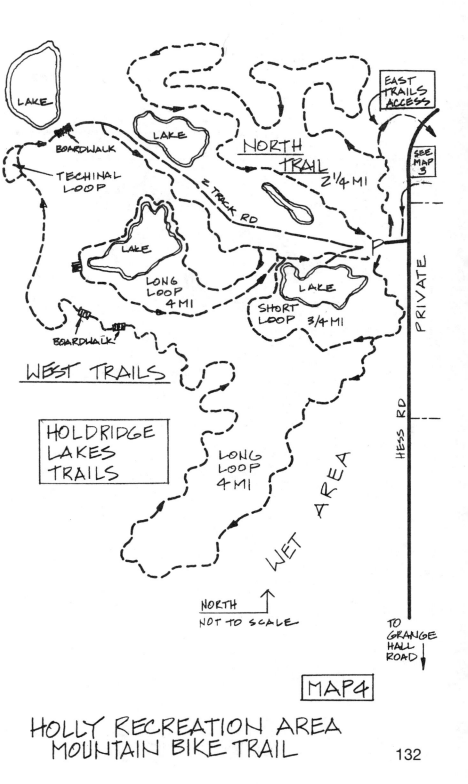

MAP 4

HOLLY RECREATION AREA
MOUNTAIN BIKE TRAIL

Labels on Map 4:

- LAKE
- BOARDWALK
- TECHINAL LOOP
- LAKE
- NORTH TRAIL 2¼ MI
- EAST TRAILS ACCESS
- SEE MAP 3
- Z TRACK RD
- LAKE
- LONG LOOP 4 MI
- BOARDWALK
- LAKE
- SHORT LOOP 3/4 MI
- PRIVATE
- WEST TRAILS
- HOLDRIDGE LAKES TRAILS
- HESS RD
- LONG LOOP 4 MI
- WET AREA
- NORTH NOT TO SCALE
- TO GRANGE HALL ROAD

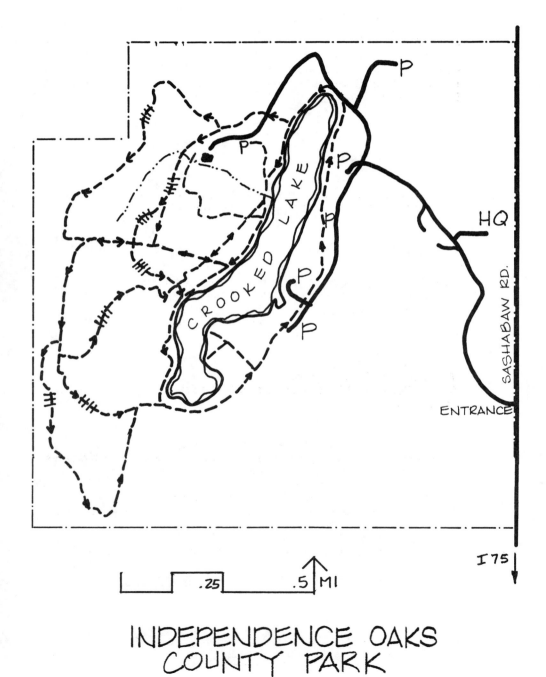

INDEPENDENCE OAKS COUNTY PARK

.25   .5 MI

Independence Oaks County Park
9501 Sashabaw Rd.
Clarkston, MI 48016

248-625-0877
248-625-6473

Oakland County Parks and Recreation Commission
2800 Watkins Lake Rd.
Waterford, MI 48328

810-858-0906

Michigan Atlas & Gazetteer Location: 41B6

County Location: Oakland

Directions To Trailhead:
North of Pontiac off I-75 at Sashabaw Rd. exit 89, then north 2.5 miles to the park entrance

Trail Type: Hiking/Walking, Cross Country Skiing, Interpretive
Trail Distance: 10+ mi   Loops: Many   Shortest: .25 mi Longest: 3+ mi
Trail Surface: Paved and natural
Trail Use Fee: None, but vehicle entry fee required
Method Of Ski Trail Grooming: Double track set
Skiing Ability Suggested: Novice to advanced
Hiking Trail Difficulty: Easy to moderate
Mountain Biking Ability Suggested: NA
Terrain: Steep 2%, Hilly 45%, Moderate 15%, Flat 38%
Camping: Youth group camping only

Operated by the Oakland County Parks and Recreation Commission
The complex trail system provides many different route options. Using different sections, over 10 miles of trails are available.
Ski rentals, warming area, snack bar, picnic grounds, fishing, boating, Rubach Sensory Garden, swimming, nature trail and center and ice skating. Some of the best cross country trails in southeast Michigan.
Open 8am to sunset daily (Closed Christmas Day)
Fishing and ice skating available.
A .3 mile "All Visitors Trail" with observation deck overlooking crooked Lake is available for visitors with disabilities.

Indian Springs Metropark
5200 Indian Trail
White Lake, MI 48386

248-625-7280
800-47-PARKS

Huron-Clinton Metropolitan Authority
13000 High Ridge Drive, PO Box 2001
Brighton, MI 48116-8001

810-227-2757

Michigan Atlas & Gazetteer Location: 41C56

County Location: Oakland

Directions To Trailhead:
Just north of Pontiac Lake State Recreation Area and south of Clarkston on White Lake Rd, between Cuthbert and Teggerdine Roads.

Trail Type: Hiking/Walking, Cross Country Skiing, Interpretive
Trail Distance: 11 mi   Loops: Many   Shortest: .3 mi   Longest: 4.2 mi
Trail Surface: Paved and natural
Trail Use Fee: None, but vehicle entry fee required
Method Of Ski Trail Grooming: Track set
Skiing Ability Suggested: Novice
Hiking Trail Difficulty: Easy
Mountain Biking Ability Suggested: NA
Terrain: Steep 0%, Hilly 5%, Moderate 35%, Flat 60%
Camping: None

Operated by the Huron-Clinton Metropolitan Authority.
Year around 2,224 acre regional recreation area with a wide variety of facilities including a nature center, golf course and picnic grounds.
Hiking trail terrain is listed above.
Mountan bikes are restricted to the paved hike/bike trail.
Cross country ski trail terrain is 5% steep, 25% hilly, 35% moderate and 35% flat. Ski rentals on weekends only.
Trails for skiing and hiking/biking are not identical.
Timberland Swamp Nature Sanctuary is located on the north border of this Metropark.
Call or write for the Metropark Guide, published each year.

SEE MAPS ON NEXT PAGE

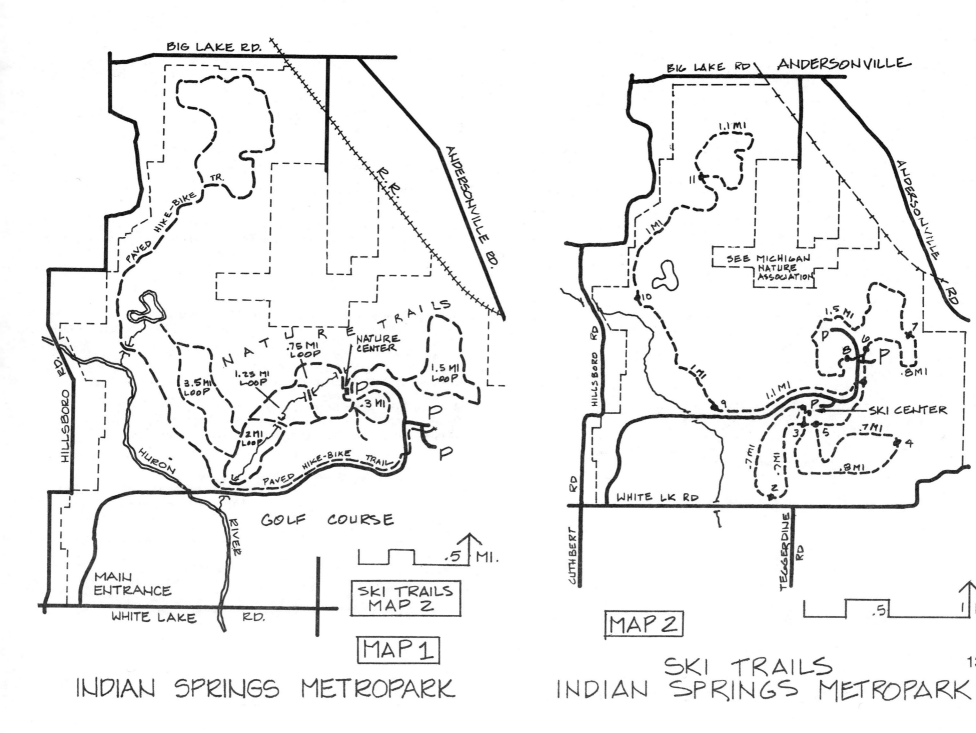

MAP 1

INDIAN SPRINGS METROPARK

MAP 2

SKI TRAILS
INDIAN SPRINGS METROPARK

135

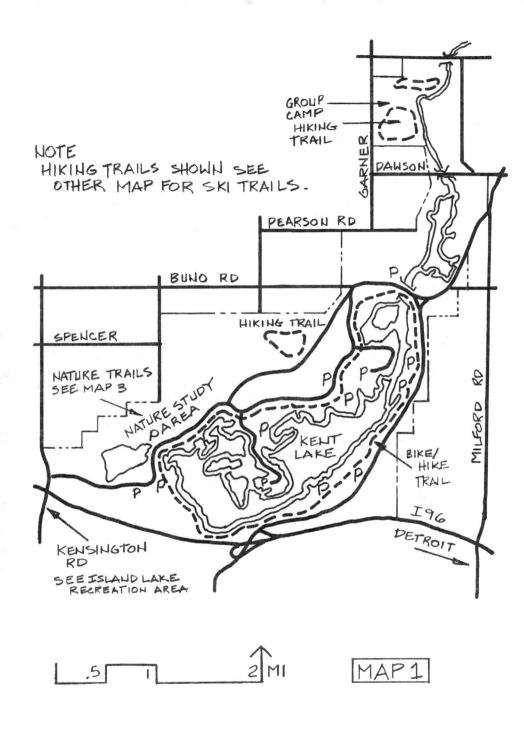

NOTE
HIKING TRAILS SHOWN SEE
OTHER MAP FOR SKI TRAILS.

GROUP CAMP HIKING TRAIL

GARNER

DAWSON

PEARSON RD

BUNO RD

HIKING TRAIL

SPENCER

NATURE TRAILS SEE MAP 3

NATURE STUDY AREA

KENT LAKE

MILFORD RD

BIKE/ HIKE TRAIL

I 96

DETROIT

KENSINGTON RD

SEE ISLAND LAKE RECREATION AREA

P

.5   1   2 MI

MAP 1

Kensington Metropark
2240 West Buno Rd.
Milford , MI 48042-9725

248-685-1561
800-47-PARKS

Huron-Clinton Metropolitan Authority
13000 High Ridge Drive, PO Box 2001
Brighton, MI 48116-8001

810-227-2757

Michigan Atlas & Gazetteer Location: 41D4

County Location: Oakland & Livingston

Directions To Trailhead:
SW of Milford and just north of I-96
Exit I-96 at Kent Lake Rd.(exit153) or Kensington Rd.(exit 151) and turn north to park

Trail Type: Hiking/Walking, Cross Country Skiing, Interpretive
Trail Distance: 25+ mi   Loops: Many   Shortest: .5 mi   Longest: 8 mi
Trail Surface: Paved, gravel and natural
Trail Use Fee: None, but vehicle entry fee required
Method Of Ski Trail Grooming: Track set as needed
Skiing Ability Suggested: Novice to intermediate
Hiking Trail Difficulty: Easy
Mountain Biking Ability Suggested: NA
Terrain: Steep 10%, Hilly 40%, Moderate 30%, Flat 20%
Camping: Youth group campground only, reservations required

Operated by the Huron-Clinton Metropolitan Authority
Warming area, rentals, lessons, snack bar, fishing, ice skating, boating, golf, nature center with trails, group camping and sledding are available in the park.
The main hiking/biking trail is paved and follows the shore of Kensington Lake.
Biking limited to the paved trail in non skiing months.
Some ski trails on the golf course.
Bike/hike trail distance is 8.2 miles. Terrain listed above.
Nature Trails: 6 loops from .5 to 3 mi; Steep 0%, Hilly 25%, Moderate 30%, Flat 45%.
Bike/hike and ski trails overlap.
Call or write for their Metropark Guide, published each year.

KENSINGTON METROPARK

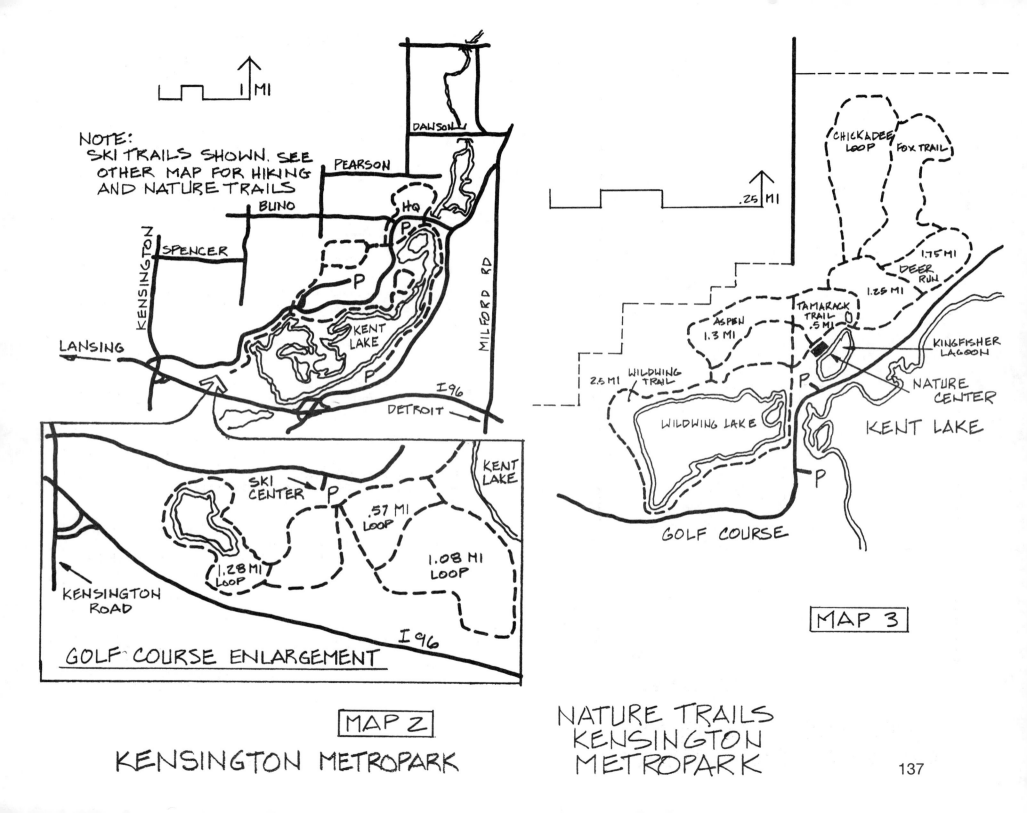

MAP 2

KENSINGTON METROPARK

NATURE TRAILS KENSINGTON METROPARK

NOTE:
SKI TRAILS SHOWN. SEE OTHER MAP FOR HIKING AND NATURE TRAILS

1 MI

DAWSON

PEARSON

BUNO

HQ

KENSINGTON

SPENCER

P

P

KENT LAKE

MILFORD RD

LANSING

P

I 96

DETROIT

GOLF COURSE ENLARGEMENT

KENT LAKE

SKI CENTER

P

.57 MI LOOP

1.08 MI LOOP

1.28 MI LOOP

KENSINGTON ROAD

I 96

.25 MI

CHICKADEE LOOP

FOX TRAIL

1.75 MI

DEER RUN

1.25 MI

ASPEN 1.3 MI

TAMARACK TRAIL .5 MI

KINGFISHER LAGOON

NATURE CENTER

WILDWING TRAIL

2.5 MI

P

WILDWING LAKE

KENT LAKE

P

GOLF COURSE

MAP 3

137

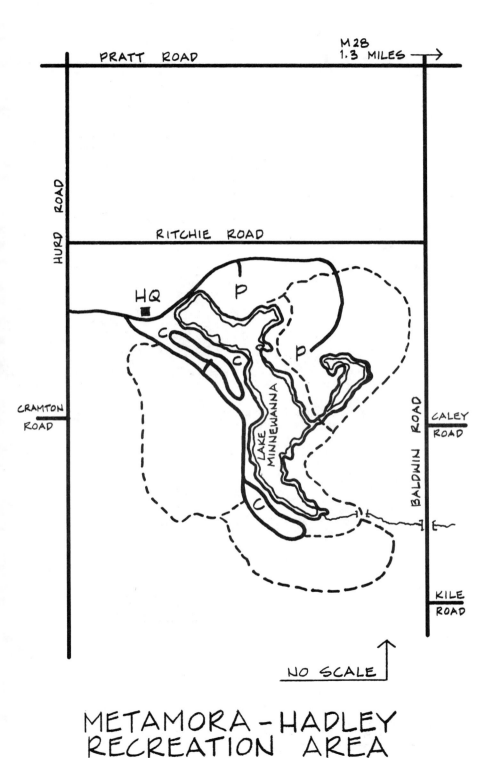

PRATT ROAD

M 28
1.3 MILES →

HURD ROAD

RITCHIE ROAD

HQ

P

LAKE MINNEWANNA

CRAMTON ROAD

BALDWIN ROAD

CALEY ROAD

KILE ROAD

NO SCALE

METAMORA-HADLEY RECREATION AREA

Metamora-Hadley Recreation Area
3871 Hurd Rd.   810-797-4439
Metamora, MI 48455

DNR Parks and Recreation Division

517-373-1270

Michigan Atlas & Gazetteer Location: 41A7

County Location: Lapeer

Directions To Trailhead:
South from Lapeer on M24 to Pratt Rd., then west 2 miles to Herd Rd., then south .7 mile to recreation area entrance. Trailheads at campground office and beach area.

Trail Type: Hiking/Walking, Cross Country Skiing, Interpretive
Trail Distance: 6 mi   Loops: 2   Shortest: 1.3 mi Longest: 2.5 mi
Trail Surface: Natural
Trail Use Fee: None, but vehicle entry fee required
Method Of Ski Trail Grooming: None
Skiing Ability Suggested: Novice to intermediate
Hiking Trail Difficulty: Easy
Mountain Biking Ability Suggested: NA
Terrain: Steep 1%, Hilly 30%, Moderate 40%, Flat 29%
Camping: Campground in recreation area

Maintained by the DNR Parks and Recreation Division.
Trails were designed for hiking but are skiable when snow depth permits.

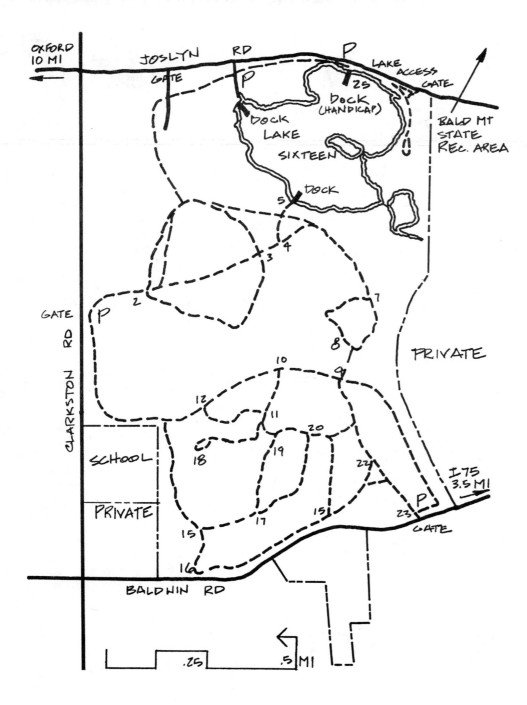

Orion Oaks County Park
2301 Clarkston Rd
Lake Orion, MI 48360

810-248-0906

Oakland County Parks and Recreation Commission
2800 Watkins Lake Rd
Waterford, MI 48328

810-248-0906

Michigan Atlas & Gazetteer Location: 41BC7

County Location: Oakland

Directions To Trailhead:
Clarkston Rd between Baldwin and Joslyn Rds north of Pontiac.

Trail Type: Hiking/Walking, Cross Country Skiing
Trail Distance: 12 mi   Loops: Many   Shortest: .5 mi   Longest: 10 mi
Trail Surface: Natural
Trail Use Fee: None but vehicle permit is required
Method Of Ski Trail Grooming: None
Skiing Ability Suggested: Novice
Hiking Trail Difficulty: Easy
Mountain Biking Ability Suggested: NA
Terrain: Steep 10%, Hilly 25%, Moderate 45%, Flat 20%
Camping: None

Maintained by Oakland County Parks
Park is under development.
Contact Oakland County Parks regarding up to date trail developments

ORION OAKS COUNTY PARK

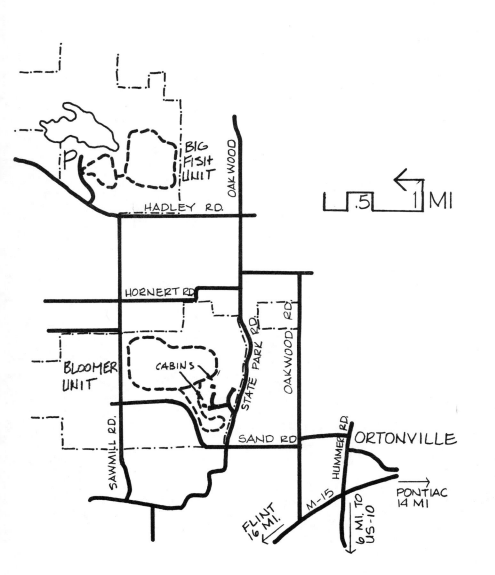

Ortonville Recreation Area
5779 Hadley Rd.   810-627-3828
Ortonville, MI 48462

DNR Parks and Recreation Division

517-373-1270

Michigan Atlas & Gazetteer Location: 41AB6

County Location: Oakland & Lapeer

Directions To Trailhead:
SE of Flint, north of Clarkston and east of M15.
Big Fish Unit - 1.5 miles NE of Ortonville 1.25 miles north of Oakwood Rd on Hadley Rd.
Bloomer Unit - .5 mile east of Sands Rd. on State Park Rd.

Trail Type: Hiking/Walking, Cross Country Skiing, Mountain Biking
Trail Distance: 4.25 mi   Loops: 2   Shortest: 1.5 mi Longest: 2.75 mi
Trail Surface: Natural
Trail Use Fee: None, but vehicle entry fee required
Method Of Ski Trail Grooming: None
Skiing Ability Suggested: Intermediate to advanced
Hiking Trail Difficulty: Moderate
Mountain Biking Ability Suggested: Novice
Terrain: Steep 10%, Hilly 30%, Moderate 30%, Flat 30%
Camping: Group campground available

Maintained by the DNR Parks and Recreation Division.
Cabins available for rent in the Bloomer Unit.

ORTONVILLE RECREATION AREA

TRAIL NOTES

Pontiac Lake Recreation Area
7800 Gale Rd, R#2   248-666-1020
Waterford, MI 48327

DNR Parks and Recreation Division

517-322-1300
517-373-1270

Michigan Atlas & Gazetteer Location: 41C56

County Location: Oakland

Directions To Trailhead:
Located just north of M-59 on the north side of Pointiac Lake, west of Pontiac, and east of Highland Recreation area. Take M-59 west from Pontiac to Williams Lake Rd, then north about 1mile to Gale Rd (at the first right curve), left on Gale Rd for about 1/2 mile(past the park HQ), then left into the Pontiac Lake Recreation Area, beach parking lot. When entering the lot, the trailhead is in the far right corner.

Trail Type: Hiking/Walking, Cross Country Skiing, Mountain Biking, Interpretive
Trail Distance: 17+ mi   Loops: Many   Shortest: .25 mi Longest: 10.7 mi
Trail Surface: Natural and gravel
Trail Use Fee: None, but vehicle entry permit required
Method Of Ski Trail Grooming: None
Skiing Ability Suggested: Novice to advanced
Hiking Trail Difficulty: Moderate to difficult
Mountain Biking Ability Suggested: Intermediate to advanced
Terrain: Steep 15%, Hilly 45%, Moderate 25%, Flat 20%
Camping: Campground in the recreation area.

Maintained by the DNR Parks and Recreation Divsion
Trail distances vary and some may overlap.
>   Hiking trails - May use mountain bike and horse trails
>   Mountain biking trails -
>   10.7 miles - outer loop
>   plus approximate 2 miles of additional connector trail
>   Skiing trails - Trails above are used for skiing.
>   (Stable in the park with horse trails throughout the park)
Large modern campground located along trail system.
Mountain bike trail maintained by the Michigan Mountain Biking Association.
This mountain bike trail is for the better intermediate and advanced riders only.
Snowmobiles are permitted in the park and may find their way onto the trails.
Revised - Spring 1998

SEE MAPS ON NEXT PAGE

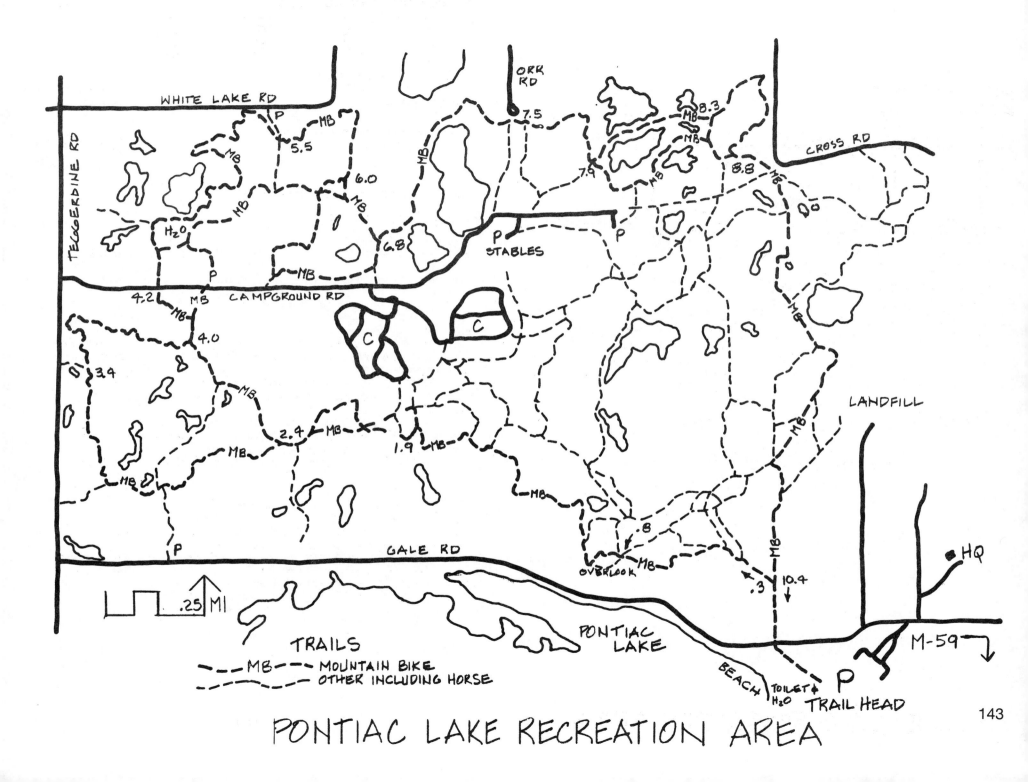

PONTIAC LAKE RECREATION AREA

TRAILS

- – – MB – – – MOUNTAIN BIKE
- – – – OTHER INCLUDING HORSE

.25 MI

143

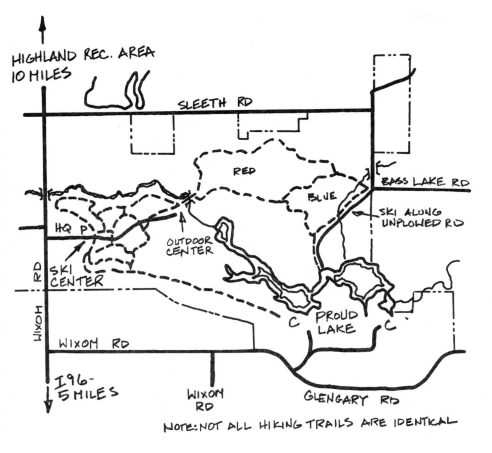

HIGHLAND REC. AREA
10 MILES

SLEETH RD

RED

BLUE

BASS LAKE RD

SKI ALONG UNPLOWED RD

HQ P

OUTDOOR CENTER

SKI CENTER

WIXOM RD

PROUD LAKE

I96-5 MILES

WIXOM RD

WIXOM RD

GLENGARY RD

NOTE: NOT ALL HIKING TRAILS ARE IDENTICAL

.5   1 MI

Proud Lake Recreation Area
3500 Wixom Rd., Rte 3
Milford, MI 48042

810-685-2433

DNR Parks and Recreation Division

517-373-1270

Michigan Atlas & Gazetteer Location: 41D5

County Location: Oakland

Directions To Trailhead:
3 miles SE of Milford on Wixom Rd. or From I-96 take Wixom Rd. north 6 miles

Trail Type: Hiking/Walking, Cross Country Skiing, Mountain Biking, Interpretive
Trail Distance: 8 mi   Loops: Several   Shortest: 1 mi   Longest: 5 mi
Trail Surface: Natural
Trail Use Fee: None, but vehicle entry fee required
Method Of Ski Trail Grooming: None
Skiing Ability Suggested: Novice
Hiking Trail Difficulty: East
Mountain Biking Ability Suggested: Novice
Terrain: Steep 0%, Hilly 0%, Moderate 40%, Flat 60%
Camping: Campground with heated restroom open all year

Maintained by the DNR Parks and Recreation Division
Nature and hiking trails provided.
Ski center located at trailhead, operated by Heavner Concessions.
Rentals, lessons, ski shop, refreshments and warming shelter .
Horse back riding trails (not shown on map) west of Nixon Rd are sometimes
use by hikers and mountain bikers.
Lodging available for groups 685-2433

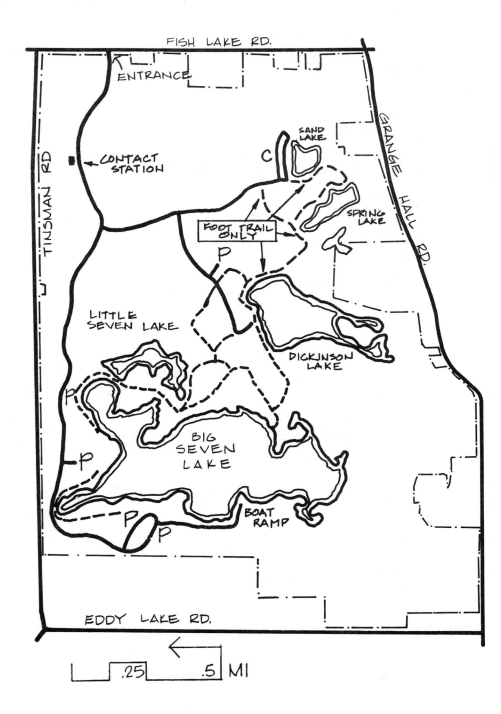

Seven Lakes State Park
2220 Tinsman Rd.
Fenton , MI 48430

248-634-7271
248-634-8811

DNR Parks and Recreation Division

517-373-1270

Michigan Atlas & Gazetteer Location: 41B45

County Location: Oakland

Directions To Trailhead:
Exit I-75 at Grange Hall Rd, then go 6 miles west to Fish Lake Rd., then north on Fish Lake Rd 1 mile to park entrance. Trailheads at boat launch and north picnic area.

Trail Type: Hiking/Walking, Cross Country Skiing, Mountain Biking, Interpretive
Trail Distance: 5.5 mi   Loops: Many   Shortest: .4 mi   Longest: 3.5 mi
Trail Surface: Natural
Trail Use Fee: None, but vehicle entry fee required
Method Of Ski Trail Grooming: None
Skiing Ability Suggested: Novice
Hiking Trail Difficulty: Easy
Mountain Biking Ability Suggested: Novice
Terrain: Steep 2%, Hilly 20%, Moderate 50%, Flat 28%
Camping: On site

Maintained by the DNR Parks and Recreation Division
All 1,400 acres are open for cross-country skiing.
Mountain biking limited to the Red, Green and Yellow trails.
Dickenson Nature Trial is not open to mountain bike use.

SEVEN LAKES STATE PARK

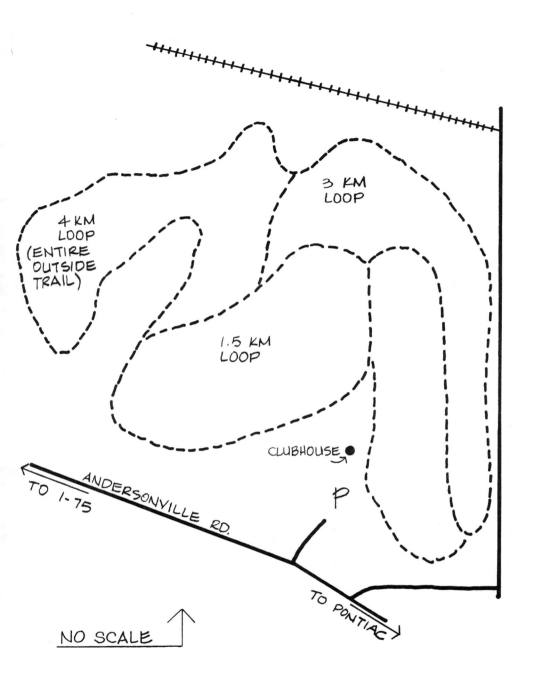

Springfield Oaks County Park
12450 Andersonville Rd.
Davisburg, MI 48019

810-625-2540

Oakland County Parks and Recreation Commission
2800 Watkins Lake Rd.
Pontiac , MI 48056

810-858-0906

Michigan Atlas & Gazetteer Location: 41C5

County Location: Oakland

Directions To Trailhead:
Just west of I-75 at Andersonville Rd. and Davisburg Rd.. in Davisburg

Trail Type: Cross Country Skiing
Trail Distance: 8.5 km   Loops: 3   Shortest: Longest:
Trail Surface: Natural
Trail Use Fee: None
Method Of Ski Trail Grooming: None
Skiing Ability Suggested: Novice to intermediate
Hiking Trail Difficulty: NA
Mountain Biking Ability Suggested: NA
Terrain: Steep 0%, Hilly 0%, Moderate 40%, Flat 60%
Camping: None

Maintained by the Oakland County Parks & Recreation Commission
Warming building available.
Trails on a golf course.

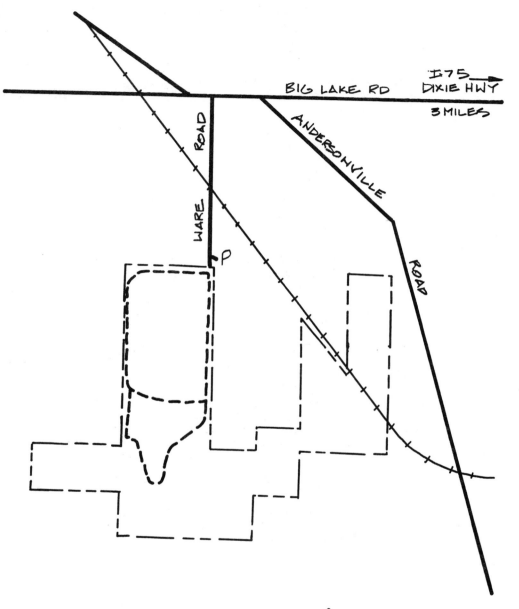

BIG LAKE RD

I75
DIXIE HWY →

3 MILES

ANDERSONVILLE ROAD

WARE ROAD

P

Michigan Nature Association
PO Box 102
Avoca, MI 48006

810-324-2626

Michigan Atlas & Gazetteer Location: 41C56

County Location: Oakland

Directions To Trailhead:
On the north side of Indian Hills Metropark off Big Lake Rd just west of Andersonville Rd. Take Ware Rd south to the trailhead.

Trail Type: Hiking/Walking, Interpretive
Trail Distance: 2.5 mi   Loops: 2   Shortest: 1.5 mi Longest: 2 mi
Trail Surface: Natural
Trail Use Fee: None
Method Of Ski Trail Grooming: NA
Skiing Ability Suggested: NA
Hiking Trail Difficulty: Moderate
Mountain Biking Ability Suggested: NA
Terrain: 100% Flat
Camping: None

Maintained by the Michigan Nature Association
A unique 245 acre sanctuary that is the Michigan Nature Association's showplace.   Other than logged, the sanctuary has never been disturbed including tilling for farmland.
Every season provides the visitor with new things to see and experience.

.25   .5 MI

TIMBERLAND SWAMP
NATURE SANCTUARY

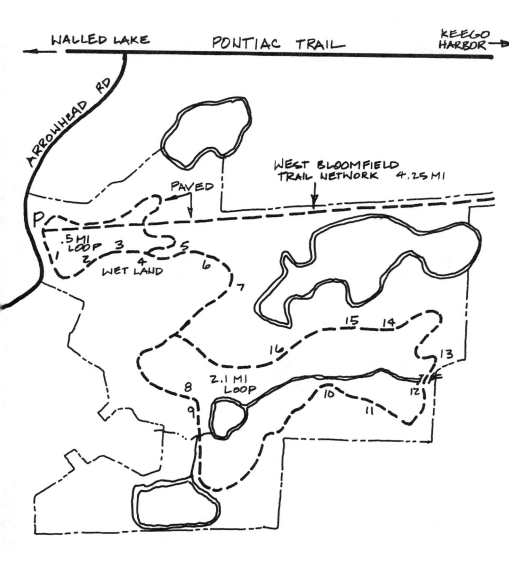

WALLED LAKE ← PONTIAC TRAIL → KEEGO HARBOR →

ARROWHEAD RD

WEST BLOOMFIELD TRAIL NETWORK 4.25 MI

PAVED

P

.5 MI LOOP 3

2

WET LAND

4

5

6

7

15 14

16

13

2.1 MI LOOP

8

9

10 12

11

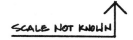
SCALE NOT KNOWN

WEST BLOOMFIELD WOODS
NATURE PRESERVE

West Bloomfield Parks and Recreation Commission
3325 Middlebelt Road
West Bloomfield, MI 48323

810-334-5660

Michigan Atlas & Gazetteer Location: 41D6

County Location: Oakland

Directions To Trailhead:
North on Orchard Lake Rd to Pontiac Trail, then west on Pontiac Trail to
Arrowhead Rd, then south on Arrowhead to trailhead parking

Trail Type: Hiking/Walking, Cross Country Skiing, Interpretive
Trail Distance: 2.6 mi   Loops: 2   Shortest: .5 mi   Longest: 2.1 mi
Trail Surface: Natural and paved(.5 mi)
Trail Use Fee: None
Method Of Ski Trail Grooming: None
Skiing Ability Suggested: Novice to intermediate
Hiking Trail Difficulty: Easy to moderate
Mountain Biking Ability Suggested: NA
Terrain: Steep 0%, Hilly 15%, Moderate 60%, Flat 20%
Camping: None

Maintained by the West Bloomfield Parks and Recreation Commission
A 16 station interpretive trail along ponds and a creek.
Adjacent to the West Bloomfield Trail Network (see other listing)

West Bloomfield Parks and Recreation Commission
3325 Middlebelt Road
West Bloomfield, MI 48323

810-334-5660

Michigan Atlas & Gazetteer Location: 41D67

County Location: Oakland

Directions To Trailhead:
North on Orchard Lake Rd to Pontiac Trail, then left(west) on Pontiac Trail to Arrowhead Rd, then left(south) on Arrowhead to trailhead.

Trail Type: Hiking/Walking, Cross Country Skiing, Mountain Biking, Interpretive
Trail Distance: 4.25 mi   Loops: NA   Shortest: NA   Longest: NA
Trail Surface: Crushed limestone
Trail Use Fee: None
Method Of Ski Trail Grooming: None
Skiing Ability Suggested: Novice
Hiking Trail Difficulty: Easy
Mountain Biking Ability Suggested: Novice
Terrain: 100% Flat
Camping: None

Maintained by the West Bloomfield Parks and Recreation Commission
Trail has 21 interpreted stations from end to end.
West Bloomfield Nature Preserve is located along this trail. (see other listing)

ORCHARD LAKE RD

PINE LK RD

LONG LAKE RD

OLD ORCHARD TRAIL

ORCHARD LAKE

UPPER STRAITS LAKE

PONTIAC TRAIL

LONE PINE

ORCHARD LAKE RD

ARROWHEAD

P

WEST BLOOMFIELD WOODS NATURE PRESERVE

HALSTED

WALNUT LK RD

.5   1 MI

WEST BLOOMFIELD TRAIL NETWORK

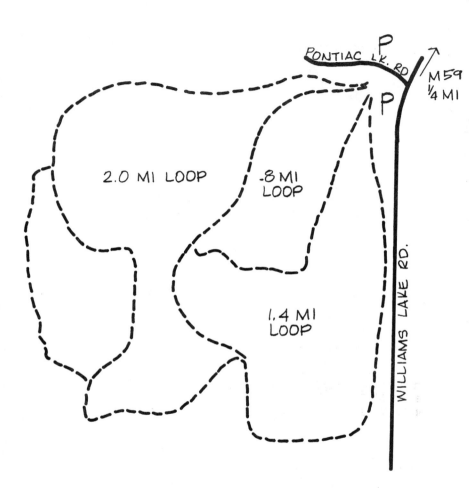

2.0 MI LOOP

.8 MI LOOP

1.4 MI LOOP

PONTIAC LK. RD.

P

P

M59 ¼ MI

WILLIAMS LAKE RD.

WHITE LAKE OAKS GOLF COURSE

White Lake Oaks County Park
991 S. Williams Lake Rd.
Pontiac, MI 48054

810-698-2700

Oakland County Parks & Recreation Commission
2800 Watkins Lake Rd.
Pontiac, MI 48054-1697

810-858-0906

Michigan Atlas & Gazetteer Location: 41C6

County Location: Oakland

Directions To Trailhead:
On Williams Lake Rd., just south of Highland Rd. (M59) and Pontiac Lake Rd.

Trail Type: Cross Country Skiing
Trail Distance: 6.6 km   Loops: 3   Shortest: Longest:
Trail Surface: Natural
Trail Use Fee: None
Method Of Ski Trail Grooming: Packed
Skiing Ability Suggested: Novice
Hiking Trail Difficulty: NA
Mountain Biking Ability Suggested: NA
Terrain: Flat to rolling
Camping: None

Maintained by the Oakland County Parks & Recreation Commission
Warming area, snack bar, lessons and rentals available.
Trails are on a golf course

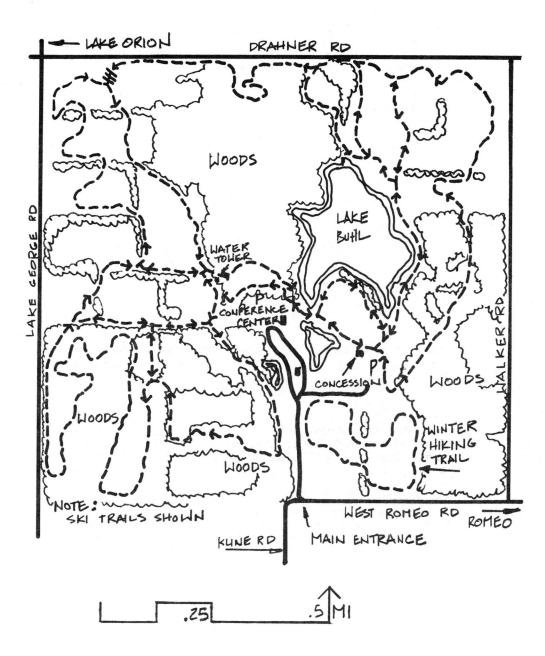

LAKE ORION →

DRAHNER RD

LAKE GEORGE RD

WOODS

LAKE BUHL

WATER TOWER

CONFERENCE CENTER

WOODS

WOODS

CONCESSION

WOODS

WINTER HIKING TRAIL

WALKER RD

NOTE: SKI TRAILS SHOWN

WEST ROMEO RD

ROMEO →

KUNE RD

MAIN ENTRANCE

.25 .5 MI

ADDISON OAKS COUNTY PARK

Addison Oaks County Park
1480 W Romeo Rd.
Leonard, MI 48367

248-693-2432

Oakland County Parks and Recreation Commission
2800 Watkins Lake Rd.
Pontiac, MI 48056

248-858-0906

Michigan Atlas & Gazetteer Location: 42B1

County Location: Oakland

Directions To Trailhead:
North on Rochester Rd. from Rochester, then west on West Romeo Rd. about 2 miles to the park entrance which is on the right.

Trail Type: Hiking/Walking, Cross Country Skiing, Mountain Biking
Trail Distance: 12+ mi   Loops: Many   Shortest: .1 mi   Longest: 5.3 mi
Trail Surface: Paved and natural
Trail Use Fee: None, but vehicle entry fee required.
Method Of Ski Trail Grooming: Track set when snow depth permits
Skiing Ability Suggested: Novice to intermediate
Hiking Trail Difficulty: Easy to moderate
Mountain Biking Ability Suggested: Novice to advanced
Terrain: Steep 8%, Hilly 15%, Moderate 57%, Flat 20%
Camping: Modern, primitive and group camping facilities in the park

Operated by the Oakland County Parks and Recreation Commission.
A complete year-round recreation area. Call for information and brochure.
Excellent trail system with a wide variety of terrain and many wooded trails.
Trail distance listed above is a combined distance for all trails.
Mountain bike trail distance is about 5 miles. Bike/helmet rentals available.
Cross country ski trail distance is about 9.75 miles.
Cross country ski trails use both the hiking trail and mountain bike trail systems.
Both cross country ski and mountain bike events held seasonally.
Lighted 1.5 mile ski trail, cross country ski lessons and ski rentals available.
 There is an open slope available for telemarking.
One hiking trail remains available throughout the winter months.

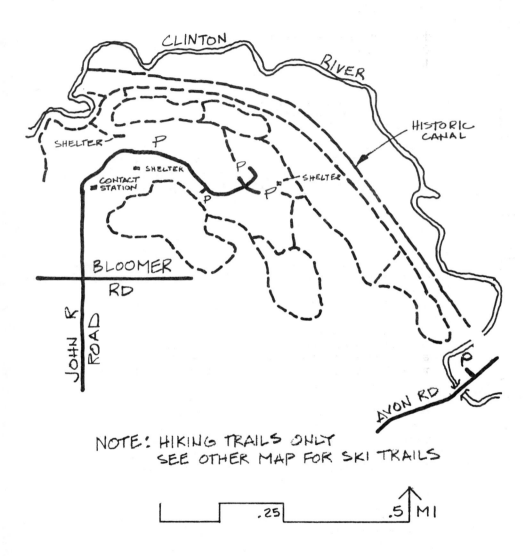

CLINTON

RIVER

HISTORIC
CANAL

SHELTER

P

SHELTER

P

CONTACT
STATION

SHELTER

P

P

BLOOMER

RD

JOHN R ROAD

P

AVON RD

NOTE: HIKING TRAILS ONLY
SEE OTHER MAP FOR SKI TRAILS

.25   .5 MI

BLOOMER PARK

Bloomer Park

City of Rochester Hills
1000 Rocherster Hills Drive
Rochester Hills, MI 48309

810-652-1321

Michigan Atlas & Gazetteer Location: 42C12

County Location: Oakland

Directions To Trailhead:
Take John R Rd north to park. About 3 miles north of M59

Trail Type: Hiking/Walking, Cross Country Skiing, Mountain Biking, Interpretive
Trail Distance: 6 mi   Loops: 6   Shortest: 1.2 mi Longest: 1.6 mi
Trail Surface: Natural
Trail Use Fee: Yes, daily or annual vehicle entry permit required
Method Of Ski Trail Grooming: None
Skiing Ability Suggested: Novice
Hiking Trail Difficulty: Easy
Mountain Biking Ability Suggested: Novice
Terrain: Steep 2%, Hilly 18%, Moderate 45%, Flat 35%
Camping: None

Owned by the City of Rochester Hills
Previously the Bloomer Unit, Rochester -Utica State Recreation Area
Continues under development by the city.

Dinosaur Hill Nature Preserve
333 North Hill Circle
Rochester, MI 48307

810-656-0999

Michigan Atlas & Gazetteer Location: 42C1

County Location: Oakland

Directions To Trailhead:
From Rochester Rd, take Tienken 2 blocks to Winry, then 2 blocks south to Axford, then 1 block to North Hill Circle and the preserve.

Trail Type: Hiking/Walking, Interpretive
Trail Distance: 2 mi   Loops: Several   Shortest: Longest:
Trail Surface: Natural
Trail Use Fee: None
Method Of Ski Trail Grooming: None
Skiing Ability Suggested: Novice
Hiking Trail Difficulty: Easy
Mountain Biking Ability Suggested: NA
Terrain: Steep 0%, Hilly 0%, Moderate 15%, Flat 85%
Camping: None

A small (17 acre) but active nature preserve in the center of Rochester
Guided walks and all types of programs available.
Adjacent to the Paint Creek Trail (see other listing)
Call for brochure and further information

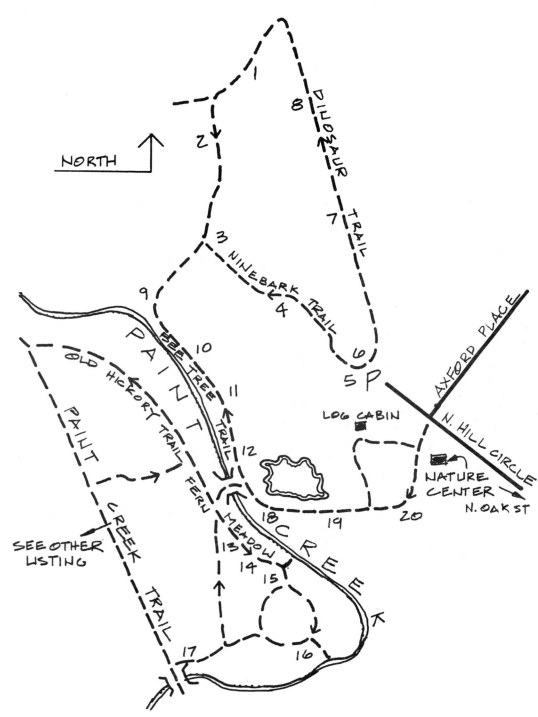

DINOSAUR HILL NATURE PRESERVE

Freedom Hill County Park
15000 Metro Parkway
Sterling Heights, MI 48077

810-979-7010
810-979-8750

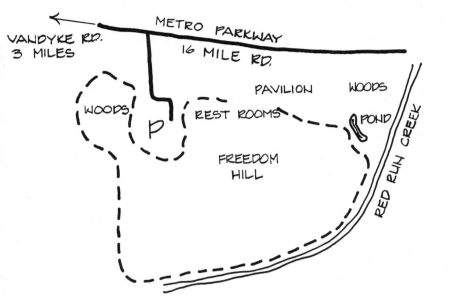

VANDYKE RD.
3 MILES

METRO PARKWAY
16 MILE RD.

WOODS

P

PAVILION

REST ROOMS

WOODS

POND

FREEDOM HILL

RED RUN CREEK

NO SCALE

FREEDOM HILL COUNTY PARK

Michigan Atlas & Gazetteer Location: 42D23

County Location: Macomb

Directions To Trailhead:
1.5 miles east of Schoenherr Rd on Metropolitan Parkway (16 Mile Rd.).

Trail Type: Cross Country Skiing
Trail Distance: 2 km   Loops: 1   Shortest: Longest:
Trail Surface: Natural
Trail Use Fee: None
Method Of Ski Trail Grooming: Track set
Skiing Ability Suggested: Novice
Hiking Trail Difficulty: Easy
Mountain Biking Ability Suggested: NA
Terrain: Steep 0%, Hilly 0%, Moderate 95%, Flat 5%
Camping: None

Operated by the Macomb County Park Parks and Recreation Commission.
Picnic area, restrooms, tot lot, multi-use building and amphitheater available.
Heated building available in winter.

Lapeer County Parks and Recreation Commission
225 Clay St
Lapeer, MI 48446

313-667-0304

Michigan Atlas & Gazetteer Location: 42A1

County Location: Lapeer

Directions To Trailhead:
From Dryden take S. Mill Rd south to the park.

Trail Type: Hiking/Walking, Cross Country Skiing, Interpretive
Trail Distance: 1 mi   Loops: 2   Shortest: Longest:
Trail Surface: Natural
Trail Use Fee: None
Method Of Ski Trail Grooming: None
Skiing Ability Suggested: Novice
Hiking Trail Difficulty: Easy
Mountain Biking Ability Suggested: NA
Terrain: Steep 0%, Hilly 0%, Moderate 70%, Flat 30%
Camping: None on site

Owned by the Lapeer County Parks and Recreation Commission
80 acre county park complete with rental hall, historic mill, fishing, picnic area, outdoor pavilions, play fields, ski and nature trails, lighted skating rink, lighted sledding and toboggan run along with other features.

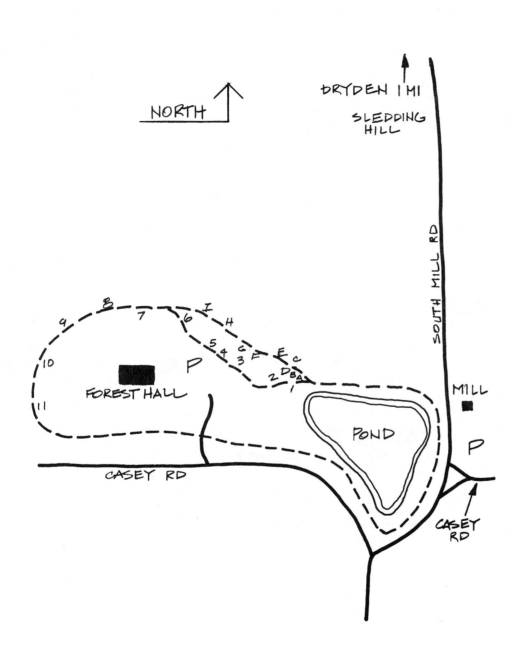

NORTH

DRYDEN 1 MI

SLEDDING HILL

SOUTH MILL RD

FOREST HALL

POND

MILL

CASEY RD

CASEY RD

GENERAL SQUIER COUNTY PARK

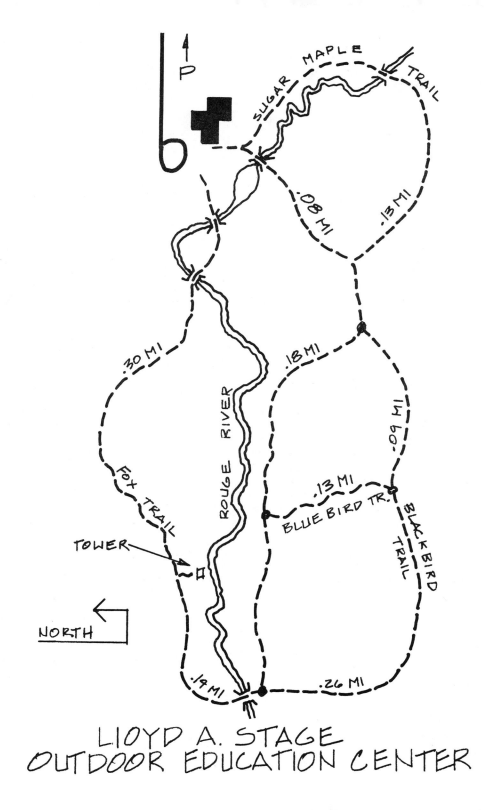

City of Troy
6685 Collidge Rd
Troy, MI 48098

810-524-3567

Michigan Atlas & Gazetteer Location: 42D1

County Location: Oakland

Directions To Trailhead:
Exit I-75 at Crooks Rd, then north to Square Lake Rd, then west to Coolidge Rd,
then north .74 mile to entrance on the west side of the road.

Trail Type: Hiking/Walking, Interpretive
Trail Distance: 1.3 mi   Loops: 4   Shortest: .4 mi   Longest: 1 mi
Trail Surface: Natrual
Trail Use Fee: None
Method Of Ski Trail Grooming: NA
Skiing Ability Suggested: NA
Hiking Trail Difficulty: Easy
Mountain Biking Ability Suggested: NA
Terrain: Steep 2%, Hilly 10%, Moderate 75%, Flat 13%
Camping: None

Owned by the City of Troy
An outdoor education center with a nature center building.

LIOYD A. STAGE
OUTDOOR EDUCATION CENTER

Paint Creek Trailways Commission
4393 Collins Rd.
Rochester, MI 48064

810-651-9260

Michigan Atlas & Gazetteer Location: 42BC1

County Location: Oakland

Directions To Trailhead:
Between Lake Orion and Utica along the Paint Creek and the City of Rochester.
Trailheads- Located at many road crossings. Some with parking lots.

Trail Type: Hiking/Walking, Cross Country Skiing, Mountain Biking, Interpretive
Trail Distance: 10.5 mi   Loops: NA   Shortest: NA   Longest: NA
Trail Surface: Paved and granular surfaces
Trail Use Fee: None
Method Of Ski Trail Grooming: None
Skiing Ability Suggested: Novice
Hiking Trail Difficulty: Easy
Mountain Biking Ability Suggested: Novice
Terrain: Steep 0%, Hilly 0%, Moderate 10%, Flat 90%
Camping: None, but camping is available nearby

Maintained by the Paint Creek Trailways Commission whos members are the
Oakland Township, Rochester Hills, Rochester and Orion Township.
Trail follows the route of a former railroad track. Development of trail facilities
continues.
Two cider mills are located along the trail.
Restaurants are located at each end of the trail.
See also the Dinosaur Hill Nature Preserve.
Only paved sections are in Rochester.
Listed as a mountain bike trail, since most is limestone surfaced. No speical
single track trail provided.

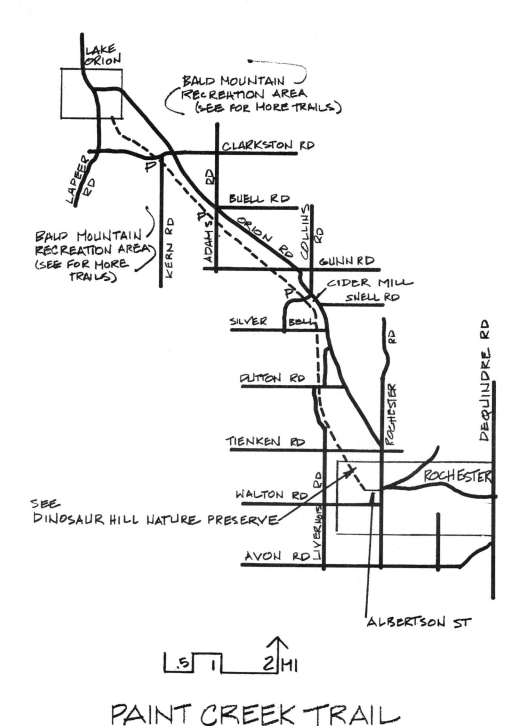

PAINT CREEK TRAIL

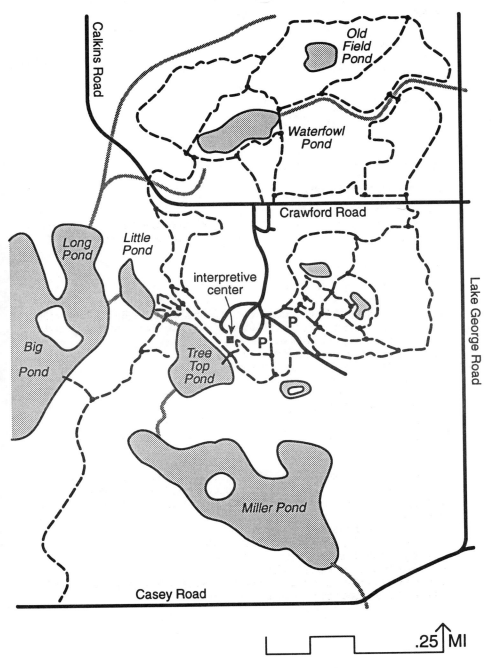

Seven Ponds Nature Center

Seven Ponds Nature Center
3854 Crawford Road   810-796-3200
Dryden, MI 48428

Michigan Atlas & Gazetteer Location: 42A1

County Location: Lapeer

Directions To Trailhead:
I-96 to M24, then south to Dryden Rd, then east 7 miles to Calkins Rd, then 1 mile south to the nature center.

Trail Type: Hiking/Walking, Cross Country Skiing, Interpretive
Trail Distance: 5 mi   Loops: 10   Shortest: .25 mi Longest: 1 mi
Trail Surface: Natural
Trail Use Fee: Yes, an entry fee is charged and memberships are available
Method Of Ski Trail Grooming: None
Skiing Ability Suggested: Novice to intermediate
Hiking Trail Difficulty: Easy
Mountain Biking Ability Suggested: NA
Terrain: Steep 0%, Hilly 25%, Moderate 25%, Flat 50%
Camping: None

Owned by the Michigan Audubon Society
An intensively used 250 acre nature center with much to offer and many programs throughout the year.
Seven Ponds was written about in the Fall 1989 issue of the "Great Lakes Skier" as an excellent place to ski.
Write or call for their brochure

Stony Creek Metropark
4300 Main Park Rd.   810-781-4242
Washington , MI 48094-9763   800-47-PARKS

Huron-Clinton Metropolitan Authority
13000 High Ridge Drive, PO Box 2001   810-227-2757
Brighton, MI 48116-8001

Michigan Atlas & Gazetteer Location: 42C2

County Location: Oakland & Macomb

Directions To Trailhead:
NE of Rochester, north of Utica off of Van Dyke Expressway (M53). From M53, take 26 Mile Rd. west 1.5 miles to park entrance

Trail Type: Hiking/Walking, Cross Country Skiing, Mountain Biking, Interpretive
Trail Distance: 20+ mi   Loops: Many   Shortest: .5 mi   Longest: 6.2 mi
Trail Surface: Paved, gravel and natural
Trail Use Fee: None, but vehicle entry fee required
Method Of Ski Trail Grooming: Track set
Skiing Ability Suggested: Novice to advanced
Hiking Trail Difficulty: Easy
Mountain Biking Ability Suggested: NA
Terrain: Below
Camping: Group campground available, reservations required

Operated by the Huron-Clinton Metropolitan Authority
Complete outdoor recreation area with almost every activity available.
Hike/bike trails overlap on some ski trails.
Hike/bike trail loop is about 6.2 miles long and is limited to a route around the lake. Terrain: Generally moderate to flat.
Cross country ski trail network is about 15 miles with 6 loops. Terrain: 30% hilly, 20% moderate, 50% flat.
Nature trials are 3 loops in 4.25 mile system with loops of .5, 1.25 and 2.5 mile loops. Terrain: Hilly 10%,Moderate 40%, Flat 50%
Mountain biking available on ski trails west of the West Branch picnic area.
Terrian is Flat to Steep.
Call or write for their Metropark Guide, published each year.

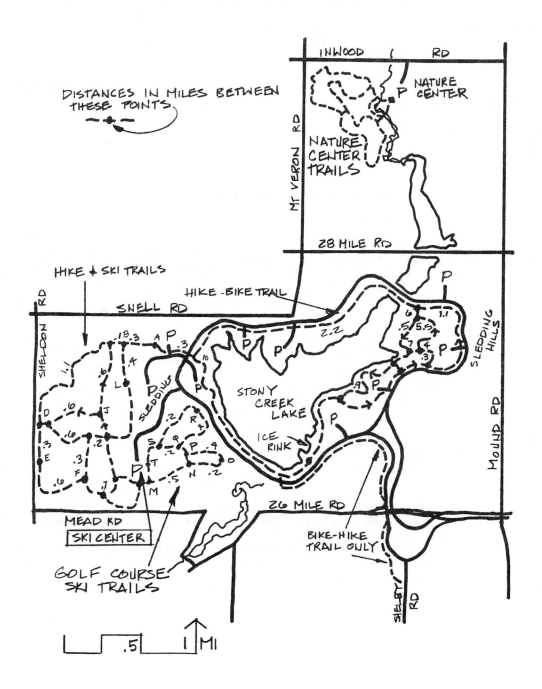

DISTANCES IN MILES BETWEEN THESE POINTS

STONY CREEK METROPARK

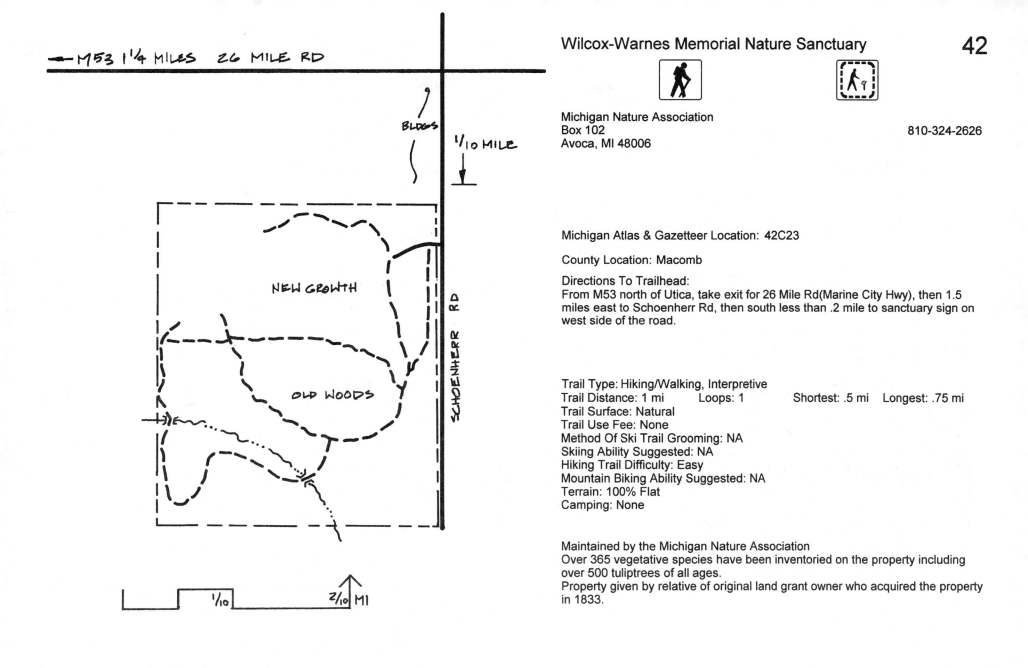

Michigan Nature Association
Box 102
Avoca, MI 48006

810-324-2626

Michigan Atlas & Gazetteer Location: 42C23

County Location: Macomb

Directions To Trailhead:
From M53 north of Utica, take exit for 26 Mile Rd(Marine City Hwy), then 1.5 miles east to Schoenherr Rd, then south less than .2 mile to sanctuary sign on west side of the road.

Trail Type: Hiking/Walking, Interpretive
Trail Distance: 1 mi   Loops: 1   Shortest: .5 mi   Longest: .75 mi
Trail Surface: Natural
Trail Use Fee: None
Method Of Ski Trail Grooming: NA
Skiing Ability Suggested: NA
Hiking Trail Difficulty: Easy
Mountain Biking Ability Suggested: NA
Terrain: 100% Flat
Camping: None

Maintained by the Michigan Nature Association
Over 365 vegetative species have been inventoried on the property including over 500 tuliptrees of all ages.
Property given by relative of original land grant owner who acquired the property in 1833.

WILCOX-WARNES
MEMORIAL NATURE SANCTUARY

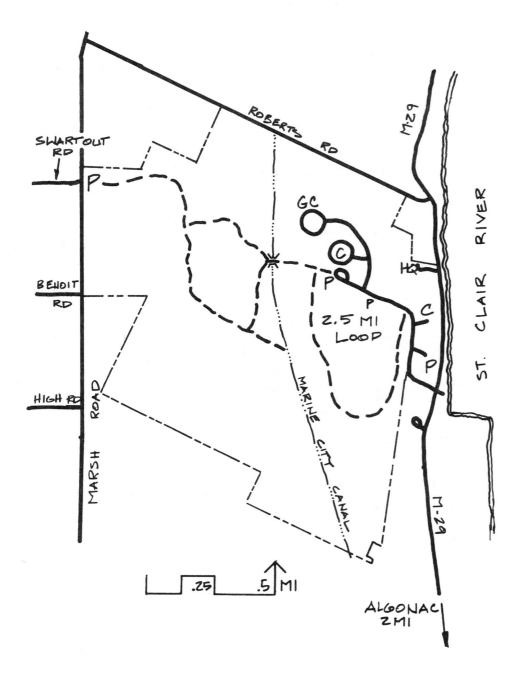

Algonac State Park
8732 River Road
Marine City, MI 48039

810-765-5605
810-327-6765

DNR Parks and Recreation Division

517-373-1270
517-322-1300

Michigan Atlas & Gazetteer Location: 43C6

County Location: St. Clair

Directions To Trailhead:
On M29 between Algonac an Marine City on the St. Clair River.

Trail Type: Hiking/Walking, Cross Country Skiing
Trail Distance: 2.5 mi   Loops: 1   Shortest: NA   Longest: 2.5 mi
Trail Surface: Natural
Trail Use Fee: None, except vehicle entry permit required
Method Of Ski Trail Grooming: None
Skiing Ability Suggested: Novice
Hiking Trail Difficulty: Easy
Mountain Biking Ability Suggested: NA
Terrain: 100% Flat
Camping: Campgrounds on site for both individuals and groups

Maintained by the DNR Parks and Recreation Division
Though relatively small with only 63 acres the park supports many varieties of plant life.

ALGONAC STATE PARK

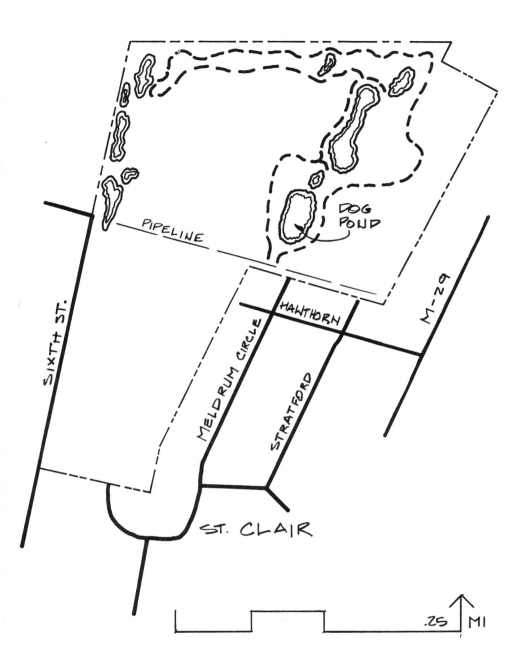

PIPELINE

SIXTH ST.

MELDRUM CIRCLE

HAWTHORN

STRATFORD

M-29

DOG POND

ST. CLAIR

.25 ↑ MI

ALICE W. MOORE WOODS
NATURE SANCTUARY

Michigan Nature Association
PO Box 102   810-324-2626
Avoca, MI 48006

Michigan Atlas & Gazetteer Location: 43B67

County Location: St Clair

Directions To Trailhead:
On the north city limits of St Clair

Trail Type: Hiking/Walking, Interpretive
Trail Distance: 1.5 mi   Loops: 1   Shortest: NA   Longest: 1.5 mi
Trail Surface: Natural
Trail Use Fee: None
Method Of Ski Trail Grooming: NA
Skiing Ability Suggested: NA
Hiking Trail Difficulty: Easy
Mountain Biking Ability Suggested: NA
Terrain: 100 % Flat
Camping: None

Owned by the Michigan Nature Association
Virgin oak-hickory forest. Some tree trunks are 3' in diameter.
Sanctuary publication available from the association

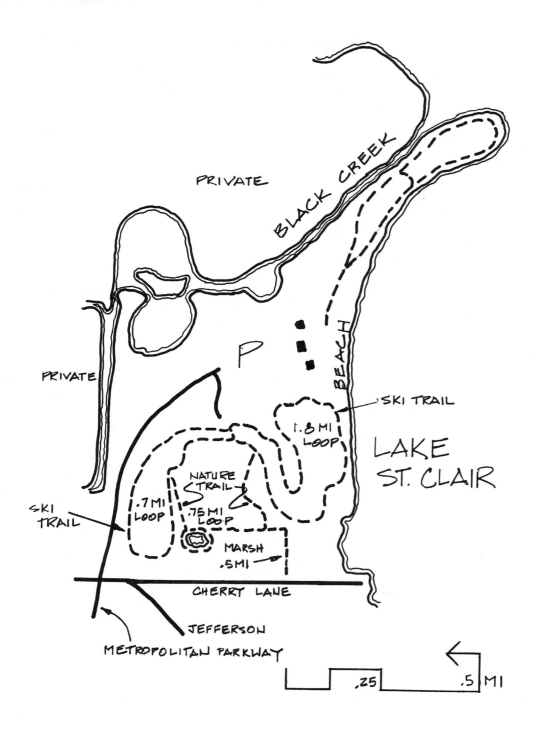

PRIVATE

BLACK CREEK

PRIVATE

P

BEACH

SKI TRAIL

1.8 MI LOOP

LAKE ST. CLAIR

SKI TRAIL

.7 MI LOOP

NATURE TRAIL

.75 MI LOOP

MARSH .5 MI

CHERRY LANE

JEFFERSON

METROPOLITAN PARKWAY

.25   .5 MI

METRO BEACH METROPARK

Metro Beach Metropark
13000 High Ridge Rd
Brighton, MI 48116-8001

810-227-2757
800-47-PARKS

Huron-Clinton Metropolitan Authority
1300 High Ridge Drive, PO Box 2001
Brighton, MI 48116-8001

810-227-2757

Michigan Atlas & Gazetteer Location: 43D4

County Location: Macomb

Directions To Trailhead:
At the east end of the Metro Parkway in Mt Clemens on Lake St. Clair
Trailhead - At the Center Plaza

Trail Type: Hiking/Walking, Cross Country Skiing, Interpretive
Trail Distance: 3.75 mi   Loops: 2   Shortest: 1.25 mi Longest: 2.5 mi
Trail Surface: Natural
Trail Use Fee: None, but vehicle entry fee required
Method Of Ski Trail Grooming: Track set
Skiing Ability Suggested: Novice
Hiking Trail Difficulty: NA
Mountain Biking Ability Suggested: NA
Terrain: 100% Flat
Camping: None

Operated by the Huron-Clinton Metropolitan Authority
Warming shelter, ski rentals and snack bar available. Special group rate for ski
rentals during the week. Complete summer recreation center with beach, par 3
golf, tennis, nature   study area, picnic grounds and much more.
Nature Trail is 1.25 miles long
Cross Country Ski Trail is 2.5 miles long
Call or write for their Metropark Guide, published each year.

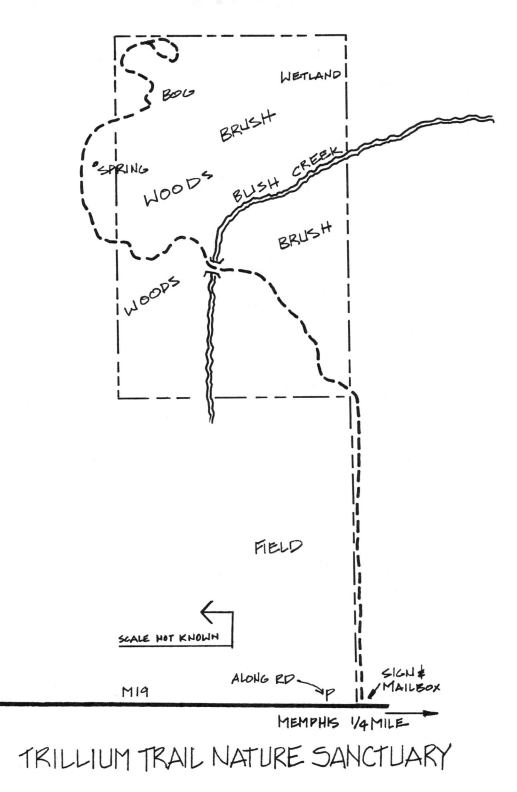

Michigan Nature Association
PO Box 102
Avoca, MI 48006

810-324-2626

Michigan Atlas & Gazetteer Location: 43A45

County Location: St. Clair

Directions To Trailhead:
From Memphis, go .25 mile north on city limits on M19, then look for sign on east side of the road.   Park on road shoulder. Walk east on 1/4 mile long easement between farmers field and neighbors yard to sanctuary.

Trail Type: Hiking/Walking, Interpretive
Trail Distance: .5 mi   Loops: NA   Shortest: NA   Longest: NA
Trail Surface: Natural
Trail Use Fee: None
Method Of Ski Trail Grooming: NA
Skiing Ability Suggested: NA
Hiking Trail Difficulty: Easy
Mountain Biking Ability Suggested: NA
Terrain: Steep 5%, Hilly 45%, Moderate 20%, Flat 30%
Camping: None

Maintained by the Michigan Nature Association
Sanctuary of mixed hardwoods with extensive areas of white trillium.
Trail is well established and should be easy to find.

TRILLIUM TRAIL NATURE SANCTUARY

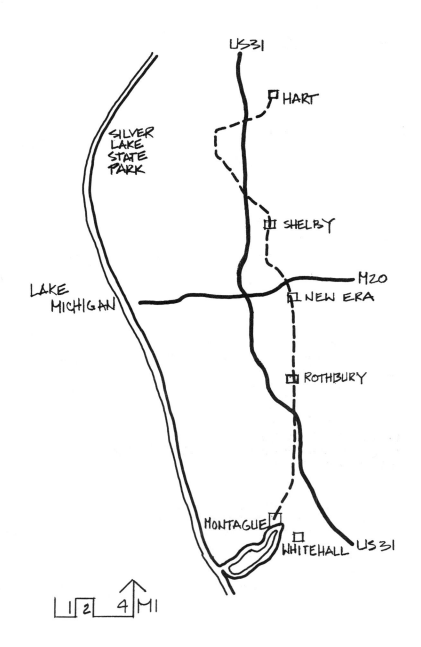

HART-MONTAGUE BICYCLE TRAIL
STATE PARK

Silver Lake State Park
Rte 1, Box 254
Mears, MI 49436

616-873-3083

DNR Parks and Recreation Division

517-373-1270
517-322-1300

Michigan Atlas & Gazetteer Location: 44A4,54CD34

County Location: Oceana & Muskegon

Directions To Trailhead:
Between Hart and Montague parallel to US-31. Trail passes through the communities of New Era, Shelby and Mears.

Trail Type: Hiking/Walking, Cross Country Skiing, Interpretive
Trail Distance: 22.5 mi   Loops: NA   Shortest: NA   Longest: NA
Trail Surface: Paved
Trail Use Fee: Yes,
Method Of Ski Trail Grooming: Not groomed
Skiing Ability Suggested: Novice
Hiking Trail Difficulty: Easy
Mountain Biking Ability Suggested: NA
Terrain: Steep 0%, Hilly 0%, Moderate 5%, Flat 95%
Camping: Campgrounds are in the area

Maintained by the DNR Parks Division and the Oceana-Muskegon Trailways Commission
Food, lodging, bike shops, picnic shelters, restrooms and water are available along the trail.
The trail is all asphalt paved. Right of Way width varies from 30 to 100 wide.
Ski and bike rental equipment is available in the area.
There are no special dirt mountain bike trails .
Ski shops are located in Pentwater and Whitehall.
A bike shop is located at the southern end of the trail in Montague
Detailed map guide book is available from White Lake C of C at 616-893-4585, Hart/Silver Lake C of C at 616-873-2247, Silver Lake Tourist Association at 616-873-5048

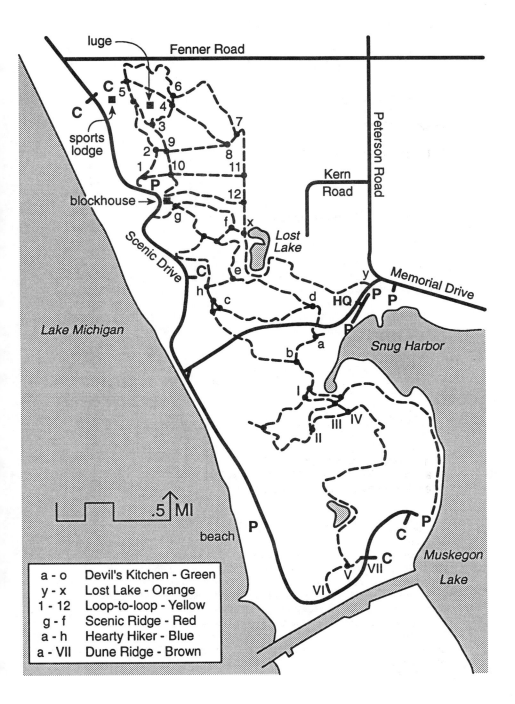

Muskegon State Park
3560 Memorial Drive
North Muskegon, MI 49445

616-744-3480

DNR Parks and Recreation Division

517-373-1270

Michigan Atlas & Gazetteer Location: 44BC4

County Location: Muskegon

Directions To Trailhead:
NW side of Muskegon. Take US31 to North Muskegon and follow signs to the state park. on Lake Michigan off Memorial Drive.

Trail Type: Hiking/Walking, Cross Country Skiing
Trail Distance: 10.5 mi   Loops: 6+   Shortest: .75 mi Longest: 5 mi
Trail Surface: Natural
Trail Use Fee: None, but vehicle entry fee required
Method Of Ski Trail Grooming: Track set
Skiing Ability Suggested: Novice to intermediate
Hiking Trail Difficulty: Moderate
Mountain Biking Ability Suggested: NA
Terrain: Steep 20%, Hilly 50%, Moderate 20%, Flat 10%
Camping: Campground in the park

Maintained by the DNR Parks and Recreation Division
Typical state park with beaches, campgounds and trails. Luge run, biathalon range, ski rentals, lessons and the customary summer facilities are available.
The luge is one of only 4 luge runs in the United States.
Large complex of trails for both hiking and cross country skiing.
The designated ski trails are a portion of the hiking trail system.
A detailed descriptive brochure of the hiking trails and a separated ski trail map are available.

Muskegon State Park

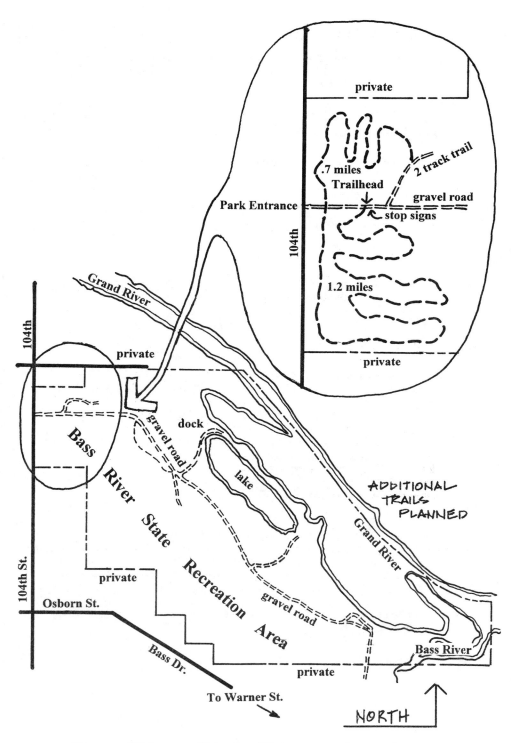

Bass River State Recreation Area

Hoffmaster State Park
6585 Lake Harbor Drive
Muskegon, MI 49441

616-798-3711

DNR Parks and Recreation Division

517-373-1270

Michigan Atlas & Gazetteer Location: 45D6

County Location: Ottawa

Directions To Trailhead:
On the Grand River, between Grand Haven and Eastmanville (68th St). From US31 about 6 miles south of Grand Haven, take Lake Michigan Drive east about 7 miles to 104th Ave., then north about 2 1/2 miles past Osborn St. to the park entrance on the west side of the road. From Allendale, take Lake Michigan Drive west about 4 1/2 miles to 104th Ave, then north to the park entrance

Trail Type: Hiking/Walking, Mountain Biking
Trail Distance: 3 mi   Loops: 1   Shortest: NA   Longest: 3 mi
Trail Surface: Natural
Trail Use Fee: None, but vehicle permit required
Method Of Ski Trail Grooming: NA
Skiing Ability Suggested: NA
Hiking Trail Difficulty: Easy
Mountain Biking Ability Suggested: Novice
Terrain: Steep 0%, Hilly 0%, Moderate 0%, Flat 100%
Camping: None

Managed by the DNR Park and Recreation Department
Undeveloped park with the exception of the mountain bike trail designed and constructed by the Michigan Mountain Biking Association (MMBA).
Additional mountain biking, hiking and cross country skiing available on the unmarked two track trails throughout this large park.
The mountain bike trail is somewhat technical but is generally on level terrain.
An excellent trail for the beginner or intermediate rider. However, the more advanced rider will equally enjoy the ride. The MMBA plans to expand the trail as volunteer support is available.
No drinking water or developed facilities at this time.
Toilets are available.

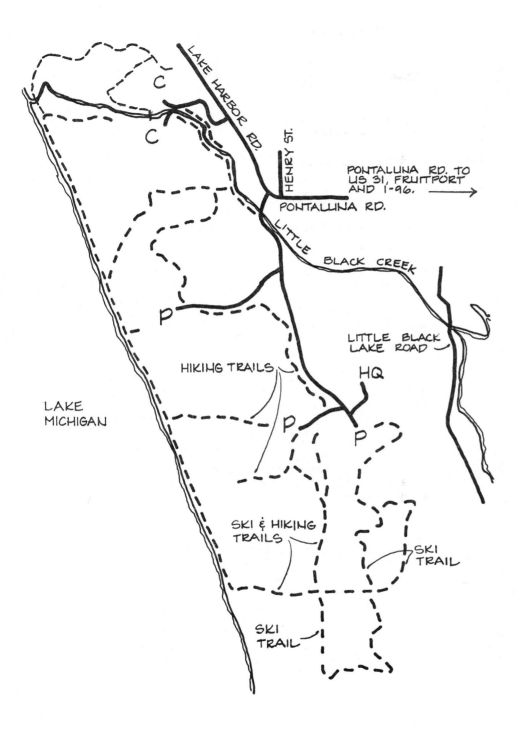

Hoffmaster State Park
6585 Lake Harbor Rd.
Muskegon, MI 49441

616-798-3573

DNR Parks and Recreation Division

517-373-1270

Michigan Atlas & Gazetteer Location: 45CD5

County Location: Muskegon

Directions To Trailhead:
South of Muskegon on Lake Michigan Take US31 south from I-69 to Pontaluna Rd., then west 3 miles to the park .

Trail Type: Hiking/Walking, Cross Country Skiing, Interpretive
Trail Distance: 10 mi   Loops: Many   Shortest: Longest:
Trail Surface: Natural - sand and some paved
Trail Use Fee: None, but vehicle entry fee required
Method Of Ski Trail Grooming: None
Skiing Ability Suggested: Novice to advanced
Hiking Trail Difficulty: Easy to moderate
Mountain Biking Ability Suggested: NA
Terrain: Rolling to hilly
Camping: Campgound in park

Maintained by the DNR Parks and Recreation Division
Ski trails are 2.5 miles long. Extensive hiking trail system throughout the park and along the shore of Lake Michigan.
The Gillette Nature Center (accessible) in the park is open daily 8am to 10pm.
For additional information contact the Gillette Nature Center at   616-798-3573

HOFFMASTER STATE PARK

Grand Haven Township
13300 168th Ave
Grand Haven, MI 49417

616-842-3515

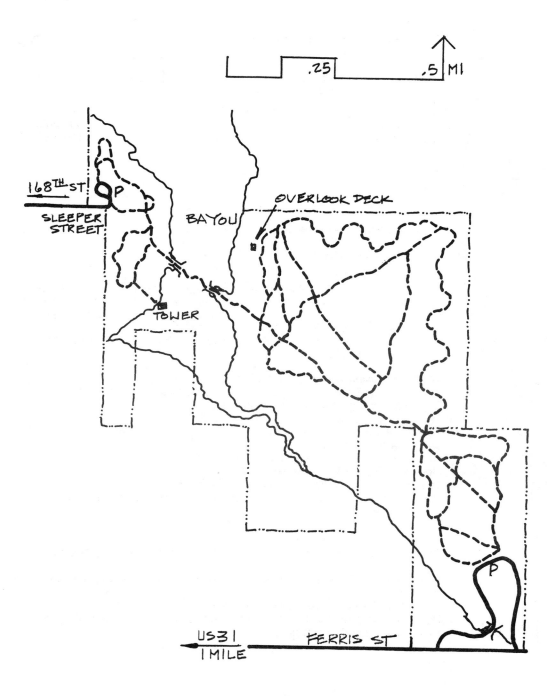

168TH ST.

SLEEPER STREET

P

BAYOU

OVERLOOK DECK

TOWER

P

US31
1 MILE

FERRIS ST

Michigan Atlas & Gazetteer Location: 45D5

County Location: Ottawa

Directions To Trailhead:
US31 south from Grand Haven 2.6 miles to Ferris St., then east on Ferris 1.5 miles to the entrance

Trail Type: Hiking/Walking, Cross Country Skiing, Mountain Biking
Trail Distance: 4.5 mi   Loops: Many   Shortest: .25 mi Longest: 1 mi
Trail Surface: Natural
Trail Use Fee: None
Method Of Ski Trail Grooming: None
Skiing Ability Suggested: Novice to intermediate
Hiking Trail Difficulty: Easy to moderate
Mountain Biking Ability Suggested: Novice to intermediate
Terrain: Steep 1%, Hilly 4%, Moderate 10%, Flat 80%
Camping: None

Owned by Grand Haven Township
Managed as a community park.

HOFMA PARK

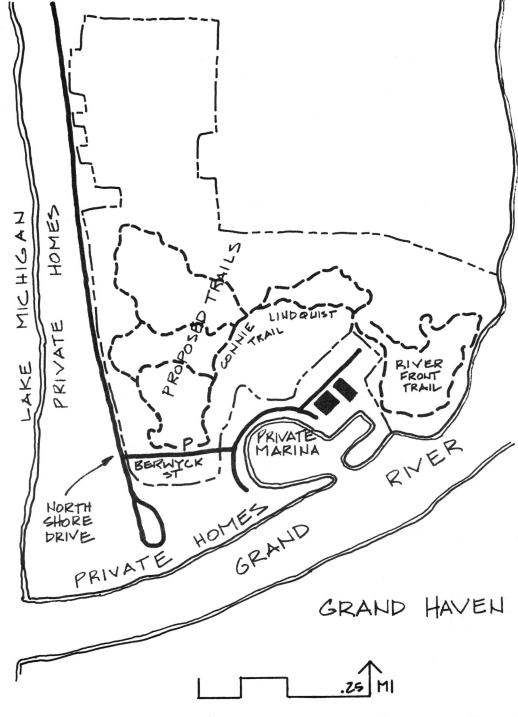

City Manager, City of Ferrysburg
408 Fifth St., PO Box 38
Ferrysburg, MI 49409

616-842-5950
616-842-5803

Michigan Atlas & Gazetteer Location: 45D5

County Location: Ottawa

Directions To Trailhead:
On US31 north from Grand Haven across the bridge for a very short distance, take the Ferrysburg exit, then left (west) at the Stop sign at the bottom of the off ramp(3rd St.), go .4 mi. to North Shore Drive(sharp curve to the north), then left (west again) on North Shore Drive, go 1.7 mi to North Beach Park, then south 1.5 mi to Berwyck St., then .2 mi on Berwyck St. to paved parking lot on the north side of the street.

Trail Type: Hiking/Walking, Interpretive
Trail Distance: 1.5 mi   Loops: 2   Shortest: Longest:
Trail Surface: Natural-sand and wood chips
Trail Use Fee: None
Method Of Ski Trail Grooming: NA
Skiing Ability Suggested: NA
Hiking Trail Difficulty: Easy to moderate
Mountain Biking Ability Suggested: NA
Terrain: Steep 0%, Hilly 0%, Moderate 95%, Flat 5%
Camping: Hoffmaster State Park is about 8 miles north on Lake Michigan

Owned by the City of Ferrysburg
This trail covers part of the 51 acre dune preserve along the shore of Lake Michigan .
Do not wander off the established trail because it will deteriorate the fragile landscape.
15 station interpretive signs are along the trail.
Paved handicapper parking and adjacent very short boardwalk at parking lot.
No extensive handicapper trails.

KITCHEL-LINDQUIST DUNES PRESERVE

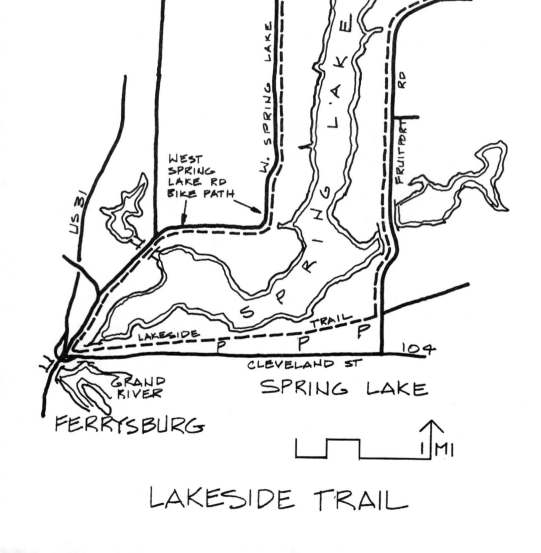

Lakeside Trail around Spring Lake

Village of Spring Lake
102 W. Savidge
Spring Lake, MI 49456

616-842-1393

City of Ferrysburg
PO Box 38, 408 5th St.
Ferrysburg, MI 49409-0038

616-842-5950

Michigan Atlas & Gazetteer Location: 45D5

County Location: Muskegon

Directions To Trailhead:
Around Spring Lake and through the communities of Spring Lake, Ferrysburg and Fruitport

Trail Type: Hiking/Walking, Cross Country Skiing
Trail Distance: 14+ mi   Loops: 1   Shortest: NA   Longest: NA
Trail Surface: Paved
Trail Use Fee: None
Method Of Ski Trail Grooming: None
Skiing Ability Suggested: Novice
Hiking Trail Difficulty: Easy
Mountain Biking Ability Suggested: NA
Terrain: 100%Flat
Camping: None, but available in the area

A cooperative project of Spring Lake Village, Ferrysburg, Fruitport and Spring Lake Township.
1.5 miles of the trail is in the Village of Spring Lake on an abandon railroad right of way. Along this section are parks and children play areas.

LAKESIDE TRAIL

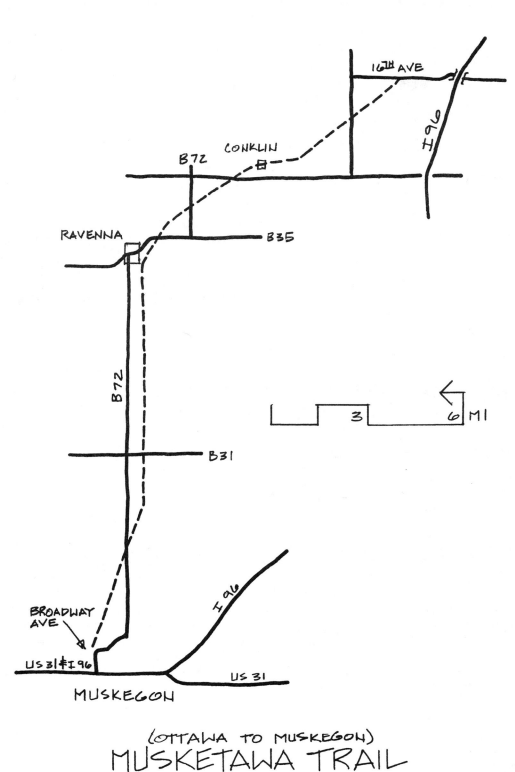

RAVENNA

B72

CONKLIN

16ᵀᴴ AVE

I 96

B72

B35

B31

I 96

BROADWAY AVE

US 31 & I 96

US 31

MUSKEGON

3   6 MI

(OTTAWA TO MUSKEGON)
MUSKETAWA TRAIL

Musketawa (Ottawa - Muskegon) Trail

DNR, Forest Mangement Division, Recreation & Trails Section
PO Box 30452   517-373-9483
Lansing, MI 48909

Michigan Atlas & Gazetteer Location: 45CD567,46D1

County Location: Ottawa

Directions To Trailhead:
Between Muskegon and Grand Rapids
North of B72 on the east side of Muskegon Heights through Ravenna then southeast to Herrington which is 2 miles north of Marne.

Trail Type: Hiking/Walking, Cross Country Skiing, Mountain Biking,
Trail Distance: 26 mi   Loops: NA   Shortest: NA   Longest: NA
Trail Surface: Ballast and existing surface
Trail Use Fee: None
Method Of Ski Trail Grooming: None
Skiing Ability Suggested: Novice
Hiking Trail Difficulty: Easy
Mountain Biking Ability Suggested: Novice
Terrain: 100% Flat
Camping: None

Managed by the DNR Forest Mangement Division, Recreation and Trails Section
Currently under development. To be open to the public in 1995 after basic improvements are made. Surfacing dependent on local support.

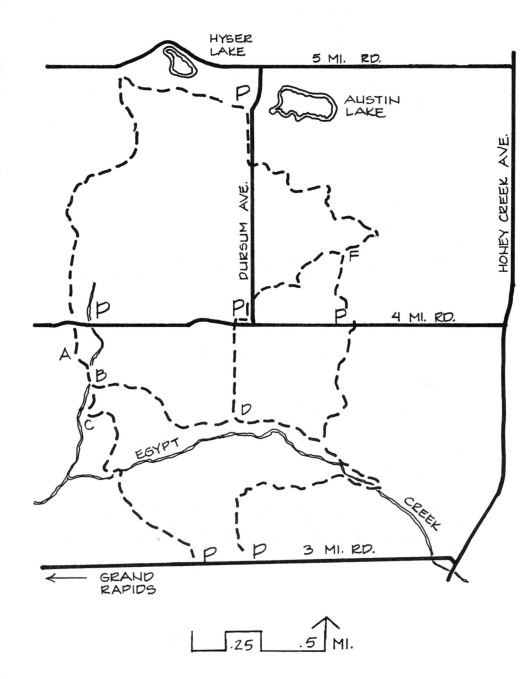

Cannonsburg State Game Area
350 Ottawa Ave NW
Grand Rapids, MI 49503

616-456-5071

DNR Wildlife Division Office

517-373-1263

Michigan Atlas & Gazetteer Location: 46D34

County Location: Kent

Directions To Trailhead:
8 miles east of Grand Rapids between 3 and 5 Mile Rds and just west of Honey Creek Ave

Trail Type: Hiking/Walking, Cross Country Skiing, Mountain Biking
Trail Distance: 10 mi   Loops: Numerous Shortest: Longest:
Trail Surface: Natural
Trail Use Fee: None
Method Of Ski Trail Grooming: None
Skiing Ability Suggested: Novice to intermediate
Hiking Trail Difficulty: Easy to moderate
Mountain Biking Ability Suggested: Novice
Terrain: Rolling to hilly
Camping: None

Maintained by the DNR Wildlife Division.
Not available for skiing before January 1st . Trail system has a variety of terrain, scenery and habitat. Connects to the Egypt Valley Trail for the winter only. Obey all "No Trespassing" signs since there are privately owned lands within the game area.

VERY IMPORTANT:This area is extremely over used by trail users. Continued additional non-hunting recreational use could close this area to mountain bikers, skiers and hikers.   Consider going to other areas more suited and designed for recreational trail use.   If you must use this area, do so less often than you have in the past.

CANNONSBURG STATE GAME AREA

Grand Rapids Parks and Recreation Department
210 Market St.
Grand Rapids, MI 49507

616-456-3696

Michigan Atlas & Gazetteer Location: 46D2

County Location: Kent

Directions To Trailhead:
Along the Grand River on the north side of Grand Rapids. US 131 to Ann St.
exit, then east 1/4 mile to Monroe Ave north. Park is on the west side at several
parking lots for the next 2 miles

NO MAP

Trail Type: Hiking/Walking, Cross Country Skiing

Trail Surface: Paved
Trail Use Fee: None
Method Of Ski Trail Grooming: Not known
Skiing Ability Suggested: Novice
Hiking Trail Difficulty: Easy
Mountain Biking Ability Suggested: NA
Terrain: Steep 0%, Hilly 0%, Moderate 0%, Flat 100%
Camping: None

Maintained by the Grand Rapids Parks and Recreation Department
Park is currently under redevelopment. Call ahead for current status.
Plans call for this park to be the southern end of the White Pine Trail (see other
listing)

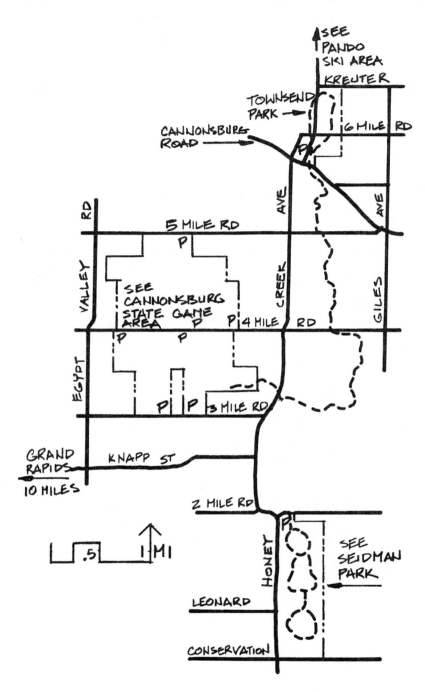

EGYPT VALLEY TRAIL

Kent County Park Commission
1500 Scribner NW
Grand Rapids, MI 49504

616-774-3697

Michigan Atlas & Gazetteer Location: 46D4

County Location: Kent

Directions To Trailhead:
9 miles NE of Grand Rapids

Trail Type: Hiking/Walking, Cross Country Skiing
Trail Distance: 5 mi   Loops: None   Shortest: Longest:
Trail Surface: Natural
Trail Use Fee: None
Method Of Ski Trail Grooming: None
Skiing Ability Suggested: Novice to intermediate
Hiking Trail Difficulty: Moderate
Mountain Biking Ability Suggested: NA
Terrain: Flat to hilly
Camping: None

Maintained by the Kent County Park Commission.
Most of the trail is on private property. Please respect the property rights of the owners whos land you are using. Trail open from 12/15 to 4/15 if 2 inches of snow are present .
The state game area section is open for skiing beginning Jan 2nd

Consumers Power Company, Hydro Operations Dept.
330 Chestnut St.
Cadillac, MI 49601

616-779-5507

Michigan Atlas & Gazetteer Location: 46A2

County Location: Newaygo

Directions To Trailhead:
At the Hardy Dam on teh Muskegon River. From US 31 north of Grand Rapids, take the Jefferson Rd exit 125, then west on Jefferson Rd about 7.5 miles to the dam. The trailhead is on the west side of the dam on the south side of Jefferson Rd.

Trail Type: Hiking/Walking, Interpretive
Trail Distance: 1.5 mi   Loops: None   Shortest: NA   Longest: NA
Trail Surface: Natural
Trail Use Fee: None
Method Of Ski Trail Grooming: NA
Skiing Ability Suggested: NA
Hiking Trail Difficulty: Moderate
Mountain Biking Ability Suggested: NA
Terrain: Steep 0%, Hilly 10%, Moderate 80%, Flat 10%
Camping: None on site but private, state and federal camprounds nearby

Maintained by the Consumers Power Company
Developed with the cooperation of the Boy Scouts of America.
This is a 26 station nature trail.
Brochures are at the trailhead and from the Consumers Power Company in Cadillac.
Round trip trail length is 3 miles.

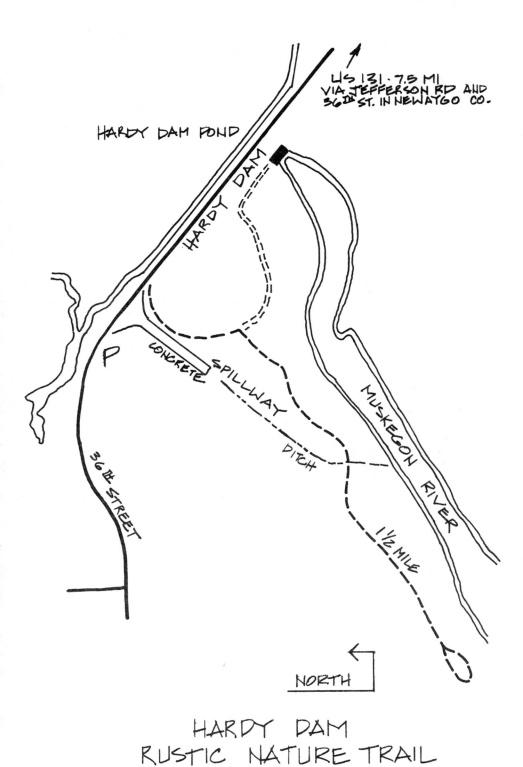

HARDY DAM
RUSTIC NATURE TRAIL

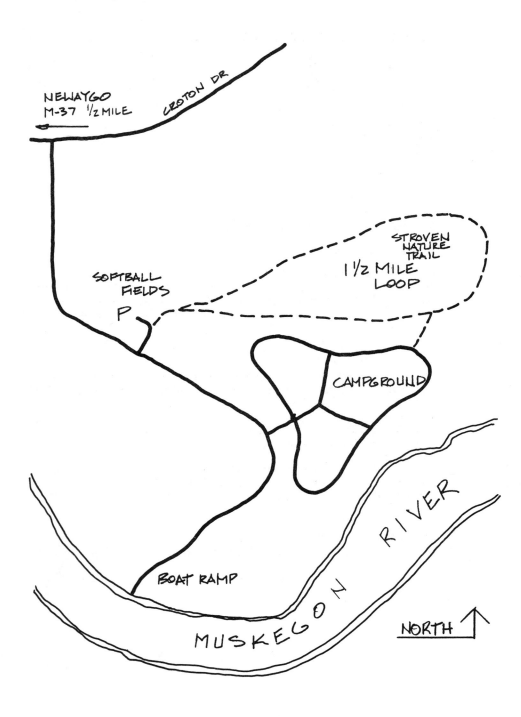

Newaygo County Parks Commission
4684 S. Evergreen Drive
Newaygo, MI 49337

616-652-9191

Michigan Atlas & Gazetteer Location: 46A1

County Location: Newaygo

Directions To Trailhead:
From M37 in Newaygo, turn right onto Croton Rd for about .25 mile to park entrance

Trail Type: Hiking/Walking, Interpretive
Trail Distance: 1.5 mi   Loops: 1   Shortest: Longest: 1.5 mi
Trail Surface: Natural
Trail Use Fee: None
Method Of Ski Trail Grooming: NA
Skiing Ability Suggested: NA
Hiking Trail Difficulty: Easy
Mountain Biking Ability Suggested: NA
Terrain: Steep 0%, Hilly 0%, Moderate 10%, Flat 90%
Camping: Campground on site

Owned by the County of Newaygo
Modern campground with all facilities including ball fields, playgrounds and boat ramp

STROVEN NATURE TRAIL
HENNING PARK

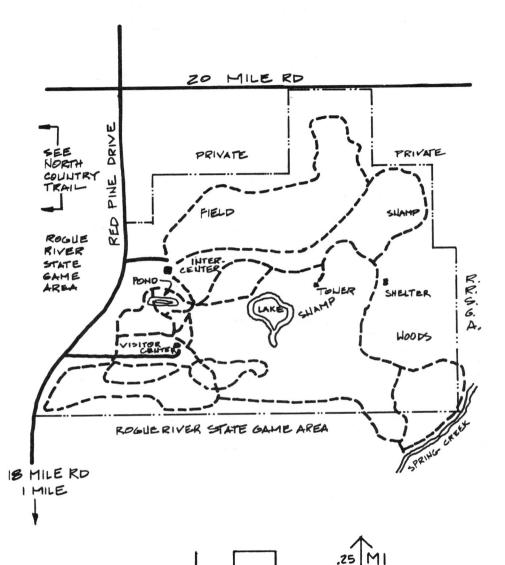

HOWARD CHRISTENSEN
NATURE CENTER

Kent Intermediate School District
16160 Red Pine Drive
Kent City, MI 49330

616-887-1852

Michigan Atlas & Gazetteer Location: 46B2

County Location: Muskegon

Directions To Trailhead:
North on M37(Alpine Ave) from Grand Rapids, onto Sparta Ave northbound through Kent City, then right on 17 or 18 Mile Rd to Red Pine, then north to the nature center. The nature center is south of 20 Mile Rd.

Trail Type: Hiking/Walking, Cross Country Skiing, Interpretive
Trail Distance: 5 mi   Loops: 8   Shortest: .25 mi Longest: 1.5 mi
Trail Surface: Paved and natural
Trail Use Fee: None
Method Of Ski Trail Grooming: None
Skiing Ability Suggested: Novice
Hiking Trail Difficulty: Easy
Mountain Biking Ability Suggested: NA
Terrain: Steep 0%, Hilly 5%, Moderate 10%, Flat 85%
Camping: None

Owned by the Kent Intermediate School District
Designed for outdoor education of school groups but the public is invited.

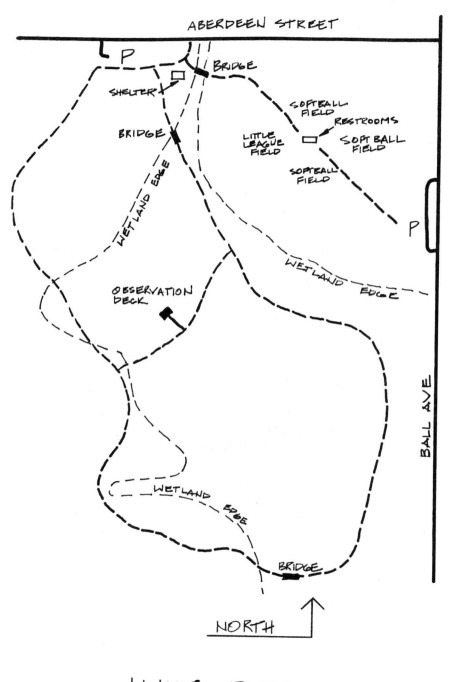

ABERDEEN STREET

P

BRIDGE

SHELTER

SOFTBALL FIELD

RESTROOMS

LITTLE LEAGUE FIELD

SOFTBALL FIELD

BRIDGE

WETLAND EDGE

SOFTBALL FIELD

P

WETLAND EDGE

OBSERVATION DECK

BALL AVE.

WETLAND EDGE

BRIDGE

NORTH

HUFF PARK
NATURE PRESERVE

Grand Rapids Parks and Recreation Department
201 Market St SW
Grand Rapids, MI 49503

616-456-3696

Michigan Atlas & Gazetteer Location: 46D3

County Location: Kent

Directions To Trailhead:
In Grand Rapids at Aberdeen and Ball Streets.
Park entrance is on Aberdeen St.

Trail Type: Hiking/Walking, Interpretive
Trail Distance: 1 mi   Loops: 2   Shortest: .6 mi   Longest: 1 mi
Trail Surface: Paved and boardwalk
Trail Use Fee: None
Method Of Ski Trail Grooming: NA
Skiing Ability Suggested: NA
Hiking Trail Difficulty: Easy
Mountain Biking Ability Suggested: NA
Terrain: Steep 0%, Hilly 0%, Moderate 0%, Flat 100%
Camping: None

Owned by the Grand Rapids Department of Parks and Recreation
Totally accessible nature trail
Restroom at trailhead
Brochure available

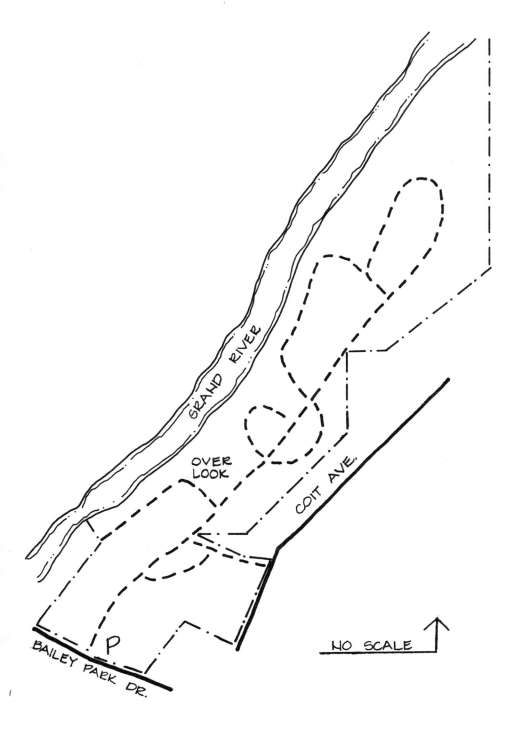

LAMOREAUX PARK

Kent County Park Commission
1500 Scribner NW
Grand Rapids, MI 49504

616-336-3697

Michigan Atlas & Gazetteer Location: 46D2

County Location: Kent

Directions To Trailhead:
North of the Grand Rapids city limits on Coit Avenue, 1 mile north of 4 Mile Rd

Trail Type: Hiking/Walking, Cross Country Skiing
Trail Distance: 3 mi   Loops: 3   Shortest: Longest:
Trail Surface: Natural
Trail Use Fee: None
Method Of Ski Trail Grooming: Track set occasionally
Skiing Ability Suggested: Novice
Hiking Trail Difficulty: Easy
Mountain Biking Ability Suggested: NA
Terrain: Steep 0%, Hilly 0%, Moderate 15%, Flat 85%
Camping: None

Maintained by the Kent County Park Commission
Parking off Bailey Park Drive and Coit Avenue

Newaygo County Community Services
4 West Oak St.   616-924-0641
Fremont, MI 49412

Michigan Atlas & Gazetteer Location: 46A1

County Location: Newaygo

Directions To Trailhead:
From Newaygo, go north 4 miles on M 37 to 40th St., then left (west) and go 2 miles to Gordon Ave at a sharp left curve (south). Take Gordan Ave 1 mile to 48th ST. Turn left(east) on 48th St and go 1.5 miles to the park trailhead which will be on your right.

Trail Type: Hiking/Walking, Interpretive
Trail Distance: .5 mi   Loops: 1   Shortest: NA   Longest: .5 mi
Trail Surface: Natural and boardwalk
Trail Use Fee: None
Method Of Ski Trail Grooming: NA
Skiing Ability Suggested: NA
Hiking Trail Difficulty: Easy
Mountain Biking Ability Suggested: NA
Terrain: Steep 0%, Hilly 0%, Moderate 0%, Flat 100%
Camping: None

Maintained by Newaygo County Coummunity Services
Small nature trail with accessible boardwalk.

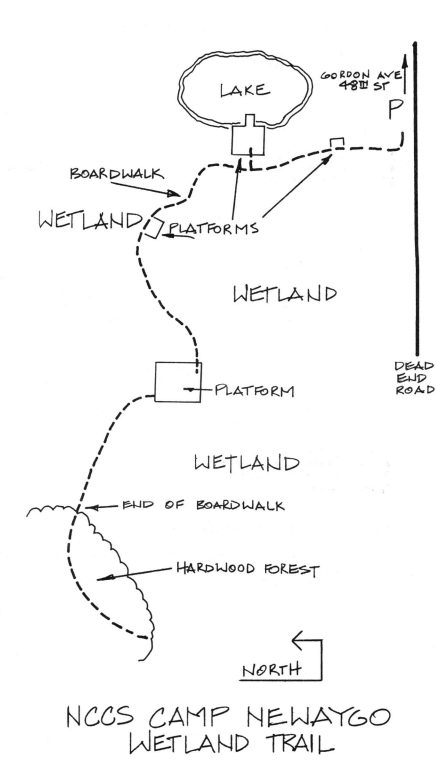

LAKE

GORDON AVE
48ᵀᴴ ST
P

BOARDWALK

WETLAND   PLATFORMS

WETLAND

DEAD
END
ROAD

PLATFORM

WETLAND

END OF BOARDWALK

HARDWOOD FOREST

NORTH

NCCS CAMP NEWAYGO
WETLAND TRAIL

DNR, Wildlife Division, District 9
State Office Bldg, 6th Floor, 350 Ottawa NW   616-456-5071
Grand Rapids, MI 49503

North Country Trail Association
49 Monroe Center, Suite 200B   616-454-5506
Grand Rapids, MI 49546

Michigan Atlas & Gazetteer Location: 46BC2

County Location: Kent

Directions To Trailhead:
North of Grand Rapids - 7 miles west of Cedar Springs and 5 miles north of Sparta.
South trail head - Division and Solon St, just north of 17 Mile Rd.
North trail head - 22 Mile Rd, between Sparta and Red Pine

Trail Type: Hiking/Walking, Cross Country Skiing
Trail Distance: 5.5 mi   Loops: NA   Shortest: NA   Longest: NA
Trail Surface: Natural
Trail Use Fee: None
Method Of Ski Trail Grooming: None
Skiing Ability Suggested: Novice
Hiking Trail Difficulty: Easy
Mountain Biking Ability Suggested: NA
Terrain: Flat to slightly rolling
Camping: None

Trail in the Rogue River State Game Area
Trail built and maintained by the North Country Trail Association.
See NCT - Michigan Section - Hiker Guide, page 15 available from the NCTA.
Recently maintained and relocated in some sections
The Howard Christensen Nature Center (see other listing) is nearby on the east side of Red Pine Drive.

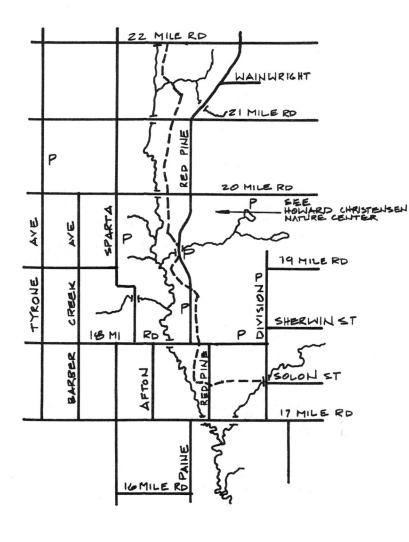

NORTH COUNTRY TRAIL
ROGUE RIVER STATE GAME AREA

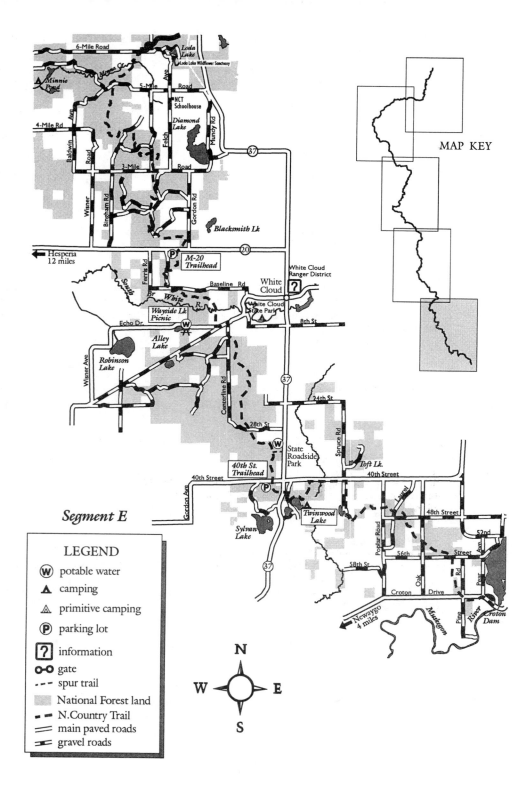

Baldwin/White Cloud Ranger Station, Huron Manistee N.F.
650 N. Michigan Ave   616-745-4631
Baldwin, MI 49304   800-821-6263

Forest Supevisor, Huron Manistee National Forest
1755 S. Mitchell St   800-821-6263
Cadillac, MI 49601

Michigan Atlas & Gazetteer Location: 46A12,56CD1

County Location: Newaygo

Directions To Trailhead:
South trailhead - E. from Newaygo on Croton Dr. to the Croton Dam.
North trailhead - Just west of the Loda Lake Wildlife Sanctuary(see other
listing)on 6 Mile Rd (6 miles north of M20), 3 miles west of M37. Also on M20, 5
miles west of M37. At roadside park, just north of 40th St on M37.

Trail Type: Hiking/Walking, Mountain Biking
Trail Distance: 27 mi   Loops: NA   Shortest: NA   Longest: NA
Trail Surface: Gravel and natural
Trail Use Fee: None
Method Of Ski Trail Grooming: NA
Skiing Ability Suggested: NA
Hiking Trail Difficulty: Easy to moderate
Mountain Biking Ability Suggested: Novice (only permitted north of M20)
Terrain: Steep 0%, Hilly 15%, Moderate 55%, Flat 30%
Camping: None along trail but several private and public nearby

Maintained by the Huron-Manistee National Forest
Varied forest cover and wetlands with stream crossings.
Closed to mountain biking south of M20.
Not very hilly but very still a very scenic section.
For further information contact the North Country Trail Association. New
members always welcome.

Pando Ski Area
8076 Belding Rd. NE
Rockford, MI 49341

616-874-8343

SEE MAPS ON NEXT PAGE

Michigan Atlas & Gazetteer Location: 46D4

County Location: Kent

Directions To Trailhead:
12 Miles northeast of Grand Rapids on M44.

Trail Type: Cross Country Skiing, Mountain Biking
Trail Distance: 5 mi   Loops: Many   Shortest: Longest:
Trail Surface: Natural
Trail Use Fee: Yes
Method Of Ski Trail Grooming: Track set when snow conditon permits.
Skiing Ability Suggested: Novice to advanced
Hiking Trail Difficulty: NA
Mountain Biking Ability Suggested: Intermediate to advanced
Terrain: Steep 2%, Hilly 18%, Moderate 50%, Flat 30%
Camping: None

Privately owned all season recreation area.
Total trail distance for mountain bike trails is about 4 miles.
Lodge, ski rentals, snack bar and instruction.
Site of annual mountain bike races.

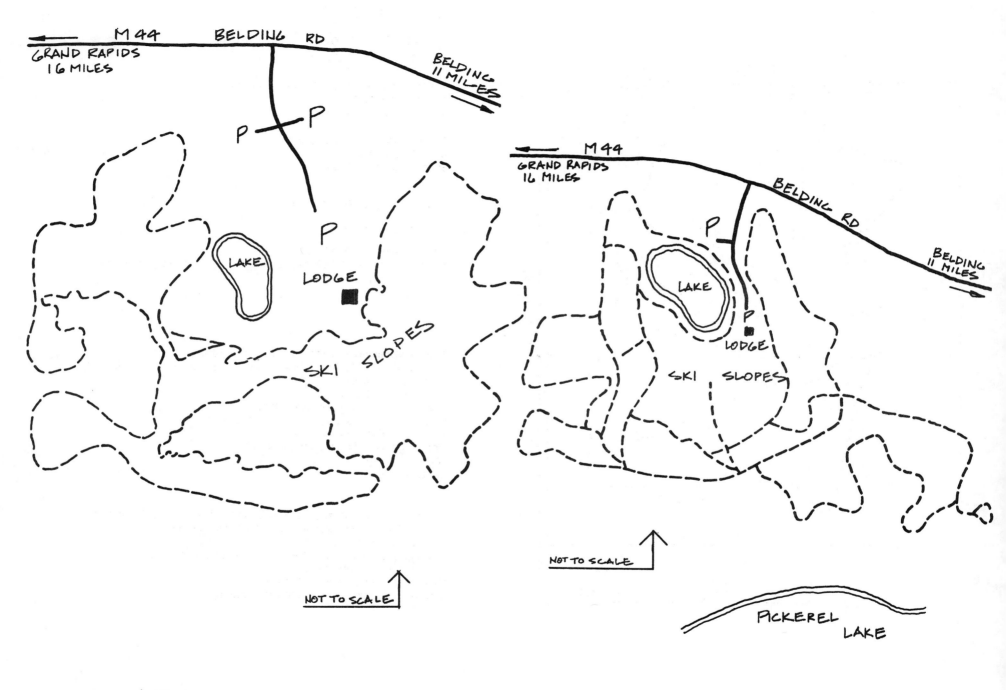

Left map:

M 44 BELDING RD

GRAND RAPIDS
16 MILES

BELDING
11 MILES

P — P

P

LAKE

LODGE

SKI SLOPES

NOT TO SCALE

MOUNTAIN BIKE TRAILS
PANDO

Right map:

M 44

GRAND RAPIDS
16 MILES

BELDING RD

BELDING
11 MILES

P

LAKE

P

LODGE

SKI SLOPES

NOT TO SCALE

PICKEREL LAKE

SKI TRAILS
PANDO

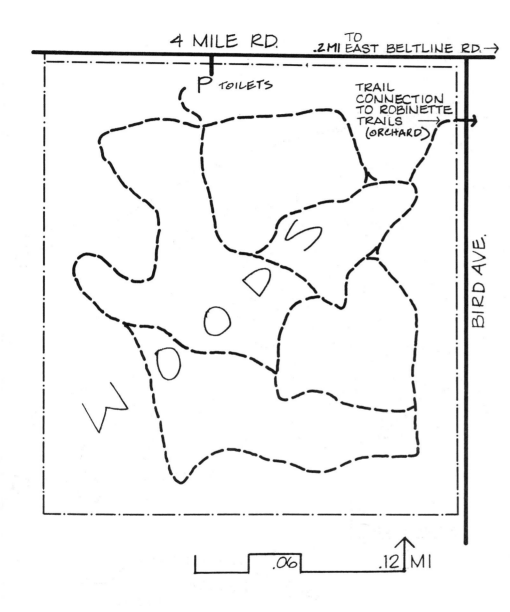

4 MILE RD.

TO
.2MI EAST BELTLINE RD. →

P TOILETS

TRAIL
CONNECTION
TO ROBINETTE
TRAILS
(ORCHARD) →

BIRD AVE.

|___|‾‾|___.06___|‾‾|___.12|MI

Provin Trails Park

Grand Rapids Parks and Recreation Department
201 Market St. SW
Grand Rapids, MI 49503

616-456-3696

Kent County Park Commission
1500 Scribner NW
Grand Rapids, MI 49504

616-774-3697

Michigan Atlas & Gazetteer Location: 46D3

County Location: Kent

Directions To Trailhead:
3/4 mile west of East Beltline at the corner of 4 Mile Rd. & Bird Ave

Trail Type: Hiking/Walking, Cross Country Skiing
Trail Distance: 1.7 mi   Loops: Many   Shortest: Longest:
Trail Surface: Natural
Trail Use Fee: None
Method Of Ski Trail Grooming: None
Skiing Ability Suggested: Intermediate to advanced
Hiking Trail Difficulty: Moderate
Mountain Biking Ability Suggested: NA
Terrain: Rolling
Camping: None

Maintained as a joint effort of the Grand Rapids Parks & Recreation, Kent
County Park Commission and Grand Rapids Township.
No facilities except for toilets.
Trails connect with Robinette's Apple Haus trails to the east.
Developed as nature trails.
Parking lot is located on 4 Mile Rd.
Extensive mature pine reforestation plantings.

PROVIN TRAILS PARK

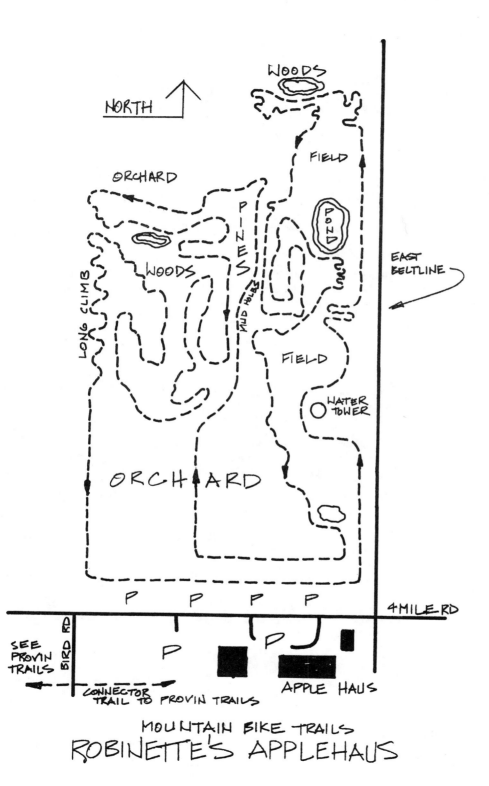

Robinette's Apple Haus
3142 4 Mile Rd
Grand Rapids, MI 49505

616-361-5567

Michigan Atlas & Gazetteer Location: 46D3

County Location: Kent

Directions To Trailhead:
At the northeast edge of Grand Rapids. Just west of East Beltline at 4 Mile Rd

Trail Type: Hiking/Walking, Cross Country Skiing, Mountain Biking
Trail Distance: 4.5 mi   Loops: 1   Shortest: NA   Longest: 4.5 mi
Trail Surface: Natural
Trail Use Fee: Yes for mountain biking only
Method Of Ski Trail Grooming: None
Skiing Ability Suggested: Novice to intermediate
Hiking Trail Difficulty: Easy
Mountain Biking Ability Suggested: Novice to advanced
Terrain: Steep 0%, Hilly 20%, Moderate 30%, Flat 50%
Camping: None

Privately operated 125 acre orchard
Trials are primarily for mountain biking but can be skied and hiked.
No ski trail grooming provided.
All trails are single track.
Trail connector to Provin Trail Park. See other listing.
Hours are 9 to 9 weekdays and 9 to 5:30 Saturday. Closed Sunday. Also closed
when it rains.
Gift store and restrooms available.

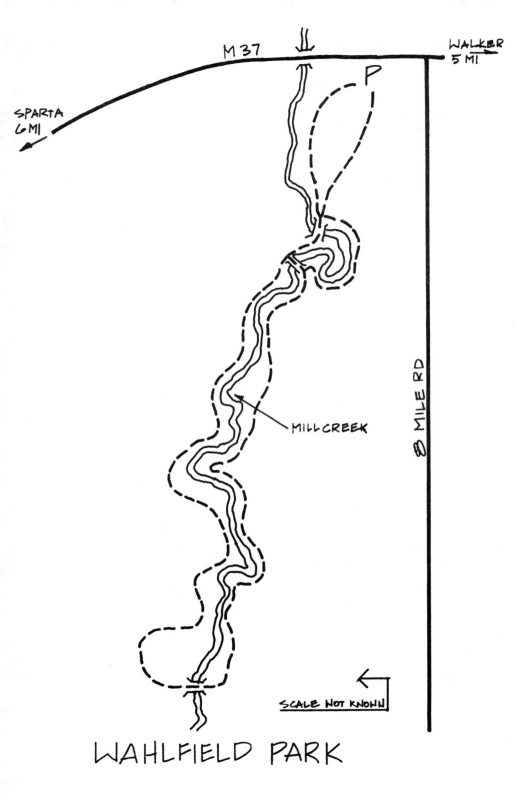

WAHLFIELD PARK

Wahlfield Park

Kent County Parks Commission
1500 Scribner Ave. NW
Grand Rapids, MI 49504-3299

616-774-3697

Michigan Atlas & Gazetteer Location: 46D2

County Location: Kent

Directions To Trailhead:
At M37 and 8 Mile Rd 7 miles north of Grand Rapids

Trail Type: Hiking/Walking, Cross Country Skiing
Trail Distance: 3 mi   Loops: 1   Shortest: NA   Longest: 3 mi
Trail Surface: Natural
Trail Use Fee: None
Method Of Ski Trail Grooming: NA
Skiing Ability Suggested: Novice
Hiking Trail Difficulty: Easy
Mountain Biking Ability Suggested: NA
Terrain: Steep 0%, Hilly 0%, Moderate 25%, Flat 75%
Camping: None

Maintained by the Kent County Park Commission

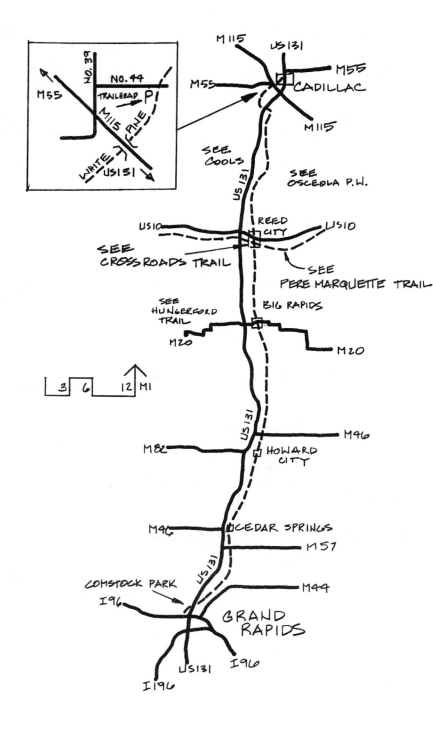

DNR Parks and Recreation Division
PO Box 30257
Lansing, MI 48909

517-373-1270

Michigan Atlas & Gazetteer Location: 46A-D234. 56A-D34,66CD4,67C4

County Location: Wexford, Osceola, Mecosta,Montcalm,Kent

Directions To Trailhead:
South trailhead - Comstock Park near Grand Rapids
North trailhead - Cadillac

Trail Type: Hiking/Walking, Cross Country Skiing, Mountain Biking
Trail Distance: 92 mi   Loops: NA   Shortest: NA   Longest: NA
Trail Surface: Ballast and natural
Trail Use Fee: Not known
Method Of Ski Trail Grooming: None
Skiing Ability Suggested: Novice
Hiking Trail Difficulty: Easy
Mountain Biking Ability Suggested: Novice
Terrain: 100% Flat
Camping: None along trail but nearby

Managed by the DNR Parks and Recreation Division
The main north-south rail trail in the state.
Intersects the Pere Marquette State Trail in Reed City.
Continues under development but very useable for hiking and mountain biking.
A detail of the Cadillac trailhead is shown on the trail map.
The Comstock Park trailhead has not yet been constructed (1997)

WHITE PINE TRAIL STATE PARK

Montcalm Conservation District
77 S. State St.
Stanton, MI 48888

517-831-8155
517-831-4606

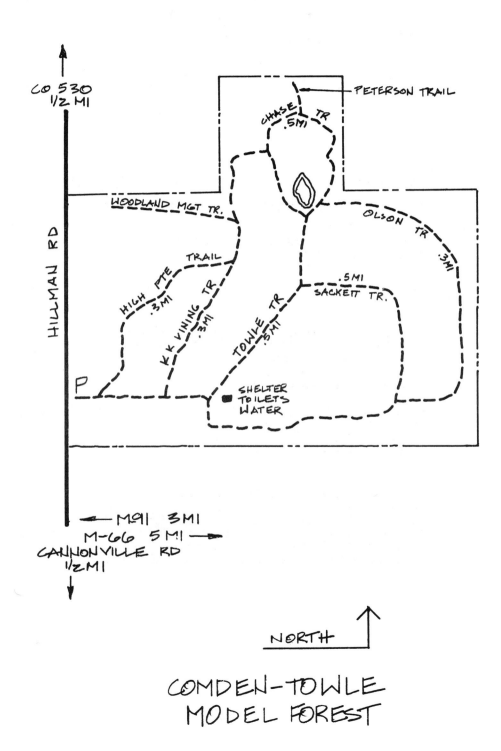

Michigan Atlas & Gazetteer Location: 47B6

County Location: Montcalm

Directions To Trailhead:
From Stanton take M 66 north to McBride Rd, then west on Co.Rd 530 through
Entrican to Hillman Rd. Then south on Hillman to the parking lot on the east side
of the road.

Trail Type: Hiking/Walking, Cross Country Skiing, Interpretive
Trail Distance: 2.7 mi   Loops: Shortest: Longest:
Trail Surface: Natural
Trail Use Fee: None
Method Of Ski Trail Grooming: None
Skiing Ability Suggested: Novice
Hiking Trail Difficulty: Easy
Mountain Biking Ability Suggested: NA
Terrain: Steep 1%, Hilly 5%, Moderate 0%, Flat 95%
Camping: None

Maintained by the Montcalm Conservation District
Comphensive nature trail guide available.
Shelter, water and restrooms available.

COMDEN-TOWLE
MODEL FOREST

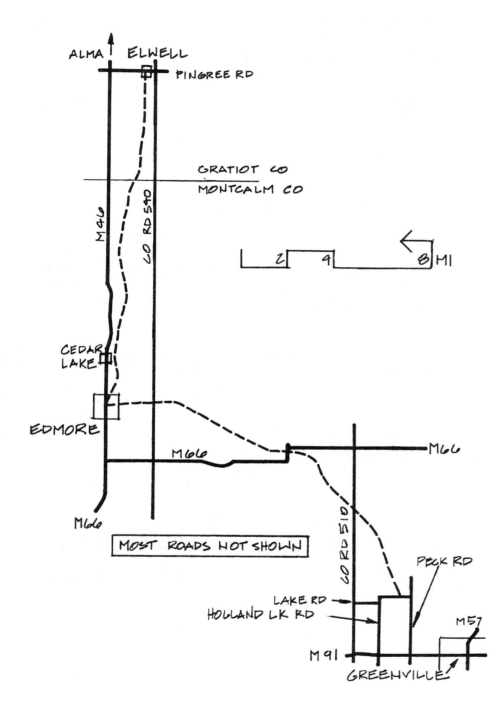

Rails to Trails Conservancy
913 W. Holmes Rd, Suite 145   517-393-6022
Lansing, MI 48901

Friends of the Heartland Trail
PO Box 233   517-427-5589
Sidney, MI 48885   517-427-3478

Michigan Atlas & Gazetteer Location: 47ABC67,48A123

County Location: Montcalm, Gratiot

Directions To Trailhead:
From just northeast of Greenville on the west to Elwell on the east.
West trailhead - Take M91 north about 2 miles to Peck Rd, then east to Lake Rd, then north to trailhead.
East trailhead - Community of Elwell, about 4 miles west of Alma

Trail Type: Hiking/Walking, Cross Country Skiing, Mountain Biking
Trail Distance: 35 mi   Loops: NA   Shortest: NA   Longest: NA
Trail Surface: Ballast and natural
Trail Use Fee:
Method Of Ski Trail Grooming:
Skiing Ability Suggested:
Hiking Trail Difficulty:
Mountain Biking Ability Suggested:
Terrain: 100%Flat
Camping: None

Owned by the Rails to Trails Conservancy
Being developed the the Friends of the Heartland Trail
This trail was recently purchased (1994) by Fred Meijer and donated to the Rails to Trails Conservancy.
No improvements have been made(1994). Contact above organizations for current status.
The Friends of the Heartland, welcome new members to work on this project.

HEARTLAND RAIL TRAIL

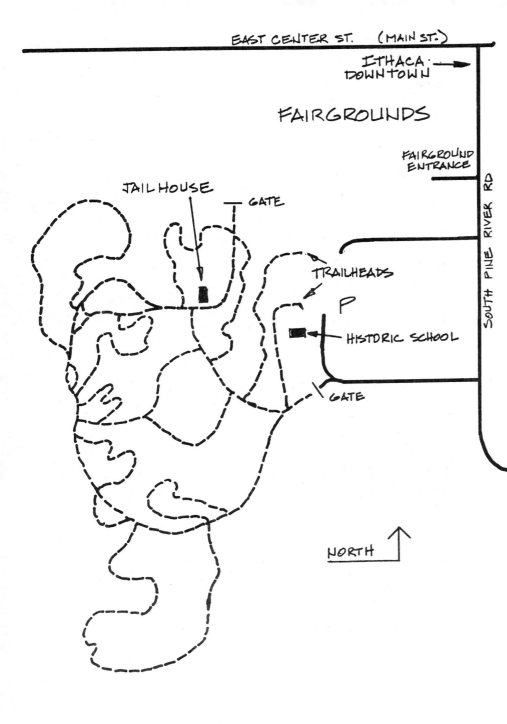

ITHACA → DOWNTOWN

FAIRGROUNDS

FAIRGROUND ENTRANCE

JAIL HOUSE — GATE

TRAILHEADS

P

HISTORIC SCHOOL

SOUTH PINE RIVER RD

GATE

NORTH ↑

ITHACA JAILHOUSE TRAIL

Ithaca Jailhouse Trail

48

City of Ithaca
129 West Emerson St
Ithaca, MI 488847

517-875-3200

Michigan Atlas & Gazetteer Location: 48B4

County Location: Gratiot

Directions To Trailhead:
From US-27 go west into downtown Ithaca on the main street which is Center St (Washington Rd out side of town), then south on South River Road past the main fairground area to the trailhead, which is across a field (parking area) to the west, next to the wooded area.

Trail Type: Hiking/Walking, Cross Country Skiing, Mountain Biking
Trail Distance: 5+ mi   Loops: 9   Shortest: .36 mi Longest: 3+ mi
Trail Surface: Natural, wet in spring
Trail Use Fee: None
Method Of Ski Trail Grooming: None
Skiing Ability Suggested: Novice
Hiking Trail Difficulty: Easy
Mountain Biking Ability Suggested: Novice to intermediate
Terrain: Steep 0%, Hilly 7%, Moderate 30%, Flat 63%
Camping: 20 camping sites near trailhead on fairgrounds

Owned by the City of Ithaca
Located in a wooded area attached to the county fair grounds.
Developed by volunteers and members of the Michigan Mountain Biking Association
Trail system developed in 1994 as a mountain bike trail.
Best to ride in dry conditions since the soil is heavy clay.
Popular riding area for Alma College and Central Michigan University students.
Site of annual mountain bike races.
Revised - Spring 1998

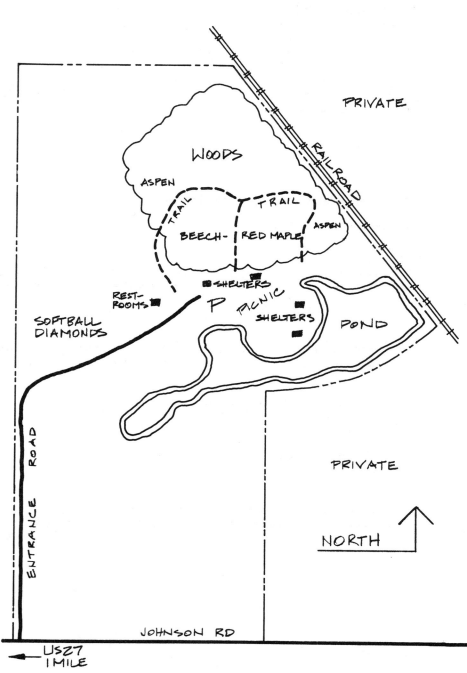

Reed County Park

Gratiot County Parks and Recreation
214 E. Center
Ithaca, MI 48847

517-875-5244

Michigan Atlas & Gazetteer Location: 49C4

County Location: Gratiot

Directions To Trailhead:
5 miles south of Ithaca on US27, take Johnson Rd east 1.5 miles to the park.

Trail Type: Hiking/Walking, Cross Country Skiing, Interpretive
Trail Distance: .5 mi   Loops: 2   Shortest: Longest:
Trail Surface: Natural
Trail Use Fee: None
Method Of Ski Trail Grooming: None
Skiing Ability Suggested: Novice
Hiking Trail Difficulty: Easy
Mountain Biking Ability Suggested: NA
Terrain: Flat
Camping: None

Maintained by the Gratiot County Parks and Recreation
A 14 acre wooded park

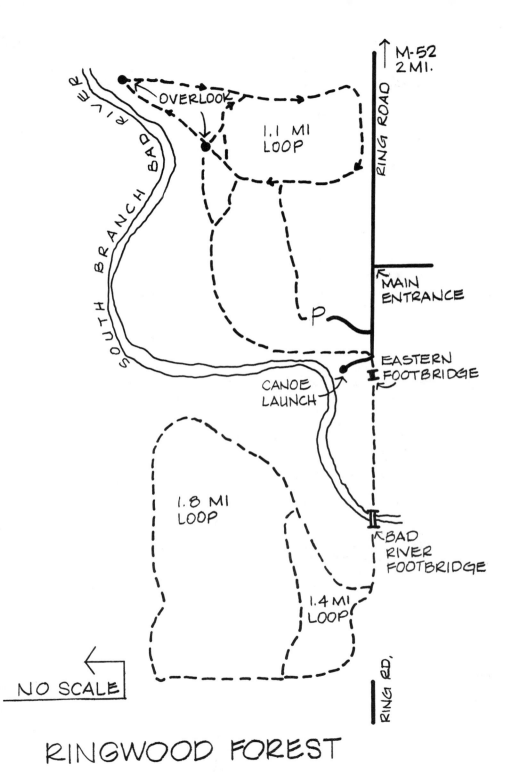

NO SCALE

RINGWOOD FOREST

Ringwood Forest

Saginaw County Parks & Recreation Commission
111 S. Michgian Ave
Saginaw, MI 48602

517-790-5280

Michigan Atlas & Gazetteer Location: 49B7

County Location: Saginaw

Directions To Trailhead:
SW of Saginaw near St Charles
Trailhead - From St Charles south on M52, 2 miles to Ring Rd., then west 2 miles to Fordney Road. Park entrance at the corner of Ring Rd. and Fordney Rd.

Trail Type: Hiking/Walking, Cross Country Skiing, Mountain Biking, Interpretive
Trail Distance: 3.5 mi   Loops: 5   Shortest: .9 mi   Longest: 1.8 mi
Trail Surface: Natural
Trail Use Fee: None
Method Of Ski Trail Grooming: Track set
Skiing Ability Suggested: Novice to intermediate
Hiking Trail Difficulty: Easy
Mountain Biking Ability Suggested: Novice
Terrain: Steep 0%, Hilly 5%, Moderate 20%, Flat 75%
Camping: None

Operated by the Saginaw County Parks & Recreation Commission.
Clinics available Park contains the oldest evergreen, a 104 year old spruce.
A 14 station interpretive trail is part of this system.

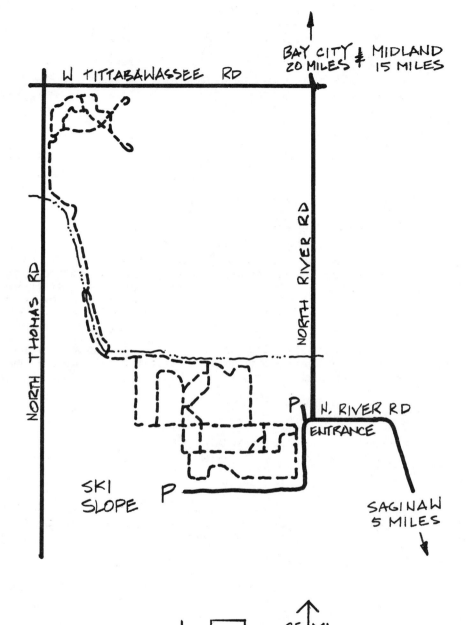

SKI
SLOPE

BINTZ APPLE MOUNTAIN

Bintz Apple Mountain Ski Area
4535 North River Rd.
Freeland , MI 48623

517-781-2550
517-781-2590

Michigan Atlas & Gazetteer Location: 50A1

County Location: Saginaw

Directions To Trailhead:
5 miles south of Freeland and 5 miles NW of Saginaw on North River Rd. I-75 to I-675 and exit at Tittabawassee Rd., then west for 7 miles and across the Tittabawassee River,then first left on River Rd to ski area.

Trail Type: Cross Country Skiing
Trail Distance: 4 mi   Loops: Several   Shortest: Longest:
Trail Surface: Natrual
Trail Use Fee: Yes, daily and annual permits
Method Of Ski Trail Grooming: None
Skiing Ability Suggested: Novice
Hiking Trail Difficulty: NA
Mountain Biking Ability Suggested: NA
Terrain: 100% Flat
Camping: None

Privately operated alpine ski area with cross country skiing.
The first completely man-made ski hill in the United States in 1961.
Lessons, rentals, ski shop, snack bar, restaurant and lounge.
Trails cover 300 acres.

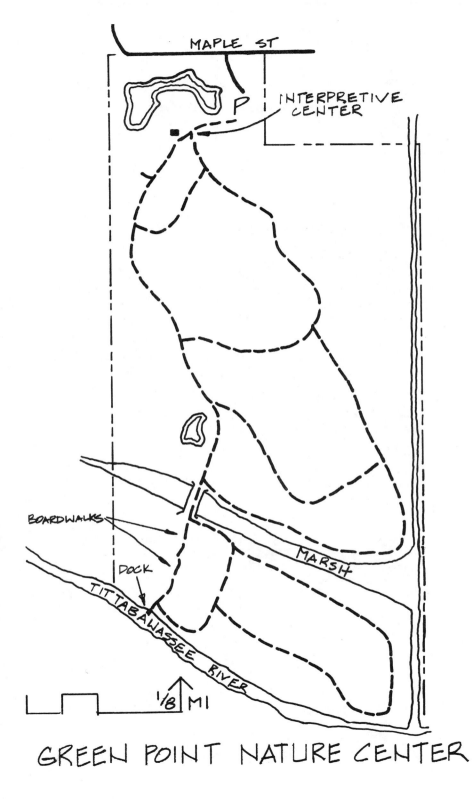

GREEN POINT NATURE CENTER

Green Point Nature Center
3010 Maple St
Saginaw, MI 48630

517-759-1669

Michigan Atlas & Gazetteer Location: 50A2

County Location: Saginaw

Directions To Trailhead:
From I-75 take M46 West Ave(Holland Ave) exit, take M46 through the city and over the Saginaw River, then turn left (south) on Mich. Ave for about 2 blocks west of the bridge, then follow Michigan until there are a set of stop lights on a curve, turn left (south)on Maple St, immediately past the stop lights, look for a brown sign. Follow Maple to the nature center. Germania Golf Course is your right.

Trail Type: Hiking/Walking, Cross Country Skiing, Interpretive
Trail Distance: 2.5 mi   Loops: 6   Shortest: .2 mi   Longest: 1.5 mi
Trail Surface: Gravel and natural
Trail Use Fee: None
Method Of Ski Trail Grooming: None
Skiing Ability Suggested: Novice
Hiking Trail Difficulty: Easy
Mountain Biking Ability Suggested: NA
Terrain: 100% Flat
Camping: None

Owned by trhe city of Saginaw in cooperation with the Fish and Wildlife Service. Visitor Center is managed and staffed by Fish and Wildlife Service.
Trails open during daylight hours.
No pets or bikes allowed.

Saginaw County Parks & Recreation Commission
111 S. Michigan Ave
Saginaw, MI 48602

517-790-5280

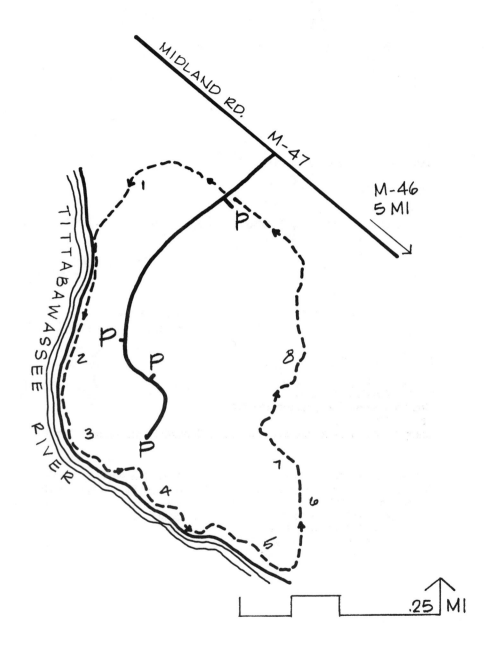

Michigan Atlas & Gazetteer Location: 50A1

County Location: Saginaw

Directions To Trailhead:
5 miles NW of Saginaw on M47 (Midland Rd.)

Trail Type: Hiking/Walking, Cross Country Skiing, Mountain Biking, Interpretive
Trail Distance: 1.5 mi   Loops: 1   Shortest: Longest:
Trail Surface: Natural
Trail Use Fee: None
Method Of Ski Trail Grooming: Track set
Skiing Ability Suggested: Novice
Hiking Trail Difficulty: Easy
Mountain Biking Ability Suggested: Novice
Terrain: 100% Flat
Camping: None

Operated by the Saginaw County Parks & Recreation Commission
Trail follows a scenic section of the Tittabawasse River
8 station interpretative trail. Brochure available
Warming shelter available during clinics
The long trail is a self guided floodplain nature trail
Just south of Bintz Apple Mountain Ski Area

IMERMAN MEMORIAL PARK

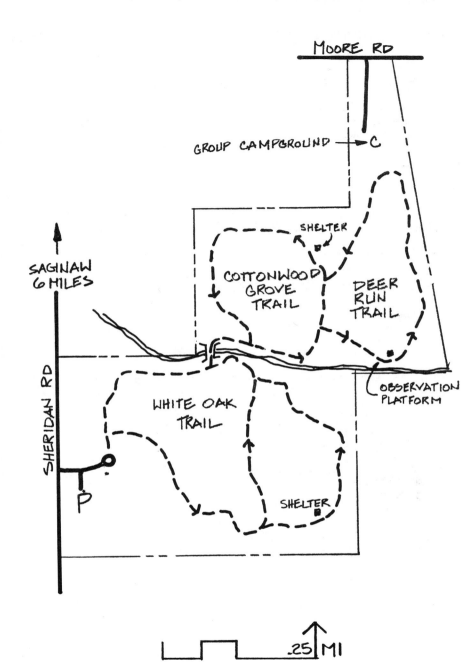

MOORE RD

GROUP CAMPGROUND → C

SAGINAW
6 MILES

SHERIDAN RD

SHELTER

COTTONWOOD GROVE TRAIL

DEER RUN TRAIL

OBSERVATION PLATFORM

WHITE OAK TRAIL

P

SHELTER

.25 MI

PRICE NATURE CENTER

Saginaw County Parks & Recreation Commission
111 S. Michigan Ave   517-790-5280
Saginaw, MI 48602

Michigan Atlas & Gazetteer Location: 50B2

County Location: Saginaw

Directions To Trailhead:
6 miles south of Saginaw on Sheridan Rd (1 mile east of M13), between Moore Rd. and Curtis Rd.

Trail Type: Hiking/Walking, Cross Country Skiing, Interpretive
Trail Distance: 2.7 mi   Loops: 3   Shortest: .7 mi   Longest: 1 mi
Trail Surface: Natural
Trail Use Fee: None
Method Of Ski Trail Grooming: Track set
Skiing Ability Suggested: Novice
Hiking Trail Difficulty: Easy
Mountain Biking Ability Suggested: NA
Terrain: 100% Flat
Camping: Available for organized groups with advance reservation

Operated by the Saginaw County Parks & Recreation Commission
Nature programs and ski clinics available with advance notice 100 year old beech/maple forest
Three loops with individual nature trail guides available
    White Oak Trail - 1 mile
    Cottonwood Grove Trail - 1 mile
    Dear Run - .7 mile

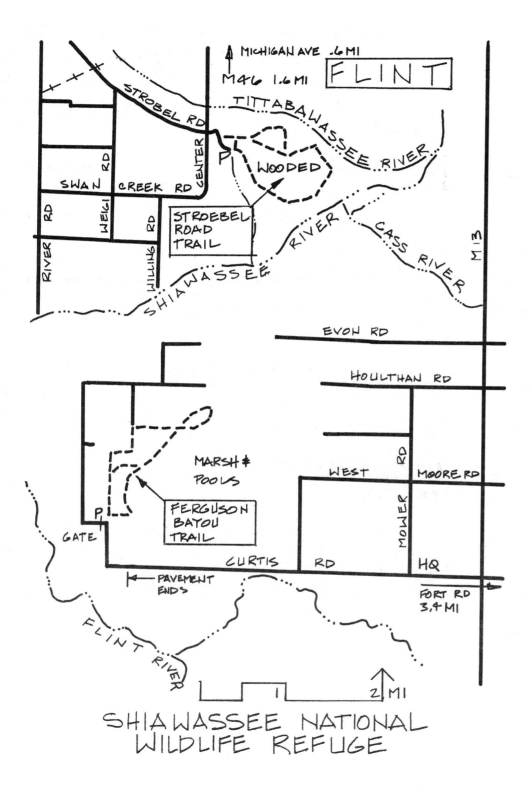

Shiawassee National Wildlife Refuge
6975 Mower Rd
Saginaw, MI 48601

517-777-5930

Michigan Atlas & Gazetteer Location: 50B1

County Location: Saginaw

Directions To Trailhead:
Ferguson Bayou Trailhead - 4 miles south of Saginaw and 4 miles west of M13 on Curtis Rd
Stroebel Road Trailhead - Center Rd south of M46(Gratiot Rd), then cross the Tittabawassee River bridge on Center to Stroebel Rd, then turn left(east) for one block to trailhead.

Trail Type: Hiking/Walking, Cross Country Skiing, Mountain Biking, Interpretive
Trail Distance: 9 mi   Loops: 4   Shortest: 1.5 mi Longest: 5 mi
Trail Surface: Natural
Trail Use Fee: None
Method Of Ski Trail Grooming: None
Skiing Ability Suggested: Novice
Hiking Trail Difficulty: Easy
Mountain Biking Ability Suggested: Novice
Terrain: 100% Flat
Camping: None

Maintained by the U.S. Fish and Wildlife Service, Department of Interior
Trails closed during specific hunting periods from October to December
Stroebel Rd Trail: 4 miles long; The trail is subject to spring and fall flooding. Good area for songbird observations; Coal mining took place in this area in the early 1900's.
Feguson Bayou Trail: 5 miles long; The trail is on dikes and well drained most of the year. However the short loop could be wet; The trail passes through bottomland hardwoods and agricultural management areas. At the half way point, there is an observation deck with a 10X spotting scope.
Trails being developed by local volunteers.

Genesee County Parks and Recreation Commission
5045 Stanley Rd   810-736-7100
Flint, MI 48506

For-Mar Nature Preserve
2142 N. Genesee Rd   810-789-8567
Burton, MI 48509

Michigan Atlas & Gazetteer Location: 51D5

County Location: Genesse

Directions To Trailhead:
East of Flint 3 miles on I69 to Belsay Rd, north 2 miles to Potter Rd, then west .3 mile to preserve entrance.
Trailhead is at the Interpretive Center.

NO MAP

Trail Type: Hiking/Walking, Cross Country Skiing, Interpretive
Trail Distance: 7 mi   Loops: 8   Shortest: Longest:
Trail Surface: Paved, gravel and natural
Trail Use Fee: None
Method Of Ski Trail Grooming: None
Skiing Ability Suggested: Novice to intermediate
Hiking Trail Difficulty: Easy
Mountain Biking Ability Suggested: NA
Terrain: Flat
Camping: None

Operated by the Genesee County Parks and Recreation Commission.
Hiking trailsare not all be identical to ski trails.
Trails start at the DeWaters Education Center.
About 400 acre preserve with many trails.
Special trails for visually impared and wheel chair users is provided.
Call or write for brochure

Genesee County Parks and Recreation Commision
5045 Stanley Rd
Flint, MI 48506

810-736-7100

NO MAP

Michigan Atlas & Gazetteer Location: 51D5

County Location: Genesee

Directions To Trailhead:
On the Flint River in the Genesee Recreation Area northeast of Flint.

Trail Type: Hiking/Walking
Trail Distance: 2.5 mi   Loops: 2   Shortest: .8 mi   Longest: 1.7 mi
Trail Surface: Paved
Trail Use Fee: None, but vehicle entry fee requried
Method Of Ski Trail Grooming: NA
Skiing Ability Suggested: NA
Hiking Trail Difficulty: NA
Mountain Biking Ability Suggested: Easy
Terrain: Steep 0%, Hilly 0%, Moderate 80%, Flat 20%
Camping: None

Owned by the Genesee Coounty Parks and Recreation Commission
Many varied facilities including beaches, boating, Crossroads Village and fishing
sites to name only a few.
Crossroads Village is a turn of the century town complete with pond, main street
and complete steam train ride outside the park.

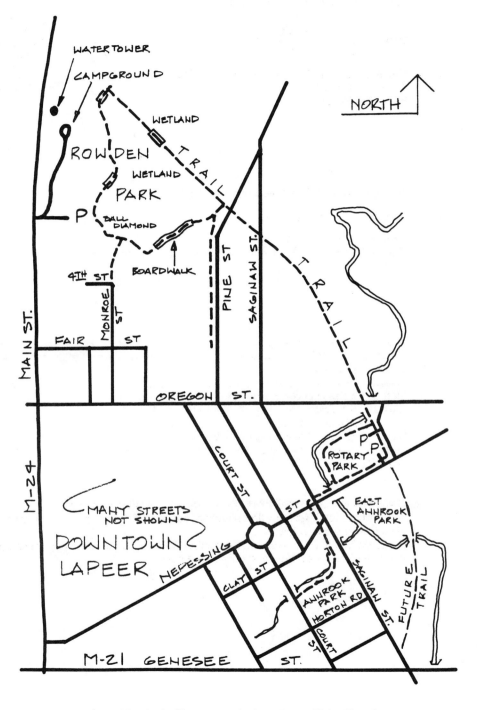

LAPEER LINEAR PARK

City of Lapeer
576 Liberty Park   810-664-5231
Lapeer, MI 48446

Michigan Atlas & Gazetteer Location: 51D7

County Location: Lapeer

Directions To Trailhead:
In the City of Lapeer between Annrook Park and Rowden Park.

Trail Type: Hiking/Walking
Trail Distance: 2.2 mi   Loops: 2   Shortest: 4. mi   Longest: 1 mi
Trail Surface: Paved
Trail Use Fee: None
Method Of Ski Trail Grooming: NA
Skiing Ability Suggested: NA
Hiking Trail Difficulty: Easy
Mountain Biking Ability Suggested: NA
Terrain: Flat
Camping: Campground along the trail

Maintained by the City of Lapeer
Trail connects 4 city parks.
The Watertower Travel Trailer Park in Rowden Park is seasonal from spring
through fall. The campground phone is 664-4296.
Expansion of the trail on the abandoned railroad track south to M-21 is planned
in the future.

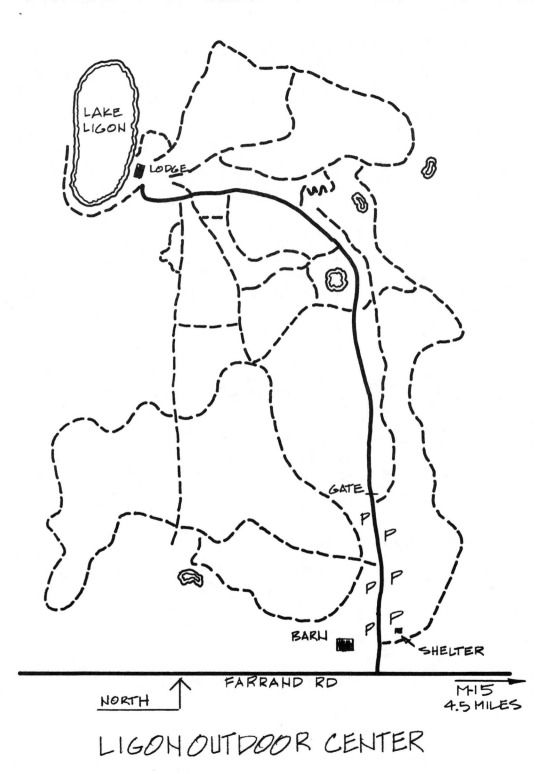

Genesee Intermediate School District
2413 West Maple Rd
Flint, MI 48507

810-687-4270

Michigan Atlas & Gazetteer Location: 51C5

County Location: Genesee

Directions To Trailhead:
From I-75 east on M57 to Genesee Rd, then north 1 mile to Farrand Rd, then east .5 mile to the center

Trail Type: Hiking/Walking, Cross Country Skiing, Interpretive
Trail Distance: 5 mi   Loops: 3   Shortest: 1mi   Longest: 3 mi
Trail Surface: Natural
Trail Use Fee: None
Method Of Ski Trail Grooming: Track set
Skiing Ability Suggested: Novice to intermediate
Hiking Trail Difficulty: Easy
Mountain Biking Ability Suggested: NA
Terrain: Steep 0%, Hilly 80%, Moderate 10%, Flat 10%
Camping: Group camping available

Owned by the Genesee Intermediate School District.
Complete outdoor center with educational programs.

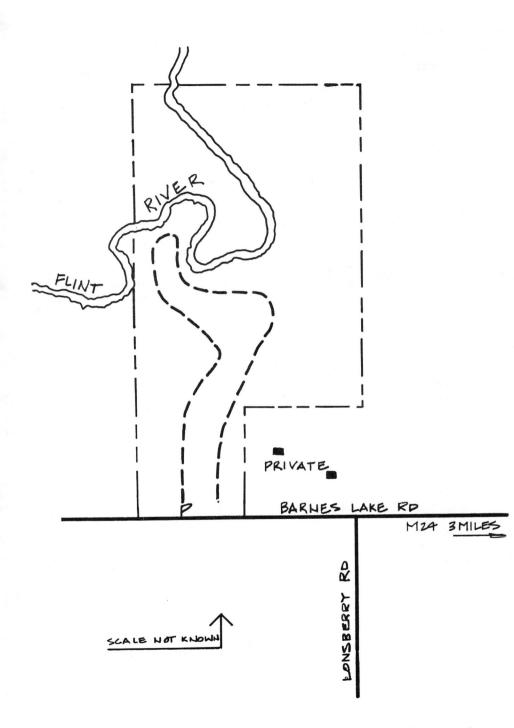

Michigan Nature Association
PO Box 102
Avoca, MI 48006

810-324-2626

Michigan Atlas & Gazetteer Location: 51C67

County Location: Lapeer

Directions To Trailhead:
From Lapeer, go 9.5 miles north on M24 to Barnes Lake Rd, then go 2 miles west to entrance which is just west of Lonsberry Rd. (some maps spell it "Lodsberry")

Trail Type: Hiking/Walking, Interpretive
Trail Distance: 1.5 mi   Loops: 1   Shortest: NA   Longest: 1.5 mi
Trail Surface: Natural
Trail Use Fee: None
Method Of Ski Trail Grooming: NA
Skiing Ability Suggested: NA
Hiking Trail Difficulty: Moderate
Mountain Biking Ability Suggested: NA
Terrain: Steep 10%, Hilly 30%, Moderate 30%, Flat 30%
Camping: None

Maintained by the Michigan Nature Association
This sanctuary is along the North Branch of the Flint River.
A detailed description of all the MNA properties is available from the association.

ZUCKER NATURE SANCTUARY

Lapeer County Parks and Recreation Commission
255 Clay St.
Lapeer, MI 48446

810-667-0304

Michigan Atlas & Gazetteer Location: 51D6

County Location: Lapeer

Directions To Trailhead:
Northwest of Lapeer. Take Oregon Rd west from Lapeer to Indian Rd, then north on Indian Rd which changes to Pero Lake Rd.. Park entrance is on the west side of the road.

Trail Type: Hiking/Walking, Cross Country Skiing, Interpretive
Trail Distance: I+ mi   Loops: 2   Shortest: Longest: 1+ mi
Trail Surface: Natural and paved
Trail Use Fee: None
Method Of Ski Trail Grooming: Not known
Skiing Ability Suggested: Novice
Hiking Trail Difficulty: Easy
Mountain Biking Ability Suggested: NA
Terrain:
Camping: None

Maintained by the Lapeer County Parks and Recreation Commission
Complete county park with waterslide, picnic area, ball fields, boat rentals, fishing, pavilions, lighted sleding hill and much more.
Separate ski and nature trails.

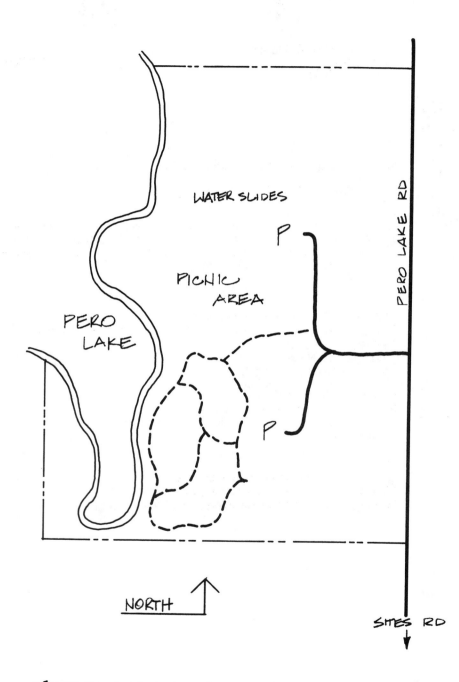

WATER SLIDES

P

PICNIC AREA

PERO LAKE

P

PERO LAKE RD

NORTH

SITES RD

TORZEWSKI COUNTY PARK

194.1

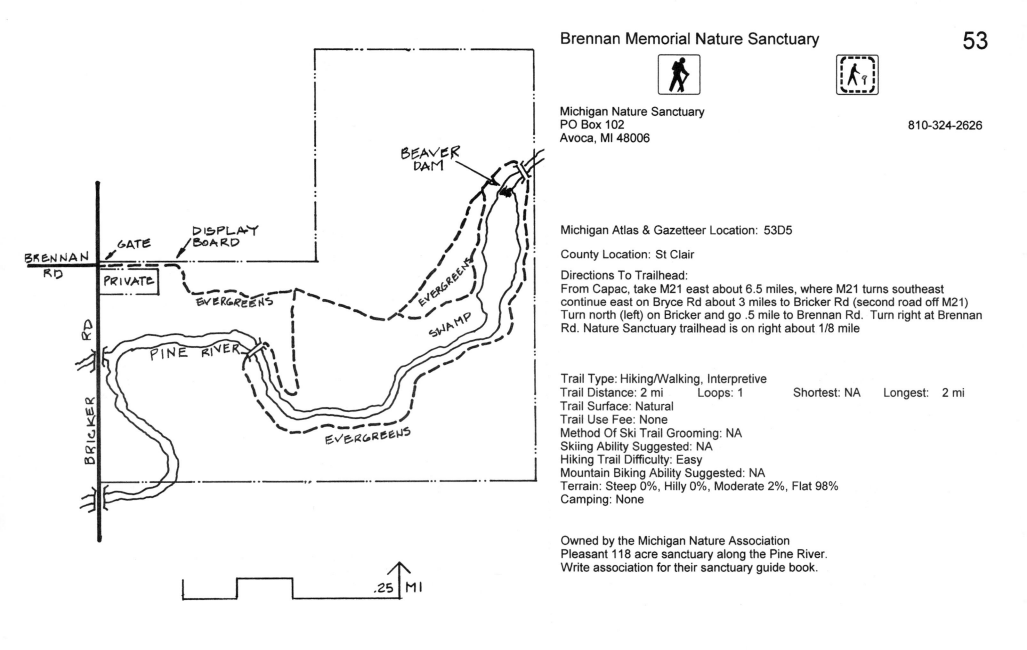

Michigan Nature Sanctuary
PO Box 102
Avoca, MI 48006

810-324-2626

Michigan Atlas & Gazetteer Location: 53D5

County Location: St Clair

Directions To Trailhead:
From Capac, take M21 east about 6.5 miles, where M21 turns southeast continue east on Bryce Rd about 3 miles to Bricker Rd (second road off M21) Turn north (left) on Bricker and go .5 mile to Brennan Rd. Turn right at Brennan Rd. Nature Sanctuary trailhead is on right about 1/8 mile

Trail Type: Hiking/Walking, Interpretive
Trail Distance: 2 mi   Loops: 1   Shortest: NA   Longest: 2 mi
Trail Surface: Natural
Trail Use Fee: None
Method Of Ski Trail Grooming: NA
Skiing Ability Suggested: NA
Hiking Trail Difficulty: Easy
Mountain Biking Ability Suggested: NA
Terrain: Steep 0%, Hilly 0%, Moderate 2%, Flat 98%
Camping: None

Owned by the Michigan Nature Association
Pleasant 118 acre sanctuary along the Pine River.
Write association for their sanctuary guide book.

BEAVER DAM

DISPLAY BOARD

GATE

BRENNAN RD

PRIVATE

EVERGREENS

EVERGREENS

SWAMP

PINE RIVER

BRICKER RD

EVERGREENS

.25 MI

BRENNAN MEMORIAL NATURE SANCTUARY

Ruby Campground
7700 Imlay City Rd
Avoca, MI 48006

810-324-2766

Michigan Atlas & Gazetteer Location: 53D5

County Location: St Clair

Directions To Trailhead:
About 17 miles west of Port Huron on M136, then south on Cribbins Rd 1 mile to
Imlay City Rd, then west 1/2 mile to the campground.

NO MAP

Trail Type: Hiking/Walking, Mountain Biking
Trail Distance: 7 mi   Loops: Shortest: Longest: 7 mi
Trail Surface: Natural
Trail Use Fee: Not known
Method Of Ski Trail Grooming: NA
Skiing Ability Suggested: NA
Hiking Trail Difficulty: Easy
Mountain Biking Ability Suggested: Intermediate to advanced
Terrain: Steep 10%, Hilly 40%, Moderate 40%, Flat 10%
Camping: Beautiful campground on the site.

Privately operated and family owned campground.
Trail is along the Mill Creek and through woods and former gravel pit.
Site of an annual mountain bike race.
Call ahead for current information about trail conditions.

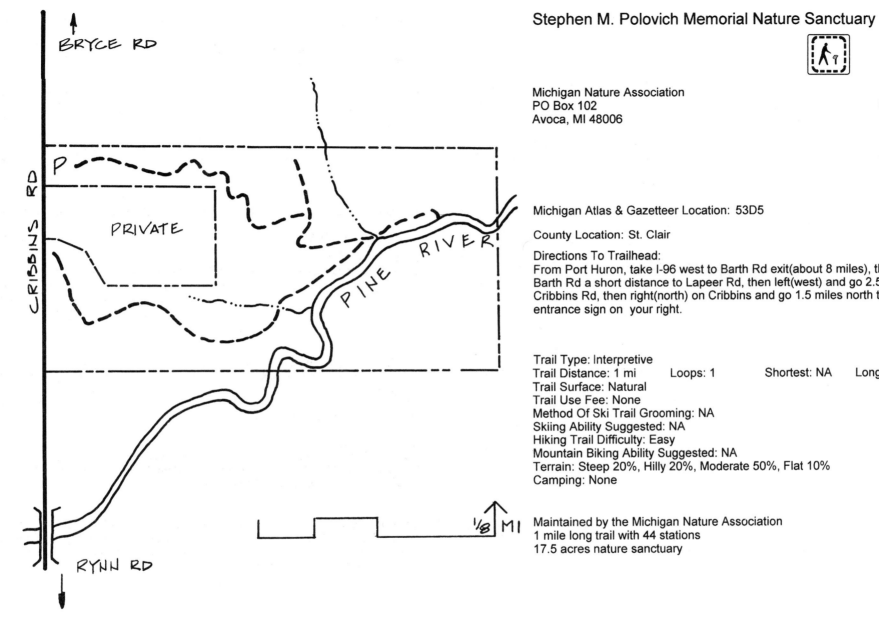

Michigan Nature Association
PO Box 102
Avoca, MI 48006

810-324-2626

Michigan Atlas & Gazetteer Location: 53D5

County Location: St. Clair

Directions To Trailhead:
From Port Huron, take I-96 west to Barth Rd exit(about 8 miles), then north on Barth Rd a short distance to Lapeer Rd, then left(west) and go 2.5 miles to Cribbins Rd, then right(north) on Cribbins and go 1.5 miles north to sanctuary entrance sign on your right.

Trail Type: Interpretive
Trail Distance: 1 mi   Loops: 1   Shortest: NA   Longest: 1 mi
Trail Surface: Natural
Trail Use Fee: None
Method Of Ski Trail Grooming: NA
Skiing Ability Suggested: NA
Hiking Trail Difficulty: Easy
Mountain Biking Ability Suggested: NA
Terrain: Steep 20%, Hilly 20%, Moderate 50%, Flat 10%
Camping: None

Maintained by the Michigan Nature Association
1 mile long trail with 44 stations
17.5 acres nature sanctuary

Ludington State Park
Box 709
Ludington , MI 49431

616-843-8671

DNR Parks and Recreation Division

517-373-1270

Michigan Atlas & Gazetteer Location: 54A3,64D23

County Location: Mason

Directions To Trailhead:
North of Ludington at the end of M116 along Lake Michigan

SEE MAPS ON NEXT PAGE

Trail Type: Hiking/Walking, Cross Country Skiing, Interpretive
Trail Distance: 22 mi   Loops: 15   Shortest: .5 mi   Longest: 2.7 mi
Trail Surface: Paved and natural
Trail Use Fee: None, but vehicle entry fee required
Method Of Ski Trail Grooming: Track set as needed
Skiing Ability Suggested: Novice to advanced
Hiking Trail Difficulty: Easy to difficult
Mountain Biking Ability Suggested: NA
Terrain: Steep 0%, Hilly 40%, Moderate 40%, Flat 20%
Camping: Campgrounds in the park

Maintained by the DNR Parks and Recreation Division
Extensive trail system.
Some hiking trails are not suitable for skiing and some ski trails are not available
for hiking In the summer.
Some trails are not well marked.
Be sure to take both hiking and ski trail maps with you in the winter.
Shelters and toilets are available along the trail system.
1,699 acres have been designated as a Wilderness Natural Area. This area
includes the park land from Big Sable Lighthouse to north the boundary (which is
the south boundary of the Nordhouse Dunes, managed by the Forest Service).
Paved trail along the river useable for bikes and handicappers.
Of the distance listed, 4 miles are designated ski trials in 4 trails(loops) from the
visitor center.

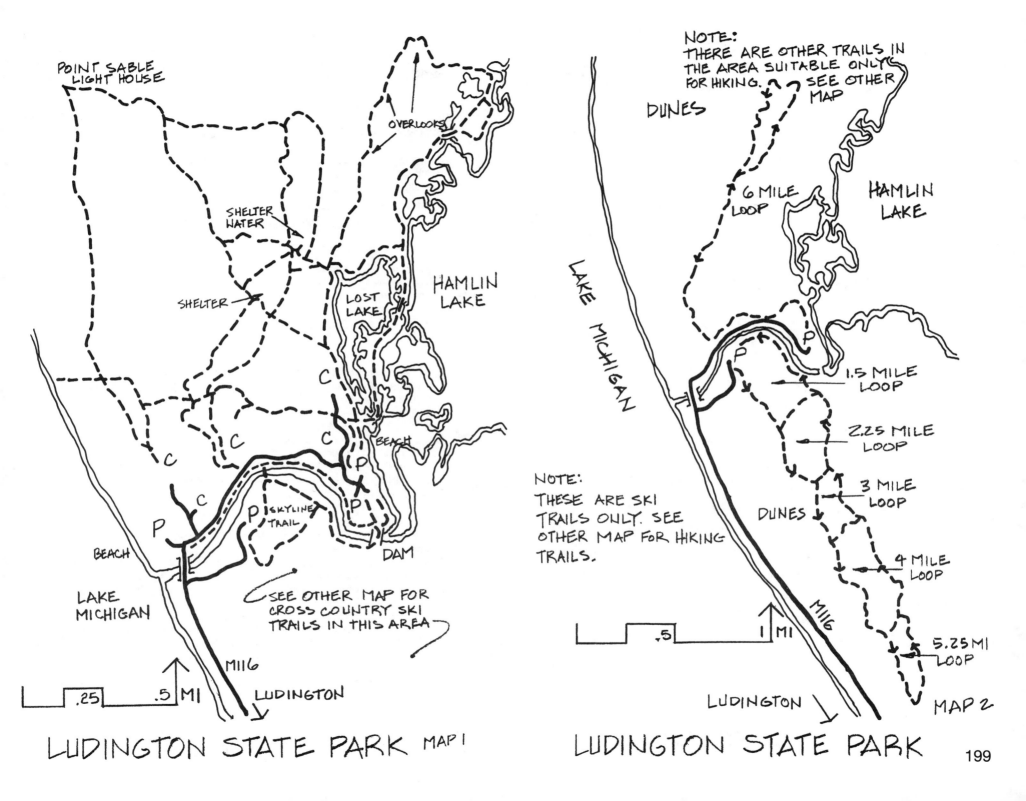

POINT SABLE
LIGHT HOUSE

OVERLOOKS

SHELTER
WATER

SHELTER

LOST
LAKE

HAMLIN
LAKE

C

C

C

C

BEACH

C

C

P

P

SKYLINE
TRAIL

P

P

DAM

BEACH

P

LAKE
MICHIGAN

SEE OTHER MAP FOR
CROSS COUNTRY SKI
TRAILS IN THIS AREA

.25   .5 MI

M116

LUDINGTON

LUDINGTON STATE PARK MAP 1

NOTE:
THERE ARE OTHER TRAILS IN
THE AREA SUITABLE ONLY
FOR HIKING. SEE OTHER
MAP

DUNES

HAMLIN
LAKE

6 MILE
LOOP

LAKE MICHIGAN

P

P

1.5 MILE
LOOP

2.25 MILE
LOOP

3 MILE
LOOP

DUNES

4 MILE
LOOP

NOTE:
THESE ARE SKI
TRAILS ONLY. SEE
OTHER MAP FOR HIKING
TRAILS.

5.25 MI
LOOP

.5   1 MI

M116

LUDINGTON

MAP 2

LUDINGTON STATE PARK

199

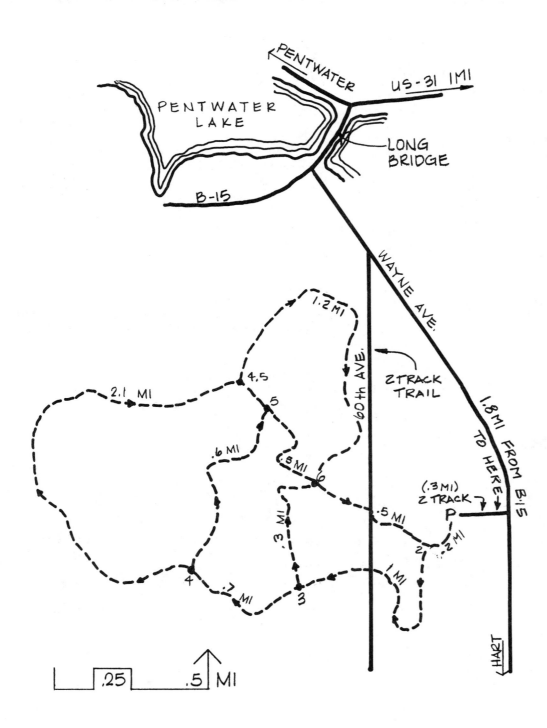

PENTWATER PATHWAY

Field Office, Baldwin Forest Area
1757 E. Hayes Rd   616-861-5636
Shelby, MI 49455

Baldwin Area Forest, Pere Marquette State Forest
Rte 2, Box 2810   616-745-4651
Baldwin, MI 49304

Michigan Atlas & Gazetteer Location: 54B3

County Location: Oceana

Directions To Trailhead:
SE of Pentwater on B15 to Wayne Ave., then south on Wayne Ave. to the
Pathway. It is southeast of Pentwater Lake.

Trail Type: Hiking/Walking, Cross Country Skiing, Mountain Biking
Trail Distance: 7.4 mi   Loops: 4   Shortest: 2.3 mi Longest: 6 mi
Trail Surface: Natural
Trail Use Fee: None
Method Of Ski Trail Grooming: None
Skiing Ability Suggested: Novice
Hiking Trail Difficulty: Easy
Mountain Biking Ability Suggested: Novice
Terrain: Flat to rolling with a hilly section.
Camping: None

Managed by the DNR Forest Management Division
Trail maintained by local volunteers.
Other contacts:
        DNR Forest Management Division Office, Lansing, 517-275-1275
        DNR Forest Management Region Office, Roscommon, 517-275-5151

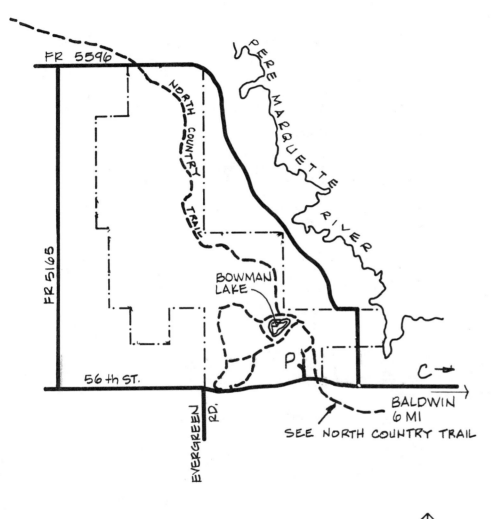

FR 5596

NORTH COUNTRY TRAIL

PERE MARQUETTE RIVER

FR 5165

BOWMAN LAKE

P

56th ST.

EVERGREEN RD.

C→

BALDWIN
6 MI

SEE NORTH COUNTRY TRAIL

.5   1 MI

BOWMAN LAKE
FOOT TRAVEL AREA

Baldwin/White Cloud Ranger Station, Huron-Manistee N.F.
650 N. Michigan Ave   616-745-4631
Baldwin, MI 49304

Forest Supervisor, Huron-Manistee National Forest
1755 S. Mitchell St   616-775-2421
Cadillac, MI 49601   800-821-6263

Michigan Atlas & Gazetteer Location: 55A6

County Location: Lake

Directions To Trailhead:
6 miles west of Baldwin on Carr Rd (56th Street)
Trailhead - Take Carrs Rd. west out of Baldwin about 2.5 miles, then left at fork
to continue on Carrs Rd, proceed across the Pere Marquette River and the road
to the parking lot is on your right about 1.5 miles past the bridge to the trailhead.

Trail Type: Hiking/Walking, Cross Country Skiing
Trail Distance: 2.25 mi   Loops: 2   Shortest: 2 mi   Longest: 2.25 mi
Trail Surface: Natural
Trail Use Fee: None
Method Of Ski Trail Grooming: None
Skiing Ability Suggested: Intermediate
Hiking Trail Difficulty: Moderate
Mountain Biking Ability Suggested:
Terrain: Steep 0%, Hilly 10%, Moderate 80%, Flat 10%
Camping: Campground nearby an primitive camping permitted

Maintained by the Baldwin Ranger District, Huron-Manistee National Forest
Many old unmarked two track roads and paths are available for wilderness skiing
and hiking in this special 1,000 acre foot travel only area.
The North Country Trail - Segment C passes through this tract of land.
If mountain biking on the NCT, stay on the trail and and do not explore the
Bowman Lake trails since mountain biking is prohibited in the foot travel area.
Mountain biking is also prohibited south of 56th Street.

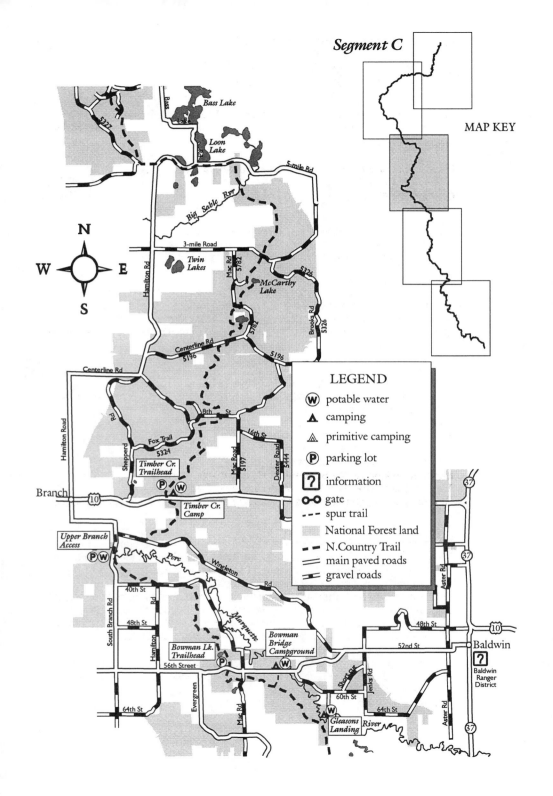

Segment C

MAP KEY

LEGEND

- Ⓦ potable water
- ▲ camping
- ⚠ primitive camping
- Ⓟ parking lot
- ? information
- o–o gate
- - - - spur trail
- ▓ National Forest land
- = = N.Country Trail
- ═ main paved roads
- ≡ gravel roads

Baldwin/White Cloud Ranger Station, Huron-Manistee N.F.
650 N. Michigan Ave   616-745-4631
Baldwin, MI 49304

Forest Supervisor, Huron-Manistee National Forest
1755 S. Mitchell St.   616-775-2421
Cadillac, MI 49601   800-821-6263

Michigan Atlas & Gazetteer Location: 55AB7,65D67

County Location: Newaygo & Lake

Directions To Trailhead:
Trailheads - From Baldwin take M37 south 3 miles to Star Lake Rd (76th St), then west 2.5 miles to the trail. On US10 just east of Branch at Timber Creek. At Bowman Lake Foot Travel Area on Carrs Rd (56th St), take M37 south from Baldwin about 1 mile, then west on Carrs Rd about 6 miles to Bowman Lake.

Trail Type: Hiking/Walking, Mountain Biking
Trail Distance: 28.9 mi   Loops: NA   Shortest: NA   Longest: NA
Trail Surface: Natural
Trail Use Fee: None
Method Of Ski Trail Grooming: NA
Skiing Ability Suggested: NA
Hiking Trail Difficulty: Easy to moderate
Mountain Biking Ability Suggested: Novice
Terrain: Steep 0%, Hilly 35%, Moderate 40%, Flat 25%
Camping: Bowman Bridge CG , Timber Creek CG and others

Maintained by the Huron-Manistee National Forest
A very easy riding and walking segment of the North Country Trail.
Because of excellent trail routing, it gives the impression of passing through a much more isolated area than actually exists.
Mountain biking is prohibited from Bowman Lake south into Segment D.
Campground at Bowman Bridge and is also permitted 200' from the trail.
For more information or membership information contact the North Country Trail Association.

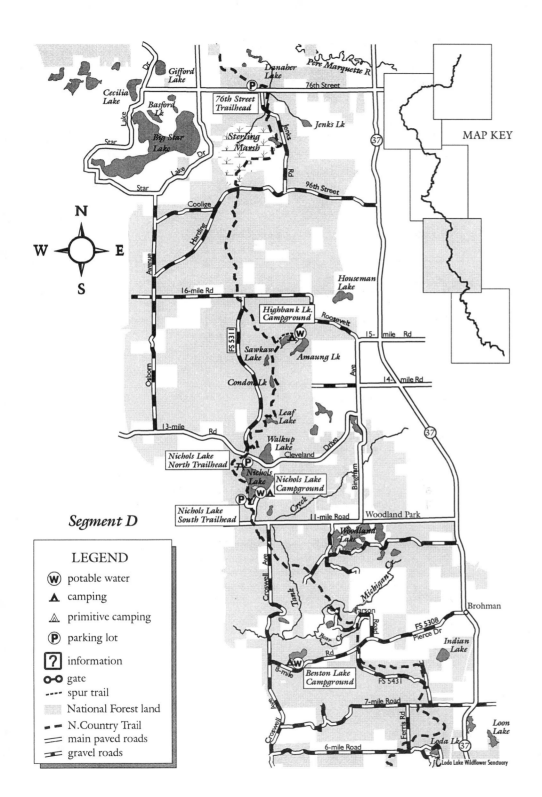

LEGEND
- (W) potable water
- ▲ camping
- △ primitive camping
- (P) parking lot
- [?] information
- o–o gate
- - - - - spur trail
- National Forest land
- – ■ – N.Country Trail
- ═══ main paved roads
- ═══ gravel roads

Segment D

Baldwin/White Cloud Ranger Station, Huron-Manistee N.F.
650 N. Michigan Ave.   616-745-4631
Baldwin, MI 49304

Forest Supervisor, Huron-Manistee National Forest
1755 S. Mitchell St.   616-775-2421
Cadillac, MI 49601   800-821-6263

Michigan Atlas & Gazetteer Location: 55BC7,56C1

County Location: Lake, Newaygo

Directions To Trailhead:
Parallel to and along about 5 miles west of M37 from 76th St. on the north to 6 Mile Rd in the Brohman and Woodland Park area on the south.
North trailhead is on 76th St. just east of Big Star Lake.
Central trailhead is at the Nichols Lake National Forest Campgrounds just west of Woodland Park

Trail Type: Hiking/Walking, Mountain Biking
Trail Distance: 23.4 mi   Loops: NA   Shortest: NA   Longest: NA
Trail Surface: Natural
Trail Use Fee: None
Method Of Ski Trail Grooming: NA
Skiing Ability Suggested: NA
Hiking Trail Difficulty: Easy to moderate
Mountain Biking Ability Suggested: Novice to intermediate
Terrain: Steep 0%, Hilly 35%, Moderate 40%, Flat 25%
Camping: At Highbank Lake and Nichols Lake National Forest campgrounds.

Maintained by the Huron-Manistee National Forest
Easy to moderate riding and walking segment of the North Country Trail.
Because of the excellent trail routing, it gives the impression of passing through a much more isolated area than actually exists.
The section between 16 Mile Rd and the Nichols Lake Campground is fravorite of mine. Give it a try and let me know what you think.
In addition to the 3 campgrounds on or nearby the trail, primative camping is permitted on national forest property more than 200' from the trail. Private campgrounds are in the area as well.
Mountain biking is prohibited from Segment E (north), south in to Nichols Lake North trailhead on Cleveland Drive. South of Cleveland Drive, the trail is open to mountain biking.
Contact the North Country Trail Association.

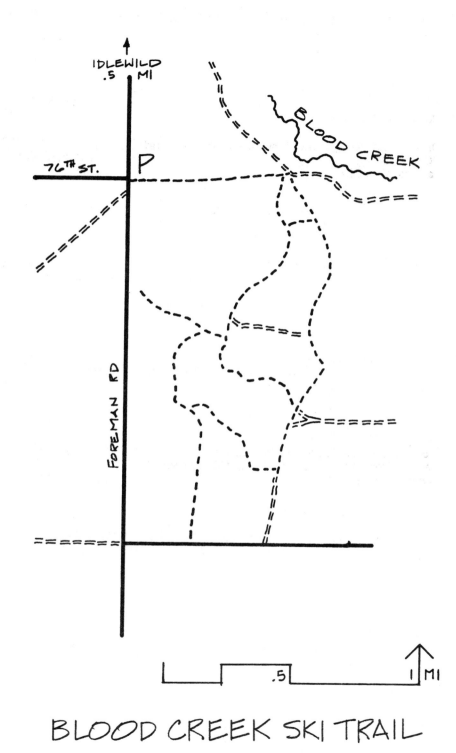

IDLEWILD .5 MI

76TH ST.

P

BLOOD CREEK

FOREMAN RD

.5   1 MI

BLOOD CREEK SKI TRAIL

Baldwin/White Cloud Ranger Station, Huron-Manistee N.F.
650 N. Michigan Ave   616-745-4631
Baldwin, MI 49304

Forest Supervisor, Huron Manistee National Forest
1755 S. Mitchell St   800-821-6263
Cadillac, MI 49601   616-775-2421

Michigan Atlas & Gazetteer Location: 56B1

County Location: Lake

Directions To Trailhead:
South of Baldwin 3.5 miles on M37 to 76th St., then east to Foreman Rd
intersection and trailhead.

Trail Type: Cross Country Skiing
Trail Distance: 4.5 mi   Loops: 3+   Shortest: 1.2 mi Longest: 3.5 mi
Trail Surface: Natural
Trail Use Fee: None
Method Of Ski Trail Grooming: None
Skiing Ability Suggested: None
Hiking Trail Difficulty: NA
Mountain Biking Ability Suggested: NA
Terrain: Steep 0%, Hilly 10%, Moderate 90%, Flat 20%
Camping: None

Maintained by the Baldwin Ranger District, Huron Manistee National Forest
Popular cross country ski area for local skiers.

Reed City Chamber of Commerce/Cross Roads Trail Committee
780 N. Park St.   616-832-5431
Reed City, MI 49677

DNR, Forest Management Division-Recreation and Trails Section
PO Box 30452   517-373-9483
Lansing, MI 48090

Michigan Atlas & Gazetteer Location: 56AB3

County Location: Osceola

Directions To Trailhead:
In downtown Reed City

Trail Type: Hiking/Walking, Cross Country Skiing,
Trail Distance: 2 mi   Loops: NA   Shortest: NA   Longest: NA
Trail Surface: Paved and wood chips
Trail Use Fee: None
Method Of Ski Trail Grooming: None
Skiing Ability Suggested: Novice
Hiking Trail Difficulty: Easy
Mountain Biking Ability Suggested: Novice
Terrain: Steep 0%, Hilly 0%, Moderate 10%, Flat 90%
Camping: None

Maintained by Reed City
Crossroads Rail Trail is paved. Reed City Linear Park is wood chip surface
Crossroads Rail Trail will become a part of the Pere Marquette Tail (Clare -
Baldwin)

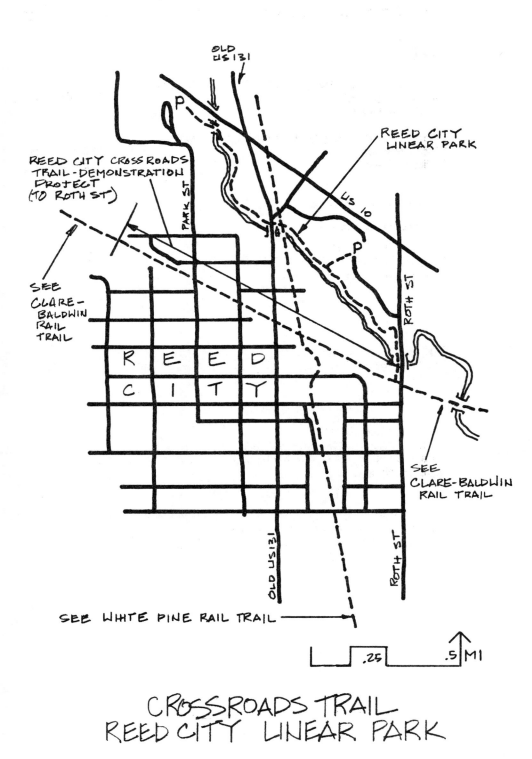

CROSSROADS TRAIL
REED CITY LINEAR PARK

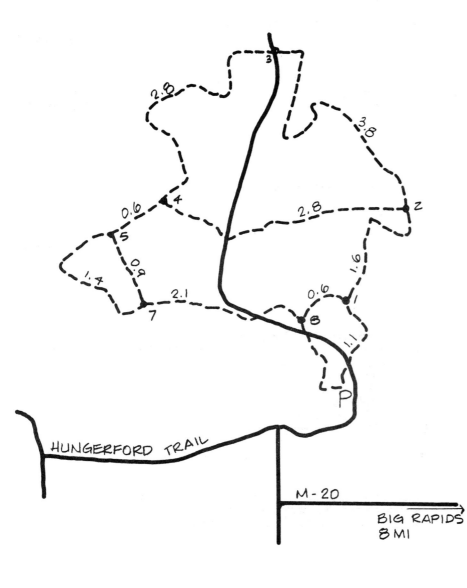

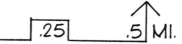

HUNGERFORD TRAIL

M-20

BIG RAPIDS
8 MI

.25 .5 MI.

Baldwin/White Cloud Ranger Station
650 N Michigan Ave
Baldwin, MI 49304

616-745-4631

Forest Supervisor, Huron-Manistee National Forest
1755 S. Mitchell Street
Cadillac, MI 49601

616-775-2421
800-821-6263

Michigan Atlas & Gazetteer Location: 56C23

County Location: Newaygo

Directions To Trailhead:
West of Big Rapids about 7 miles and NE of White Cloud about 18 miles
Trailhead - West from Big Rapids 8.5 miles to the Norwitch Township Hall turn
north on Cypress Ave. .5 mile to cemetery, then east .5 mile, then north on
FH5134 for .25 mile to the trailhead .

Trail Type: Hiking/Walking, Cross Country Skiing, Mountain Biking
Trail Distance: 20.8 km   Loops: 4   Shortest: 3.1 mi Longest: 13 mi
Trail Surface: Natural
Trail Use Fee: None
Method Of Ski Trail Grooming: None
Skiing Ability Suggested: Novice to intermediate
Hiking Trail Difficulty: Easy
Mountain Biking Ability Suggested: Novice to intermediate
Terrain: Steep 0%, Hilly 35%, Moderate 40%, Flat 25%
Camping: Primitive campground along the trail

Maintained by the White Cloud Ranger District, Huron-Manistee National Forest
Benches are located at some intersections.
Trail maps are located at intersections
Bike and ski shop in Big Rapids.

HUNGERFORD TRAIL

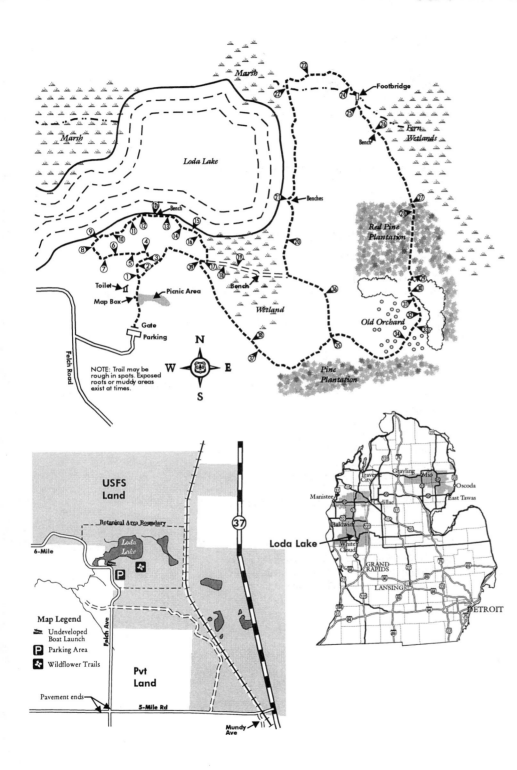

Baldwin/White Cloud Ranger Station, Huron Manistee N.F.
650 N. Michigan Ave   616-745-4631
Baldwin, MI 49304

Forest Supervisor, Huron Manistee National Forest
1755 S. Mitchell St   616-775-2421
Cadillac, MI 49601   800-821-6263

Michigan Atlas & Gazetteer Location: 56C1

County Location: Newaygo

Directions To Trailhead:
On M37 south of Brohman to 5 Mile Rd, then west 1 mile to Felch, then north to the trailhead.

Trail Type: Hiking/Walking, Interpretive
Trail Distance: 1.5 mi   Loops: 1   Shortest: NA   Longest: 1.5 mi
Trail Surface: Natural and boardwalk
Trail Use Fee: None
Method Of Ski Trail Grooming: NA
Skiing Ability Suggested: NA
Hiking Trail Difficulty: Easy
Mountain Biking Ability Suggested: NA
Terrain: 100% Flat
Camping: Nichols Lake NFCG about 10 miles away

Maintained by the Baldwin Ranger District, Huron Manistee National Forest
Trail through a small wildflower sanctuary.
North Country Trail is about 1 mile to the west.

DNR - Forest Mangement Division, Recreation and Trails Section
POB 30452
Lansing, MI 48909

517-373-1275

Michigan Atlas & Gazetteer Location: 56B4,57AB4567,58B12

County Location: Clare, Lake, Osceola

Directions To Trailhead:
From Clare to Baldwin. Parallel to and on the south side of US10.
West trailhead - M37
East trailhead - Next to Old US10 near Harrison Ave about 3 miles west of Clare

Trail Type: Hiking/Walking, Cross Country Skiing, Mountain Biking
Trail Distance: 55 mi   Loops: NA   Shortest: NA   Longest: NA
Trail Surface: Ballast and natural
Trail Use Fee: None
Method Of Ski Trail Grooming: NA
Skiing Ability Suggested: Novice
Hiking Trail Difficulty: Easy
Mountain Biking Ability Suggested: Novice
Terrain: 100% Flat
Camping: None

Currently under development by the DNR Forest Management Division
See also Crossroads Trail in Reed City.
In the future, this trail should connect with the Pere Marquette Trail of Mid-Michigan at Clare.

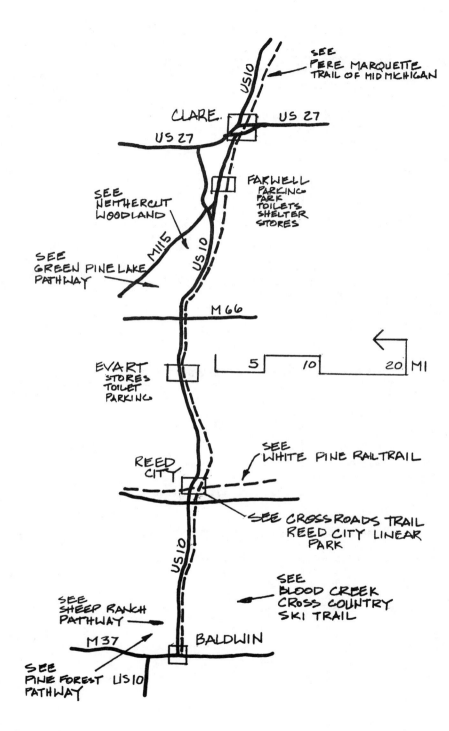

PERE MARQUETTE STATE TRAIL

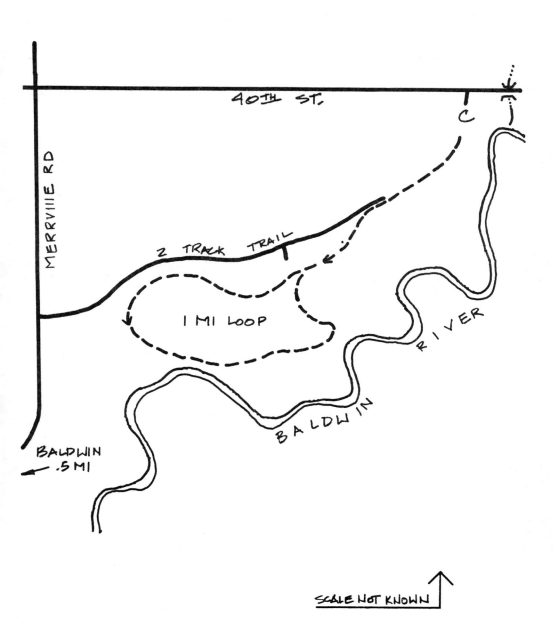

Baldwin Forest Area, Pere Marquette State Forest
Rte 2, Box 2810   616-745-4651
Baldwin, MI 49304

District Forest Manager, Pere Marquette State Forest
Rte 1, 8015 South US131   616-775-9727
Cadillac, MI 49601

Michigan Atlas & Gazetteer Location: 56A1

County Location: Lake

Directions To Trailhead:
At the Bray Creek State Forest Campgound NE from Baldwin on Dog Track Rd.
for 1.5 miles then east on 40th St. for about .5 mile

Trail Type: Hiking/Walking, Cross Country Skiing
Trail Distance: 1 mi   Loops: 1   Shortest: Longest:
Trail Surface: Natural
Trail Use Fee: None
Method Of Ski Trail Grooming: None
Skiing Ability Suggested: Novice
Hiking Trail Difficulty: Easy
Mountain Biking Ability Suggested: NA
Terrain: Steep 0%, Hilly 0%, Moderate 80%, Flat 20%
Camping: Campgound at trailhead

Maintained by the DNR Forest Management Division
Part of the trail follows the Baldwin River.
Short and pleasant nature trail from the campground.
Sheep Ranch Pathway is just across the river.

PINE FOREST PATHWAY

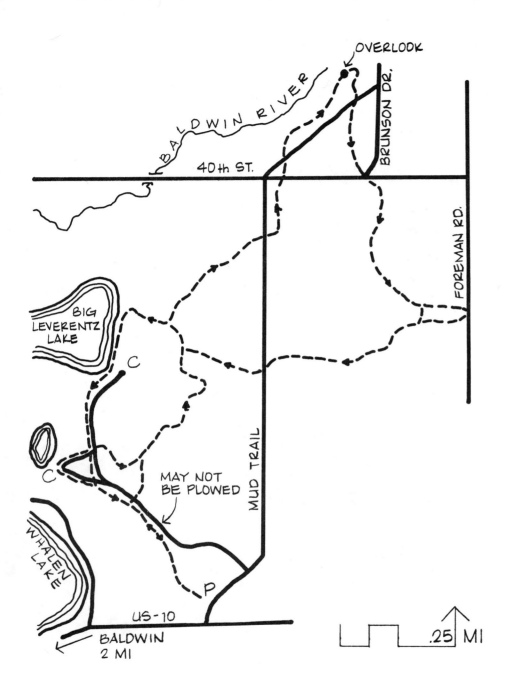

Baldwin Forest Area, Pere Marquette Forest Area
Rte 2, Box 2810
Baldwin, MI 49304   616-745-4651

District Forest Manager, Pere Marquette State Forest
Rte 1, 8015 South US131   616-775-9727
Cadillac, MI 49601

Michigan Atlas & Gazetteer Location: 56A1

County Location: Lake

Directions To Trailhead:
2 miles east of Baldwin on US10, then north on Mud Trail, parking lot
immediately on the left (west).

Trail Type: Hiking/Walking, Cross Country Skiing, Mountain Biking
Trail Distance: 4.5 mi   Loops: 2   Shortest: 1 mi   Longest: 2.3 mi
Trail Surface: Natural
Trail Use Fee: None
Method Of Ski Trail Grooming: None
Skiing Ability Suggested: Novice
Hiking Trail Difficulty: Easy
Mountain Biking Ability Suggested: Novice
Terrain: Steep 0%, Hilly 0%, Moderate 10%, Flat %90%
Camping: Campgrounds along trail but with limited facilities in winter

Maintained by the DNR Forest Management Division
Swamps, low hills, Baldwin River, two lakes and small creeks will be found
along this trail Snowmobilers may be present in the area. Pit toilet at parking lot.
Other contacts:
        DNR Forest Management Division Office, Lansing, 517-373-1275
        DNR Forest Management Region Office, Roscommon, 517-275-5151

SHEEP RANCH PATHWAY

TRAIL NOTES

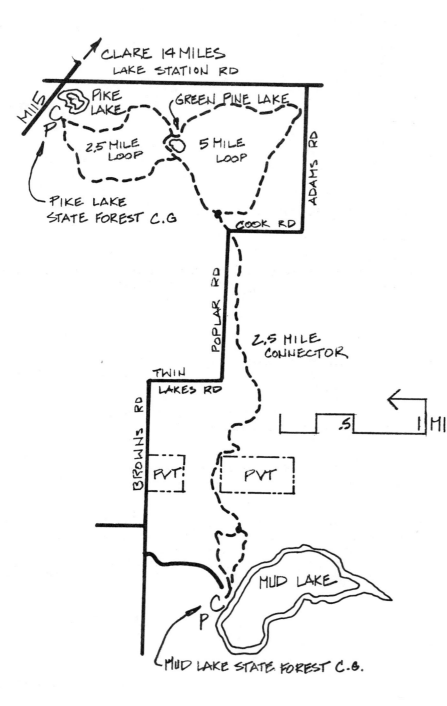

GREEN PINE LAKE PATHWAY

Gladwin Forest Area, Au Sable State Forest
801 N. Silver Leaf, PO Box 337   517-426-9205
Gladwin, MI 48624

District Forest Manager, Au Sable State Forest
191 S. Mt. Tom Rd., PO Box 939   517-826-3211
Mio, MI 48647

Michigan Atlas & Gazetteer Location: 57A7

County Location: Clare

Directions To Trailhead:
14 miles NW of Clare on M115 at the Pike Lake State Forest Campground

Trail Type: Hiking/Walking, Cross Country Skiing, Mountain Biking
Trail Distance: 8.5 mi   Loops: 3   Shortest: 1 mi   Longest: 5 mi
Trail Surface: Natural
Trail Use Fee: None
Method Of Ski Trail Grooming: None
Skiing Ability Suggested: Novice
Hiking Trail Difficulty: Easy
Mountain Biking Ability Suggested: Novice
Terrain: Flat to slightly rolling
Camping: Campground available at trailhead

Maintained by the DNR Forest Management Division
About 4 miles north from the new Pere Marquette Trail (Clare to Baldwin)
Other contacts:
          DNR Forest Management Division Office, Lansing, 517-373-1275
          DNR Forest Management Region Office, Roscommon, 517-275-5151

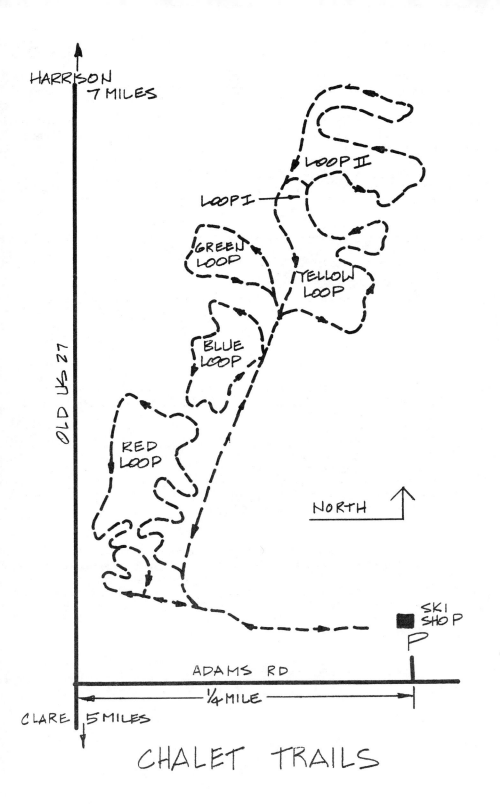

Chalet Cross Country
4275 Adams Rd
Clare, MI 48617

517-386-9697

Michigan Atlas & Gazetteer Location: 58A2

County Location: Clare

Directions To Trailhead:
6 miles north of Clare on old US27. From the north US10/27 Clare exit, take Clare Ave (Old 27) north 5 miles to Adams Rd., then right (east) .25 mile to the trailhead.

Trail Type: Cross Country Skiing
Trail Distance: 10 km   Loops: 4   Shortest: 2.2 km Longest: 2.8 km
Trail Surface: Natural
Trail Use Fee: Yes
Method Of Ski Trail Grooming: Track set with skating trails
Skiing Ability Suggested: Novice to advanced
Hiking Trail Difficulty: NA
Mountain Biking Ability Suggested: NA
Terrain: Steep 5%, Hilly 30%, Moderate 50%, Flat 15%
Camping: None

Privately operated ski touring center
Warming area, lessons, candlelight skiing, rentals and ski shop.
Enjoyable trail system that is certianly worth a visit.
Open weekends from 10 to 6 and Thursday-Friday, but call ahead.

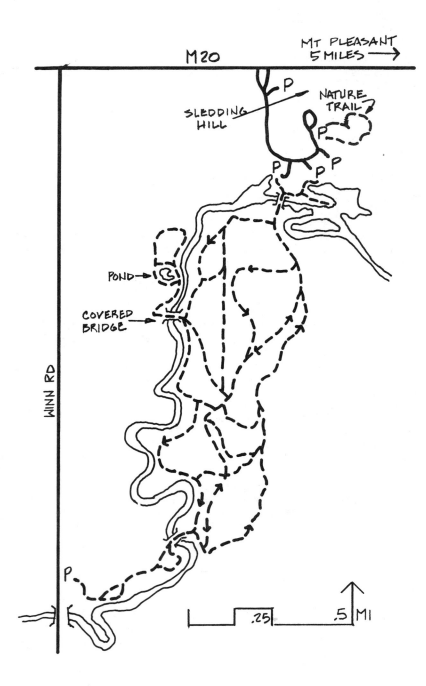

MT PLEASANT
5 MILES →

M20

SLEDDING HILL

NATURE TRAIL

P P P P P

POND →

COVERED BRIDGE →

WINN RD

P

.25   .5 MI

DEERFIELD NATURE PARK

Deerfield Nature Park

Isabella County Parks Department
200 N. Main St.
Mt Pleasant , MI 48858

517-772-0911
x233

Deerfield Nature Park
2445 W Remus Rd.
Mt Pleasant, MI 48858

517-772-2879

Michigan Atlas & Gazetteer Location: 58D1

County Location: Isabella

Directions To Trailhead:
5.5 miles west of Mt Pleasant on M-20

Trail Type: Hiking/Walking, Cross Country Skiing, Mountain Biking
Trail Distance: 7.5 mi   Loops: 10   Shortest: .1 mi   Longest: 2.6 mi
Trail Surface: Natrual
Trail Use Fee: None but park entry fee required
Method Of Ski Trail Grooming: Track set
Skiing Ability Suggested: Novice
Hiking Trail Difficulty: Easy
Mountain Biking Ability Suggested: Novice
Terrain: Steep 0%, Hilly 0%, Moderate 5%, Flat 95%
Camping: Ten canoe and hike-in camping sites

Operated by the Isabella County Parks Department
Over 591 acres of all season recreational facilities. Picnic area, ponds for
swimming and fishing, sledding, ice fishing, tubing and field game areas are
available. Two suspension bridges and a wooden covered bridge are in the
park.
Ski trails are always well groomed.
Ski shop with ski rentals available in Mt. Pleasant.

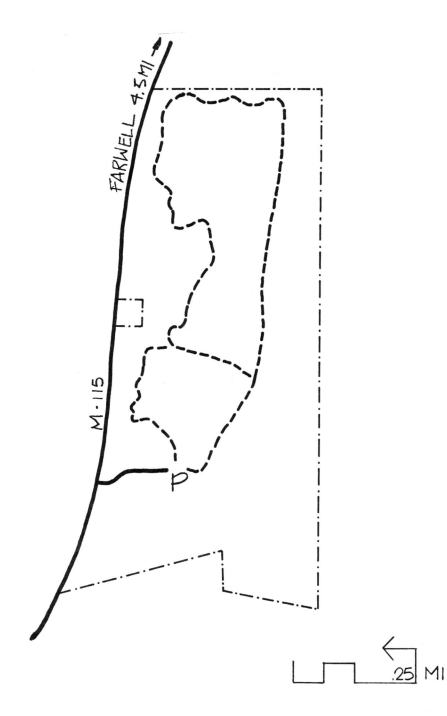

Neithercut Woodland
Department of Biology, Central Michigan University   517-774-3412
Mt. Pleasant, MI 48859

Michigan Atlas & Gazetteer Location: 58A1

County Location: Clare

Directions To Trailhead:
4.5 miles west of Farwell on M115, on the south side of the road Property starts just west of US10/M115 intersection (the west end of the divided section of US10). The entrance is about 1 mile farther west.

Trail Type: Hiking/Walking, Cross Country Skiing
Trail Distance: 2.5 mi   Loops: 3   Shortest: Longest:
Trail Surface: Natural
Trail Use Fee: Donations accepted
Method Of Ski Trail Grooming: None
Skiing Ability Suggested: Novice
Hiking Trail Difficulty: Easy
Mountain Biking Ability Suggested: NA
Terrain: Rolling
Camping: None

Maintained by Central Michigan University, Department of Biology
This is primarily an outdoor classroom with trails for hiking and skiing containing 250 acres

NEITHERCUT WOODLAND

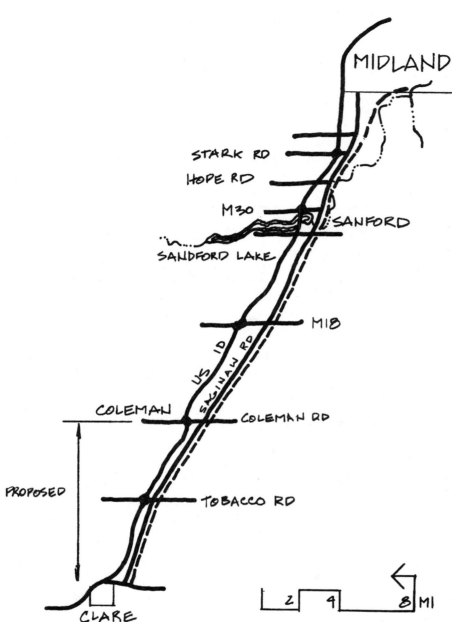

STARK RD
HOPE RD
M30
SANFORD
SANDFORD LAKE
M18
US 10
SAGINAW RD
COLEMAN
COLEMAN RD
PROPOSED
TOBACCO RD
CLARE

SEE PERE MARQUETTE TRAIL WEST OF CLARE

PERE MARQUETTE TRAIL OF MID-MICHIGAN

MIDLAND

2 4 8 MI

Midland County Parks and Recreation Commission
220 W. Ellsworth   517-832-6870
Midland, MI 48640

Michigan Atlas & Gazetteer Location: 58BC34,59CD4567

County Location: Midland, Isabella

Directions To Trailhead:
East trailhead - Exit US10 at the Eastman Rd exit then take Eastman Rd south. After it curves to the left, take a right on Ashman and follow it to the trailhead in downtown Midland.
West trailhead - The east city limit of Coleman. This may move to the west in the future.

Trail Type: Hiking/Walking, Cross Country Skiing, Mountain Biking
Trail Distance: 23 mi   Loops: NA   Shortest: NA   Longest: NA
Trail Surface: Paved, existing ballast, natural
Trail Use Fee: None
Method Of Ski Trail Grooming: None
Skiing Ability Suggested: Novice
Hiking Trail Difficulty: Easy
Mountain Biking Ability Suggested: NA
Terrain: 100%Flat
Camping: None

Maintained by Midland County Parks and Recreation
Asphalt 12' wide for first 3 miles from Midland and 14' wide for the next 20 miles to Coleman.
Additional parking available at Emerson Park on the west side of Midland
Future expansion to Clare is planned.
The 3 mile section at the east end of the rail trail is owned by the City of Midland.

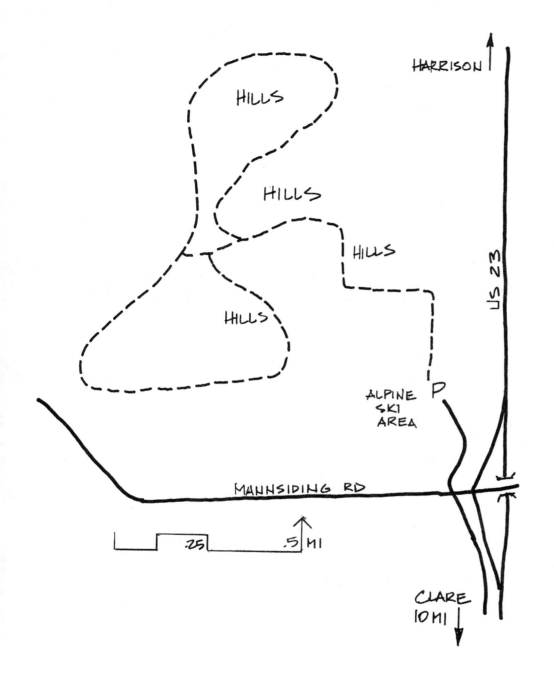

Snow Snake Mountain Inc.
3407 E. Mannsiding Rd
Harrison, MI 48625

517-539-6583

Michigan Atlas & Gazetteer Location: 58A2

County Location: Clare

Directions To Trailhead:
From Clare, take US27 north 9 miles to the Lake George/Mannsiding Rd exit, then west to the mountain which borders the west side US27 on the north side of Mannsiding Rd.

Trail Type: Cross Country Skiing
Trail Distance: 3 mi   Loops: 2   Shortest: 1.5 mi Longest: 2 mi
Trail Surface: Natural
Trail Use Fee: Yes
Method Of Ski Trail Grooming: Track set
Skiing Ability Suggested: Intermediate
Hiking Trail Difficulty: NA
Mountain Biking Ability Suggested: NA
Terrain: Steep 0%, Hilly 80%, Moderate 10%, Flat 10%
Camping: None, but campgrounds available nearby

Privately operated alpine ski area and golf course.
Day lodge with food service available.
Cross country ski rentals available

SNOW SNAKE MOUNTAIN

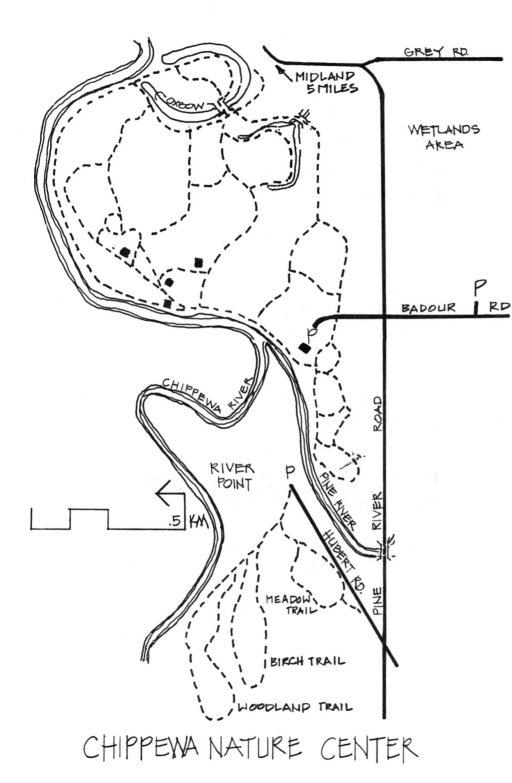

Chippewa Nature Center
400 South Badour Rd
Midland, MI 48640

517-631-0830

Michigan Atlas & Gazetteer Location: 59D6

County Location: Midland

Directions To Trailhead:
From M20 west of Midland, south on Homer Rd, East on Prairie Rd to sign at entrance(follow brown/white signs from M20. From Business US10 in Midland, west on Poseyville Rd to St. Charles (cross Tittabawassee River) follow signs.

Trail Type: Hiking/Walking, Cross Country Skiing, Interpretive
Trail Distance: 12 mi   Loops: 8   Shortest: .4 mi   Longest: 3.1 mi
Trail Surface: Paved and natural
Trail Use Fee: None
Method Of Ski Trail Grooming: None
Skiing Ability Suggested: Novice to intermediate
Hiking Trail Difficulty: Easy
Mountain Biking Ability Suggested: NA
Terrain: Steep 0%, Hilly 0%, Moderate 05%, Flat 95%
Camping: None

A private, non-profit educational organization open to the public.
Very popular area for cross country skiing.
Trails are open seven days a week all year long from dawn to dusk..
Only minutes from Midland on the Pine and Chippewa Rivers, this is without a doubt an outstanding nature center.
Historical buildings; a visitor center that houses museums, gift shop, library classrooms; arboretum; enviornmental study area and 900 acres of beautiful land to explore. The visitor center was designed by famous Michigan architect Alden Dow.
Year around programs for the entire family.
Visitor Center is staffed from 8-5 M-F, 9-5 Sat. and 1-5 Sun.
Write or call for information and brochure.
Please - no pets, smoking or bicycles.

CHIPPEWA NATURE CENTER

Midland - Mackinac Trail

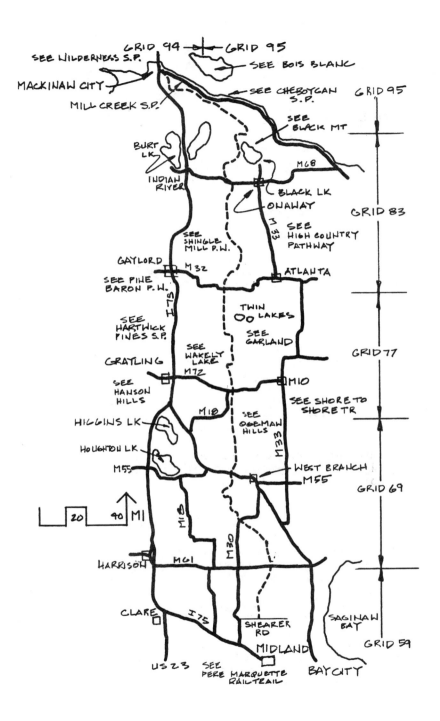

Midland-Mackinac Trail Commission
1211 Kingsbury Court
Midland, Mi 48640

517-631-5230

District Ranger, Mio Ranger District, HMNF
401 Court St
Mio, MI 48647

517-826-3252

Michigan Atlas & Gazetteer Location: 59AB67.69A-D57,77A-D,83A-D56,94BC3
4,95CD56

County Location: Midland, Gladwin, Ogemaw,Oscoda, plus more

Directions To Trailhead:
Southern trailhead - 11 miles north of Midland at the Mills Community Center on Shearer Rd, 2 miles west of Herner Rd.
Northern trailhead- Mackinaw City

Trail Type: Hiking/Walking, Cross Country Skiing, Mountain Biking
Trail Distance: 200+ mi   Loops: Shortest: Longest:
Trail Surface: Natural
Trail Use Fee: None
Method Of Ski Trail Grooming: None
Skiing Ability Suggested: Intermediate to advanced
Hiking Trail Difficulty: Easy to moderate
Mountain Biking Ability Suggested: Novice to advanced
Terrain: Steep 0%, Hilly 10%, Moderate 10%, Flat 80%
Camping: Many campgounds along the trail

Developed and maintained by the Mackinaw Trail Commission, Boy Scouts of America and the Huron-Manistee National Forest
Follows the approximate route of the old Saginaw & Mackinaw native american trail.
12 miles passes through the Huron Manistee National Forest.
Due to the isolated nature of this trail, only experienced skiers with good winter survial skills should ski this trail.
Other counties: Montmorency, Otsego, Cheboygan, Crawford

MIDLAND-MACKINAC TRAIL

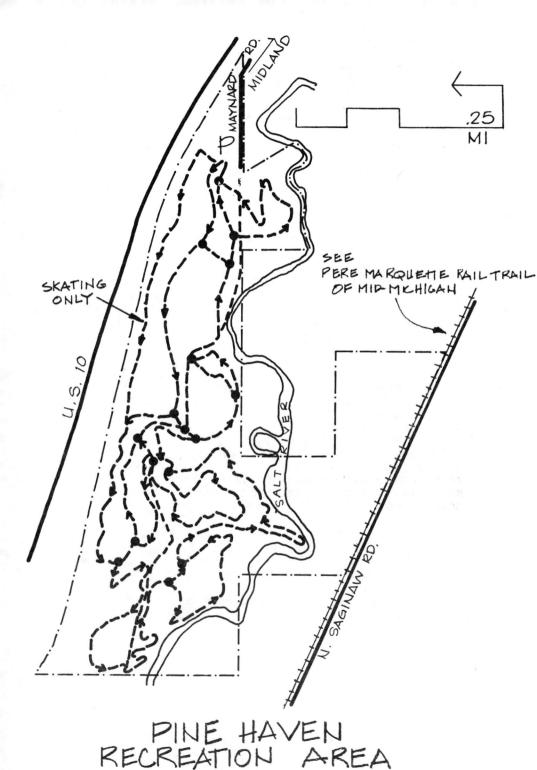

SKATING ONLY

U.S. 10

SEE
PERE MARQUETTE RAIL TRAIL
OF MID-MICHIGAN

SALT RIVER

N. SAGINAW RD.

MIDLAND RD.

MAYNARD RD.

.25 MI

PINE HAVEN
RECREATION AREA

Midland County Parks & Recreation Commission
220 W. Ellsworth   517-832-6870
Midland, MI 48640

Michigan Atlas & Gazetteer Location: 59C5

County Location: Midland

Directions To Trailhead:
NW of Midland and the Village of Sanford, adjacent to and south of US10 Exit at West River Rd., turn south to Maynard Rd., then west on Maynard to the end of the road.

Trail Type: Hiking/Walking, Cross Country Skiing, Mountain Biking, Interpretive
Trail Distance: 8/5 mi   Loops: 9   Shortest: .2 mi   Longest: 2.3 mi
Trail Surface: Natural
Trail Use Fee: None, but donations accepted at trailhead
Method Of Ski Trail Grooming: Track set
Skiing Ability Suggested: Novice to advance
Hiking Trail Difficulty: Easy to moderate
Mountain Biking Ability Suggested: Novice to intermediate
Terrain: Steep 10%, Hilly 10%, Moderate 50%, Flat 30%
Camping: None

Maintained by the Midland County Parks and Recreation Commission
Food concession on site during ski season.
Site of cross country ski races throughout the winter.
A very pleasant wooded trail system designed for cross country skiing.
The Pere Marquette Rail Trail of Mid Michigan is along the south border of the park property.

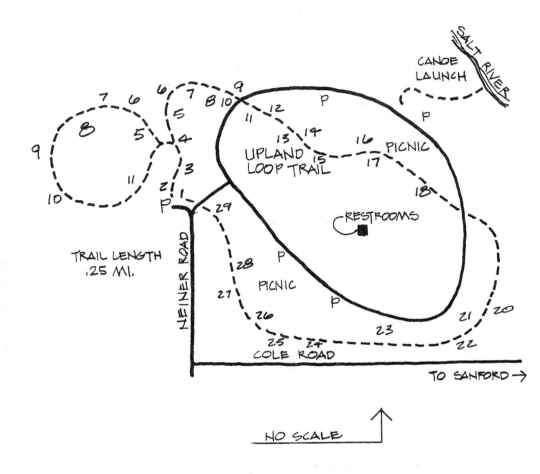

Midland County Parks and Recreation Commission
220 W. Ellsworth
Midland MI 48640

517-832-6870

Michigan Atlas & Gazetteer Location: 59C5

County Location: Midland

Directions To Trailhead:
Take US10 10 miles west of Midland to the west River Rd exit, then left one mile to Saginaw Rd, then left again and go about .25 mile to M30, then right about .25 mile to Cole Rd, then right on Cole Rd to the park.

Trail Type: Hiking/Walking, Interpretive
Trail Distance: 1.15 mi   Loops: 2   Shortest: .25 mi Longest: 1 mi
Trail Surface: Natural
Trail Use Fee: None
Method Of Ski Trail Grooming: NA
Skiing Ability Suggested: NA
Hiking Trail Difficulty: Easy
Mountain Biking Ability Suggested: NA
Terrain: Steep 0%, Hilly 0%, Moderate 95%, Flat 5%
Camping: None

Maintained by the Midland Country Parks and Recreation Commission
Two nature trails are in the system.
        Veterans Grove Trail with 12 stations
        Upland Loop Trail with 30 stations.
Additional park property is undeveloped.
Trail brochure is available.

VETERANS MEMORIAL PARK

Bay City State Park
3582 State Park Drive
Bay City, MI 48706

517-667-0717
517-684-3020

DNR Parks and Recreation Division
PO Box 30028
Lansing, MI 48909

517-373-1270
517-322-1300

Michigan Atlas & Gazetteer Location: 60C2

County Location: Bay

Directions To Trailhead:
I-75 to exit 168(Beaver Rd), turn east and follow Beaver Rd for 5 miles to the state park.

Trail Type: Hiking/Walking, Cross Country Skiing, Mountain Biking, Interpretive
Trail Distance: 5 mi   Loops: 4   Shortest: .75 mi Longest: 3 mi
Trail Surface: Paved, gravel and natural
Trail Use Fee: None, but vehicle entry permit required
Method Of Ski Trail Grooming: None
Skiing Ability Suggested: Novice
Hiking Trail Difficulty: Easy
Mountain Biking Ability Suggested: NA
Terrain: Steep 0%, Hilly 0%, Moderate 5%, Flat 95%
Camping: Available on site

Maintained by the DNR Parks and Recreation Division
Several nature trails, observation towers, campground and nature center are available in this complex. The trails wind through a decidious forest, cattail marsh and the Lake Huron beach. The Chickadee Trail next to the Jennison Nature Center and Frank D. Andersen Nature Trail provides accessible trails for handicappers. Interpretive signs, benches , toilets and shelter areas are located along the trails. The Jennison Nature Center, constructed in 1949 is the center of nature study for the park and wildlife refuge. The Frank D. Andersen Nature Trail has two specialized areas. One is for bird observation with a covered viewing area and the other is a marsh overlook with another covered viewing area. The Tobico Marsh provides an excellent opportunity to view many varieties of waterfowl from the two 30' observation towers.

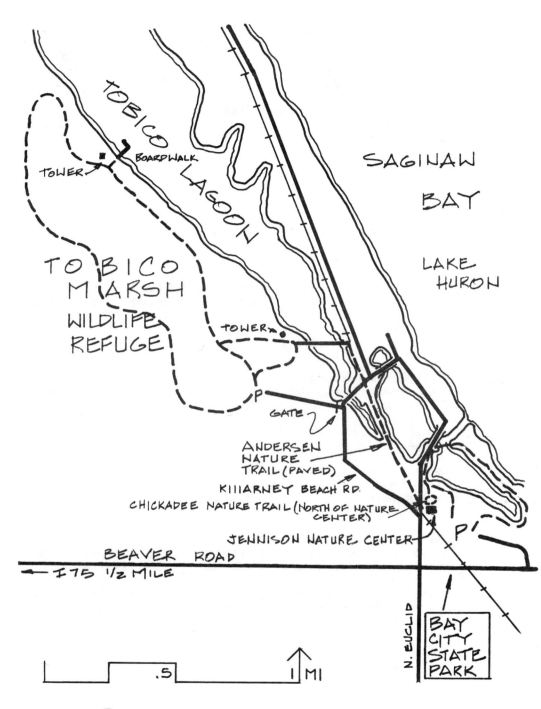

TOBICO LAGOON

TOWER

BOARDWALK

SAGINAW

BAY

LAKE
HURON

TO BICO
M ARSH

WILDLIFE
REFUGE

TOWER

P

GATE

ANDERSEN
NATURE
TRAIL (PAVED)

KIIIARNEY BEACH RD.

CHICKADEE NATURE TRAIL (NORTH OF NATURE
CENTER)

JENNISON NATURE CENTER

P

BEAVER   ROAD

I75 ½ MILE

N. EUCLID

BAY
CITY
STATE
PARK

.5   1 MI

BAY CITY STATE PARK
TOBICO MARSH WILDLIFE REFUGE

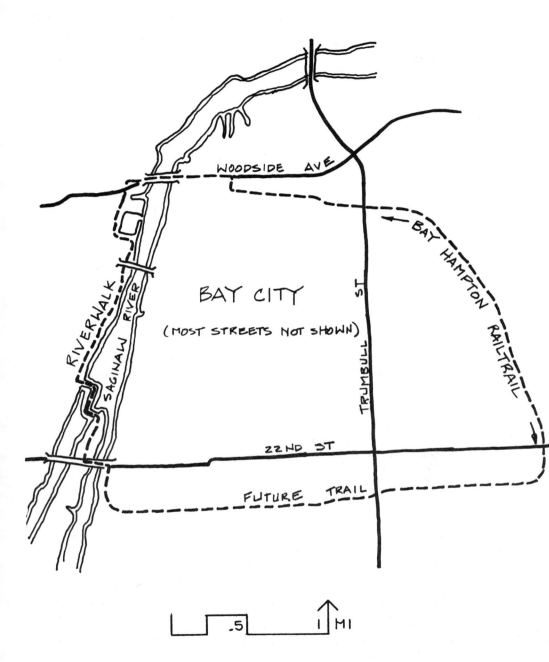

BAY CITY RIVERWALK
BAY HAMPTON RAILTRAIL

Bay County Convention and Visitors Bureau
901 Saginaw St
Bay City, Mi 48708

517-893-1222

Michigan Atlas & Gazetteer Location: 60D23

County Location: Bay

Directions To Trailhead:
Downtown Bay City. Riverwalk is on the west side of the Saginaw River between Salxburg Ave on the south and Midland St. on the north. Bay Hampton Rail Trail is between N. Johnson at 1st St to Youngs Ditch Rd in Hampton Township

Trail Type: Hiking/Walking
Trail Distance: 4.3 mi　　Loops: NA　　　Shortest: NA　　Longest:　NA
Trail Surface: Paved, gravel and ballast
Trail Use Fee: None
Method Of Ski Trail Grooming: NA
Skiing Ability Suggested: NA
Hiking Trail Difficulty: Easy
Mountain Biking Ability Suggested: Novice
Terrain: 100% Flat
Camping: None

Owned by Bay City
Currently 2 separate trails. Riverwalk is 2 miles and the Bay Hampton Rail Trail is 2.3 miles. Plans call for additional sections to make the two trails a loop trail of over 10 miles.
The Riverwalk is a well developed paved trail along the Saginaw River with many recreational features inlcuding a fishing pier, exercise course and picnic areas
No special mountain bike trail is provided. General biking is allowed.

Bay County Recreation Department
800 John F Kennedy Drive
Bay City, MI 48706

517-893-5531

Michigan Atlas & Gazetteer Location: 60B2

County Location: Bay

Directions To Trailhead:
I-75 to the Pinconning exit, then east on Pinconning Rd to the Saginaw Bay and the park.

Trail Type: Hiking/Walking, Cross Country Skiing, Interpretive
Trail Distance: 3.5 mi   Loops: 4   Shortest: .25 mi Longest: .75 mi
Trail Surface: Natural
Trail Use Fee: Yes
Method Of Ski Trail Grooming: None
Skiing Ability Suggested: Novice
Hiking Trail Difficulty: Easy
Mountain Biking Ability Suggested: NA
Terrain: Steep 0%, Hilly 0%, Moderate 30%, Flat 70%
Camping: Campground on the site

Maintained by the Bay County Recreation Department
Boat launch and general recreation facilities are provided
Observation tower along the trail at the bay

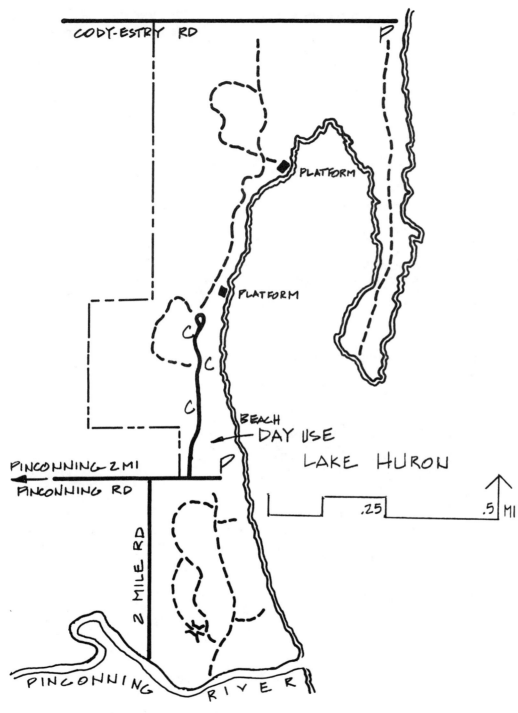

PINCONNING COUNTY PARK

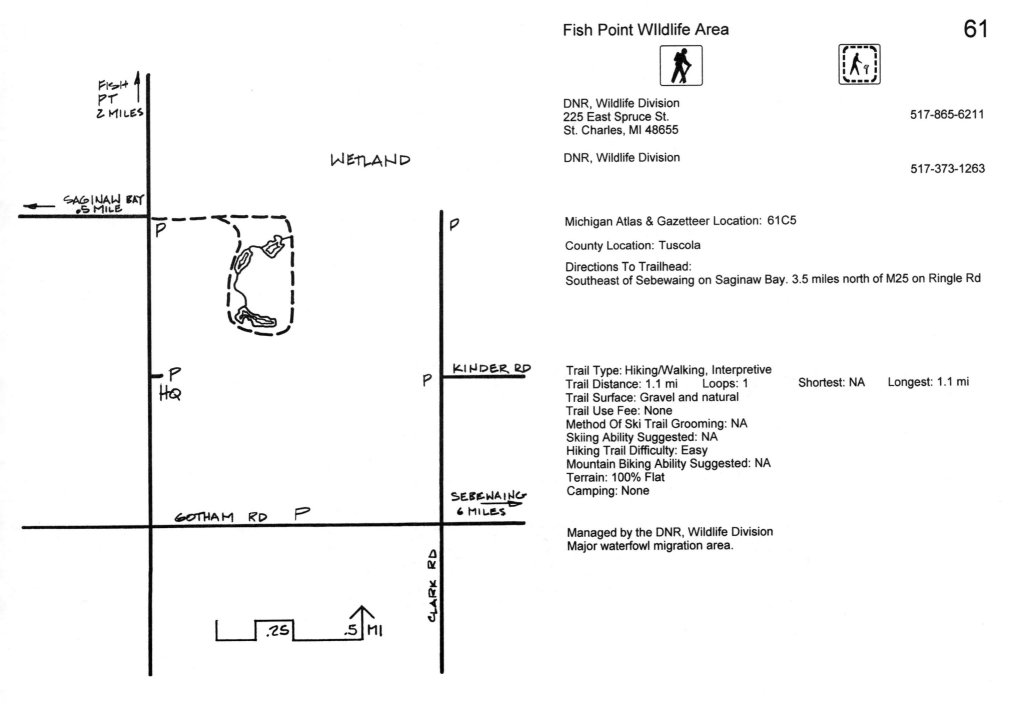

DNR, Wildlife Division
225 East Spruce St.
St. Charles, MI 48655

517-865-6211

DNR, Wildlife Division

517-373-1263

Michigan Atlas & Gazetteer Location: 61C5

County Location: Tuscola

Directions To Trailhead:
Southeast of Sebewaing on Saginaw Bay. 3.5 miles north of M25 on Ringle Rd

Trail Type: Hiking/Walking, Interpretive
Trail Distance: 1.1 mi   Loops: 1   Shortest: NA   Longest: 1.1 mi
Trail Surface: Gravel and natural
Trail Use Fee: None
Method Of Ski Trail Grooming: NA
Skiing Ability Suggested: NA
Hiking Trail Difficulty: Easy
Mountain Biking Ability Suggested: NA
Terrain: 100% Flat
Camping: None

Managed by the DNR, Wildlife Division
Major waterfowl migration area.

FISH POINT
STATE WILDLIFE AREA

Sebewaing Sportsmans Club
Bay Rd
Sebewaing, MI 48759

800-358-4862

Michigan Atlas & Gazetteer Location: 61C6

County Location: Huron

Directions To Trailhead:
From Sebewaing south on M 25, turn west on Bay St to the end. The trail on north side of street across from the VFW.

Trail Type: Hiking/Walking, Cross Country Skiing, Interpretive
Trail Distance: 1 mi   Loops: 1   Shortest: NA   Longest: 1 mi
Trail Surface: Natural
Trail Use Fee: None
Method Of Ski Trail Grooming: Packed
Skiing Ability Suggested: Novice
Hiking Trail Difficulty: Easy
Mountain Biking Ability Suggested: NA
Terrain: Steep 0%, Hilly 0%, Moderate 0%, Flat 100%
Camping: None but available nearby

Maintained locally by citizens in the area.
Call ahead for current status of the trail.
Trail follows the shoreline of Saginaw Bay of Lake Huron

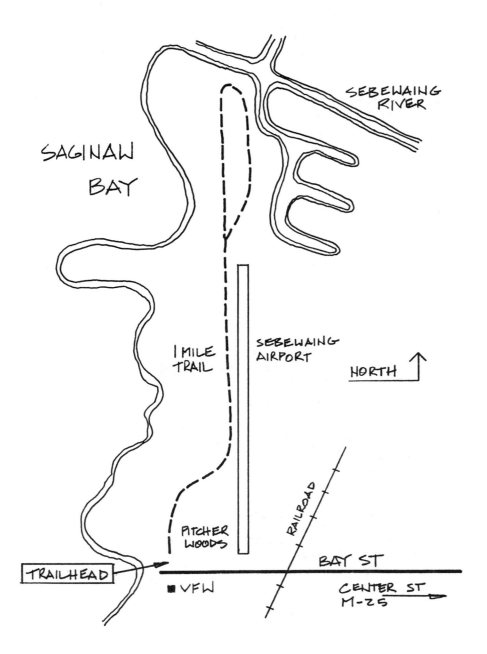

SEBEWAING NATURE TRAIL

Village of Cass City
6737 Church St.
Cass City, MI 48726

517-872-2911

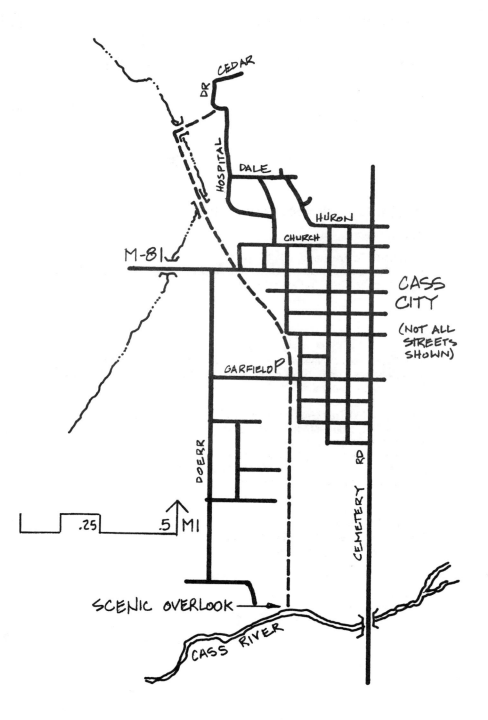

M-81

CASS
CITY

(NOT ALL
STREETS
SHOWN)

CEDAR
DR
HOSPITAL
DALE
HURON
CHURCH
GARFIELD P
DOERR
CEMETERY RD

.25 .5 MI

SCENIC OVERLOOK

CASS RIVER

Michigan Atlas & Gazetteer Location: 62D1

County Location: Tuscola

Directions To Trailhead:
In the village of Cass City. Trail crosses M81

Trail Type: Hiking/Walking, Interpretive
Trail Distance: 1.6 mi   Loops: NA   Shortest: NA   Longest: NA
Trail Surface: Gravel
Trail Use Fee: None
Method Of Ski Trail Grooming: NA
Skiing Ability Suggested: NA
Hiking Trail Difficulty: Easy
Mountain Biking Ability Suggested: NA
Terrain: 100% Flat
Camping: None

Owned by the Village of Cass City
This is a rail trail project.
Scenic overlook at the Cass River end.
Parking at Garfield Ave.

CASS CITY HIKING TRAIL

Sanilac County Parks
2820 N. Lakeshore
Carsonville, MI 48491

810-622-8715

Michigan Atlas & Gazetteer Location: 62D2

County Location: Sanilac

Directions To Trailhead:
About 6 miles southeast of Cass City on M53 between Pringle Rd and
Severance Rd

NO MAP

Trail Type: Hiking/Walking
Trail Distance: 3 mi   Loops: 4   Shortest: Short   Longest: 1 mi
Trail Surface: Natural
Trail Use Fee: None
Method Of Ski Trail Grooming: NA
Skiing Ability Suggested: NA
Hiking Trail Difficulty: Easy
Mountain Biking Ability Suggested: NA
Terrain: Steep 0%, Hilly 0%, Moderate 25%, Flat 75%
Camping: None

Maintained by the Sanilac County Parks
A riverside (Cass River) day use park with pavilion and picnic area.

Huron County Commissioners
250 E. Huron, Rm 211
Bad Axe, MI 48413

800-358-4862
517-269-6431

Michigan Atlas & Gazetteer Location: 62A2

County Location: Huron

Directions To Trailhead:
Located along Saginaw Bay between Port Austin and Caseville next to Sleeper State Park.
From M 25 take Oak Beach Rd south to Loosemoore Rd, then left(east) on Loosemoore to the parking lot on the left side of the road.

Trail Type: Hiking/Walking, Interpretive
Trail Distance: 1.25 mi   Loops: 2   Shortest: .5 mi   Longest: .75 mi
Trail Surface: Natural and boardwalk
Trail Use Fee: None
Method Of Ski Trail Grooming: NA
Skiing Ability Suggested: NA
Hiking Trail Difficulty: Easy
Mountain Biking Ability Suggested: NA
Terrain: Steep 0%, Hilly 0%, Moderate 0%, Flat 100%
Camping: None but state parks are nearby

Owned by the Huron County Commissioners
280 acre property with developed nature trail.
28 station nature trail. Trail guide available.
Additional devlopment of the trail is planned to establish a third loop.
Memberships available for this non profit support organization.

Map

M-25

NOT COMPLETED

BENCH
15
OVERLOOK   17   16
19 18   14
20   13
BENCH   .75 MI
LOOP   BRIDGE
12

HANDICAPPER LOOP
21
22
BENCH   11
9   10
.5 MI
LOOP   8   7
GAZEBO
4   5
WATER 2   6
3
P   TOILET
LOOSEMOORE RD

OAK BEACH RD

NORTH ↑

HURON COUNTY NATURE CENTER
WILDERNESS ARBORETUM

Michigan Department of State, History Department
717   West Allegan
Lansing, MI 48919-1847

517-373-1979

Michigan Atlas & Gazetteer Location: 62C2

County Location: Sanilac

Directions To Trailhead:
3 miles north of M81 or 11 miles south of Bad Axe on Germania Rd

Trail Type: Interpretive
Trail Distance: 1 mi   Loops: 1   Shortest: NA   Longest: 1 mi
Trail Surface: Natural
Trail Use Fee: None
Method Of Ski Trail Grooming: NA
Skiing Ability Suggested: NA
Hiking Trail Difficulty: Easy
Mountain Biking Ability Suggested: NA
Terrain:
Camping: None

Managed by the History Department, Michigan Department of State
1000 year old prehistoric rock carvings in limestone
Interpretive trail includes 10 stations explaining various historical points along
the trail.

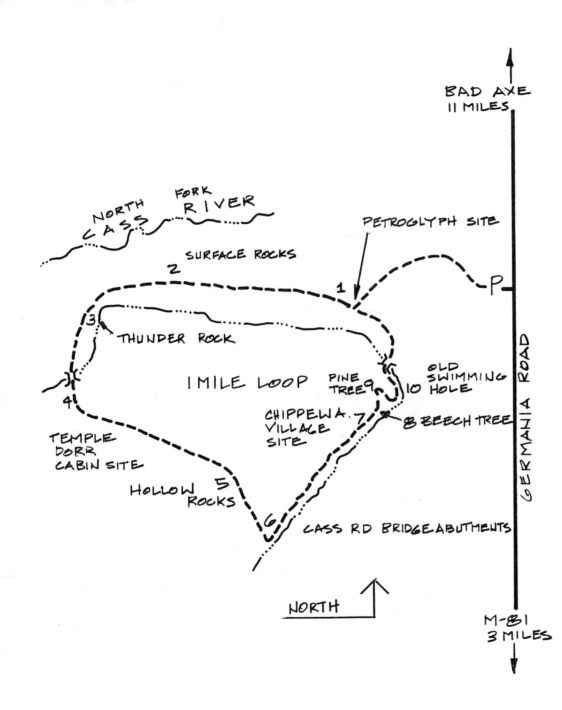

PETROGLYPH PARK NATURE TRAIL

Port Crescent State Park
1776 Port Austin Rd.
Port Austin , MI 48467

517-738-8663

DNR Parks and Recreation Division

517-373-1270

Michigan Atlas & Gazetteer Location: 62A2

County Location: Huron

Directions To Trailhead:
On Saginaw Bay, 5 miles west of Port Austin. Ski trail accessible from the west end of Port Crescent Rd at M25 when gates are open and snow depth is adequate. Hiking/nature trails are accessible from main park day use area.

Trail Type: Hiking/Walking, Cross Country Skiing, Interpretive
Trail Distance: 5.3 mi   Loops: 7   Shortest: 2.3 mi Longest: 3 mi
Trail Surface: Naatural
Trail Use Fee: None, but vehicle entry fee required
Method Of Ski Trail Grooming: Not known
Skiing Ability Suggested: Novice
Hiking Trail Difficulty: Easy
Mountain Biking Ability Suggested: NA
Terrain: Steep 0%, Hilly 0%, Moderate 10%, Flat 90%
Camping: Campground available in the park

Maintained by the DNR Parks and Recreation Division.
Separate trails for hiking and skiing.
Overlooks of Saginaw Bay from trail.
Ski trails are accessable from the west end of Port Crescent Rd at M25, when gates are open and snow depth is adequate for skiiing. Candlelight ski tours scheduled throughout the winter. Ski rentals available locally.
Very popular campground in the summer requiring reservation or arrive during the early weekdays.

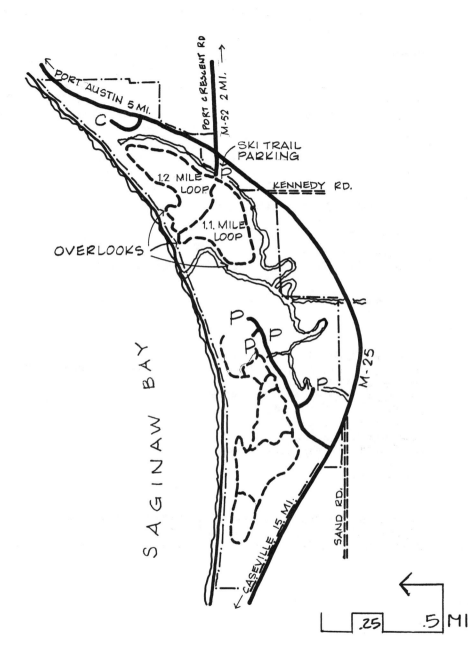

PORT CRESCENT STATE PARK

Sleeper State Park
6573 State Park Rd.
Caseville, MI 48725

517-856-4411

DNR Parks and Recreation Division

517-373-1270

Michigan Atlas & Gazetteer Location: 62A1

County Location: Huron

Directions To Trailhead:
4 miles east of Caseville on M25 at the north tip of the thumb
Ski trailhead - Headqarters building on State Park Rd., just east of main park entrance
Summer trailheads - From campground

Trail Type: Hiking/Walking, Cross Country Skiing, Mountain Biking, Interpretive
Trail Distance: 4 mi   Loops: 2   Shortest: 1.5 mi Longest: 2.5 mi
Trail Surface: Natural
Trail Use Fee: None, but vehicle entry fee required
Method Of Ski Trail Grooming: Track set
Skiing Ability Suggested: Novice
Hiking Trail Difficulty: Easy
Mountain Biking Ability Suggested: Novice
Terrain: 100% Flat
Camping: Campground in the park

Maintained by the DNR Parks and Recreation Division
The Ridges Nature Trail has 14 stations that explains various features of both natural and historical interest.

SAGINAW BAY

M-25

← CASEVILLE

P   P

PT. AUSTIN →

C   C

1   7 FOR SKI TRAILS ONLY

← HIKING TRAILS ONLY →

6   → P

2   1.5 MI.

3   4   5   SKI TRAIL ONLY

1.5 MI. LOOP
RIDGES NATURE TRAIL

STATE PARK RD.

OUTDOOR CENTER

8

P

2.5 MI. LOOP
DEER RUN TRAIL

9

NO SCALE

SLEEPER STATE PARK

Sanilac County Parks
2820 N. Lakeshore
Carsonville, MI 48419

810-622-8715

Michigan Atlas & Gazetteer Location: 63D6

County Location: Sanilac

Directions To Trailhead:
On Lake Huron north of Port Huron
11 miles north of Port Sanilac on the east side of M25

NO MAP

Trail Type: Hiking/Walking, Interpretive
Trail Distance: 2 mi   Loops: 2   Shortest: .5 mi   Longest: 1 mi
Trail Surface: Natural
Trail Use Fee: None
Method Of Ski Trail Grooming: NA
Skiing Ability Suggested: NA
Hiking Trail Difficulty: Easy
Mountain Biking Ability Suggested: NA
Terrain: Steep 0%, Hilly 0%, Moderate 15%, Flat 85%
Camping: None

Maintained by the Sanilac County Parks
A lakeside day use park

Sanilac County Parks
2820 N. Lakeshore
Carsonville, MI 48419

810-622-8715

Michigan Atlas & Gazetteer Location: 63D6

County Location: Sanilac

Directions To Trailhead:
On Lake Huron north of Port Huron
6.5 miles north of Port Sanilac on the east side of M25

NO MAP

Trail Type: Hiking/Walking, Interpretive
Trail Distance: 1 mi   Loops: 3   Shortest: Short   Longest: Short
Trail Surface: Natural
Trail Use Fee: None
Method Of Ski Trail Grooming: NA
Skiing Ability Suggested: NA
Hiking Trail Difficulty: Easy
Mountain Biking Ability Suggested: NA
Terrain: Moderate
Camping: A modern 171 site campround is in the park

Maintained by the Sanilac County Parks
A complete lakeside park and wooded campground with all facilities.
Reservations available.

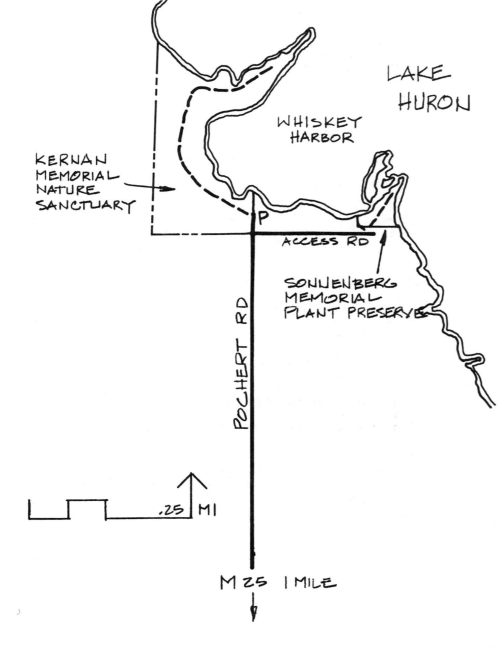

LAKE
HURON

WHISKEY
HARBOR

KERNAN
MEMORIAL
NATURE
SANCTUARY

P

ACCESS RD

SONNENBERG
MEMORIAL
PLANT PRESERVE

POCHERT RD

.25 MI

M 25 1 MILE

Michigan Nature Association
PO Box 102
Avoca, MI 48006

810-324-2626

Michigan Atlas & Gazetteer Location: 63A5

County Location: Huron

Directions To Trailhead:
From Port Hope, take US25 north about 2.5 miles, then turn right on Pochert Rd
about 1.5 miles to dead end and park. Preserves are east and west of parking
location.

Trail Type: Interpretive
Trail Distance: 1.25 mi   Loops: NA   Shortest: NA   Longest: NA
Trail Surface: Natural
Trail Use Fee: None
Method Of Ski Trail Grooming: NA
Skiing Ability Suggested: NA
Hiking Trail Difficulty: Easy
Mountain Biking Ability Suggested: NA
Terrain: Steep 0%, Hilly 0%, Moderate 10%, Flat 90%
Camping: None

Maintained by the Michigan Nature Association
The complete name is Kernan Memorial Sanctuary and Thelma Sonnenberg
Memorial Plant Preserve
Access between the two facilities can be on the beach or the access road.
Complete written descriptions of the preserves are available from the MNA.

KERNAN MEMORIAL NATURE SANCTUARY
SONNENBERG MEMORIAL PLANT PRESERVE

Huron County Parks
417 S. Hanselman St
Bad Axe, MI

517-269-6404

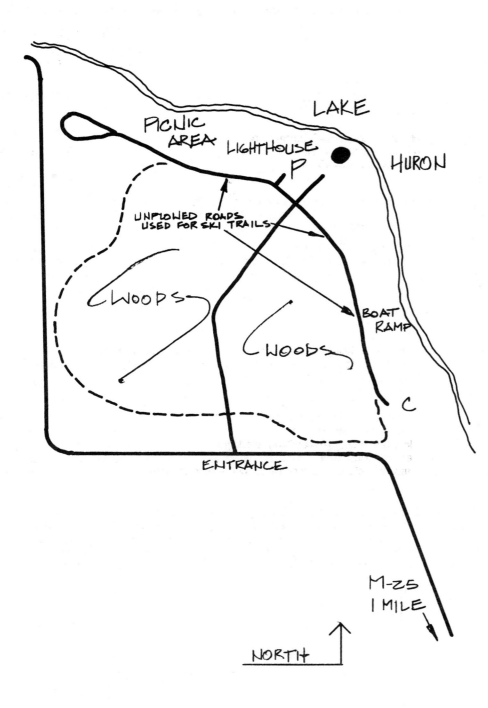

Michigan Atlas & Gazetteer Location: 63A7

County Location: Huron

Directions To Trailhead:
Between Port Austin and Port Hope on Lake Huron just east from the tip of the thumb. From M 25, take lighthouse Rd north about 1.5 miles to the trailhead and lighthouse.

Trail Type: Hiking/Walking, Cross Country Skiing
Trail Distance: 1 mi   Loops: 1   Shortest: NA   Longest: 1 mi
Trail Surface: Natural
Trail Use Fee: None
Method Of Ski Trail Grooming: Not known
Skiing Ability Suggested: Novice
Hiking Trail Difficulty: Easy
Mountain Biking Ability Suggested: NA
Terrain: Steep 0%, Hilly 0%, Moderate 0%, Flat 100%
Camping: Campground on site

Owned by Huron County
120 acre park with a complete campground on the shore of Lake Huron

LIGHTHOUSE COUNTY PARK

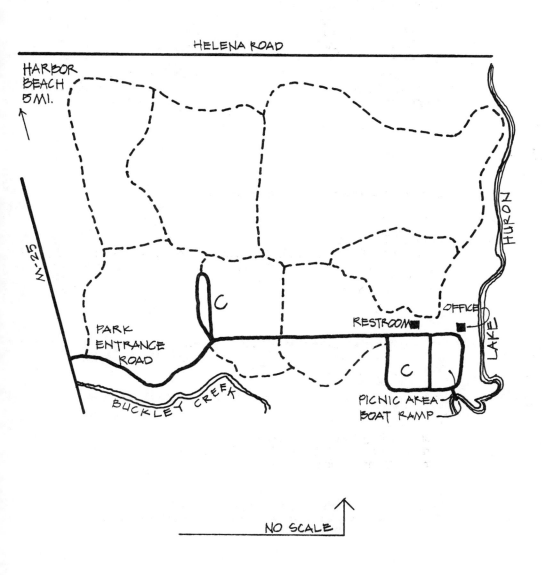

Wagener County Park
2671 Lakeshore (M-25)
Harbor Beach, MI 48441

517-479-9131

Huron County Road Commission
417 S. Hanselman St.
Bad Axe, MI 48413

517-269-6404

Michigan Atlas & Gazetteer Location: 63B5

County Location: Huron

Directions To Trailhead:
5 miles south of Harbor Beach on Lake Huron

Trail Type: Hiking/Walking, Cross Country Skiing, Interpretive
Trail Distance: 5 mi   Loops: 4   Shortest: .2 mi   Longest: 1.5 mi
Trail Surface: Natural
Trail Use Fee: None
Method Of Ski Trail Grooming: none
Skiing Ability Suggested: Novice
Hiking Trail Difficulty: Easy
Mountain Biking Ability Suggested: NA
Terrain: 100% Flat
Camping: Modern campground available in the park

Maintained by the Huron County Road Commission
A seasonal (May 1st to Oct. 1st) campground with trails.
The campground is full service Skiing permitted during the winter but, no
facilities except pit toilets are available.
The park contains 139 acres

Manistee Ranger Station, Huron Manistee National Forest
412 Red Apple Rd   616-723-2211
Manistee, MI 49660

Forest Supervisor, Huron Manistee National Forest
1755 S. Mitchell St.   616-775-2421
Cadillac, Mi 49601   800-821-6263

Michigan Atlas & Gazetteer Location: 64D3

County Location: Manistee

Directions To Trailhead:
Follow signs west from US31 about 8 miles south of Manistee

Trail Type: Hiking/Walking, Mountain Biking
Trail Distance: 3+ mi   Loops: 2   Shortest: .5 mi   Longest: 2.5 mi
Trail Surface: Gravel
Trail Use Fee: None
Method Of Ski Trail Grooming: NA
Skiing Ability Suggested: NA
Hiking Trail Difficulty: Easy
Mountain Biking Ability Suggested: Novice
Terrain: Steep 0%, Hilly 05%, Moderate 20%, Flat 80%
Camping: Campground at trailhead

Maintained by the Manistee Ranger District, Huron Manistee National Forest
Bike/walking trail that is routed around the campground.
Reported that road bicycles can ride on the gravel trail.

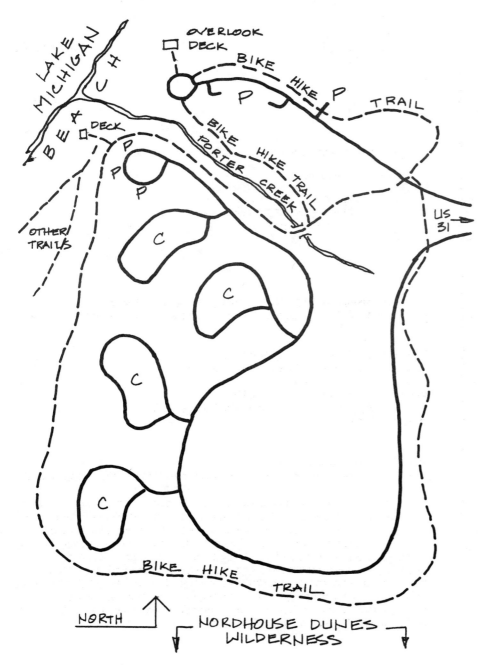

LAKE MICHIGAN RECREATION AREA

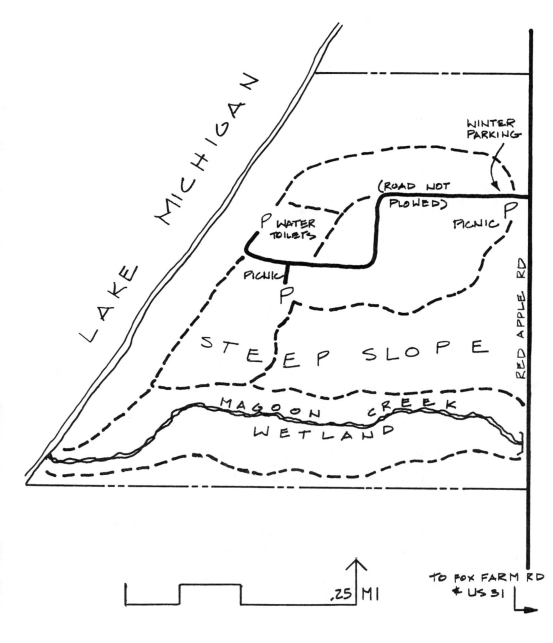

Filer Township
2107 Red Apple Rd
Manistee, MI 49660

616-723-2073

Michigan Atlas & Gazetteer Location: 64C4

County Location: Manistee

Directions To Trailhead:
Take US31 4.5 miles south of Manistee, then 3 miles west on Fox Farm Rd, then .5 mile north on Red Apple Rd to natural area entrance.

Trail Type: Hiking/Walking, Cross Country Skiing, Interpretive
Trail Distance: 2.5 mi   Loops: Several   Shortest: .5 mi   Longest: 2 mi
Trail Surface: Natural
Trail Use Fee: None
Method Of Ski Trail Grooming: None
Skiing Ability Suggested: Novice to intermediate
Hiking Trail Difficulty: Easy
Mountain Biking Ability Suggested: NA
Terrain: Steep 0%, Hilly 25%, Moderate 0%, Flat 75%
Camping: None

Owned by Filer Township
Community recreation and natural area along the shore of Lake Michigan and Magoon Creek.
Plant and animal enthusiasts are attacted to the several eco-systems in less than 100 acres. "It combines 2,300' of Lake Michigan shoreline of young dune formation including the mouth of Magoon Creek. The creek environs are a temperate rain forest bordered by thickets opening to rolling meadows affording each its own distinct flora and fauna. Second growth white pines, a climax beech/maple forest, old orchards and cedar stands afford variety and beauty. This small parcel of rolling hills provides glorious views of Lake Michigan. It is a sheltered valley for evening and winter deer; the quiet of a deep woods and temperate rain forest; the sun of an open meadow; the ripple of a gentle stream and the crash of waves on a sandy beach."

MAGOON CREEK NATURAL AREA

Manistee Ranger Station, Huron-Manistee National Forest
412 Red Apple Rd   616-723-2211
Manistee, MI 49660

Forest Supervisor, Huron-Manistee National Forest
1755 S. Mitchell St   616-775-2421
Cadillac, MI 49601   800-821-6263

Michigan Atlas & Gazetteer Location: 64CD3

County Location: Mason

Directions To Trailhead:
Between Ludington and Manistee on Lake Michigan
South trailhead - At west end of Nurnberg Rd., 6 miles west of Quarterline Rd.
North trailhead - Lake Michigan Recreation Area which is at the west end of FH
5629, 7.5 miles from US31 (9 miles south of Manistee)

Trail Type: Hiking/Walking, Cross Country Skiing
Trail Distance: 15 mi   Loops: Many   Shortest: 1 mi   Longest: 3 mi
Trail Surface: Natural
Trail Use Fee: None
Method Of Ski Trail Grooming: None
Skiing Ability Suggested: Intermediate to advanced
Hiking Trail Difficulty: Moderate
Mountain Biking Ability Suggested: NA
Terrain: Steep 5%, Hilly 60%, Moderate 20%, Flat 15%
Camping: Campground available at Lake Michigan Recreation Area

Maintained by Manistee Ranger District, Huron-Manistee National Forest
Trails not designed for skiing but are skiable for experience skiers only. Some
trails in dune area along Lake Michigan shore. Lake Michigan Recreation Area is
located at the north trailhead off FR 5629, 7.5 miles west of US31. FR 5629 is
not plowed. Access must be gained via Nurnberg Rd. The Wilderness is 1200
acres of wooded sand dunes 700 acres of open sand 4 miles of beach on Lake
Michigan. Because it is a wilderness area, all trail markings have been
removed.

SEE MAP ON NEXT PAGE

WILDERNESS REGULATIONS

These regulations meet wilderness management objectives, and will be enforced.

- Group size of ten or fewer.

- Mechanical and motorized vehicles and equipment *are not permitted*; this includes *bikes* and wheeled carts. Wheelchairs are permitted.

- Campsites and campfires must be more than *400 feet* from Lake Michigan, *200 feet* from Nordhouse Lake, and away from trails.

- No Beach fires! Driftwood and dunewood must not be removed from the Wilderness.

- The use of *horses and other pack stock* is prohibited in the Nordhouse Dunes.

- Public nudity is not allowed, and is illegal.

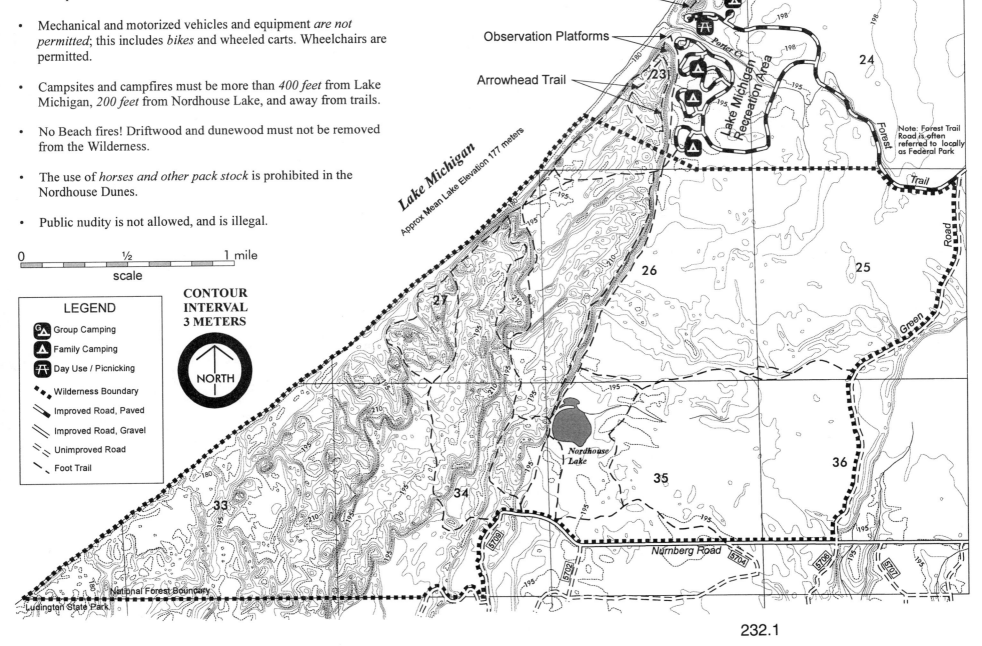

NORDHOUSE DUNES WILDERNESS AREA

Observation Platform
Stairs
Observation Platforms
Arrowhead Trail

Lake Michigan
Approx Mean Lake Elevation 177 meters

Porter Cr
Lake Michigan Recreation Area

Note: Forest Trail Road is often referred to locally as Federal Park

Forest Trail Road
Green Road

Nordhouse Lake
Nürnberg Road

National Forest Boundary
Ludington State Park

0 ½ 1 mile
scale

CONTOUR INTERVAL 3 METERS

NORTH

LEGEND
- Group Camping
- Family Camping
- Day Use / Picnicking
- Wilderness Boundary
- Improved Road, Paved
- Improved Road, Gravel
- Unimproved Road
- Foot Trail

Ludington State Park
PO Box 709
Ludington, MI 49431

616-843-8671

Michigan Atlas & Gazetteer Location: 64B4

County Location: Manistee

Directions To Trailhead:
From Manistee, take M110 west off on US31 2 miles to the Park

Trail Type: Hiking/Walking, Cross Country Skiing, Interpretive
Trail Distance: 2.3 mi   Loops: 4   Shortest: .6 mi   Longest: 1.7 mi
Trail Surface: Natural
Trail Use Fee: None, but vehicle entry fee required
Method Of Ski Trail Grooming: None
Skiing Ability Suggested: Novice
Hiking Trail Difficulty: Easy
Mountain Biking Ability Suggested: NA
Terrain: Steep 0%, Hilly 30%, Moderate 30%, Flat 40%
Camping: Campground on site

Maintained by the DNR Parks and Recreation Division
Park on Lake Michigan with beautiful beach and lakeside campground.
Multi loop hiking trail.
Nature trail with guide available.

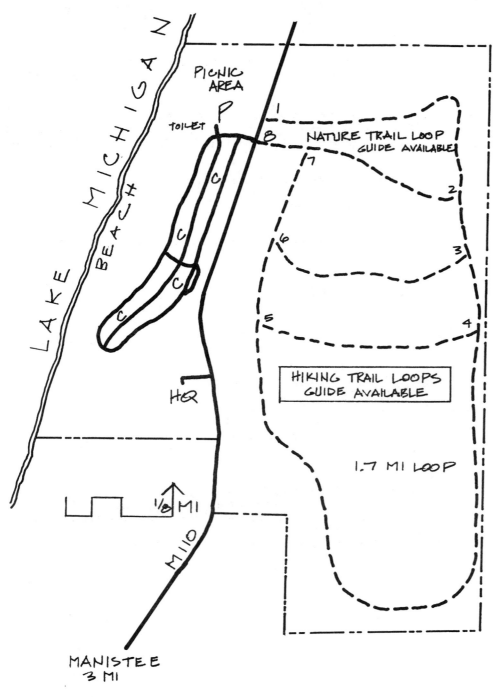

ORCHARD BEACH STATE PARK

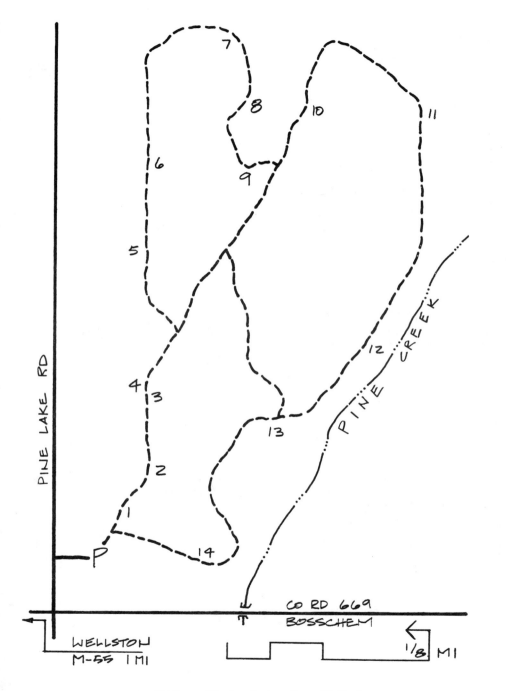

Manistee Ranger Station, Huron Manistee National Forest
412 Red Apple Rd
Manistee, MI 49660   616-732-2211

Forest Supervisor, Huron Manistee National Forest
1755 S. Mitchell St
Cadillac, MI 49601   616-775-2421
     800-821-6263

Michigan Atlas & Gazetteer Location: 65C7

County Location: Manistee

Directions To Trailhead:
From Wellston, go west on M55 1 mile to Bosschem Rd, then south 1 mile to parking lot trailhead

Trail Type: Hiking/Walking, Interpretive
Trail Distance: .84 mi   Loops: 3   Shortest: .2 mi   Longest: .65 mi
Trail Surface: Natural
Trail Use Fee: None
Method Of Ski Trail Grooming: None
Skiing Ability Suggested: NA
Hiking Trail Difficulty: Easy
Mountain Biking Ability Suggested: NA
Terrain: Steep 0%, Hilly 0%, Moderate 10%, Flat 90%
Camping: None nearby

Managed by the Huron Manistee National Forest
This is a demonstration arboretum developed by the USDA Forest Service.
The trail passes through trees that were planted in 1940 to test their growth potential in this climate.
Trees from Europe, Asia and various parts of the USA are planted here.

ARBORETUM TRAIL

Manistee Cross Country Ski Council
PO Box 196   616-723-2575
Manistee, MI 49660   616-723-6062

Manistee Ranger District, Manistee National Forest
412 Red Apple Rd   616-732-2211
Manistee, MI 49660   800-821-6263

Michigan Atlas & Gazetteer Location: 65C6

County Location: Manistee

Directions To Trailhead:
About 18 miles east of Manistee and 7 miles west of Wellston on M55, then
 south 3.5 miles on Udell Hills Rd.

SEE MAP ON NEXT PAGE

Trail Type: Cross Country Skiing, Mountain Biking
Trail Distance: 46 mi   Loops: 6   Shortest: .5 mi   Longest: 28 mi
Trail Surface: Natural
Trail Use Fee: Yes, donation for ski grooming only
Method Of Ski Trail Grooming: Track set
Skiing Ability Suggested: Novice to advanced
Hiking Trail Difficulty: NA
Mountain Biking Ability Suggested: Intermediate to advanced
Terrain: See text below.
Camping: None, but private and federal campgrounds are nearby

Developed and maintained by the Manistee Cross Country Ski Council and the
Michigan Mountain Biking Association in cooperation with the Huron-Manistee
National Forest.
On the site of the former Big M alpine ski area. A very scenic trail system. Day
use cabin on site at the trailhead that is open on winter weekends. Well
designed and groomed classic trail system that is very popular by local and state
wide skiers alike. Cross country terrain is Steep 15%, Hilly 35%, Moderate 35%
and Flat 15%. Extensive mountain bike trail system is being added (1997) to the
existing ski trail system. 16 miles are expected by the end of 1997 and the
balance in 1998. Mountain bike terrian rating has not been established. Call for
current trail information.

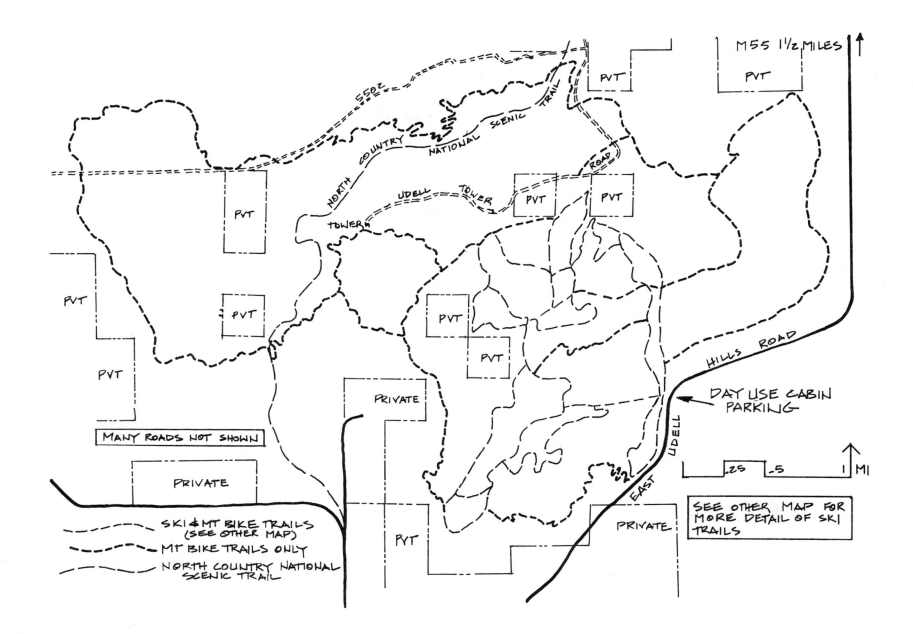

M55 1½ MILES

PVT

PVT

5502

NORTH COUNTRY NATIONAL SCENIC TRAIL

PVT

ROAD

PVT

UDELL   TOWER

TOWER

PVT   PVT

PVT

PVT

PVT

PRIVATE

PVT

HILLS ROAD

DAY USE CABIN PARKING

MANY ROADS NOT SHOWN

PRIVATE

EAST UDELL

PRIVATE

.25   .5   1 MI

SEE OTHER MAP FOR MORE DETAIL OF SKI TRAILS

- - - - SKI & MT BIKE TRAILS (SEE OTHER MAP)
- - - - MT BIKE TRAILS ONLY
- - - - NORTH COUNTRY NATIONAL SCENIC TRAIL

BIG "M" MOUNTAIN BIKE & SKI TRAILS

235.1

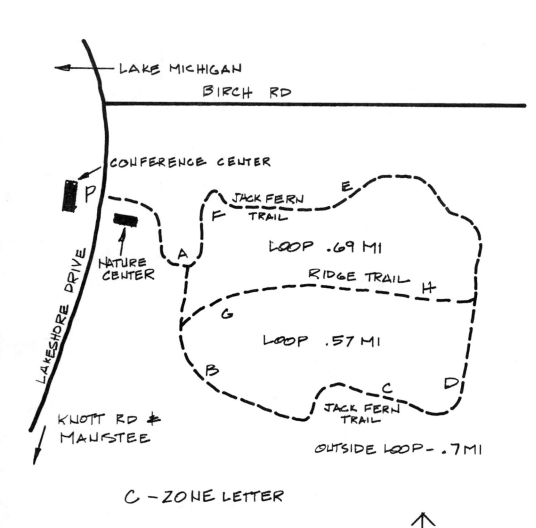

Lake Bluff Audubon Center
4374 W. Fox Farm
Manistee, MI 49660

616-723-2872
616-723-2625

Michigan Atlas & Gazetteer Location: 65B4

County Location: Manistee

Directions To Trailhead:
From US31 north, take M110(Lake Shore Dirve) along the Lake Michigan shoreline past Orchard Beach State Park about 1 mile to the center.

Trail Type: Hiking/Walking, Interpretive
Trail Distance: 1 mi   Loops: 2   Shortest: .57 mi   Longest: .7 mi
Trail Surface: Natural (wood chips)
Trail Use Fee: None
Method Of Ski Trail Grooming: NA
Skiing Ability Suggested: NA
Hiking Trail Difficulty: Easy
Mountain Biking Ability Suggested: NA
Terrain: Steep 0%, Hilly 25%, Moderate 40%, Flat 35%
Camping: None

Owned by the Michigan Audubon Society
Small but very interesting interpretive trail.

Map labels

LAKE MICHIGAN
BIRCH RD
CONFERENCE CENTER
LAKESHORE DRIVE
P
NATURE CENTER
JACK FERN TRAIL
E
F
A
LOOP .69 MI
RIDGE TRAIL H
G
LOOP .57 MI
B
C D
JACK FERN TRAIL
OUTSIDE LOOP - .7 MI
KNOTT RD & MANISTEE
C - ZONE LETTER

LAKE BLUFF AUDUBON CENTER

TRAIL NOTES

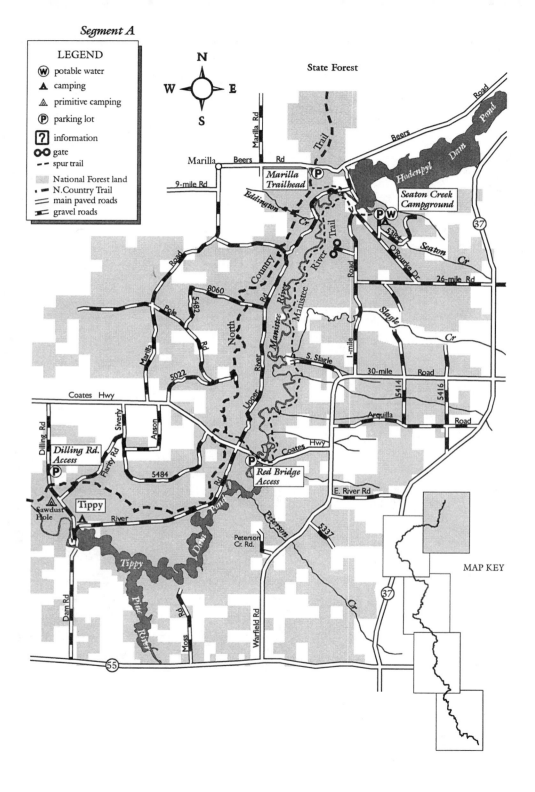

Segment A

LEGEND
- Ⓦ potable water
- ▲ camping
- △ primitive camping
- Ⓟ parking lot
- ? information
- ∞ gate
- - - spur trail
- National Forest land
- N.Country Trail
- main paved roads
- gravel roads

Manistee Ranger Station, Huron-Manistee National Forest
412 Red Apple Rd
Manistee, MI 49660
616-723-2211

Forest Supervisor, Huron-Manistee National Forest
1755 S. Mitchell St.
Cadillac, MI 49601
616-775-2421
800-821-6263

Michigan Atlas & Gazetteer Location: 65B7, 66AB1

County Location: Manistee

Directions To Trailhead:
Between Manistee and Cadillac.
Some trailheads - From Marilla east on Beers Rd 2 miles to the trailhead or about 6 miles west on Beers Rd from M115. From Brethren go east on Coates Hwy 7 miles to trail.
From Brethren go south 2.5 miles to the bridge and trailhead. On M55 about 7 miles west of Wellston.

Trail Type: Hiking/Walking, Mountain Biking
Trail Distance: 15.6 mi   Loops: NA   Shortest: NA   Longest: NA
Trail Surface: Natural
Trail Use Fee: None
Method Of Ski Trail Grooming: NA
Skiing Ability Suggested: NA
Hiking Trail Difficulty: Moderate
Mountain Biking Ability Suggested: Novice to advanced
Terrain: Steep 10%, Hilly 30%, Moderate 40%, Flat 20%
Camping: Camping is permitted 200' from trail

Maintained by Huron-Manistee National Forest.
Part of the trail follows a ridge that parallels the Manistee River. Excellent scenic views of the Hodenpyl Pond, Manistee River valley and the Udell Hills in the spring and fall. Trail is marked with gray diamond blazes.
The section west of Dilling Rd is closed to mountain bikes.
Trail connects to the Manistee Trail (see other listing) just below the dam at a spectactular 245' long suspension bridge and just north of Coates Hwy (hiking permitted only).
For further information contact the North Country Trail Association.

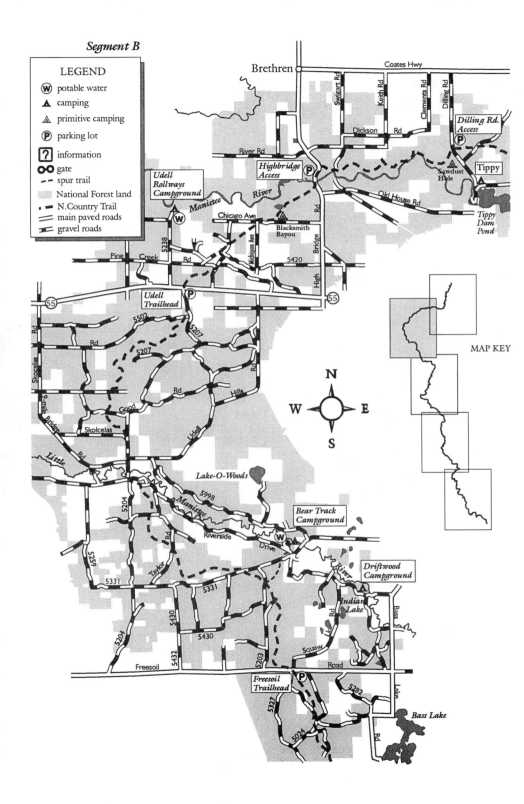

Manistee Ranger Station, Huron-Manistee National Forest
412 Red Apple Rd.   616-723-2211
Manistee, MI 49660

Forest Supervisor, Manistee National Forest
1755 S. Mitchell St.   616-775-2421
Cadillac, MI 49601   800-821-6263

Michigan Atlas & Gazetteer Location: 65BCD567

County Location: Manistee, Mason, Lake

Directions To Trailhead:
East of Manistee on M55, just west of the Wellston
North trailhead - Tippy Dam Pond at Dilling Rd
Central trailhead- M55 at the Udell Hills just west of Wellston
South trailhead- Freesoil Rd about 2.5 miles west of Bass Lake Rd.

Trail Type: Hiking/Walking, Mountain Biking
Trail Distance: 26.5 mi   Loops: NA   Shortest: NA   Longest: NA
Trail Surface: Natural
Trail Use Fee: None
Method Of Ski Trail Grooming: NA
Skiing Ability Suggested: NA
Hiking Trail Difficulty: Easy to moderately difficult
Mountain Biking Ability Suggested: Intemediate
Terrain: Steep 10%, Hilly 30%, Moderate 40%, Flat 20%
Camping: No campgrounds along the trail but several nearby.

Maintained by the Huron-Manistee National Forest
The northern section follows the Manistee River between Dilling Rd and Higbridge.
The section between HIghbridge and M55 is flat and not very interesting.
The section between M55 and the Little Manistee River is in the Udell Hills. This section is great for hiking or mountain biking. In the spring and fall, before the trees have leaves, nice views are possible to the west towards Manistee.
The section south of the Manistee River is again quite flat but more isolated and quite enjoyable.
The trail north of M55 to Segment A is closed to mountain bikes.

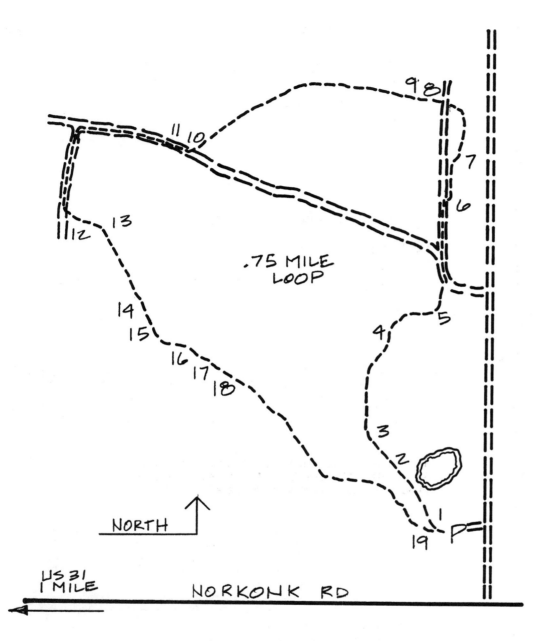

.75 MILE
LOOP

NORTH

US 31
1 MILE

NORKONK RD

Manistee Soil and Water Conservaton District
8840 Chippewa Hwy
Bear Lake, MI 49614

616-889-4761

Michigan Atlas & Gazetteer Location: 65A6

County Location: Manistee

Directions To Trailhead:
Take US31 about 5 miles north of Bear Lake to Norkonk Rd, then east 1 mile to trailhead parking lot.

Trail Type: Interpretive
Trail Distance: .75 mi   Loops: 1   Shortest: NA   Longest: .75 mi
Trail Surface: Natural
Trail Use Fee: None
Method Of Ski Trail Grooming: NA
Skiing Ability Suggested: NA
Hiking Trail Difficulty: Easy
Mountain Biking Ability Suggested: NA
Terrain: Moderate
Camping: None

A cooperative project of the Manistee Soil Conservation Service District, Michigan Youth Corp, USDA Forest Service-NE Area, State and PRivate Forestry and the DNR Forest Management Division
A 19 station interpretive trail of woodland mangement techniques.

WOODLAND MANAGEMENT TRAIL

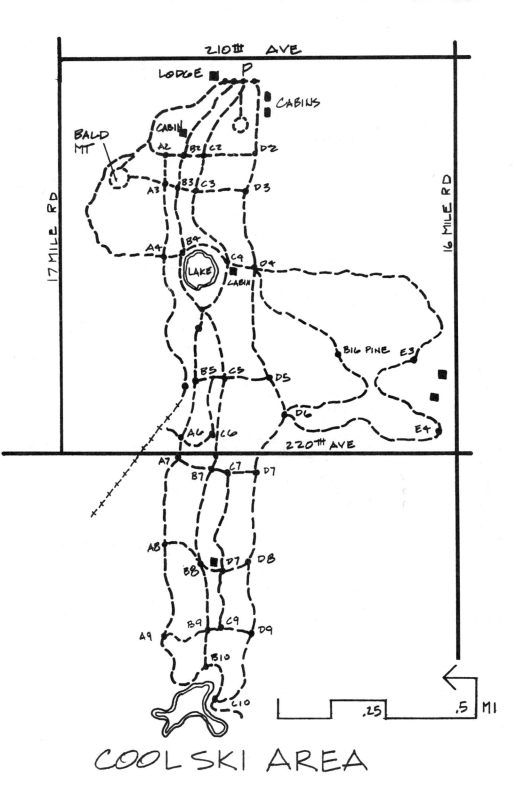

COOL SKI AREA

Cool Cross Country Ski Area
5557 N 210th Ave
Le Roy, MI 49655

616-768-4624

Michigan Atlas & Gazetteer Location: 66D34

County Location: Osceola

Directions To Trailhead:
16 miles south of Cadillac and 8 miles north of Reed City east of US131. Exit US131 at exit 162, then west t o 210th St., then north 2.5 miles to the ski area.

Trail Type: Hiking/Walking, Cross Country Skiing, Mountain Biking, Interpretive
Trail Distance: 40 km   Loops: Many   Shortest: 1 mi   Longest: 6 mi
Trail Surface: Natural
Trail Use Fee: Yes
Method Of Ski Trail Grooming: Track set with skating lanes
Skiing Ability Suggested: Novice to advanced
Hiking Trail Difficulty: Easy to moderate
Mountain Biking Ability Suggested: Novice to advanced
Terrain: Steep 15%, Hilly 25%, Moderate 40%, Flat 25%
Camping: Camping area available on site

Family owned touring center since 1976. One of the best touring centers in the state, with something for everyone. Mountain biking added several years ago. Mountain bike and ski races held annually. Lodging of all kinds from cabins to a bunk house and lakeside camping. Pro shop, rentals, restaurant, warming house, lessons, moonlight & guided tours, snowshoe rental, ice skating pond and clinics. The trails are delightful with ammenities of benches, fire pits and a portion of the trail is lighted. Trails pass through a variety of terrain and vegatation. Some trails are double tracked and all are continually well groomed. Write or call for brochure and reservations.

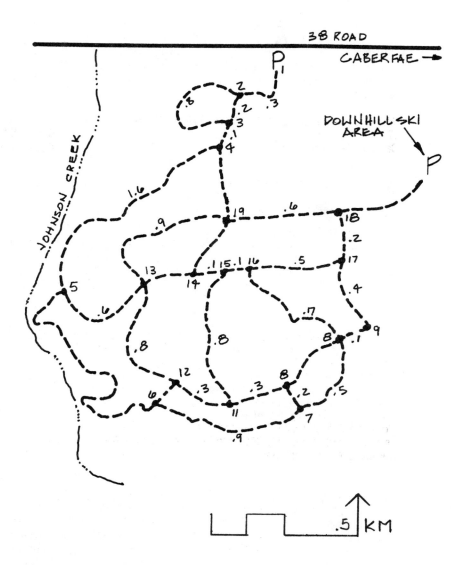

DISTANCES IN KILOMETERS

Manistee Ranger Station, Huron-Manistee National Forest
412 Red Apple Rd
Manistee, MI 49660

616-723-2211

Forest Supervisor, Huron-Manistee National Forest
1755 S. Mitchell St.
Cadillac , MI 49601

616-774-2421
800-821-6263

Michigan Atlas & Gazetteer Location: 66C2

County Location: Wexford

Directions To Trailhead:
From M55/115 junction take M55 west 13 miles to Caberfae Rd., then north 2 miles to trailhead
Trailhead - About 1 mile west of the downhill ski area on 38 Rd to parking lot on the south side of the road.

Trail Type: Hiking/Walking, Cross Country Skiing, Mountain Biking
Trail Distance: 18 km   Loops: Many   Shortest: 1.8 km Longest:
Trail Surface: Natural
Trail Use Fee: None
Method Of Ski Trail Grooming: Trails range from track set to no grooming
Skiing Ability Suggested: Novice to intermediate
Hiking Trail Difficulty: Easy
Mountain Biking Ability Suggested: Novice to intermediate
Terrain: Steep 3%, Hilly 15%, Moderate 50%, Flat 32%
Camping: Backcountry camping permitted along trail

Maintained by Cadillac Ranger District, Huron-Manistee National Forest
Ski shop, first aid, rentals and lodging at the adjacent downhill ski area.
Trail system is perfect for intermediate skiers and novice mountain bikers. However, novice skiers and advanced mountain bikers will enjoy the trails as well. Some trails are not groomed. But since this trail is very popular, usually those trails not groomed are well skied in by others. The trail system connects to the downhill ski area.

MACKENZIE TRAIL

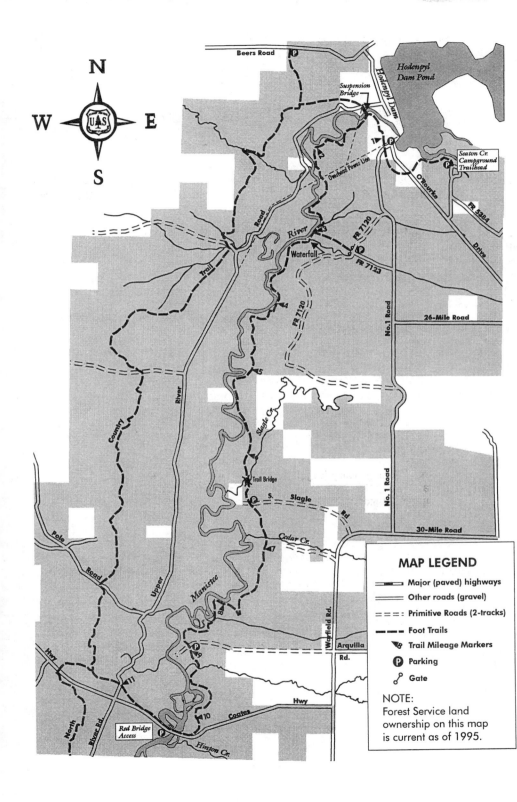

Manistee Ranger Station, Huron Manistee National Forest
412 Red Apple Rd   616-723-2211
Manistee, MI 49660

Forest Supervisior, Huron Manistee National Forest
1755 S. Mitchell St.   616-775-2421
Cadillac, MI 49601   800-821-6263

Michigan Atlas & Gazetteer Location: 66B1

County Location: Manistee

Directions To Trailhead:
From the north: From Mesick, take M37 south 6 miles to 26 Rd., then west on 26 Rd for 3 miles to O'Rourke Dr. (stay to the right fork), then right on O'Rourke Dr. for about 1 mile to Seaton Creek Campground.
From the south: From junction of M37 and M55, follow M37 north 9 miles to 26 Rd, then left on 26 Rd and follow instructions above

Trail Type: Hiking/Walking
Trail Distance: 11 mi   Loops: NA   Shortest: NA   Longest: NA
Trail Surface: Natural
Trail Use Fee: None
Method Of Ski Trail Grooming: NA
Skiing Ability Suggested: NA
Hiking Trail Difficulty: Moderate
Mountain Biking Ability Suggested: NA
Terrain: Steep 15%, Hilly 30%, Moderate 45%, Flat 10%
Camping: At north trailhead

Maintained by the Huron Manistee National Forest.
This hiking trail was built in 1991along the east side of the Manistee River just below Hodenpyl Dam and north of Red Bridge, connecting to the North Country Trail on both ends. At the north end, a 245' long suspension bridge crosses the Manistee River just below the dam. The trail offers hikers the opportunity to experience the riverlands along the beautiful Manistee River, which is a nationally designated Wild and Scenic River. The trail meanders through native hardwoods and pine and low areas along the river. Overlooks are abundant for viewing wildlife along the trail. The trail is marked with gray colored diamonds. There is a 60' bridge over Stagle Creek that was built in 1992. At mile post 3 is a fragile water fall formed by clay and gravel. Please do not climb around on the waterfall, since any activity could accelerate erosion and distroy the falls. There is also a bridge across the Manistee River, making a 26 mile loop with the North Country Trail. THIS TRAIL IS ONLY FOR HIKING. IT IS NOT OPEN FOR MOUNTAIN BIKING.

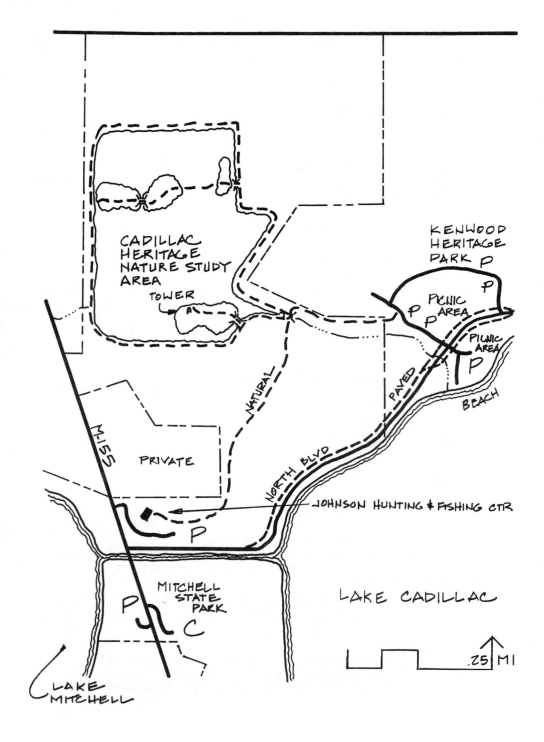

Mitchell State Park
6093 E. M115
Cadillac, MI 49601

616-775-7911

DNR Parks and Recreation Division
POB 30257
Lansing, MI 48909

517-373-1270

Michigan Atlas & Gazetteer Location: 66B4

County Location: Wexford

Directions To Trailhead:
South trailhead - Just north of main campground on M115 between Lake Mitchell and Lake Cadillac.
East trailheads - On North Boulevard .75 mile east of M 115 and a short time farther at the Kenwood Heritage Park

Trail Type: Hiking/Walking, Cross Country Skiing, Interpretive
Trail Distance: 2.25 mi   Loops: 2   Shortest: 1.75 mi Longest: 2 mi
Trail Surface: Paved and natural
Trail Use Fee: None but the Fishing & Hunting Center has an admission fee
Method Of Ski Trail Grooming: None
Skiing Ability Suggested: Novice
Hiking Trail Difficulty: Easy
Mountain Biking Ability Suggested: NA
Terrain: 100% Flat
Camping: On site

Maintained by the DNR Parks and Recreation Divsion
Adjacent to the Johnson Hunting & Fishing Center.
Additional paved trail follows next to North Boulevard to Kenwood Heritage Park (township park).

MITCHELL STATE PARK

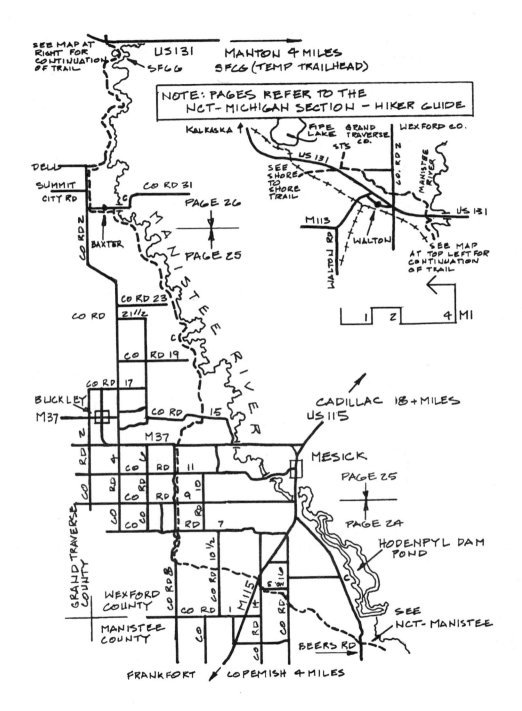

District Forest Manager, Pere Marquette State Forest
8015 Mackinaw Trail   616-775-9727
Cadillac, MI 49601

North Country Trail Association
PO Box 311   616-689-1912
White Cloud, MI 49349

Michigan Atlas & Gazetteer Location: 66AB1-5,67A4,74D34,75D4

County Location: Wexford, Grand Traverse

Directions To Trailhead:
Southwest trailhead - Beers Rd, just west of the Hodenpyl Dam east of Mesick
East trailhead - About 1.5 miles north of the M113/US131 intersection

Trail Type: Hiking/Walking, Mountain Biking
Trail Distance: 45.15   Loops: NA   Shortest: NA   Longest: NA
Trail Surface: Natural
Trail Use Fee: None
Method Of Ski Trail Grooming: NA
Skiing Ability Suggested: NA
Hiking Trail Difficulty: Moderate to difficult
Mountain Biking Ability Suggested: Intermediate to advanced
Terrain: Rolling to steep
Camping: Some campgrounds nearby

Trail located in the Pere Marquette State Forest
Trail built and maintained by members of the North Country Trail Association
Very scenic views of the Manistee River Valley and surrounding area.
Varied forest cover.
Trail follows old ORV trails, two-tracks and constructed single track trails
Contact the North Country Trail Association for the detailed map book of the
entire Michigan Section which is updated periodically. See pages 24,25 & 26
Trail marked with blue blazes
Campgrounds:
       Private campground on Hodenpyl Dam Pond at No.3 1/2 Rd
       Baxter Bridge SFCG at Co Rd 31 just south of the Manistee River
       Old US131 SFCG just west of US131 at the Manistee River

Pine Valleys Pathway

Baldwin Forest Area, Pere Marquette State Forest
Rte 2, Box 2810
Baldwin, MI 49304

616-745-4651

District Forest Manager, Pere Marquette State Forest
Rte 1, 8015 South US131
Cadillac, MI 49601

616-775-9727

Michigan Atlas & Gazetteer Location: 66D1

County Location: Clare

Directions To Trailhead:
Between Baldwin and M55 on M37 17 miles north of Baldwin and 9 miles south of M55, then east on 7 Mile Rd .2 mile to parking lot

Trail Type: Hiking/Walking, Cross Country Skiing, Mountain Biking
Trail Distance: 8.2 mi   Loops: 4   Shortest: 1.8 mi Longest: 6.1 mi
Trail Surface: Natural
Trail Use Fee: None
Method Of Ski Trail Grooming: None
Skiing Ability Suggested: Novice
Hiking Trail Difficulty: Easy
Mountain Biking Ability Suggested: Novice
Terrain: Steep 0%, Hilly 10%, Moderate 40%, Flat 50%
Camping: None

Maintained by the DNR Forest Management Division
The southern loops are more interesting than the northern loop that passes through a recent clear cut area
ORV and horse trails nearby and crossing this trail system
Popular cross country ski trail.
Other contacts:
        DNR Forest Management Division Office, Lansing, 517-373-1275
        DNR Forest Management Region Office, Roscommon, 517-275-5151

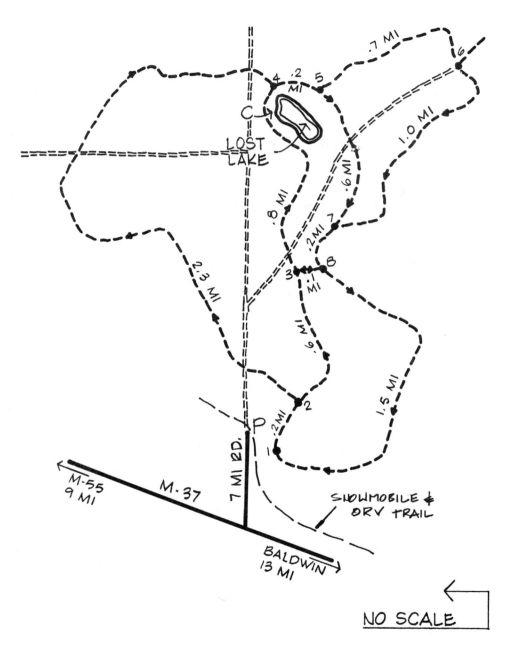

PINE VALLEYS PATHWAY

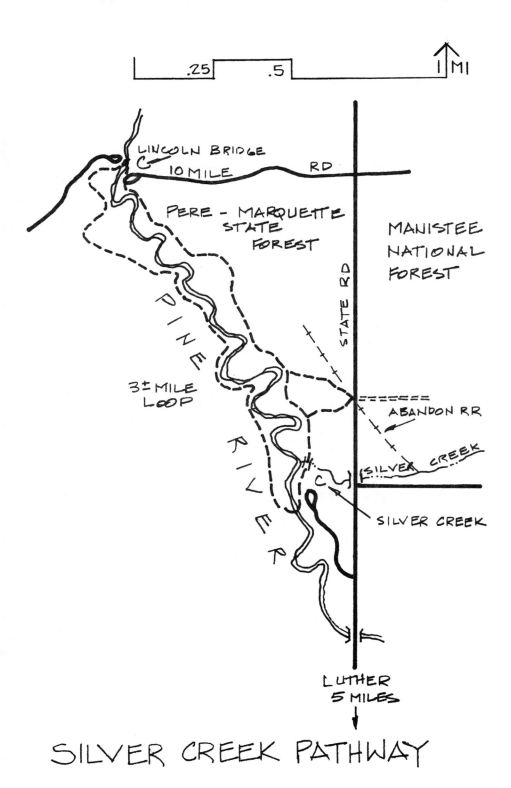

SILVER CREEK PATHWAY

Baldwin Forest Area, Pere Marquette State Forest
Rte 2, Box 2810
Baldwin, MI 49304

616-745-4651

District Forest Manager, Pere Marquette State Forest
8015 Mackinaw Trail
Cadillac, MI 49601

616-775-9727

Michigan Atlas & Gazetteer Location: 66C2

County Location: Lake

Directions To Trailhead:
5.5 miles north of Luther via State Rd to SFCG

Trail Type: Hiking/Walking, Cross Country Skiing, Mountain Biking
Trail Distance: 3+ mi   Loops: 1   Shortest: NA   Longest: 3+ mi
Trail Surface: Natural
Trail Use Fee: None
Method Of Ski Trail Grooming: None
Skiing Ability Suggested: Novice
Hiking Trail Difficulty: Easy
Mountain Biking Ability Suggested: Novice
Terrain: Steep 0%, Hilly 0%, Moderate 40%, Flat 60%
Camping: At Lincoln Bridge and Silver Creek SFCG's

Maintained by the DNR Forest Management Division
Trail loops both sides of Silver Creek with a SFCG at the half way point.

Kalkaska Forest Area, Pere Marquette State Forest
2089 N. Birch   616-258-2711
Kalkaska, MI 49464

District Forest Manager, Pere Marquette State Forest
Rte 1, 8015 South US131   616-775-9727
Cadillac, MI 49601

Michigan Atlas & Gazetteer Location: 67B5

County Location: Wexford

Directions To Trailhead:
Trailhead - North from Cadillac on US131, then right on 13th St. for 1.5 miles to the point where the road turns south (at playground) Trailhead at edge of the playground.
Trailhead - North from Cadillac on US131, then right on 34 Mile Rd.(Boon Rd.) 3.5 miles to Seeley Rd (the road turns north) and the parking lot will be found just past the turn on the right.

Trail Type: Hiking/Walking, Cross Country Skiing, Mountain Biking
Trail Distance: 11.3 mi   Loops: 6   Shortest: 1.2 mi Longest: 9.75 mi
Trail Surface: Natural
Trail Use Fee: None
Method Of Ski Trail Grooming: Track set
Skiing Ability Suggested: Novice to intermediate
Hiking Trail Difficulty: Easy
Mountain Biking Ability Suggested: Novice
Terrain: Steep 0%, Hilly 10%, Moderate 60%, Flat 30%
Camping: Campgrounds in the Cadillac area

Maintained by the DNR Forest Management Division
The west loops are more challenging then the east loops. The east loops off Boon Rd are over more level terrain. Parking for access to the trailhead for the west loops is on 13th St is at the Wexford-Missaukee Intermediate School District building. The trailhead is at the edge of the playground.
A rather good ski trail.   A very enjoyable trail that I usually try to ski every year.
Other contacts:
      DNR Forest Management Division Office, Lansing, 517-373-1275
      DNR Forest Management Region Office, Roscommon, 517-275-5151

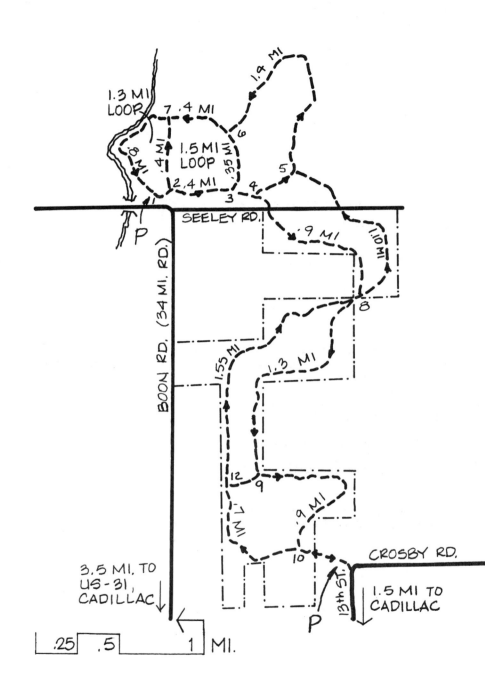

CADILLAC PATHWAY

City of Cadillac
200 Lake St
Cadillac, MI 49601

616-775-0181

Michigan Atlas & Gazetteer Location: 67C4

County Location: Wexford

Directions To Trailhead:
Along Lake Cadillac on the northeast shore in Cadillac

Trail Type: Hiking/Walking
Trail Distance: 1 mi   Loops: NA   Shortest: NA   Longest: NA
Trail Surface: Paved
Trail Use Fee: None
Method Of Ski Trail Grooming: NA
Skiing Ability Suggested: NA
Hiking Trail Difficulty: Easy
Mountain Biking Ability Suggested: NA
Terrain: 100% Flat
Camping: Campground nearby

Owned by the City of Cadillac
The trail follows the shoreline.

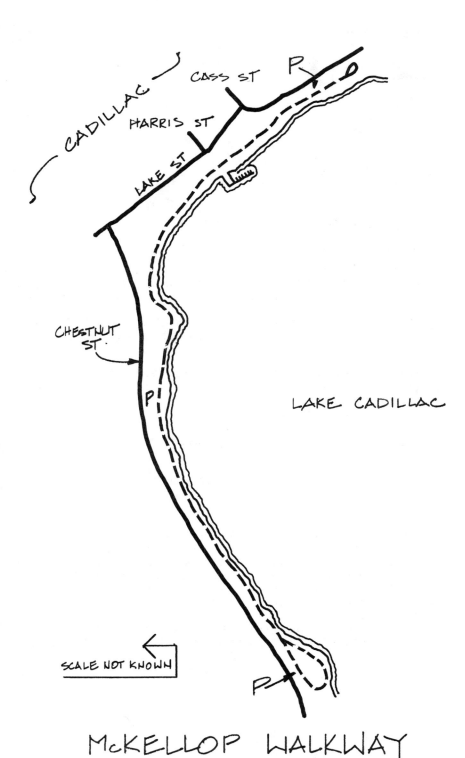

CADILLAC

CASS ST   P

HARRIS ST

LAKE ST

CHESTNUT ST.

P

LAKE CADILLAC

SCALE NOT KNOWN

P

McKELLOP WALKWAY

McGuire's Resort
7880 Mackinaw Trail
Cadillac, MI 49601

616-775-9947
800-632-7302

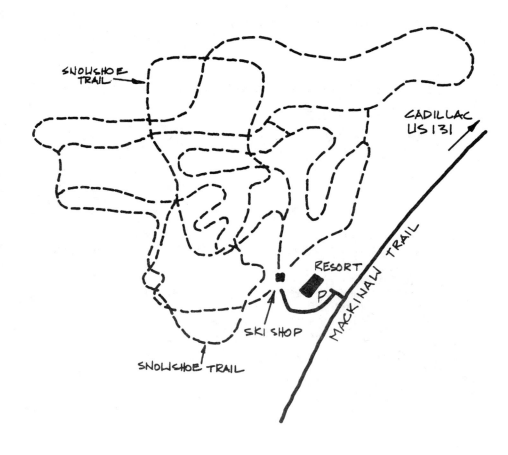

SNOWSHOE
TRAIL

CADILLAC
US 131

RESORT

SKI SHOP

SNOWSHOE TRAIL

MACKINAW TRAIL

Michigan Atlas & Gazetteer Location: 67C4

County Location: Wexford

Directions To Trailhead:
1 mile southwest of Cadillac on Mackinaw Trail between US 131 and M 115

Trail Type: Hiking/Walking, Cross Country Skiing
Trail Distance: 14 km   Loops: 6   Shortest: 1 km   Longest: 9 km
Trail Surface: Natural and paved
Trail Use Fee: Yes, but complimentary for guests
Method Of Ski Trail Grooming: Track set
Skiing Ability Suggested: Novice to intermediate
Hiking Trail Difficulty: Easy
Mountain Biking Ability Suggested: NA
Terrain: Steep 1%, Hilly 0%, Moderate 25%, Flat 74%
Camping: None on site but campgrounds in the area

Privately operated complete four season resort
Ski trails on the golf course
Outstanding occomodations with all amenities
Lighted 3 km ski trail

NORTH

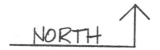

MCGUIRES RESORT

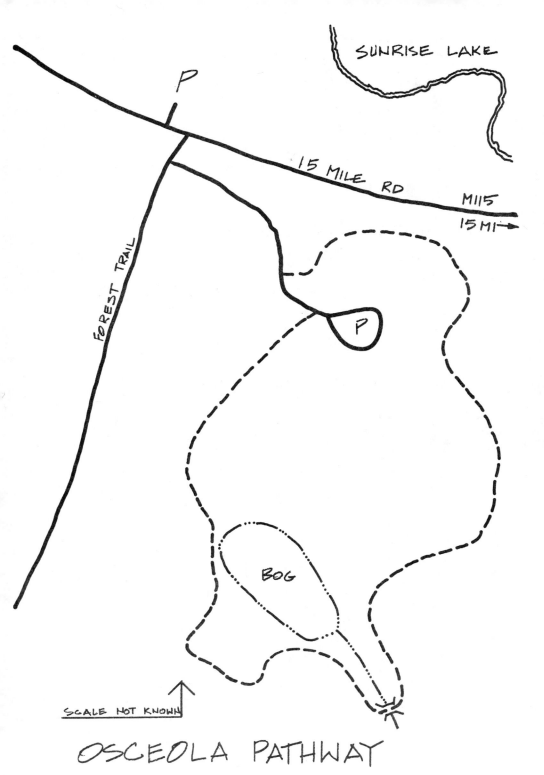

SUNRISE LAKE

P

15 MILE RD

M115

15 MI →

FOREST TRAIL

P

BOG

SCALE NOT KNOWN

OSCEOLA PATHWAY

Osceola Pathway

Baldwin Forest Area, Pere Marquette State Forest
Rte 2, Box 2810
Baldwin, MI 49304

616-745-4651

District Forest Manager, Pere Marquette State Forest
8015 Mackinaw Trail
Cadillac, MI 49601

616-775-9727

Michigan Atlas & Gazetteer Location: 67D5

County Location: Osceola

Directions To Trailhead:
6 miles east of LeRoy via Sunrise Lake Rd and 15 Mile Rd south Cadillac at Sunrise Lake SFCG

Trail Type: Hiking/Walking
Trail Distance: .5 mi   Loops: 1   Shortest: Longest: .5 mi
Trail Surface: Natural
Trail Use Fee: None
Method Of Ski Trail Grooming: NA
Skiing Ability Suggested: NA
Hiking Trail Difficulty: Easy
Mountain Biking Ability Suggested: NA
Terrain:
Camping: Campground at trailhead

Maintained by the DNR Forest Management Divsion

Michigan Trail Riders Association Inc
Chamber of Commerce
Traverse City, MI 49684

616-947-5075

DNR Forest Management Division, Recreation and Trails Section
PO Box 30452
Lansing, MI 48909

517-373-9483

Michigan Atlas & Gazetteer Location: 67,70,71,73,74,75,76,77,78

County Location: Many

Directions To Trailhead:
Extends from Empire to Oscoda with spurs north from Frederick to M33 and south from Mayfield to Cadillac

• CAMGROUNDS

NOTE:
SEE SEGMENTS IN MORE
DETAIL ELSEWHERE IN
ATLAS.

Trail Type: Hiking/Walking, Mountain Biking
Trail Distance: 302 mi   Loops: NA   Shortest: NA   Longest: NA
Trail Surface: Natural with lots of sand
Trail Use Fee: None
Method Of Ski Trail Grooming: NA
Skiing Ability Suggested: NA
Hiking Trail Difficulty: Easy to difficult
Mountain Biking Ability Suggested: Intermediate
Terrain: Steep 2%, Hilly 10%, Moderate 50%, Flat 38%
Camping: Campgounds along trail(see map)

Maintained by the DNR Forest Management and Parks and Recreation Division
and the Michigan Trail Riders Association(horseback riders user group).
Connects with sections maintained by the Huron-Manistee National Forest in
the Oscoda to Mio area. See other listings for more detail. Used heavily by
horseback riders. Some sections may not be suitable for hiking because of
extensive loose sand. Other trails near or along this trail: Mackinaw Trail, Mason
Tract Pathway, Muncie Lakes Pathway Wakeley Lake Non-Motorized Area,
Corsair Trail, Highbanks Trail, Sand Lakes Quiet Area and Loud Creek Pathway.
This is a point to point trail across the state from Lake Michigan to Lake Huron
with spurs north and south. Part used for the North Country Trail.
Detailed trail maps available from the Michigan Trail Riders Association, 1650
Ormond Rd, White Lake, MI 48383-2344. Memberships also available.

SHORE TO SHORE TRAIL

Cross Country Ski Headquarters
9435 Co Rd 100, Higgins Lake
Roscommon, MI 48653

517-821-6661

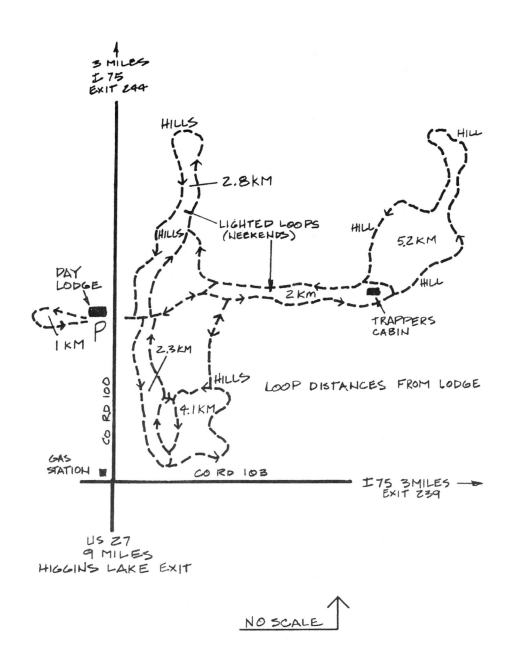

Michigan Atlas & Gazetteer Location: 68A3

County Location: Roscommon

Directions To Trailhead:
On the east side of Higgins Lake on Co Rd 100 From NB I75 take exit 239, turn left over overpass, then right on Co Rd 103. Continue 3.5 miles to stop and blinker, then right .5 mile to shop From US27 take Higgins Lake Rd. exit, go towards Higgins Lake 3.5 miles past the South Park(9.1 miles from US27)

Trail Type: Hiking/Walking, Cross Country Skiing, Interpretive
Trail Distance: 17.4 km   Loops: 8   Shortest: 1 km   Longest: 8 km
Trail Surface: Natural
Trail Use Fee: None, but donations accepted*
Method Of Ski Trail Grooming: Track set with skating lanes
Skiing Ability Suggested: Novice to advanced
Hiking Trail Difficulty: Easy
Mountain Biking Ability Suggested: NA
Terrain: Steep 0% Hilly 15%, Moderate 40%, Flat 45%
Camping: None

Privately operated touring center.
Ski shop, lodge with sundeck, snack bar and restrooms.
Owners, Bob and Lynne Frye are very knowledgeable in the proper selection of ski equipment for every level of skier.
Trails are constantly groomed very well.
Lighted trail.
Races and events held throughout the ski season.
Newsletter available.

CROSS COUNTRY SKI HEADQUARTERS

Roscommon Forest Area, Au Sable State Forest
Box 158
Houghton Lake Heights, MI 48630

517-422-5522

District Forest Manager, Au Sable State Forest
1919 S. Mt. Tom Rd.
Mio, MI 48647

517-826-3211

Michigan Atlas & Gazetteer Location: 68C3

County Location: Roscommon

Directions To Trailhead:
7 miles south of M55 (Houghton Lake) on Reserve Rd. (Co Rd 400)
(McDonalds's is on the corner of M55 and Reserve Rd.) Trailhead is not well marked.

Trail Type: Hiking/Walking, Cross Country Skiing, Mountain Biking
Trail Distance: 3 mi   Loops: 1   Shortest: NA   Longest: 1 mi
Trail Surface: Natrual
Trail Use Fee: None
Method Of Ski Trail Grooming: None
Skiing Ability Suggested: Intermediate to advanced
Hiking Trail Difficulty: Moderate to difficult
Mountain Biking Ability Suggested: Novice
Terrain: Very hilly
Camping: None

Maintained by the DNR Forest Management Division
Other contacts:
        DNR Forest Manggement Division Office, Lansing, 517-373-1275
        DNR Forest Management Region Office, Roscommon, 517-275-5151

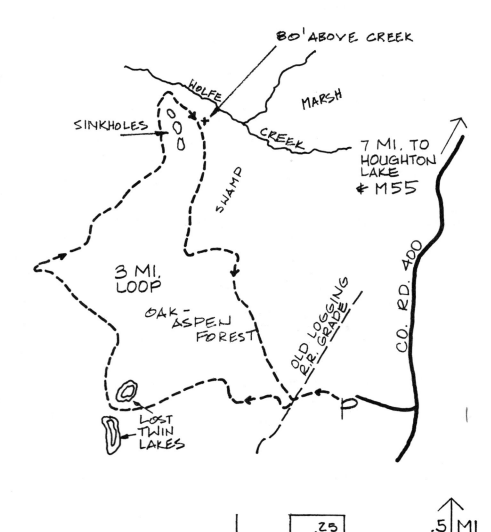

80' ABOVE CREEK

WOLFE

MARSH

CREEK

SINKHOLES

SWAMP

7 MI. TO HOUGHTON LAKE & M55

CO. RD. 400

3 MI. LOOP

OAK-ASPEN FOREST

OLD LOGGING R.R. GRADE

P

LOST TWIN LAKES

.25   .5 MI

LOST TWIN LAKES PATHWAY

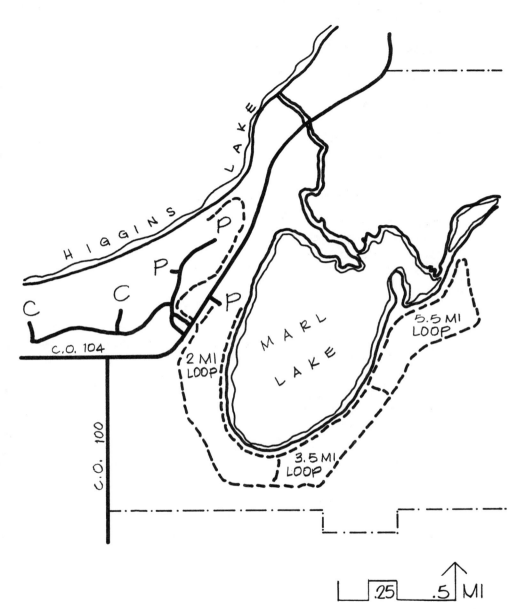

South Higgins Lake State Park
106 State Park Drive
Roscommon , MI 48653

517-821-6374

DNR Parks and Recreation Division

517-373-1270

Michigan Atlas & Gazetteer Location: 68A3

County Location: Roscommon

Directions To Trailhead:
On the south end of Higgins Lake on Co Rd 100

Trail Type: Hiking/Walking, Cross Country Skiing, Mountain Biking
Trail Distance: 5.8 mi   Loops: 3   Shortest: 2 mi   Longest: 5.5 mi
Trail Surface: Natural
Trail Use Fee: None, but vehicle entry fee required
Method Of Ski Trail Grooming: Track set
Skiing Ability Suggested: Novice to intermediate
Hiking Trail Difficulty: Easy
Mountain Biking Ability Suggested: Novice
Terrain: Steep 0%, Hilly 0%, Moderate 20%, Flat 80%
Camping: Campground in the park open throughout the year

Maintained by the DNR Parks and Recreation Division
Trails designed for skiing
Rentals available from nearby private ski shops.

SOUTH HIGGINS LAKE STATE PARK

Gladwin Forest Area, Au Sable State Forest
801 North Silverleaf
Gladwin, MI 48624

517-426-9205

District Forest Manager, Au Sable State Forest
191 S. Mt. Tom Rd., PO Box 939
Mio, MI 48647

517-826-3211

Michigan Atlas & Gazetteer Location: 68C4,69C4

County Location: Gladwin

Directions To Trailhead:
In the NW corner of Gladwin County, 2 miles east of Meridith 1 mile north of M18 off the Meridith Grade

Trail Type: Hiking/Walking, Cross Country Skiing, Mountain Biking
Trail Distance: 2.7 mi   Loops: 2   Shortest: 1.2 mi Longest: 1.7 mi
Trail Surface: Natural
Trail Use Fee: None
Method Of Ski Trail Grooming: None
Skiing Ability Suggested: Novice
Hiking Trail Difficulty: Easy
Mountain Biking Ability Suggested: Novice
Terrain: 100% Flat
Camping: Available along the trail

Maintained by the DNR Forest Management Division
A nice easy day hike for families.
The trail connects several state forest campgrounds.

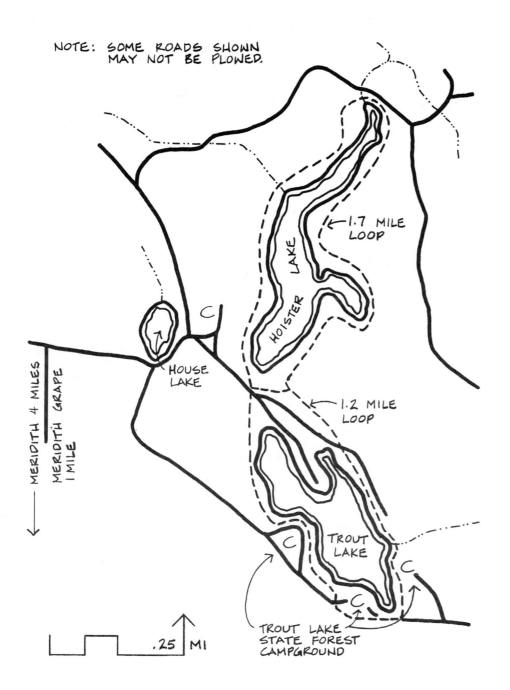

NOTE: SOME ROADS SHOWN MAY NOT BE PLOWED.

1.7 MILE LOOP

HOISTER LAKE

HOUSE LAKE

MERIDITH 4 MILES

MERIDITH GRADE 1 MILE

1.2 MILE LOOP

TROUT LAKE

TROUT LAKE STATE FOREST CAMPGROUND

.25 MI

TROUT LAKE PATHWAY

Au Sable Valley Nordic Ski Club

Cross Country Ski Headquarters
9435 Co Rd 100, Higgins Lake
Roscommon, MI 48653

517-821-6661

Michigan Atlas & Gazetteer Location: 68A2

County Location: Roscommon

Directions To Trailhead:
Exit US27 northbound at Higgins Lake Rd. (South Higgins Lake State Park), then east .25 mile to Old 27, then north about 4 miles to a parking lot on the west side of the road .

Trail Type: Cross Country Skiing
Trail Distance: 3 mi   Loops: 1   Shortest: 3mi   Longest: 3 mi
Trail Surface: Natural
Trail Use Fee: Donation accepted
Method Of Ski Trail Grooming: Track set as needed
Skiing Ability Suggested: Novice to intermediate
Hiking Trail Difficulty: NA
Mountain Biking Ability Suggested: NA
Terrain: Steep 0%, Hilly 15%, Moderate 40%, Flat 45%
Camping: None

Developed and maintained by the Au Sable Valley Nordic Ski Club
Trail maintained strictly on a volunteer basis with volunteer equipment and labor. Only gas and oil are paid for by the club from memberships, donations and profits from the Beaver Creek Challenge Ski Race held the 1st Sunday in February at the nearby North Higgins Lake State Park.

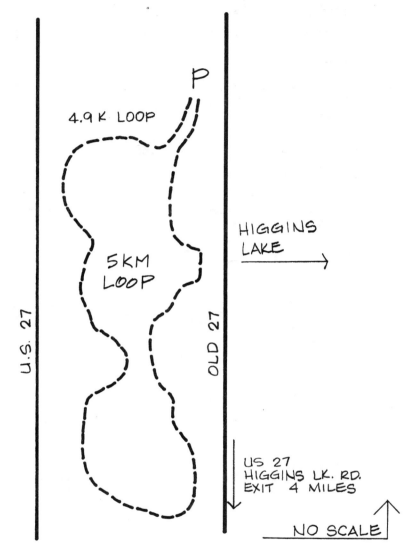

4.9 K LOOP

5KM LOOP

U.S. 27

OLD 27

P

HIGGINS LAKE →

US 27
HIGGINS LK. RD.
EXIT 4 MILES

NO SCALE

WEST HIGGINS LAKE TRAIL

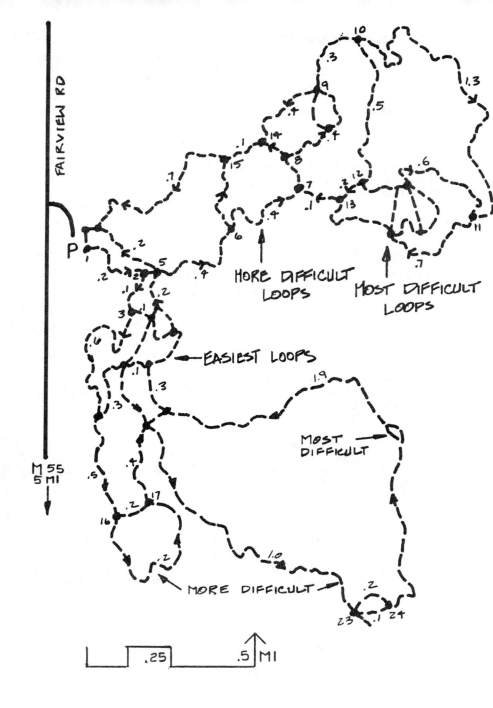

West Branch Area Chamber of Commerce
422 W. Houghton Ave   517-345-2821
West Branch, MI 48661

Roscommon Forest Area, Au Sable State Forest
Box 218, 8717 N. Roscommon Rd.   517-275-5151
Roscommon , MI 48653

Michigan Atlas & Gazetteer Location: 69B7

County Location: Ogemaw

Directions To Trailhead:
5.5 miles north of West Branch on Fairview Rd. (F7) Use exit 212 off I-75

Trail Type: Hiking/Walking, Cross Country Skiing, Mountain Biking
Trail Distance: 13.6 mi   Loops: 12   Shortest: .5 mi   Longest: 5 mi
Trail Surface: Natural
Trail Use Fee: None, but donations accepted
Method Of Ski Trail Grooming: Track set weekly
Skiing Ability Suggested: Intermediate to advanced
Hiking Trail Difficulty: Moderate
Mountain Biking Ability Suggested: Intermediate
Terrain: Hilly
Camping: Available in the area seasonally

Developed by the West Branch Kiwanis and Optimist Clubs, Michigan Youth
Corps, DNR, Ogemaw Ski Council and many local volunteers
Maintained by the Ogemaw Ski Council.
Well designed, marked and groomed trail system.
Good trail for mountain biking.
Rentals available in West Branch.

OGEMAW HILLS PATHWAY

Roscommon Forest Area, Au Sable State Forest
Box 218
Roscommon, MI 48653

616-275-8512

District Forest Manger, Au Sable State Forest
191 S. Mt. Tom, PO Box 939
Mio, MI 48947

517-826-3211

Michigan Atlas & Gazetteer Location: 69A5

County Location: Roscommon

Directions To Trailhead:
8 miles north of St. Helen on Co Rd F97 then east on Sunset Drive about 1 mile
to trailhead

Trail Type: Hiking/Walking, Interpretive
Trail Distance: 1.5 mi   Loops: 1   Shortest: NA   Longest: 1.5 mi
Trail Surface: Natural
Trail Use Fee: None
Method Of Ski Trail Grooming: NA
Skiing Ability Suggested: NA
Hiking Trail Difficulty: Easy
Mountain Biking Ability Suggested: NA
Terrain: 100% Flat
Camping: None

Maintained by the DNR Forest Management Division
Site of former largest Red Pine in Michigan(died around 1982)
8 station interpretative trail, Brochure available from Area office only

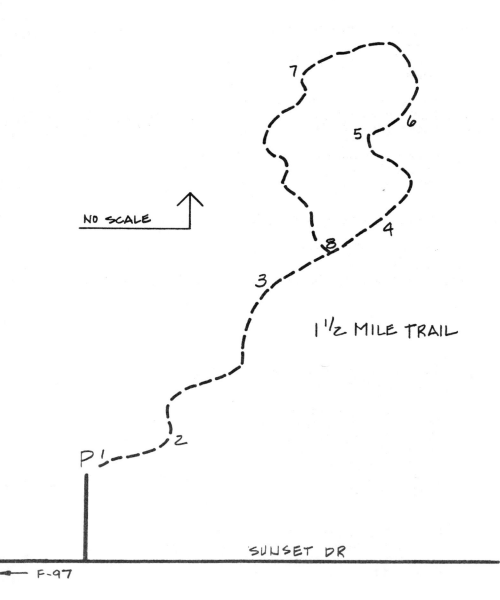

NO SCALE

1 1/2 MILE TRAIL

P!

SUNSET DR

F-97

RED PINE NATURAL AREA

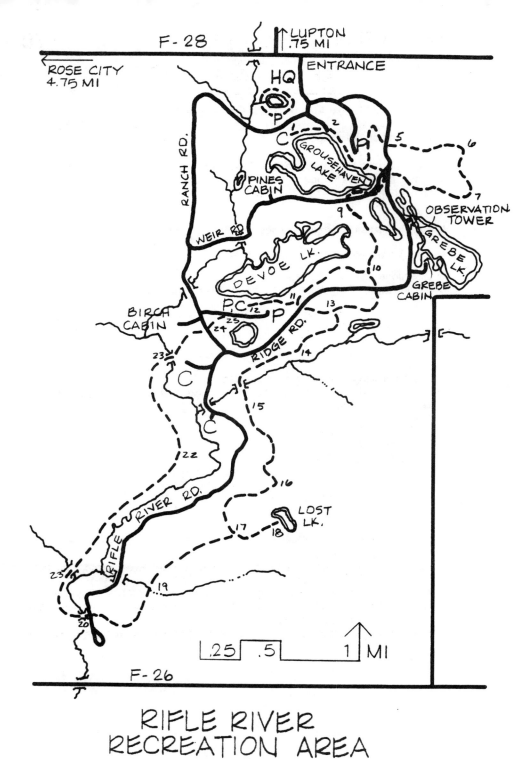

F-28

↑ LUPTON
.75 MI

ROSE CITY
4.75 MI

ENTRANCE

HQ
P

C

GROUSEHAVEN
LAKE

2

5

6

7

PINES
CABIN

RANCH RD.

WEIR RD.

9

OBSERVATION
TOWER

GREBE
LK.

DEVOE LK.

10

GREBE
CABIN

BIRCH
CABIN

PC 12

11

P

13

23

25

24

RIDGE RD.

14

C

15

C

22

RIFLE RIVER RD.

16

LOST
LK.

17

18

23

19

20

.25 .5 1 MI

F-26

T

RIFLE RIVER
RECREATION AREA

Rifle River Recreation Area
2550 East Rose City Rd
Lupton, MI 48635

517-437-2258

DNR Parks and Recreation Division

517-373-1270
517-322-1300

Michigan Atlas & Gazetteer Location: 70AB12

County Location: Ogemaw

Directions To Trailhead:
4.75 miles east of Rose City on F28 (Rose City Rd)

Trail Type: Hiking/Walking, Cross Country Skiing, Mountain Biking, Interpretive
Trail Distance: 13. 5 mi   Loops: 2   Shortest: Longest: 13.5 mi
Trail Surface: Natural
Trail Use Fee: None, but vehicle entry fee required
Method Of Ski Trail Grooming: None
Skiing Ability Suggested: Novice
Hiking Trail Difficulty: Easy to moderate
Mountain Biking Ability Suggested: Novice
Terrain: Steep 0%, Hilly 25%, Moderate 25%, Flat 50%
Camping: Campground in recreation area

Maintained by the DNR Parks and Recreation Division
Extensive trail system.
Trails south of Ridge Rd(south half of the park) are flat. Trails east of
Grousenhaven and Devoe Lake are hilly.
Excellent for wildlife observations

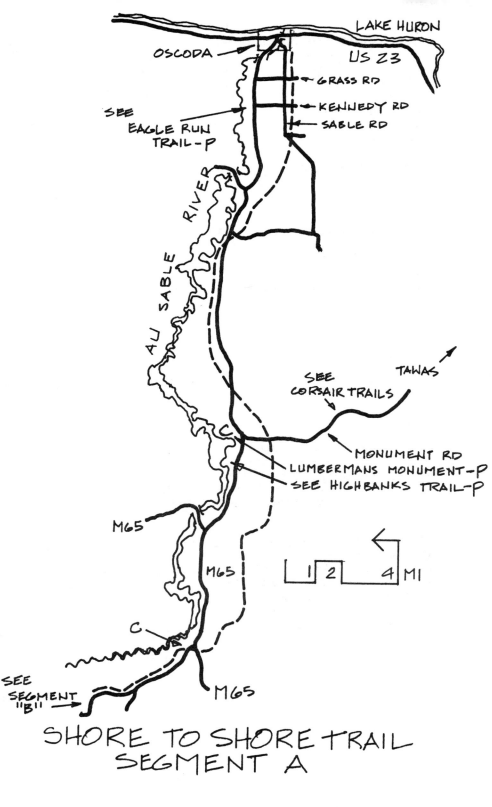

SHORE TO SHORE TRAIL
SEGMENT A

Huron Shores Ranger Station, Huron-Manistee National Forest
5761 N. Skeel Rd.   517-739-0728
Oscoda, MI 48750

Forest Supervisor, Huron-Manistee National Forest
1755 N. Mitchell St.   616-775-2421
Cadillac, MI 49601   800-821-6263

Michigan Atlas & Gazetteer Location: 70A34, 71A567, 78D3

County Location: Iosco

Directions To Trailhead:
East trailhead - South edge of Au Sable (adjacent to the south side of Oscoda).

West trailhead - Iosco/ Alcona county line on Curtisville Rd. About 2.5 north of the South Branch Trail Camp.

Trail Type: Hiking/Walking, Mountain Biking
Trail Distance: 45 mi   Loops: No   Shortest: NA   Longest: NA
Trail Surface: Natural
Trail Use Fee: None
Method Of Ski Trail Grooming: None
Skiing Ability Suggested: NA
Hiking Trail Difficulty: Easy to moderate
Mountain Biking Ability Suggested: Novice but sand present
Terrain: Steep 0%, Hilly 0%, Moderate 50%, Flat 50%
Camping: Campgrounds along the trail

Maintained by the Tawas Ranger District, Huron-Manistee National Forest
Primarily a equistrian trail.
Campgrounds at Rollways and South Branch with wilderness camping pemitted more than 200' from the trail.
Drinking water available at the campgrounds and Rollways Picnic Areas. For detailed maps of the entire trail contact: Michigan Trail Riders Association, 1650 Ormond Rd, White Lake, MI 48383
Mountain biking is difficult because of loose sand conditions on much of the trail.

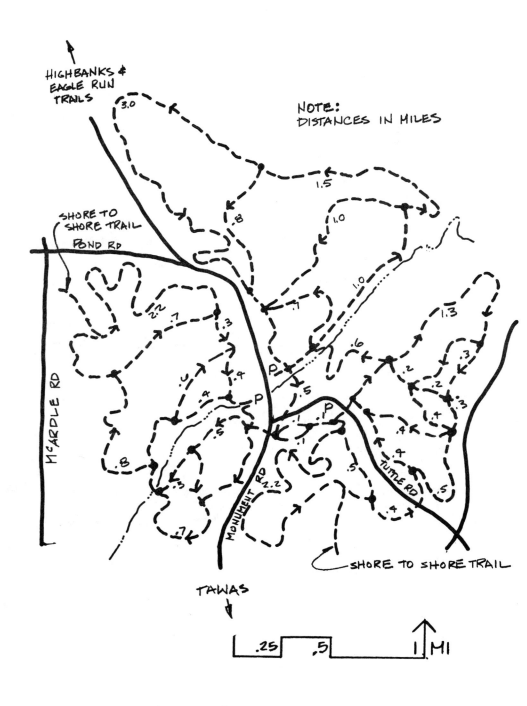

HIGHBANKS & EAGLE RUN TRAILS

SHORE TO SHORE TRAIL

POND RD

McARDLE RD

MONUMENT RD 2.2

TUTTLE RD

NOTE: DISTANCES IN MILES

SHORE TO SHORE TRAIL

TAWAS

.25 .5 1 MI

CORSAIR TRAILS

Corsair Trail Council
PO Box 608
Tawas City, MI 48763

800-558-2927
517-362-2001

Huron Shores Ranger Station, Huron-Manistee National Forest
5761 N. Skeel Rd
Oscoda, MI 48750

517-739-0728

Michigan Atlas & Gazetteer Location: 71A5

County Location: Iosco

Directions To Trailhead:
From M55 & US23 intersection take M55 west about .8 mile to Wilbur Rd, then north on Wilbur Rd to 1.2 miles to Monument Rd, then NW on Monument Rd about 7 miles to trails. Trailheads on both sides of the road for the 3 systems, Corsair, Wright's Lake and Silver Valley .

Trail Type: Hiking/Walking, Cross Country Skiing, Interpretive
Trail Distance: 26.2 mi   Loops: 19   Shortest: 1.3 mi Longest: 7.2 mi
Trail Surface: Natural
Trail Use Fee: None
Method Of Ski Trail Grooming: Track set with 10 km for skating
Skiing Ability Suggested: Novice to advanced
Hiking Trail Difficulty: Easy to moderate
Mountain Biking Ability Suggested: NA
Terrain: Steep 15%, Hilly 35%, Moderate 30%, Flat 20%
Camping: Many campgrounds in the general area

Developed by the local community in cooperation with the Huron-Manistee National Forest
A well goomed excellent trail system for all skill levels.
The Silver Valley section is the site of an old toboggan and alpine ski area of the 1940's. Site of the annual Silver Creek Challenge citizen race held the last Saturday of January each year.
Excellent lodging packages are available from the local motels. Ski rentals and ski equipment are available from Nordic Sports in East Tawas at 218 West Bay St., 517-362-2001.
Write or call the tourist bureau for lodging information and reservations
Many other trails in the area.

Huron Shores Ranger Station, Huron-Manistee National Forest
5761 N. Skeel Rd   517-739-0728
Oscoda, MI 48750

Oscoda Chamber of Commerce
100 W Michigan   800-235-4625
Oscoda, MI 48750

Michigan Atlas & Gazetteer Location: 71A6

County Location: Iosco

Directions To Trailhead:
NW from East Tawas on Monument Rd. to River Rd., then east 13 miles, or west from Oscoda 2 1/2 miles on River Rd. to the trail.

SEE MAP ON NEXT PAGE

Trail Type: Hiking/Walking, Cross Country Skiing, Mountain Biking
Trail Distance: 7 mi   Loops: 4   Shortest: 2.5 mi   Longest: 5 mi
Trail Surface: Natural
Trail Use Fee: None
Method Of Ski Trail Grooming: Track set
Skiing Ability Suggested: Novice
Hiking Trail Difficulty: Easy
Mountain Biking Ability Suggested: Novice
Terrain: 100% Flat
Camping: Campgrounds nearby

Maintained by the Huron-Manistee National Forest with community support
Scenic views of the Au Sable River from the trail
Local ski shop - Nordic Sports Ski Shop, 218 West Bay St., East Tawas, 362-2001
For information contact the Oscoda Chamber of Commerce.

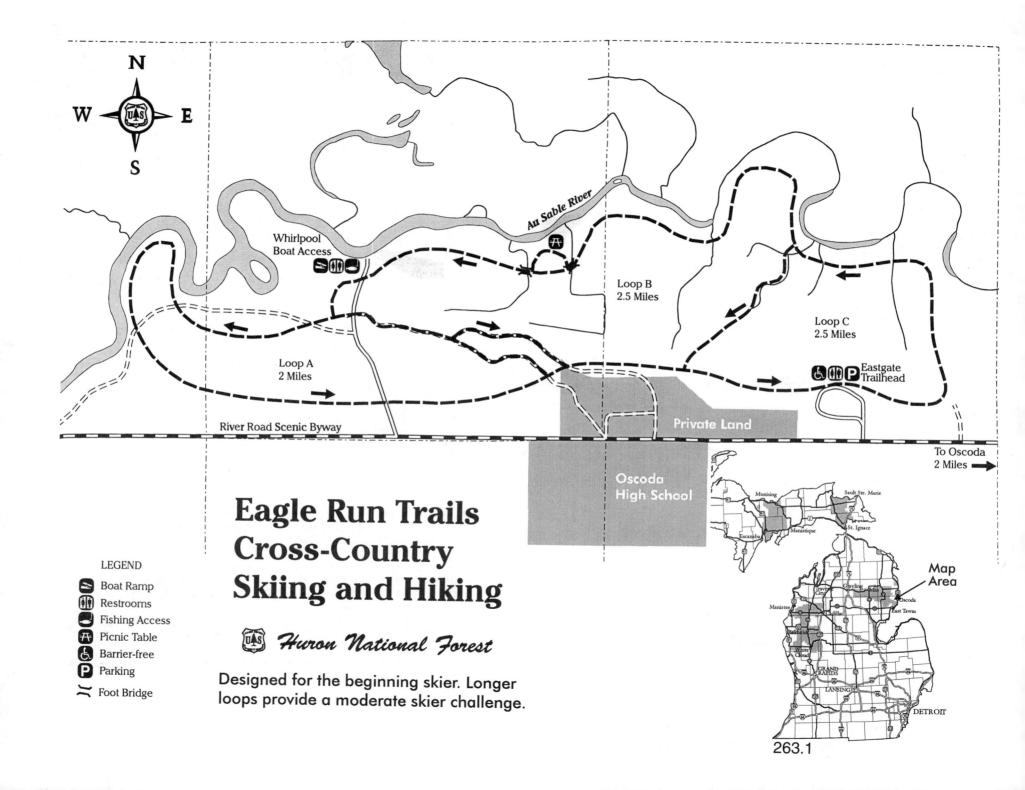

**Eagle Run Trails
Cross-Country
Skiing and Hiking**

Au Sable River

Whirlpool
Boat Access

Loop B
2.5 Miles

Loop C
2.5 Miles

Loop A
2 Miles

Eastgate
Trailhead

River Road Scenic Byway

Private Land

To Oscoda
2 Miles →

Oscoda
High School

LEGEND

- Boat Ramp
- Restrooms
- Fishing Access
- Picnic Table
- Barrier-free
- Parking
- Foot Bridge

Huron National Forest

Designed for the beginning skier. Longer
loops provide a moderate skier challenge.

Map
Area

263.1

Corsair Ski Council
PO Box 608
Tawas City , MI 48763

800-558-2927
517-362-2001

Huron Shores Ranger Station, Huron-Manistee National Forest
5761 N. Skeel Rd
Oscoda, MI 48750

517-739-0728

Michigan Atlas & Gazetteer Location: 71A45

County Location: Iosco

Directions To Trailhead:
Take Monument Rd. past the Corsair Trails north until it ends at River Rd. The trailhead is in the parking lot directly across from that intersection.

Trail Type: Hiking/Walking, Cross Country Skiing, Interpretive
Trail Distance: 10 km   Loops: NA   Shortest: NA   Longest: NA
Trail Surface: Natural
Trail Use Fee: None
Method Of Ski Trail Grooming: None
Skiing Ability Suggested: Novice to intermediate
Hiking Trail Difficulty: Easy to moderate
Mountain Biking Ability Suggested: NA
Terrain: Steep 0%, Hilly 0%, Moderate 30%, Flat 70%
Camping: None

Developed by the local community in cooperation with the Huron-Manistee National Forest The trail is rather flat but the scenery of the Au Sable River is outstanding
The Lumbermans Monument is located at the trailhead. Recently renovated the monument now as a pavilion, interpretive center and historical displays and bathrooms. A deck over the "Highbanks" 120' above the river affords an outstanding view of the area.
largo Springs (the west end of the trail) has been completely renovated. Cantlevered deck over the Highbanks provides another view of the AuSable River valley.
River Road, the road that parallels the ski trail is designated a National Scenic Byway.

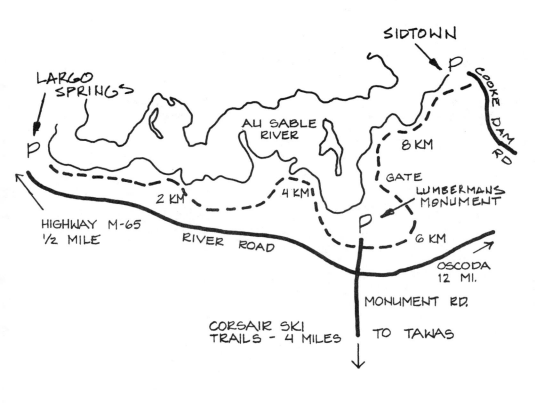

HIGHBANKS TRAIL

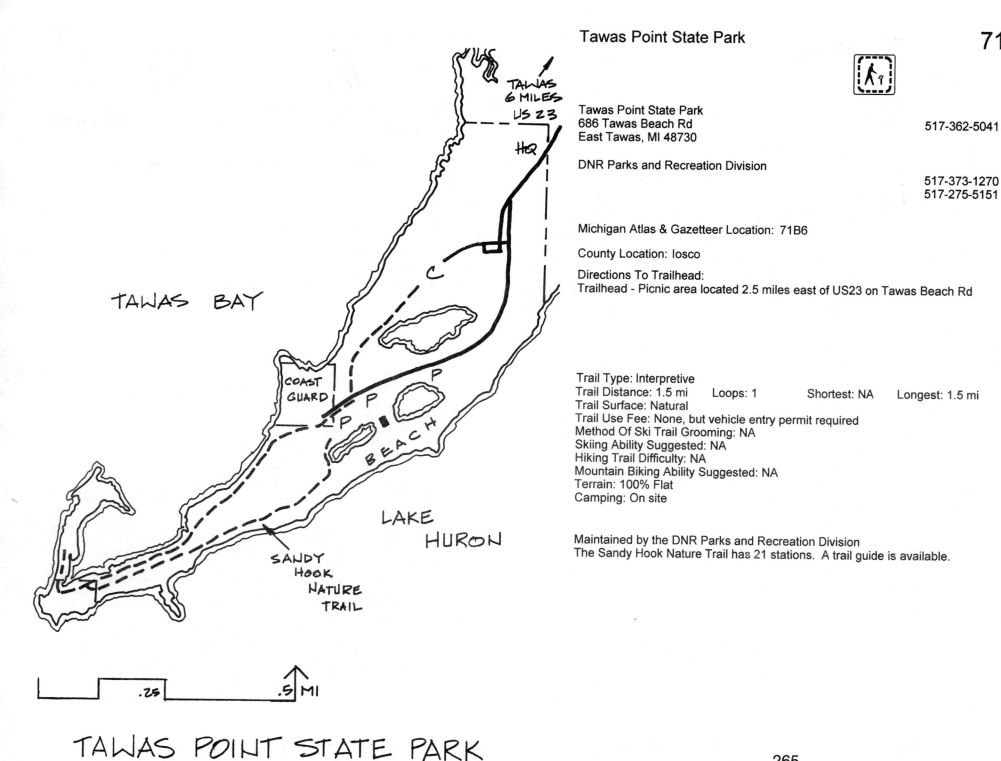

TAWAS BAY

TAWAS 6 MILES
US 23

HQ

COAST GUARD

P P P

BEACH

LAKE HURON

SANDY HOOK NATURE TRAIL

.25   .5 MI

TAWAS POINT STATE PARK

Tawas Point State Park
686 Tawas Beach Rd
East Tawas, MI 48730

517-362-5041

DNR Parks and Recreation Division

517-373-1270
517-275-5151

Michigan Atlas & Gazetteer Location: 71B6

County Location: Iosco

Directions To Trailhead:
Trailhead - Picnic area located 2.5 miles east of US23 on Tawas Beach Rd

Trail Type: Interpretive
Trail Distance: 1.5 mi   Loops: 1   Shortest: NA   Longest: 1.5 mi
Trail Surface: Natural
Trail Use Fee: None, but vehicle entry permit required
Method Of Ski Trail Grooming: NA
Skiing Ability Suggested: NA
Hiking Trail Difficulty: NA
Mountain Biking Ability Suggested: NA
Terrain: 100% Flat
Camping: On site

Maintained by the DNR Parks and Recreation Division
The Sandy Hook Nature Trail has 21 stations. A trail guide is available.

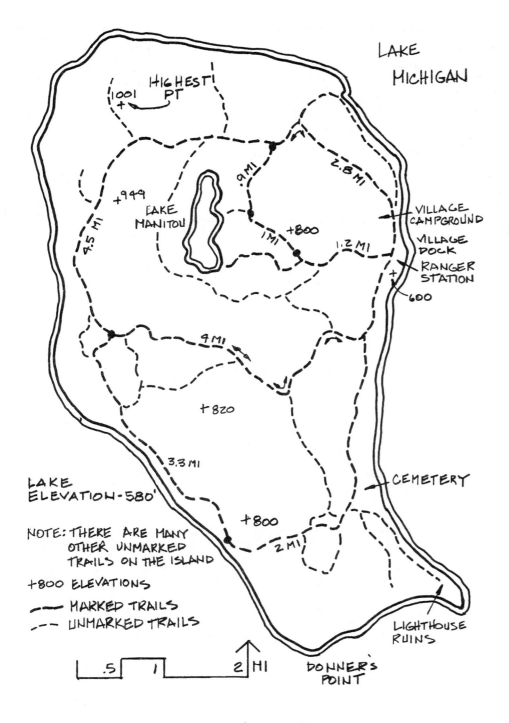

LAKE MICHIGAN

HIGHEST PT.
1001 +

+949

LAKE MANITOU

8.5 MI

.9 MI

2.8 MI

1 MI
+800

1.2 MI

VILLAGE CAMPGROUND

VILLAGE DOCK

RANGER STATION

+ 600

.9 MI

+820

3.3 MI

LAKE ELEVATION - 580'

CEMETERY

NOTE: THERE ARE MANY OTHER UNMARKED TRAILS ON THE ISLAND

+800 ELEVATIONS

--- MARKED TRAILS
--- UNMARKED TRAILS

+800

2 MI

LIGHTHOUSE RUINS

.5   1   2 MI

DONNER'S POINT

NORTH MANITOU ISLAND

Sleeping Bear Dunes National Lakeshore
PO Box 277, 9922 Front St. (M72)
Empire, MI 49630

616-326-5134

Michigan Atlas & Gazetteer Location: 72A2

County Location: Leelanau

Directions To Trailhead:
In Lake Michigan, west of Leland, 12 miles offshore

Trail Type: Hiking/Walking, Interpretive
Trail Distance: 50+ mi   Loops: Many   Shortest: Longest:
Trail Surface: Natural
Trail Use Fee: None
Method Of Ski Trail Grooming: NA
Skiing Ability Suggested: NA
Hiking Trail Difficulty: Easy to difficult
Mountain Biking Ability Suggested: NA
Terrain: Steep 0%, Hilly 5%, Moderate 40%, Flat 55%
Camping: One developed campground with wilderness camping permitted

Maintained by Sleeping Bear Dunes National Lakeshore
A wilderness area with very minimal developed facilities. Recommended for campers with some backcountry experience. Season 5/30 to 11/15 Since there are a minimum of marked trails and available maps do not show all trails and roads, backcountry hiking experience is required. A very unique island that is worth the effort to reach. This island is rich in history of the late 1800's to the 1940's. All campers must register at the Ranger Station on the island There is a special deer hunt from 10/15 - 11/15 Write for brochure and more detailed map needed for hiking. Low impact camping methods are required to protect this fragile environment. Cooking must be done on portable stoves. Daily ferry service is available from Leland at 10am returning to Leland by 5pm. Call 616-256-9061 or 616-271-4217 for information and reservations.

Sleeping Bear Dunes National Lakeshore
PO Box 277, 9922 Front St.(M72)
Empire, MI 49630

616-326-5134

Michigan Atlas & Gazetteer Location: 72B1

County Location: Leelanau

Directions To Trailhead:
In Lake Michigan, west of Leland, 17 miles off shore

Trail Type: Hiking/Walking, Interpretive
Trail Distance: 15 mi   Loops: Many   Shortest: Longest:
Trail Surface: Gravel roads and natural
Trail Use Fee: None
Method Of Ski Trail Grooming: NA
Skiing Ability Suggested: NA
Hiking Trail Difficulty: Easy to moderate
Mountain Biking Ability Suggested: NA
Terrain: Steep 0%, Hilly 0%, Moderate 20%, Flat 80%
Camping: Some campgrounds on the island with designated site camping

Maintained by the Sleeping Bear Dunes National Lakeshore
Two track roads are used for hiking trails, as well as many miles of foot paths
that form a network that reaches every corner of the island. A very unique island
with a very fragile ecosystem that should be experienced with great care.
Outstanding spring wildflower displays. All campers must register at the Ranger
Station located at the Visitor Center .
Low impact camping methods are required to protect this fragile enviornment..
Season - Memorial Day through 10/15. Daily ferry service available from Leland
at 10am returning back to Leland by 5:30pm call 616-256-9061 for information
and reservations.

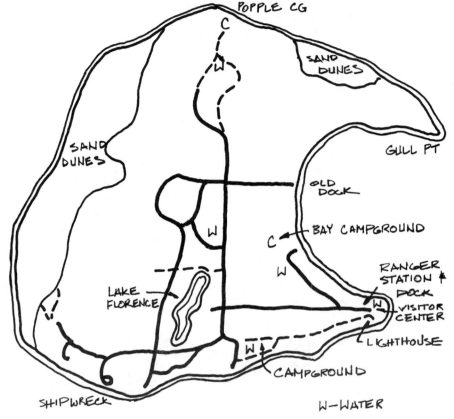

POPPLE CG

C

SAND
DUNES

SAND
DUNES

GULL PT

OLD
DOCK

W

BAY CAMPGROUND
C

RANGER
STATION &
DOCK

W

VISITOR
CENTER

LAKE
FLORENCE

W

W

LIGHTHOUSE

W

CAMPGROUND

SHIPWRECK

W-WATER

NOTE: PLEASE RESPECT RIGHTS OF
PRIVATE PROPERTY OWNERS

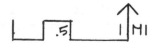
.5   1 MI

SOUTH MANITOU ISLAND

Sleeping Bear Dunes National Lakeshore
PO Box 277, 9922 Front St. (M72)
Empire, MI 49630

616-326-5134

Michigan Atlas & Gazetteer Location: 73A67

County Location: Leelanau

Directions To Trailhead:
Between Glen Haven and Glen Arbor, just south of M109 on Lake Michigan.
Trailhead - 1 mile east of M109 on Day Forest Rd, where Day Forest Rd intersects Stocking Rd or take Stocking Rd south from M109 just east of the DH Day campground entrance.

Trail Type: Hiking/Walking, Cross Country Skiing
Trail Distance: 8.6 mi   Loops: 3   Shortest: 2.5 mi Longest: 6.7 mi
Trail Surface: Natural
Trail Use Fee: None
Method Of Ski Trail Grooming: None
Skiing Ability Suggested: Novice to advanced
Hiking Trail Difficulty: Moderate
Mountain Biking Ability Suggested: NA
Terrain: Steep 0%, Hilly 30%, Moderate 55%, Flat 15%
Camping: Camping at 2 locations in the park and backcountry camping permitted

Maintained by the Sleeping Bear Dunes National Lakeshore.
Very scenic overlooks of Glen Haven, Lake Michigan and Glen Lake.
Trail has gradual but long climbs end in long downhill runs.
The wide trails attest to the fact that this site was originally planned as a subdivision before it was rescued for public recreation.
Hunting in season: 9/15 to 12/15, please wear bright clothing.
Many other trails in the Sleeping Bear Dunes National Lakeshore.

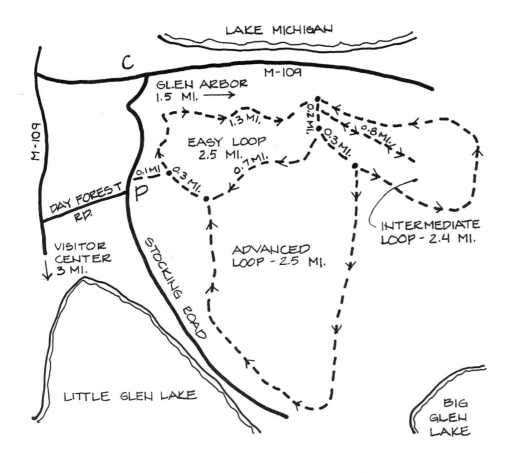

NOTE: OTHER UNMARKED TRAILS IN AREA.

NO SCALE

ALLIGATOR HILL TRAIL

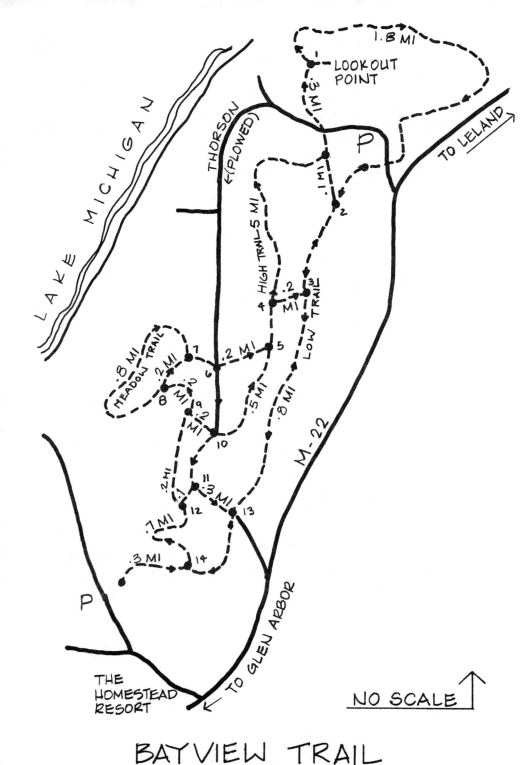

BAYVIEW TRAIL

Sleeping Bear Dunes National Lakeshore
PO Box 277, 9922 Front St. (M72)
Empire, MI 49630

616-326-5134
616-334-3756

Homestead
Wood Ridge Rd.
Glen Arbor, MI 49636

616-334-5000

Michigan Atlas & Gazetteer Location: 73A7

County Location: Leelanau

Directions To Trailhead:
Trailhead - About .5 mile west of M22 on Thorson Rd between Glen Arbor and Leland, just north of the Homestead .
Trailhead - Just inside the main entrance of the Homestead on the right near the reception center.

Trail Type: Hiking/Walking, Cross Country Skiing
Trail Distance: 15 km   Loops: 8   Shortest: 1km   Longest: 15 km
Trail Surface: Natural
Trail Use Fee: Fri., Sat. & Sun. when groomed
Method Of Ski Trail Grooming: Track set Fridays and weekends
Skiing Ability Suggested: Novice to advanced
Hiking Trail Difficulty: Moderate
Mountain Biking Ability Suggested: NA
Terrain: Steep 23%, Hilly 34%, Moderate 25%, Flat 18%
Camping: Campground available in park at 2 locations

Maintained by the Homestead under permit from the Sleeping Bear Dunes National Lakeshore.
Varied and interesting trail for the intermediate and above skier. Novice skiers will find the trail quite challenging.
From the lookout, a panoramic view of both Manitou islands, South Fox Island, and Pyramid Point are visable.

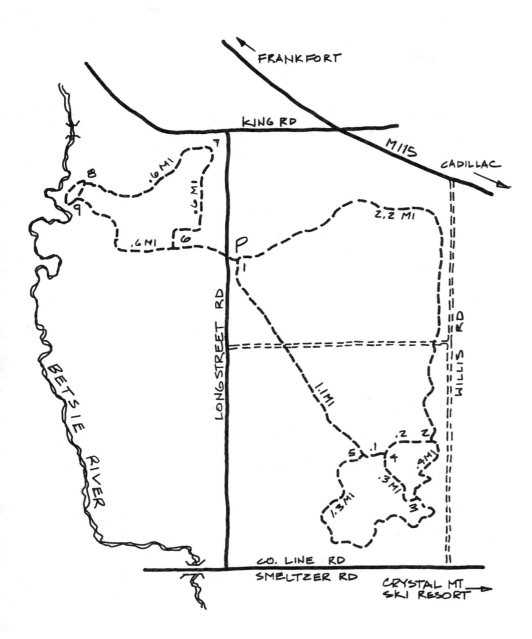

Betsie River Pathway

Traverse City Forest Area, Pere Marquette State Forest
404 W 14th St.   616-964-4920
Traverse City, MI 49684

District Forest Manager, Pere Marquette State Forest
Rte 1, 8015 South US131   616-775-9727
Cadillac, MI 49601

Michigan Atlas & Gazetteer Location: 73D6

County Location: Benzie

Directions To Trailhead:
Between Frankfort and Thompsonville on M115
Trailhead - West from Thompsonville 5 miles (just beyond Crystal Mt), then bear
left(south) on King Rd. .5 mile to Longstreet Rd., then left again for .75 miles to
parking lot.

Trail Type: Hiking/Walking, Cross Country Skiing, Mountain Biking
Trail Distance: 7.9 mi   Loops: 5   Shortest: 2.2 mi Longest: 7.54 mi
Trail Surface: Natural
Trail Use Fee: None
Method Of Ski Trail Grooming: None
Skiing Ability Suggested: Novice to intermediate
Hiking Trail Difficulty: Easy to moderate
Mountain Biking Ability Suggested: Novice to intermediate
Terrain: Steep 0%, Hilly 20%, Moderate 30%, Flat 50%
Camping: None, but campgrounds available 16 miles away at Platte River

Maintained by the DNR Forest Management Division.
Some trail segments were redesigned in 1997.
Trails west of the parking lot are more difficult than the loops toward the east.
Trails connect to Crystal Mountain Resort (trail use fee area) (see other entry).
The combination of the DNR and Crystal Mountain trails makes for a very
enjoyable day of skiing.
The connecting trail may not be signed.

BETSIE RIVER PATHWAY

Friends of the Betsie Valley Trail
POB 474
Beulah, MI 49617

DNR - Forest Management Division
POB 30028
Lansing, MI 48909

517-373-1275

Michigan Atlas & Gazetteer Location: 73CD457

County Location: Benzie

Directions To Trailhead:
Between Frankfort and Thompsonville approximately along M115

Trail Type: Hiking/Walking, Cross Country Skiing, Mountain Biking
Trail Distance: 22 mi   Loops: None   Shortest: NA   Longest: NA
Trail Surface: Ballast and natural
Trail Use Fee: None
Method Of Ski Trail Grooming: None
Skiing Ability Suggested: Novice
Hiking Trail Difficulty: Easy
Mountain Biking Ability Suggested: Novice
Terrain: 100% Flat
Camping: None, but campgrounds are in the area

Trail currently underdevelopment
Contact the DNR for current status

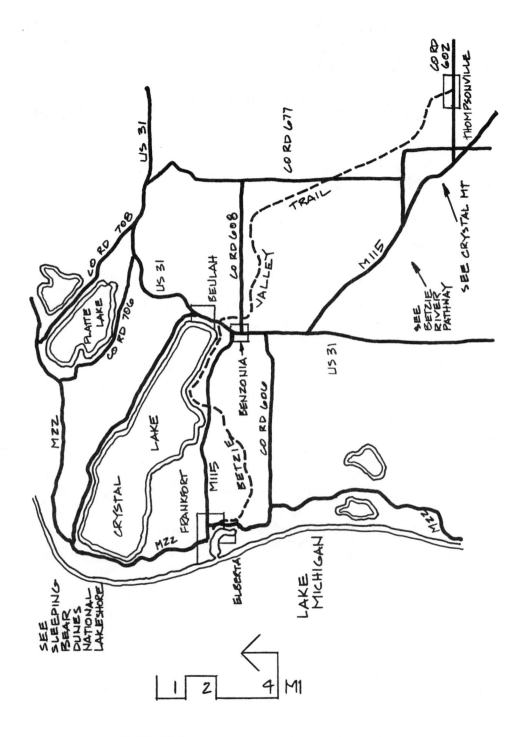

BETSIE VALLEY TRAIL

Sleeping Bear Dunes National Lakeshore
PO Box 277, 9922 Front St   616-326-5134
Empire, MI 49630

Michigan Atlas & Gazetteer Location: 73AB6

County Location: Leelanau

Directions To Trailhead:
Along the Pierce Stocking Scenic Drive south of Glen Haven off M109

Trail Type: Hiking/Walking
Trail Distance: 1.5 mi   Loops: 1   Shortest: NA   Longest: 1.5 mi
Trail Surface: Natural and boardwalk
Trail Use Fee: None
Method Of Ski Trail Grooming: NA
Skiing Ability Suggested: NA
Hiking Trail Difficulty: Moderate
Mountain Biking Ability Suggested: NA
Terrain: Moderate
Camping: Nearby in the National Lakeshore

Managed by the Sleeping Bear Dunes National Lakeshore
A 9 station dune interpretive trail.
A trail guide is available.

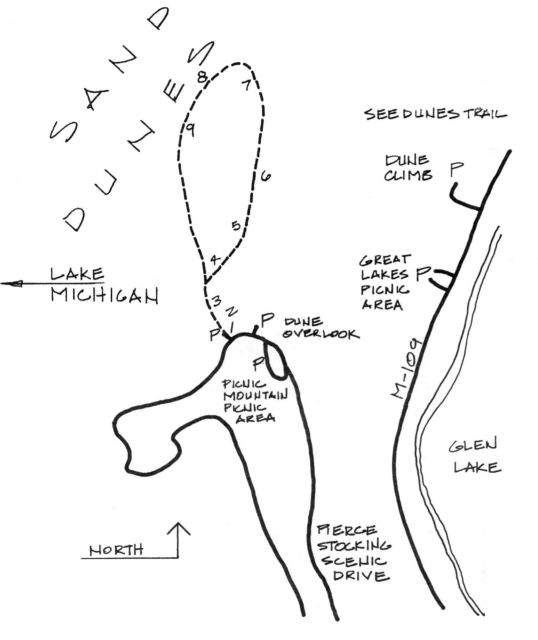

SAND DUNES

LAKE
MICHIGAN

SEE DUNES TRAIL

DUNE
CLIMB P

GREAT
LAKES P
PICNIC
AREA

M-109

GLEN
LAKE

P DUNE
OVERLOOK

PICNIC
MOUNTAIN
PICNIC
AREA

PIERCE
STOCKING
SCENIC
DRIVE

NORTH

COTTONWOOD TRAIL

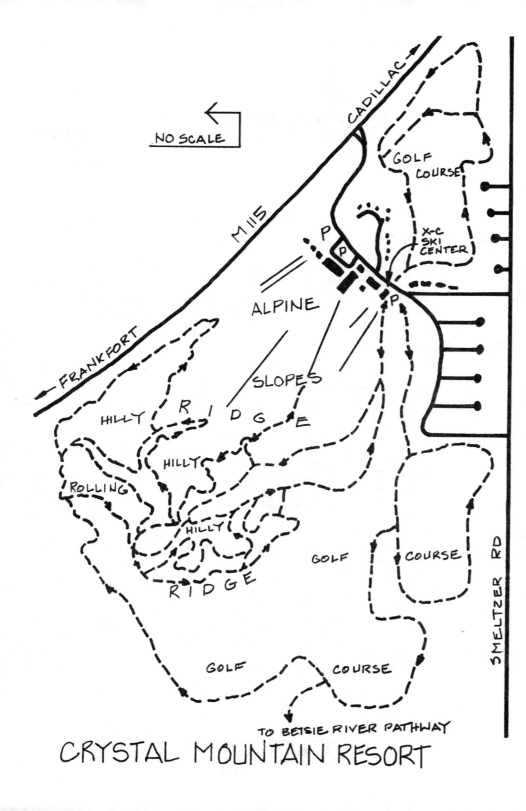

CRYSTAL MOUNTAIN RESORT

Crystal Mountain Resort

Crystal Mountain Resort

Thompsonville, MI 49683

616-378-2911
800-321-4637

Michigan Atlas & Gazetteer Location: 73D67

County Location: Benzie

Directions To Trailhead:
On M115, 36 miles NW of Cadillac 28 miles SW of Traverse City via county roads

Trail Type: Hiking/Walking, Cross Country Skiing, Mountain Biking
Trail Distance: 26 km   Loops: 12   Shortest: 1 km   Longest: 7 km
Trail Surface: Natural
Trail Use Fee: Yes, $5.00 with lift ticket privileges
Method Of Ski Trail Grooming: Double track set with skating lanes
Skiing Ability Suggested: Novice to advanced
Hiking Trail Difficulty: NA
Mountain Biking Ability Suggested: Novice to advanced
Terrain: Steep 15%, Hilly 25%, Moderate 40%, Flat 20%
Camping: None

Privately operated 4 season alpine ski area with extensive cross country trail system.
Lodging, restaurant, instruction, rentals, ski shop, entertainment and an outdoor pool.
Trails were expertly designed by John Capper.
Trail system connects to the Betsie River Pathway to the west.
Very scenic views westward from the trail.
10 km lighted trails.
Quality skating and classic ski rentals available.
Trail access can be gained from the Cheers Chairlift.
The cross country ski center is at the golf course clubhouse.
An exceptional nordic center with terrific trails and expert grooming.

Sleeping Bear Dunes National Lakeshore
PO Box 277, 9922 Front St. (M72)   616-326-5134
Empire, MI 49630

Michigan Atlas & Gazetteer Location: 73A6

County Location: Leelanau

Directions To Trailhead:
South trailhead - On M109 near the Dune Climb, south of Glen Haven
North trailhead - Near Sleeping Bear Dunes Point Coast Guard Station west of Glen Haven

Trail Type: Hiking/Walking
Trail Distance: 3.6 mi   Loops: 2   Shortest: 2.8 mi Longest: 3.5 mi
Trail Surface: Natural sand
Trail Use Fee: None
Method Of Ski Trail Grooming: NA
Skiing Ability Suggested: NA
Hiking Trail Difficulty: Difficult
Mountain Biking Ability Suggested: NA
Terrain: Varies
Camping: Available at 2 locations in the park

Maintained by the Sleeping Bear Dunes National Lakeshore.
South trail is a point to point trail of 3.5 miles round trip leading to the Lake Michigan shoreline from the Dune Climb.
North trail is a 2.8 mile loop with a point to point spur of .4 mile just west of the Maritime Museum west of Glen Haven.
Groups and families are strongly cautioned to stay togather since distances on the dunes are deceiving and its easy to become disoriented and lost.
Wear bright clothing during the hunting season 9/15 to 12/15

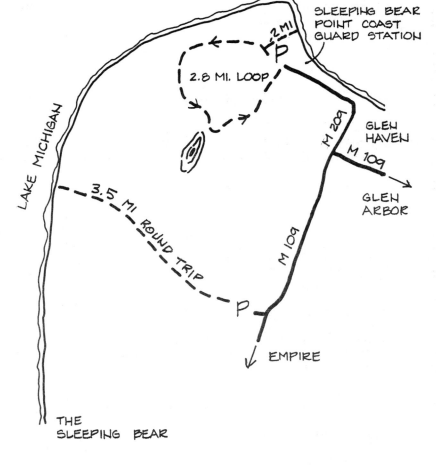

DUNES TRAIL

Empire Bluff Trail

Sleeping Bear Dunes National Lakeshore
PO Box 277, 9922 Front St. (M72)
Empire, MI 49630

616-326-5134

Michigan Atlas & Gazetteer Location: 73B6

County Location: Leelanau

Directions To Trailhead:
1 mile south of Empire on Wilco Rd. along Lake Michigan

Trail Type: Hiking/Walking, Cross Country Skiing, Interpretive
Trail Distance: .75 mi   Loops: NA   Shortest: NA   Longest: NA
Trail Surface: Natural
Trail Use Fee: None
Method Of Ski Trail Grooming: None
Skiing Ability Suggested: Intermediate to advanced
Hiking Trail Difficulty: Moderate
Mountain Biking Ability Suggested: NA
Terrain: Steep 0%, Hilly10%, Moderate 85%, Flat 5%
Camping: Available at two locations in the park

Maintained by the Sleeping Bear Dunes National Lakeshore
This is a point to point trail.
Brochure available explaining the 6 stations of this trail.
Very impressive overlook of Lake Michigan from the end of the trail.
Wear bright clothing during hunting season 9/15 - 12/15.
The trail has some challenging sections.

LAKE MICHIGAN

EMPIRE BLUFF

EMPIRE

M-22

WILCO RD.

FRANKFORT
AND HONOR

NO SCALE

EMPIRE BLUFF TRAIL

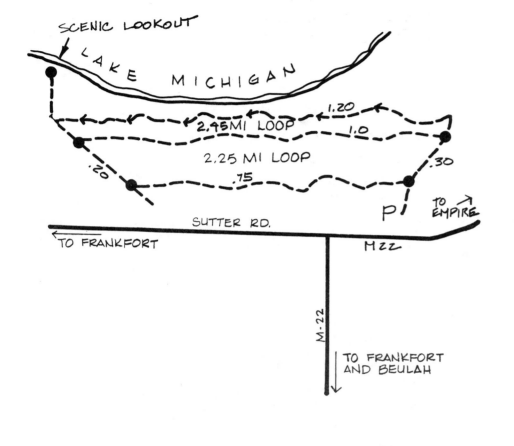

SCENIC LOOKOUT

LAKE MICHIGAN

1.20

2.45 MI LOOP

1.0

2.25 MI LOOP

.30

.20

.75

SUTTER RD.

P

TO EMPIRE

TO FRANKFORT

M22

M-22

TO FRANKFORT AND BEULAH

NO SCALE

OLD INDIAN TRAIL

Old Indian Trail

Sleeping Bear Dunes National Lakeshore
PO Box 277, 9922 Front St. (M72)
Empire, MI 49630

616-326-5134

Michigan Atlas & Gazetteer Location: 73C5

County Location: Benzie

Directions To Trailhead:
Between Frankfort and Empire on the north side of Crystal Lake near the west end of Long Lake
Trailhead - At the intersection of M22 and Sutter Rd.

Trail Type: Hiking/Walking, Cross Country Skiing
Trail Distance: 3.55 mi   Loops: 2   Shortest: 2.25 mi Longest: 2.3 mi
Trail Surface: Natural
Trail Use Fee: None
Method Of Ski Trail Grooming: None
Skiing Ability Suggested: Novice
Hiking Trail Difficulty: Easy
Mountain Biking Ability Suggested: NA
Terrain: Flat to rolling with one steep hill
Camping: Available at two locations in the park

Maintained by the Sleeping Bear Dunes National Lakeshore.
Scenic view of Lake Michigan along the trail.
Wear bright clothing during hunting season 9/15 - 12/15

Platte Plains Trail

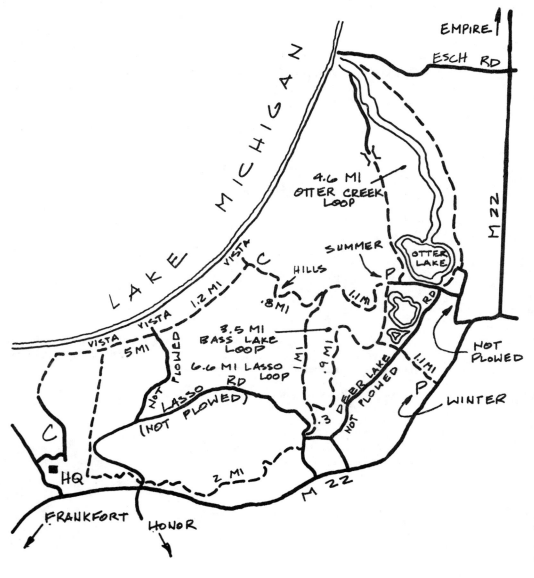

EMPIRE

ESCH RD

LAKE MICHIGAN

M 22

4.6 MI OTTER CREEK LOOP

SUMMER
HILLS
VISTA
C
1.2 MI VISTA
VISTA
.5 MI
.8 MI
OTTER LAKE
P
1.1 MI
3.5 MI BASS LAKE LOOP
6.6 MI LASSO LOOP
LASSO RD (NOT PLOWED)
.9 MI
1 MI
DEER LAKE
.3
NOT PLOWED
1.1 MI
A
RD
P
NOT PLOWED
WINTER

C
■ HQ
2 MI
M 22

FRANKFORT   HONOR

SCALE NOT KNOWN

Sleeping Bear Dunes National Lakeshore
PO Box 277, 9922 Front St.(M72)
Empire, MI 49630

616-326-5134

Michigan Atlas & Gazetteer Location: 73C6

County Location: Benzie

Directions To Trailhead:
North of Platte Lake off M22
South trailhead - At Platte River Campground
North trailhead - At the west end of Esch Rd., 1 mile west of M22 and 3.5 miles south of Empire
Central trailhead - Just south of Trails End Rd. and M22 intersection

Trail Type: Hiking/Walking, Cross Country Skiing
Trail Distance: 18.3 mi   Loops: 3   Shortest: 3.5 mi Longest: 6.6 mi
Trail Surface: Gravel and natural
Trail Use Fee: None
Method Of Ski Trail Grooming: None
Skiing Ability Suggested: Novice to intermediate
Hiking Trail Difficulty: Easy to moderate
Mountain Biking Ability Suggested: NA
Terrain: Steep 0%, Hilly 10%, Moderate 50%, Flat 40%
Camping: Campground at south trailhead and along trail on Lake Michigan

Maintained by the Sleeping Bear Dunes National Lakeshore
Several overlooks of Lake Michigan Extensive trail system of diverse habitat.
Wear bright clothing during hunting season 9/15 - 12/15.
Skiing on unplowed roads provides additional trail length not listed above.
Detailed trail maps available from Sleeping Bear Dunes National Lakeshore.

PLATTE PLAINS TRAIL

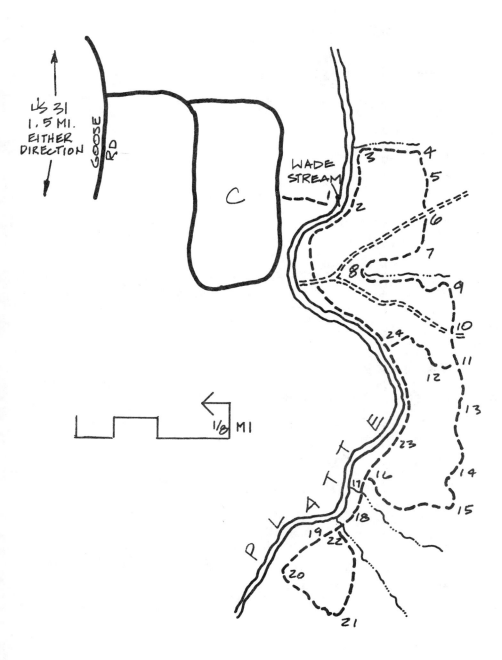

Traverse City Forest Area, Pere Marquette State Forest
404 West 14th Street
Traverse City, MI 49684

616-922-5280

District Forest Manager, Pere Marquette State Forest
8015 Mackinaw Trail
Cadillac, MI 49601

616-775-9727

Michigan Atlas & Gazetteer Location: 73C7

County Location: Benzie

Directions To Trailhead:
2.5 miles southeast of Honor via US31 and Goose Rd. (MUST WADE RIVER TO GET TO PATHWAY)

Trail Type: Hiking/Walking, Interpretive
Trail Distance: 2.5 mi   Loops: 3   Shortest: .5 mi   Longest: 2.5 mi
Trail Surface: Natural and water
Trail Use Fee: None
Method Of Ski Trail Grooming: NA
Skiing Ability Suggested: NA
Hiking Trail Difficulty: Easy
Mountain Biking Ability Suggested: NA
Terrain: Steep 0%, Hilly 70%, Moderate 20%, Flat 10%
Camping: At trailhead

Maintained by the DNR Forest Management Division
This is a 26 station interpretive trail.
Brochure available

PLATTE SPRINGS PATHWAY

Sleeping Bear Dunes National Lakeshore
PO Box 277, 9922 Front St. (M72)   616-326-5134
Empire, MI 49630

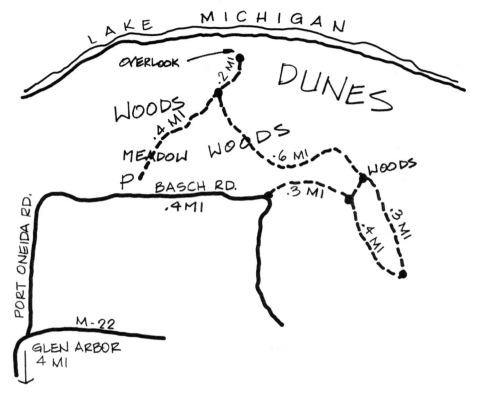

Michigan Atlas & Gazetteer Location: 73A7

County Location: Leelanau

Directions To Trailhead:
Between Glen Arbor and Leland, north of M22 on Lake Michigan
Trailhead - 5 miles north of Glen Arbor, turn north on Port Oneida Rd., parking
area is on the north side of the road, about .5 mile after Point Oneida Rd. turns
east..

Trail Type: Hiking/Walking
Trail Distance: 2.8 mi   Loops: 1   Shortest: NA   Longest: 2.7 mi
Trail Surface: Natural and gavel road
Trail Use Fee: None
Method Of Ski Trail Grooming: NA
Skiing Ability Suggested: NA
Hiking Trail Difficulty: Moderate
Mountain Biking Ability Suggested: NA
Terrain: Hilly
Camping: Available at 2 locations in the park

Maintained by the Sleeping Bear Dunes National Lakeshore
Quite varied environments along the trail, including a meadow, beech-maple
forest, an open sand dune and an outstanding vista of Lake Michigan.
Part of the loop trail is on a vehicle road.
Trail can be hiked in either direction.
Wear bright clothing during hunting season 9/15 - 12/15.

PYRAMID POINT TRAIL

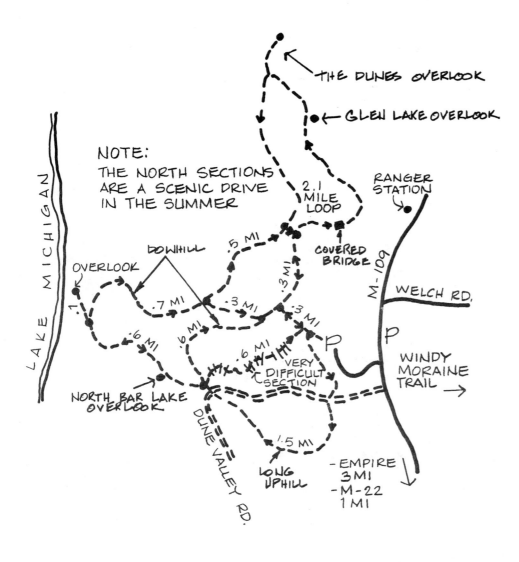

NOTE:
THE NORTH SECTIONS ARE A SCENIC DRIVE IN THE SUMMER

THE DUNES OVERLOOK

GLEN LAKE OVERLOOK

RANGER STATION

2.1 MILE LOOP

COVERED BRIDGE

M-109

WELCH RD.

DOWNHILL

.5 MI

OVERLOOK

.7 MI

.3 MI

.3 MI

.3 MI

.6 MI

.6 MI

.6 MI

.1

P

P

WINDY MORAINE TRAIL →

VERY DIFFICULT SECTION

NORTH BAR LAKE OVERLOOK

DUNE VALLEY RD.

LONG UPHILL

1.5 MI

- EMPIRE 3 MI
- M-22 1 MI

LAKE MICHIGAN

.5   1 MI

SCENIC DRIVE CROSS COUNTRY SKI TRAIL

Sleeping Bear Dunes National Lakeshore
PO Box 277, 9922 Front St. (M72)   616-326-5134
Empire, MI 49630

Michigan Atlas & Gazetteer Location: 73AB6

County Location: Leelanau

Directions To Trailhead:
SW of Glen Lake on M109 Trailhead - 3 miles north of Empire on M109 just south of Welch Rd. then a short distance to the trailhead parking lot on the west side of the road .

Trail Type: Cross Country Skiing
Trail Distance: 7.2 mi   Loops: 5+   Shortest: 2.1 mi Longest: 6 mi
Trail Surface: Natural
Trail Use Fee: None
Method Of Ski Trail Grooming: None
Skiing Ability Suggested: Novice and advanced
Hiking Trail Difficulty: Moderate to difficult
Mountain Biking Ability Suggested: NA
Terrain: Steep 5%, Hilly 40%, Moderate 40%, Flat 15%
Camping: Available at two locations in the park

Maintained by the Sleeping Bear Dunes National Lakeshore
An advanced return trail is very difficult and should only be attempted by experienced skiers . Spectacular scenic overlook of the shore of Lake Michigan and the dunes.
Across the road from the Windy Moraine Trail.
Sandy snow may be encountered near overlooks. Previously this trail was known as the Shauger Hill Trail. Scenic views of Glen Lake, Lake Michigan and the dunes. Parts of the trail are the Pierce Stocking Scenic Drive used in the snowless months. These sections can be skied in both directions.
The downhill sections of the drive are great for telemarking.
Wear bright clothing during hunting season 9/15 - 12/15.

Sleeping Bear Dunes National Lakeshore
PO Box 277, 9922 Front St.
Empire, MI 49630

616-326-5134

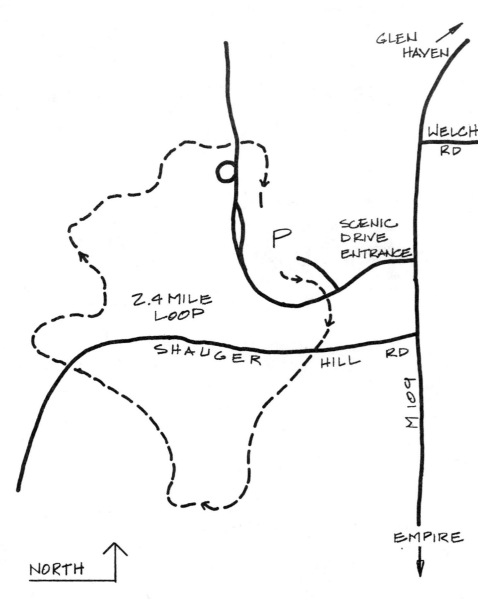

Michigan Atlas & Gazetteer Location: 73B6

County Location: Leelanau

Directions To Trailhead:
Between Empire and Glen Haven on M109. Trailhead at the first parking lot on the Stocking Scenic Drive

Trail Type: Hiking/Walking
Trail Distance: 2.4 mi   Loops: 1   Shortest: NA   Longest: 2.4 mi
Trail Surface: Natural
Trail Use Fee: None
Method Of Ski Trail Grooming: NA
Skiing Ability Suggested: NA
Hiking Trail Difficulty: Moderate
Mountain Biking Ability Suggested: NA
Terrain: Steep 30%, Hilly 30%, Moderate 25%, Flat 15%
Camping: Campgrounds in the National Lakeshore and surrounding area

Maintained by the Sleeping Bear Dunes National Lakeshore
This is part of the Scenic Drive Cross Country Ski Trail system

SHAUGER HILL HIKING TRAIL

Grand Traverse Regional Land Conservancy
624 Third St.
Traverse City, MI 49684

616-929-7911

Michigan Atlas & Gazetteer Location: 73C6

County Location: Benzie

Directions To Trailhead:
Located on the edge of Beulah, just west US 31 and north of Narrow Guage Rd

Trail Type: Hiking/Walking, Interpretive
Trail Distance: 1.5 mi   Loops: 2   Shortest: .75 mi Longest: 1 mi
Trail Surface: Natural
Trail Use Fee: None
Method Of Ski Trail Grooming: NA
Skiing Ability Suggested: NA
Hiking Trail Difficulty: Easy
Mountain Biking Ability Suggested: NA
Terrain: Steep 0%, Hilly 0%, Moderate 0%, Flat 100%
Camping: None, but camprounds are nearby

Maintained by the Grnd Traverse Regional Land Conservancy
This 132 acre preserve was once a vegetable farm until 1982.

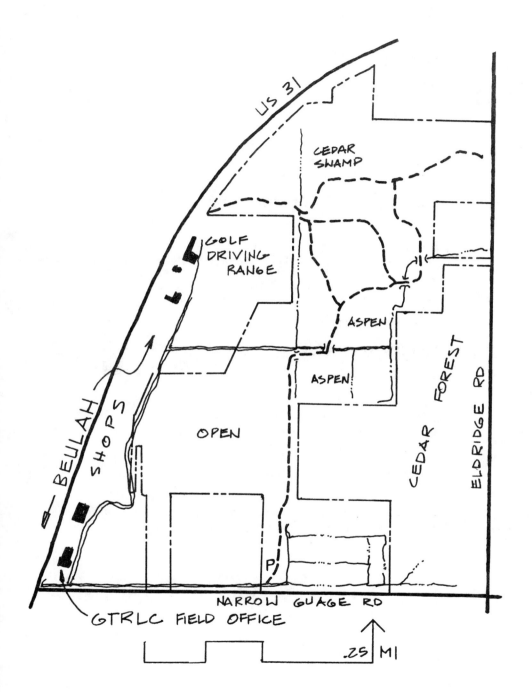

US 31

CEDAR SWAMP

GOLF DRIVING RANGE

ASPEN

ASPEN

CEDAR FOREST

ELDRIDGE RD

OPEN

BEULAH SHOPS

P

NARROW GUAGE RD

GTRLC FIELD OFFICE

.25 MI

TRAPP FARM NATURE PRESERVE

Grand Traverse Regional Land Conservancy
624 Third St
Traverse City, MI 49684

616-929-7911

Michigan Atlas & Gazetteer Location: 73D5

County Location: Benzie

Directions To Trailhead:
From Benzonia, take Grace Rd west. Follow Grace Rd to M22. Take M22 south about 1 mile south of the M 22 and Herron Rd intersection. Sign on east side of the road marks the trailhead location. Trail starts as a 2 track dirt path through a field.

Trail Type: Hiking/Walking, Cross Country Skiing, Interpretive
Trail Distance: .5 mi   Loops: NA   Shortest: NA   Longest: NA
Trail Surface: Natural
Trail Use Fee: None
Method Of Ski Trail Grooming: None
Skiing Ability Suggested: Novice
Hiking Trail Difficulty: Easy
Mountain Biking Ability Suggested: NA
Terrain: Steep 0%, Hilly 0%, Moderate 0%, Flat 100%
Camping: None

Maintained by the Grand Traverse Regional Land Conservancy
Property borders the west shore of Upper Herring Lake.
The Preserve is 122 acres.

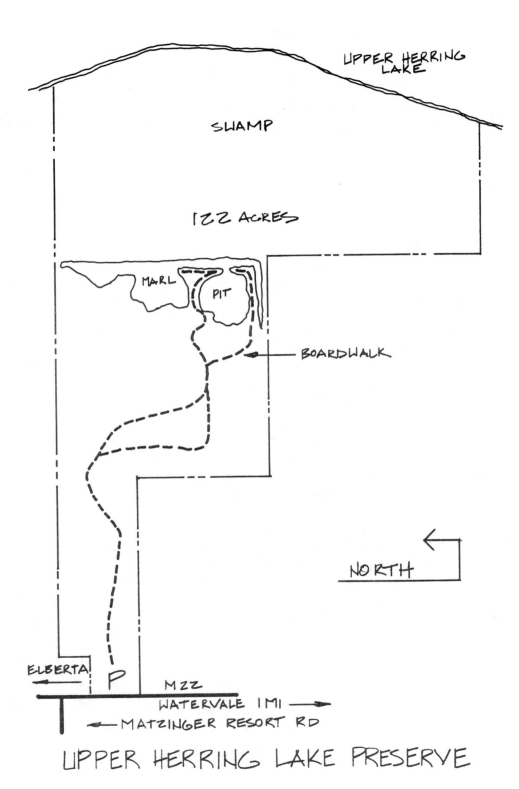

UPPER HERRING LAKE
SWAMP
122 ACRES
MARL
PIT
BOARDWALK
NORTH
ELBERTA
P
M22
WATERVALE 1MI →
← MATZINGER RESORT RD

UPPER HERRING LAKE PRESERVE

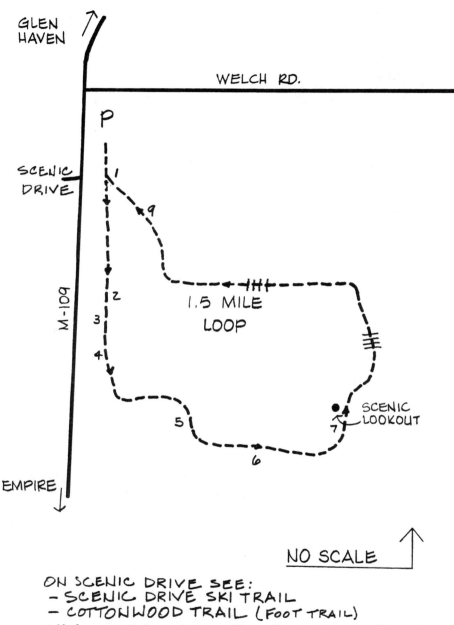

GLEN HAVEN

WELCH RD.

P

SCENIC DRIVE

M-109

1
9
2
3
4
5
6
7

1.5 MILE LOOP

SCENIC LOOKOUT

EMPIRE

NO SCALE

ON SCENIC DRIVE SEE:
- SCENIC DRIVE SKI TRAIL
- COTTONWOOD TRAIL (FOOT TRAIL)
SEE MANY OTHER TRAILS IN THE S.B.D.N.L.

WINDY MORAINE TRAIL

Sleeping Bear Dunes National Lakeshore
PO Box 277, 9922 Front St. (M72)
Empire, MI 49630

616-326-5134

Michigan Atlas & Gazetteer Location: 73B6

County Location: Leelanau

Directions To Trailhead:
SW of Glen Lake on M109
Trailhead - 3 miles north of Empire on Welch Rd. just east of M109.

Trail Type: Hiking/Walking, Interpretive
Trail Distance: 1.5 mi   Loops: 1   Shortest: Longest: 1.5 mi
Trail Surface: Natural
Trail Use Fee: None
Method Of Ski Trail Grooming: None
Skiing Ability Suggested: Novice
Hiking Trail Difficulty: Easy
Mountain Biking Ability Suggested: NA
Terrain: Rolling
Camping: Available at two locations in the park

Maintained by the Sleeping Bear Dunes National Lakeshore
Across M109 from the Scenic Drive Cross Country Ski Trail.
The trail consists of 1/3 downhill, 1/3 flat and 1/3 uphill.
Wear bright clothing during hunting season 9/15 - 12/15.

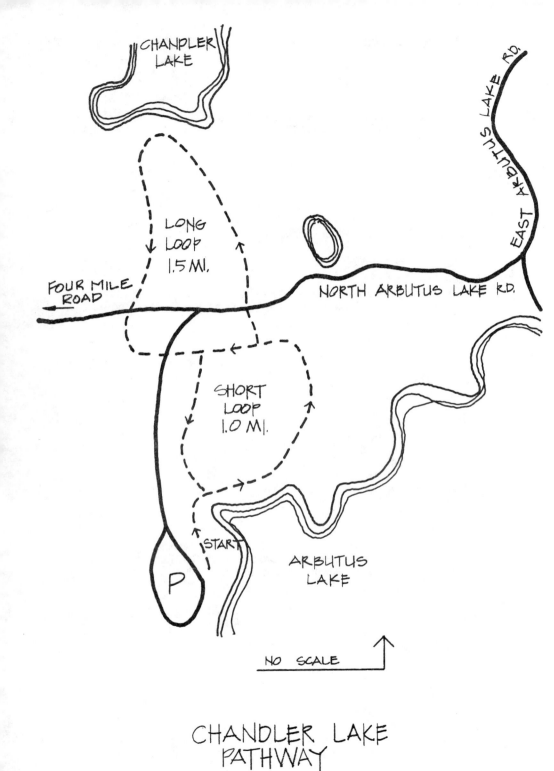

Chandler Lake Pathway

Traverse City Forest Area, Pere Marquette State Forest
404 W. 14th St   616-922-5280
Traverse City, MI 49684

District Forest Manger, Pere Marquette State Forest
8015 Mackinaw Trail   616-775-9727
Cadillac, MI 49601

Michigan Atlas & Gazetteer Location: 74C3

County Location: Grand Traverse

Directions To Trailhead:
10 miles southeast of Traverse City via Garfield Rd, east on Potter Rd, south on
4 Mile Rd, east on N. Arbutus Rd

Trail Type: Hiking/Walking, Cross Country Skiing, Mountain Biking
Trail Distance: 2.5 mi   Loops: 2   Shortest: 1 mi   Longest: 1.5 mi
Trail Surface: Natural
Trail Use Fee: None
Method Of Ski Trail Grooming: None
Skiing Ability Suggested: Novice
Hiking Trail Difficulty: Easy
Mountain Biking Ability Suggested: Novice
Terrain: Steep 0%, Hilly 0%, Moderate 20%, Flat 80%
Camping: State Forest Campground at trailhead

Maintained by the DNR Forest Management Division

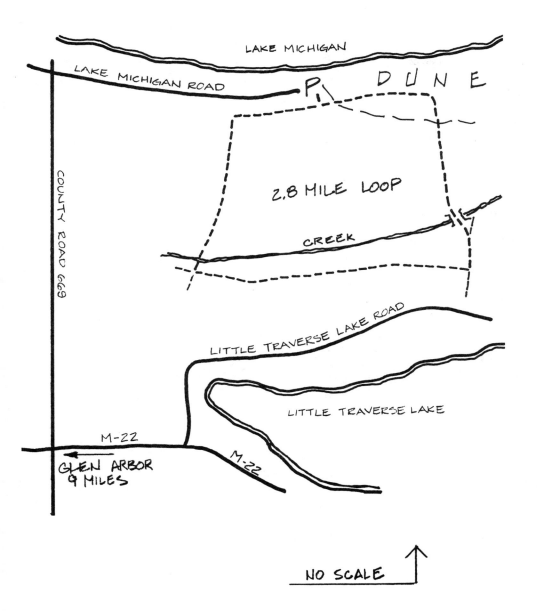

Good Harbor Bay Ski Trail

Sleeping Bear Dunes National Lakeshore
PO Box 277, 9922 Front St. (M72)   616-326-5134
Empire, MI 49630

Michigan Atlas & Gazetteer Location: 74A1

County Location: Leelanau

Directions To Trailhead:
Between Glen Arbor and Leland, north of M22 on Lake Michigan.
Trailhead - On M22 between Little Traverse Lake and Bass Lake, take Co Rd
669 to Lake Michigan and turn right and proceed to end of the road

Trail Type: Hiking/Walking, Cross Country Skiing
Trail Distance: 2.8 mi   Loops: 1   Shortest: NA   Longest: 2.8 mi
Trail Surface: Natural
Trail Use Fee: None
Method Of Ski Trail Grooming: None
Skiing Ability Suggested: Novice
Hiking Trail Difficulty: Easy
Mountain Biking Ability Suggested: NA
Terrain: Flat
Camping: Available at 2 locations in the park

Maintained by the Sleeping Bear Dunes National Lakeshore
Trailhead along the shore of Lake Michigan

GOOD HARBOR BAY SKI TRAIL

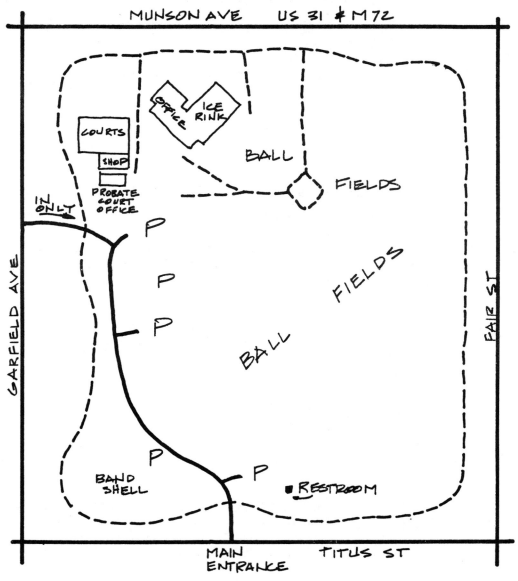

MUNSON AVE   US 31 & M 72

GARFIELD AVE

IN ONLY

COURTS

SHOP

PROBATE COURT OFFICE

OFFICE

ICE RINK

BALL

FIELDS

P

P

P

BALL   FIELDS

P

P

BAND SHELL

RESTROOM

FAIR ST

MAIN ENTRANCE   TITUS ST

NORTH

GRAND TRAVERSE COUNTY CIVIC CENTER

Grand Traverse County Parks and Recreation Department.
1125 W. Civic Center Drive
Traverse City, MI 49684   616-922-4818

Michigan Atlas & Gazetteer Location: 74B3

County Location: Grand Traverse

Directions To Trailhead:
In downtown Traverse City at the county Civic Center

Trail Type: Hiking/Walking, Cross Country Skiing
Trail Distance: 1 mi   Loops: 1   Shortest: NA   Longest: 1 mi
Trail Surface: Paved 8' wide
Trail Use Fee: None
Method Of Ski Trail Grooming: Yes
Skiing Ability Suggested: Novice
Hiking Trail Difficulty: Easy
Mountain Biking Ability Suggested: NA
Terrain: Steep 0%, Hilly 0%, Moderate 5%, Flat 95%
Camping: None

Maintained by the Grand Traverse County Parks and Recreation Department
Part of a multi recreational facility complex .

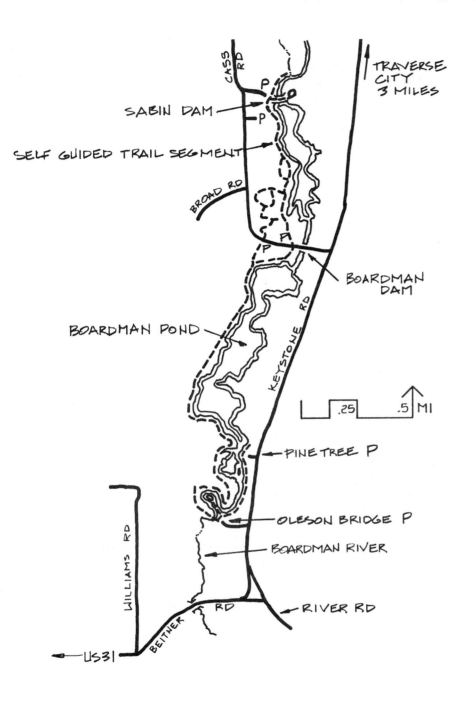

SABIN DAM

SELF GUIDED TRAIL SEGMENT

CASS RD

BROAD RD

TRAVERSE CITY 3 MILES

P

P

P

P

BOARDMAN DAM

BOARDMAN POND

KEYSTONE RD

PINE TREE P

OLESON BRIDGE P

BOARDMAN RIVER

WILLIAMS RD

BEITHER RD

RIVER RD

US 31

.25 .5 MI

GRAND TRAVERSE
NATURAL EDUCATION PRESERVE

Grand Traverse County Parks and Recreation Department
1125 W. Civic Center Drive
Traverse City, MI 49684

616-922-4818

Michigan Atlas & Gazetteer Location: 74C23

County Location: Grand Traverse

Directions To Trailhead:
South of Traverse City on the Boardman River at Sabin and Boardman Dams.
Trailheads off Cass Rd and Keystone Road at Sabin Dam, Boardman Dam,
Pine Tree and Oleson Bridge.

Trail Type: Hiking/Walking, Cross Country Skiing, Interpretive
Trail Distance: 6 mi   Loops: Many   Shortest: .25 mi Longest: 2 mi
Trail Surface: Wood chips
Trail Use Fee: None
Method Of Ski Trail Grooming: None
Skiing Ability Suggested: Novice
Hiking Trail Difficulty: Easy
Mountain Biking Ability Suggested: NA
Terrain: Steep 0%, Hilly 40%, Moderate 40%, Flat 20%
Camping: None

Owned by Grand Traverse County as a park and teaching facility
374 acres along the Boardman River
The self guided nature trail off Cass Rd has 9 stations.
Trail guide is available.
Surprisingly secluded area very close to Traverse City.

Grand Traverse Resort Village
PO Box 404
Acme, MI 49610-0404

616-938-2100
800-748-0303

Michigan Atlas & Gazetteer Location: 74B4

County Location: Grand Traverse

Directions To Trailhead:
Near M72 and US31 intersection 6 miles NE of Traverse City

Trail Type: Hiking/Walking, Cross Country Skiing
Trail Distance: 11+ mi   Loops: Many   Shortest: .5 mi   Longest: 5 mi
Trail Surface: Paved, gravel and natural
Trail Use Fee: Yes
Method Of Ski Trail Grooming: Track set
Skiing Ability Suggested: Novice to intermediate
Hiking Trail Difficulty: Easy to moderate
Mountain Biking Ability Suggested: Novice to intermediate
Terrain: Steep 0%, Hilly 15%, Moderate 60%, Flat 25%
Camping: Campground available at Traverse City State Park

A luxury 4 seasons resort with all facilities including golf courses, pool, tennis courts, racketball courts to name a few. The resort is large with over 750 rooms. Ski center is at the golf course started building on M72.
Lighted ski trail available.
Added in 1995, a 5.4 mile network of trails explore the resort property between US31 and the Grand Traverse Bay. Open to hiking and mountain bikes, this trail passes through woods, meadows and orchards. Picnic areas are also along this trail. The trail connects to the The Music House on US31.
A separate walking/jogging trail around the resort is 2 miles long.

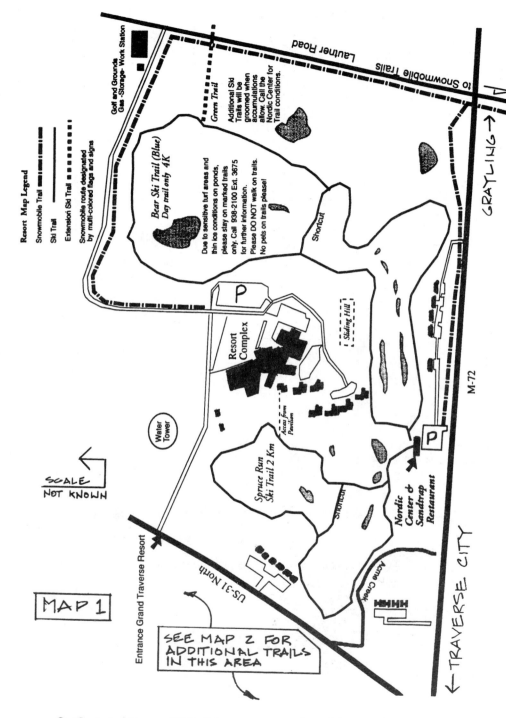

MAP 1

SEE MAP 2 FOR ADDITIONAL TRAILS IN THIS AREA

GRAND TRAVERSE RESORT

SCALE NOT KNOWN

Resort Map Legend
Snowmobile Trail
Ski Trail
Extension Ski Trail
Snowmobile route designated by multi-colored flags and signs

Golf and Grounds
Gas -Storage- Work Station

Green Trail

Additional Ski Trails will be groomed when accumulations allow. Call the Nordic Center for Trail conditions.

Due to sensitive turf areas and thin ice conditions on ponds, please stay on marked trails only. Call 938-2100 Ext. 3675 for further information.
Please DO NOT walk on trails. No pets on trails please!

Bear Ski Trail (Blue)
Day trail only 4K

Lautner Road

to Snowmobile Trails

GRAYLING →

Shortcut

Resort Complex

Skiing Hill

P

Water Tower

Access from Pavilion

Spruce Run Ski Trail 2 Km

Shortcut

Nordic Center & Sandtrap Restaurant

P

M-72

← TRAVERSE CITY

Entrance Grand Traverse Resort

US-31 North

Acme Creek

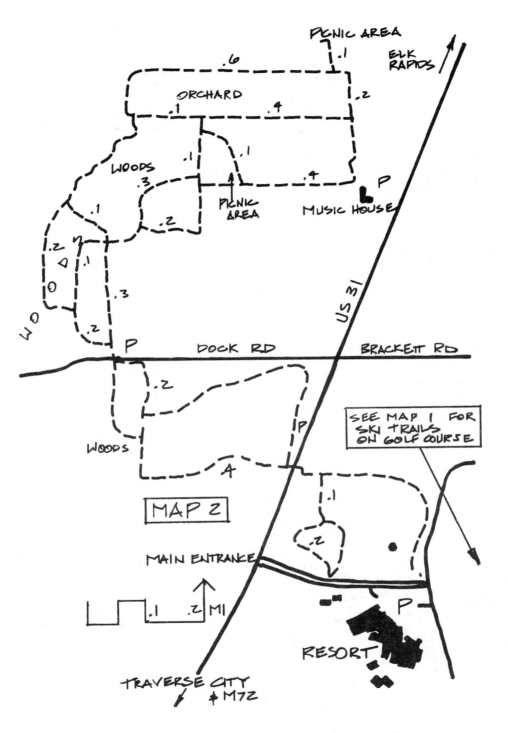

PICNIC AREA

ELK RAPIDS

.6

.1

ORCHARD

.2

.1

.4

WOODS

.1

.1

.4

.3

P

.2

PICNIC AREA

MUSIC HOUSE

.1

US 31

.2

W O O D S

.1

.3

.2

P

DOCK RD

BRACKETT RD

.2

SEE MAP 1 FOR SKI TRAILS ON GOLF COURSE

WOODS

P

MAP 2

.4

.1

.2

MAIN ENTRANCE

.1

.2 MI

RESORT

P

TRAVERSE CITY & M72

GRAND TRAVERSE RESORT

286.1

Traverse City Recreation Department
625 Woodmere St.
Traverse City, MI 49684

616-922-4910
616-947-8566

Michigan Atlas & Gazetteer Location: 74B2

County Location: Grand Traverse

Directions To Trailhead:
One mile west of the Traverse City city limit, at the end of Randolph St. in the
hills overlooking Traverse City

Trail Type: Hiking/Walking, Cross Country Skiing
Trail Distance: 2.5 km   Loops: 2   Shortest: 1 km   Longest: 1.5 km
Trail Surface: Natural
Trail Use Fee: Yes,
Method Of Ski Trail Grooming: Track set daily
Skiing Ability Suggested: Novice to advanced
Hiking Trail Difficulty: NA
Mountain Biking Ability Suggested: NA
Terrain: Steep 0%, Hilly 20%, Moderate 20%, Flat 60%
Camping: None

Downhill ski area operated by Traverse City Recreation Department
Warming area, rentals and snack bar
Loops are relatively short but most are very challenging
Lighted for cross country ski trails and downhill slopes

NO MAP

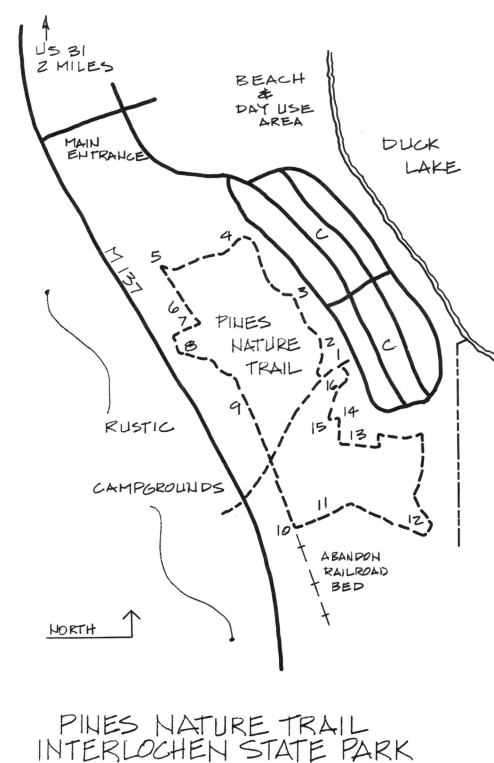

US 31
2 MILES

M 137

MAIN
ENTRANCE

BEACH
&
DAY USE
AREA

DUCK
LAKE

C

4

5

3

6 7

8

PINES
NATURE
TRAIL

C

2
1

16

9

14

15   13

11

10

12

RUSTIC

CAMPGROUNDS

ABANDON
RAILROAD
BED

NORTH

PINES NATURE TRAIL
INTERLOCHEN STATE PARK

Interlochen State Park
M137
Interlochen, Mi 49643

616-276-9511

DNR Parks and Recreation Division

616-992-5270
517-275-5151

Michigan Atlas & Gazetteer Location: 74C1

County Location: Grand Traverse

Directions To Trailhead:
Interlochen is located southwest of Traverse City via US31, then south at
Interlochen Corners for 2 miles to the park.

Trail Type: Hiking/Walking, Cross Country Skiing, Interpretive
Trail Distance: 3 mi   Loops: Several   Shortest: Longest:
Trail Surface: Natural and gravel
Trail Use Fee: None, but vehicle entry permit required
Method Of Ski Trail Grooming: None
Skiing Ability Suggested: Novice
Hiking Trail Difficulty: Easy
Mountain Biking Ability Suggested: NA
Terrain: Steep 0%, Hilly 0%, Moderate 20%, Flat 80%
Camping: On site

Maintained by the DNR Parks and Recreation Division
A popular state park with swimming and boating.
This is a interpretive trail of the history and nature of the area.
A trail guide is available for the 16 station trail.

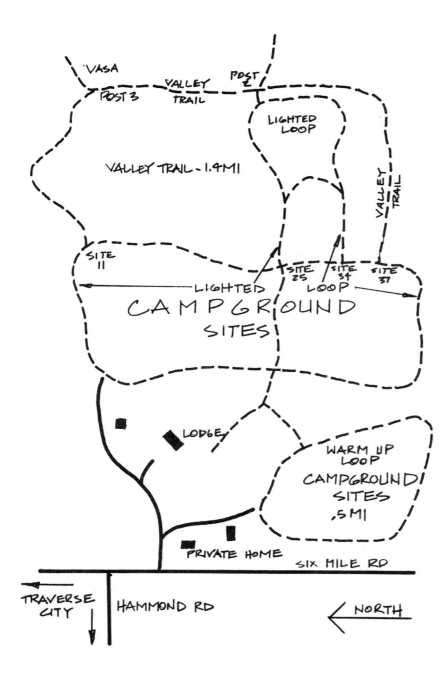

Jellystone Park Camp Resort
4050 Hammond Rd
Traverse City, MI 49684

616-947-2770

Michigan Atlas & Gazetteer Location: 74C4

County Location: Grand Traverse

Directions To Trailhead:
East of Traverse City and 2 miles south of East Grand Traverse Bay. From US31/M72, take 3 Mile Rd south to the end (Hammond Rd), then left (east) on Hammond Rd to the resort at the end of the road.

Trail Type: Hiking/Walking, Cross Country Skiing, Mountain Biking, Interpretive
Trail Distance: 2 mi   Loops: Shortest: Longest:
Trail Surface: Natural, paved and gravel
Trail Use Fee: Yes
Method Of Ski Trail Grooming: Track set
Skiing Ability Suggested: Novice to intermediate
Hiking Trail Difficulty: Easy
Mountain Biking Ability Suggested: Novice to intermediate
Terrain: Steep 0%, Hilly 0%, Moderate 20%, Flat 80%
Camping: Complete private campground on site

Privately operated campgound
Total camp resort with all facilities including a pool, playground, complete hookups, day lodge and camp store.
Trails connect with the Vasa Trail (see other listing).
Popular starting point for skiing and mountain biking on the Vasa Trail.
Ideal camping area for mountain biking on the Vasa trail.
Some ski trails in the resort are campground roads in the summer.
Lighted ski trails provided.

JELLYSTONE PARK

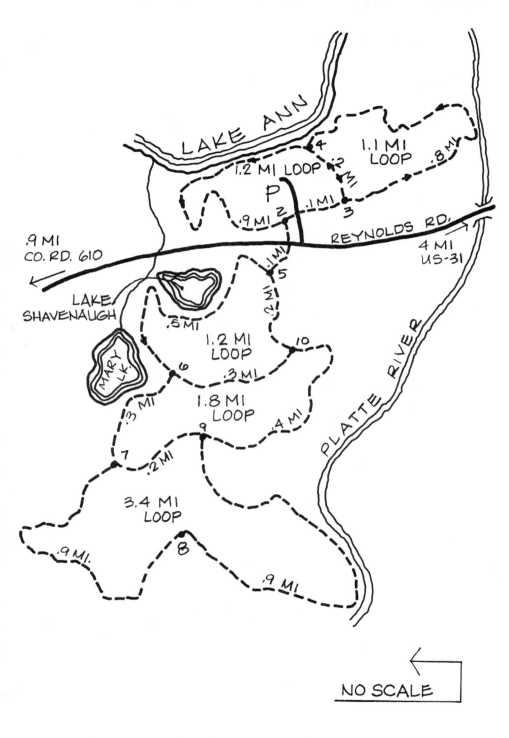

Lake Ann Pathway

Traverse City Forest Area, Pere Marquette State Forest
404 W 14th St.   616-922-5280
Traverse City, MI 49684

District Forest Manager, Pere Marquette State Forest
Rte. 1, 8015 South US131   616-775-9727
Cadillac, MI 49601

Michigan Atlas & Gazetteer Location: 74C1

County Location: Benzie

Directions To Trailhead:
West of Traverse City between M72 and US31 near Lake Ann
Trailhead - From Lake Ann west on Almira Rd. to Reynolds Rd., then south 2.5
miles to Lake Ann State Forest   Campground

Trail Type: Hiking/Walking, Cross Country Skiing, Mountain Biking
Trail Distance: 5.8 mi   Loops: 5   Shortest: 1 mi   Longest: 3 mi
Trail Surface: Natural
Trail Use Fee: None
Method Of Ski Trail Grooming: Track set
Skiing Ability Suggested: Novice to advanced
Hiking Trail Difficulty: Easy to moderate
Mountain Biking Ability Suggested: Novice to intermediate
Terrain: Steep 0%, Hilly 10%, Moderate 40%, Flat 50%
Camping: Campground at trailhead

Maintained by the DNR Forest Management Division
Loops provide interesting skiing for skiers of all skill levels.
The loops west of Reynolds Rd are some of the best designed in the DNR
system. Simply a joy to ski!!!
Other contacts:
        DNR Forest Management Division Office, Lansing, 517-373-1275
        DNR Forest Management Region Office, Roscommon, 517-275-5151

LAKE ANN PATHWAY

Traverse City Area Forest, Pere Marquette State Forest
404 14th St.   616-946-4920
Traverse City, MI 49684

District Forest Manager, Pere Marquette State Forest
Rte 1, 8015 South US131   616-775-9727
Cadillac, MI 49601

Michigan Atlas & Gazetteer Location: 74C1

County Location: Grand Traverse

Directions To Trailhead:
12 miles SW of Traverse City on US31 at near Interlochen
Trailhead - West 1.5 miles from Interlochen on US31 to Wildwood Rd., then
north 1 mile to state forest campground

Trail Type: Hiking/Walking, Cross Country Skiing, Mountain Biking, Interpretive
Trail Distance: 6.3 mi   Loops: 3   Shortest: 2.4 mi Longest: 6.15 mi
Trail Surface: Natural
Trail Use Fee: None
Method Of Ski Trail Grooming: Track Set
Skiing Ability Suggested: Novice
Hiking Trail Difficulty: Easy
Mountain Biking Ability Suggested: Novice to intermediate
Terrain: Steep 0%, Hilly 0%, Moderate 50%, Flat 50%
Camping: Campground available at trailhead

Maintained by the DNR Forest Management Division
Lake DuBonnet is an artifical lake with a floating island.
21 station interpretive trail
Trail reviewed in the Great Lakes Skier, fall 1989.
Other contacts:
       DNR Forest Management Division Office, Lansing, 517-373-1275
       DNR Forest Management Region Office, Roscommon, 517-275-5151

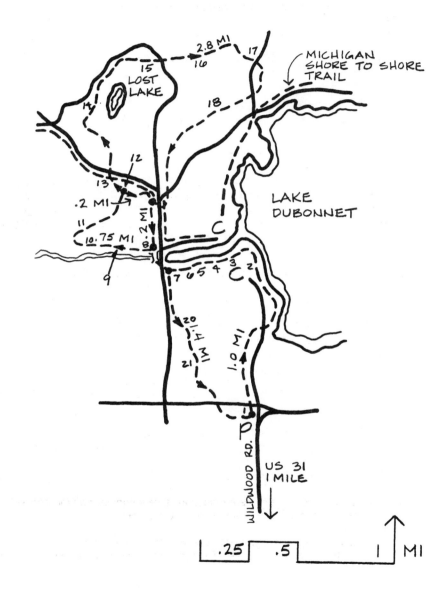

LOST LAKE PATHWAY

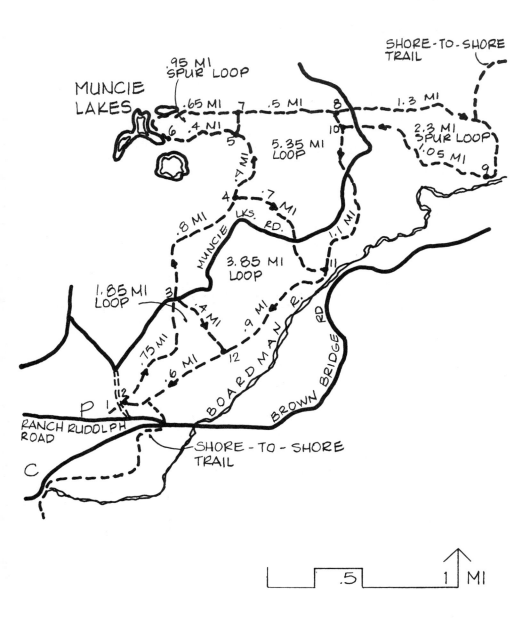

SHORE-TO-SHORE TRAIL

.95 MI SPUR LOOP

MUNCIE LAKES

.65 MI 7 .5 MI 8 1.3 MI

.6 .4 MI 5 10 2.3 MI SPUR LOOP

.05 MI 9

5.35 MI LOOP

.7 MI

4 .7 MI

.8 MI

MUNCIE LKS. RD.

1.1 MI

3.85 MI LOOP

11

1.85 MI LOOP 3

.4 MI .9 MI

.75 MI 12 .6 MI

BOARDMAN R.

BROWN BRIDGE RD.

P 1 2

RANCH RUDOLPH ROAD

C

SHORE-TO-SHORE TRAIL

.5   1 MI

MUNCIE LAKES PATHWAY

Muncie Lakes Pathway

Traverse City Forest Area, Pere Marquette State Forest
404 W 14th St.   616-946-4920
Traverse City, MI 49684

District Forest Manager, Pere Marquette State Forest
Rte 1, 8015 South US131   616-775-9727
Cadillac, MI 49601

Michigan Atlas & Gazetteer Location: 74C4,75C4

County Location: Grand Traverse

Directions To Trailhead:
SE of Traverse City about 13 miles near Ranch Rudolf resort. From Traverse City take Garfield Ave south to Hammond Rd., then east on Hammond Rd to High Lake Rd, south .5 mile to Supply Rd., then east on Supply Rd. about 3 miles to Rennie Lake Rd., then turn south until it dead ends, turn left and the parking lot is about 2 miles away .

Trail Type: Hiking/Walking, Cross Country Skiing, Mountain Biking
Trail Distance: 11.5 mi   Loops: 5   Shortest: .95 mi Longest: 5.35 mi
Trail Surface: Natural
Trail Use Fee: None
Method Of Ski Trail Grooming: Track set
Skiing Ability Suggested: Novice
Hiking Trail Difficulty: Easy
Mountain Biking Ability Suggested: Novice
Terrain: Steep 0%, Hilly 5%, Moderate 60%, Flat 35%
Camping: State forest CG are nearby and Jellystone Campground on 5 Mile Rd

Maintained by the DNR Forest Management Division
The first cross country ski trail developed by the DNR in the early 1970's. Numerous refinements have been made since that time to make this a delightful trail that passes by the beautiful Boardman River.
A trail connects to Ranch Rudolf with its food and lodging facilities.
Many hills throughout the system makes for a very popular trail for local skiers.
Sand Lakes Quiet Area is only a few miles to the east.
Other contacts:
        DNR Forest Management Division Office, Lansing, 517-373-1275
        DNR Forest Management Region Office, Roscommon, 517-275-5151

74

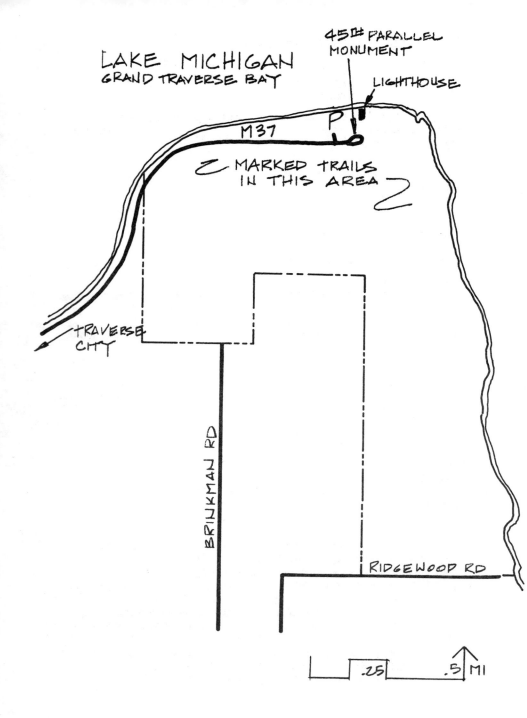

LAKE MICHIGAN
GRAND TRAVERSE BAY

45ᵗʰ PARALLEL
MONUMENT

LIGHTHOUSE

M37

MARKED TRAILS
IN THIS AREA

TRAVERSE
CITY

BRINKMAN RD

RIDGEWOOD RD

.25 .5 MI

Old Mission State Park

DNR Parks and Recreation Division
PO Box 30028
Lansing, MI 48909

517-373-1270

Michigan Atlas & Gazetteer Location: 74A4

County Location: Grand Traverse

Directions To Trailhead:
North end of Old Mission peninsula on M37.

Trail Type: Hiking/Walking, Cross Country Skiing
Trail Distance: 3 mi?   Loops: Shortest: Longest:
Trail Surface: Natural
Trail Use Fee: None
Method Of Ski Trail Grooming: None
Skiing Ability Suggested: Novice
Hiking Trail Difficulty: Easy
Mountain Biking Ability Suggested: NA
Terrain: Steep 0%, Hilly 0%, Moderate 15%, Flat 85%
Camping: None

Owned by the state of Michigan
Managed by the DNR Parks and Recreation Division
Northern portion - Leased to Peninsula Township for park purposes
Southern portion - DNR plans to lease remainder of land to the township for park purposes.

Some trails exist around the tip near the lighthouse. Some casual trail marking has been done but may not be marked well.

OLD MISSION STATE PARK

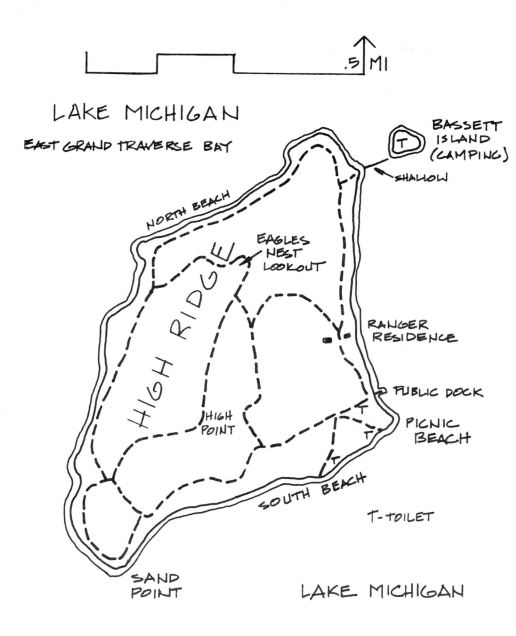

LAKE MICHIGAN

EAST GRAND TRAVERSE BAY

BASSETT ISLAND (CAMPING)

T

SHALLOW

NORTH BEACH

EAGLES NEST LOOKOUT

HIGH RIDGE

RANGER RESIDENCE

PUBLIC DOCK

HIGH POINT

PICNIC BEACH

T

T

T

SOUTH BEACH

T - TOILET

SAND POINT

LAKE MICHIGAN

POWER ISLAND WILDERNESS PARK

Grand Traverse County Parks and Recreation Departme Department
1125 W.Civic Center Drive
Traverse City, MI 49684

616-922-4818

Michigan Atlas & Gazetteer Location: 74B3

County Location: Grand Traverse

Directions To Trailhead:
In Grand Traverse Bay (west arm), just off shore near Bowers Harbor

Trail Type: Hiking/Walking
Trail Distance: 5 mi   Loops: Many   Shortest: Longest:
Trail Surface: Natural
Trail Use Fee: None
Method Of Ski Trail Grooming: NA
Skiing Ability Suggested: NA
Hiking Trail Difficulty: Easy to difficult
Mountain Biking Ability Suggested: NA
Terrain: Steep 5%, Hilly 10%, Moderate 35%, Flat 50%
Camping: Campground on the island

Maintained by the Grand Traverse County Parks and Recreation Department
The island is also known as Marion Island.
Power Island has a beach, toilets and picnic area.
A campground is located on the adjacent Bassett Island which is connected to Power Island by a narrow Isthmus. Depending on the water level of Grand Traverse Bay the isthmus may be above or just below water level.
The two islands have a colorful past. Bassett Island was named after a hermit of the same name that lived on the island in the 1890's.
Henry Ford bought both islands in 1917 for the site of a future summer home that was never built. He may have camped on the island in August of 1923 with Thomas Edison and Harvey Firestone. In the 1960's the island was bought by Eugene Power of Ann Arbor and given to Grand Traverse County for a public park.

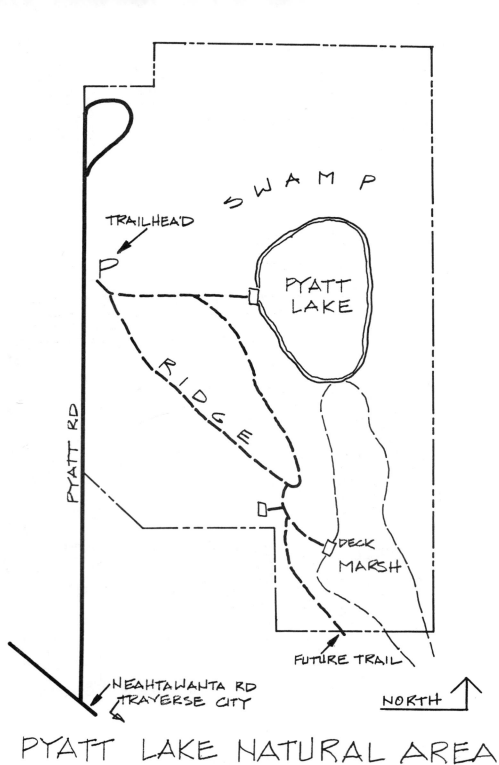

Grand Traverse Regional Land Conservancy
624 Third Street
Traverse City, MI 49684

616-929-7911

Michigan Atlas & Gazetteer Location: 74A3

County Location: Grand Traverse

Directions To Trailhead:
Take Peninsula Drive north out of Traverse City on Old Mission Peninsula about 10 miles to Neahtawanta Rd, then west .25 mile to Pyatt Rd(seasonal), then north .25 mile to trailhead parking lot.

Trail Type: Hiking/Walking, Cross Country Skiing, Interpretive
Trail Distance: 1 mi   Loops: 1   Shortest: NA   Longest: 1 mi
Trail Surface: Natural
Trail Use Fee: None
Method Of Ski Trail Grooming: None
Skiing Ability Suggested: Novice
Hiking Trail Difficulty: Easy
Mountain Biking Ability Suggested: NA
Terrain: 100%Flat
Camping: None

Owned by the Grand Traverse Regional Land Conservancy
Trail is to be completed by 6/1/95
Trail not designed for skiing but permitted.
Trail has two observation decks.
The natural area contains 135 acres

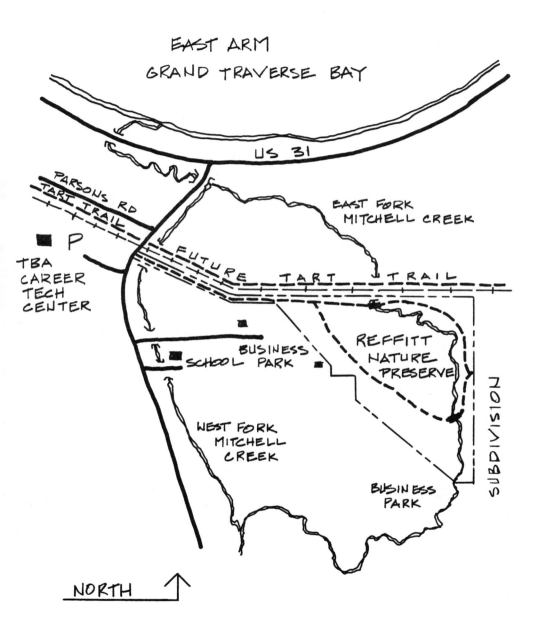

EAST ARM
GRAND TRAVERSE BAY

US 31

PARSONS RD

TART TRAIL

P

TBA
CAREER
TECH
CENTER

FUTURE TART TRAIL

EAST FORK
MITCHELL CREEK

SCHOOL BUSINESS PARK

REFFITT
NATURE
PRESERVE

SUBDIVISION

WEST FORK
MITCHELL
CREEK

BUSINESS
PARK

NORTH ↑

REFFITT NATURE PRESERVE

Reffitt Nature Preserve

Grand Traverse Regional Land Conservancy
624 Third St.
Traverse City, MI 49684

616-929-7911

Michigan Atlas & Gazetteer Location: 74C3

County Location: Grand Traverse

Directions To Trailhead:
Take 3 Mile south from US31 off East Grand Traverse Bay, to Parsons Rd., turn west (right) into the Traverse Bay Area Vocational Center parking lot. Park there. Pick up the TART trail located on the north side of the parking lot and take the trail east across 3 Mile Rd., then cross the railroad tracks to the preserve sign at the trailhead.

Trail Type: Hiking/Walking, Cross Country Skiing, Interpretive
Trail Distance: ! mi   Loops: 1   Shortest: NA   Longest: 1 mi
Trail Surface: Natural and boardwalk
Trail Use Fee: None
Method Of Ski Trail Grooming: None
Skiing Ability Suggested: Novice
Hiking Trail Difficulty: Easy
Mountain Biking Ability Suggested: NA
Terrain: 100% Flat
Camping: State Park nearby

Owned by the Grand Traverse Regional Land Conservancy
Located along the Mitchell Creek, a state designated trout stream.
The preserve was acquired in 1992.
The trail including boardwalks are scheduled for installation by 6/1/95.
The trail is not designed for skiing but is permitted.

Grand Traverse Regional Land Conservancy
624 Third St.
Traverse City, MI 49684

616-929-7911

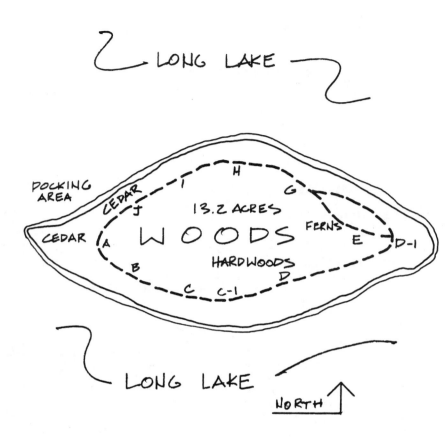

LONG LAKE

PARKING AREA

CEDAR

CEDAR

H

I

J

G

13.2 ACRES

W O O D S

FERNS

E

D-1

A

B

HARDWOODS

D

C

C-1

LONG LAKE

NORTH

Michigan Atlas & Gazetteer Location: 74C2

County Location: Grand Traverse

Directions To Trailhead:
Located Long Lake southwest of Traverse City. Small public park is located on the northeast side of the lake.

Trail Type: Hiking/Walking, Interpretive
Trail Distance: 2/3 mi   Loops: 1   Shortest: NA   Longest: 2/3 mi
Trail Surface: Natural
Trail Use Fee: None
Method Of Ski Trail Grooming: NA
Skiing Ability Suggested: NA
Hiking Trail Difficulty: Easy
Mountain Biking Ability Suggested: NA
Terrain: Steep 0%, Hilly 25%, Moderate 50%, Flat 25%
Camping: NOne

Maintained by the Grand Traverse City Regional Land Conservancy
Being on an island this is one of the most unique trail locations in the region.
Trail guide available from the Conservancy
13.2 acre island with 3,400 ft shoreline

SOUTH ISLAND NATURE PRESERVE

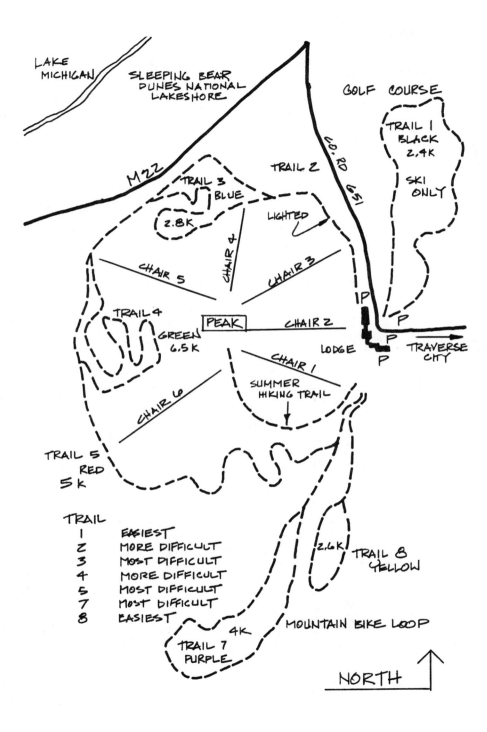

LAKE MICHIGAN

SLEEPING BEAR DUNES NATIONAL LAKESHORE

M22

GOLF COURSE

CO. RD 651

TRAIL 2

TRAIL 3 BLUE

2.8K

LIGHTED

TRAIL 1 BLACK 2.4K

SKI ONLY

CHAIR 4

CHAIR 5

CHAIR 3

TRAIL 4

PEAK

GREEN 6.5K

CHAIR 2

LODGE

P P P P P

TRAVERSE CITY

SUMMER HIKING TRAIL

CHAIR 1

CHAIR 6

TRAIL 5 RED 5K

TRAIL
1   EASIEST
2   MORE DIFFICULT
3   MOST DIFFICULT
4   MORE DIFFICULT
5   MOST DIFFICULT
7   MOST DIFFICULT
8   EASIEST

2.6K TRAIL 8 YELLOW

MOUNTAIN BIKE LOOP

4K

TRAIL 7 PURPLE

NORTH

SUGAR LOAF RESORT

Sugar Loaf Resort

Sugar Loaf Resort
Route 1
Cedar, MI 49621

616-228-5461
800-968-0576

Michigan Atlas & Gazetteer Location: 74A1

County Location: Leelanau

Directions To Trailhead:
From Traverse City, take M72 west for 7 miles, then turn right (north) on Co Rd 651and follow the signs

Trail Type: Hiking/Walking, Cross Country Skiing, Mountain Biking
Trail Distance: 26 km   Loops: 8   Shortest: 1 km   Longest: 5.6 km
Trail Surface: Natural
Trail Use Fee: Yes, for skiing
Method Of Ski Trail Grooming: Double track set daily with skating lane
Skiing Ability Suggested: Novice to advanced
Hiking Trail Difficulty: Easy to moderate
Mountain Biking Ability Suggested: Intermediate to advanced
Terrain: Flat to very hilly
Camping: Available in the nearby Sleeping Bear Dunes National Lakeshore

Privately operated 4 season alpine ski resort with an extensive well designed and maintained trail system. Original trail system designed by John Capper. Lodging, ski shop, lessons, restaurants to name only a few features. Breathtaking views of Lake Michigan, off shore islands and surrounding landscape from   the top of Sugar Loaf.
Chair lift rides.
1/2 mile marked hiking trail to the top of the loaf.
Mountain bike trail is 4 km.

TART
PO Box 252
Traverse City, MI 49685-0252

616-933-TART

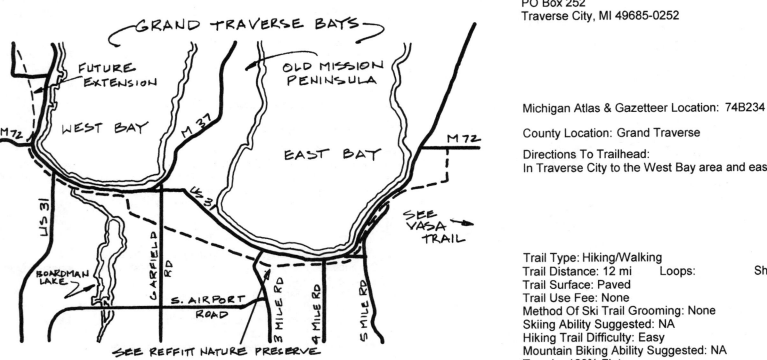

Michigan Atlas & Gazetteer Location: 74B234

County Location: Grand Traverse

Directions To Trailhead:
In Traverse City to the West Bay area and east to Acme.

Trail Type: Hiking/Walking
Trail Distance: 12 mi   Loops: Shortest: Longest:
Trail Surface: Paved
Trail Use Fee: None
Method Of Ski Trail Grooming: None
Skiing Ability Suggested: NA
Hiking Trail Difficulty: Easy
Mountain Biking Ability Suggested: NA
Terrain: 100% Flat
Camping: Traverse City State Park

Maintained by TART
Bike and roller blade rentals and repairs are available in Traverse City
Trail is 8' wide asphalt pavement and within view of the Grand Traverse Bays
going east-west through downtown Traverse City
Popular urban trail from west bay Traverse City parks to M72 near the Grand
Traverse Resort.
The Leelanau Trail connects to this trail.
Resturants (including fast food) are along this trail.
Bike rentals including pedal "cars" are available for rent along the trail

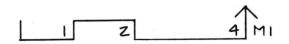

TRAVERSE CITY RECREATION TRAIL

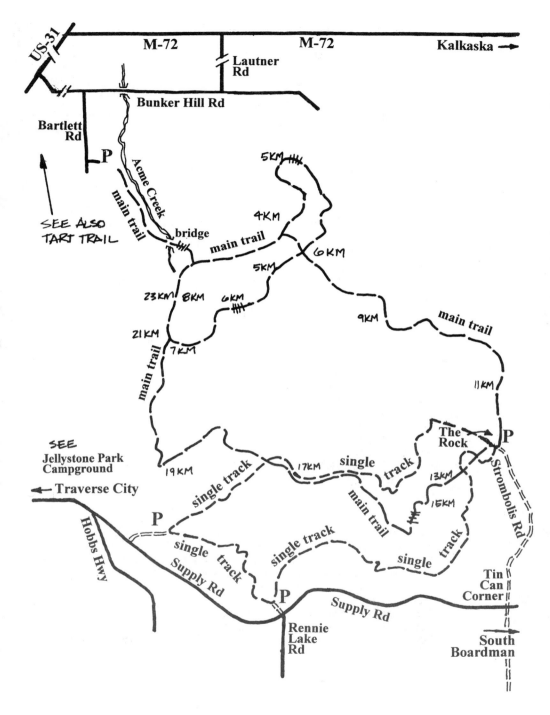

North American Vasa, Inc.
PO Box 500   616-938-4400
Acme, MI 49610-0550

Traverse City Forest Area, Pere Marquette State Forest
404 West 14th St   616-946-4920
Traverse City, MI 49864

Michigan Atlas & Gazetteer Location: 74C4,75C4

County Location: Grand Traverse

Directions To Trailhead:
M72 south from Acme to Bunker Hill Rd, then to Bartlett Rd, then south on Bartlett to trailhead on left (east) side of the road. Also access off Supply Rd. near Hobbs Hwy intersection and east of the intersection.

Trail Type: Hiking/Walking, Cross Country Skiing, Mountain Biking
Trail Distance: 35+ km   Loops: 4   Shortest: 3 km   Longest: 26 km
Trail Surface: Natural
Trail Use Fee: None, but donations accepted at the trailhead
Method Of Ski Trail Grooming: Track set with skating lane
Skiing Ability Suggested: Novice to intermediate
Hiking Trail Difficulty: Easy but long
Mountain Biking Ability Suggested: Novice to intermediate
Terrain: Steep 5%, Hilly 25%, Moderate 50%, Flat 20%
Camping: State Forest Campgrounds, Traverse City S.P. and Jellystone Park

Maintained by the North American Vasa, Inc a non-profit organization, DNR Forest Mangement Division and MMBA.
Site of several annual races including the Iceman mountain bike race held in November and the North American Vasa cross country ski race held in February
Heated restrooms at the trailhead on Bartlett Rd
The premier trail in the lower peninsula
The Vasa course and many other forest roads and trails are used for mountain biking.

VASA PATHWAY

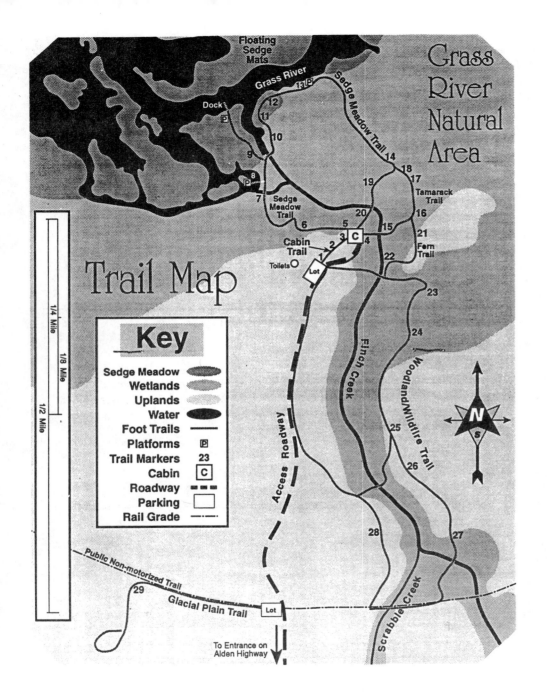

Trail Map

Key

Sedge Meadow	
Wetlands	
Uplands	
Water	
Foot Trails	—
Platforms	P
Trail Markers	23
Cabin	C
Roadway	- - -
Parking	☐
Rail Grade	-·-·-

Grass River Natural Area, Inc
PO Box 231
Bellaire, MI 49615-0231

616-533-8576
616-533-8314

Michigan Atlas & Gazetteer Location: 75A6

County Location: Antrim

Directions To Trailhead:
Between Lake Bellaire and Clam Lake, 8.5 miles west of Mancelona via M88 and Co Rd 618 (Alden Hwy) 1.5 miles east of Crystal Springs Rd. and .5 mile west of Comfort Rd. on Co Rd 618 (Alden Hwy).

Trail Type: Hiking/Walking, Cross Country Skiing, Interpretive
Trail Distance: 3 mi   Loops: 5   Shortest: .25 mi Longest: 2.25 mi
Trail Surface: Natural and boardwalks
Trail Use Fee: None, donations accepted (tax deductable)
Method Of Ski Trail Grooming: None
Skiing Ability Suggested: Novice
Hiking Trail Difficulty: Easy
Mountain Biking Ability Suggested: NA
Terrain: 100% flat
Camping: Not permitted

Maintained by Grass River Natural Area, Inc a non profit corporation
The Natural Area covers over 1,000 acres.
Interpretive Center phone answered in the summer only.
Limited skiing because of narrow boardwalks.
Additional 5 miles of old railroad right-of-way from Crystal Springs Rd to Brake Rd. is available for skiing and hiking (closed to motorized vehicles).
A 3/4 mile long access road from Co Rd 618 is not plowed.
Please leave your smoking, pets and food at home when visiting this natural area.
Call or write for the Trail Guide.

GRASS RIVER NATURAL AREA

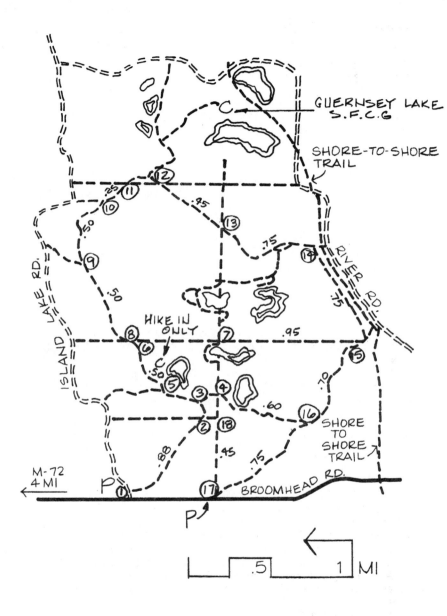

SAND LAKES
QUIET AREA

Traverse City Forest Area, Pere Marquette State Forest
404 W. 14th St.   616-946-4920
Traverse City, MI 49684

District Forest Manager, Pere Marquette State Forest
8015 Mackinaw Trail   616-775-9727
Cadillac, MI 49601

Michigan Atlas & Gazetteer Location: 75C5

County Location: Grand Traverse and Kalkaska

Directions To Trailhead:
Between Kalkaska and Traverse City, south of M72.
Trailhead - (For skiers) 1.5 miles east of Williamsburg on M72 take Broomhead Rd. south for about 4 miles to parking lot on the left.
Trailhead -(For hikers) Take Island Lake Rd. west from Kalkaska for about 9 miles to Guernsey Lake State Forest Campground (follow signs).

Trail Type: Hiking/Walking, Cross Country Skiing, Mountain Biking
Trail Distance: 10.98+ mi Loops: Several   Shortest: Longest: 8.6 mi
Trail Surface: Natural
Trail Use Fee: None
Method Of Ski Trail Grooming: None, but well skied all of the time
Skiing Ability Suggested: Novice
Hiking Trail Difficulty: Easy to moderate
Mountain Biking Ability Suggested: NA
Terrain: Flat to very hilly
Camping: Campground in the quiet area is open during snowless months

Maintained by the DNR Forest Management Division
This 2,800 acre quiet area is closed to motorized vehicles, making it a very delightful ski, hiking and mountain bike area.
The Shore to Shore Trail passes through the area but not on the trails.
The circular route around the quiet area is best for biking and skiing since the EW and NS trails are on section lines and ignore the difficult terrain that is very difficult to ski.
A hike/bike-in camping site is provided with pit toilets and a water well. This area is a favorite of the local skiers and mountain bikers.

TRAIL NOTES

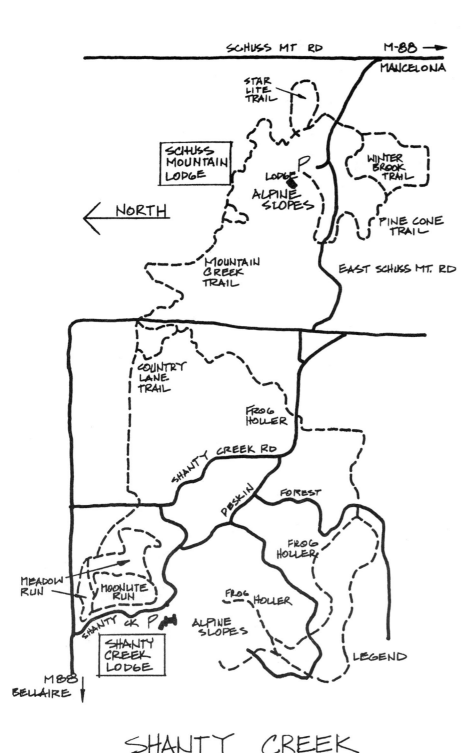

SHANTY CREEK

Shanty Creek

Bellaire, MI 49615

616-533-8621
800-678-4111

E-mail: info@ shantycreek.com
Web: shantycreek.com

Michigan Atlas & Gazetteer Location: 75A67

County Location: Antrim

Directions To Trailhead:
Between Mancelona and Bellaire north and east of M88 (follow signs) Schuss Village is just west of Mancelona and Summit Village (formerly Shanty Creek Lodge) is just southeast of Bellaire.

Trail Type: Hiking/Walking, Cross Country Skiing, Mountain Biking
Trail Distance: 20 mi   Loops: Many   Shortest: .75 mi Longest: 10 mi
Trail Surface: Paved, gravel, natural
Trail Use Fee: Yes, varies with season and trail use
Method Of Ski Trail Grooming: Track set
Skiing Ability Suggested: Novice to advanced
Hiking Trail Difficulty: Easy to difficult
Mountain Biking Ability Suggested: Novice
Terrain: Steep 5%, Hilly 15%, Moderate 55%, Flat 25%
Camping: Campgrounds nearby

Privately operated 2 lodge (including Schuss Mountain), 4 season full service resort complex with all amenities.
SKIING-Site of the annual White Pine Stampede held the first Saturday of February . This unique 2 lodge trail system allows for some very unique trail opportunities with an interconnecting trail between the lodges. Lighted ski trail. Some trails on golf courses. Trail fee includes shuttle bus service between resorts. Longer downhill runs on the ski trail from Schuss Village to Summit Village (Shanty Creek) then the reverse.
MOUNTAIN BIKING-Resort trails for mountain biking are mostly 2 track roads between the two lodges. A beginner riding experience. Nothing very technical. A moderate amount of sand may be encountered. The fromer NORBA race course was closed when the area was developed for condo's and more downhill skiing. However, some single track may be developed in the future. Call for current trail information. Mountain bike trail facilities seem to change from year to year at this resort.

TRAIL NOTES

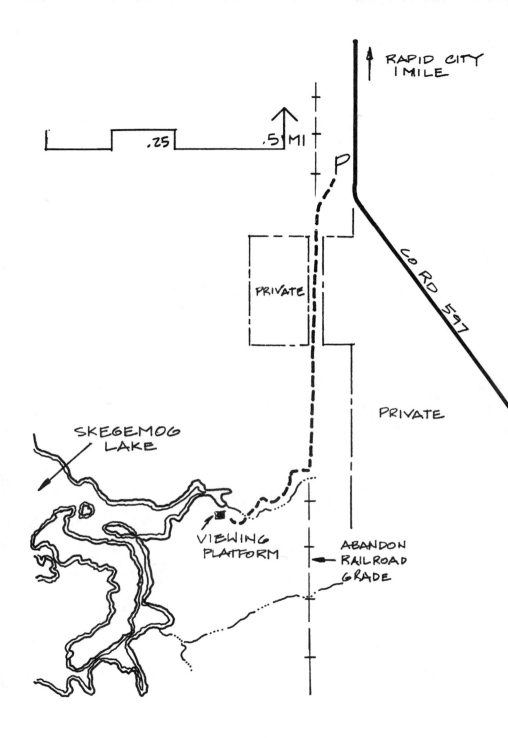

Skegemog Lake Pathway

Kalkaska Forest Area, Pere Marquette State Forest
2089 N. Birch
Kalkaska, MI 49646

616-258-2711

District Forest Manager, Pere Marquette State Forest
8015 Mackinaw Trail
Cadillac, MI 49601

616-775-9727

Michigan Atlas & Gazetteer Location: 75B5

County Location: Antrim

Directions To Trailhead:
From Kalkaska take M72 west about 4.5 miles, then north on Co. Rd. 597 (Rapid City Rd) about 5 miles to trail head. Trailhead - On west side just after a bend in the road.

Trail Type: Hiking/Walking, Cross Country Skiing, Mountain Biking, Interpretive
Trail Distance: 1.75 mi   Loops: NA   Shortest: NA   Longest: NA
Trail Surface: Natural
Trail Use Fee: None
Method Of Ski Trail Grooming: None
Skiing Ability Suggested: Novice
Hiking Trail Difficulty: Easy
Mountain Biking Ability Suggested: Novice
Terrain: 100% Flat
Camping: None

Maintained by the DNR Forest Management Division
Part of the trail is on an abandon railroad bed.
Viewing platform at end of trail overlooking Skegemog Lake shoreline

SKEGEMOG LAKE PATHWAY

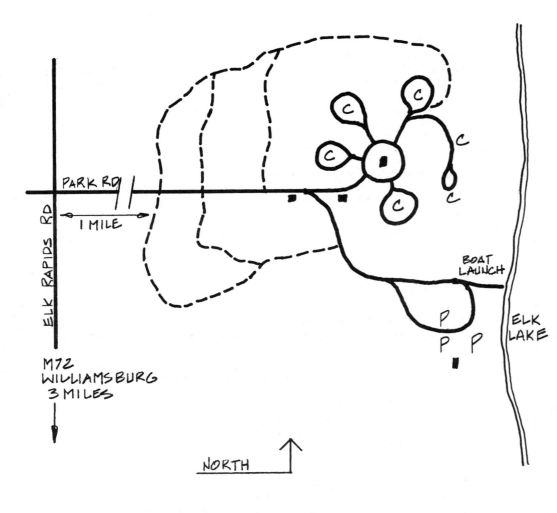

PARK RD

1 MILE

ELK RAPIDS RD

M72
WILLIAMSBURG
3 MILES

BOAT
LAUNCH

ELK
LAKE

P
P P

NORTH

Whitewater Township Park
9500 Park Rd.
Williamsburg, MI 49690

616-267-9321

Michigan Atlas & Gazetteer Location: 75B4

County Location: Grand Traverse

Directions To Trailhead:
M72, 10 miles east from Traverse City to Williamsburg, north on Elk Lake Rd 3 miles to Park Rd., then east on Park Rd to the park.

Trail Type: Hiking/Walking, Cross Country Skiing, Interpretive
Trail Distance: 1.5 mi   Loops: 2   Shortest: .5 mi   Longest: 1 mi
Trail Surface: Wood chips and natural
Trail Use Fee: None
Method Of Ski Trail Grooming: None
Skiing Ability Suggested: Novice to intermediate
Hiking Trail Difficulty: Easy
Mountain Biking Ability Suggested: NA
Terrain: Steep 0%, Hilly 0%, Moderate 80%, Flat 20%
Camping: Campground at trailhead

Owned by Whitewater Township
Very nice campground with boat launch on the shore of Elk Lake.
Total park is 117 acres.

WHITEWATER PARK

Cross Country Ski Shop

Cross Country Ski Shop
PO Box 745
Grayling, MI 49738

517-348-8558
517-821-6559

Michigan Atlas & Gazetteer Location: 76C3

County Location: Roscommon

Directions To Trailhead:
On I-75 Business Loop behind the Holiday Inn on the south side of Grayling

Trail Type: Cross Country Skiing
Trail Distance: 2.5 mi   Loops: 3   Shortest: .3 mi   Longest: 2.5 mi
Trail Surface: Natural
Trail Use Fee: None
Method Of Ski Trail Grooming: Track set with skating lanes
Skiing Ability Suggested: Novice
Hiking Trail Difficulty: NA
Mountain Biking Ability Suggested: NA
Terrain: Steep 0%, Hilly 0%, Moderate 5%, Flat 95
Camping: None

Complete ski shop with rentals.
Owned and staffed by expert nordic skiers.
Excellent place to try out equipment before purchasing.
One of the most knowledgeable shops for racing and touring equipment in the state.
A .8 mile lighted trail on site.

4KM LOOP

GRAYLING

SKI SHOP

HOLIDAY INN

P

P

P

RIDGE RUN

LIGHTED LOOP 1.3 KM

BUS. 75 LOOP

NO SCALE

CROSS COUNTRY SKI SHOP

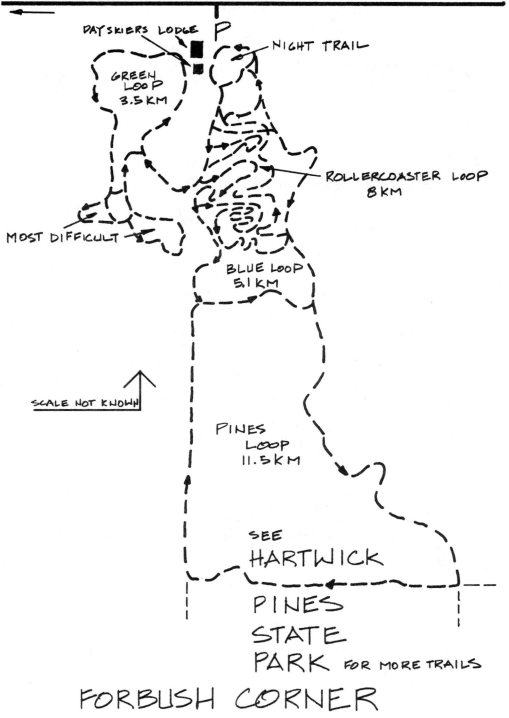

I·75
EXIT 264 .5MI (FREDERIC-LEWISTON)

DAYSKIERS LODGE

P

NIGHT TRAIL

GREEN LOOP 3.5KM

ROLLERCOASTER LOOP 8KM

MOST DIFFICULT

BLUE LOOP 5.1KM

SCALE NOT KNOWN

PINES LOOP 11.5KM

SEE HARTWICK PINES STATE PARK FOR MORE TRAILS

FORBUSH CORNER

Dave Forbush
4971 Co. Rd. 612, PO Box 327
Frederic , MI 49733

517-348-5989

Michigan Atlas & Gazetteer Location: 76B3

County Location: Crawford

Directions To Trailhead:
9 miles north of Grayling on I-75, then .25 mile east of exit 264
(Lewiston/Fredric) to the ski area

Trail Type: Cross Country Skiing
Trail Distance: 36+ km   Loops: 5   Shortest: 1 km   Longest: 11.5 km
Trail Surface: Natural
Trail Use Fee: Yes
Method Of Ski Trail Grooming: Expertly track set and groomed space for skating
Skiing Ability Suggested: Novice to advanced
Hiking Trail Difficulty: NA
Mountain Biking Ability Suggested: NA
Terrain: Steep 5%, Hilly 45%, Moderate 35%, Flat 15%
Camping: Campground available at Hartwick Pines State Park

A privately operated touring center.
Brown bag eating area, limited food service(weekends only), lessons, lodging,
quality ski shop with rentals.
Owner, Dave Forbush prides himself in the expertly goomed trails accomplished
by three Snowcat grooming machines.
Lighted trail available. Trails connect with Hartwick Pines State Park.
Scheduled ski instruction with Scott Hartwig.
Ski clinics held by Olympic Gold Medalist, Nikolai Anikin, former head coach of
the Soviet team.
Write for a free brochure.

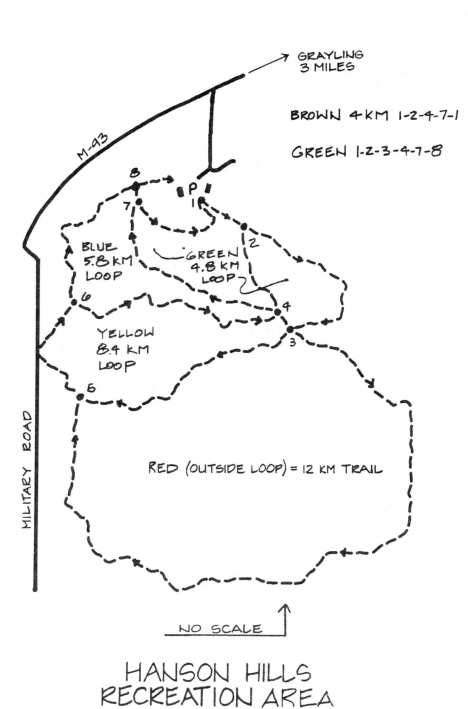

GRAYLING
3 MILES

M-93

BROWN 4 KM 1-2-4-7-1

GREEN 1-2-3-4-7-8

BLUE
5.8 KM
LOOP

GREEN
4.8 KM
LOOP

YELLOW
8.4 KM
LOOP

RED (OUTSIDE LOOP) = 12 KM TRAIL

MILITARY ROAD

NO SCALE

HANSON HILLS
RECREATION AREA

Hanson Hills Recreation Park
PO Box 361
Grayling, MI 49738

517-348-9266

Michigan Atlas & Gazetteer Location: 76CD23

County Location: Crawford

Directions To Trailhead:
Takes M72/M93 west 1.5 miles to the M93 cutoff, then south on M93 to the park 1.5 miles west of Grayling

Trail Type: Hiking/Walking, Cross Country Skiing, Mountain Biking
Trail Distance: 35 km   Loops: 5   Shortest: 4 km   Longest: 12 km
Trail Surface: Natural
Trail Use Fee: Yes, daily and seasonal passes available
Method Of Ski Trail Grooming: Track set
Skiing Ability Suggested: Novice to intermediate
Hiking Trail Difficulty: Easy to moderate
Mountain Biking Ability Suggested: Novice to intermediate
Terrain: Steep 0%, Hilly 60%, Moderate 30%, Flat 10%
Camping: None

Maintained by a local community group on the Hanson State Game Refuge
Ski rentals, snack bar, warming area and alpine skiing.
Orginally developed in the 1930's for cross-country skiing.
Some of the original trail signs are still visable.
All trails completely redone in 1986.
Site of races held annually.
Skating trail available.
Write for the brochure.

TRAIL NOTES

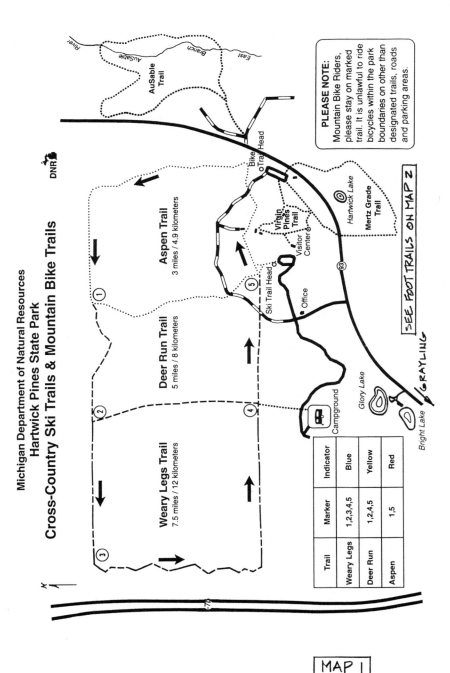

Michigan Department of Natural Resources
Hartwick Pines State Park
Cross-Country Ski Trails & Mountain Bike Trails

AuSable Trail

East Branch AuSable River

DNR

Aspen Trail
3 miles / 4.9 kilometers

Deer Run Trail
5 miles / 8 kilometers

Weary Legs Trail
7.5 miles / 12 kilometers

Bike Trail Head

Virgin Pines Trail

Hartwick Lake

Mertz Grade Trail

Visitor Center

Ski Trail Head

Office

93

Campground

Glory Lake

Bright Lake

GRAYLING

I-75

PLEASE NOTE:
Mountain Bike Riders, please stay on marked trail. It is unlawful to ride bicycles within the park boundaries on other than designated trails, roads and parking areas.

SEE FOOT TRAILS ON MAP 2

Trail	Marker	Indicator
Weary Legs	1,2,3,4,5	Blue
Deer Run	1,2,4,5	Yellow
Aspen	1,5	Red

MAP 1

Hartwick Pines State Park
Rte 3, Box 3840
Grayling, MI 49738

517-348-7068

DNR Park and Recreation Division

517-373-1270

Michigan Atlas & Gazetteer Location: 76BC3

County Location: Crawford

Directions To Trailhead:
7.5 miles NE of Grayling on M 93
East of I-75 (exit 259) about 3 miles

Trail Type: Hiking/Walking, Cross Country Skiing, Mountain Biking, Interpretive
Trail Distance: 18+ mi   Loops: Many   Shortest: 1 mi   Longest: 7.5+ mi
Trail Surface: Natural
Trail Use Fee: None, but vehicle entry fee required
Method Of Ski Trail Grooming: Designated ski trails are track set
Skiing Ability Suggested: Novice to intermediate
Hiking Trail Difficulty: Easy to moderate
Mountain Biking Ability Suggested: Easy to moderate
Terrain: Steep 3%, Hilly 7%, Moderate 60%, Flat 30%
Camping: Campground in park year open all year

Maintained by the DNR Parks and Recreation Division
A unique state park with a stand of virgin White Pine, one over 300 years old.
Site of the Logging Museum and Interpreative Center
Some trails connect with Forbush Corner cross country ski area on the north.
Marked Nature Trails:
        Virgin Pines Nature Trail -1 mile loop
        Mertz Grande Nature Trail -2 mile loop
        AuSable River Foot (nature) Trail - 3 mile loop
Marked Hiking/Mountain Biking Trails:
        Aspen - 3 mile loop
        Deer Run - 5 mile loop
        Weary Legs - 7.5 mile loop
Many additional unmarked trails in the park.

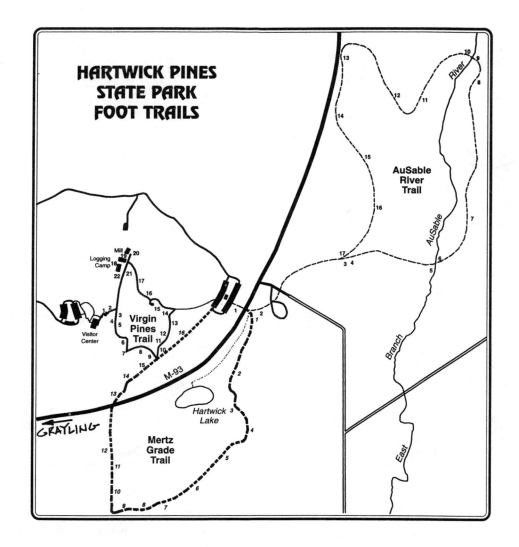

HARTWICK PINES
STATE PARK
FOOT TRAILS

AuSable
River
Trail

Mill
Logging
Camp

Virgin
Pines
Trail

Visitor
Center

M-93

GRAYLING

Mertz
Grade
Trail

Hartwick
Lake

AuSable

Branch

East

River

NORTH

MAP 2

HARTWICK PINES STATE PARK

311

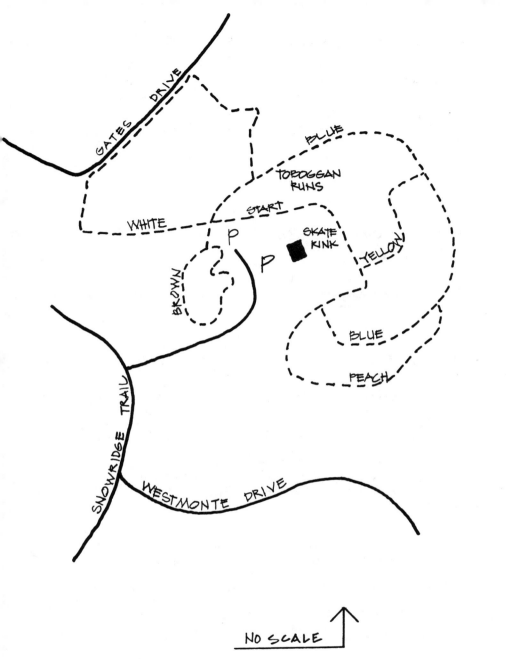

Lakes of the North
541 Skytrails Court
Mancelona, MI 49656

616-585-6155
616-585-6000

Michigan Atlas & Gazetteer Location: 76A2

County Location: Otsego

Directions To Trailhead:
4 miles west of Alba on C42, then 2 miles on Olds Rd to winter sports area

Trail Type: Cross Country Skiing
Trail Distance: 15 km   Loops: 7   Shortest: Longest:
Trail Surface: Natural
Trail Use Fee: Yes
Method Of Ski Trail Grooming:
Skiing Ability Suggested: Novice
Hiking Trail Difficulty: NA
Mountain Biking Ability Suggested: NA
Terrain: Flat to rolling
Camping: On site

Privately operated cross country ski area in a planned recreational community.

LAKES OF THE NORTH

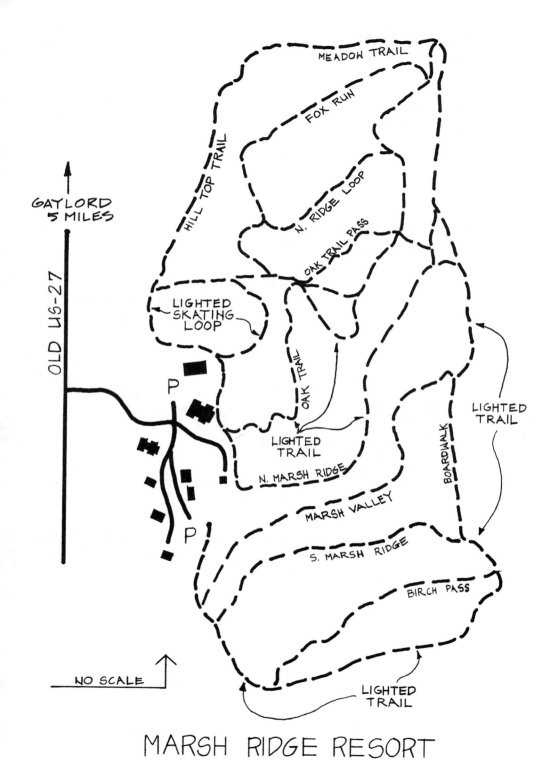

Marsh Ridge
4815 Historic 27, PO Box 623
Gaylord, MI 49735

800-624-7518
517-732-6794

Michigan Atlas & Gazetteer Location: 76A3

County Location: Otsego

Directions To Trailhead:
5 miles south of Gaylord I-75 to exit 279, then south on Old 27 about 1.5 miles
to the entrance on the east side of the highway.

Trail Type: Cross Country Skiing
Trail Distance: 28 km   Loops: 10   Shortest: 3 km   Longest: 10 km
Trail Surface: Nastural
Trail Use Fee: Yes, guests are free
Method Of Ski Trail Grooming: Track set
Skiing Ability Suggested: Novice to advanced
Hiking Trail Difficulty: NA
Mountain Biking Ability Suggested: NA
Terrain: Steep 10%, Hilly 20%, Moderate 30%, Flat 40%
Camping: None

Privately operated resort and conference center
The resort includes 32 jacuzzi suites, pool, sauna, whirlpool, exerise and tanning
facilities.
Eight double jacuzzi theme suites available.
This trail system is small but never the less a delight to ski.
All trails are well groomed with 3.5 km are lighted.
Lodges are elaborately decorated with theme decorating . Four Diamond and
AAA rated. Breakfast included with each room.
Golf and ski packages available as well as group rates .

Michaywe Resort
1535 Opal Lake Rd.
Gaylord, MI 49735

517-939-8919
517-939-8800

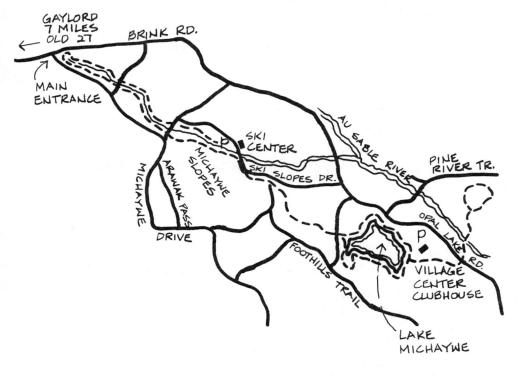

Michigan Atlas & Gazetteer Location: 76A3

County Location: Otsego

Directions To Trailhead:
7 miles south of Gaylord on old US27, then east on Charles Brink Rd to Michaywe main entrance, then follow signs to Ski Center at the base of the alpine slopes.

Trail Type: Hiking/Walking, Cross Country Skiing
Trail Distance: 11 mi   Loops: 6   Shortest: 1 mi   Longest: 2 mi
Trail Surface: Natural
Trail Use Fee: None
Method Of Ski Trail Grooming: Double track set
Skiing Ability Suggested: Novice to advanced
Hiking Trail Difficulty: NA
Mountain Biking Ability Suggested: NA
Terrain: Steep 20%, Hilly 20%, Moderate 30%, Flat 30%
Camping: Available on site and at a nearby KOA

Privately operated alpine and nordic resort
Lessons, rentals, lodging, restaurant, snack bar, entertainment and bar.
Telemark area with lifts and lessons available.
Very nice well groomed beginner trail system.
Light trail on weekends.

NO SCALE

MICHAYWE RESORT

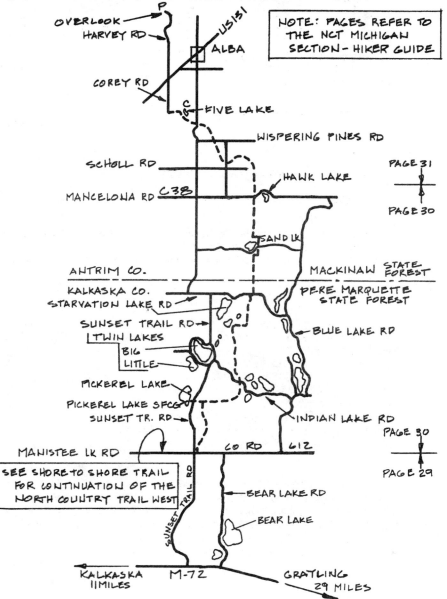

Kalkaska Forest Area, Pere Marquette State Forest
2089 North Birch St   616-258-2711
Kalkaska, MI 49646

Gaylord Forest Area, Mackinaw State Forest
1732 West M32, Box 667   517-732-3541
Gaylord, MI 49735

Michigan Atlas & Gazetteer Location: 76AB1

County Location: Kalkaska, Antrim

Directions To Trailhead:
South Trailhead - Co. Rd. 612 about 100 yards east of Sunrise Trail
North Trailhead - Landside Overlook of the Jordan River Valley on the north
end of Harvey Rd (overlook located 1 mile west of Alba on Co. Rd. 620, then
1.5 miles north on Harvey Rd.)

Trail Type: Hiking/Walking, Mountain Biking
Trail Distance: 21.7 mi   Loops: NA   Shortest: NA   Longest: NA
Trail Surface: Natural
Trail Use Fee: None
Method Of Ski Trail Grooming: NA
Skiing Ability Suggested: NA
Hiking Trail Difficulty: Easy
Mountain Biking Ability Suggested: Easy
Terrain: Rolling to hilly
Camping: Pickerel Lake, Five Lake and Pinney Bridge SFCG's

Trail located in the Pere Marquette and Mackinaw State Forest
Built and maintained by North Country Trail Association members and
volunteers
Contact the North Country Trail Association for the Hiker Guide at PO Box 311,
White Cloud, MI 49349 616-689-1912
Trail marked with blue blazes
See NCNST - Michigan Section - Hiker Guide, pages 30 and 31.

NORTH COUNTRY TRAIL-
PERE MARQUETTE 2/MACKINAW 1 STATE FORESTS

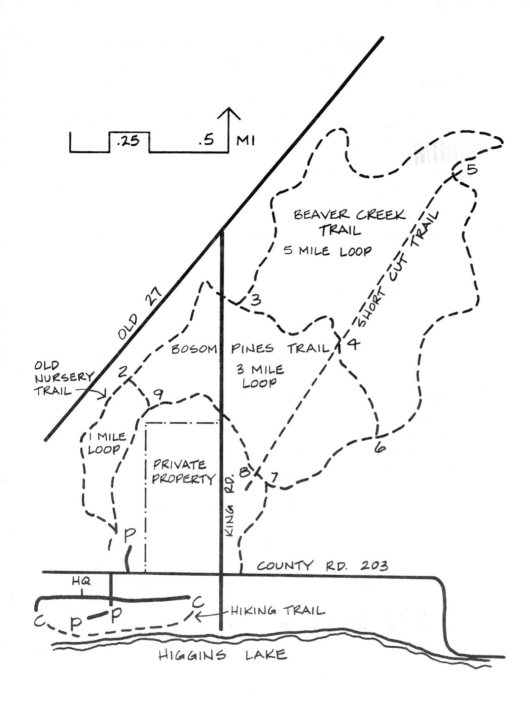

North Higgins Lake State Park
11511 W. Higgins Lake Drive
Roscommon, MI 48653

517-821-6125

DNR Parks and Recreation Division

517-373-1270

Michigan Atlas & Gazetteer Location: 76D23

County Location: Crawford

Directions To Trailhead:
1.5 miles east of US27 or 4.5 miles west of I75 on Co Rd 200 (Roscommon Rd.)
at the north end of Higgins Lake .
Trailhead - Parking lot of CCC Museum and historical exhibit on the north side
of the road.

Trail Type: Hiking/Walking, Cross Country Skiing, Mountain Biking, Interpretive
Trail Distance: 7.5 mi   Loops: 3   Shortest: 1 mi   Longest: 6 mi
Trail Surface: Natural
Trail Use Fee: None, but vehicle entry fee required
Method Of Ski Trail Grooming: Track set
Skiing Ability Suggested: Novice to intermediate
Hiking Trail Difficulty: Easy
Mountain Biking Ability Suggested: Novice
Terrain: Steep 0%, Hilly 20%, Moderate 30%, Flat 50%
Camping: Available in the park

Maintained by the DNR Parks and Recreation Division
Site of the Beaver Creek Challenge held in February
Hanson Hill, Cross Country Ski Headquarters and Tisdale Triangle are other
trails nearby . Most trails are double width. Some are single with a skating lane.
The 1 and 3 mile loops have the most hills.
A nature and fitness trail are also part of the system.

NORTH HIGGINS LAKE STATE PARK

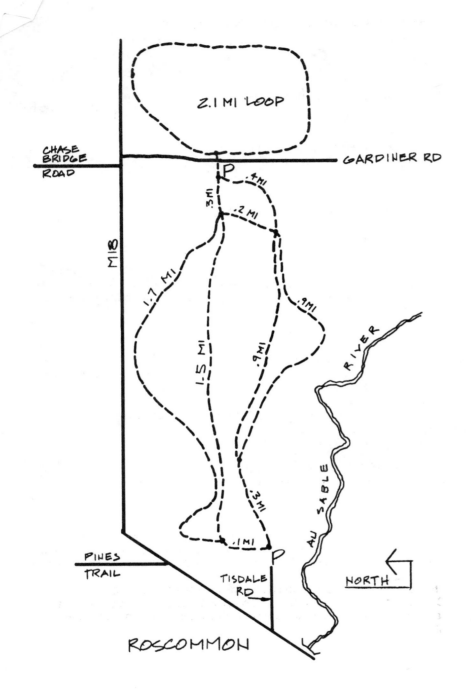

Roscommon Forest Area, Au Sable State Forest
Box 218, 8717 N. Roscommon Rd.   517-275-5151
Roscommon, MI 48635

District Forest Manager, Au Sable State Forest
191 S. Mt. Tom Rd.   517-826-3211
Mio, MI 48647

Michigan Atlas & Gazetteer Location: 76D4, 77D4

County Location: Roscommon

Directions To Trailhead:
Trailhead - At the east end of Tisdale Rd. .5 mile east of Roscommon on M18.
Trailhead - .5 mile south of M18, on Gardiner Rd .

Trail Type: Hiking/Walking, Cross Country Skiing, Mountain Biking
Trail Distance: 8.4 mi   Loops: 4   Shortest: 3 mi   Longest: 6 mi
Trail Surface: Natural
Trail Use Fee: None
Method Of Ski Trail Grooming: Track set
Skiing Ability Suggested: Novice to intermediate
Hiking Trail Difficulty: Easy
Mountain Biking Ability Suggested: Novice
Terrain: Steep 0%, Hilly 0%, Moderate 80%, Flat 20%
Camping: None along the trail but public and private campgrounds in the area

Maintained by the DNR Forest Management Division
Popular with local residents of Roscommon and the surrounding area
Other contacts:
        DNR Forest Management Division Office, Lansing, 517-373-1275
        DNR Forest Management Region Office, Roscommon, 517-275-5151

TISDALE TRIANGLE PATHWAY

Wilderness Valley   Attn. Dave Smith
7519 Mancelona Rd.   616-585-7090
Gaylord, MI 49735

Michigan Atlas & Gazetteer Location: 76A2

County Location: Otsego

Directions To Trailhead:
10 miles SW of Gaylord via Old US27 to the south end of Otsego Lake, then west on C-38(Mancelona Rd) 5 miles then south on Mt. Fredrick Rd about 2 miles, then west a short distance to the trailhead lodge (golf course clubhouse).

Trail Type: Cross Country Skiing
Trail Distance: 18 km   Loops: 6   Shortest: 1km   Longest: 18 km
Trail Surface: Natural
Trail Use Fee: Yes
Method Of Ski Trail Grooming: Double track set daily with skating lane
Skiing Ability Suggested: Novice to expert
Hiking Trail Difficulty: Easy to moderate
Mountain Biking Ability Suggested: NA
Terrain: Steep 20%, Hilly 60%, Moderate 15%, Flat 5%
Camping: None

Privately operated ski touring center.
Ski lodge, rentals, ski shop, restaurant and lodging are available on site.
Completely new trail system for 1994 on the 36 hole Black Forest championship golf course south of Co Rd C38. Expansion of the 18km course will take place in coming years.
The golf course club house is used as the ski lodge in the winter.
Consistantly well groomed trails, a reputation for outstanding trail design and reliable snow should continue to make this touring center one of the best in the state.

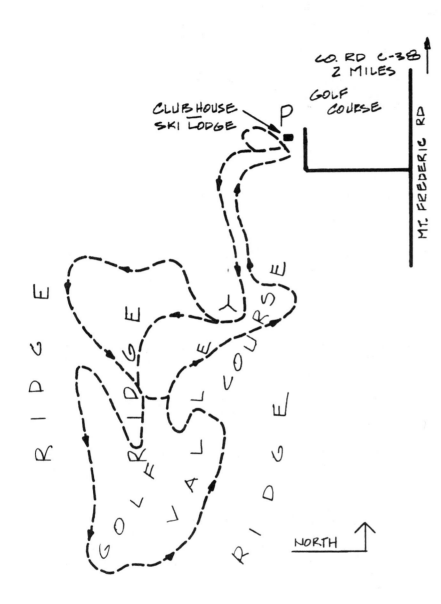

WILDERNESS VALLEY
CROSS COUNTRY SKI CENTER

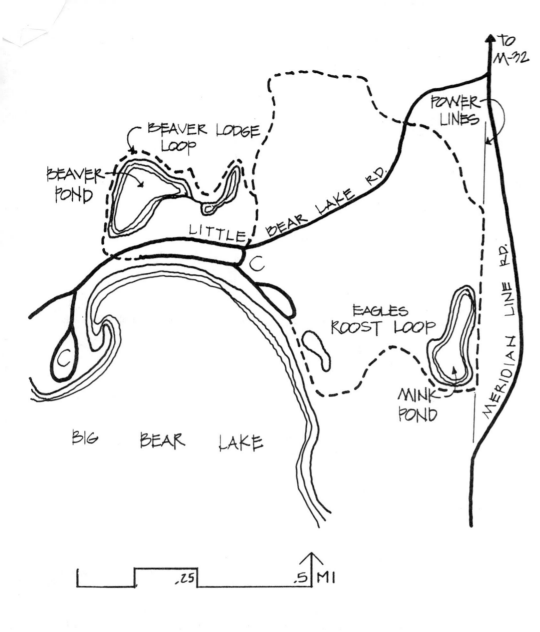

Gaylord Forest Area, Mackinaw State Forest
West M32, PO Box 667
Gaylord, Mi 49735

517-732-3541

District Forest Manger, Mackinaw State Forest
West M32, PO Box 667
Gaylord, MI 49725

517-732-3541

Michigan Atlas & Gazetteer Location: 77A6

County Location: Otsego

Directions To Trailhead:
From Gaylord take M32 east to Co Rd 495(Meridian Line Rd), then south 1.5 miles to the Bear Lake SFCG or,
3 miles south of Veinna Corners to Bear Lake Rd, then west 2 miles to Bear Lake SFCG
Trailheads are between site 36 and the Day Use Area and at across the road from the main entrance

Trail Type: Hiking/Walking, Interpretive
Trail Distance: 2.5 mi   Loops: 2   Shortest: .6   Longest: 2.2 mi
Trail Surface: Natural
Trail Use Fee: None
Method Of Ski Trail Grooming: NA
Skiing Ability Suggested: NA
Hiking Trail Difficulty: Easy
Mountain Biking Ability Suggested: NA
Terrain: Steep 0%, Hilly 5%, Moderate 80%, Flat 20%
Camping: Campground on site

Maintained by the DNR Forest Management Division
Part of the trail was the AuSable and Northwest Railroad that hauled logs to Lewiston and Oscoda in the late 1800's.
The trail passes through a wide variety of flora including upland hardwoods, pines, aspen and others. Also the trail passes a pond used by beavers.
Trail brochure is available.

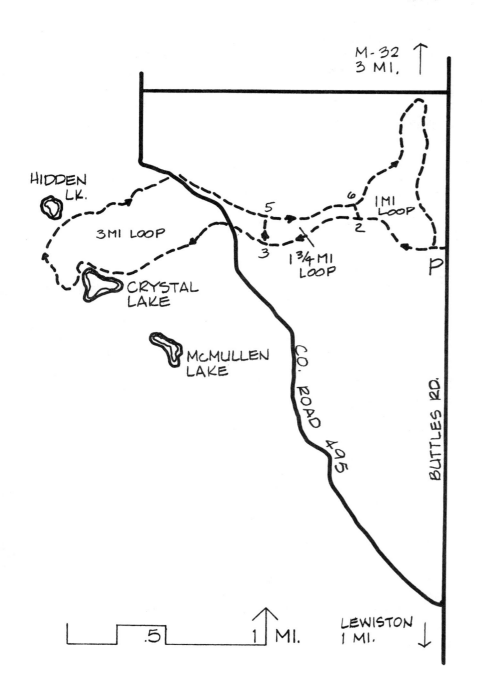

Atlanta Area Forest, Mackinaw State Forest
HCR 74, Box 30
Atlanta, MI 49709

517-785-4251

District Forest Manager, Mackinaw State Forest
Box 667, 1732 West M32
Gaylord, MI 49735

517-732-3541

Michigan Atlas & Gazetteer Location: 77A6

County Location: Montmorency

Directions To Trailhead:
Between Lewiston and M32 on Buttles Rd.(1 mile west of Co Rd 491) Take
Buttles Rd., north about 3 miles to the parking lot at the trailhead on the west
side of the road. Ellsworth Rd. is about 1 mile north of the trailhead.

Trail Type: Hiking/Walking, Cross Country Skiing, Mountain Biking
Trail Distance: 6 mi   Loops: 3   Shortest: 1.2 mi Longest: 3 mi
Trail Surface: Natural
Trail Use Fee: None
Method Of Ski Trail Grooming: None
Skiing Ability Suggested: Novice to intermediate
Hiking Trail Difficulty: Easy
Mountain Biking Ability Suggested: Novice
Terrain: Steep 0%, Hilly 2%, Moderate 30%, Flat 68%
Camping: None

Maintained by the DNR Forest Management Division
An good trail for the beginning skier.
Since much of the trail is in open terrian, this trail should be avoided on windy
winter days.
Other contacts:
        DNR Forest Management Division Office, Lansing, 517-373-1275
        DNR Forest Management Region Office, Roscommon, 517-275-5151

BUTTLES ROAD PATHWAY

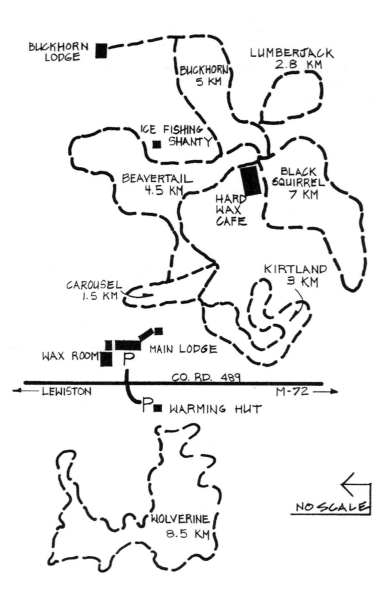

Garland
HCR-1, Box 364-M
Lewiston, MI 49756

517-786-2211
800-968-0042

Michigan Atlas & Gazetteer Location: 77B6

County Location: Oscoda

Directions To Trailhead:
On Co Rd 489, 4.5 miles south of Lewiston and 12 miles north of Luzerne.

Trail Type: Cross Country Skiing
Trail Distance: 32.3 km   Loops: 7   Shortest: 1.5 km Longest: 8.5 km
Trail Surface: Natural
Trail Use Fee: Yes
Method Of Ski Trail Grooming: Track set
Skiing Ability Suggested: Novice to intermediate
Hiking Trail Difficulty: NA
Mountain Biking Ability Suggested: NA
Terrain: Steep 0%, Hilly 0%, Moderate 30%, Flat 70%
Camping: None

Privately operated 3,000 acre, four seasons resort
Ski shop, rentals, lodging, lessons, skating rink, restaurant, sauna, pool and jacuzzi are available. 5000 foot airstrip is on the property with charter air service available.
Very elegant lodge with other accomodations available.
Trails are on the golf course and rolling hills of the surrounding area.

GARLAND

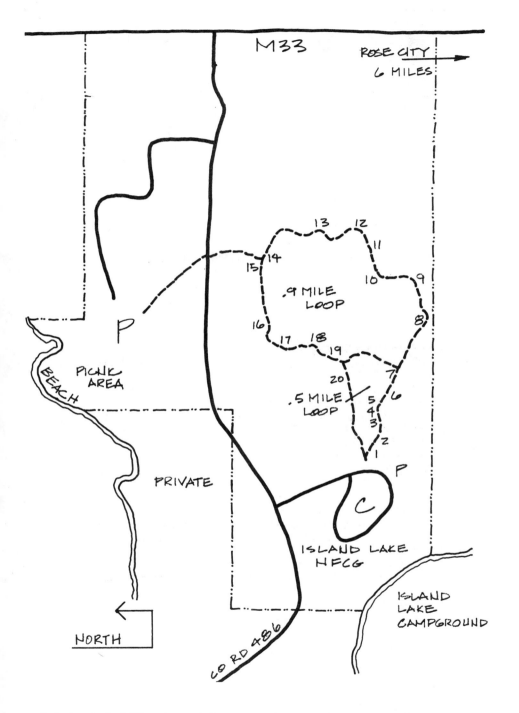

ISLAND LAKE NATURETRAIL

Mio Ranger Station, Huron Manistee National Forest
401 Court St
Mio, MI 48647

517-826-3252

Forest Supervisor, Huron Manistee National Forest
1755 S. Mitchell St.
Cadillac, MI 49691

616-775-2421
800-821-6263

Michigan Atlas & Gazetteer Location: 77D7

County Location: Oscoda

Directions To Trailhead:
North of M33 about 6 miles from Rose City, then west on Co Rd 486 about .7 mile to the campground where the trailhead is located. The main trailhead is not located at the day use area, but there is a feeder trail to the main loop from the day use area.

Trail Type: Hiking/Walking, Interpretive
Trail Distance: 1.4 mi   Loops: 2   Shortest: .5 mi   Longest: .9 mi
Trail Surface: Natural
Trail Use Fee: None
Method Of Ski Trail Grooming: NA
Skiing Ability Suggested: NA
Hiking Trail Difficulty: Easy
Mountain Biking Ability Suggested: NA
Terrain: Steep 5%, Hilly 85%, Moderate 10%, Flat 0%
Camping: At trailhead

Maintained by the Mio Ranger District, Huron Manistee National Forest
The Island Lake Nature Trail is a self guided 20 station interpretive trail.
A trail guide is available.

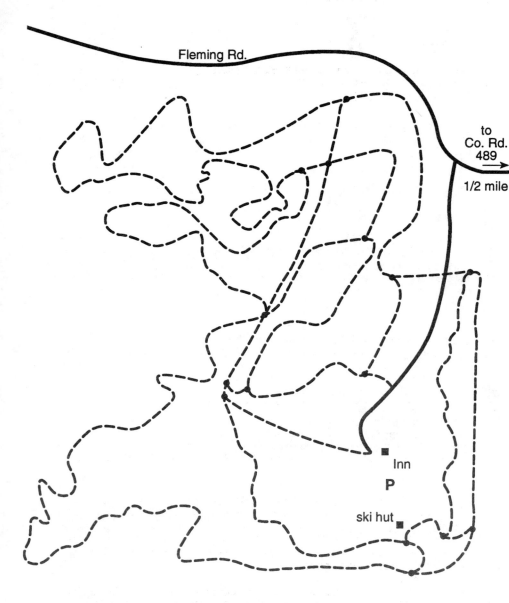

LakeView Hills Country Inn and Nordic Ski Center
PO Box 365
Lewiston, MI 49756

517-786-2000
517-786-3445

Michigan Atlas & Gazetteer Location: 77B6

County Location: Oscoda

Directions To Trailhead:
3 miles south of Lewiston on Co Rd 489, then west on Fleming Rd to resort

Trail Type: Hiking/Walking, Cross Country Skiing, Mountain Biking, Interpretive
Trail Distance: 20 km   Loops: Many   Shortest: Longest:
Trail Surface: Gravel and natural
Trail Use Fee: Yes, free to guests
Method Of Ski Trail Grooming: Track set
Skiing Ability Suggested: Novice to advanced
Hiking Trail Difficulty: Easy to difficult
Mountain Biking Ability Suggested: Novice to Advanced
Terrain: Steep 45%, Hilly 10%, Moderate 30%, Flat 15%
Camping: None

Privately operated bed and breakfast with additional lake front resort nearby.
A beautiful hill top bed and breakfast with very challenging trails
The trails are open to the public without being overnight guests.
Site of nordic ski race annually.

Lakeview Hills Country Inn
Nordic Ski Center

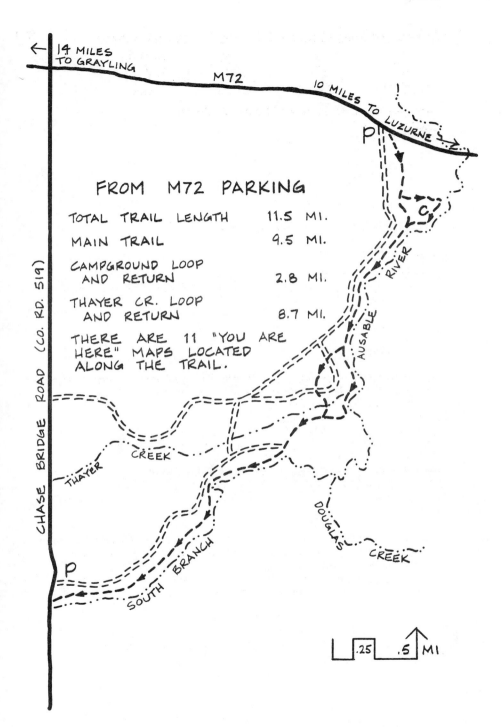

← 14 MILES TO GRAYLING

M72

10 MILES TO LUZURNE →

FROM M72 PARKING

TOTAL TRAIL LENGTH	11.5 MI.
MAIN TRAIL	9.5 MI.
CAMPGROUND LOOP AND RETURN	2.8 MI.
THAYER CR. LOOP AND RETURN	8.7 MI.

THERE ARE 11 "YOU ARE HERE" MAPS LOCATED ALONG THE TRAIL.

CHASE BRIDGE ROAD (CO. RD. 519)

P

C

AUSABLE RIVER

THAYER CREEK

DOUGLAS CREEK

P

SOUTH BRANCH

.25   .5 MI

MASON TRACT PATHWAY

Roscommon Forest Area, Au Sable State Forest
Box 218, 8717 N. Roscommon Rd   517-275-5151
Roscommon, MI 48635

District Forest Manager, Au Sable State Forest
191 S. Mt. Tom Rd.   517-826-3211
Mio, MI 48647

Michigan Atlas & Gazetteer Location: 77D45

County Location: Crawford

Directions To Trailhead:
North trailhead - On M72 about 15 miles east of Grayling
South trailhead - 15 miles east of Grayling turn south on Chase Bridge Rd., then continue about 10 miles to South Branch Au Sable River bridge. Trailhead is on the north side of the bridge.

Trail Type: Hiking/Walking, Cross Country Skiing
Trail Distance: 11.3 mi   Loops: NA   Shortest: NA   Longest: NA
Trail Surface: Natural
Trail Use Fee: None
Method Of Ski Trail Grooming: Track set
Skiing Ability Suggested: Novice to intermediate
Hiking Trail Difficulty: Easy
Mountain Biking Ability Suggested: NA
Terrain: Steep 0%, Hilly 5%, Moderate 85%, Flat 10%
Camping: Campground on Au Sable River along trail at Canoe Harbor

Maintained by the DNR Forest Mananagment Division
This is a point to point trail along the east side of the scenic South Branch, Au Sable River.
There are many summer trailheads since a county road passes within sight of the pathway. However, in the winter the road is not plowed and therefore the only trailheads are listed above.
Other contacts:
        DNR Forest Management Division Office, Lansing, 517-373-1275
        DNR Forest Management Region Office, Roscommon, 517-275-5151

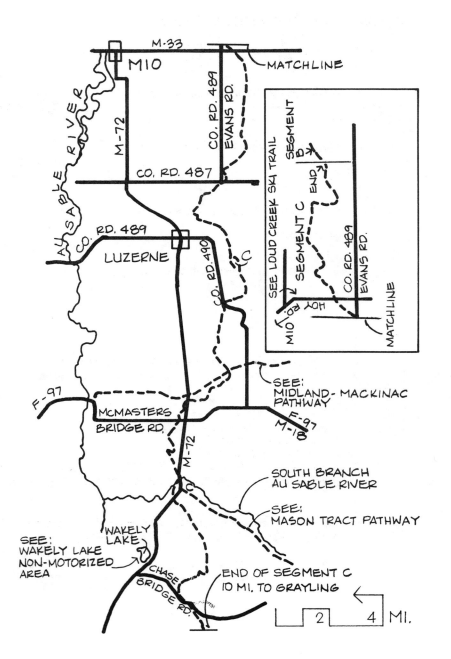

SHORE TO SHORE TRAIL
SEGMENT C

Mio Ranger Station, Huron-Manistee National Forest
401 Court St.
Mio, MI 48647

517-826-3252

Forest Supervisor, Huron-Manistee National Forest
1755 S. Mitchell St
Cadillac, MI 49601

616-775-2421
800-821-6263

Michigan Atlas & Gazetteer Location: 77D4567

County Location: Oscoda/Crawford

Directions To Trailhead:
From a point 6 miles SE of Mio to about 8 miles SE of Grayling.
Luzerne Trail Camp-Mio west on M72 8 miles to Luzerne, then south on Co Rd 490 for 2 miles, then continue south on Durfree (FR 4153) for about 1 mile to the camp.

Trail Type: Hiking/Walking, Mountain Biking
Trail Distance: 41 mi   Loops: No   Shortest: Longest:
Trail Surface: Natural
Trail Use Fee: None
Method Of Ski Trail Grooming: None
Skiing Ability Suggested: NA
Hiking Trail Difficulty: Moderate
Mountain Biking Ability Suggested: Novice but sand present
Terrain: Steep 0%, Hilly 20%, Moderate 20%, Flat 60%
Camping: Campground at Luzerne Trail Camp and backcountry camping permitted

Maintained by the Mio Ranger District, Huron-Manistee National Forest and the Michigan Trail Riders Association.
Trail is primarily for horse back riding.
For maps of the entire trail contact: Michigan Trail Riders Association, 1650 Ormond Rd, White Lake, MI 48383.

Mio Ranger Station, Huron Manistee National Forest
401 Court St.   517-826-3252
Mio, MI 48647

Forest Supervisor, Huron-Manistee National Forest
1755 S. Mitchell St.   616-775-2421
Cadillac, MI 49601   800-821-6263

Michigan Atlas & Gazetteer Location: 77C45

County Location: Crawford

Directions To Trailhead:
10 miles east Grayling and 22 miles west of Mio on M72

Trail Type: Hiking/Walking, Cross Country Skiing, Mountain Biking
Trail Distance: 16.5 mi   Loops: 3   Shortest: 4.5 mi Longest: 7 mi
Trail Surface: Natural
Trail Use Fee: None
Method Of Ski Trail Grooming: None
Skiing Ability Suggested: Novice to advanced
Hiking Trail Difficulty: Easy to moderate
Mountain Biking Ability Suggested: Novice
Terrain: Steep 0%, Hilly 25%, Moderate 55%, Flat 20%
Camping: Permitted but no developed campgrounds in area

Maintained by the Mio Ranger District, Huron-Manistee National Forest
Part of the area is closed from March 1 -July 1 for Loon Nesting

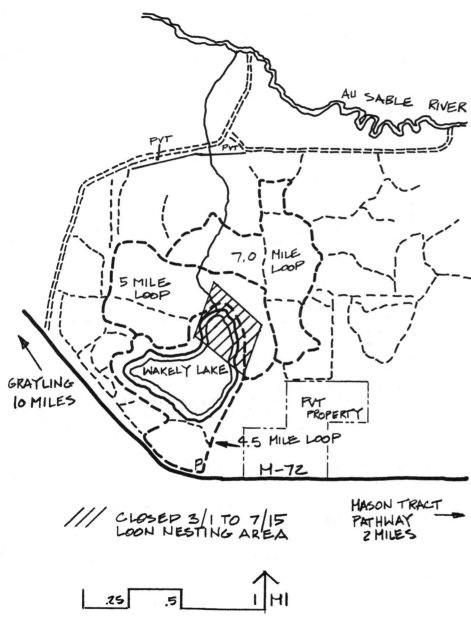

WAKELY LAKE NON-MOTORIZED AREA

Hinchman Acres Resort
702 N. Morenci (M33), PO Box 220
Mio, MI 48647

517-826-3267
800-438-0203

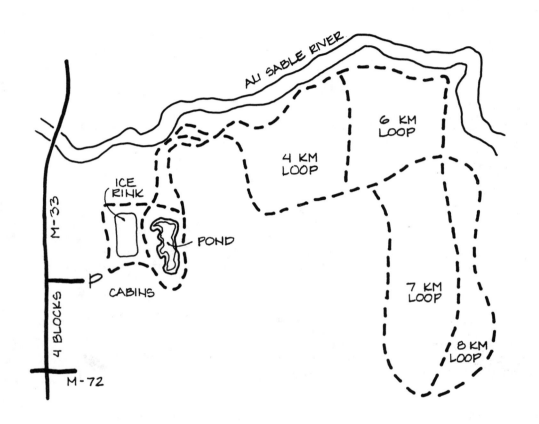

Michigan Atlas & Gazetteer Location: 78D1

County Location: Oscoda

Directions To Trailhead:
North end of Mio, just south of the Au Sable River on the east side of M33

Trail Type: Hiking/Walking, Cross Country Skiing, Mountain Biking
Trail Distance: 20+ km   Loops: 4   Shortest: 4 km   Longest: 8 km
Trail Surface: Natural
Trail Use Fee: Yes, free for guests of the resort
Method Of Ski Trail Grooming: Double track set
Skiing Ability Suggested: Novice
Hiking Trail Difficulty: Easy
Mountain Biking Ability Suggested: Novice
Terrain: Steep 0%, Hilly 0%, Moderate 40%, Flat 60%
Camping: None

Privately operated 4 season resort since 1933.
Warming area, snack bar, lodging, rentals, ski shop and night skiing Ice skating rink on the property.
Lodging available - 13 cottages, 6 with fireplaces.
Scenic trails in the Huron National Forest with views of the Au Sable River.
Free ski rental, no trail fee and free instruction when staying at the resort.
Great family ski resort.
TRAILS FOR HIKING AND MOUNTAIN BIKING AVAILABLE ONLY FOR GUESTS.
Call for more information on these "special packages" AAA approved resort

HINCHMAN ACRES RESORT

Huron Shores Ranger Station, Huron Manistee National Forest
5761 N. Skeel Rd.   517-724-6471
Oscoda, MI 48750

Forest Supervisor, Huron-Manistee National Forest
1755 S. Mitchell St.   616-775-2421
Cadillac, MI 49601   800-821-6263

Michigan Atlas & Gazetteer Location: 78C34

County Location: Alcona

Directions To Trailhead:
22 miles west of Harrisville on M72 at M65 Jct.
East trailhead - .25 mile south of Jct on M65
West trailhead - On F32(FR4516) just north of the Au Sable Rd intersection

Trail Type: Hiking/Walking, Cross Country Skiing
Trail Distance: 20 mi   Loops: Many   Shortest: 1 mi   Longest: 18 mi
Trail Surface: Natural
Trail Use Fee: None
Method Of Ski Trail Grooming: None
Skiing Ability Suggested: Intermediate to advanced
Hiking Trail Difficulty: Moderate to difficult
Mountain Biking Ability Suggested: NA
Terrain: Rolling to hilly
Camping: Off trail camping permitted

Maintained by the Harrisville Ranger District, Huron-Manistee National Forest
An extensive area of 10,600 acres restricted for use by hikers, skiers and
snowshoers only
Tow hand pumps are along the trails at each end of the area and useable year
around.
Write for brochure

SEE MAP ON NEXT PAGE

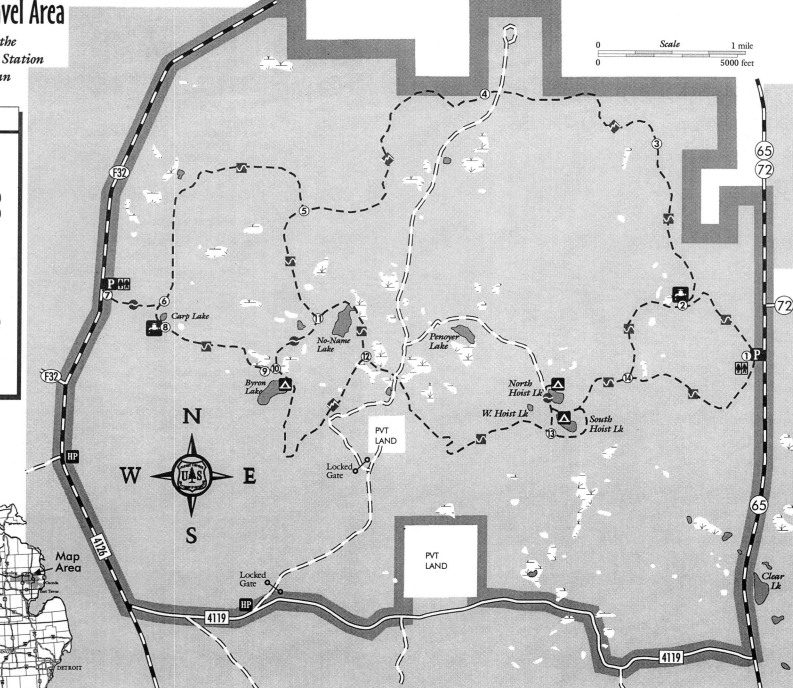

Hoist Lakes Foot Travel Area

Administered by the
Huron Shores Ranger Station
Oscoda, Michigan

Segment	Distance
1-2	¾ mi (1.2 km)
2-3	¾ mi (1.2 km)
3-4	1¼ mi (2 km)
4-5	2¼ mi (3.6 km)
5-6	2¼ mi (3.6 km)
6-7	½ mi (.8 km)
6-8	¼ mi (.4 km)
8-9	1 mi (1.6 km)
9-10	1/10 mi
10-11	½ mi (.8 km)
11-12	¼ mi (.4 km)
10-12	1½ mi (2.4 km)
12-13	3 mi (4.8 km)
13-14	1 mi (1.6 km)
14-2	¾ mi (1.2 km)
14-1	12 mi (2.4 km)

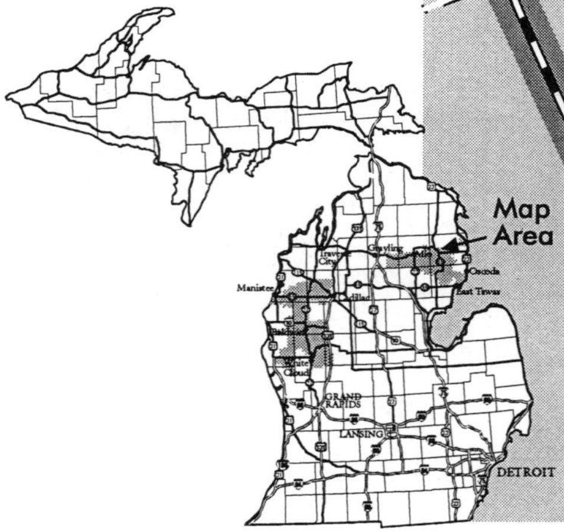

Carp Lake

No-Name Lake

Penoyer Lake

Byron Lake

North Hoist Lk

W. Hoist Lk

South Hoist Lk

PVT LAND

Locked Gate

PVT LAND

Locked Gate

Clear Lk

Map Area

F32

4126

4119

65

72

Huron Shores Ranger Station, Huron Manistee National Forest
5761 N. Skeel Rd
Oscoda, MI 47850

517-724-6471

Forest Supervisor, Huron Manistee National Forest
1755 S. Mitchell St.
Cadillac, MI 49601

616-775-2421
800-821-6263

Michigan Atlas & Gazetteer Location: 78D4

County Location: Alcona

Directions To Trailhead:
From the intersection of M72 and M65 go south 3.3 miles to FR 4124, then right 1 mile to campground and trailhead

Trail Type: Hiking/Walking, Interpretive
Trail Distance: 1 MI   Loops: 1   Shortest: NA   Longest: 1 mi
Trail Surface: Natural
Trail Use Fee: None
Method Of Ski Trail Grooming: None
Skiing Ability Suggested: Novice
Hiking Trail Difficulty: Easy
Mountain Biking Ability Suggested: NA
Terrain: Steep 0%, Hilly 0%, Moderate 95%, Flat 5%
Camping: At trailhead

Maintained by the Harrisville Ranger District, Huron Manistee National Forest
Short campground hiking trail along the shore of Horseshoe Lake

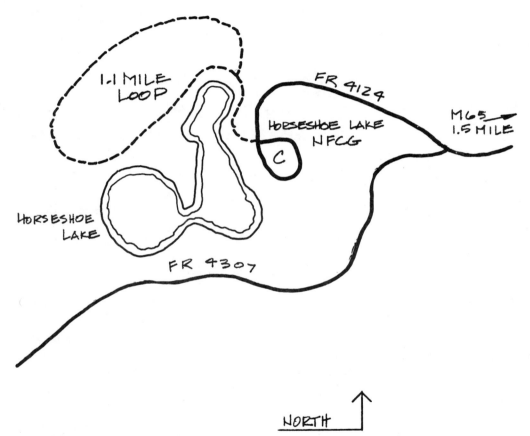

1.1 MILE LOOP

FR 4124

HORSESHOE LAKE NFCG

C

M65 1.5 MILE

HORSESHOE LAKE

FR 4307

NORTH

HORSESHOE LAKE NATURE TRAIL

Loud Creek Cross Country Ski Trail

Mio Ranger Station, Huron-Manistee National Forest
401 Court St.   517-826-3252
Mio, MI 48647

Forest Supervisor, Huron-Manistee National Forest
1755 S. Mitchell St.   616-775-2421
Cadillac, MI 49601   800-821-6263

Michigan Atlas & Gazetteer Location: 78CD1

County Location: Ogemaw

Directions To Trailhead:
From East 14th St. in Mio, south 1 mile on Hoy Rd., then east .5 mile on Cauchy Rd. to parking lot

SEE MAP ON NEXT PAGE

Trail Type: Hiking/Walking, Cross Country Skiing
Trail Distance: 9.8 km   Loops: 6   Shortest: 1.3 km Longest: 2.2 km
Trail Surface: Natural
Trail Use Fee: None
Method Of Ski Trail Grooming: Packed
Skiing Ability Suggested: Intermediate
Hiking Trail Difficulty: Easy
Mountain Biking Ability Suggested: NA
Terrain: Steep 0%, Hilly 40%, Moderate 40%, Flat 20%
Camping: Backcountry camping permitted

Maintained by the Mio Ranger District, Huron-Manistee National Forest
A total of 12 miles of ski loops are planned for this system in coming years
The trail system will be designed for the intermediate to advanced skier
Strong local support from the Loud Creek Nordic Club built and maintains this trail system.
For information about the club, contact the district ranger for the name and address of the current club president.

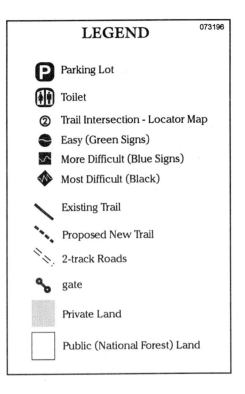

LEGEND

073196

P Parking Lot

🚻 Toilet

② Trail Intersection - Locator Map

● Easy (Green Signs)

▨ More Difficult (Blue Signs)

◆ Most Difficult (Black)

— Existing Trail

--- Proposed New Trail

⫶⫶ 2-track Roads

⊶ gate

▨ Private Land

☐ Public (National Forest) Land

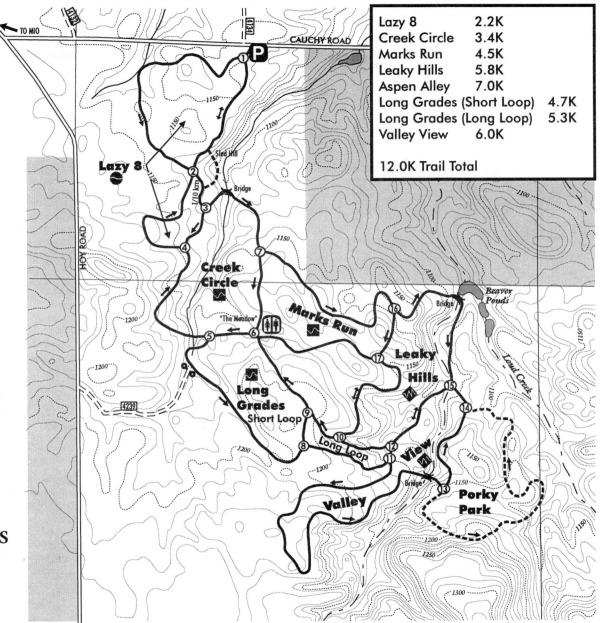

Lazy 8	2.2K
Creek Circle	3.4K
Marks Run	4.5K
Leaky Hills	5.8K
Aspen Alley	7.0K
Long Grades (Short Loop)	4.7K
Long Grades (Long Loop)	5.3K
Valley View	6.0K

12.0K Trail Total

LOUD CREEK SKI - HIKING TRAILS

Mio Ranger District
Huron National Forest

NORTH

Scale:

0   402 mtr   1/2 mile
.8 km

330.1

Huron Shores Ranger Station, Huron-Manistee National Forest
5761 N. Skeel Rd   517-724-6471
Oscoda, MI 48750

Forest Supervisor, Huron-Manistee National Forest
1755 S. Mitchell St.   616-775-2421
Cadillac, MI 49601   800-821-6263

Michigan Atlas & Gazetteer Location: 78D123

County Location: Alcona

Directions To Trailhead:
From the Iosco Co line near the Au Sable River west to a point about 4 miles
SW of McKinley near Co Rd 602.
West trailhead - McKinley Trail Camp-From Mio east on Co Rd 602 for 9 miles
to the camp
Trail access-From M65 in Glennie, take Bamfield Rd west 6 miles to the
Curtisville Store. The trail is across the road from the store

Trail Type: Hiking/Walking, Mountain Biking
Trail Distance: 25 mi   Loops: No   Shortest: NA   Longest: NA
Trail Surface: Natural
Trail Use Fee: None
Method Of Ski Trail Grooming: None
Skiing Ability Suggested: NA
Hiking Trail Difficulty: Moderate
Mountain Biking Ability Suggested: Novice but sand present
Terrain: Steep 0%, Hilly 0%, Moderate 70%, Flat 30%
Camping: McKinley Trail Camp and wilderness camping permitted

Maintained by the Harrisville Ranger District, Huron-Manistee National Forest
and the Michigan Trail Riders Association
Primarily a horse back riding trail.
Can be used for backcountry skiing for experienced skiers with good winter
survival skills
A portion of the trail follows the ridge along the Au Sable River.
Several wood bridges cross streams along the trail.
For detailed maps of the entire trail contact: Michigan Trail Riders Association,
1650 Ormond Rd. White Lake, MI 48383

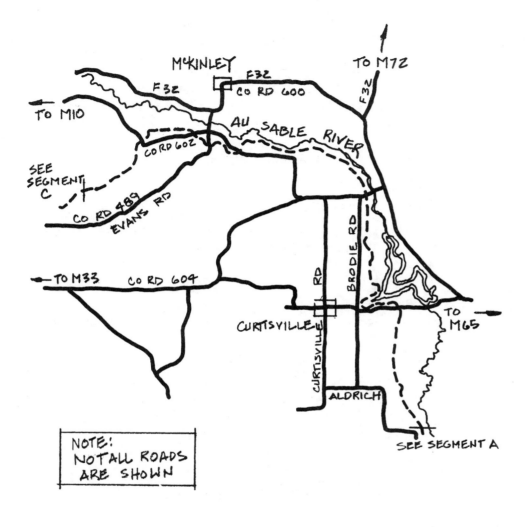

NOTE:
NOT ALL ROADS
ARE SHOWN

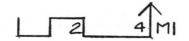

SHORE TO SHORE TRAIL
SEGMENT B

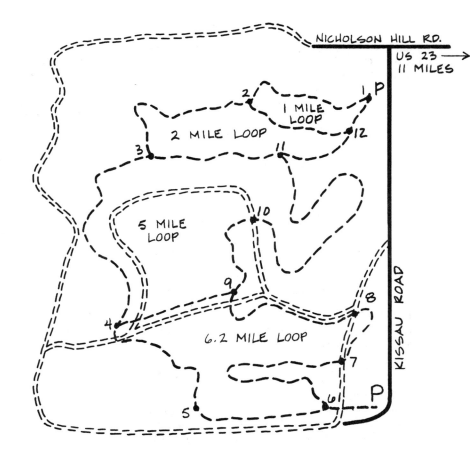

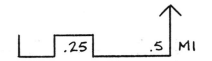

CHIPPEWA HILLS PATHWAY

Chippewa Hills Pathway

Atlanta Forest Area, Mackinaw State Forest
HCR 74, Box 30   517-785-4252
Atlanta, MI 49709

District Forest Manager, Mackinaw State Forest
Box 667, 1732 West M32   517-732-3541
Gaylord, MI 49735

Michigan Atlas & Gazetteer Location: 79A4

County Location: Alpena

Directions To Trailhead:
Between Harrisville and Alpena, 11 miles west of Ossineke (US23) on Nicholson Hill Rd. Trailhead - Just south of Nicholson Hill Rd. on Kissau Rd. Overflow parking available on Nicholson Hill Rd., just west of Kissau Rd.

Trail Type: Hiking/Walking, Cross Country Skiing, Mountain Biking
Trail Distance: 8 mi   Loops: 4   Shortest: 1 mi   Longest: 2.9 mi
Trail Surface: Natural
Trail Use Fee: None
Method Of Ski Trail Grooming: Track set
Skiing Ability Suggested: Novice to intermediate
Hiking Trail Difficulty: Easy
Mountain Biking Ability Suggested: Novice to intermediate
Terrain: Steep 3%, Hilly 5%, Moderate 60%, Flat 32%
Camping: None

Maintained by the DNR Forest Management Division
Waxing and sitting benches provided along trail.
Trail maps and directional arrows are at all intersections.
Scenic overlook along trail.
Popular local ski trail.
Other contacts:
        DNR Forest Management Division Office, Lansing, 517-373-1275
        DNR Forest Management Region Office, Roscommon, 517-275-5151

HARRISVILLE

US 23

C

C

CEDAR RUN
NATURE
TRAIL

P

DAY
USE

BEACH

LAKE
HURON

SCALE NOT KNOWN

Tawas Point State Park
686 Tawas Point State Park
East Tawas, MI 48730

517-362-5041

Harrisville State Park
PO Box 326
Harrrisville, MI 48740

517-724-5126

Michigan Atlas & Gazetteer Location: 79C7

County Location: Alcona

Directions To Trailhead:
Along Lake Huron off US23 on the south edge of Harrisville

Trail Type: Interpretive
Trail Distance: 1 mi   Loops: 1   Shortest: NA   Longest: 1 mi
Trail Surface: Natrual
Trail Use Fee: None, except vehicle permit required
Method Of Ski Trail Grooming: NA
Skiing Ability Suggested: NA
Hiking Trail Difficulty: NA
Mountain Biking Ability Suggested: NA
Terrain: Flat 100%
Camping: Modern campground on site

Maintained by the DNR Parks and Recreation Division.
The Cedar Run Nature Trail has 14 interpretated stations.

HARRISVILLE STATE PARK

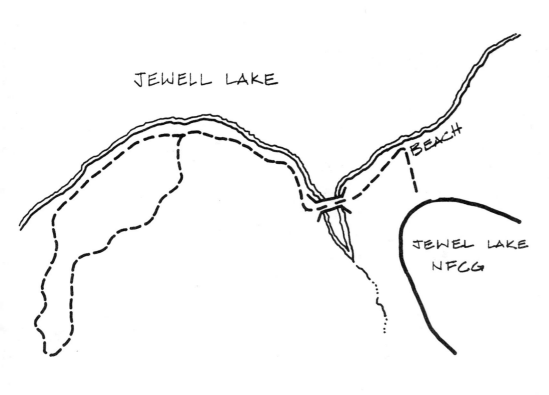

JEWELL LAKE

BEACH

JEWEL LAKE
NFCG

.25 MI

JEWELL LAKE TRAIL

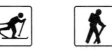

Huron Shores Ranger Station, Huron Manistee National Forest
5761 N. Skeel Rd   517-724-6471
Oscoda, MI 48750

Forest Supervisor, Huron Manistee National Forest
1755 S. Mitchell St.   616-775-2421
Cadillac, MI 49601   800-821-6263

Michigan Atlas & Gazetteer Location: 79C5

County Location: Alcona

Directions To Trailhead:
14.5 miles west of Harrisville on M72 then north 1.7 miles on Sanborn Rd, then left on Trask Lake Rd for .7 mile, then left on FR 4601 to campground and trailhead

Trail Type: Hiking/Walking, Cross Country Skiing
Trail Distance: 1 mi   Loops: 1   Shortest: NA   Longest: 1 mi
Trail Surface: Natural
Trail Use Fee: None
Method Of Ski Trail Grooming: None
Skiing Ability Suggested: Novice
Hiking Trail Difficulty: Easy
Mountain Biking Ability Suggested: NA
Terrain: 100%Flat
Camping: Campground at trailhead

Maintained by the Harrisville Ranger District, Huron Manistee National Forest
The trail winds through a variety of vegetation types and interesting forest features. The topography is generally flat for a leisurely walk.

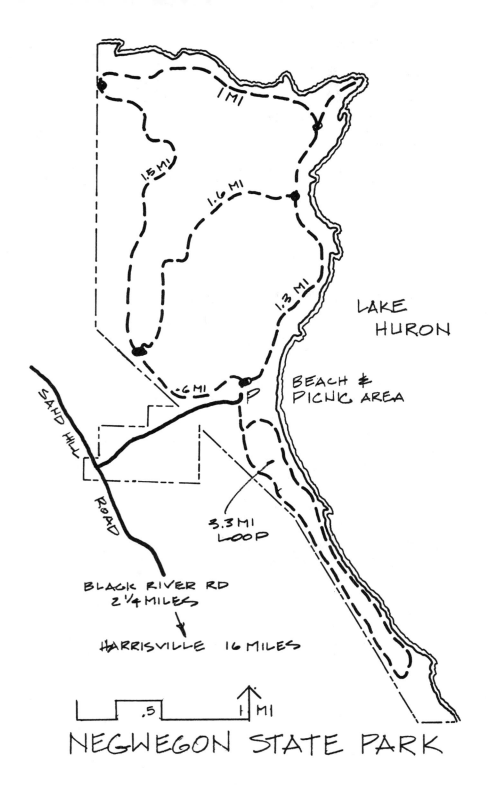

Tawas Point State Park
686 Tawas Beach Rd
East Tawas, MI 48730

517-362-5041

Michigan Atlas & Gazetteer Location: 79AB67

County Location: Alcona

Directions To Trailhead:
12 miles north on US23 from Harrisville to Black River Rd., then east (right) on Black River Rd about 1.5 miles to Sand Hill Rd, then turn left and go 2.5 miles to a gravel road, travel east about 1.25 miles to a parking lot.

Trail Type: Hiking/Walking, Mountain Biking
Trail Distance: 10 mi   Loops: 3   Shortest: 3.3 mi Longest: 5.2 mi
Trail Surface: Natural including sand
Trail Use Fee: None
Method Of Ski Trail Grooming: NA
Skiing Ability Suggested: NA
Hiking Trail Difficulty: Easy
Mountain Biking Ability Suggested: Easy
Terrain: 100% Flat
Camping: At Harrisville State Park

Maintained by the DNR Parks and Recreation Division
Relatively new and undeveloped park. Park development is in the planning stages.
Along the shore of Lake Huron
Very isolated area.

LAKE HURON

BEACH & PICNIC AREA

SAND HILL ROAD

3.3 MI LOOP

BLACK RIVER RD 2¼ MILES

HARRISVILLE 16 MILES

.5   1 MI

NEGWEGON STATE PARK

Atlanta Forest Area, Mackinaw State Forest
4343 M32 West
Alpena, MI 49707   517-354-2209

District Forest Manager, Mackinaw State Forest
1732 West M32 PO Box 667
Gaylord, MI 49735   517-732-3541

Michigan Atlas & Gazetteer Location: 79A6

County Location: Alpena

Directions To Trailhead:
South of Alpena on Lake Huron at Ossineke SFCG

Trail Type: Hiking/Walking, Cross Country Skiing, Interpretive
Trail Distance: 1 mi   Loops: 1   Shortest: NA   Longest: NA
Trail Surface: Natural
Trail Use Fee: None
Method Of Ski Trail Grooming: None
Skiing Ability Suggested: Novice
Hiking Trail Difficulty: Easy
Mountain Biking Ability Suggested: NA
Terrain: 100% Flat
Camping: Campground at the trailhead

Maintained by the DNR Forest Management Division
Trail along the Lake Huron shoreline.

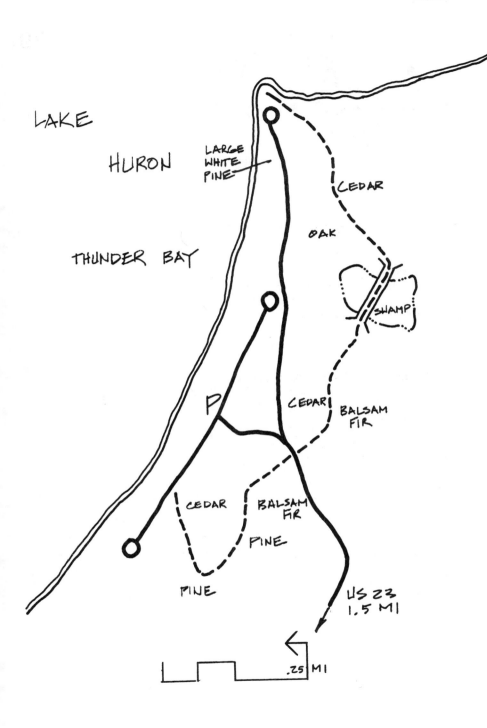

LAKE

HURON

THUNDER BAY

LARGE WHITE PINE

CEDAR

OAK

SWAMP

P

CEDAR

BALSAM FIR

CEDAR

BALSAM FIR

PINE

PINE

US 23
1.5 MI

.25 MI

OSSINEKE PATHWAY

Huron Shores Ranger Station. Huron-Manistee National Forest
5761 N. Skeel Rd   517-724-6471
Oscoda, MI 48750

Forest Supervisor, Huron-Manistee National Forest
1755 S. Mitchell St.   616-775-2421
Cadillac, MI 49601   800-821-6263

Michigan Atlas & Gazetteer Location: 79C4

County Location: Alcona

Directions To Trailhead:
19 miles west of Harrisville on M72 Trailhead is located on the south side of the road

SEE MAP ON NEXT PAGE

Trail Type: Hiking/Walking, Cross Country Skiing
Trail Distance: 6 mi   Loops: 4   Shortest: 3 mi   Longest: 5.6 mi
Trail Surface: Natural
Trail Use Fee: None
Method Of Ski Trail Grooming: None
Skiing Ability Suggested: Novice to intermediate
Hiking Trail Difficulty: Moderate
Mountain Biking Ability Suggested: NA
Terrain: Steep 0%, Hilly 0%, Moderate 25%, Flat 75%
Camping: Primitive campground available

Maintained by the Harrisville Ranger District, Huron-Manistee National Forest
Pleasant area for back country skiing and hiking.
Near the Hoist Lakes Foot Travel Area.
Mountain biking is prohibited in this area.

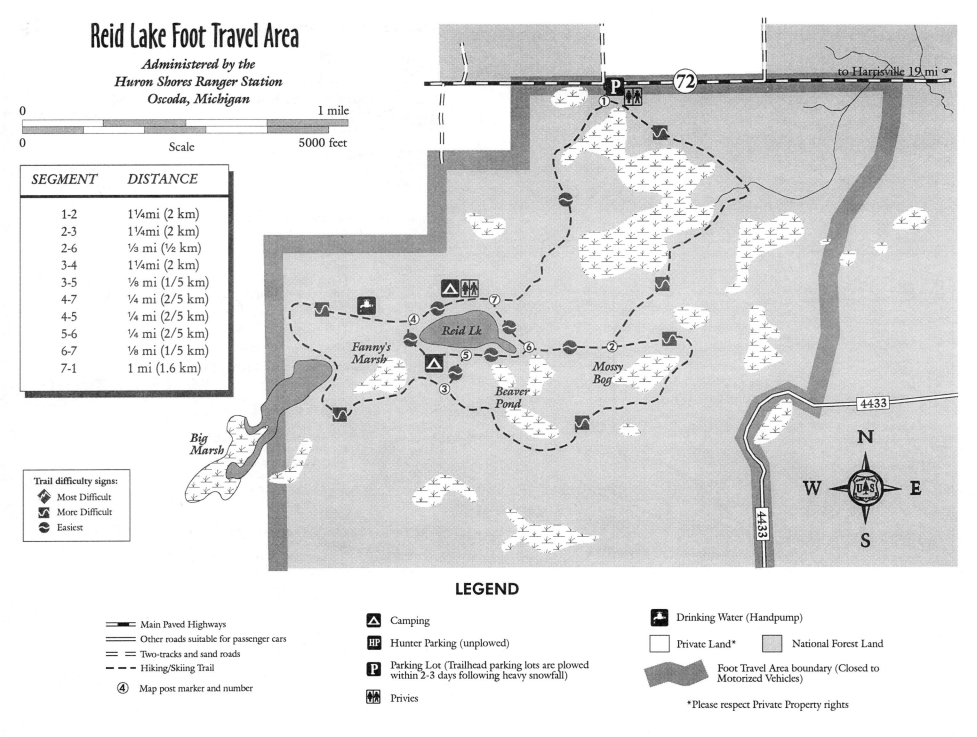

Reid Lake Foot Travel Area

Administered by the
Huron Shores Ranger Station
Oscoda, Michigan

to Harrisville 19 mi

SEGMENT	DISTANCE
1-2	1¼mi (2 km)
2-3	1¼mi (2 km)
2-6	⅓ mi (½ km)
3-4	1¼mi (2 km)
3-5	⅛ mi (1/5 km)
4-7	¼ mi (2/5 km)
4-5	¼ mi (2/5 km)
5-6	¼ mi (2/5 km)
6-7	⅛ mi (1/5 km)
7-1	1 mi (1.6 km)

Reid Lk

Fanny's Marsh

Mossy Bog

Beaver Pond

Big Marsh

Trail difficulty signs:
◆ Most Difficult
▨ More Difficult
⬤ Easiest

N W S E

LEGEND

▰▰▰ Main Paved Highways
═══ Other roads suitable for passenger cars
= = Two-tracks and sand roads
- - - Hiking/Skiing Trail
④ Map post marker and number

△ Camping
HP Hunter Parking (unplowed)
P Parking Lot (Trailhead parking lots are plowed within 2-3 days following heavy snowfall)
🚻 Privies

🚰 Drinking Water (Handpump)
☐ Private Land*
▦ National Forest Land
〰 Foot Travel Area boundary (Closed to Motorized Vehicles)

*Please respect Private Property rights

337.1

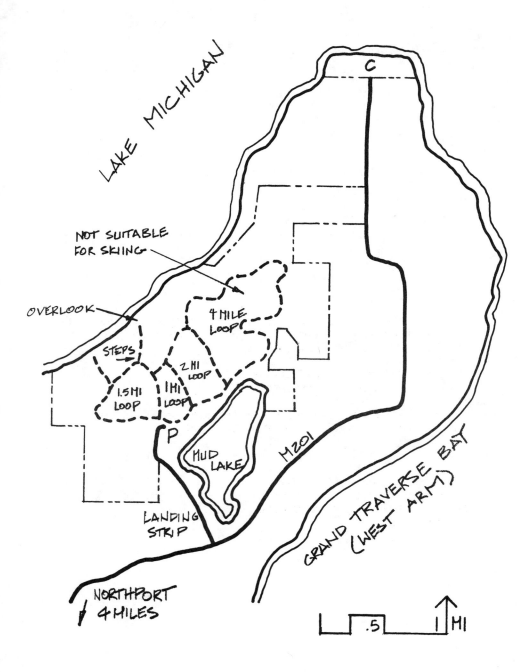

LAKE MICHIGAN

NOT SUITABLE
FOR SKIING

OVERLOOK

STEPS

4 MILE
LOOP

2 MI
LOOP

1.5 MI
LOOP

1 MI
LOOP

P

MUD
LAKE

M201

LANDING
STRIP

GRAND TRAVERSE BAY
(WEST ARM)

NORTHPORT
4 MILES

.5   1 MI

LEELANAU STATE PARK

Leelanau State Park
Rte 1 Box 49
Northport, Mi 49670

616-386-5422

Traverse City State Park
1132 US31 North
Traverse City, MI 49684

616-947-7193

Michigan Atlas & Gazetteer Location: 80C3

County Location: Leelanau

Directions To Trailhead:
At the north end of the Leelanau Peninsula, 36 miles north of Traverse City.
Take Co Rd 629 north out of Northport 3 miles to Densmore Rd (Airport Rd),
then left to the parking lot.

Trail Type: Hiking/Walking, Cross Country Skiing, Interpretive
Trail Distance: 8.5 mi   Loops: 6   Shortest: 1.2 mi Longest: 3.5 mi
Trail Surface: Natural
Trail Use Fee: None, but vehicle entry fee required
Method Of Ski Trail Grooming: None
Skiing Ability Suggested: Intermediate to advanced
Hiking Trail Difficulty: Easy to moderate
Mountain Biking Ability Suggested: NA
Terrain: Steep 10%, Hilly 45%, Moderate 35%, Flat 10%
Camping: Campground available 4 miles north of trailhead

Maintained by the DNR Parks and Recreation Division
Scenic views of Lake Michigan are provided from an overlook and beach.
The trail passes through a dune area, hardwoods, pines and along the shore of
an inland lake to provide plenty of variety.
A pleasant trail system for both hiking and skiing.
The 4 mile loop is not suitable for skiing.

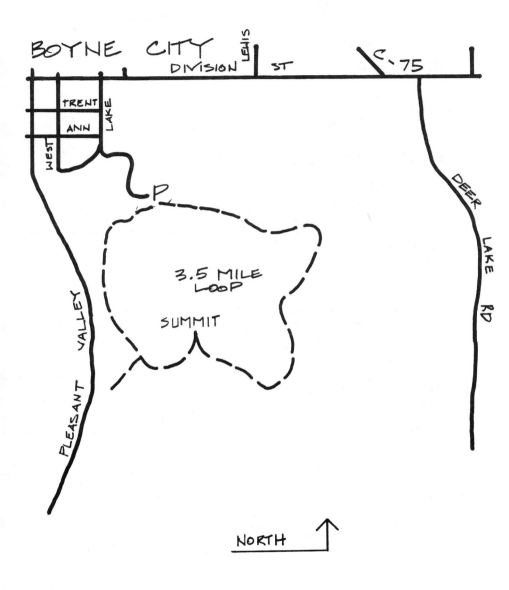

BOYNE CITY

DIVISION

LEWIS ST

C-75

TRENT

LAKE

ANN

WEST

P

DEER LAKE RD

3.5 MILE LOOP

SUMMIT

PLEASANT VALLEY

NORTH ↑

AVALANCHE PRESERVE

Avalanche Preserve

Boyne City Chamber of Commerce
28 S. Lake St.
Boyne City, Mi 49712

616-582-6222

Michigan Atlas & Gazetteer Location: 81C7

County Location: Charlevoix

Directions To Trailhead:
In Boyne City, turn south on Lake St. and proceed to end of the road.

Trail Type: Hiking/Walking, Cross Country Skiing, Mountain Biking, Interpretive
Trail Distance: 4.5 mi   Loops: 2   Shortest: 1.5 mi Longest: 3 mi
Trail Surface: Gravel and natural surfaces
Trail Use Fee: None
Method Of Ski Trail Grooming: Track set
Skiing Ability Suggested: Intermediate
Hiking Trail Difficulty: Moderate
Mountain Biking Ability Suggested: Intermediate to advanced
Terrain: Steep 0%, Hilly 80%, Moderate 15%, Flat 5%
Camping: None

Maintained by the City of Boyne City
Spectacular view of Lake Charlevoix and Boyne City from the trail.
Moderately challenging trail for mountain biking and skiing.
Trail map is approximate only.

Grand Traverse Regional Land Conservancy
624 Third St
Traverse City, MI 49684

616-929-7911

Michigan Atlas & Gazetteer Location: 81D6

County Location: Antrim

Directions To Trailhead:
From Traverse City, take US 31 north to Eastport, then east on M 88 through Central Lake, then turn east on Co. Rd. 624 about 5 miles. About 1/2 mile pat Six Mile Rd, turn left on Wilson Rd. Continue on Wilson Rd to its end past a log cabin to the parking lot.

Trail Type: Hiking/Walking, Interpretive
Trail Distance: 1 mi   Loops: 1   Shortest: NA   Longest: 1 mi
Trail Surface: Natural
Trail Use Fee: None
Method Of Ski Trail Grooming: NA
Skiing Ability Suggested: NA
Hiking Trail Difficulty: Moderate to difficult
Mountain Biking Ability Suggested: NA
Terrain: Steep 10%, Hilly 60%, Moderate 30%, Flat 0%
Camping: None

Maintained by the Grand Traverse Regional Land Conservancy
Wonderful small natural area.
Boardwalk planned in the next few years

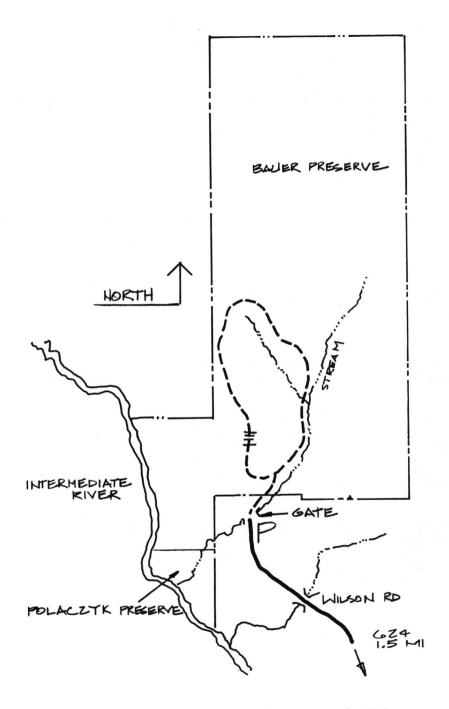

BAUER - POLACZYK
NATURE PRESERVE

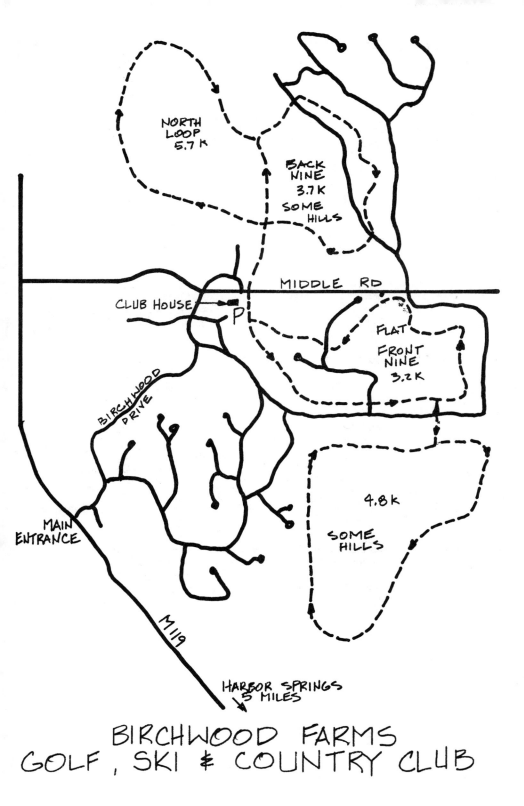

NORTH LOOP 5.7 K

BACK NINE 3.7 K SOME HILLS

MIDDLE RD

CLUB HOUSE

P

FLAT FRONT NINE 3.2 K

BIRCHWOOD DRIVE

4.8 K

SOME HILLS

MAIN ENTRANCE

M119

HARBOR SPRINGS 5 MILES

BIRCHWOOD FARMS
GOLF, SKI & COUNTRY CLUB

Birchwood Farms Golf and Country Club
600 Birchwood Drive
Harbor Springs, MI 49740

616-526-2166

Michigan Atlas & Gazetteer Location: 81A7

County Location: Emmet

Directions To Trailhead:
East of Harbor Springs on M119

Trail Type: Cross Country Skiing
Trail Distance: 3.5 mi   Loops: 4   Shortest: 3.2 km Longest: 5.7 km
Trail Surface: Natural
Trail Use Fee: None
Method Of Ski Trail Grooming: ?
Skiing Ability Suggested: ?
Hiking Trail Difficulty: NA
Mountain Biking Ability Suggested: NA
Terrain: ?
Camping: None

Privately owned residential resort community with trails open to the public.

Little Traverse Conservancy
3264 Powell Rd
Harbor Springs, MI 49740

616-347-0991

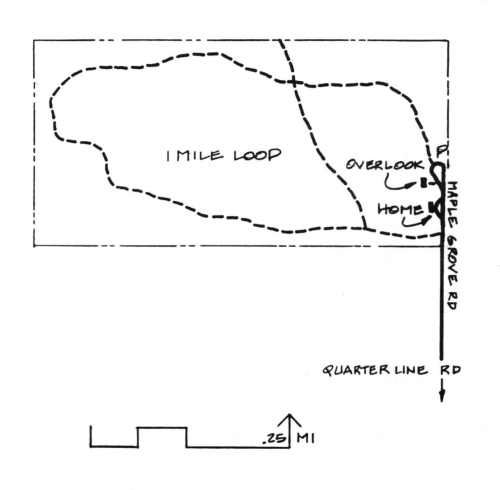

I MILE LOOP

OVERLOOK

HOME

MAPLE GROVE RD

QUARTER LINE RD

.25 MI

Michigan Atlas & Gazetteer Location: 81B6

County Location: Charlevoix

Directions To Trailhead:
From US31 between Charlevoix and Petoskey, take Burgess Rd 3.5 miles to Quarterline, then left 1 mile east to Maple Grove Rd., then left on Maple Grove and continue about .75 mile to parking area and trailhead.

Trail Type: Hiking/Walking, Cross Country Skiing, Interpretive
Trail Distance: 1.8 mi   Loops: 2   Shortest: .3 mi   Longest: 1.5 mi
Trail Surface: Natural
Trail Use Fee: None
Method Of Ski Trail Grooming: None
Skiing Ability Suggested: Novice to intermediate
Hiking Trail Difficulty: Moderate
Mountain Biking Ability Suggested: NA
Terrain: Steep 0%, Hilly 35%, Moderate 35%, Flat 30%
Camping: None on site but Fisherman's Island State Park south of Charlevoix

Owned by the Little Traverse Conservancy
Though it is a small parcel of 80 acres since is located over 300 above Lake Michigan, it has a panoramic view of the Leelanau Peninsula and Beaver Island. A brochure is available for the self guided nature trail.

CHARLES RANSOM NATURE PRESERVE

Fisherman's Island State Park
PO Box 456
Charlevoix, MI 49720

616-547-6641

DNR Parks and Recreation Division

517-373-1270
517-275-5151

Michigan Atlas & Gazetteer Location: 81B5

County Location: Charlevoix

Directions To Trailhead:
2 miles SW of Charlevoix on US31, turn west on Bell's Bay Rd. for about 1 mile to park entrance

Trail Type: Hiking/Walking, Cross Country Skiing, Mountain Biking, Interpretive
Trail Distance: 5 mi   Loops: 2   Shortest: 2 mi   Longest: 4.5 mi
Trail Surface: Natural
Trail Use Fee: None, but vehicle entry fee required $2/day, $10/year
Method Of Ski Trail Grooming: None $4 $20
Skiing Ability Suggested: Novice to intermediate
Hiking Trail Difficulty: Easy
Mountain Biking Ability Suggested: Novice to intermediate
Terrain: Steep 15%, Hilly 15%, Moderate 50%, Flat 20%
Camping: Rustic campground available in park

Maintained by the DNR Parks Division On the shore of Lake Michigan
Also many miles of unmarked two track roads and trails in this 2,763 acres park are available for use.

our walk

Map

Fisherman's Island

P
C
C

BELL'S BAY RD.

MC GEACH CR.

H-31

TO CHARLEVOIX 5 MILES

C

P

CLIPPERVIEW RD.

1 MI.

FISHERMAN'S ISLAND
STATE PARK

Hayo-Went-Ha
RR1 Box 30
Central Lake, MI 49622

616-544-5915
616-544-2916

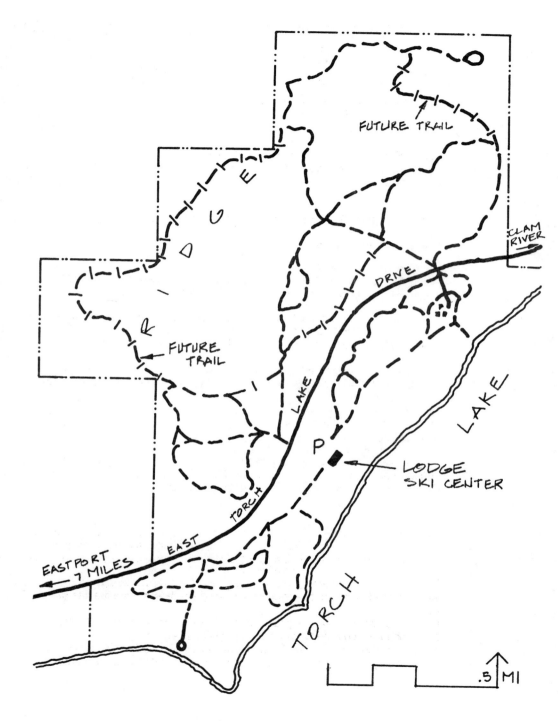

Michigan Atlas & Gazetteer Location: 81D5

County Location: Antrim

Directions To Trailhead:
5 miles south of Eastport on East Torch Lake Drive or 5 miles west of Central Lake on East Torch Lake Drive

Trail Type: Cross Country Skiing
Trail Distance: 18 km   Loops: 5   Shortest: 1 mi   Longest: 3.5 mi
Trail Surface: Natural and gravel
Trail Use Fee: Yes, day, annual, senior and childrens special rates
Method Of Ski Trail Grooming: Track set
Skiing Ability Suggested: Novice to advanced
Hiking Trail Difficulty: NA
Mountain Biking Ability Suggested: NA
Terrain: Steep 5%, Hilly 25%, Moderate 40%, Flat 30%
Camping: None

Owned by the State YMCA of Michigan
Ski rentals, lodge and instruction available.
Modern camp lodge available for overnight groups during the fall, winter and spring seasons.
Scenic views of Torch Lake from the trail.

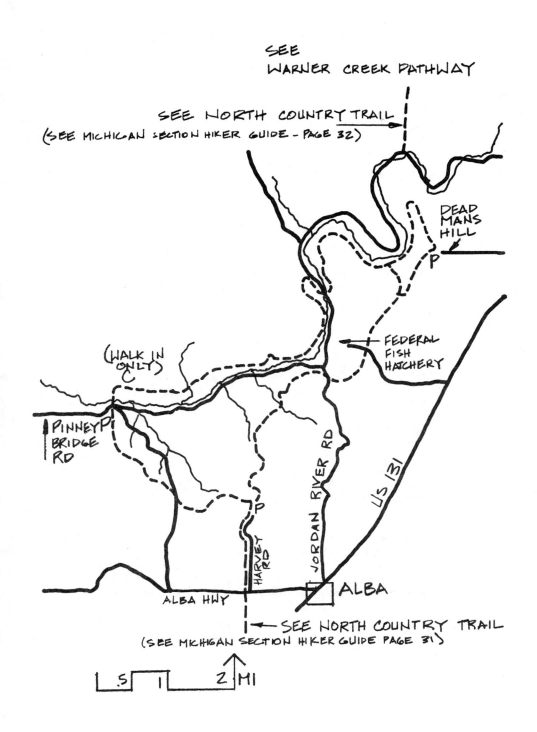

SEE
WARNER CREEK PATHWAY

SEE NORTH COUNTRY TRAIL
(SEE MICHIGAN SECTION HIKER GUIDE - PAGE 32)

DEAD MANS HILL

P

FEDERAL FISH HATCHERY

(WALK IN ONLY)

PINNEY BRIDGE RD

JORDAN RIVER RD

US 131

HARVEY HARD

P

ALBA

ALBA HWY

SEE NORTH COUNTRY TRAIL
(SEE MICHIGAN SECTION HIKER GUIDE PAGE 31)

.5 1 2 MI

JORDAN RIVER PATHWAY

Jordan River Pathway

Gaylord Forest Area, Mackinaw State Forest
1732 West M32, PO Box 667   517-732-3541
Gaylord, MI 49735

District Forest Manager, Mackinaw State Forest
 1732 West M32, PO Box 667   517-732-3541
Gaylord, MI 49735

Michigan Atlas & Gazetteer Location: 81D7, 82D7

County Location: Antrim

Directions To Trailhead:
West of US131; 6 miles north of Mancelona; 9 miles south of Boyne Falls
Trailhead 1 - 1 mile west of Alba on Alba Rd, then north to trail. and valley overlook.
Trailhead 2 - 1.5 miles south of the intersection of M32 and US131, turn west on Deadmans Hill Rd. to overlook .
Trailhead 3 - 2 miles west from M66 on Pinney Bridge Rd. to SFCG

Trail Type: Hiking/Walking, Interpretive
Trail Distance: 18.2 mi   Loops: 2   Shortest: 3 mi   Longest: 18 mi
Trail Surface: Natural
Trail Use Fee: None
Method Of Ski Trail Grooming: NA
Skiing Ability Suggested: NA
Hiking Trail Difficulty: Moderate to difficult
Mountain Biking Ability Suggested: NA
Terrain: Steep 5%, Hilly 70%, Moderate 20%, Flat 5%
Camping: At Pinney Bridge hike in campground only

Maintained by the DNR Forest Management Division
Not suitable for skiing because there are no outruns and sharp turns in the trail.
Mountain biking prohibited by the Director of the DNR.
One of the most scenic river valley's in the state.
The loop is most rewarding with an overnight stay at the hike-in campground which is sited nicely on the edge of a clearing which was once the site of a CCC camp.
Portions of the trail are designated as the North Country National Scenic Trail.
Much of the trail on the north side of the river usually wet.
The trail section south side of river the trail follows a course that is much higher up the valley wall which makes the trail much drier and with more scenic views.

City of Charlevoix, Mt. McSauba Ski Area,
210 State St.   616-547-3267
Charlevoix, MI 49720

City of Charlevoix, Recreation Department
210 State St.   616-547-3253
Charlevoix, Mi 49720

Michigan Atlas & Gazetteer Location: 81B5

County Location: Charlevoix

Directions To Trailhead:
1 mile north of Charlevoix, west of US31 near Lake Michigan. Take Mercer St. north from US31 to Pleasant St. then west on Pleasant to the ski hill lodge or further west to the parking lot at the end of the street in the Mt. McSauba Recreation Area.

Trail Type: Hiking/Walking, Cross Country Skiing
Trail Distance: 2 mi   Loops: 1   Shortest: Longest: 2 mi
Trail Surface: Natural
Trail Use Fee: None
Method Of Ski Trail Grooming: Track set
Skiing Ability Suggested: Novice to intermediate
Hiking Trail Difficulty: Easy to moderate
Mountain Biking Ability Suggested: NA
Terrain: Rolling to hilly
Camping: None

Owned by the City of Charlevoix
Downhill and cross country ski area and summer recreation program take place here.
Warming area and snack bar at base lodge.
Trails connect to the North Point Nature Preserve (see other listing)
The entire trail is lighted for night skiing.

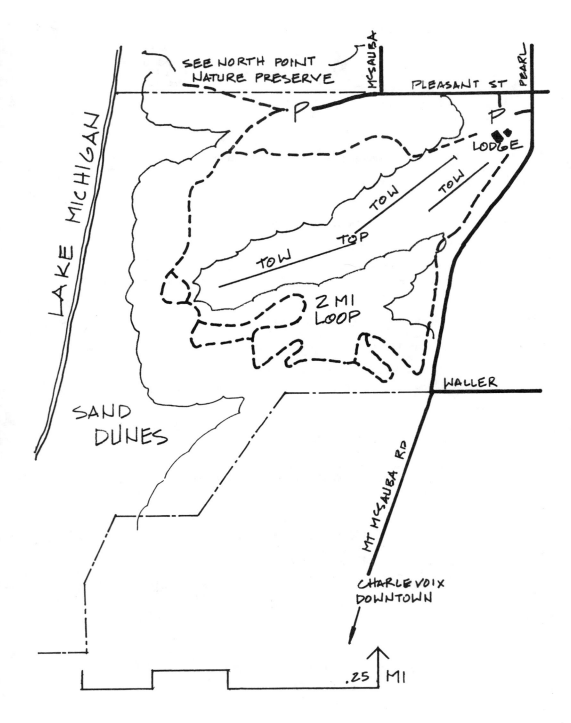

MT MCSAUBA RECREATION AREA

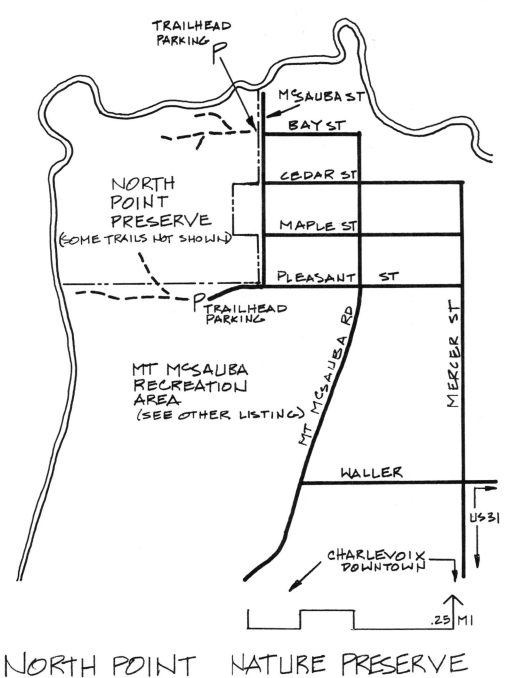

LAKE MICHIGAN

TRAILHEAD PARKING

P

MᶜSAUBA ST

BAY ST

CEDAR ST

NORTH POINT PRESERVE
(SOME TRAILS NOT SHOWN)

MAPLE ST

PLEASANT ST

P Trailhead Parking

MT MᶜSAUBA RECREATION AREA
(SEE OTHER LISTING)

MT MᶜSAUBA RD

MERCER ST

WALLER

US 31

CHARLEVOIX DOWNTOWN

.25 MI

NORTH POINT NATURE PRESERVE

North Point Nature Preserve

Little Traverse Conservancy
3264 Powell Rd
Harbor Springs, MI 49740

616-347-0991

Charlevoix Township

Michigan Atlas & Gazetteer Location: 81B6

County Location: Charlevoix

Directions To Trailhead:
From US31 in Charlevois, takeMercer Rd north to Pleasant St.,then left to the preserve

Trail Type: Hiking/Walking, Cross Country Skiing, Interpretive
Trail Distance: 1.5 mi   Loops: 1   Shortest: NA   Longest: 1.5 mi
Trail Surface: Natural
Trail Use Fee: None
Method Of Ski Trail Grooming: Track set (planned for 1994/95)
Skiing Ability Suggested: Novice
Hiking Trail Difficulty: Easy to moderate
Mountain Biking Ability Suggested: Novice
Terrain: Steep 0%, Hilly 0%, Moderate 35%, Flat 65%
Camping: None

Owned by the Little Traverse Converancy
Adjacent to Mt. McSauba Recreation Area.
2,800 lf of shoreline and 28 acres.
Many trails lace the preserve.
Groomed ski trails connect with the Mt. McSauba Recreation Area trails.

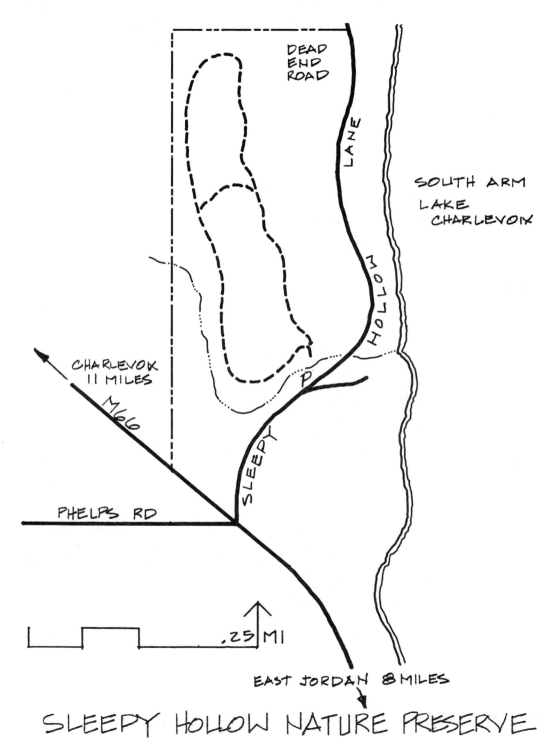

DEAD END ROAD

SOUTH ARM LAKE CHARLEVOIX

HOLLOW

LANE

CHARLEVOIX 11 MILES

M66

P

SLEEPY

PHELPS RD

.25 MI

EAST JORDAN 8 MILES

SLEEPY HOLLOW NATURE PRESERVE

Little Traverse Conservancy
3264 Powell Rd
Harbor Springs, MI 49740

616-347-0991

Michigan Atlas & Gazetteer Location: 81C6

County Location: Charlevoix

Directions To Trailhead:
M66 south of Charlevoix about 11 miles, then left on Sleepy Hollow Lane (across from Phelps Rd), then park about .12 miles on left side of road.

Trail Type: Hiking/Walking, Cross Country Skiing, Interpretive
Trail Distance: 1+mi   Loops: 2   Shortest: Longest:
Trail Surface: Natural
Trail Use Fee: None
Method Of Ski Trail Grooming: None
Skiing Ability Suggested: Novice
Hiking Trail Difficulty: Easy
Mountain Biking Ability Suggested: NA
Terrain: Steep 0%, Hilly 3%, Moderate 70%, Flat 27%
Camping: None

Owned by the Little Traverse Conservancy
A fifty acre parcel with a dense mature forest and spring fed stream.

Thorne Swift Nature Preserve
6696 Lower Shore Drive
Harbor Springs, MI 49740

616-526-6401

Michigan Atlas & Gazetteer Location: 81A7

County Location: Emmet

Directions To Trailhead:
4 miles west of Harbor Springs on Lower Shore Drive via M119

Trail Type: Interpretive
Trail Distance: 1.25 mi   Loops: 2   Shortest: Longest:
Trail Surface: Natural
Trail Use Fee: None, but parking fee for non-township residents
Method Of Ski Trail Grooming: None
Skiing Ability Suggested: NA
Hiking Trail Difficulty: NA
Mountain Biking Ability Suggested: NA
Terrain: 100%Flat
Camping: None

Owned by the Little Traverse Conservancy and leased to West Traverse Township.
Nature preserve complete with a nature center building and resident manager with   naturalist staff. Extensive programs provided.
Beautiful (although small) sandy beach on the north shore of Little Traverse Bay available for swimming and sun bathing.
Open daily from Memorial Day to Labor Day.
A trail guide brochure is available.

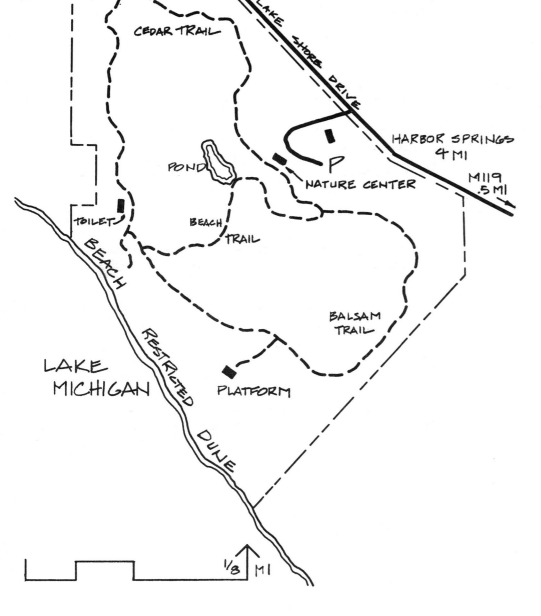

THORNE SWIFT NATURE PRESERVE

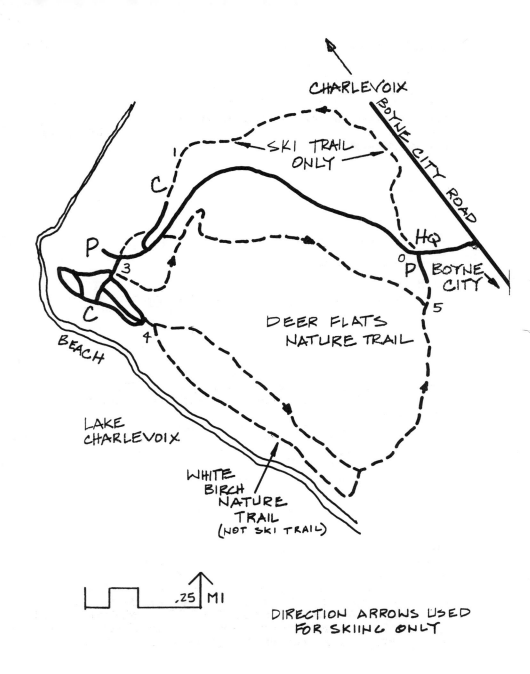

CHARLEVOIX

BOYNE CITY ROAD

SKI TRAIL ONLY

C

P

3

C

BEACH

4

LAKE CHARLEVOIX

DEER FLATS NATURE TRAIL

HQ

P BOYNE CITY

5

WHITE BIRCH NATURE TRAIL (NOT SKI TRAIL)

.25 MI

DIRECTION ARROWS USED FOR SKIING ONLY

YOUNG STATE PARK

Young State Park
Boyne City Rd, PO Box 3651
Boyne City , Mi 49712

616-582-7523

DNR Parks and Recreation Division

517-373-1270
517-275-5151

Michigan Atlas & Gazetteer Location: 81C7

County Location: Charlevoix

Directions To Trailhead:
3 miles north of Boyne City on the north side of Lake Charlevoix on Boyne City Rd.

Trail Type: Hiking/Walking, Cross Country Skiing, Interpretive
Trail Distance: 7.5 mi   Loops: 2   Shortest: 3.5 mi Longest: 5 mi
Trail Surface: Natural
Trail Use Fee: None, but vehicle entry fee required
Method Of Ski Trail Grooming: Track set
Skiing Ability Suggested: Novice
Hiking Trail Difficulty: Easy
Mountain Biking Ability Suggested: NA
Terrain: Steep 5%, Hilly 5%, Moderate 10%, Flat 80%
Camping: Campground available in park

Maintained by the DNR Parks and Recreation Division
The White Birch Nature Trail is not groomed for skiing.
An additional trail is groomed in the winter to provide two loops.
Although the park is very popular, considerable wildlife and flora can be observed along the trails.

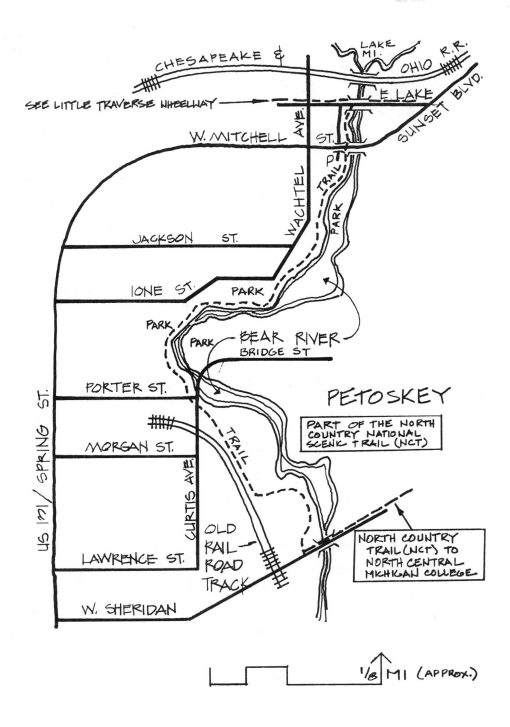

Bear River Park

City of Petoskey, Parks and Recreation Department
100 W. Lake St.
Petoskey, MI 49770

616-347-2500

Michigan Atlas & Gazetteer Location: 82AB1

County Location: Emmet

Directions To Trailhead:
From US31, turn on Lake St west to City Hall. Trail across from City Hall.

Trail Type: Hiking/Walking, Cross Country Skiing, Mountain Biking
Trail Distance: 1.75 mi   Loops: NA   Shortest: NA   Longest: NA
Trail Surface: Natural
Trail Use Fee: None
Method Of Ski Trail Grooming: None
Skiing Ability Suggested: Novice to intermediate
Hiking Trail Difficulty: Easy
Mountain Biking Ability Suggested: Novice
Terrain: Steep 0%, Hilly 20%, Moderate 20%, Flat 60%
Camping: Mangus Park in Petoskey

Owned by the City of Petoskey
In this a city park in the middle of town along the Bear River.
About 1 mile of the trail can be used by mountain bikes.
Trail connects with the Little Traverse Wheelway (see other listing) at Lake St.
The trail is just south and across the street from the fire station on Lake St.
Part of the North Country National Scenic Trail (NCT). The NCT continues south
through the North Central Michigan College Campus Natural Area (see other
listing) on Howard St. and northwest through Petoskey to Lake Michigan

BEAR RIVER PARK

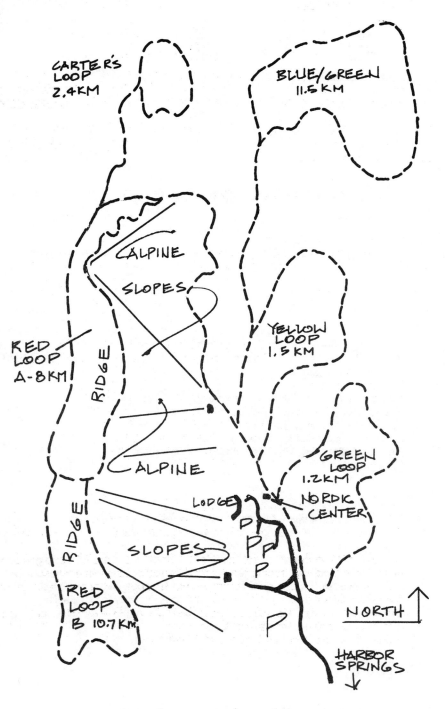

Boyne USA Resorts
Boyne Highlands
Harbor Springs, MI 49740

616-526-3029
800-GOBOYNE

Michigan Atlas & Gazetteer Location: 82A1

County Location: Emmet

Directions To Trailhead:
Between Harbor Springs and Petoskey on Pleasantview Rd (follow signs).

Trail Type: Cross Country Skiing
Trail Distance: 20 mi   Loops: 8   Shortest: .5 mi   Longest: 3 mi
Trail Surface: Natural
Trail Use Fee: Yes
Method Of Ski Trail Grooming: Track set
Skiing Ability Suggested: Novice to advanced
Hiking Trail Difficulty: NA
Mountain Biking Ability Suggested: NA
Terrain: Steep 10%, Hilly 40%, Moderate 40%, Flat 10%
Camping: Available at Petoskey State Park in summer months only

Privately operated luxury 4 seasons ski and golf resort with all facilities.
New trail system for 1997 with loops on top of the mountain and surrounding lowlands.
A 5 mile skating trail provided in the trail system.
Plans for expansion of the ski trails in coming years.

BOYNE HIGHLANDS

Boyne USA Resorts
Boyne Mountain
Boyne Falls, MI 49713

616-549-6088
800-GOBOYNE

Cross Country Ski Director
Boyne Mountain
Boyne Falls, MI 49713

same as above

Michigan Atlas & Gazetteer Location: 82C1

County Location: Charlevoix

Directions To Trailhead:
15 miles south of Petoskey at Boyne Falls, just SW of US131and M75
intersection at the south edge of Boyne Falls

SEE MAP ON NEXT PAGE

Trail Type: Cross Country Skiing, Mountain Biking
Trail Distance: 35 km   Loops: Many   Shortest: .5 km   Longest: 20 km
Trail Surface: Natural
Trail Use Fee: Yes
Method Of Ski Trail Grooming: Track set with skating lanes
Skiing Ability Suggested: Novice to advanced
Hiking Trail Difficulty: Moderate
Mountain Biking Ability Suggested: Intemediate to advanced
Terrain: Steep 10%, Hilly 30%, Moderate 30%, Flat 30%
Camping: None

Privately operated 4 season ski resort.
Lodging, restaurant, snack bar, lessons, rentals, pool and shops.
Great trails for cross country skiing and mountain biking.   Site of mountain bike races.
One trail goes to the top of the mountain. Others are in the hills and golf course of the resort. Special events are planned throughout the winter season,
including races, guided picnic tours, nordic demo-days, hot dog roasts and wine & cheeze tours.
Cross country skiing/lodging packages available. Packages include lodging ood, lessons, trail passes, and apres' ski activities.
About 10 miles of trails are open to mountain biking.

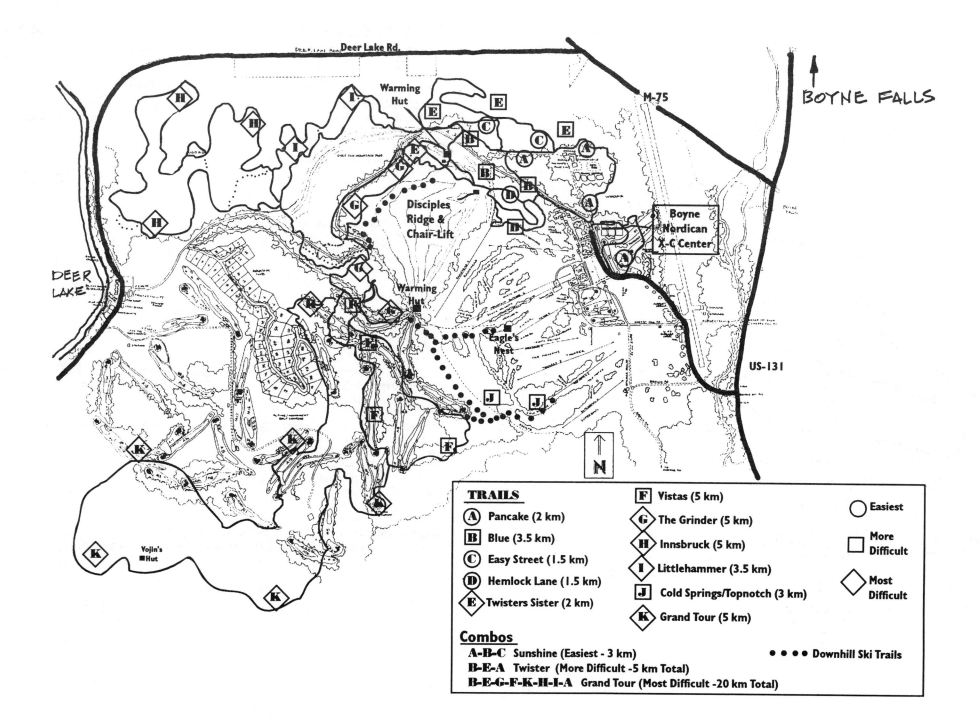

TRAILS

Ⓐ Pancake (2 km)

Ⓑ Blue (3.5 km)

Ⓒ Easy Street (1.5 km)

Ⓓ Hemlock Lane (1.5 km)

◈Ⓔ Twisters Sister (2 km)

Ⓕ Vistas (5 km)

◈Ⓖ The Grinder (5 km)

◈Ⓗ Innsbruck (5 km)

◈Ⓘ Littlehammer (3.5 km)

Ⓙ Cold Springs/Topnotch (3 km)

◈Ⓚ Grand Tour (5 km)

○ Easiest

□ More Difficult

◇ Most Difficult

Combos

A-B-C Sunshine (Easiest - 3 km)

B-E-A Twister (More Difficult -5 km Total)

B-E-G-F-K-H-I-A Grand Tour (Most Difficult -20 km Total)

●●●● Downhill Ski Trails

BOYNE NORDICAN

352.1

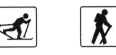

Burt Lake State Park
6635 State Park Drive
Indian River, MI 49749

616-238-9392

DNR Parks and Recreation Divison

517-373-1270
517-275-5151

Michigan Atlas & Gazetteer Location: 82A4

County Location: Cheboygan

Directions To Trailhead:
1 mile south of Indian River on Old US27

Trail Type: Hiking/Walking, Cross Country Skiing, Interpretive
Trail Distance: 1.5 mi　　Loops: 1　　　Shortest: NA　　Longest: 1.5 mi
Trail Surface: Natural
Trail Use Fee: None
Method Of Ski Trail Grooming: None
Skiing Ability Suggested: Novice
Hiking Trail Difficulty: Easy
Mountain Biking Ability Suggested: NA
Terrain: Steep 0%, Hilly 0%, Moderate 20%, Flat 80%
Camping: Campground on site

Maintained by the DNR Parks and Recreation Division
The park has a large sandy beach and is along the shore for a beautiful lake.

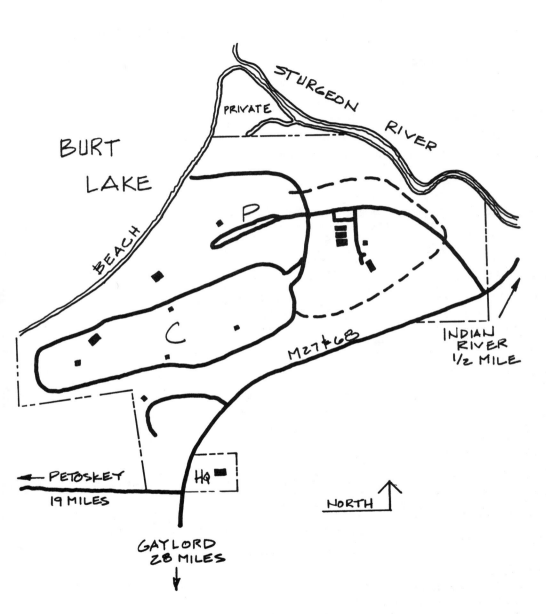

BURT LAKE

BEACH

STURGEON RIVER

PRIVATE

P

C

M27&68

INDIAN RIVER ½ MILE

PETOSKEY 19 MILES

HQ

NORTH

GAYLORD 28 MILES

BURT LAKE STATE PARK

Camp Petosega

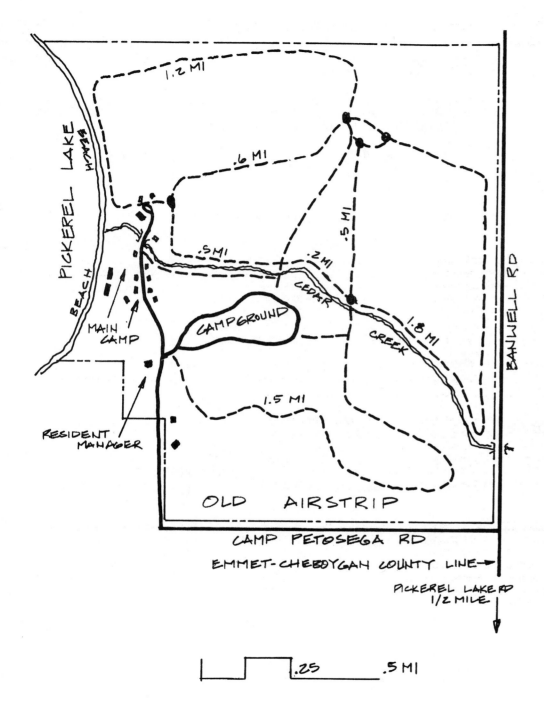

Emmet County
200 Division St.
Petoskey, MI 49770

616-348-1702
616-348-1731

Michigan Atlas & Gazetteer Location: 82A2

County Location: Emmet

Directions To Trailhead:
Located between Petoskey and Indian River on the east side of Pickerel Lake.
Park entrance on the west side of Banwell Rd. From M 68 take Miller Rd (county line) south, continue south onto Banwell Rd to the park (about 4 miles south of M 68).

Trail Type: Hiking/Walking, Cross Country Skiing, Interpretive
Trail Distance: 6 mi   Loops: 6   Shortest: 1 mi   Longest: 4 mi
Trail Surface: Natural
Trail Use Fee: None
Method Of Ski Trail Grooming: None
Skiing Ability Suggested: Novice
Hiking Trail Difficulty: East
Mountain Biking Ability Suggested: NA
Terrain: Steep 10%, Hilly 0%, Moderate 0%, Flat 90%
Camping: Available on the site with 33 sites. 10 with electric

Owned by Emmet County
Facility under redevelopment. Planned operation to resume in 1997.
Park open but no facilities available. Call ahead for current status.
The park is 300 acres, 2,200 ft of sandy beach, 4,000 ft trout stream, 4 rental cabins, 33 improved camp sites, restrooms with showers, RV dump station, picnic grounds, recreaton hall and park store and nature trail.

CAMP PETOSEGA

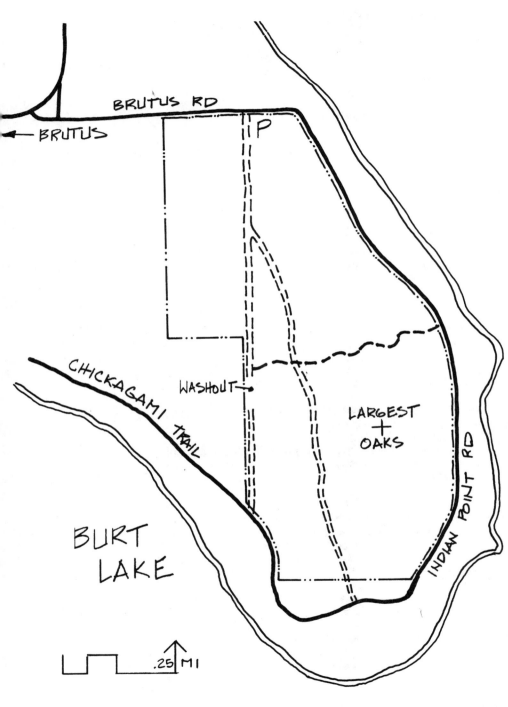

Colonial Point Memorial Forest

Little Traverse Conservancy
3264 Powell Rd
Harbor Springs, MI 49740

616-347-0091

Michigan Atlas & Gazetteer Location: 82A3

County Location: Cheboygan

Directions To Trailhead:
Us 31 north from Petoskey to Brutus Rd, then east on Brutus and continue onto gravel surface. Follow signs to the forest.

Trail Type: Hiking/Walking, Cross Country Skiing, Interpretive
Trail Distance: 2 mi   Loops: Shortest: Longest:
Trail Surface: Natural
Trail Use Fee: None
Method Of Ski Trail Grooming: None
Skiing Ability Suggested: Novice to intermediate
Hiking Trail Difficulty: Easy
Mountain Biking Ability Suggested: MA
Terrain: Steep 0%, Hilly 5%, Moderate 70%, Flat 25%
Camping: Maple Bay SFCG just west of the forest on Burt Lake shoreline.

Owned by the Universtiy of Michigan Biological Station as a gift from the Little Traverse Conservancy and The Nature Conservancy.
The largest stand of old growth Red Oaks in the lower peninsula. Average age is between 100 and 150 years old. Also stands of impressive maple, beech, white pine, basswood, white ash and black cherry are throughout the forest.

COLONIAL POINT MEMORIAL FOREST

Hidden Valley Resort
M32 East, PO Box 556
Gaylord, MI 49735

800-752-5510
517-732-5181

NO MAP

Michigan Atlas & Gazetteer Location: 82D34

County Location: Otsego

Directions To Trailhead:
Just east of Gaylord 1 mile on M32.

Trail Type: Mountain Biking

Trail Surface: Natural
Trail Use Fee: Yes
Method Of Ski Trail Grooming: NA
Skiing Ability Suggested: NA
Hiking Trail Difficulty: NA
Mountain Biking Ability Suggested: Novice to advanced
Terrain:
Camping: None

Privately owned resort open to mountain biking in the summer.
The resort is a private club in the winter and therefore not open to cross country
skiing, except on special occasions.

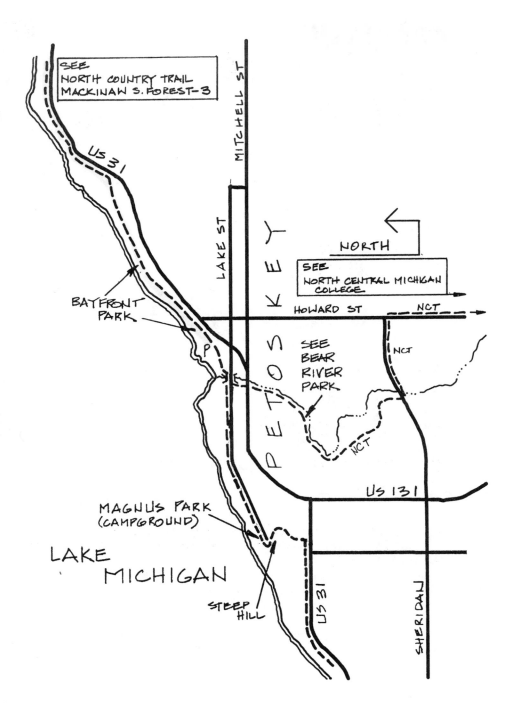

City of Petoskey, Parks and Recreation Department
100 West Lake St
Petoskey, MI 49770

616-347-2500

Michigan Atlas & Gazetteer Location: 82AB1

County Location: Emmet

Directions To Trailhead:
Along US 31 in Petoskey between the highway and Lake Michigan.
Park at Bayfront Park near the History Museum

Trail Type: Hiking/Walking, Cross Country Skiing
Trail Distance: 1.75 mi   Loops: NA   Shortest: NA   Longest: NA
Trail Surface: Paved
Trail Use Fee: None
Method Of Ski Trail Grooming: None
Skiing Ability Suggested: Novice
Hiking Trail Difficulty: Easy
Mountain Biking Ability Suggested: NA
Terrain: Steep 15%, Hilly 10%, Moderate 0%, Flat 75%
Camping: Mangus Park on the bay in Petoskey

Maintained by the City of Petoskey
The trail is along the waterfront on Little Traverse Bay
The Wheelway from Petoskey to Harbor Springs will be a replica of a bikeway
that existed in the 1890's.
The Wheelway is connected to the Bear River Park (see other listing)
The Wheelway, Bear River Park and North Central Michigan College nature
trails are all part of the North Country National Scenic Trail (see other listings)

LITTLE TRAVERSE WHEELWAY

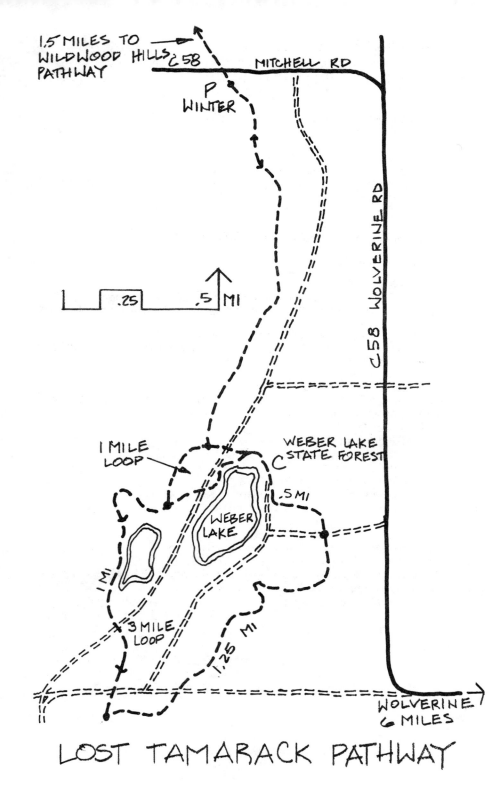

1.5 MILES TO WILDWOOD HILLS PATHWAY

C 58

MITCHELL RD

P WINTER

C 58 WOLVERINE RD

.25 | .5 MI

1 MILE LOOP

WEBER LAKE STATE FOREST

.5 MI

WEBER LAKE

1 MI

3 MILE LOOP

1.25 MI

WOLVERINE 6 MILES

LOST TAMARACK PATHWAY

Lost Tamarack Pathway

Indian River Forest Area, Mackinaw State Forest
6984 M68, PO Box 10   616-238-9313
Indian River, MI 49749

District Forest Manager, Mackinaw State Forest
 1732 West M32, PO Box 667   517-732-3541
Gaylord, MI 49735

Michigan Atlas & Gazetteer Location: 82B3

County Location: Cheboygan

Directions To Trailhead:
6.5 miles west of Wolverine in C58 at Weber Lake State Forest Campground

Trail Type: Hiking/Walking, Cross Country Skiing, Mountain Biking
Trail Distance: 4.75 mi   Loops: 2   Shortest: 1 mi   Longest: 3 mi
Trail Surface: Natural
Trail Use Fee: None
Method Of Ski Trail Grooming: NA
Skiing Ability Suggested: NA
Hiking Trail Difficulty: Easy to moderate
Mountain Biking Ability Suggested: Novice
Terrain: Rolling
Camping: Campground at trailhead

Maintained by the DNR Forest Management Division
Includes a 1.25 mile point to point trail.
The point to point trial is connected to a 1.5 mile trail that connects to to the Wildwood Hills Pathway.
Not well maintained in recent years. Anyone interested in some volunteer work?
Other contacts:
        DNR Forest Management Division Office, Lansing, 517-373-1275
        DNR Forest Management Region Office, Roscommon, 517-275-5151

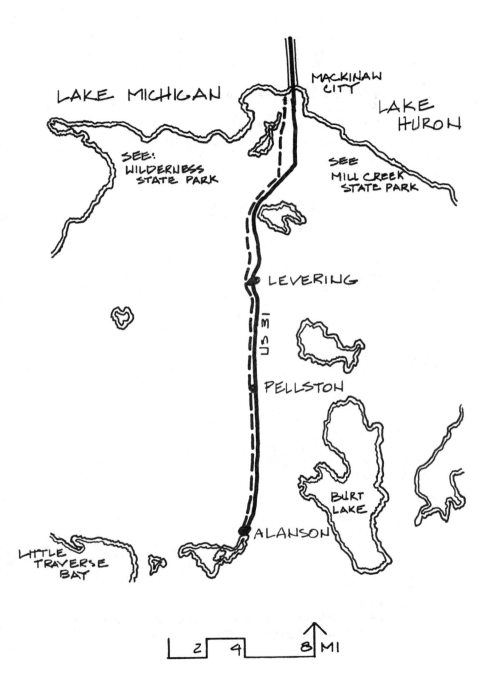

MACKINAW/ALANSON RAIL TRAIL

Indian River Forest Area, Mackinaw State Forest
6984 M68, PO Box 10
Indian River, MI 49749

616-238-9313

District Forest Manger, Mackinaw State Forest
1732 West M32, PO Box 667
Gaylord, MI 49735

517-732-3541

Michigan Atlas & Gazetteer Location: 82A2, 94BCD23

County Location: Emmet,

Directions To Trailhead:
North trailhead - In Mackinaw City, west of I-75 behind the Chalet House Motel and Shepler's Ferry parking lot.. May park in the Chalet House Motel lot, but check in with them first.
Southern trailhead- Hillside Gardens in Alanson
Suggested southern trailhead at this time(1994) due to overgrown condition of the trail - Levering

Trail Type: Hiking/Walking, Mountain Biking
Trail Distance: 24 mi   Loops: NA   Shortest: NA   Longest: NA
Trail Surface: Gravel, ballast and natural
Trail Use Fee: None
Method Of Ski Trail Grooming: NA
Skiing Ability Suggested: NA
Hiking Trail Difficulty: Easy
Mountain Biking Ability Suggested: Novice
Terrain: 100% Flat
Camping: None

Maintained by the Forest Management Division
Used mostly as a snowmobile trail.
Because of loose surface, this trail may be difficult to ride and hike at his time.
Check conditions of the trail surface before starting.

Little Traverse Conservancy
3264 Powell Rd
Harbor Springs, Mi 49740

616-347-0991

Michigan Atlas & Gazetteer Location: 82B2

County Location: Emmet

Directions To Trailhead:
From US31 east of Petoskey, take Mitchell Rd(C58) east to Maxwell Rd, then right approximately .75 mil to the Preserve. Sign on the west (right) side of the road.

Trail Type: Hiking/Walking, Cross Country Skiing, Interpretive
Trail Distance: 1.5 mi   Loops: 2   Shortest: Longest:
Trail Surface: Natural
Trail Use Fee: None
Method Of Ski Trail Grooming: NA
Skiing Ability Suggested: NA
Hiking Trail Difficulty: Easy
Mountain Biking Ability Suggested: NA
Terrain: Steep 0%, Hilly 5%, Moderate 15%, Flat 80%
Camping: None

Owned by the Little Traverse Conservancy
168 acres donated in 1984
Two branches of the Minnehaha Creek which is spring fed, flow across the property.

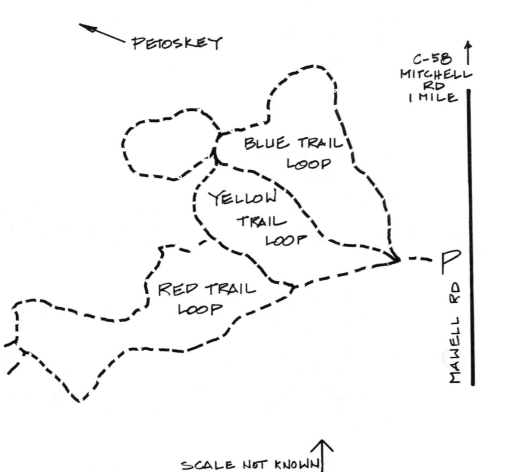

PETOSKEY

C-58
MITCHELL
RD
1 MILE

BLUE TRAIL LOOP

YELLOW TRAIL LOOP

RED TRAIL LOOP

P

MAWELL RD

SCALE NOT KNOWN

McCUNE NATURE PRESERVE

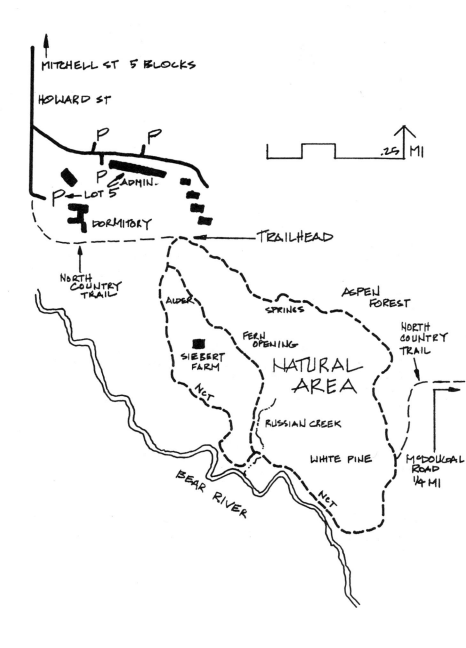

North Central Michigan College
1515 Howard
Petoskey, MI 49770

616-348-6641

Michigan Atlas & Gazetteer Location: 82B1

County Location: Emmet

Directions To Trailhead:
From Mitchell St. in downtown Petoskey, take Howard St south about 9 blocks to the end of the street and the College. Park in Parking Lot 5. Walk east around the south side of the dorm to the trailhead. A trailhead sign designates the beginning of the trail.

Trail Type: Hiking/Walking, Cross Country Skiing, Interpretive
Trail Distance: 2.15 mi　　Loops: 2　　　Shortest: 1.75 mi Longest: 1.85 mi
Trail Surface: Natural
Trail Use Fee: None
Method Of Ski Trail Grooming: None
Skiing Ability Suggested: Novice to intermediate
Hiking Trail Difficulty: Easy
Mountain Biking Ability Suggested: NA
Terrain: Steep 2%, Hilly 8%, Moderate 20%, Flat 70%
Camping: None

Owned by the North Central Michigan College
Short but pleasant ski trails on the edge of town.
The natural area features a variety of habitats including the Bear River and a 52 acre Northern White Cedar swamp. Wet areas are crossed with boardwalks.
A self guided brochure is available at the trailhead.

The North Country National Scenic Trail uses part of this trail system.

NORTH CENTRAL MICHIGAN COLLEGE

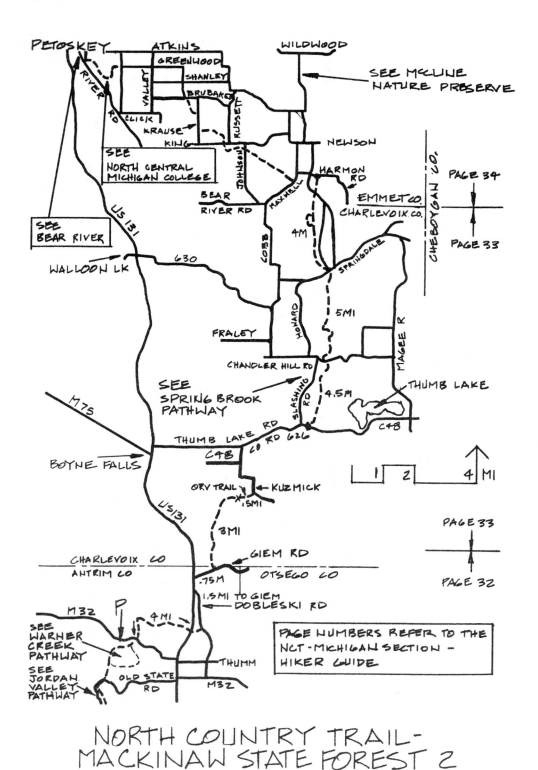

Gaylord Forest Area, Mackinaw State Forest
1732 West M31, PO Box 667   517-732-3541
Gaylord, MI 49735

Indian River Forest Area, Mackinaw State Forest
PO Box 10   616-238-9313
Indian River, MI 49749

Michigan Atlas & Gazetteer Location: 82BCD12

County Location: Antrim, Charlevoix, Emmet

Directions To Trailhead:
South Trailhead - The Jordan River Pathway to the Warner Creek Pathway on M32
North Trailhead - Bear River Trail in Petoskey (see other listing)
Trailhead - On Thumb Lake Rd, about 5 miles east of Boyne Falls
Trailhead - North Central Michigan College Natural Area in Petoskey at the south end of Howard St.

Trail Type: Hiking/Walking, Mountain Biking
Trail Distance: 52+ mi   Loops: NA   Shortest: NA   Longest: NA
Trail Surface: Natural, gravel and paved
Trail Use Fee: None
Method Of Ski Trail Grooming: NA
Skiing Ability Suggested: NA
Hiking Trail Difficulty: Easy to moderate
Mountain Biking Ability Suggested: Novice to intermediate
Terrain: Flat to hilly
Camping: No established campgrounds nearby. Off trail camping permitted.

This section is in the Mackinaw State Forest and on county roads
The route generally parallels US131 to the east except were is crosses US131 at each end of this section near M32 and in Petoskey.
Off road sections of the trail are very scenic.
Some short sections of the trail follows county roads.
For the section south, see NCT- Pere Marquette State Forest 2/Mackinaw State Forest 1
For the section north, see NCT - Mackinaw State Forest 3
For more information and the detailed Hiker Guide map book contact the North Country Trail Association

NORTH COUNTRY TRAIL -
MACKINAW STATE FOREST 2

Indian River Forest Area, Mackinaw State Forest
POB 10   616-238-9313
Indian River, MI 49749

North Country Trail Association
49 Monroe Center, Suite 200B   616-454-5506
Grand Rapids, MI 49503

Michigan Atlas & Gazetteer Location: 82A1,94CD1

County Location: Emmet

Directions To Trailhead:
South Trailhead - Little Traverse Wheelway in Petoskey (see other listing)
North Trailhead - Wilderness State Park just west of Mackinaw City (see other listing)

Trail Type: Hiking/Walking
Trail Distance: 33.2 mi   Loops: NA   Shortest: NA   Longest: NA
Trail Surface: Natural
Trail Use Fee: None
Method Of Ski Trail Grooming: NA
Skiing Ability Suggested: NA
Hiking Trail Difficulty: Moderate
Mountain Biking Ability Suggested: Intermediate to advanced
Terrain: Steep 0%, Hilly 30%, Moderate 60%, Flat 10%
Camping: None along trail but available nearby. See below.

Trail in the Mackinaw State Forest
Some sections along county roads Built and maintained by the North Country Trail Association. Members always welcome.
Very scenic section of northern Michigan. Varied terrian from rolling to hilly and open to deep woods. Northern section follows near the Lake Michigan sand dunes.
Camping near the trail at Petoskey State Park. Camping on the trail at Wycamp State Forest Campground and Wilderness State Park near the north end of this section.No established campgrounds in the middle of this section. However, wilderness camping is pemitted 200' off the trail on state forest property.
For more detailed trail information see the Michigan Section Hiker Guide available from the North Country Trail Association.

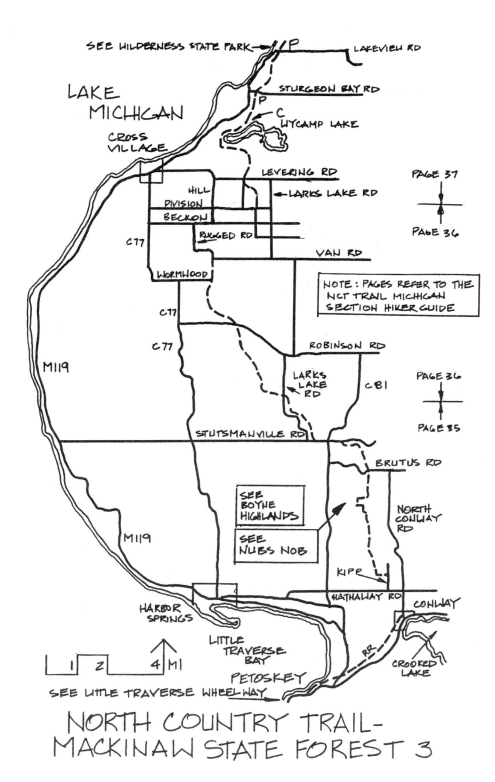

SEE WILDERNESS STATE PARK → P   LAKEVIEW RD

LAKE MICHICAN

STURGEON BAY RD
P
C WYCAMP LAKE

CROSS VILLAGE

LEVERING RD

HILL DIVISION ← LARKS LAKE RD
BECKON

C77   RUGGED RD

VAN RD

WORMWOOD

C77

C77

ROBINSON RD

LARKS LAKE RD   C81

M119

STUTSMANVILLE RD

BRUTUS RD

SEE BOYNE HIGHLANDS

NORTH CONWAY RD

SEE NUBS NOB

M119

KIPP

HARBOR SPRINGS

HATHAWAY RD

CONWAY

LITTLE TRAVERSE BAY

RR

CROOKED LAKE

PETOSKEY

PAGE 37

PAGE 36

NOTE: PAGES REFER TO THE NCT TRAIL MICHIGAN SECTION HIKER GUIDE

PAGE 36

PAGE 35

1 2   4 MI

SEE LITTLE TRAVERSE WHEEL WAY

NORTH COUNTRY TRAIL- MACKINAW STATE FOREST 3

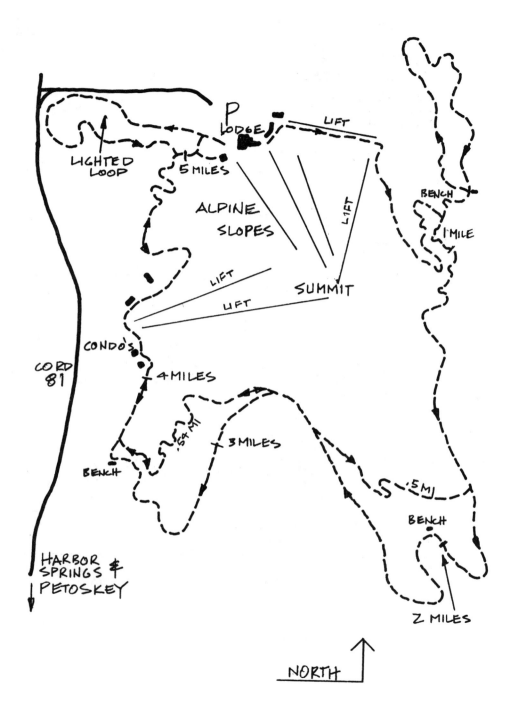

Nub's Nob
4021 Nubs Nob Rd.
Harbor Springs, MI 49740

616-526-2131
800-ski-haus

Michigan Atlas & Gazetteer Location: 82A1

County Location: Emmet

Directions To Trailhead:
Northeast of Harbor Springs on C81. Follow the signs

Trail Type: Cross Country Skiing
Trail Distance: 14 km   Loops: 2   Shortest: 2 km   Longest: 12 km
Trail Surface: Natural
Trail Use Fee: Yes
Method Of Ski Trail Grooming: Track set and skating lanes
Skiing Ability Suggested: Novice and advanced
Hiking Trail Difficulty: NA
Mountain Biking Ability Suggested: NA
Terrain: Steep 5%, Hilly 40%, Moderate 50%, Flat 5%
Camping: None

Privately operated downhill ski resort
Restaurant, lodge, and rentals available.
The main loop several hundred feet of elevation change.
Detailed trail map available when paying trail fee.
(*) Includes optional routes and internal loops.
2km lighted flat trail available
Especially for skate skiers, the trail is 16' wide!

NUB'S NOB

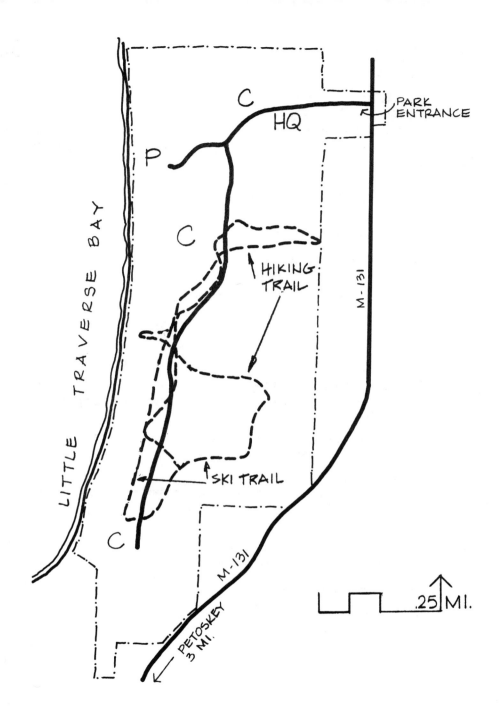

PETOSKEY STATE PARK

Petoskey State Park

Petoskey State Park
2475 Harbor-Petoskey Rd.
Petoskey, MI 49770

616-347-2311

DNR Parks and Recreation Division

517-373-1270

Michigan Atlas & Gazetteer Location: 82A1

County Location: Emmet

Directions To Trailhead:
West of Petoskey via US31, then north on M119 (Harbor-Petoskey Rd.) to the park which will be on your left

Trail Type: Hiking/Walking, Cross Country Skiing, Interpretive
Trail Distance: 5 mi   Loops: 2   Shortest: 2 mi   Longest: 4 mi
Trail Surface: Natural
Trail Use Fee: None, but vehicle entry fee required
Method Of Ski Trail Grooming: None
Skiing Ability Suggested: Novice
Hiking Trail Difficulty: Moderate
Mountain Biking Ability Suggested: NA
Terrain: Steep 1%, Hilly 15%, Moderate 40%, Flat 44%
Camping: Campground available in park

Maintained by the DNR Parks and Recreation Division
Beautiful beach on Little Traverse Bay.
The compact trail system is a real joy to ski. It's surprisingly protected from the lake winds.

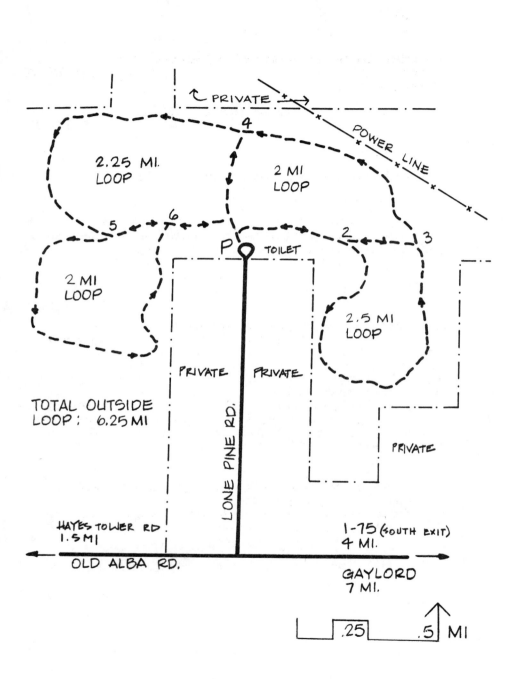

TOTAL OUTSIDE
LOOP : 6.25 MI

PINE BARON PATHWAY

Gaylord Forest Area, Mackinaw State Forest
1732 West M32, PO Box 667   517-732-3541
Gaylord, MI 49735

District Forest Manager, Mackinaw State Forest
1732 West M32, PO Box Box 667   517-732-3541
Gaylord, MI 49735

Michigan Atlas & Gazetteer Location: 82D2

County Location: Otsego

Directions To Trailhead:
About 6 miles southwest of Gaylord on Old Alba Rd.
Trailhead: West from downtown Gaylord on M32 just past I-75 to Dickerson Rd, south on Dickerson to West Otsego Lake Drive, then right for about 1/2 mile to Old Alba Rd, then right for 2 1/2 miles to Lone Pine Rd., then right(north) 1 1/2 miles to the end of the road and the trailhead

Trail Type: Hiking/Walking, Cross Country Skiing
Trail Distance: 6.25 mi   Loops: 4   Shortest: 2 mi   Longest: 2.5 mi
Trail Surface: Natural
Trail Use Fee: None, but donations for trail maintenance
Method Of Ski Trail Grooming: Double track set
Skiing Ability Suggested: Novice only
Hiking Trail Difficulty: Easy
Mountain Biking Ability Suggested: NA
Terrain: Steep 0%, Hilly 5%, Moderate 20%, Flat 75%
Camping: Camground available at Otsego Lake State Park and private campgrounds

Maintained by the DNR Forest Management Division
Forested trail system of second growth trees.
No steep hills on the trail.
Good trail for the beginning skier.
Pit toilet at parking lot
Also contact the DNR Forest Management Division Office, Lansing, 517-373-1275

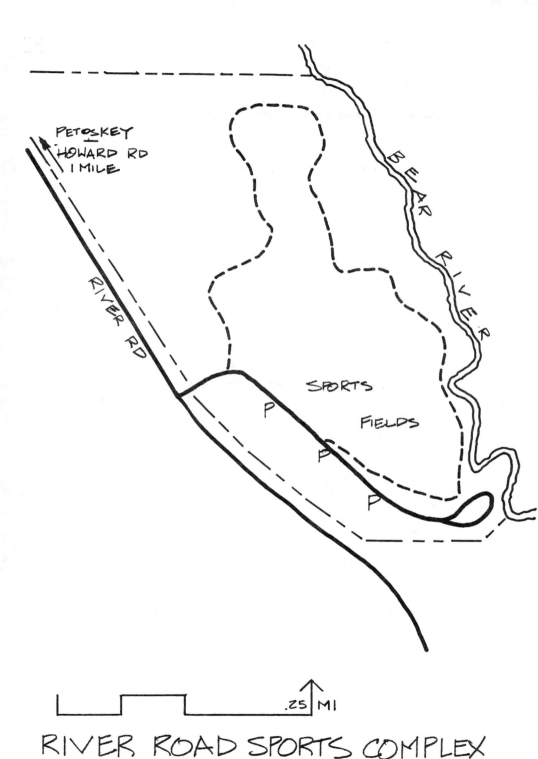

City of Petoskey, Department of Parks and Recreation
100 W. Lake St
Petoskey, MI 49770

616-347-2500

Michigan Atlas & Gazetteer Location: 82AB1

County Location: Charlevoix

Directions To Trailhead:
US131south of Petoskey, turn east on Sheridan to Clarion St., then turn south onClarion to Riverbend Rd. Continue south .5 mile to the complex.

Trail Type: Hiking/Walking, Cross Country Skiing
Trail Distance: 1.5 mi   Loops: 1   Shortest: Longest: 1.5 mi
Trail Surface: Natural
Trail Use Fee: None
Method Of Ski Trail Grooming: Track set
Skiing Ability Suggested: Novice
Hiking Trail Difficulty: Easy
Mountain Biking Ability Suggested: NA
Terrain: 100% Flat
Camping: None

Maintained by the City of Petoskey Department of Parks and Recreation
Ball fields and fishing available.

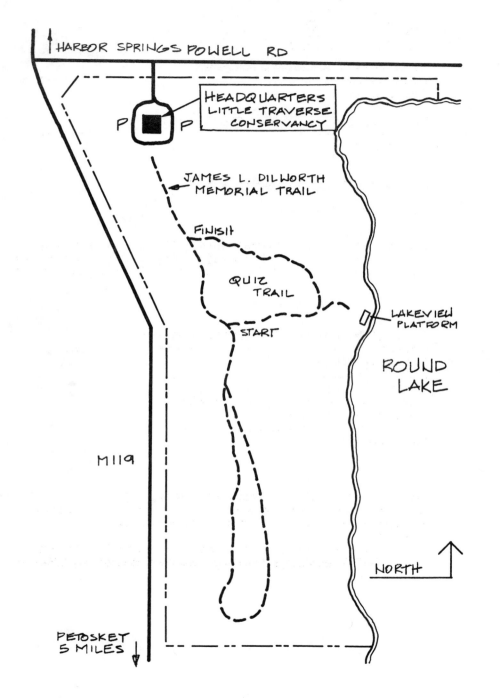

Little Traverse Conservancy
3264 Powell Rd
Harbor Springs, MI 49740

616-347-0991

Michigan Atlas & Gazetteer Location: 82A1

County Location: Emmet

Directions To Trailhead:
From Petoskey take US31 north to M119, then left for about 4 miles to Powell Rd, then right and take first driveway on right into parking lot.

Trail Type: Hiking/Walking, Cross Country Skiing, Interpretive
Trail Distance: 1 mi   Loops: 2   Shortest: Longest:
Trail Surface: Natural
Trail Use Fee: None
Method Of Ski Trail Grooming: None
Skiing Ability Suggested: Novice
Hiking Trail Difficulty: Easy
Mountain Biking Ability Suggested: NA
Terrain: 100%Flat
Camping: None

Owned by the Little Traverse Conservancy
Site of the headquarters building for the organization.
Self guided trail brochure available.

ROUND LAKE NATURE PRESERVE

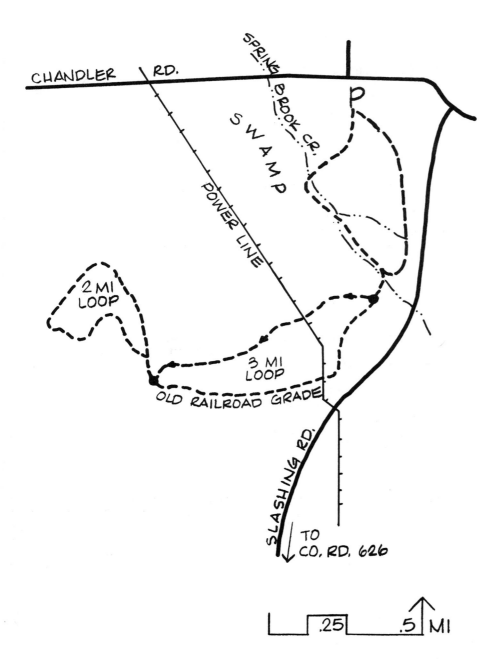

CHANDLER RD.

SPRING BROOK CR.

SWAMP

POWER LINE

P

2 MI LOOP

3 MI LOOP

OLD RAILROAD GRADE

SLASHING RD.

TO CO. RD. 626

.25 .5 MI

SPRING BROOK PATHWAY

Spring Brook Pathway

Gaylord Forest Area, Mackinaw State Forest
1732 West M32, PO Box 667   517-732-3541
Gaylord, MI 49735

District Forest Manager, Mackinaw State Forest
1732 West M32, PO Box 667   517-732-3541
Gaylord, MI 49735

Michigan Atlas & Gazetteer Location: 82C2

County Location: Charlevoix

Directions To Trailhead:
Just east of Boyne Falls on Thumb Lake Rd. (C48) for 5 miles to Slashing Rd.,
then north 2.5 miles to the end of the road, then west on Chandler Rd. .4 miles
to parking lot on the south side (you will pass the old Thunder Mountain ski area
on Slashing Rd.)

Trail Type: Hiking/Walking, Cross Country Skiing, Mountain Biking
Trail Distance: 5 mi   Loops: 3   Shortest: Longest:
Trail Surface: Natural
Trail Use Fee: None
Method Of Ski Trail Grooming: None
Skiing Ability Suggested: Novice to intermediate
Hiking Trail Difficulty: Moderate
Mountain Biking Ability Suggested: Easy
Terrain: Flat to hilly
Camping: None

Maintained by the DNR Forest Management Division
The loops contain more difficult terrain the farther away from the trailhead the
user travels. Habitat varies from cedar lowlands to upland hardwoods.
Other contacts:
        DNR Forest Management Division Office, Lansing, 517-373-1275
        DNR Forest Management Region Office, Roscommon, 517-275-5151

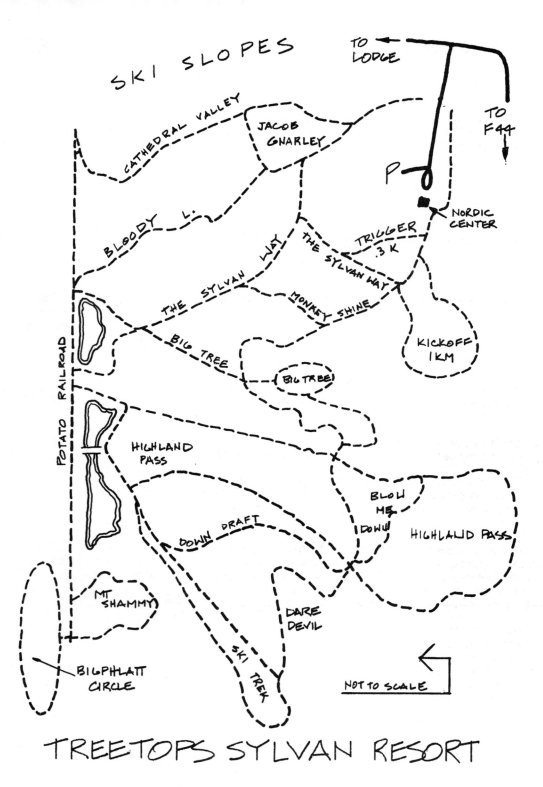

SKI SLOPES

CATHEDRAL VALLEY

JACOB GNARLEY

TO LODGE

TO F44

P

NORDIC CENTER

BLOODY L.

THE SYLVAN WAY

TRIGGER .3 K

THE SYLVAN WAY

MONKEY SHINE

KICKOFF 1KM

BIG TREE

BIG TREE

POTATO RAILROAD

HIGHLAND PASS

BLOW ME DOWN

HIGHLAND PASS

DOWN DRAFT

MT SHAMMY

DARE DEVIL

SKI TREK

BIGPHLATT CIRCLE

NOT TO SCALE

TREETOPS SYLVAN RESORT

Treetops Sylvan Resort
3962 Wilkinson Rd.
Gaylord, MI 49735

800-444-6711
517-732-6711

Michigan Atlas & Gazetteer Location: 82D4

County Location: Otsego

Directions To Trailhead:
7 miles east of Gaylord via M32 and Wilkinson Rd (follow signs).

Trail Type: Cross Country Skiing
Trail Distance: 20.1 km   Loops: Many   Shortest: 1 km   Longest: 15 km
Trail Surface: Natural
Trail Use Fee: Yes
Method Of Ski Trail Grooming: Single and double track set plus telemark
Skiing Ability Suggested: Novice to advanced
Hiking Trail Difficulty: NA
Mountain Biking Ability Suggested: NA
Terrain: Steep 10%, Hilly 25%, Moderate 35%, Flat 30%
Camping: None

Privately operated full service alpine ski area with cross country ski trails.
All services available including instruction, rentals, ski shop, 128 room hotel,
entertainment and complete food service.
Lighted trail available on weekends.
Though most of the trails are on golf course fairways, the terrain is very hilly and
many fairways are protected from the wind.
The open steep slopes of the fairways are excellent for telemarking.
There are several hilly wooded trails between the fairways and around the golf
course that make for an interesting trail system.
A different kind of trail system that allows for a full variety of techniques including
telemarking, classic and skating.
A great place to spend an afternoon on well groomed trails.

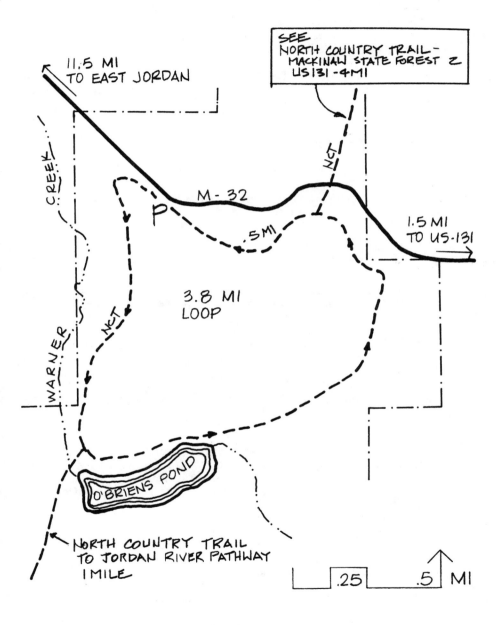

11.5 MI
TO EAST JORDAN

SEE
NORTH COUNTRY TRAIL –
MACKINAW STATE FOREST 2
US131 – 4 MI

CREEK

NCT

M-32

P

.5 MI

1.5 MI
TO US-131

3.8 MI
LOOP

WARNER

NCT

O'BRIENS POND

NORTH COUNTRY TRAIL
TO JORDAN RIVER PATHWAY
1 MILE

.25   .5 | MI

WARNER CREEK PATHWAY

Warner Creek Pathway

Gaylord Forest Area, Mackinaw State Forest
PO Box 667, 1732 West M32   517-732-3541
Gaylord, MI 49735

District Forest Manager, Mackinaw State Forest
PO Box667, 1732 West M32   517-732-3541
Gaylord, MI 49735

Michigan Atlas & Gazetteer Location: 82D1

County Location: Antrim

Directions To Trailhead:
Between US131 and East Jordan on M32, just north of Mancelona
Trailhead - 1.5 miles west of US131 on M32

Trail Type: Hiking/Walking, Cross Country Skiing, Mountain Biking
Trail Distance: 3.8 mi   Loops: 1   Shortest: Longest:
Trail Surface:
Trail Use Fee: None
Method Of Ski Trail Grooming: Track set
Skiing Ability Suggested: Novice to intermediate
Hiking Trail Difficulty: Easy
Mountain Biking Ability Suggested: Novice
Terrain: Steep 0%, Hilly 20%, Moderate 40%, Flat 405%
Camping: None

Maintained by the DNR Forest Management Division
Developed for skiers because the nearby Jordan River Pathway is not suitable
for skiing
The North Country Trail is routed along part of this pathway.
(See other listing > North Country Trail - Mackinaw State Forest 2)

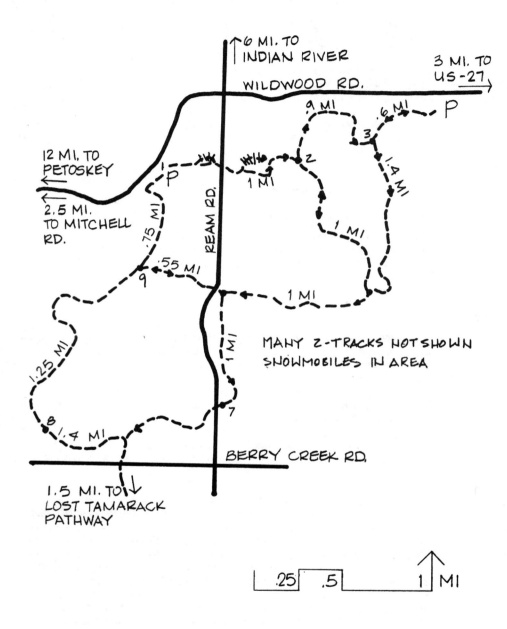

WILDWOOD HILLS PATHWAY

(Map labels:)

.6 MI. TO INDIAN RIVER

3 MI. TO US-27

WILDWOOD RD.

.9 MI

.6 MI

P

12 MI. TO PETOSKEY

2.5 MI. TO MITCHELL RD.

P

3

2

.75 MI

REAM RD.

1 MI

.4 MI

1 MI

.55 MI

9

1 MI

.25 MI

1 MI

MANY 2-TRACKS NOT SHOWN SNOWMOBILES IN AREA

.4 MI

8

7

BERRY CREEK RD.

1.5 MI. TO LOST TAMARACK PATHWAY

.25   .5   1 MI

Indian River Forest Area, Mackinaw State Forest
6984 M68, PO Box 10   616-238-9313
Indian River, MI 49749

District Forest Manager, Mackinaw State Forest
1732 West M32, PO Box 667   517-732-3541
Gaylord, MI 49735

Michigan Atlas & Gazetteer Location: 82B3

County Location: Emmet, Cheboygan

Directions To Trailhead:
Between Indian River and Petoskey on Wildwood Rd.
Trailhead - From Indian River on M68 turn south on old US27, then south 2 miles to Wildwood Rd., then west 3 miles to parking lot (south side)
Trailhead - From Petoskey on C58 (Mitchell Rd.) for about 9.5 miles, then pick up Wildwood Rd. (left fork), for 3 miles to parking lot

Trail Type: Hiking/Walking, Cross Country Skiing, Mountain Biking
Trail Distance: 9.3 mi   Loops: 3   Shortest: 4.5 mi Longest: 7 mi
Trail Surface: Natural
Trail Use Fee: None, but donation accepted to groom trail
Method Of Ski Trail Grooming: Track set
Skiing Ability Suggested: Novice to intermediate
Hiking Trail Difficulty: Easy
Mountain Biking Ability Suggested: Novice to intermediate
Terrain: Steep 20%, Hilly 20%, Moderate 40%, Flat 20%
Camping: Available in Alanson and Indian River

Maintained by the DNR Forest Management Division
A very enjoyable trail system for skiers of most skill levels including beginners.
Some snowmobiles are in the area but because of the heavy use this trail receives, they seldom if ever cause problems with the trails except for the east parking lot area.
All difficult hills can be by-passed.
One of the better trails developed for skiing by the DNR.
Somewhat difficult trail to locate in the summer because of the open fields that it crosses.
Toilets available at the parking lots.
The Lost Tamarack Pathway(see other listing) connects to the south.
Groomed with donated funds. Please contribute at the parking lot pipes.
Other contacts:
    DNR Forest Management Division Office, Lansing, 517-373-1275
    DNR Forest Management Region Office, Roscommon, 517-275-5151

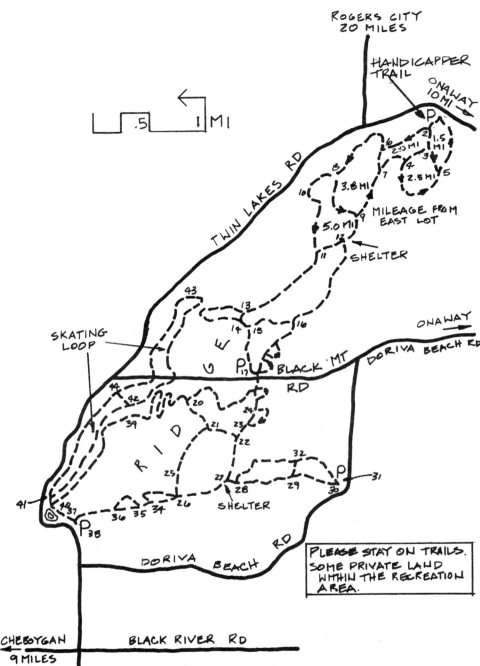

ROGERS CITY
20 MILES

HANDICAPPER
TRAIL

ONAWAY
10 MI →

.5   1 MI

TWIN LAKES RD

6   2 1.5
2.0 MI   MI
8   4   3
3.8 MI   7 2.5 MI 5
10
9
5.0 MI
11   SHELTER

MILEAGE FROM
EAST LOT

43
13
14 15   16
SKATING
LOOP

ONAWAY →

G E
17 BLACK MT   DORIVA BEACH RD
RD

18
19 19   20   24
39   21   23
25   22
R I D
32
27   28   29   30   31
41 40 37 36 35 34 26   SHELTER
P 38

DORIVA BEACH   RD

PLEASE STAY ON TRAILS.
SOME PRIVATE LAND
WITHIN THE RECREATION
AREA.

CHEBOYGAN
9 MILES

BLACK RIVER RD

BLACK MOUNTAIN
RECREATION AREA

Atlanta Forest Area, Mackinaw State Forest
HCR 74, Box 30   517-785-4251
Atlanta, MI 49709-9605

District Forest Manager, Mackinaw State Forest
1732 West M32, PO Box 667   517-732-3541
Gaylord, MI 49735

Michigan Atlas & Gazetteer Location: 83A7,95D67

County Location: Cheboygan, Presque Isle

Directions To Trailhead:
North of Onaway on M211 to Co Rd 489 to trailhead.
From Rogers City go north on US23 to Co Rd 646 then west to trailhead

Trail Type: Hiking/Walking, Cross Country Skiing, Mountain Biking, Interpretive
Trail Distance: 32   Loops: 12+   Shortest: 1 mi   Longest: 15 mi
Trail Surface: Natural and asphalt handicapper trail
Trail Use Fee: None
Method Of Ski Trail Grooming: Track set with skating loop
Skiing Ability Suggested: Novice to intermediate
Hiking Trail Difficulty: Easy to moderate
Mountain Biking Ability Suggested: Moderate to advanced
Terrain: Steep 15%, Hilly 40%, Moderate 30%, Flat 15%
Camping: Campgrounds at Black Lake SFCG, Twin Lake SFCG and Bluff
campground

Maintained by the DNR Forest Management Division
Black Mountain is the only significant topography in the area therefore, views
from the trails on the top of the mountain are quite nice. The trailheads at the
east and west end of the complex are in the lower elevations. The trailhead on
Black Mountain Rd is at the top of the mountain. None of the trails are difficult,
however some grades can be quite long though not steep. Along the trail there
are several short and fast ski loops near the Black Mountain Rd trailhead.
Snowmobile and ORV trails are also in the area. The gated trails are only to
restrict ORV and snowmobile use and not to stop non-motorized trail users.
Some sand could make mountain biking more difficult in some sections.
Excellent large multi colored trail map is available. A 1.2 mile asphalt
handicapper trail with shorter .7 mile loop. Black Lake SFCG is fully accessible.

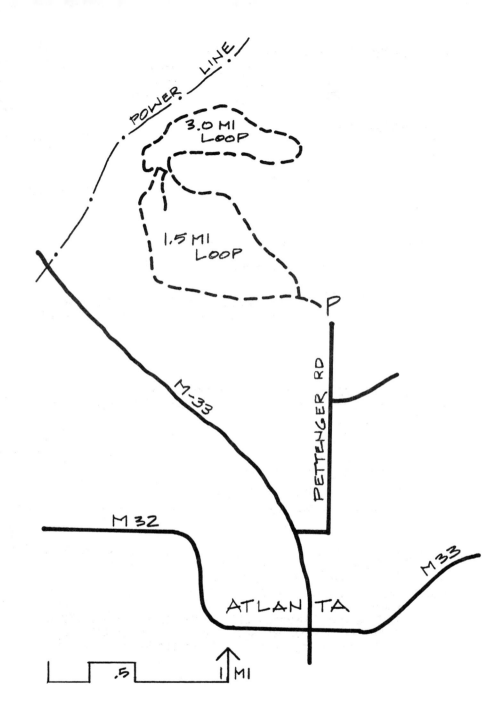

Briley Township
PO Box 207
Atlanta, MI 49709

517-785-4186

Michigan Atlas & Gazetteer Location: 83D7

County Location: Montmorency

Directions To Trailhead:
In Atlanta go north at blinker light, then .5 mile turn right at Pettinger Rd, then about .5 mile ahead is trailhead entrance

Trail Type: Cross Country Skiing
Trail Distance: 3 mi   Loops: 2   Shortest: 1.5 mi Longest: 3 mi
Trail Surface: Natural
Trail Use Fee: None
Method Of Ski Trail Grooming: Track set
Skiing Ability Suggested: Novice to intermediate
Hiking Trail Difficulty: NA
Mountain Biking Ability Suggested: NA
Terrain: Steep 0%, Hilly 50%, Moderate 25%, Flat 25%
Camping: None but Clear Lake SP and state forest campgrounds are nearby

Maintained by Briley Township
Trails in wooded area on the north side of Atlanta.

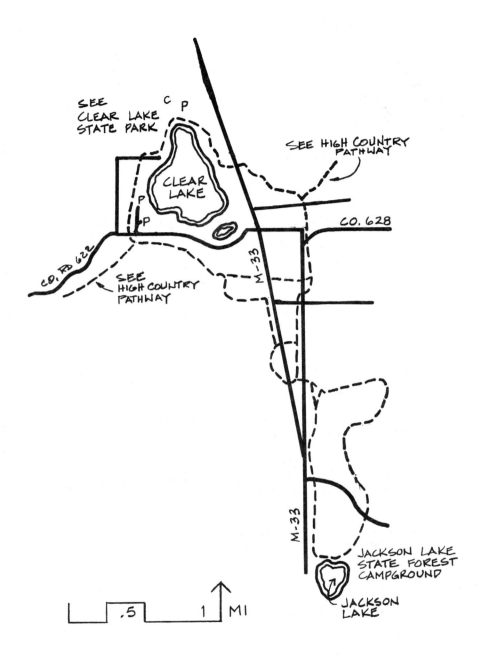

CLEAR LAKE -
JACKSON LAKE PATHWAY

Clear Lake State Park
Rte 1   517-785-4388
Atlanta, MI 49709

Atlanta Forest Area, Mackinaw State Forest
HCR 74, Box 30   517-785-4252
Atlanta, MI 49709

Michigan Atlas & Gazetteer Location: 83CD7

County Location: Presque Isle, Montmorency

Directions To Trailhead:
Trailhead - 10 miles north of Atlanta on M33 at the Clear Lake State Park.
Trailhead - Jackson Lake State Forest Campground, 3 miles south of the state park.

Trail Type: Hiking/Walking, Mountain Biking, Interpretive
Trail Distance: 7.5 mi   Loops: 3   Shortest: 2 mi   Longest: 7 mi
Trail Surface: Natural
Trail Use Fee: None, but vehicle entry permit required
Method Of Ski Trail Grooming: NA
Skiing Ability Suggested: NA
Hiking Trail Difficulty: Easy to moderate
Mountain Biking Ability Suggested: Novice to intermediate
Terrain: Steep 0%, Hilly 25%, Moderate 50%, Flat 25%
Camping: Campground at north trailhead at Clear Lake State Park

Maintained by DNR Parks and Recreation and Forest Management Divisions.
This is a 25 station interpretive trail.
A section is part of the High Country Pathway.
May not always be well maintained due to infrequent use of some sections
Other contacts:
        DNR Parks and Recreation Division Office, Lansing, 517-373-1270
        DNR Forest Management Region Office, Roscommon, 517-275-5151
        DNR Forest Management Division Office, Lansing, 517-373-1275

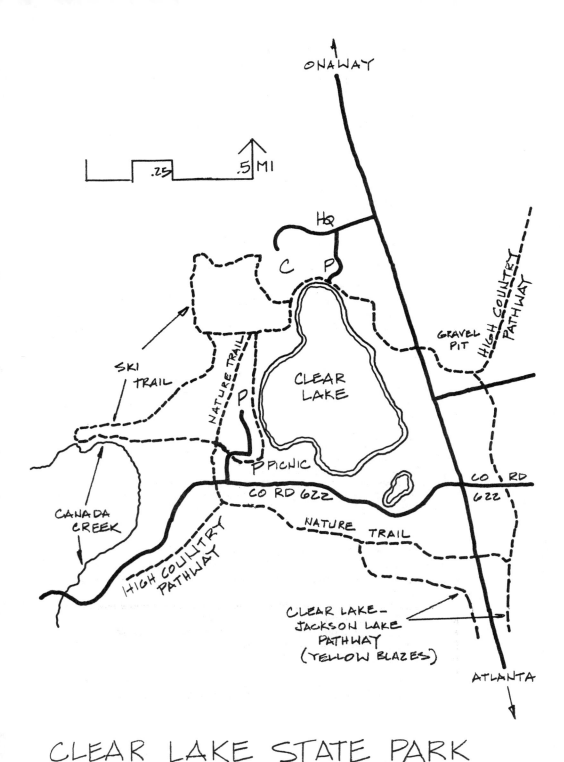

Clear Lake State Park
Rte 1, Box 51
Atlanta, MI 49709

517-785-4388

DNR Parks and Recreation Division

517-373-1270
517-275-5151

Michigan Atlas & Gazetteer Location: 83CD7

County Location: Montmorency

Directions To Trailhead:
Between Onaway and Atlanta on M33

Trail Type: Hiking/Walking, Cross Country Skiing, Interpretive
Trail Distance: 4 mi   Loops: 2   Shortest: 1.5 mi Longest: 3.5 mi
Trail Surface: Natural
Trail Use Fee: None, but vehicle entry permit required
Method Of Ski Trail Grooming: Track set
Skiing Ability Suggested: Novice
Hiking Trail Difficulty: Easy to moderate
Mountain Biking Ability Suggested: NA
Terrain: Steep 0%, Hilly 2%, Moderate 3%, Flat 95%
Camping: On site

Maintained by the DNR Parks and Recreation Division
Ski trail is separate from the hiking trail.
The trail has 13 interpreted stations.
Trail guide available.
Hiking trail system connects with the High Country Pathway and the Clear Lake
-Jackson Lake Pathway. (see other trails)

CLEAR LAKE STATE PARK

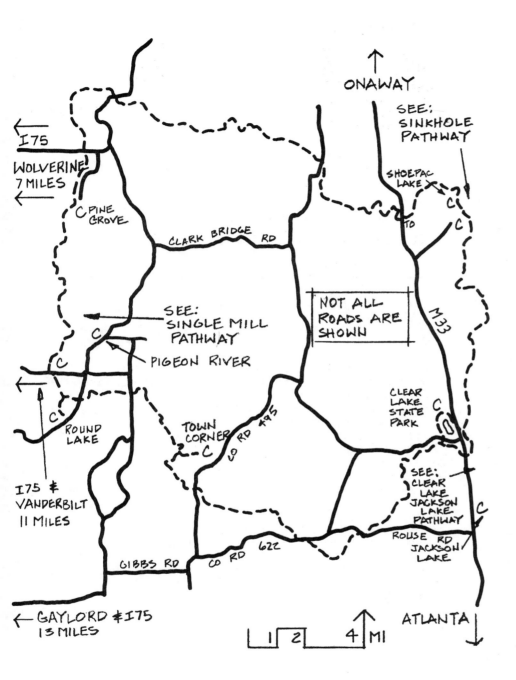

Pigeon River Country Forest Area, Mackinaw State Forest
9966 Twin Lakes Rd.   517-983-4101
Vanderbilt, MI 49795

District Forest Manager, Mackinaw State Forest
1732 West M32, PO Box 667   517-732-3541
Gaylord, MI 49735

Michigan Atlas & Gazetteer Location: 83BCD5678

County Location: Cheboygan,Otsego,Montmorency,Presque Isle

Directions To Trailhead:
Northeast of Gaylord,southwest of Onaway and northwest of Atlanta.
Trailheads - West from Vanderbilt about 9 & 12 miles on Sturgeon Valley Rd
Trailhead - Clear Lake State Park on M33 between Onaway and Atlanta
Trailhead - Sinkhole Pathway, 10 miles south of Onaway via M33 and east on
Tomahawk Lake Hwy

Trail Type: Hiking/Walking, Mountain Biking
Trail Distance: 70+ mi   Loops: 1   Shortest: NA   Longest: NA
Trail Surface: Natural
Trail Use Fee: None
Method Of Ski Trail Grooming: NA
Skiing Ability Suggested: NA
Hiking Trail Difficulty: Moderate to difficult
Mountain Biking Ability Suggested: Intermediate to advanced ONLY!
Terrain: Steep 2%, Hilly 8%, Moderate 60%, Flat 30%
Camping: Numerous campgrounds along the trail

Maintained by the DNR Forest Management Division
The High Country Pathway is part of the Shingle Mill Pathway and the Clear
Lake-Jackson Lake Pathway. It also passes through the Sinkhole Pathway
area. See those trails for more detail.
There is as much variety in terrain and habitat as can be found anywhere in the
lower peninsula. Several scenic vista's along the trail.
A very descriptive trail guide that is well worth the money is available from the
Pigeon River Country Association, PO Box 122, Gaylord, MI 49735. Annual
memberships available .,
Other contacts:
    DNR Forest Management Division Office, Lansing, 517-373-1275
    DNR Forest Management Region Office, Roscommon, 517-275-5151

HIGH COUNTRY PATHWAY

DNR - Forest Management Division
POB 30028
Lansing, MI 48909

517-373-1275

Michigan Atlas & Gazetteer Location: 83AB567, 84B12, 95BC34, 95CD5

County Location: Cheboygan, Presque Isle

Directions To Trailhead:
A former railroad from Mackinaw City to Hawks (about 15 miles south of Rogers City)
Trail passes through Cheboygan, Onaway and Millersburg

Trail Type: Hiking/Walking, Cross Country Skiing, Mountain Biking
Trail Distance: 55 mi   Loops: None   Shortest: NA   Longest: NA
Trail Surface: Ballast and natural
Trail Use Fee: None
Method Of Ski Trail Grooming: None
Skiing Ability Suggested: Novice
Hiking Trail Difficulty: Easy
Mountain Biking Ability Suggested: Novice
Terrain: 100% Flat
Camping: None, but trail passes through Aloha State Park on Mullett Lake

Managed by the DNR Forest Management Division
Under active development. Call ahead for current trail conditions.
Passes through Mill Creek and Aloha State parks.
Passes through very scenic northern Michigan landscape of woods, inland lakes, Lake Huron, rivers and wetlands. A trail not to be missed.

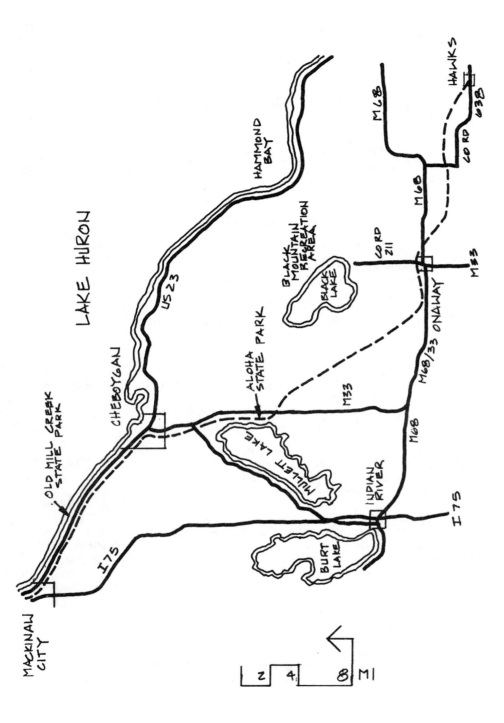

MACKINAW CITY TO HAWKS TRAIL

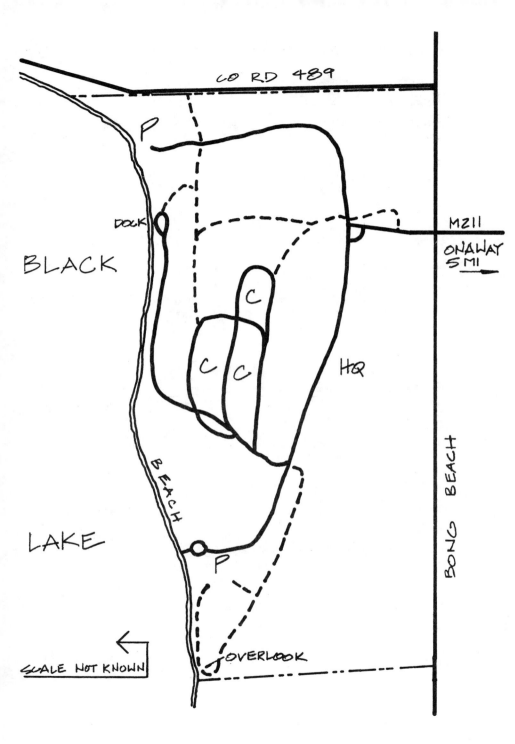

CO RD 489

P

DOCK

BLACK

C

C C

HQ

BEACH

P

LAKE

OVERLOOK

BONG BEACH

M211

ONAWAY 5 MI

SCALE NOT KNOWN

ONAWAY STATE PARK

Onaway State Park
Rte 1, Box 188
Onaway, MI 49765

517-733-8279

Clear Lake State Park
PO Box 51
Atlanta, MI 49709

517-785-4388

Michigan Atlas & Gazetteer Location: 83A7

County Location: Presque Isle

Directions To Trailhead:
Trailhead is located in the campground in the park

Trail Type: Hiking/Walking
Trail Distance: 3 mi   Loops: 2   Shortest: 1 mi   Longest: 2 mi
Trail Surface: Natural
Trail Use Fee: None, but vehicle entry permit required
Method Of Ski Trail Grooming: NA
Skiing Ability Suggested: NA
Hiking Trail Difficulty: Easy to moderate
Mountain Biking Ability Suggested: NA
Terrain: Steep 5%, Hilly 10%, Moderate 65%, Flat 20%
Camping: Campground on site

Maintained by the DNR Parks and Recreation Division
158 acre park

Pickerel Lake Pathway

Pigeon River Country Forest Area, Mackinaw State Forest
9966 Twin Lakes Road   517-983-4101
Vanderbilt, MI 49795

District Forest Manger, Mackinaw State Forest
1732 West M32, PO Box 667   517-732-3541
Gaylord, MI 49735

Michigan Atlas & Gazetteer Location: 83C4

County Location: Otsego

Directions To Trailhead:
At Pickerel Lake SFCG, east from Vanderbilt 8 miles to Pickerel Lake Rd., then north 2 miles to the day use area in the campground.

Trail Type: Hiking/Walking, Cross Country Skiing,
Trail Distance: 2 mi   Loops: 1   Shortest: NA   Longest: 2 mi
Trail Surface: Natural
Trail Use Fee: None
Method Of Ski Trail Grooming: None
Skiing Ability Suggested: Novice
Hiking Trail Difficulty: Easy
Mountain Biking Ability Suggested: NA
Terrain: Steep 0%, Hilly 0%, Moderate 15%, Flat 85%
Camping: At trailhead

Maintained by the DNR Forest Management Division
The closest campground to the Green Timbers tract.

PICKEREL LAKE

1.9 MILE LOOP

SEE
HIGH COUNTRY P.W.
SHINGLE MILL P.W.

PICKEREL LAKE RD

STURGEON VALLEY RD
3 MILES

SCALE NOT KNOWN

PICKEREL LAKE PATHWAY

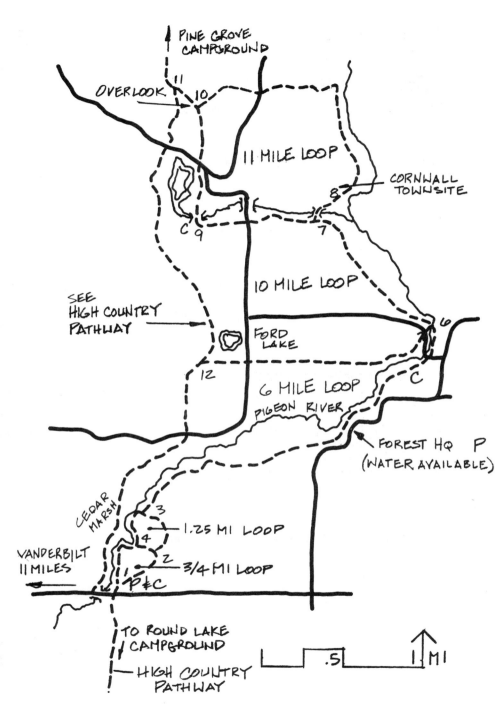

Pigeon River Country Forest Area, Mackinaw State Forest
9966 Twin Lakes Rd.   517-983-4101
Vanderbilt, MI 49759

District Forest Manager, Mackinaw State Forest
1732 West M32, PO Box 667   517-732-3541
Gaylord, MI 48735

Michigan Atlas & Gazetteer Location: 83C5

County Location: Otsego, Cheboygan

Directions To Trailhead:
9 miles east of Vanderbilt on Sturgeon Valley Rd.

Trail Type: Hiking/Walking, Cross Country Skiing, Mountain Biking
Trail Distance: 18 mi   Loops: 5   Shortest: .75 mi Longest: 11 mi
Trail Surface: Natural
Trail Use Fee: None
Method Of Ski Trail Grooming: Track set on occasion
Skiing Ability Suggested: Novice to advanced
Hiking Trail Difficulty: Easy to moderate
Mountain Biking Ability Suggested: Novice to intermediate
Terrain: Steep 2%, Hilly 5%, Moderate 48%, Flat 45%
Camping: Several campgrounds are located along the trail

Maintained by the DNR Forest Management Division
A very popular trail system that can absorb many users without becoming
crowded because of its size.
Pigeon River Country Forest Area HQ with its resident Area Forester, is located
along the trail.
A scenic overlook is along the 10 mile loop.
Drinking water is available all year at the headquarters bldg and seasonally at
the campgrounds
Part of the North Country Pathway which enters the trail at Pigeon Bridge SFCG
from the south and leaves the trail at Point 11 to the north heading to Pine Grove
SFCG
Other contacts:
        DNR Forest Management Division Office, Lansing, 517-373-1275
        DNR Forest Management Region Office, Roscommon, 517-275-5151

SHINGLE MILL PATHWAY

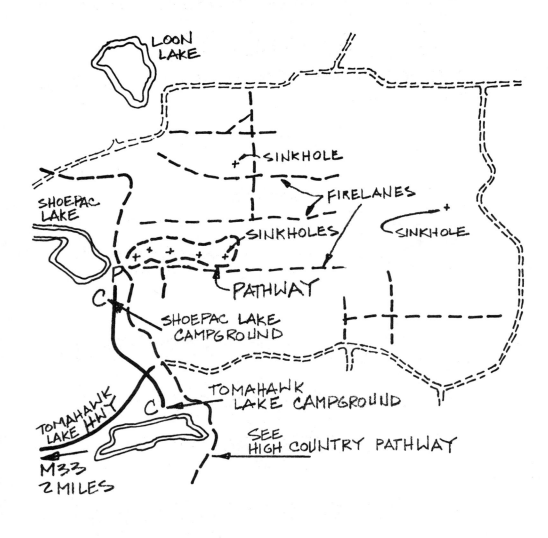

Atlanta Forest Area, Mackinaw State Forest
Rte 1, Box 30
Atlanta, MI 49709   517-785-4251

District Forest Manager, Mackinaw State Forest
Box 667, 1732 M32   517-732-3541
Gaylord, MI 49735

Michigan Atlas & Gazetteer Location: 83BC7

County Location: Presque Isle

Directions To Trailhead:
Between Onaway (8 miles) and Atlanta (16 miles) off M33 via Tomahawk Lake Hwy

Trail Type: Hiking/Walking, Cross Country Skiing, Mountain Biking
Trail Distance: 2.5 mi   Loops: 2   Shortest: .75 mi Longest: 1.5 mi
Trail Surface: Natural
Trail Use Fee: None
Method Of Ski Trail Grooming: None
Skiing Ability Suggested: Novice
Hiking Trail Difficulty: Easy
Mountain Biking Ability Suggested: Novice to intermediate
Terrain: Steep 0%, Hilly 0%, Moderate 80%, Flat 20%
Camping: Shoepac and Thomahawk State Forest Campgounds are nearby

Maintained by the DNR Forest Management Division
The Sinkhole Area contains 2,600 acres that are closed to motorized vehicles. There are many miles of fire lines within this area that area suitable for skiing & hiking beyond that which is listed above.
It's recommended that the user take along a compass since there are no maps or trail makings on the interior of this area.
This area has a unique geological formation from the result of dissolving bed rock limestone. Shoepac Lake is a result of this dissolving limestone .
Other contacts:
      DNR Forest Management Division Office, Lansing, 517-373-1275
      DNR Forest Management Region Office, Roscommon, 517-275-5151

SINKHOLE PATHWAY

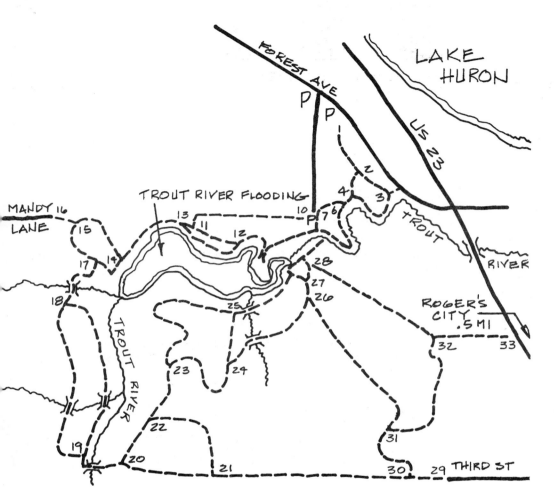

LAKE HURON

FOREST AVE

US 23

TROUT RIVER FLOODING

MANDY LANE

TROUT RIVER

TROUT RIVER

ROGER'S CITY .5 MI

THIRD ST

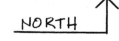

NORTH ↑

HERMAN VOGLER
CONSERVATION AREA

Herman Vogler Conservation Area

Presque Isle Soil Conservation District
240 W. Erie St.
Rogers City, MI 49779

517-734-4000

Michigan Atlas & Gazetteer Location: 84A23

County Location: Presque Isle

Directions To Trailhead:
North 1/2 mile from intersection of US 23 and Bus. US23, then west on Forest Ave about .5 mile to parking lot

Trail Type: Hiking/Walking, Cross Country Skiing, Mountain Biking, Interpretive
Trail Distance: 5.25 mi   Loops: Many   Shortest: .75 mi Longest: 2.5 mi
Trail Surface: Natural
Trail Use Fee: None, but donations are accepted
Method Of Ski Trail Grooming: Track set
Skiing Ability Suggested: Novice to intermediate
Hiking Trail Difficulty: Easy to moderate
Mountain Biking Ability Suggested: Novice to intermediate
Terrain: Steep 0%, Hilly 10%, Moderate 20%, Flat 70%
Camping: None

Maintained by the Presque Isle Soil Conservation District
Developed by many individuals and local groups as a conservation education center.

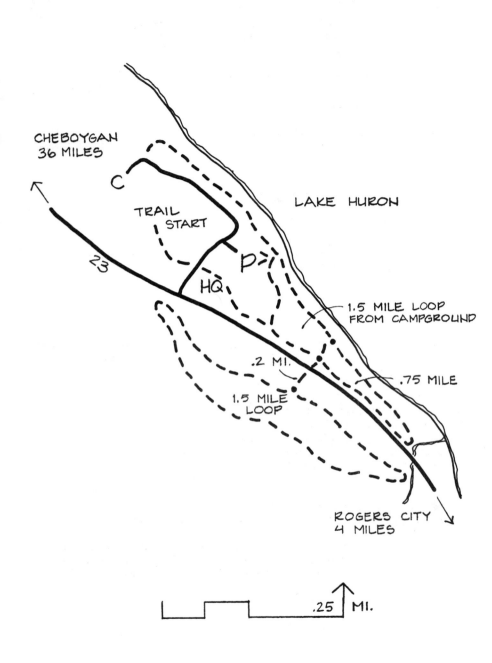

CHEBOYGAN
36 MILES

C

TRAIL START

23

HQ

P

LAKE HURON

1.5 MILE LOOP
FROM CAMPGROUND

.2 MI.

.75 MILE

1.5 MILE
LOOP

ROGERS CITY
4 MILES

.25 MI.

HOEFT STATE PARK

Hoeft State Park
US23
Rogers City, MI 49779

517-734-2543

DNR Parks and Recreation Division

517-373-1270
517-275-5151

Michigan Atlas & Gazetteer Location: 84A2

County Location: Presque Isle

Directions To Trailhead:
On US23, 5 miles north of Rogers City on Lake Huron

Trail Type: Hiking/Walking, Cross Country Skiing, Interpretive
Trail Distance: 4 mi   Loops: 2   Shortest: .75 mi Longest: 1.5 mi
Trail Surface: Natural
Trail Use Fee: None, but vehicle entry fee required
Method Of Ski Trail Grooming: Track set
Skiing Ability Suggested: Novice
Hiking Trail Difficulty: Easy
Mountain Biking Ability Suggested: NA
Terrain: Flat
Camping: Available in the park (plowed in winter as needed)

Maintained by the DNR Parks and Recreation Division
Trail in the Huron Dunes area.
A portion of the trail passes along Lake Huron.
Food and lodging available in Rogers City.
Ski rental available in Rogers City.

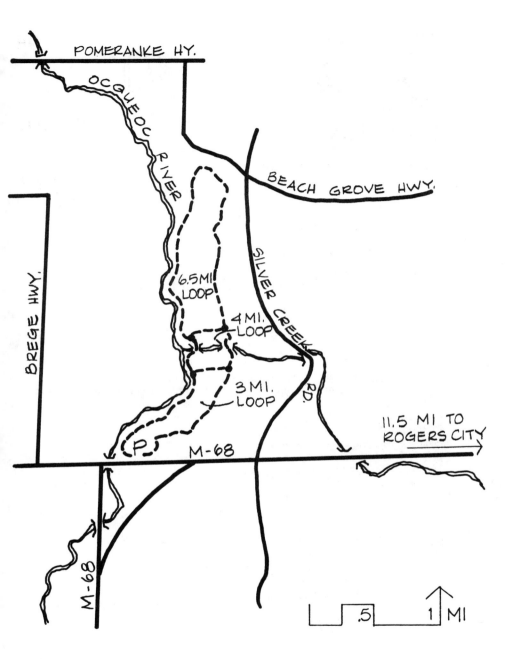

OCQUEOC FALLS
BICENTENNIAL PATHWAY

Atlanta Forest Area, Mackinaw State Forest
HCR 74, Box 30   517-785-4251
Atlanta , MI 49709-9605

District Forest Manager, Mackinaw State Forest
1732 West M32, PO Box 667   517-732-3541
Gaylord, MI 49735

Michigan Atlas & Gazetteer Location: 84A1

County Location: Presque Isle

Directions To Trailhead:
On M68, 12 miles west of Rogers City at Ocqueoc Falls Rd. where M68 turns
south 11 miles east of Onaway on M68.

Trail Type: Hiking/Walking, Cross Country Skiing, Mountain Biking, Interpretive
Trail Distance: 4 mi   Loops: 3   Shortest: 3 mi   Longest: 6 mi
Trail Surface: Natural
Trail Use Fee: Donation accepted for trail grooming
Method Of Ski Trail Grooming: Track set
Skiing Ability Suggested: Novice to advanced
Hiking Trail Difficulty: Moderate
Mountain Biking Ability Suggested: Intermediate
Terrain: Steep 2%, Hilly 10%, Moderate 88%, Flat 0%
Camping: SF campground at trailhead

Maintained by the DNR Forest Management Division
Falls are at the trailhead Rolling hills in area with scenic overlooks.
Other contacts:
        DNR Forest Management Division Office, Lansing, 517-373-1275
        DNR Forest Management Onaway Field Office, Onaway, 517-733-8775
        DNR Forest Management Region Office, Roscommon, 517-275-5151

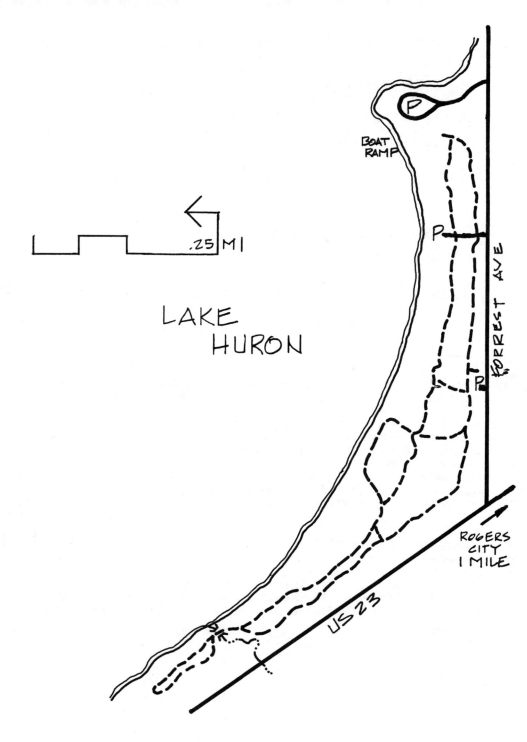

LAKE
HURON

.25 MI

BOAT
RAMP

P

FORREST AVE

P
P

ROGERS
CITY
1 MILE

US 23

SEAGULL POINT PARK

Seagull Point Park

City of Rogers City
191 E. Michigan Ave
Rogers City, MI 49779

517-734-2191

Michigan Atlas & Gazetteer Location: 84A23

County Location: Presque Isle

Directions To Trailhead:
Along the shoreline of Lake Huron at the north end of town.

Trail Type: Hiking/Walking, Cross Country Skiing, Interpretive
Trail Distance: 2.25 mi   Loops: 5   Shortest: .25 mi Longest: 2.25 mi
Trail Surface: Wood chips
Trail Use Fee: None
Method Of Ski Trail Grooming: None
Skiing Ability Suggested: Novice
Hiking Trail Difficulty: Easy
Mountain Biking Ability Suggested: NA
Terrain: Steep 0%, Hilly 0%, Moderate 95%, Flat 5%
Camping: Campgrounds nearby

Owned by the City of Rogers City
Beautiful 43 acre lakeside park on the shore of Lake Huron with an extensive
trail system for its size.

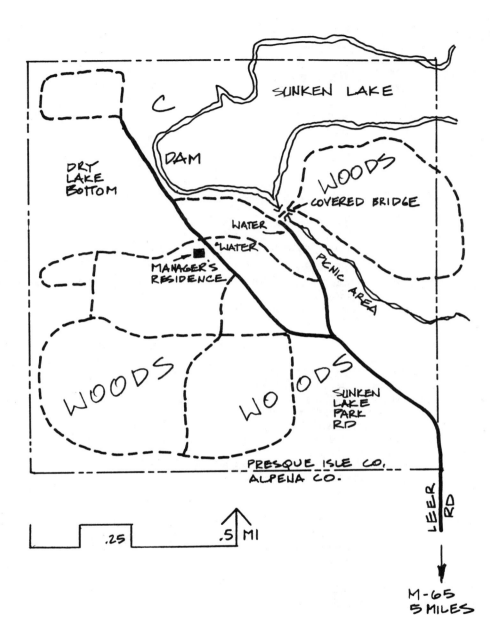

SUNKEN LAKE PARK

Alpena County Parks
10300 Leer Rd
Posen, MI 49776

517-379-3055

Michigan Atlas & Gazetteer Location: 84C4

County Location: Presque Isle

Directions To Trailhead:
Actually this Alpena County Park is located just inside Presque Isle County at the north end of Leer Rd, 1 mile west of M65.

Trail Type: Hiking/Walking, Mountain Biking, Interpretive
Trail Distance: 5 mi   Loops: 4   Shortest: 1   Longest: 2 mi
Trail Surface: Natural
Trail Use Fee: None
Method Of Ski Trail Grooming: None
Skiing Ability Suggested: Novice
Hiking Trail Difficulty: Easy
Mountain Biking Ability Suggested: Novice
Terrain: Steep 15%, Hilly 5%, Moderate 20%, Flat 60%
Camping: Campground on site

Maintained by the Alpena County Parks
A 160 acres park with 55 site campground with electricity, bathrooms and showers.
54 acre man made lake.

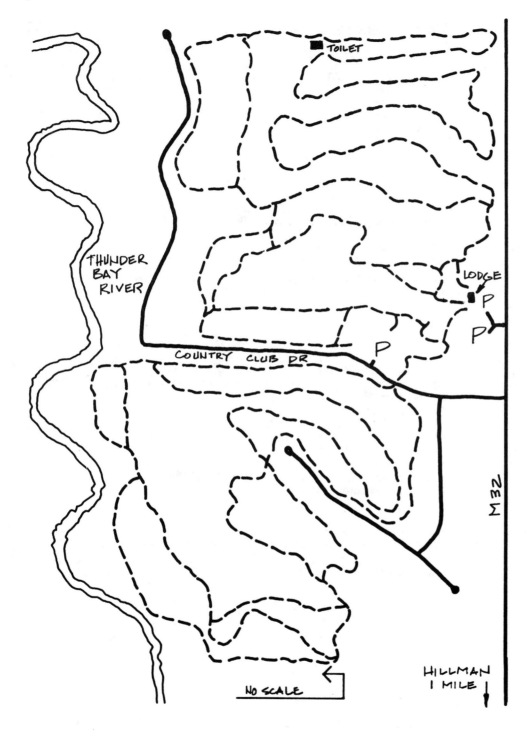

Thunder Bay Resort
One Village Corner
Hillman, MI 49746

800-729-9375
517-742-4732

Michigan Atlas & Gazetteer Location: 84D2

County Location: Montmorency

Directions To Trailhead:
Exit I-75 at exit 202(M33), then take M33 north through Rose City, Mio, Fairview and Comins to M32. At M33 turn east (right) to Hillman. Take M33 east out of Hillman to the resort just past Hillman

Trail Type: Hiking/Walking, Cross Country Skiing
Trail Distance: 15 km   Loops: 10   Shortest: .25 km Longest: 7 km
Trail Surface: Natural
Trail Use Fee: Yes for skiing
Method Of Ski Trail Grooming: Track set
Skiing Ability Suggested: Novice to intermediate
Hiking Trail Difficulty: Easy
Mountain Biking Ability Suggested: NA
Terrain: Steep 0%, Hilly 10%, Moderate 40%, Flat 50%
Camping: None

Privately operated golf resort along Thunder Bay River.
Complete extensive facilities avaiable.
Brochure available.

THUNDER BAY RESORT

City of Alpena
208 N. Second St.
Alpena, MI 49707

517-354-4158

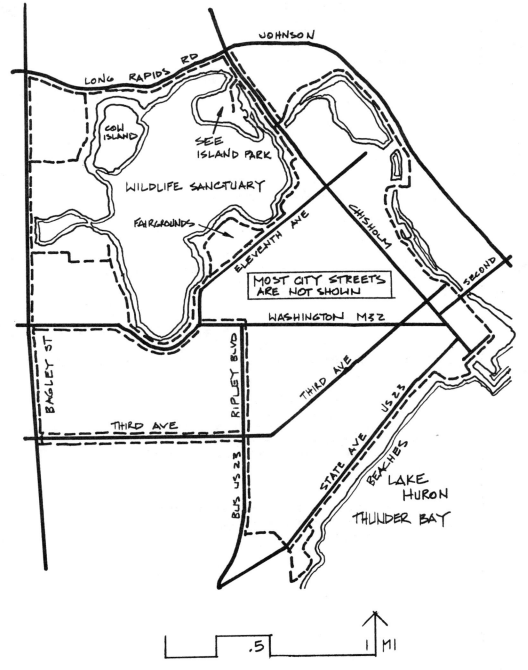

Michigan Atlas & Gazetteer Location: 85D56

County Location: Alpena

Directions To Trailhead:
Throughout the City of Alpena.

Trail Type: Hiking/Walking
Trail Distance: 10 mi   Loops: 2   Shortest: 4 mi   Longest: 8 mi
Trail Surface: Hard surface
Trail Use Fee: None
Method Of Ski Trail Grooming: NA
Skiing Ability Suggested: NA
Hiking Trail Difficulty: Easy
Mountain Biking Ability Suggested: NA
Terrain: Steep 0%, Hilly 0%, Moderate 0%, Flat 100%
Camping: Private camping in the area

Maintained by the City of Alpena
Paved trail system throughout the city connecting downtown, waterfront,
fairgrounds, Island Park and the wildlife sanctuary.
Island Park is listed separately.

ALPENA PATHWAY SYSTEM

Atlanta Forest Area, Mackinaw State Forest
Rte 1, Box 30   517-785-4252
Atlanta, MI 49709-9605

District Forest Manager, Mackinaw State Forest
1732 West M32, PO Box 667   517-732-3541
Gaylord, MI 49735

Michigan Atlas & Gazetteer Location: 85BC6

County Location: Presque Isle

Directions To Trailhead:
Between Alpena and Rogers City.
From US23, about 8 miles north of Alpena to Co Rd 405 (Grand Lake Rd.)(near Lakewood) then north on Co Rd 405 to parking lot.

Trail Type: Hiking/Walking, Interpretive
Trail Distance: 1 mi   Loops: 1   Shortest: NA   Longest: 1 mi
Trail Surface: Natural
Trail Use Fee: None
Method Of Ski Trail Grooming: None
Skiing Ability Suggested: NA
Hiking Trail Difficulty: Easy
Mountain Biking Ability Suggested: NA
Terrain: 100% Flat
Camping: None

Maintained by the DNR Forest Management Division
This is a nature with several points of interest
Trail passes near the site of the former village of Bell that once was a logging town of about 100 people.
Other contacts:
        DNR Forest Management Division Office, Lansing, 517-373-1275
        DNR Forest Management Region Office, Roscommon, 517-275-5151

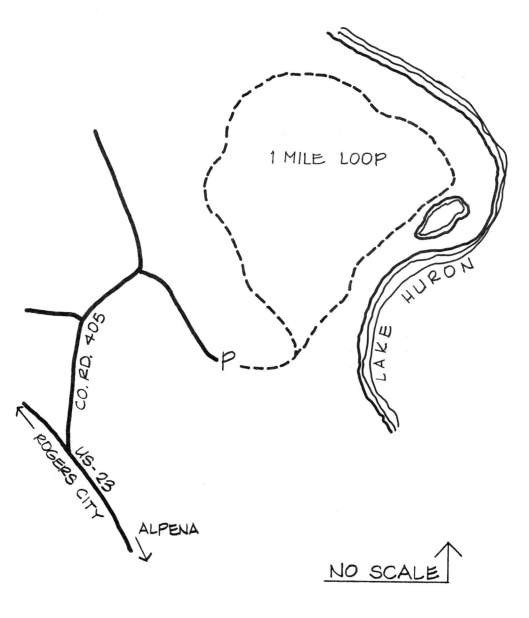

BESSER BELL PATHWAY

City of Alpena
208 N. First
Alpena, MI 49707

800-4-ALPENA

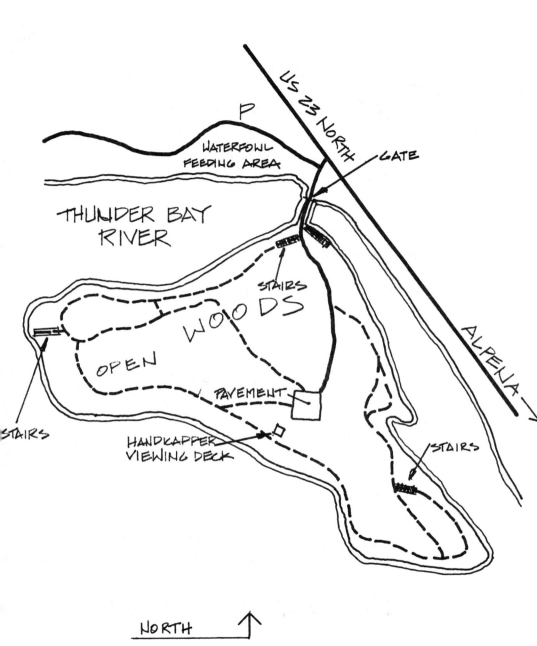

Michigan Atlas & Gazetteer Location: 85D5

County Location: Alpena

Directions To Trailhead:
In Alpena at the corner of US 23 and Johnson St. along the Thunder Bay River.

Trail Type: Hiking/Walking, Interpretive
Trail Distance: 1.5 mi   Loops: 2   Shortest: .5 mi   Longest: 1 mi
Trail Surface: Natural with handicapper viewing deck
Trail Use Fee: None
Method Of Ski Trail Grooming: NA
Skiing Ability Suggested: NA
Hiking Trail Difficulty: Easy
Mountain Biking Ability Suggested: NA
Terrain: Steep 0%, Hilly 0%, Moderate 10%, Flat 90%
Camping: Nearby

Maintained by the City of Alpena
Adjcent to wildlife area.
Viewing platform for handicappers accessible by vehicle. Obtain key from the
Holiday Inn which is located .25 mi north of US23

ISLAND PARK

Norway Ridge Pathway

Atlanta Forest Area, Mackinaw State Forest
Rte 1, Box 30
Atlanta, MI 49709

517-785-4251

District Forest Manager, Mackinaw State Forest
1732 West M32, PO Box667
Gaylord, MI 49735

517-732-3541

Michigan Atlas & Gazetteer Location: 85D5

County Location: Alpena

Directions To Trailhead:
4.5 miles SW of Alpena on Werth Road

Trail Type: Hiking/Walking, Cross Country Skiing, Mountain Biking
Trail Distance: 3 mi   Loops: 3   Shortest: .5 mi   Longest: 5.5 mi
Trail Surface: Natural
Trail Use Fee: None
Method Of Ski Trail Grooming: Track set
Skiing Ability Suggested: Novice
Hiking Trail Difficulty: Easy
Mountain Biking Ability Suggested: Novice
Terrain: Steep 0%, Hilly 0%, Moderate 20%, Flat 80%
Camping: None

Maintained by the DNR Forest Management Division
A very popular ski trail with the local skiers.

Other contacts:
     DNR Forest Management Division Office, Lansing, 517-373-1275
     DNR Forest Management Region Office, Roscommon, 517-275-5151

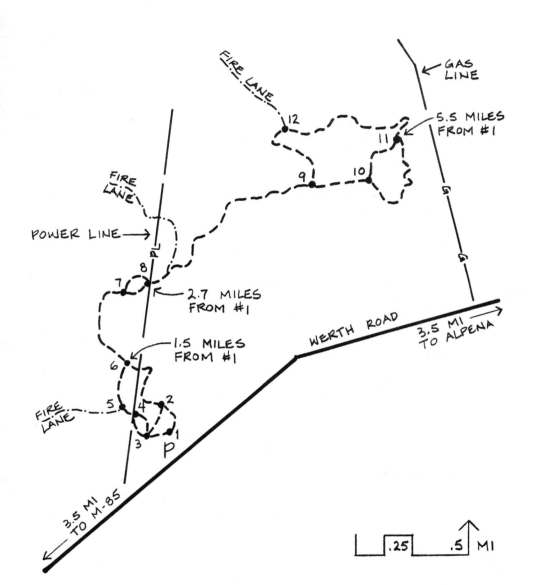

NORWAY RIDGE PATHWAY

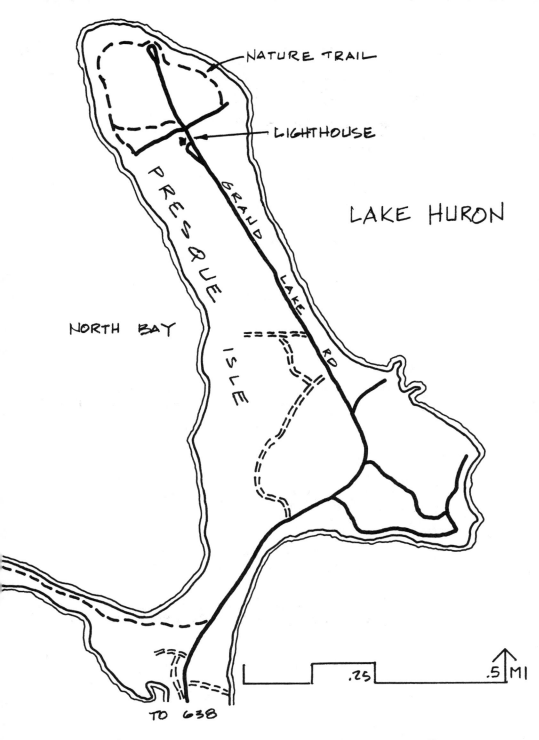

Presque Isle Lighthouse Park

Presque Isle Area Chamber of Commerce
4500 E. Grand Lake Rd
Presque Isle, MI 49777

517-595-5095
517-595-6970

517-595-2059

Michigan Atlas & Gazetteer Location: 85A5

County Location: Presque Isle

Directions To Trailhead:
US23 between Alpena and Rogers City, then take Co Rd 638 east to Grand Lake Rd, then north to lighthouse

Trail Type: Hiking/Walking, Interpretive
Trail Distance: 1 mi   Loops: 1   Shortest: NA   Longest: 1 mi
Trail Surface: Natural
Trail Use Fee: None
Method Of Ski Trail Grooming: NA
Skiing Ability Suggested: NA
Hiking Trail Difficulty: Easy
Mountain Biking Ability Suggested: NA
Terrain: 100% Flat
Camping: Campground nearby

Lighthouse maintained by the local community
Events held annually.
Trail along shore.

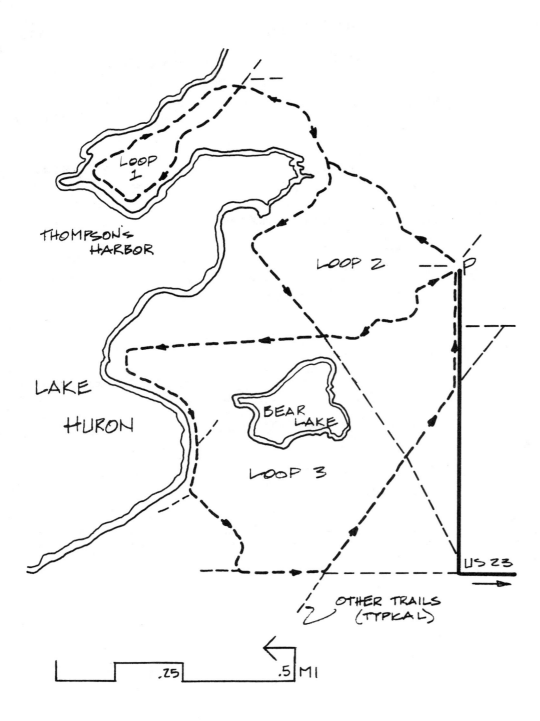

Hoeft State Park
US 23 North
Rogers City, MI 49779

517-734-2543

DNR Parks and Recreation Division

517-373-1263
517-275-5151

Michigan Atlas & Gazetteer Location: 85B45

County Location: Presque Isle

Directions To Trailhead:
12 miles southeast of Rogers City on US 23

Trail Type: Hiking/Walking, Cross Country Skiing, Mountain Biking
Trail Distance: 6 mi   Loops: 3   Shortest: 1.4 mi Longest: 2.6 mi
Trail Surface: Natural
Trail Use Fee: None, but vehicle entry permit required
Method Of Ski Trail Grooming: None
Skiing Ability Suggested: Novice
Hiking Trail Difficulty: Easy
Mountain Biking Ability Suggested: Novice to intermediate
Terrain: Steep 0%, Hilly 0%, Moderate 20%, Flat 80%
Camping: Available at Hoeft State Park

Maintained by the DNR Parks and Recreation Division
Substantially undeveloped park with many 2 tracks and trails.

THOMPSON'S HARBOR STATE PARK

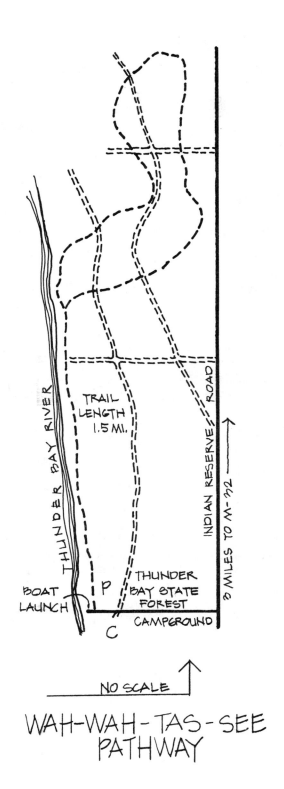

WAH-WAH-TAS-SEE
PATHWAY

NO SCALE

Alpena Field Office, Atlanta Forest Area
4343 M32 West   517-356-2209
Alpena, MI 49707

District Forest Manager, Mackinaw State Forest
1732 West M32, PO Box 667   517-732-3541
Gaylord, MI 49707

Michigan Atlas & Gazetteer Location: 85D5

County Location: Alpena

Directions To Trailhead:
5 miles west of Alpena on M32 to Indian Reserve Rd., then 3 miles south to the
Thunder Bay River SFCG and the trailhead.

Trail Type: Hiking/Walking, Cross Country Skiing, Interpretive
Trail Distance: 1.5 mi   Loops: 1   Shortest: NA   Longest: 1.5 mi
Trail Surface: Natural
Trail Use Fee: None
Method Of Ski Trail Grooming: None
Skiing Ability Suggested: Novice
Hiking Trail Difficulty: Easy
Mountain Biking Ability Suggested: NA
Terrain: 100% Flat
Camping: Campground at the trailhead

Maintained by the DNR Forest Management Division
9 station interpretive trail built in 1976 by the Youth Conservation Corps
Trail brochure is available.

USDA - Natural Resources Conservation Service
E 106 South Drive
Stephenson, MI 49887

906-753-2513

Michigan Atlas & Gazetteer Location: 86D3

County Location: Menominee

Directions To Trailhead:
In Menominee at Henes Park off M35 on Lake Michigan

Trail Type: Hiking/Walking, Interpretive
Trail Distance: .5 mi   Loops: 1   Shortest: NA   Longest: Short
Trail Surface: Natural
Trail Use Fee: None
Method Of Ski Trail Grooming: NA
Skiing Ability Suggested: NA
Hiking Trail Difficulty: Easy
Mountain Biking Ability Suggested: NA
Terrain: Flat
Camping: None

Maintaind by the Henes Park Board
An 18 station nature trail with emphasis on tree idendification. Quotes from
Shakespeare are presented that mention the trees identified.

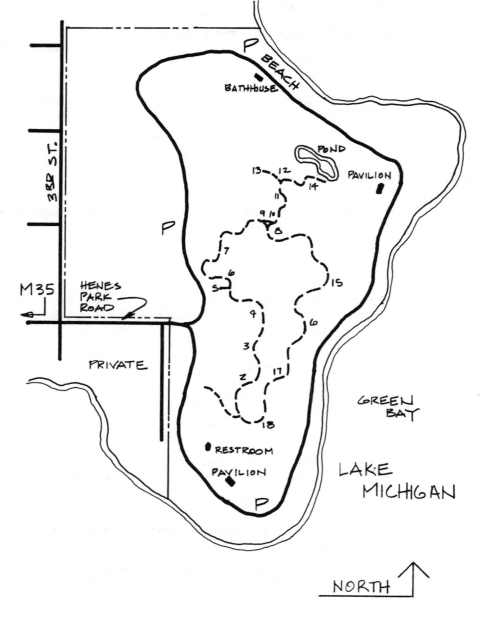

NORTH

HENES PARK
SHAKESPEARE NATURE TRAIL

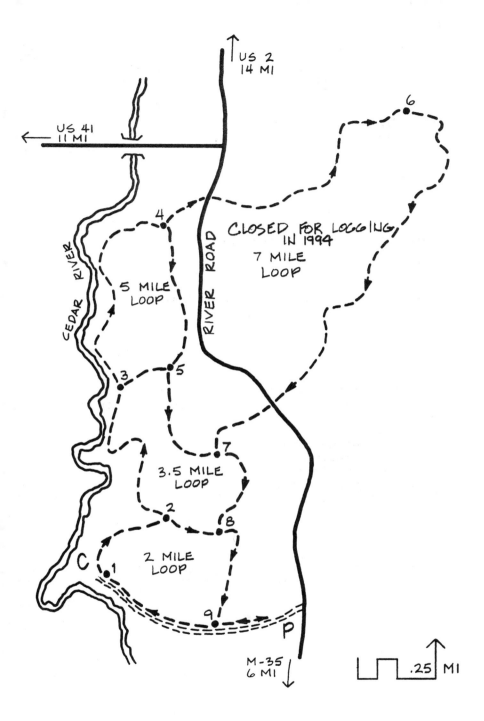

CEDAR RIVER PATHWAY

Stephenson Field Office, Escanaba River State Forest
Rte 1, Box 31B   906-753-6317
Stephenson, MI 49987

District Forest Manager, Escanaba River State Forest
6833 US41/2 & M35   906-786-2351
Gladstone, MI 49837

Michigan Atlas & Gazetteer Location: 87A5

County Location: Menominee

Directions To Trailhead:
1.5 miles north of Cedar River (town) on M35. Then north on Co Rd 551(River Rd) for 6 miles to the trailhead.

Trail Type: Hiking/Walking, Cross Country Skiing, Mountain Biking
Trail Distance: 8+ mi   Loops: 4   Shortest: 2 mi   Longest: 7 mi
Trail Surface: Natural
Trail Use Fee: None, but donations accepted for trail grooming
Method Of Ski Trail Grooming: Track set
Skiing Ability Suggested: Novice
Hiking Trail Difficulty: Easy
Mountain Biking Ability Suggested: Novice
Terrain: Steep 0%, Hilly 0%, Moderate 5%, Flat 95%
Camping: Campground along trail (ski-in only)

Managed by the DNR Forest Management Division
Trails touch on the Cedar River at several locations and pass through a variety of forest cover including pine, birch and aspen.
Campgrounds also available at Wells State Park on Lake Michigan near the town of Cedar River.
In 1993 the longest loop was temporarily closed because of a timber sale. Call ahead for current trail status.
Other contacts:
        DNR Forest Management Division Office, Lansing, 517-373-1275
        DNR Forest Management Region Office, Marquette, 906-228-6561

Iron Mountain City Park

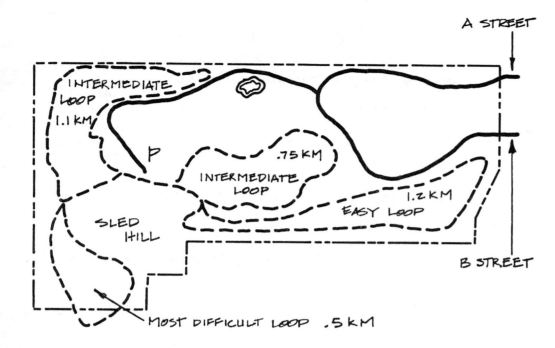

A STREET

INTERMEDIATE
LOOP
1.1 KM

P

.75 KM

INTERMEDIATE
LOOP

1.2 KM

EASY LOOP

SLED
HILL

B STREET

MOST DIFFICULT LOOP .5 KM

NORTH

Tourism Association of Dickinson County Area
600 S. Stephenson
Iron Mountain, MI 49801

906-774-2945
800-236-2447

Michigan Atlas & Gazetteer Location: 87B8

County Location: Dickinson

Directions To Trailhead:
From M95 (Carpenter Rd) take A Street west to the end of the street, watch for entrance to the park.

Trail Type: Hiking/Walking, Cross Country Skiing, Mountain Biking
Trail Distance: 3.5 km   Loops: 4   Shortest: .5 km   Longest: 1.2 km
Trail Surface: Natural
Trail Use Fee: None
Method Of Ski Trail Grooming: Track set
Skiing Ability Suggested: Novice
Hiking Trail Difficulty: Easy
Mountain Biking Ability Suggested: Novice
Terrain: Steep 0%, Hilly 10%, Moderate 50%, Flat 40%
Camping: None

Maintained by City of Iron Mountain
Ski rentals available nearby.

IRON MOUNTAIN - CITY PARK

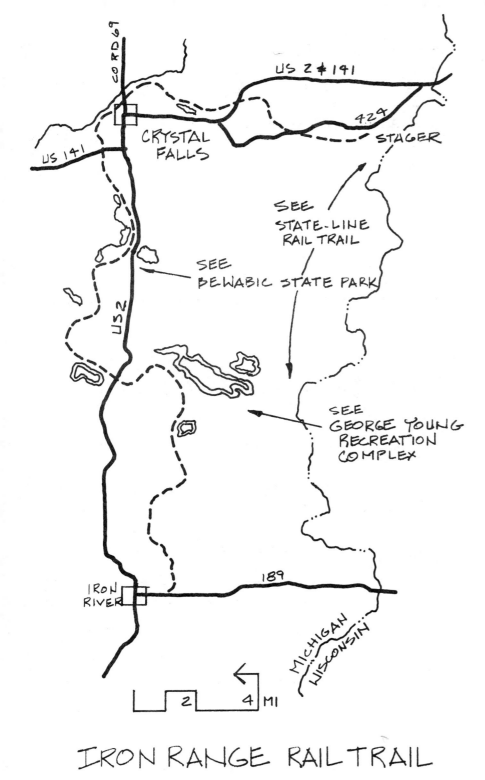

Iron Range Rail Trail

Crystal Fall Forest Area, Copper Country State Forest
1420 East US 2 West
Crystal Falls, MI 49920

906-875-6622

Iron County Road Commission
Fairgrounds
Iron River, MI 49920

906-265-4622

Michigan Atlas & Gazetteer Location: 87A6,98D34,99D56

County Location: Iron

Directions To Trailhead:
South side of Iron River through Crystal Falls and south to Stager near the Wisconsin/Michigan state line.

Trail Type: Hiking/Walking, Mountain Biking
Trail Distance: 36 mi   Loops: NA   Shortest: NA   Longest: NA
Trail Surface: Ballast, sand and natural
Trail Use Fee: None
Method Of Ski Trail Grooming: NA
Skiing Ability Suggested: NA
Hiking Trail Difficulty: Easy
Mountain Biking Ability Suggested: Intermediate
Terrain: 100% Flat
Camping: Campgrounds nearby

Maintained by the DNR Forest Management Division and the Iron Co. Road Commission
No development planned in the near future.
Used as a snowmobile trail.
Gates across trail are to restrict motor vehicle access. Non motorized use is not limited.
Connects to the State Line Rail Trail at two points to form a loop trail system.
Other contacts:
    DNR Forest Management Division 517-373-1275, Lansing
    DNR Forest Management Division 906-353-6651, Baraga
    DNR Forest Management Divsion 906-228-6561, Marquette

IRON RANGE RAIL TRAIL

Dickinson County Parks
N3393 Lake Antoine Rd
Iron Mountain, MI 49801

906-774-8875

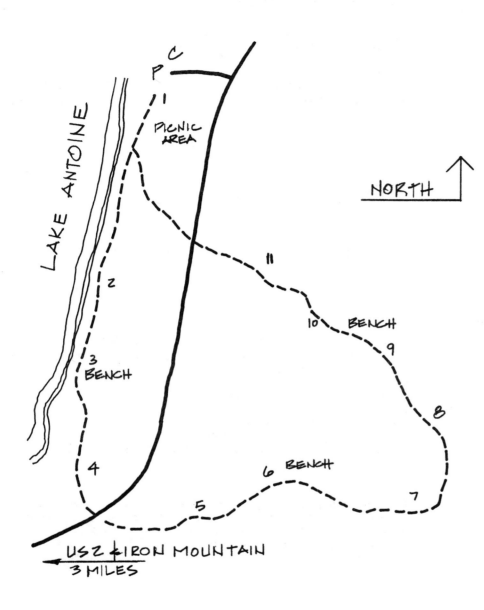

NORTH ↑

Michigan Atlas & Gazetteer Location: 87B8

County Location: Dickinson

Directions To Trailhead:
East of M 95, US 141 & 2 on South Lake Antoine Rd. About 3 miles from Iron Mountain

Trail Type: Hiking/Walking, Cross Country Skiing, Interpretive
Trail Distance: .5 mi   Loops: 1   Shortest: NA   Longest: .5 mi
Trail Surface: Natural
Trail Use Fee: None
Method Of Ski Trail Grooming: None
Skiing Ability Suggested: Novice
Hiking Trail Difficulty: Easy
Mountain Biking Ability Suggested: NA
Terrain: Steep 0%, Hilly 0%, Moderate 0%, Flat 100%
Camping: Available on site

Maintained by Dickinson County Parks
Complete campground at the trailhead.
11 station nature trail. Written guide available
Lake Antoine is a beautiful sand bottom lake which is great for swimming.

LAKE ANTOINE PARK
NATURE TRAIL

393.1

Pine Mountain Lodge
N3332 Pine Mountain Rd.
Iron Mountain, MI 49801

906-774-2747
800-321-6298

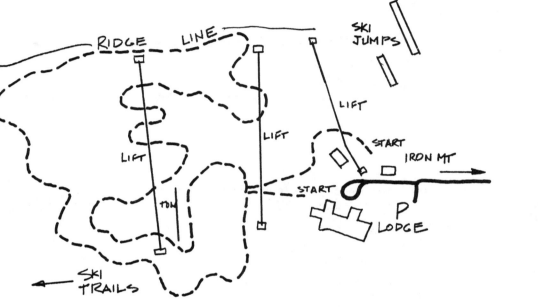

Michigan Atlas & Gazetteer Location: 87B8

County Location: Dickinson

Directions To Trailhead:
2 miles northeast of Iron Mountain on Pine Mountain Rd.

Trail Type: Hiking/Walking, Cross Country Skiing, Mountain Biking
Trail Distance: 4 mi   Loops: 1   Shortest: Longest: 4 mi
Trail Surface: Natural
Trail Use Fee: None
Method Of Ski Trail Grooming: No
Skiing Ability Suggested: Intermediate
Hiking Trail Difficulty: Moderate
Mountain Biking Ability Suggested: NA
Terrain: Steep 0%, Hilly 85%, Moderate 15%, Flat 0%
Camping: Available nearby

Privately operated full facility alpine ski area
Lodging,restaurant, tennis courts, indoor pool, golf course and convention
facilities.
90 meter ski jump in view of the trails.

MOUNTAIN BIKE TRAIL
PINE MOUNTAIN SKI & RECREATION

Crystal Falls Forest Area, Copper Country State Forest
1420 US2 West
Crystal Falls, MI 49920   906-875-6622

District Forest Manager, Copper Country State Forest
Box 440, US 41
Baraga, MI 49908   906-353-6651

Michigan Atlas & Gazetteer Location: 87A5,96AB3,97B5678,98CD1234,99D5

County Location: Gogebic, Iron

Directions To Trailhead:
East trailhead - Stager, west of US2, just north of Florence.
West trailhead - Korpela Rd, .4 mile south of US2, 4.7 miles east of Wakefield.

Trail Type: Hiking/Walking, Mountain Biking
Trail Distance: 102.2 mi   Loops: NA   Shortest: NA   Longest: NA
Trail Surface: Natural and original ballast
Trail Use Fee: None
Method Of Ski Trail Grooming: NA
Skiing Ability Suggested: NA
Hiking Trail Difficulty: Easy to moderate
Mountain Biking Ability Suggested: Novice to intermediate
Terrain: 100% Flat
Camping: None on the trail but many nearby

Maintained by the DNR Forest Management Division
Rough and rugged trail for mountain biking but can be done
36 mile section between Watersmeet and Iron River is quite nice with rock
escarpment, bridges, bridges, rivers, beaver ponds
The book "Great Rail Trails" available from the Rail to Trails Conservency is an
excellent resourse for this and other rail trails listed in this atlas.

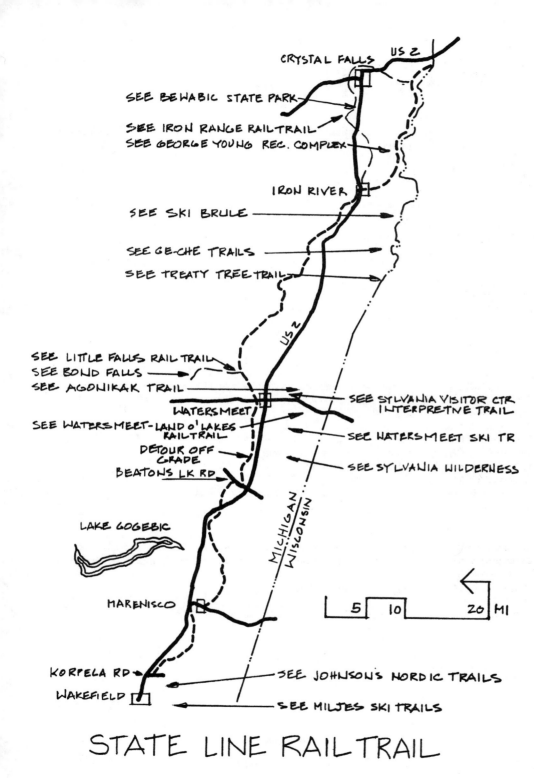

CRYSTAL FALLS — US 2
SEE BEWABIC STATE PARK
SEE IRON RANGE RAIL TRAIL
SEE GEORGE YOUNG REC. COMPLEX
IRON RIVER
SEE SKI BRULE
SEE GE-CHE TRAILS
SEE TREATY TREE TRAIL
US 2
SEE LITTLE FALLS RAIL TRAIL
SEE BOND FALLS
SEE AGONIKAK TRAIL
WATERSMEET
SEE SYLVANIA VISITOR CTR INTERPRETIVE TRAIL
SEE WATERSMEET-LAND O' LAKES RAIL TRAIL
SEE WATERSMEET SKI TR
DETOUR OFF GRADE
BEATONS LK RD
SEE SYLVANIA WILDERNESS
MICHIGAN / WISCONSIN
LAKE GOGEBIC
5 10 20 MI
MARENISCO
KORPELA RD
SEE JOHNSON'S NORDIC TRAILS
WAKEFIELD
SEE MILJES SKI TRAILS

STATE LINE RAIL TRAIL

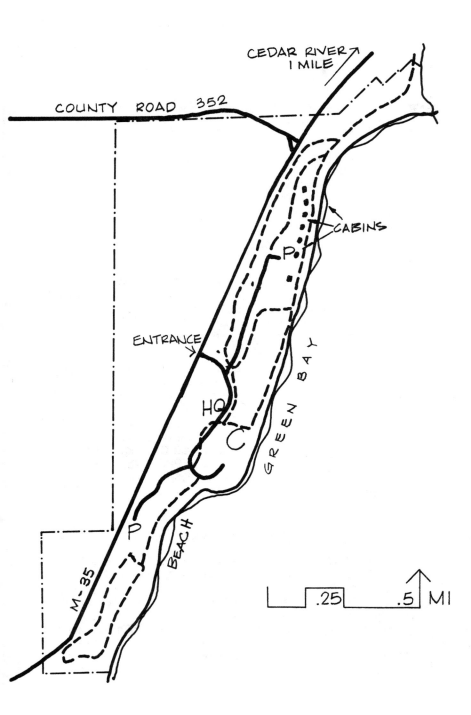

CEDAR RIVER
1 MILE

COUNTY ROAD 352

CABINS

P

ENTRANCE

HQ

C

GREEN BAY

BEACH

M-35

|___.25|___.5| MI

WELLS STATE PARK

Wells State Park

Wells State Park
M35
Cedar River, MI 49813

906-863-9747

DNR Parks and Recreation Division

517-373-1270
906-228-6561

Michigan Atlas & Gazetteer Location: 87B5

County Location: Menominee

Directions To Trailhead:
South of Escanaba and 1 mile south of Cedar River on Lake Michigan on M35

Trail Type: Hiking/Walking, Cross Country Skiing
Trail Distance: 5 mi   Loops: 4   Shortest: Longest:
Trail Surface: Natural
Trail Use Fee: None, but vehicle entry fee required
Method Of Ski Trail Grooming: Track set when grooming equipment is provided
Skiing Ability Suggested: Novice to intermediate
Hiking Trail Difficulty: Easy to moderate
Mountain Biking Ability Suggested: NA
Terrain: Steep 0%, Hilly 10%, Moderate 20%, Flat 70%
Camping: Campground in park. Open all year

Maintained by the DNR Parks and Recreation Division
Hiking and ski trails are not be identical.
6 very rustic cabins are available for rent that house up to 16 people.
Snowmobiling permitted in park except on ski trails.
Ski rentals available in Escanaba and Menominee.
Virgin forest throughout park.
3 miles of Lake Michigan shoreline.
Established in 1925 by the children of John Wells, a local lumberman, who donated the land. Many of the buildings were constructed by the CCC in the 1930's & 1940's

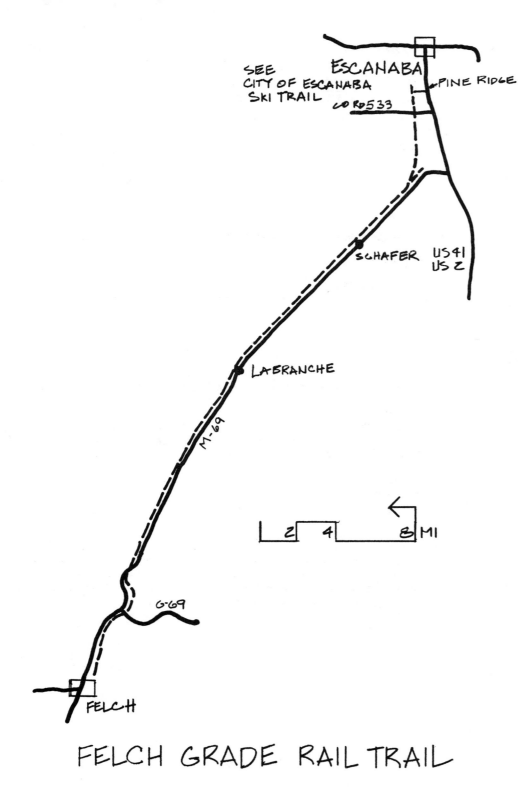

Escanaba Forest Area, Escanaba River State Forest
6833 Hwy US2,41 & M35   906-786-2354
Gladstone, MI 49837

District Forest Manager, Escanaba River State Forest
6833 Hwy2,41 & M35   906-786-2351
Gladstone, MI 49837

Michigan Atlas & Gazetteer Location: 88A234,89BC567

County Location: Delta, Menominee,Dickinson

Directions To Trailhead:
Between Felch and the western edge of Escanaba near Pine Ridge.
West trailhead - Felch Township Community Center on M69. Take Andy's Lane, then turn right on Van Lear Drive, turn left on Old Dump Rd, go 2 blocks, turn left and then make a right onto the trail grade.
East trailhead - From US2, north on Pine Ridge about 1.5 miles to the trail or Co Rd 553 1.75 miles to the trail

Trail Type: Hiking/Walking, Mountain Biking
Trail Distance: 40 mi   Loops: NA   Shortest: NA   Longest: NA
Trail Surface: Natural, ballast and gravel
Trail Use Fee: None
Method Of Ski Trail Grooming: NA
Skiing Ability Suggested: NA
Hiking Trail Difficulty: Easy
Mountain Biking Ability Suggested: Intermediate
Terrain: Steep 0%, Hilly 0%, Moderate 0%, Flat 100%
Camping: None

Managed by the DNR Forest Management Divsion.
Seasonally maintained by local group.
Very rough rail trail. Use M69 when necessary.
A little of everything can be found along this trail. Sand, water, creeks, rivers and a little of everything else.
Along the trail, the Village of LaBranche has a small store and bar and the Village of Schafter has a small store.
No parking at eastern trailheads. Suggest using the park and ride lot at M69 and US2.
ORV's and snowmobiles are permitted use of this trail.

FELCH GRADE RAIL TRAIL

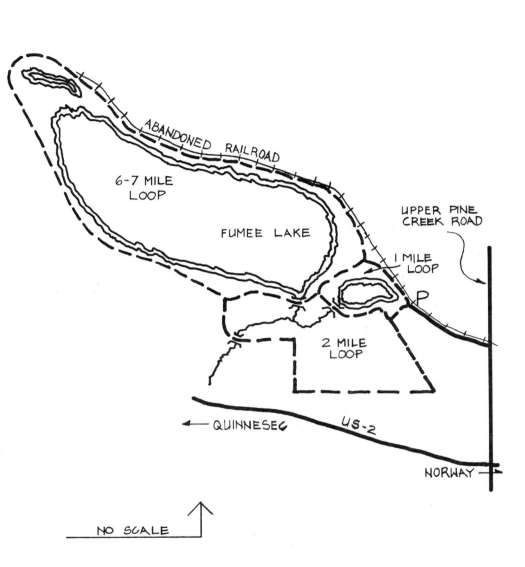

6-7 MILE
LOOP

ABANDONED RAILROAD

FUMEE LAKE

UPPER PINE
CREEK ROAD

1 MILE
LOOP

P

2 MILE
LOOP

← QUINNESEC

US-2

NORWAY →

NO SCALE

Fumee Lake Trail

Dickinson County Tourism Association
600 S. Stephenson
Iron Mountain, MI 49801

800-236-2447
906-774-2945

Michigan Atlas & Gazetteer Location: 88B1

County Location: Dickinson

Directions To Trailhead:
North of US2 between Norway and Quinnesec, take Upper Pine Creek Rd for 1 mile.

Trail Type: Hiking/Walking, Cross Country Skiing, Mountain Biking, Interpretive
Trail Distance: 8 mi   Loops: 3   Shortest: 1   Longest: 6 mi
Trail Surface: Natural
Trail Use Fee: None
Method Of Ski Trail Grooming: Track set
Skiing Ability Suggested: Novice to intermediate
Hiking Trail Difficulty: Easy
Mountain Biking Ability Suggested: Novice to intermediate
Terrain: Steep 0%, Hilly 15%, Moderate 75%, Flat 10%
Camping: Some camping nearby.

Owned by Dickinson County
Fumee Lake Natural Area has two lakes with 5 miles of undeveloped shoreline. The natural area contains, 270 species of plants, mature trees, 137 species of birds, 7 species of fish, 26 species of mammals, 6 species of anphibians, 6 species of reptiles and historical Indiana Mine.

FUMEE LAKE TRAIL

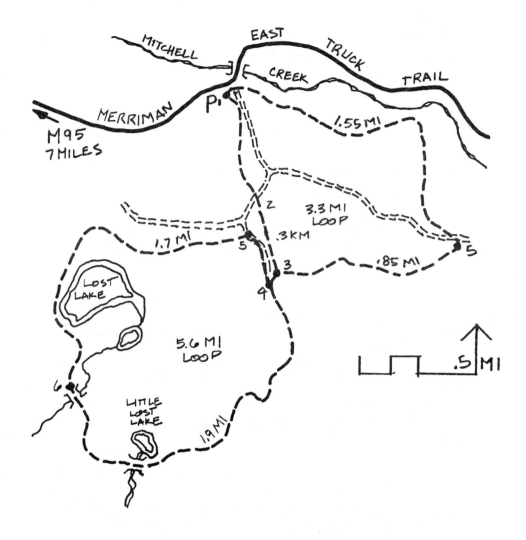

MITCHELL EAST TRUCK TRAIL

CREEK

MERRIMAN P.

M95 7 MILES

1.55 MI

2

3.3 MI LOOP

1.7 MI

.3 KM

5

5

3

.85 MI

4

LOST LAKE

5.6 MI LOOP

LITTLE LOST LAKE

1.9 MI

.5 MI

Norway Forest Area, Copper Country State Forest
PO Box 126
Norway, MI 49870

906-563-9247

District Forest Manager, Copper Country State Forest
US41 North, Box 440
Baraga, MI 49908

906-353-6651

Michigan Atlas & Gazetteer Location: 88A1

County Location: Dickinson

Directions To Trailhead:
North of Iron Mountain about 6 miles to the Merriman Truck Trail, then east about 7 miles to trailhead located just before the Mitchell Creek bridge

Trail Type: Hiking/Walking, Cross Country Skiing, Mountain Biking
Trail Distance: 6.7 mi   Loops: 2   Shortest: 3 mi   Longest: 5.6 mi
Trail Surface: Natural
Trail Use Fee: None
Method Of Ski Trail Grooming: None
Skiing Ability Suggested: Novice to intermediate
Hiking Trail Difficulty: Moderate
Mountain Biking Ability Suggested: Novice
Terrain: Steep 0%, Hilly 20%, Moderate 80%, Flat 0%
Camping: Developed campground not available nearby

Maintained by the DNR Forest Management Division
Skiers should have some winter survival skills since this trail is somewhat isolated and is not groomed.
Other contacts:
        DNR Forest Management Division Office, Lansing, 517-373-1275
        DNR Forest Management Region Office, Marquette, 906-228-6561

MERRIMAN EAST PATHWAY

City of Escanaba, Department of Recreation
121 S. 11th St.   906-786-4141
Escanaba, MI 49829

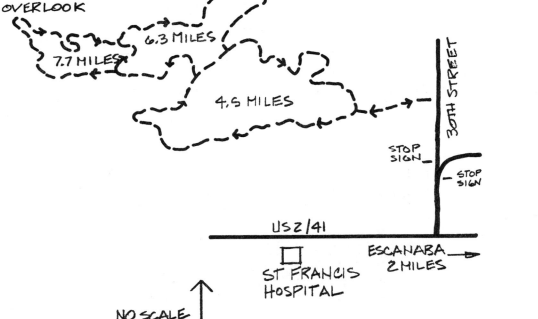

Michigan Atlas & Gazetteer Location: 89BC8

County Location: Delta

Directions To Trailhead:
On N. 30th St. (dead end street) in Escanaba, .5 mile north of US2/41 on the west side of town, just before St. Francis Hospital located on US2/41.

Trail Type: Cross Country Skiing
Trail Distance: 4.6 mi   Loops: 3   Shortest: .75 mi Longest: 2.2 mi
Trail Surface: Natural
Trail Use Fee: Yes, daily and annual permits available
Method Of Ski Trail Grooming: Track set daily or as needed
Skiing Ability Suggested: Novice to advanced
Hiking Trail Difficulty: NA
Mountain Biking Ability Suggested: NA
Terrain: Steep 10%, Hilly 40%, Moderate 40%, Flat 10%
Camping: None in area

Maintained by the City of Escanaba
Within the city limits but in a very heavily forested area.
Within 15 miles of 4 other trails; Days River Pathway, Rapid River Cross-Country Ski Trail. Cedar River Pathway and Gladstone Cross Country Ski Trail.

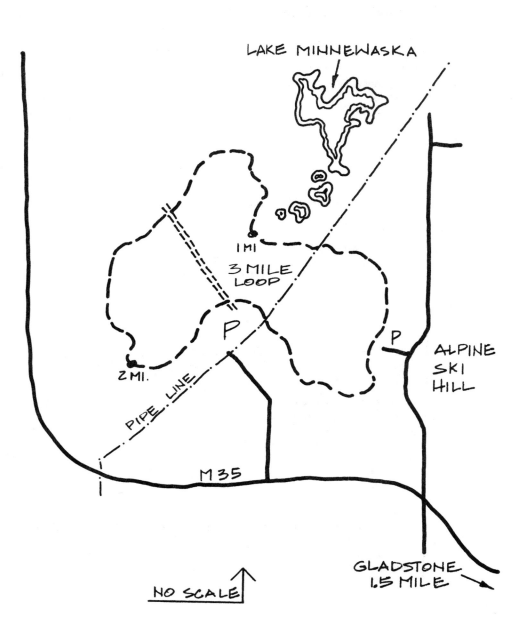

Gladstone Cross Country Ski Trail

Gladstone Sports Park
45 North Bluff Drive
Gladstone, MI 49837

906-428-2311

Michigan Atlas & Gazetteer Location: 89B8

County Location: Delta

Directions To Trailhead:
From Gladstone follow US2/41, then north on M35 2 miles, then west 1/4mile on North Bluff Drive.

Trail Type: Hiking/Walking, Cross Country Skiing, Mountain Biking
Trail Distance: 5 km   Loops: 1   Shortest: NA   Longest: NA
Trail Surface: Natural
Trail Use Fee: None
Method Of Ski Trail Grooming: Double track set
Skiing Ability Suggested: Novice tp intermediate
Hiking Trail Difficulty: Easy
Mountain Biking Ability Suggested: Novice
Terrain: Steep 0%, Hilly 0%, Moderate 90%, Flat10%
Camping: Campground available within 3 miles of the park

Municipally operated recreation area by City of Gladstone
Warming area and snack bar, sledding, tubing and downhill ski hills available.

GLADSTONE CROSS COUNTRY SKI TRAIL

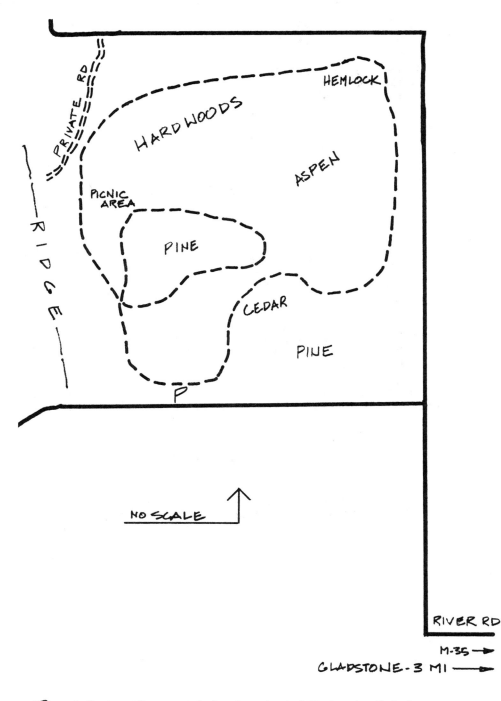

RIVER BLUFF NATURE TRAIL

Mead Paper, Woodlands Department
PO Box 1008
Escanaba, MI 49829

906-786-1660
ext 2180

Michigan Atlas & Gazetteer Location: 89B8

County Location: Delta

Directions To Trailhead:
North from Gladstone on M35 to 22st Rd (River Rd)

Trail Type: Hiking/Walking, Cross Country Skiing, Interpretive
Trail Distance: .87 mi   Loops: 2   Shortest: .2 mi   Longest: .75 mi
Trail Surface: Natrual
Trail Use Fee: None
Method Of Ski Trail Grooming: NA
Skiing Ability Suggested: NA
Hiking Trail Difficulty: Easy
Mountain Biking Ability Suggested: NA
Terrain: Not known
Camping: None

Owned by Mead Paper Company
Trail developed by Mead Paper and built by Bay De Noc Naturalists, Audubon
Society and Boy Scouts.
A 38 station interpretive trail.
Trail guide available.

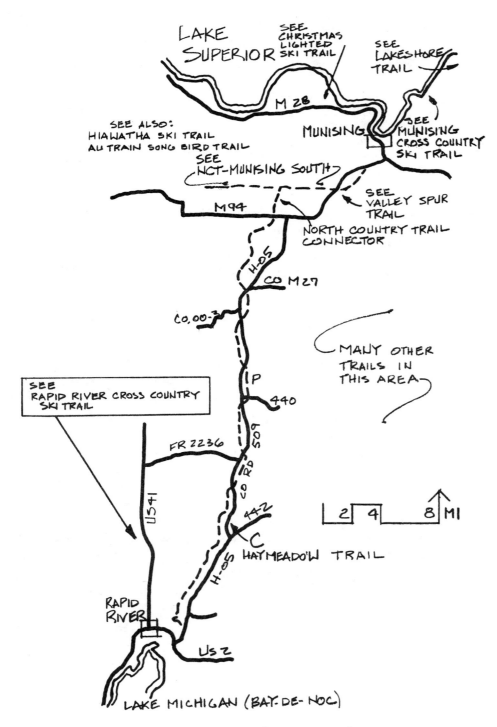

BAY DE NOC -GRAND ISLAND TRAIL

Munising Ranger District, Hiawatha National Forest
RR 2, Box 400   906-387-2512
Munising, MI 48962

Rapid River/Manistique Ranger District, Hiawatha N.F.
8181 US2   906-474-6442
Rapid River, MI 49878

Michigan Atlas & Gazetteer Location: 90A12,102BCD2

County Location: Alger, Delta

Directions To Trailhead:
Between Forest Lake on M94and Rapid River on US2. From M-28 and M94
intersection 1 mile east of Munising, take M94 9 miles west to trailhead at
Ackerman Lake. From Rapid River, take US2 east to Co Rd 509, north on Co
Rd 509 for 1.5 miles to trailhead parking lot. Also same direction out of Rapid
River but continue north on Co Rd 509 for 16 miles to parking lot on east side of
road.

Trail Type: Hiking/Walking, Mountain Biking
Trail Distance: 40 mi   Loops: NA   Shortest: NA   Longest: NA
Trail Surface: Natural with considerable sand
Trail Use Fee: None
Method Of Ski Trail Grooming: NA
Skiing Ability Suggested: NA
Hiking Trail Difficulty: Easy
Mountain Biking Ability Suggested: Intermediate to advanced
Terrain: Steep 10%, Hilly 30%, Moderate 30%, Flat 30%
Camping: Haymeadow NFCG and anywhere more than 200' from the trail

Managed by the Hiawatha National Forest.
Used mostly as a horse back riding trail which makes the trail open to mountain
bikes but sections may not be very enjoyable because of loose sand.
Water and toilet facilities available at the three trailhead locations.

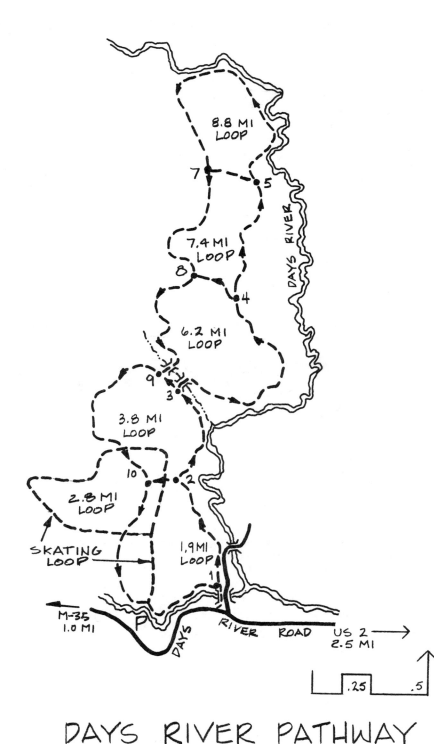

Escanaba Forest Area, Escanaba River State Forest
6833 US2/41 & M35   906-786-2354
Gladstone, MI 49835

District Forest Manager, Escanaba River State Forest
6833 US2/41 & M35   906-786-2351
Gladstone, MI 49835

Michigan Atlas & Gazetteer Location: 90A1, 102D1

County Location: Delta

Directions To Trailhead:
3 miles north of Gladstone on US2/41, then west 2 miles on Days River Rd.

Trail Type: Hiking/Walking, Cross Country Skiing, Mountain Biking
Trail Distance: 9.1 mi   Loops: 5   Shortest: 1.9 mi Longest: 8.8 mi
Trail Surface: Natural
Trail Use Fee: Donations accepted for trail grooming
Method Of Ski Trail Grooming: Track set
Skiing Ability Suggested: Novice to advanced
Hiking Trail Difficulty: Easy to moderate
Mountain Biking Ability Suggested: Novice
Terrain: Steep 5%, Hilly 10%, Moderate 50%, Flat 35%
Camping: None

Maintained by the DNR Forest Management Division
Overlooks the Days River at several locations. Deer usually seen along the trail.
A 2.8 mile skating loop in the system.
Other contacts:
        DNR Forest Management Division Office, Lansing, 517-373-1275
        DNR Forest Management Region Office, Marquette, 906-228-6561

DAYS RIVER PATHWAY

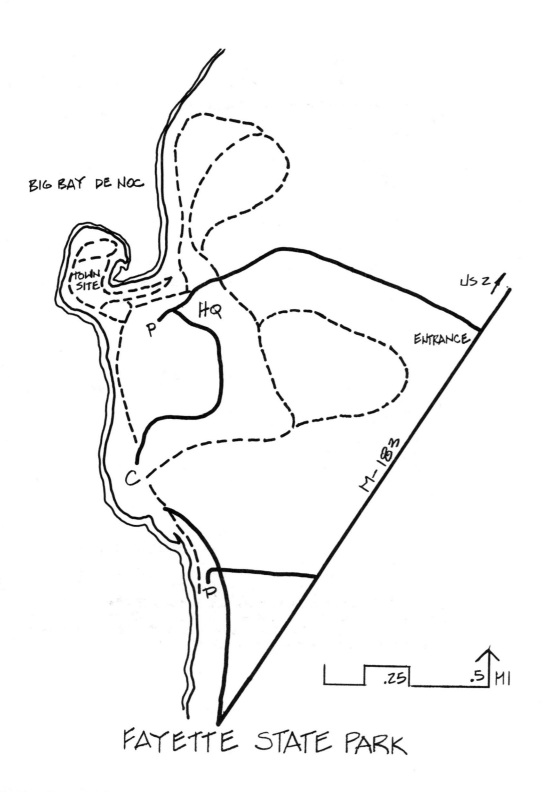

BIG BAY DE NOC

TOWN SITE

P   HQ

US 2

ENTRANCE

M-183

C

P

.25   .5 MI

FAYETTE STATE PARK

Fayette State Park
13700 13.25 Lane
Garden, MI 49835

906-644-2603

DNR Parks and Recreation Division

517-373-1270
906-228-6561

Michigan Atlas & Gazetteer Location: 90C3

County Location: Delta

Directions To Trailhead:
SW of Manistique via US2 and M183. On the west shore of the Garden
Peninsula near its south end.

Trail Type: Hiking/Walking, Cross Country Skiing, Interpretive
Trail Distance: 7 mi   Loops: Several   Shortest: 1.5 mi Longest: 4 mi
Trail Surface: Gravel and natural
Trail Use Fee: None, but vehicle entry fee required
Method Of Ski Trail Grooming: Track set
Skiing Ability Suggested: Novice to intermediate
Hiking Trail Difficulty: Easy
Mountain Biking Ability Suggested: NA
Terrain: Steep 0%, Hilly 0%, Moderate 10%, Flat 90%
Camping: Campground is open all year

Maintained by the DNR Parks and Recreation Division
Scenic overlook along trail. A unique restored village of the 1800's, settled to
house the iron smelting workers who worked there.
Annual events include:
        The Blessing of the Fleet event is held on the last Saturday in June.
        Heritage Days are held on on the first weekend of August.
Modern visitor center, 15 restored buildings, dock, campground, swimming
beach and picnic area.
Self guided tour maps available to tour the townsite.

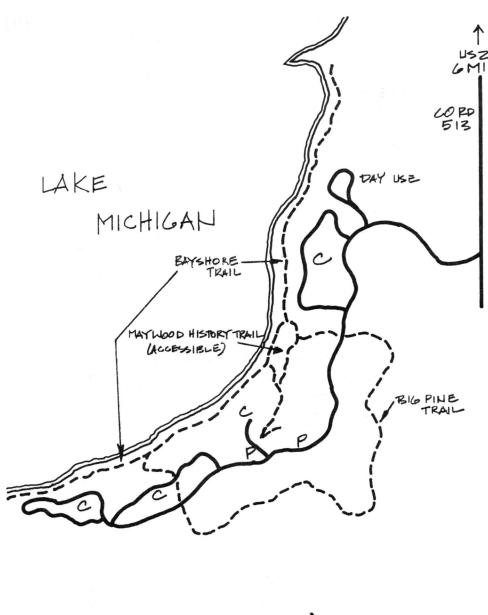

LAKE MICHIGAN

BAYSHORE TRAIL

MAYWOOD HISTORY TRAIL (ACCESSIBLE)

DAY USE

BIG PINE TRAIL

C

C

C

C

P

P

US2 6 MI

CO RD 513

.25   .5 MI

Rapid River/Manistique Ranger District, Hiawatha N.F.
8181 US2
Rapid River, MI 49878

906-474-6442

Forest Supervisor, Hiawatha National Forest
2727 N. Lincoln Rd
Escanaba, MI 49829

906-786-4062

Michigan Atlas & Gazetteer Location: 90B1

County Location: Delta

Directions To Trailhead:
East of Rapid River on US2 to Co Rd 513, then 6 miles south to recreation area

Trail Type: Hiking/Walking, Mountain Biking
Trail Distance: 3.2 mi   Loops: 1   Shortest: NA   Longest: .6 mi
Trail Surface: Paved and natural
Trail Use Fee: A day use fee may be charged in the future
Method Of Ski Trail Grooming: NA
Skiing Ability Suggested: NA
Hiking Trail Difficulty: Easy
Mountain Biking Ability Suggested: Novice
Terrain: Note below for each trail
Camping: Campground on site

Maintained by the Rapid River Ranger District, Hiawatha National Forest
Beautiful recreation area on Little Bay De Noc developed in 1990.
Trail Specifications:
Maywood History Trail - accessible, .6 mi, interpretive, benches,Flat
          This trail 200 ft tall Hemlocks along the trail
Bayshore Trail - point to point, 1.2 miles, 30% moderate, 70% flat
Big Pines Trail - point to point, 1.3 miles, 10% moderate, 90% flat
A hotel and cottages were located on the site in the 1800's. The area was also a
popular picnic area for Gladstone residents at that time.

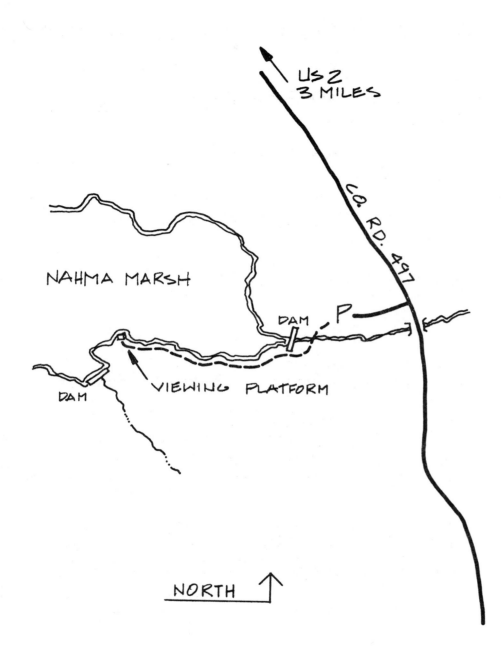

NAHMA MARSH

US 2
3 MILES

CO. RD. 497

DAM   P

VIEWING PLATFORM

DAM

NORTH

Nahma Marsh Hiking Trail

Rapid River/Manistique Ranger District, Hiawatha N.F.
8181 US 2
Rapid River, MI 49878   906-474-6442

Forest Supervisor, Hiawatha National Forest
2727 N. Lincoln Rd
Escanaba, MI 49829   906-786-4062

Michigan Atlas & Gazetteer Location: 90B3

County Location: Delta

Directions To Trailhead:
From Escanaba, take US2 east about 30 miles to Nahma Junction, then south 3 miles on Co Rd 497 to the trail.

Trail Type: Hiking/Walking
Trail Distance: .3 mi   Loops: NA   Shortest: NA   Longest: NA
Trail Surface: Packed crushed limestone & boardwalks
Trail Use Fee: None
Method Of Ski Trail Grooming: NA
Skiing Ability Suggested: NA
Hiking Trail Difficulty: Easy
Mountain Biking Ability Suggested: NA
Terrain: 100% Flat
Camping: Campground located 6 miles north on FH13 at Flowing Well NFCG

Maintained by the Rapid River Ranger District, Hiawatha National Forest
This trail was designed as a fully accessible hiking trail that ends at a two tierd wildlife viewing platform overlooking the Nahma Marsh. One tier is accessible. Rest areas with benches are located every 200 feet along the trail.
The maximum grade of the trail is 8%.

NAHMA MARSH HIKING TRAIL

(FAYETTE STATE PARK NEARBY)

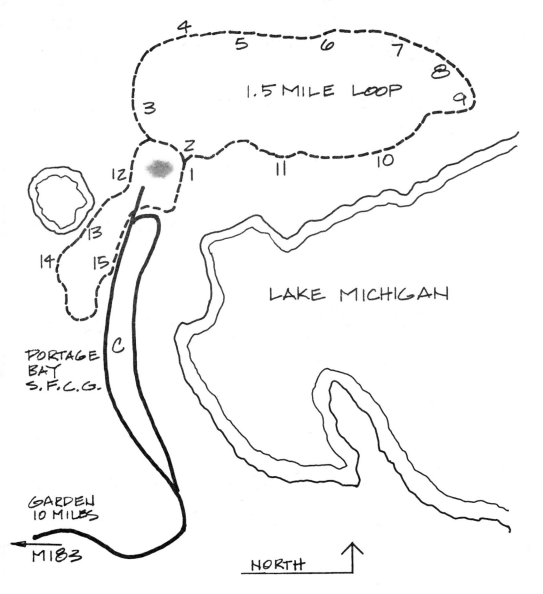

4
5 6 7
8
1.5 MILE LOOP 9
3
2
12 1
11 10
13
14 15

LAKE MICHIGAN

PORTAGE BAY S.F.C.G.

C

GARDEN 10 MILES

M183

NORTH ↑

Shingleton Forest Area, Lake Superior State Forest
PO Box 67
Shingleton, MI 49884

906-452-6227

District Forest Manager, Lake Superior State Forest
PO Box 77
Newberry, MI 49868

906-293-5131

Michigan Atlas & Gazetteer Location: 90C4

County Location: Delta

Directions To Trailhead:
10 miles southeast of Garden via M183 on the Garden Peninsula.

Trail Type: Hiking/Walking, Interpretive
Trail Distance: 2 mi   Loops: 2   Shortest: .5 mi   Longest: 1.5 mi
Trail Surface: Natural
Trail Use Fee: None
Method Of Ski Trail Grooming: NA
Skiing Ability Suggested: NA
Hiking Trail Difficulty: Easy
Mountain Biking Ability Suggested: NA
Terrain: Not known
Camping: At trailhead

Maintained by the DNR Forest Management Division
This is a native american interpretive trail of the Ojibwa Indians.

NINGA AKI PATHWAY

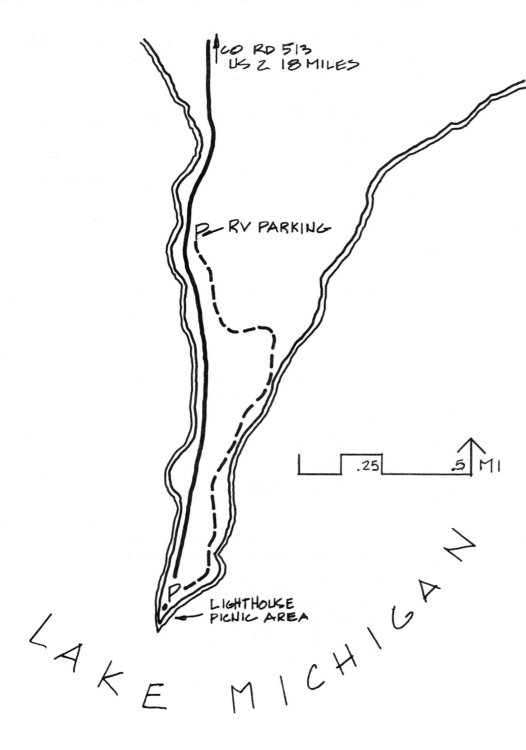

Rapid River/Manistique Ranger District, Hiawatha N. F.
8181 US2   906-474-6442
Rapid River, MI 49878

Forest Supervisor, Hiawatha National Forest
2727 N. Lincoln Rd   906-786-4062
Escanaba, MI 49829

Michigan Atlas & Gazetteer Location: 90C1

County Location: Delta

Directions To Trailhead:
At the Peninsula Point national historical lighthouse.
From Rapid River, take US2 east for 3 miles to Co Rd 513, then south for 18 miles to the trailhead.

Trail Type: Hiking/Walking, Interpretive
Trail Distance: 1 mi   Loops: NA   Shortest: NA   Longest: NA
Trail Surface: Natural
Trail Use Fee: None
Method Of Ski Trail Grooming: NA
Skiing Ability Suggested: NA
Hiking Trail Difficulty: Easy
Mountain Biking Ability Suggested: NA
Terrain: 100% Flat
Camping: Little Bay De Noc Recreation Area

Maintained by the Rapid River Ranger District, Hiawatha National Forest
Trail has inerpretive signs and benches along with vistas of the lake.
The focal point of the trail is a lighthouse built in 1865.

PENINSULA POINT HIKING TRAIL

Rapid River/Manistique Ranger District, Hiawatha N.F.
8181 US 2   906-474-6442
Rapid River, MI 49878

Forest Supervisor, Hiawatha National Forest
2727 N. Lincoln Rd.   906-786-4062
Escanaba, MI 49829

Michigan Atlas & Gazetteer Location: 90A1,102D1

County Location: Delta

Directions To Trailhead:
North of Escanaba and 7 miles north of Rapid River on US41

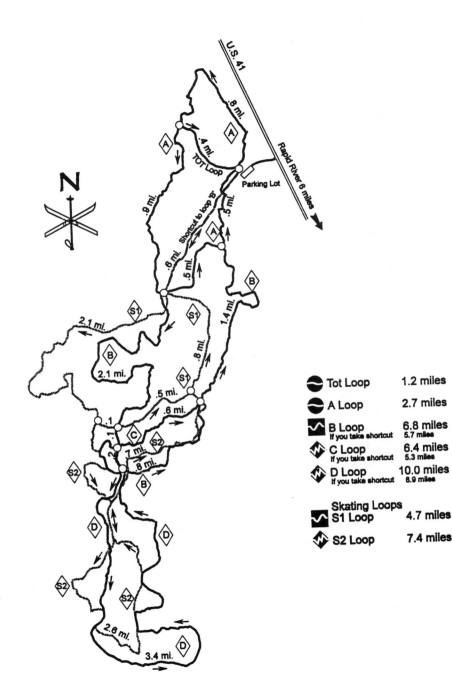

Tot Loop	1.2 miles
A Loop	2.7 miles
B Loop	6.8 miles
If you take shortcut	5.7 miles
C Loop	6.4 miles
If you take shortcut	5.3 miles
D Loop	10.0 miles
If you take shortcut	8.9 miles
Skating Loops	
S1 Loop	4.7 miles
S2 Loop	7.4 miles

Trail Type: Hiking/Walking, Cross Country Skiing
Trail Distance: 19.1mi   Loops: 4   Shortest: 1.2 mi Longest: 10 mi
Trail Surface: Natural
Trail Use Fee: None
Method Of Ski Trail Grooming: Track set
Skiing Ability Suggested: Novice to advanced
Hiking Trail Difficulty: NA
Mountain Biking Ability Suggested: NA
Terrain: Steep 27%, Hilly 28%, Moderate 25%, Flat 20%
Camping: None

Maintained by the Rapid River Ranger District, Hiawatha National Forest
Designed for cross country skiing. Well marked and maintained trail.
Loops:

       Tot loop - 1.2 mi - Easy - Classic
       A loop - 2.7 mi - Easy - Classic
       B loop - 6.8 mi - More difficult - Classic
       C loop - 6.4 mi - Most Difficult - Classic
       D loop - 10 mi - Most Difficult - Classic
       S1 loop - 4.7 mi - More difficult - Skating
       S2 loop - 7.4 mi - Most difficult - Skating

RAPID RIVER
NATIONAL CROSS COUNTRY SKI TRAIL

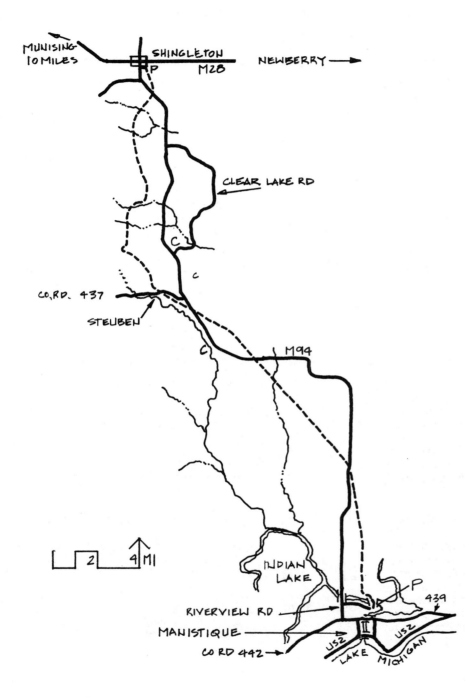

HAYWIRE RAIL TRAIL

Munising Ranger District, Hiawatha National Forest
RR 2, Box 400
Munising, MI 49862

906-387-2512

Shingleton Forest Area, Lake Superior State Forest
PO Box 67
Shingleton, MI 49884

906-452-6227`

Michigan Atlas & Gazetteer Location: 91A457,103BCD567

County Location: Alger, Schoolcraft

Directions To Trailhead:
North trailhead - East side of M-94 just south of Shingleton. Take .3 mile access trail to rail trail.
South trailhead - North of Manistique M94 to Riverview Rd. Right (east) on Riverview to parking lot just east of the water intake plant.

Trail Type: Hiking/Walking, Mountain Biking
Trail Distance: 33 mi   Loops: NA   Shortest: NA   Longest: NA
Trail Surface: Ballast, gravel and sand
Trail Use Fee: None
Method Of Ski Trail Grooming: NA
Skiing Ability Suggested: NA
Hiking Trail Difficulty: Easy
Mountain Biking Ability Suggested: Novice to intermediate
Terrain: Flat 100%
Camping: Indian River Camp and Picnic Grounds and wilderness camping

Managed by both the DNR Forest Management Divison and the Hiawatha National Forest
No development has been done to this trail.
Surface is ballast, sand and gravel.
Considerable beaver activity and sand traps will make this a challenge for mountain bikers.
A truely isolated trail with only the village of Steuben along the rail trail to provide a source of drinking water and food.
Most of its use is as a snowmobile and ORV trail.
If you are up for a challenge, try this one.

Indian Lake Pathway

Shingleton Forest Area, Lake Superior State Forest
M28 West, PO Box 67
Shingleton, MI 49884

906-452-6236
906-341-6917

District Forest Manager, Lake Superior State Forest
South M123, PO Box 77
Newberry, MI 49868

906-239-5131

Michigan Atlas & Gazetteer Location: 91A5, 103D5

County Location: Schoolcraft

Directions To Trailhead:
9 miles NW of Thompson on M149 and 1 mile west of Palms Brook State Park

Trail Type: Hiking/Walking, Cross Country Skiing, Mountain Biking
Trail Distance: 8 mi   Loops: 3   Shortest: 1 mi   Longest: 4.5 mi
Trail Surface: Natural
Trail Use Fee: None
Method Of Ski Trail Grooming: Track set
Skiing Ability Suggested: Novice to advanced
Hiking Trail Difficulty: Moderate
Mountain Biking Ability Suggested: Novice to intermediate
Terrain: Steep 0%, Hilly 25%, Moderate 75%, Flat 0%
Camping: None at trail but available nearby

Maintained by the DNR Forest Management Division
Other contacts:
      DNR Forest Management Division Office, Lansing, 517-373-1275
      DNR Forest Management Region Office, Marquette, 906-228-6561

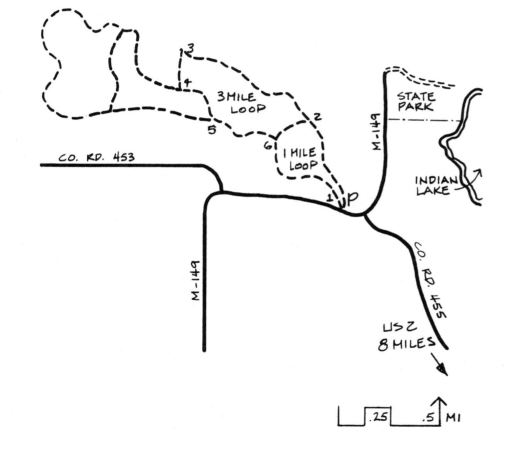

INDIAN LAKE PATHWAY

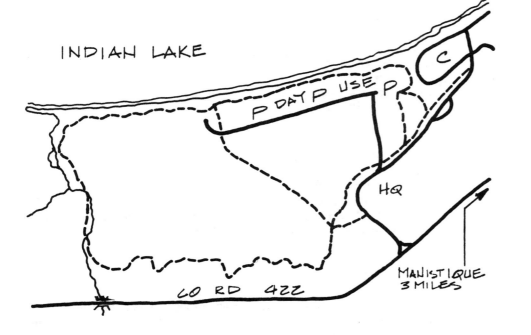

INDIAN LAKE

P DAY P USE P

C

HQ

CO RD 422

MANISTIQUE
3 MILES

NORTH

Indian Lake State Park
Rte 2, Box 2500
Manistique, MI 49854

906-341-2355

DNR Parks and Recreation Divsion

906-228-6561
517-373-1270

Michigan Atlas & Gazetteer Location: 91A6

County Location: Schoolcraft

Directions To Trailhead:
6 miles west of Manistique on US2 to Thompson, then 3 miles north on M149 ,
then .5 mile east on Co Rd 442 to the park

Trail Type: Hiking/Walking, Interpretive
Trail Distance: 4 mi   Loops: 3   Shortest: .25 mi Longest: 2 mi
Trail Surface: Natural
Trail Use Fee: None, but vehicle entry fee required
Method Of Ski Trail Grooming: NA
Skiing Ability Suggested: NA
Hiking Trail Difficulty: Easy
Mountain Biking Ability Suggested: NA
Terrain: 100% Flat
Camping: Campground at trailhead

Maintained by the DNR Parks and Recreation Division
The park contains typical facilities found in Michigan state parks

INDIAN LAKE STATE PARK

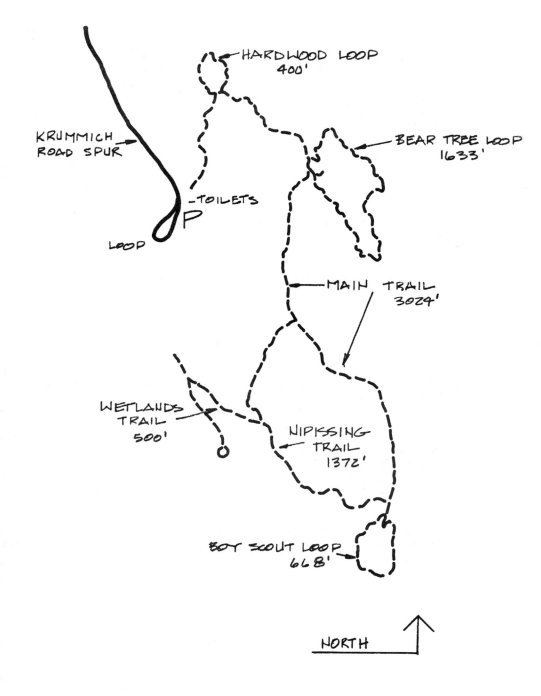

KRUMMICH ROAD SPUR

HARDWOOD LOOP 400'

BEAR TREE LOOP 1633'

TOILETS

P

LOOP

MAIN TRAIL 3024'

WETLANDS TRAIL 500'

NIPISSING TRAIL 1372'

BOY SCOUT LOOP 668'

NORTH

SCHOOLCRAFT COUNTY ENVIROMENTAL LAB.

MSU Cooperative Extension Service
Schoolcraft County Court House, Rm 218   906-341-5050
Manistique, MI 49854

Michigan Atlas & Gazetteer Location: 91A7

County Location: Schoolcraft

Directions To Trailhead:
3 miles east of Manistique to Co Rd 433 (River Rd), then north about 2 miles to Krumich Rd, then west about 2 mile to the trailhead.

Trail Type: Hiking/Walking, Cross Country Skiing, Interpretive
Trail Distance: 1.4 mi   Loops: Shortest: Longest:
Trail Surface: Natural
Trail Use Fee: None
Method Of Ski Trail Grooming: None
Skiing Ability Suggested: Novice
Hiking Trail Difficulty: Easy
Mountain Biking Ability Suggested: NA
Terrain: Steep 0%, Hilly 10%, Moderate 90%, Flat 0%
Camping: None

Managed by the Michigan State University Cooperative Extension Service

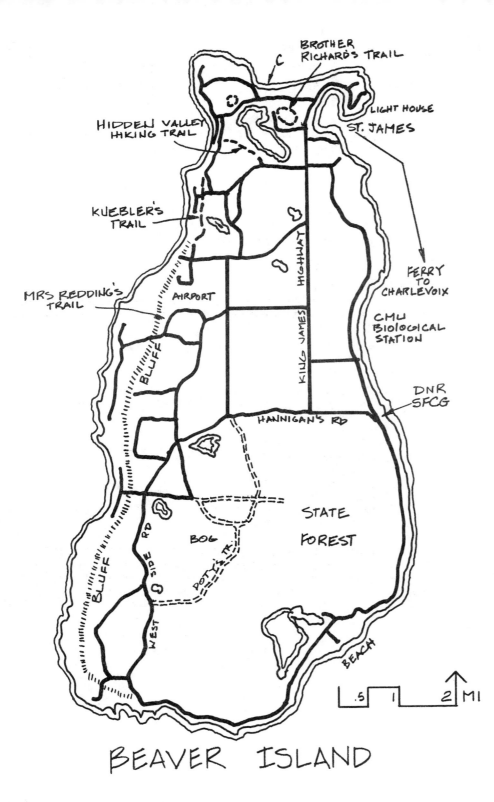

BEAVER ISLAND

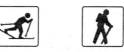

Beaver Island Chamber of Commerce
PO Box 153   616-448-2933
Beaver Island, MI 49782   616-448-2396

Michigan Atlas & Gazetteer Location: 92CD4,93CD5

County Location: Charlevoix

Directions To Trailhead:
Offshore in Lake Michigan between Charlevoix and Petoskey. Ferry service from Charlevoix.

Trail Type: Hiking/Walking, Cross Country Skiing, Mountain Biking
Trail Distance: 50+ mi   Loops: Many   Shortest: Short   Longest: Long
Trail Surface: Paved, gravel and natural
Trail Use Fee: None
Method Of Ski Trail Grooming: None
Skiing Ability Suggested: Novice to intermediate
Hiking Trail Difficulty: Easy
Mountain Biking Ability Suggested: Novice
Terrain: Steep 0%, Hilly 5%, Moderate 70%, Flat 25%
Camping: Two campgrounds on the island

Ferry service available from the Beaver Island Boat Company, 616-547-2311
A beautiful 53 square mile island with little vehicle traffic.
All roads most of which are gravel surfaced and less developed roads and trails are open to the public.
No trails specifically developed for mountain biking but the island is ideally suited for the activity.
Many miles of isolated shore accessible for hiking.
Camping available at a township campground in St. James and a state forest campground along the east shore.
About 1/3 of the island is state forest.
Write or call for complete information and a large map of the island.

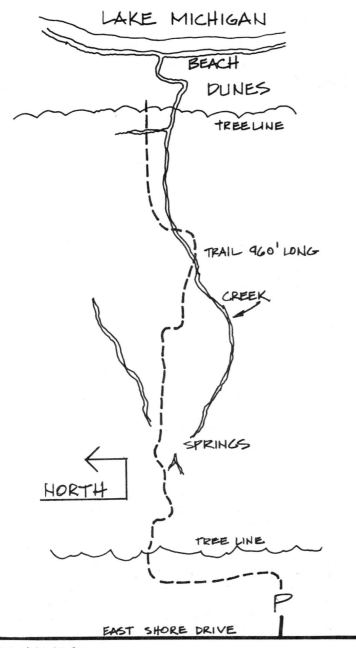

LAKE MICHIGAN

BEACH

DUNES

TREELINE

TRAIL 960' LONG

CREEK

SPRINGS

NORTH

TREE LINE

P

EAST SHORE DRIVE

← ST. JAMES

LITTLE SAND BAY TRAIL

Little Traverse Conservancy
3264 Powell Rd
Harbor Springs, MI 49740

616-347-0991

Michigan Atlas & Gazetteer Location: 92C4

County Location: Charlevoix

Directions To Trailhead:
On Beaver Island. From St. James, take Kings Hwy to East Shore Drive, then south on East Shore Drive about 1 mile to the trailhead. Across from the airport.

Trail Type: Hiking/Walking, Interpretive
Trail Distance: .1 mi   Loops: NA   Shortest: NA   Longest: NA
Trail Surface: Natural
Trail Use Fee: None
Method Of Ski Trail Grooming: NA
Skiing Ability Suggested: NA
Hiking Trail Difficulty: Easy
Mountain Biking Ability Suggested: NA
Terrain: Steep 0%, Hilly 0%, Moderate 2%, Flat 98%
Camping: Not allowed on the property

Maintained by the Little Traverse Conservancy
Point to point nature trail to Lake Michigan on Beaver Island
Contains 60 acres and 1,300 of undeveloped shoreline on Lake Michigan
Habitats include hardwood forest, cedar swamp, dunes, wetlands and beach.

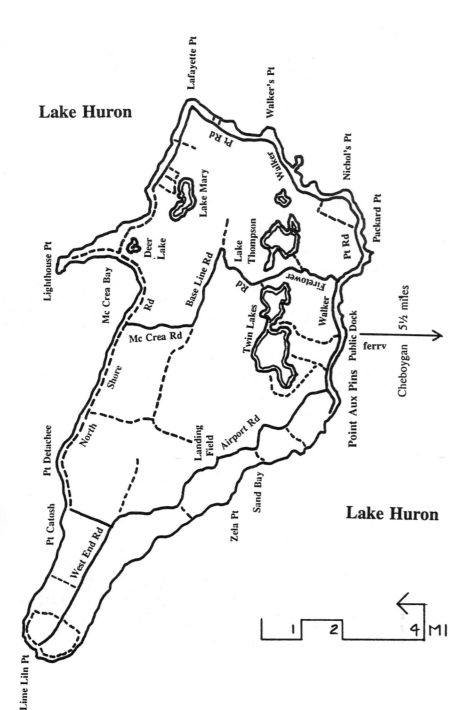

Lake Huron

Lafayette Pt

Walker's Pt

Pt Rd

Nichol's Pt

Walker

Packard Pt

Lake Mary

Lake Thompson

Pt Rd

Lighthouse Pt

Deer Lake

Base Line Rd

Firetower

Mc Crea Bay

Rd

Lake

Twin Lakes

Walker

Public Dock

Rd

Mc Crea Rd

ferry

Cheboygan   5½ miles

Shore

Point Aux Pins

North

Landing Field

Airport Rd

Lake Huron

Pt Detachee

Sand Bay

Pt Catosh

Zela Pt

West End Rd

Lime Liln Pt

BOIS BLANC ISLAND

1   2   4 MI

Cheboygan Area Chamber of Commerce
PO Box 69   616-627-7183
Cheboygan, MI 49721

Michigan Atlas & Gazetteer Location: 94B4, 95BC5

County Location: Mackinac

Directions To Trailhead:
In the north end of Lake Huron near Mackinac Island off Cheboygan

Trail Type: Mountain Biking
Trail Distance: 50+ mi   Loops: Many   Shortest: Longest:
Trail Surface: Gravel and natural
Trail Use Fee: None
Method Of Ski Trail Grooming: NA
Skiing Ability Suggested: NA
Hiking Trail Difficulty: Easy
Mountain Biking Ability Suggested: Novice to intermediate
Terrain: Varied
Camping: Primitive campground available.

Somewhat isolated island in the north end of Lake Huron
About 50% of the island is managed by the DNR Forest Management Division.
Numerous gravel and dirt roads along with almost non-existant traffic make this
island excellent for mountain biking. Many miles of roads to explore. Best to
visit before or after bug season, ie April and early May or October.
See Fall 1992 issue of Michigan Cyclist for article about the island
Ferry Services:
        Boblo Islander 616-627-9445
        Plaunt Transportation 616-627-2345/643-7300
Motel and only restaurant (reservations suggested) 616-634-7291

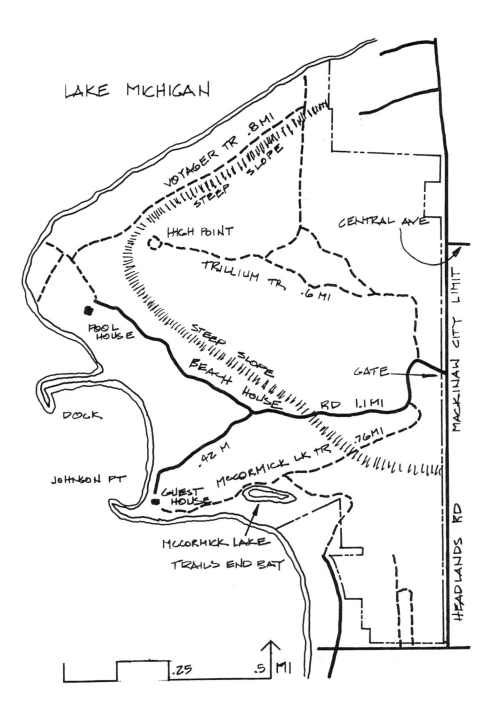

LAKE MICHIGAN

VOYAGER TR .8 MI

STEEP SLOPE

HIGH POINT

CENTRAL AVE

TRILLIUM TR. .6 MI

POOL HOUSE

STEEP SLOPE

BEACH HOUSE RD I.I MI

GATE

MACKINAW CITY LIMIT

DOCK

.42 M

.76 MI

JOHNSON PT

GUEST HOUSE

McCORMICK LK TR

McCORMICK LAKE

TRAIL'S END BAY

HEADLANDS RD

.25   .5 MI

THE HEADLANDS

Headlands

Emmet County Parks and Recreation Commission
200 Division
Petoskey, MI 49770

616-348-1702
616-348-1731

Michigan Atlas & Gazetteer Location: 94B2

County Location: Emmet

Directions To Trailhead:
West of Mackinaw City at the city limit boundary on Lake Michigan. At I 75 exit 338 (Welcome Center), turn left onto Nicolet St., then from Nicolet St., turn left onto Central Ave. Follow Central Ave. west to the end of the road which East Wilderness Park Drive (Headlands Rd). Turn left (south). The park entrance is on the right.

Trail Type: Hiking/Walking, Cross Country Skiing, Mountain Biking, Interpretive
Trail Distance: 5   Loops: 2   Shortest: 1.8 mi Longest: 2.7 mi
Trail Surface: Natural and gravel
Trail Use Fee: None
Method Of Ski Trail Grooming: Not known
Skiing Ability Suggested: Novice and intermediate
Hiking Trail Difficulty: Moderate
Mountain Biking Ability Suggested: Novice
Terrain: Steep 5%, Hilly 0%, Moderate 35%, Flat 60%
Camping: None, site but private and public facilities located in Mackinaw City

Owned by Emmet County
Former 600 acre private estate with over 2 miles of prestine shoreline.
Formerly owned by Roger McCormick of the Deering-McCormick family who owned the International Harvester Corporation.
An absolutely beautiful site on Lake Michigan with a view of the Mackinaw Bridge Recently purchased property with no development other than that which existed under private ownership.
Marked trails should be completed in 1997.
Call for current information about the park.

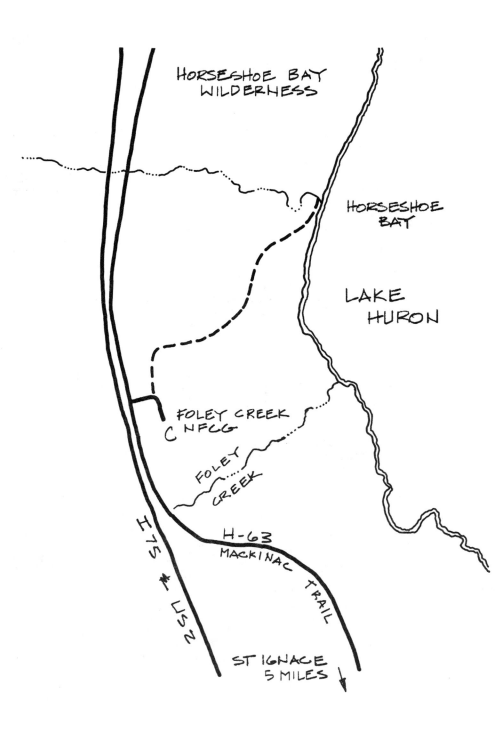

St. Ignace Ranger District, Hlawatha National Forest
Rte 2, Box 101   906-643-7900
St. Ignace, MI 49781

Forest Supervisor, Hiawatha National Forest
2727 N. Lincoln Rd   906-786-4062
Escanaba, MI 49826

Michigan Atlas & Gazetteer Location: 94A3

County Location: Mackinac

Directions To Trailhead:
Trailhead located at Foley Creek NFCG on Mackinac Trail about 5 miles north of St.. Ignace

Trail Type: Hiking/Walking
Trail Distance: 1 mi   Loops: NA   Shortest: NA   Longest: NA
Trail Surface: Natural
Trail Use Fee: None
Method Of Ski Trail Grooming: None
Skiing Ability Suggested: Novice
Hiking Trail Difficulty: Easy
Mountain Biking Ability Suggested: NA
Terrain: 100% Flat
Camping: At trailhead

Maintained by the St. Ignace Ranger District
This is a hiking trail only into the Horseshoe Bay Wilderness that was established in 1987 to protect the sensitive ecology and secluded character of this section of the Lake Huron shoreline.
To preserve this wilderness this trail is for walking only.
Camp in dispersed locations, travel in small groups, carry out your trash, be quiet, use stove instead of wood, move your campsite frequently naturalizing the area when you leave and do not disturb the area any more than absolutely necessary.
An information sheet for the trail and area is available.

HORSESHOE BAY HIKING TRAIL

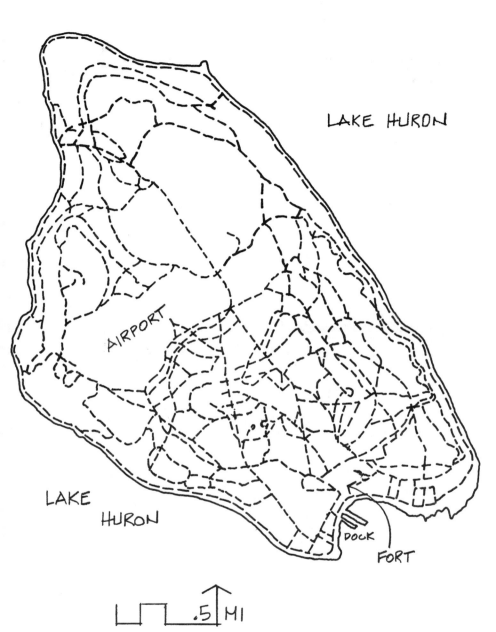

LAKE HURON

AIRPORT

LAKE
HURON

DOCK

FORT

.5 MI

MACKINAC ISLAND STATE PARK

Mackinac Island Chamber of Commerce
Box 451
Mackinac Island, MI 49757

906-847-3783
906-4-lilacs

Mackinac Island State Park Commission
PO Box 30028
Lansing, MI 48909

906-847-3328
517-373-4296

Michigan Atlas & Gazetteer Location: 94AB34

County Location: Mackinac

Directions To Trailhead:
Located in the Straits of Mackniac By ferry from St Ignace or Mackinaw City from March through November By plane from St Ignace year-around

Trail Type: Hiking/Walking, Cross Country Skiing, Mountain Biking, Interpretive
Trail Distance: 50+ mi   Loops: Many   Shortest: Longest:
Trail Surface: Paved, gravel and natural
Trail Use Fee: None
Method Of Ski Trail Grooming: Track set occasionally
Skiing Ability Suggested: Novice to advanced
Hiking Trail Difficulty: Easy to moderate
Mountain Biking Ability Suggested: Novice
Terrain: Steep 0%, Hilly 50%, Moderate 40%, Flat 10%
Camping: None

Maintained by the Mackinac Island State Park Commission
A fabulous ski area. All the trails used in the summer for carriages, horses, bikes and hiking are available for skiing in the winter. Snowmobiles are restricted to the west half of the island, leaving the best trails for the skiers. However, the snowmobiles do an excellent job of grooming the remaining roads for skating. Hiking opportunities are throughout the island. Biking is likewise great on the island. There are several hard surfaced bike trails for road bikes. One takes the shoreline of the island, while two others are more difficult following an interior route. For mountain bike riders, the options are many. I suggest visiting the island in the spring for fall, when the island is less crowded. This way you can explore all the trails the island has to offer. Mountain bikes are limited to paved trails and gravel roads. Hiking and horse trails are not open to mountain bikes. Accomodations are available year around on the island. Always call ahead.

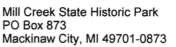

Mill Creek State Historic Park
PO Box 873
Mackinaw City, MI 49701-0873

616-436-5203

DNR Parks and Recreation Division

517-373-1270
517-275-5151

Michigan Atlas & Gazetteer Location: 94B3

County Location: Cheboygan

Directions To Trailhead:
Three miles southeast from Mackinaw City on US23

Trail Type: Hiking/Walking, Cross Country Skiing, Interpretive
Trail Distance: 3+ mi   Loops: 5   Shortest: .3 mi   Longest: 2 mi
Trail Surface: Paved, gravel and natural
Trail Use Fee: Addmission charge
Method Of Ski Trail Grooming: None
Skiing Ability Suggested: Novice
Hiking Trail Difficulty: Easy
Mountain Biking Ability Suggested: NA
Terrain: Steep 0%, Hilly 2%, Moderate 88%, Flat 10%
Camping: Available nearby

Maintained by the Parks and Recreation Divsion
Historical restoration of the a saw mill used from the 1780's to 1873.
Large restoration of the grounds around the sawmill have been developed.
Much of the lumber for structures on Mackinac Island were sawed at this location.
Brochure available.

LAKE HURON

MACKINAW CITY
3 MI.

US 23

P

VISITOR CENTER

MILL

LOOP 1

LOOP 2

LOOP 3

MAPLE SUGAR SHACK

BEAVER POND

SCALE NOT KNOWN

MILL CREEK STATE HISTORIC PARK

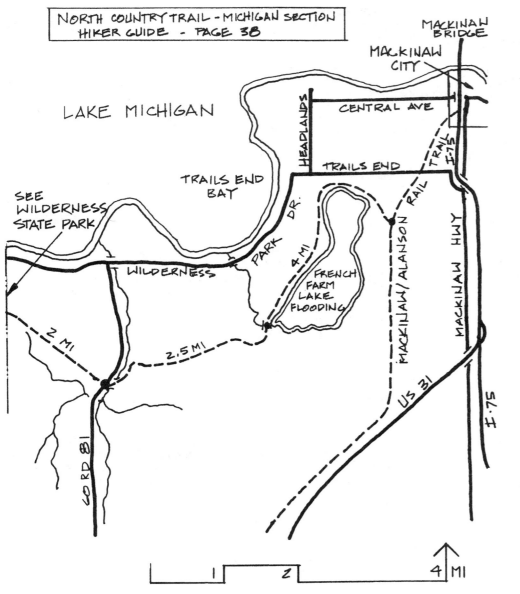

NORTH COUNTRY TRAIL - MICHIGAN SECTION
HIKER GUIDE - PAGE 38

MACKINAW BRIDGE

MACKINAW CITY

LAKE MICHIGAN

CENTRAL AVE

HEADLANDS

TRAILS END

RAIL TRAIL

I-75

TRAILS END BAY

SEE WILDERNESS STATE PARK

PARK DR.

MACKINAW / ALANSON RAIL TRAIL

MACKINAW HWY

4 MI

FRENCH FARM LAKE FLOODING

WILDERNESS

2 MI

2.5 MI

US 31

I-75

CO RD 81

4 MI

NORTH COUNTRY TRAIL - MACKINAW STATE FOREST 4

Indian River Forest Area, Mackinaw State Forest
PO Box 10
Indian River, Mi 49749

616-238-9313

North Country Trail Association
PO Box 311
White Cloud, MI 49349

616-689-1912

Michigan Atlas & Gazetteer Location: 94BC2

County Location: Emmet

Directions To Trailhead:
Between the east boundary of Wilderness State Park (see other listing) and the Mackinaw / Alanson Rail Trail (see other listing)
West trail head - East boundary of Wilderness State Park about 1 mile south of Wilderness Park Drive
East trail head - Mackinaw / Alanson Rail Trail about 1 mile south of Trails End Rd, just west of Mackinaw Hwy

Trail Type: Hiking/Walking, Mountain Biking
Trail Distance: 8.5 mi   Loops: NA   Shortest: NA   Longest: NA
Trail Surface: Natural
Trail Use Fee: None
Method Of Ski Trail Grooming: NA
Skiing Ability Suggested: NA
Hiking Trail Difficulty: Easy
Mountain Biking Ability Suggested: Novice
Terrain: Flat to rolling
Camping: Wilderness State Park

This trail section is in the Mackinaw State Forest
Trail built and maintained by the North Country Trail Association.
The Michigan Section Hiker Guide map book is available from the North Country Trail Association.
See Wilderness State Park for NCT section west of this section. In the park, NCT uses existing park trails marked as the NCT.
See NCT-St. Ignace for the section north of this section.

St. Ignace Ranger District, Hiawatha National Forest
1498 West US2   906-643-7900
St. Ignace , MI 49781

Forest Supervisor, Hiawatha National Forest
2727 N. Lincoln Rd.   906-786-4062
Escanaba, MI 49829

Michigan Atlas & Gazetteer Location: 94A123, 106CD12

County Location: Mackinac

Directions To Trailhead:
North and east of St Ignace
South trailhead - Rail trail in St Ignace
North trailhead - Just east of East Lake Rd. (NE of East Lake) on FR 3323
Lake Michigan trailhead - 11 miles west of St Ignace on US2, then 1.8 miles
north on Co Rd H57 (Brevoort Lake Rd.)

Trail Type: Hiking/Walking
Trail Distance: 35 mi   Loops: NA   Shortest: NA   Longest: NA
Trail Surface: Natural
Trail Use Fee: None
Method Of Ski Trail Grooming: NA
Skiing Ability Suggested: NA
Hiking Trail Difficulty: Moderate
Mountain Biking Ability Suggested: NA
Terrain: Rolling
Camping: Campgounds along trail

Maintained by the St. Ignace Ranger District, Hiawatha National Forest
Developed campground is located at Brevoort Lake National Forest
Campground with 70 sites, toilets and drinking water. The Ridge Trail is located
at this campground. (See other listing)
Primitive campgrounds are located on the south side of the trail near the Pt.
Aux Chenes River, on the south side of Lake Brevoort and 20 feet from the trail,
1/4 mile east of FR3119.
Wilderness camping is permitted 200' from the trail. Like the entire North
Country Trail, this is a point to point trail.
For more information contact the North Country Trail Association

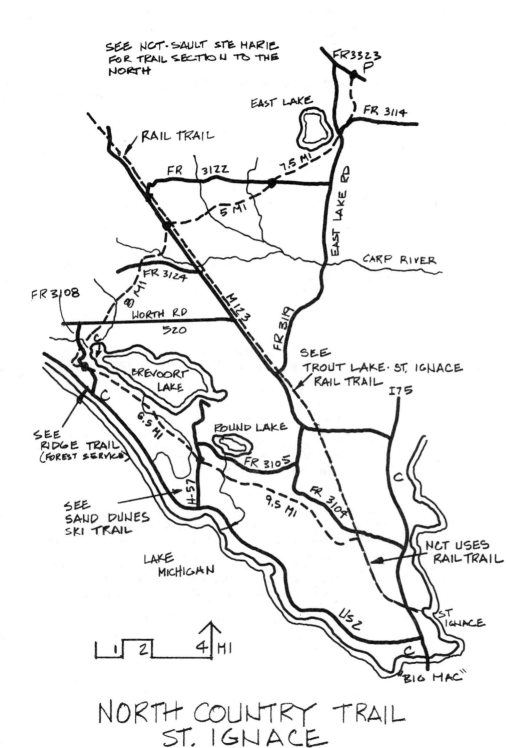

SEE NCT-SAULT STE MARIE
FOR TRAIL SECTION TO THE
NORTH

FR3323
P

EAST LAKE

FR 3114

RAIL TRAIL

FR 3122

7.5 MI

5 MI

EAST LAKE RD

CARP RIVER

FR 3124

FR 3108

8 MI

WORTH RD
520

M123

FR 3119

SEE
TROUT LAKE · ST. IGNACE
RAIL TRAIL

I75

BREVOORT
LAKE

6.5 MI

SEE
RIDGE TRAIL
(FOREST SERVICE)

ROUND LAKE

FR 3105

C

SEE
SAND DUNES
SKI TRAIL

H-57

9.5 MI

FR 3104

NCT USES
RAIL TRAIL

LAKE
MICHIGAN

US2

ST
IGNACE

C

1 2   4 MI

"BIG MAC"

NORTH COUNTRY TRAIL
ST. IGNACE

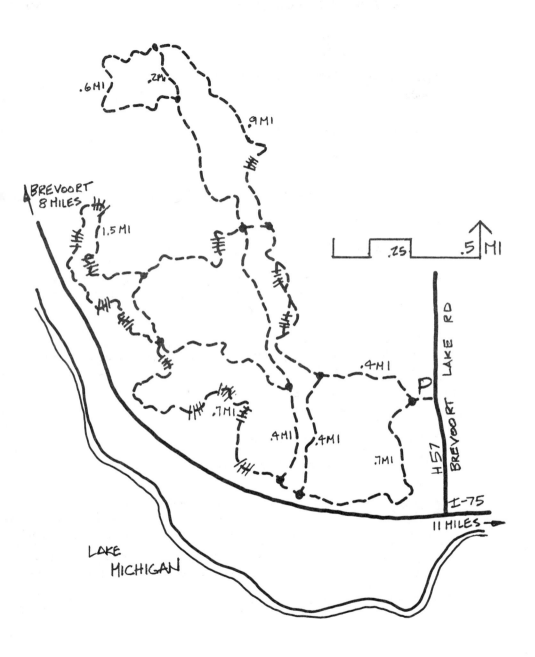

Sand Dunes Cross Country Ski Trail

94

St. Ignace Ranger District, Hiawatha National Forest
1498 West US2
St Ignace, MI 49781

906-643-7900

Forest Supervisor, Hiawatha National Forest
2727 North Lincoln Rd
Escanaba, MI 49829

906-786-4062

Michigan Atlas & Gazetteer Location: 94A1

County Location: Mackinac

Directions To Trailhead:
11 miles west of I75 (St. Ignace) on US2, then north on Brevoort Lake Rd.(H57)
.5 miles to parking lot .

Trail Type: Hiking/Walking, Cross Country Skiing
Trail Distance: 15.6 km   Loops: 7   Shortest: 2.4 km Longest: 12.3 km
Trail Surface: Natural
Trail Use Fee: Donations accepted to cover grooming costs
Method Of Ski Trail Grooming: Track set as needed
Skiing Ability Suggested: Novice to advanced
Hiking Trail Difficulty: Easy to moderate
Mountain Biking Ability Suggested: NA
Terrain: Steep 5%, Hilly 20%, Moderate 60%, Flat 15%
Camping: Seasonal camping available at the NF campground 7 miles west

Built by the St. Ignace Ranger District, Hiawatha National Forest, Silver
Mountain Cross Country Ski Club and 12 other local groups.
Excellent ski trail with varied forest cover and well designed loops with scenic
overlooks of Lake Michigan.
The entire trail was contoured to provide for a delightful skiing experience By
passes for difficult sections are provided on the intermediate loops.
The open area at the trailhead was the site of the Round Lake Civilian
Conservation Corps Camp that started in 1935.
Site of the annual Dunes Day Loppet held the first Saturday in March.

SAND DUNES
CROSS COUNTRY SKI TRAIL

422

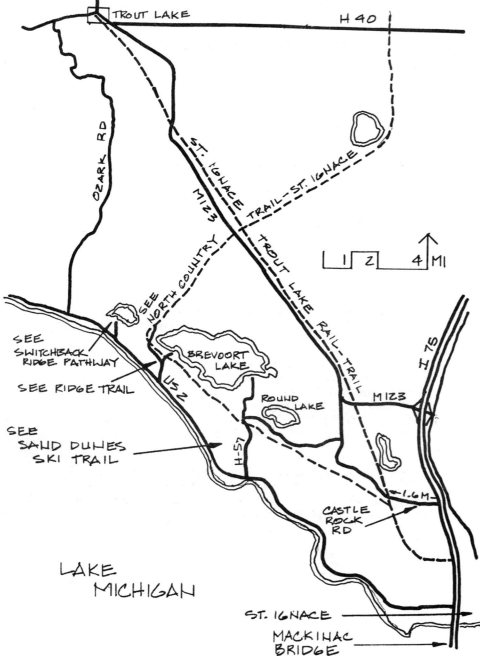

SEE
SWITCHBACK
RIDGE PATHWAY

SEE RIDGE TRAIL

SEE
SAND DUNES
SKI TRAIL

LAKE
MICHIGAN

ST. IGNACE/TROUT LAKE RAIL TRAIL

St. Ignace Ranger District, Hiawatha National Forest
1498 West US2
St. Ignace, MI 49781

906-643-7900

Forest Supervisor, Hiawatha National Forest
2727 N. Lincoln Rd
Escanaba, MI 49829

906-786-4062

Michigan Atlas & Gazetteer Location: 94AB23,105C8,106CD12

County Location: Mackinac

Directions To Trailhead:
From St. Ignace on the south to Trout Lake on the north.

Trail Type: Hiking/Walking, Mountain Biking
Trail Distance: 27 mi   Loops: NA   Shortest: NA   Longest: NA
Trail Surface: Natural and ballast
Trail Use Fee: None
Method Of Ski Trail Grooming: NA
Skiing Ability Suggested: NA
Hiking Trail Difficulty: Easy
Mountain Biking Ability Suggested: Intermediate
Terrain: 100% Flat
Camping: Campgrounds nearby

Managed by the St. Ignace Ranger District, Hiawatha National Forest
The south end of the trail is also part of the North Country Trail - St. Ignace

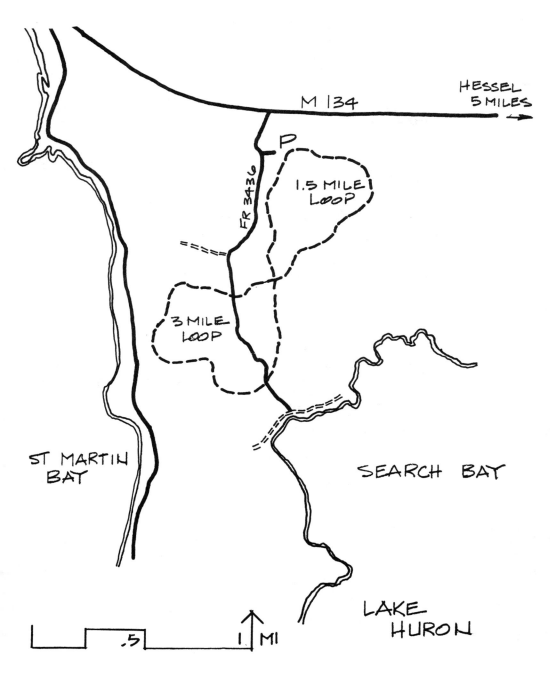

M 134

HESSEL
5 MILES →

P

FR 3436

1.5 MILE
LOOP

3 MILE
LOOP

ST MARTIN
BAY

SEARCH BAY

LAKE
HURON

.5   1 MI

ST MARTIN
CROSS COUNTRY SKI TRAIL

St. Ignace Ranger District, Hiawatha National Forest
1498 West US2   906-643-7900
St. Ignace, MI 49781

Forest Supervisor, Hiawatha National Forest
2727 N. Lincoln Rd   906-786-4062
Escanaba, MI 49829

Michigan Atlas & Gazetteer Location: 94A4,106D4

County Location: Mackinac

Directions To Trailhead:
6 miles west of Hessel on M134.

Trail Type: Hiking/Walking, Cross Country Skiing
Trail Distance: 3 mi   Loops: 2   Shortest: 1.5 mi Longest: 3 mi
Trail Surface: Natural
Trail Use Fee: None
Method Of Ski Trail Grooming: Track set
Skiing Ability Suggested: Novice
Hiking Trail Difficulty: Easy
Mountain Biking Ability Suggested: NA
Terrain: Steep 0%, Hilly 0%, Moderate 40%, Flat 60%
Camping: Dispersed camping allowed

Maintained by the St. Ignace Ranger District, Hiawatha National Forest
Hiking the trail could be difficult since it is not maintained in the summer.
Tall grass and no defined treadway makes locating the trail difficult.
Wildlife viewing including eagles, hawks, and deer.

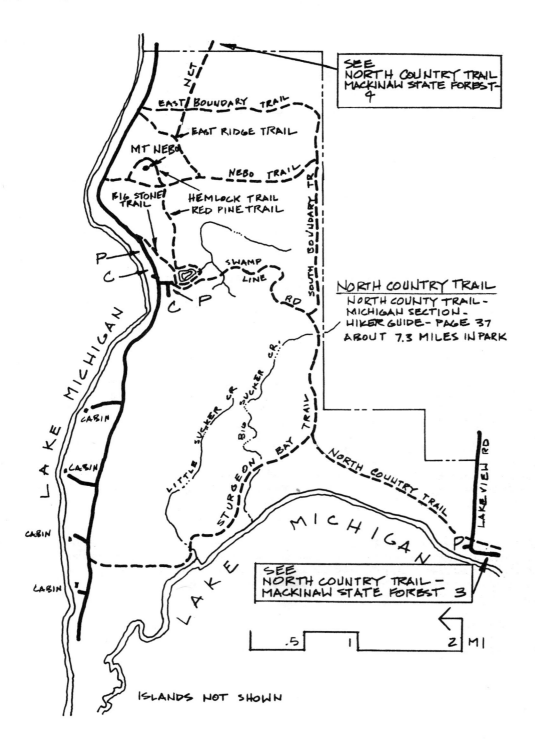

Wilderness State Park
Wilderness Park Drive
Carp Lake, MI 49718

616-436-5381

DNR Parks and Recreation Division

517-373-1270

Michigan Atlas & Gazetteer Location: 94BC12

County Location: Emmet

Directions To Trailhead:
West of Mackinaw City on C81 and Wilderness Park Drive on Lake Michigan

Trail Type: Hiking/Walking, Cross Country Skiing, Mountain Biking, Interpretive
Trail Distance: 35 mi   Loops: Many   Shortest: Longest:
Trail Surface: Natural and gravel
Trail Use Fee: None, but vehicle entry fee required
Method Of Ski Trail Grooming: None
Skiing Ability Suggested: Novice to intermediate
Hiking Trail Difficulty: Easy to moderate
Mountain Biking Ability Suggested: Novice to intermediate
Terrain: Steep 0%, Hilly 0%, Moderate 10%, Flat 90%
Camping: Available in park

Maintained by the DNR Parks and Recreation Division
Ski in cabins available for rent on a reservations only basis (bookings for
weekends should be made well in advance) Great back country skiing area.

Mountain biking trails limited to: Boundary Trail, Sturgeon Bay Trail, Nebo Trail,
Swamp line Rd and Park Drive only.
The North Country Trail passes through this park. To the west is North Country
Trail - Mackinaw State Forest 3 and to the east see North Country Trail -
Mackinaw State Forest 4

WILDERNESS STATE PARK

Cheboygan State Park
4490 Beach Rd.
Cheboygan, MI 49721

616-627-2811

DNR Parks and Recreation Division

517-373-1270
517-275-5151

Michigan Atlas & Gazetteer Location: 95C5

County Location: Cheboygan

Directions To Trailhead:
5 miles east of Cheboygan on US23, then turn left on Seffern Rd and follow the signs

Trail Type: Hiking/Walking, Cross Country Skiing, Interpretive
Trail Distance: 6 mi   Loops: 3   Shortest: .5 mi   Longest: 2 mi
Trail Surface: Natural
Trail Use Fee: None, but vehicle entry fee required
Method Of Ski Trail Grooming: Track set
Skiing Ability Suggested: Novice
Hiking Trail Difficulty: Easy
Mountain Biking Ability Suggested: NA
Terrain: Steep 0%, Hilly 5%, Moderate 15%, Flat 80%
Camping: Camping on site from April through November

Maintained by the DNR Parks and Recreation Division
Rustic cabins are available for rent all year around.
In the winter cabins can only be reached by skis. Contact the park manager to make reservations, which are required.
Park covers over 1,200 acres
The first lighthouse, the Cheboygan Light, was built in 1857. It was later relocated to the shore and operated until 1930.

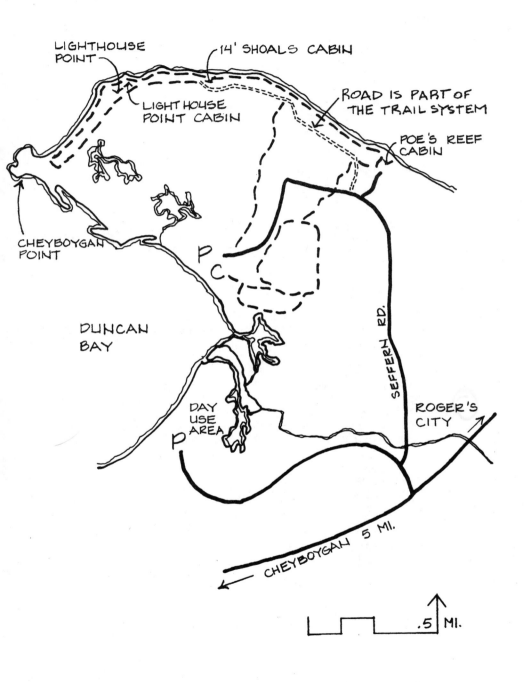

CHEYBOYGAN. STATE PARK

DeTour Cross Country Ski Trail

DeTour Area Chamber of Commerce
PO Box 161
DeTour, MI 49725

906-297-5987

Michigan Atlas & Gazetteer Location: 95A8,116B1

County Location: Chippewa

Directions To Trailhead:
5 miles west of DeTour off M134 at Detour State Forest Campground

Trail Type: Cross Country Skiing
Trail Distance: 3.3 mi   Loops: 1   Shortest: NA   Longest: 3.3 mi
Trail Surface: Natural
Trail Use Fee: None
Method Of Ski Trail Grooming: None
Skiing Ability Suggested: Novice
Hiking Trail Difficulty: NA
Mountain Biking Ability Suggested: NA
Terrain: Steep 0%, Hilly 0%, Moderate 30%, Flat 70%
Camping: Campground on site in the summer only

Maintained by the local volunteers

Map

DETOUR 5 MILES

M-134

P

C

3.3 MI LOOP

LAKE HURON

NO SCALE

DETOUR AREA
CROSS COUNTRY SKI TRAIL

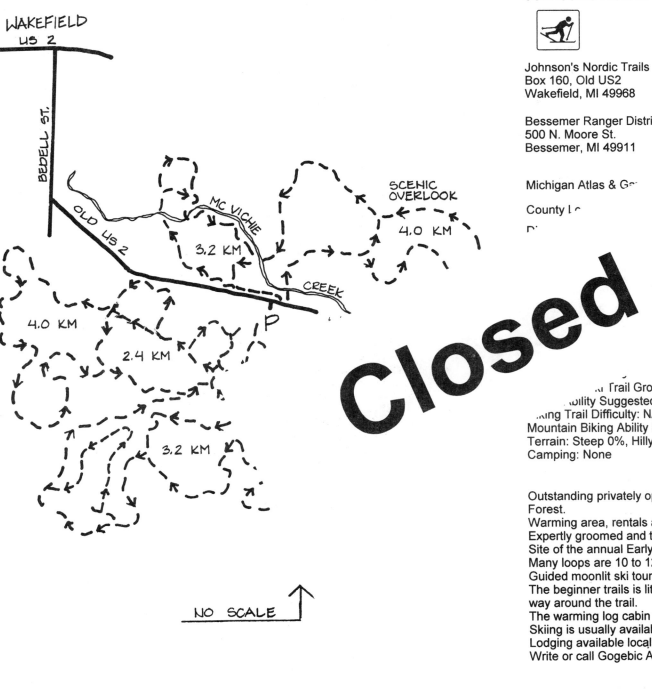

WAKEFIELD
US 2

BEDELL ST.

OLD US 2

MC VICHE

SCENIC
OVERLOOK

4.0 KM

3.2 KM

CREEK

P

4.0 KM

2.4 KM

3.2 KM

NO SCALE

JOHNSON'S NORDIC SKI TRAILS

Johnson's Nordic Trails

Johnson's Nordic Trails
Box 160, Old US2
Wakefield, MI 49968

906-224-4711
906-224-2731

Bessemer Ranger District - Ottawa National Forest
500 N. Moore St.
Bessemer, MI 49911

906-667-0261

Michigan Atlas & G⁀   · 96A1

County I⁀

⁀

⁀t of Wakefield Turn right off US2 on
⁀ed   1 mile on old US2 to the

⁀ps: 8   Shortest: .4 km   Longest: 4.8 km

⁀ Trail Grooming: Track set with skating lane
⁀ility Suggested: Novice to advanced
⁀ing Trail Difficulty: NA
Mountain Biking Ability Suggested: NA
Terrain: Steep 0%, Hilly 50%, Moderate 25%, Flat 25%
Camping: None

Outstanding privately operated cross country ski area in the Ottawa National Forest.
Warming area, rentals and ski shop available.
Expertly groomed and track set trails with beautiful scenery.
Site of the annual Early Season Classic 10km Race, held in mid-December.
Many loops are 10 to 12 feet wide for skating.
Guided moonlit ski tours on every full moon during the ski season.
The beginner trails is lit with candles blocked in ice with a bon fire about half way around the trail.
The warming log cabin was built in 1906.
Skiing is usually available from Thanksgiving into April.
Lodging available locally:
Write or call Gogebic Area Convention & Visitor Bureau. (see listing elsewhere)

Porcupine Mountains Wilderness State Park
412 South Boundary Rd.   906-885-5275
Ontonagon, MI 49953

Lake Gogebic State Park
HC 1, Box 139   906-842-3341
Marenisco, MI 48847

Michigan Atlas & Gazetteer Location: 96A4

County Location: Gogebic

Directions To Trailhead:
13 miles NE of Marenisco on the west shore of Lake Gogebic on M64 14 miles south of Bergland on M64

Trail Type: Hiking/Walking, Interpretive
Trail Distance: 2 mi   Loops: 1   Shortest: NA   Longest: 2 mi
Trail Surface: Natural
Trail Use Fee: None, but vehicle entry fee required
Method Of Ski Trail Grooming: Packed
Skiing Ability Suggested: Intermediate
Hiking Trail Difficulty: Moderate
Mountain Biking Ability Suggested: NA
Terrain: Hilly
Camping: Campground in park. Limited facilities in the winter

Maintained by the DNR Parks and Recreation Division
Trail is a self-guided nature trail.
All types of forest cover is present along trail.

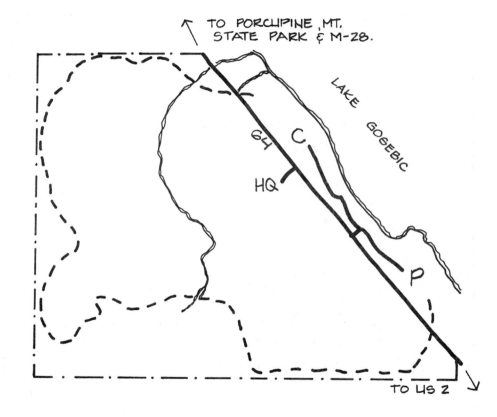

NO SCALE

LAKE GOGEBIC STATE PARK

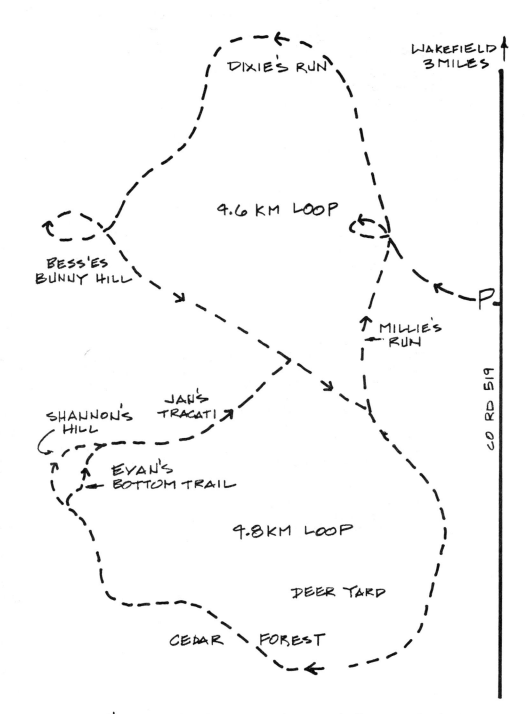

BESS'ES
BUNNY HILL

DIXIE'S RUN

4.6 KM LOOP

MILLIE'S
RUN

SHANNON'S
HILL

JAN'S
TRACATI

EVAN'S
BOTTOM TRAIL

4.8KM LOOP

DEER YARD

CEDAR FOREST

Milje's Cross Country Ski Trails

Rollie Miljevich
205 Smith St.
Wakefield, MI 49968

906-229-5267

Michigan Atlas & Gazetteer Location: 96A1

County Location: Gogebic

Directions To Trailhead:
2 miles south of Wakefield on Co Rd 519

WAKEFIELD
3 MILES

CO RD 519

Trail Type: Cross Country Skiing
Trail Distance: 11 km   Loops: 2   Shortest: 5 km   Longest: 6 km
Trail Surface: Natural
Trail Use Fee: Yes, donation
Method Of Ski Trail Grooming: Track set classic only
Skiing Ability Suggested: Novice to advanced
Hiking Trail Difficulty: NA
Mountain Biking Ability Suggested: NA
Terrain: Steep 0%, Hilly 20%, Moderate 60%, Flat 20%
Camping: None

Privately operated ski trail system
Free hot chocolate, hot coffee, hot tea and cookies to skiers.
Deer seen daily along the trails.

MILJE'S CROSS COUNTY TRAILS

Bessemer Ranger District, Ottawa National Forest
500 N. Moore St.   906-667-0261
Bessemer, MI 49911

Recreation Staff Officer, Ottawa National Forest
2100 E. Cloverland Drive   906-932-1330
Ironwood, MI 49938

Michigan Atlas & Gazetteer Location: 96AB1234, 97B5

County Location: Gogebic

Directions To Trailhead:
South of US2, east and west of Marenisco and south to Wisconsin border.

Trail Type: Mountain Biking
Trail Distance: 50+ mi   Loops: Many   Shortest: Longest:
Trail Surface: Gravel, sand and natural
Trail Use Fee: None
Method Of Ski Trail Grooming: NA
Skiing Ability Suggested: NA
Hiking Trail Difficulty: NA
Mountain Biking Ability Suggested: Novice to advanced
Terrain: Steep 10%, Hilly 25%, Moderate 25%, Flat 40%
Camping: Many campgrounds throughout the area

Maintained by the Ottawa National Forest
Trails designated in 1994. Currently under further development.

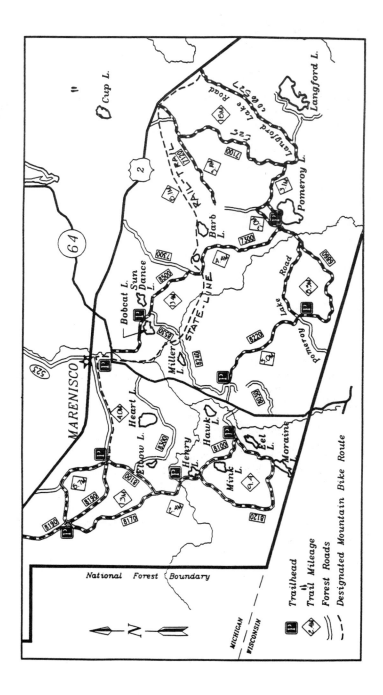

POMEROY/ HENRY LAKE
MOUNTAIN BIKE COMPLEX

Porcupine Mountain Wilderness State Park
412 South Boundary Rd
Ontonagon, MI 49953

906-885-5275

DNR Parks and Recreation Division

517-373-1270

Michigan Atlas & Gazetteer Location: 97A8

County Location: Ontonagon

Directions To Trailhead:
4 miles west of Trout Creek on M28.

Trail Type: Hiking/Walking
Trail Distance: 1 mi   Loops: 1   Shortest: NA   Longest: 1 mi
Trail Surface: Natural
Trail Use Fee: None
Method Of Ski Trail Grooming: NA
Skiing Ability Suggested: NA
Hiking Trail Difficulty: Difficult
Mountain Biking Ability Suggested: NA
Terrain: Steep 50%, Hilly 0%, Moderate 0%, Flat 50%
Camping: None

Maintained by the DNR Parks and Recreation Division
Recent purchase.
No plans to develop site at this time.
Short trail to very scenic water falls.
Bond Falls Trail is nearby.

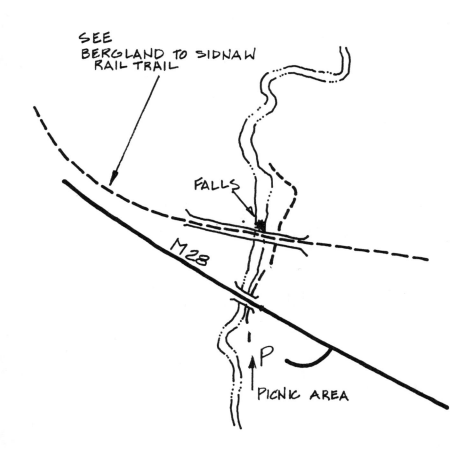

.5 MI

SEE
BERGLAND TO SIDNAW
RAIL TRAIL

FALLS

M28

P

PICNIC AREA

AGATE FALLS

Watersmeet Ranger District, Ottawa National Forest
Box 276   906-358-4551
Watersmeet, MI 49969   906-358-4756

Recreation Staff Officer, Ottawa National Forest
2100 E. Cloverland Drive   906-932-1330
Ironwood, MI 49938

Michigan Atlas & Gazetteer Location: 97BC7

County Location: Gogebic

Directions To Trailhead:
North trailhead is at the USDA - Forest Service Watersmeet Visitor Center
located at the intersection of US 2 and US 45.
South trailhead is on the east side of US 45 about .5 mile north of the
Wisconsin border at the roadside park.

Trail Type: Hiking/Walking, Cross Country Skiing, Mountain Biking
Trail Distance: 10.5 mi   Loops: None   Shortest: NA   Longest: NA
Trail Surface: Natural
Trail Use Fee: None
Method Of Ski Trail Grooming: None
Skiing Ability Suggested: Novice to intermediate
Hiking Trail Difficulty: Easy to moderate
Mountain Biking Ability Suggested: Novice to intermediate
Terrain: Steep 2%, Hilly 15%, Moderate 75%, Flat 5%
Camping: Campgrounds within 5 miles in the national forest

Maintained by the Watersmeet Ranger District, Ottawa National Forest
Sections of this trail are shared with motorized trail users.
This point to point trail can be combined with the Watersmeet-Land 0' Lakes Rail
Trail to make a 26 mile loop.
The Watersmeet Ski Trail is not suitable as a return route to Watersmeet for
mountain biking because of marsh land and beaver dams throughout the area of
the ski trail.
The community of Land O' Lakes is just .5 mile south of the south end of the
trail.

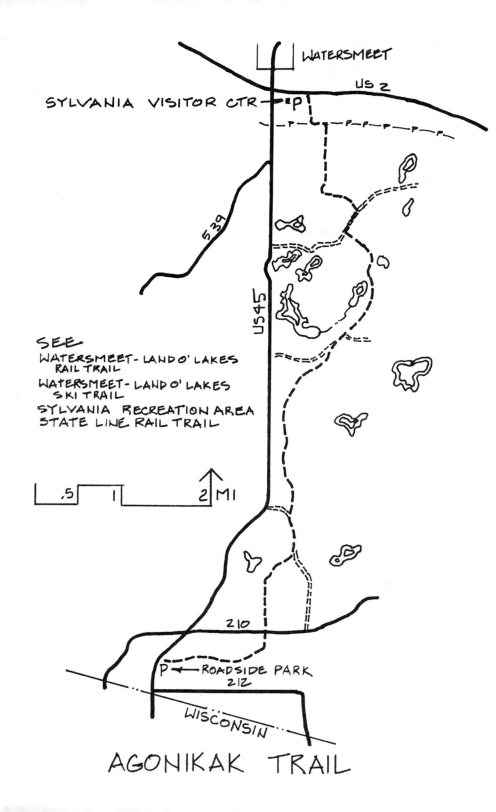

WATERSMEET

US 2

SYLVANIA VISITOR CTR — P

539

US 45

SEE
WATERSMEET- LAND O' LAKES
RAIL TRAIL
WATERSMEET- LAND O' LAKES
SKI TRAIL
SYLVANIA RECREATION AREA
STATE LINE RAIL TRAIL

.5   1   2 MI

210

P ← ROADSIDE PARK
212

WISCONSIN

AGONIKAK TRAIL

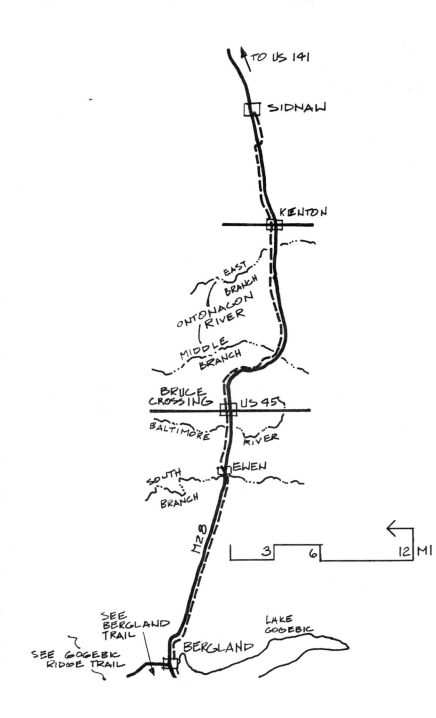

Baraga Forest Area, Copper Country State Forest
PO Box 440   906-353-6651
Baraga, MI 49908

District Forest Manager, Copper Country State Forest
PO Box 440   906-353-6651
Baraga, MI 49908

Michigan Atlas & Gazetteer Location: 97A8,98A12,108D4,109D56,110D2

County Location: Ontonagon, Houghton

Directions To Trailhead:
From Bergland to Sidnaw.
West trailhead - East on M28 from Bergland 2 miles to East Shore Rd.(2 track).
Right(south) .5 miles to the railroad grade. Left on grade (east bound).
East trailhead - Eire St in Sidnaw.

Trail Type: Hiking/Walking, Mountain Biking
Trail Distance: 42.8 mi   Loops: NA   Shortest: NA   Longest: NA
Trail Surface: Gravel, ballast and natural
Trail Use Fee: None
Method Of Ski Trail Grooming: NA
Skiing Ability Suggested: NA
Hiking Trail Difficulty: Moderate
Mountain Biking Ability Suggested: Intermediate
Terrain: 100% Flat
Camping: None on trail but public township campground in Bergland

Maintained by the DNR Forest Mangement Division
Several spectacular bridges along the trail
Agate Falls is within view from the trail. See Agate Falls Trail.

BERGLAND TO SIDNAW RAIL TRAIL

Porcupine Mountain Wilderness State Park
412 South Boundary Rd
Ontonagon, MI 49953

906-885-5275

DNR Parks and Recreation Division

517-373-1270

Michigan Atlas & Gazetteer Location: 97A7

County Location: Ontonagon

Directions To Trailhead:
Between Watersmeet and Bruce Crossing on US45, then east from Paulding 4 miles on Bond Falls Rd

Trail Type: Hiking/Walking
Trail Distance: .5 MI   Loops: 1   Shortest: NA   Longest: .5 mi
Trail Surface: Natural
Trail Use Fee: None
Method Of Ski Trail Grooming: NA
Skiing Ability Suggested: NA
Hiking Trail Difficulty: Easy to moderate
Mountain Biking Ability Suggested: NA
Terrain: Steep 0%, Hilly 0%, Moderate 95%, Flat 5%
Camping: Avaialble nearby

Maintained by the DNR Parks and Recreation Division.
Short trail along the creek to the very scenic falls.
No development planned in the near future.

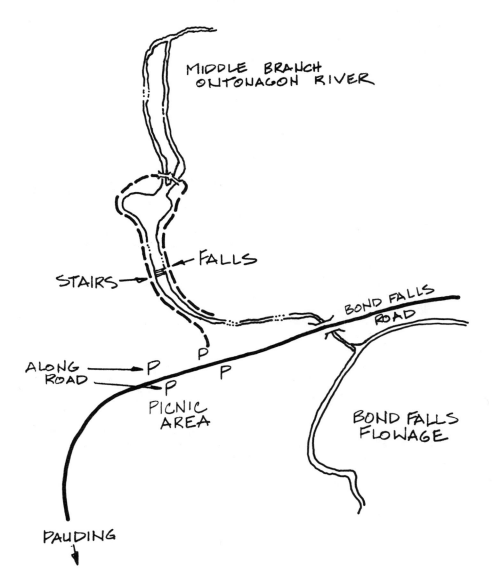

.25 MI

MIDDLE BRANCH ONTONAGON RIVER

FALLS

STAIRS

BOND FALLS ROAD

ALONG ROAD

P P P P

PICNIC AREA

BOND FALLS FLOWAGE

PAUDING

BOND FALLS

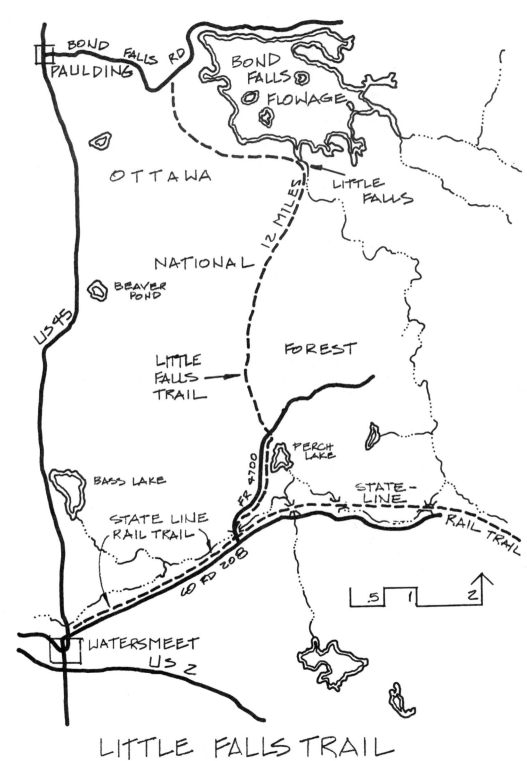

Watersmeet Ranger District, Ottawa National Forest
PO Box 276
Watersmeet, MI 49969

906-358-4551

Recreation Staff Officer, Ottawa National Forest
2100 Cloverland Drive
Ironwood, Mi 49938

906-932-1330

Michigan Atlas & Gazetteer Location: 97B8

County Location: Gogebic, Ontonagon

Directions To Trailhead:
South trailhead - 3 miles east of Watersmeet on the State-Line Rail Trail, then north on Buck Lake Rd (also known as Peach Lake Rd). The trail veers to the right from Buck Lake Rd and runs parallel to the road on the east side.   Just after passing Perch Lake the trail crosses Buck Lake Rd and continues north.
North trailhead - About 2.3 miles east of Paulding on Bond Falls Rd

Trail Type: Hiking/Walking, Mountain Biking
Trail Distance: 12 mi   Loops: NA   Shortest: NA   Longest: NA
Trail Surface: Natural and ballast
Trail Use Fee: None
Method Of Ski Trail Grooming: NA
Skiing Ability Suggested: NA
Hiking Trail Difficulty: Moderate
Mountain Biking Ability Suggested: Advanced
Terrain: Steep 0%, Hilly 0%, Moderate 10%, Flat 90%
Camping: Marion Lake, Bond Falls Flowage and Imp Lake

Managed by the Watersmeet Ranger District, Ottawa National Forest
Rugged rail trail with beaver dam lakes and logging operations.
Used as a snowmobile trail in the winter.
ORV's use this trail as well.

LITTLE FALLS TRAIL

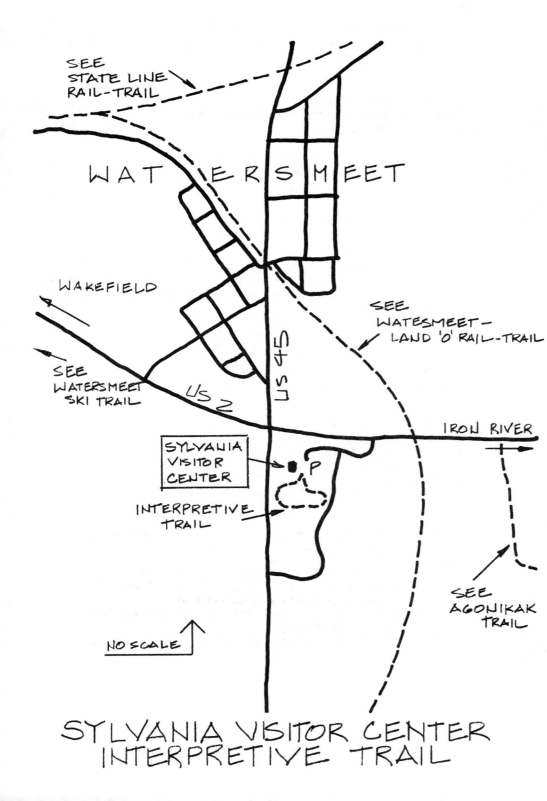

Watersmeet Ranger District, Ottawa National Forest
PO Box 276
Watersmeet, MI 49969

906-358-4551
906-358-4756

Recreation Staff Officer, Ottawa National Forest
2100 E. Cloverland Drive
Ironwood, MI 49938

906-932-1330

Michigan Atlas & Gazetteer Location: 97B7

County Location: Gogebic

Directions To Trailhead:
Just southeast of the intersection of US2 and US45

Trail Type: Hiking/Walking, Interpretive
Trail Distance: 1 mi　　　Loops: 1　　　Shortest: NA　　　Longest: 1 mi
Trail Surface: Natural
Trail Use Fee: None
Method Of Ski Trail Grooming: NA
Skiing Ability Suggested: NA
Hiking Trail Difficulty: Easy
Mountain Biking Ability Suggested: NA
Terrain: 100% Flat
Camping: With in 5 miles

Maintained by the Watersmeet Ranger District , Ottawa National Forest
Many other trails nearby.

SEE STATE LINE RAIL-TRAIL

W A T E R S M E E T

WAKEFIELD

SEE WATERSMEET SKI TRAIL

US 45

US 2

SEE WATESMEET – LAND 'O' RAIL-TRAIL

SYLVANIA VISITOR CENTER

INTERPRETIVE TRAIL

IRON RIVER

P

SEE AGONIKAK TRAIL

NO SCALE

SYLVANIA VISITOR CENTER INTERPRETIVE TRAIL

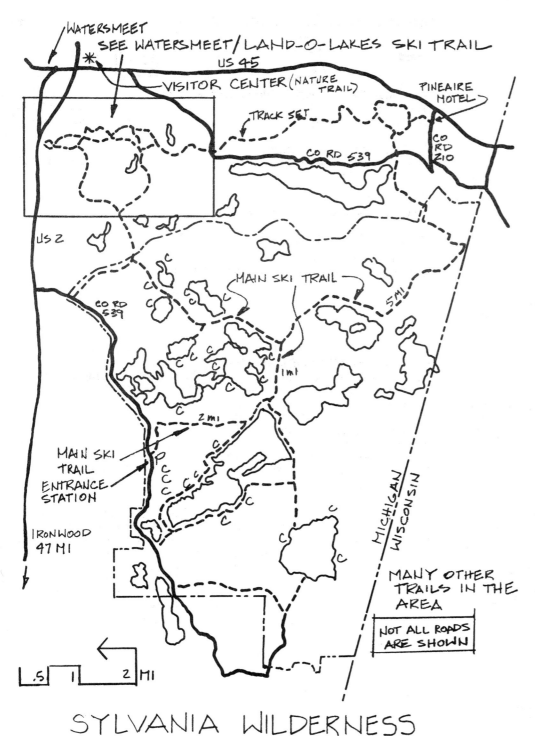

Sylvania Recreation Area
Watersmeet Ranger District, Ottawa National Forest   906-358-4551
Watersmeet , MI 49969

Recreation Staff Officer, Ottawa National Forest
2100 East Cloverland Drive   906-932-1330
Escanaba, MI 49938

Michigan Atlas & Gazetteer Location: 97BC567

County Location: Gogebic

Directions To Trailhead:
4 miles west of Watersmeet to Hwy 535, then south 4 miles(watch for signs) to entrance station where main trailhead is located. Other trailheads further into the Wilderness.

Trail Type: Hiking/Walking, Cross Country Skiing
Trail Distance: 26 mi   Loops: NA   Shortest: NA   Longest: NA
Trail Surface: Natural
Trail Use Fee: None
Method Of Ski Trail Grooming: None
Skiing Ability Suggested: Intermediate to advanced
Hiking Trail Difficulty: Easy to moderate
Mountain Biking Ability Suggested: NA
Terrain: Steep 0%, Hilly 0%, Moderate 80%, Flat 20%
Camping: Available in recreation area. Limited facilites in winter

Maintained by the Watersmeet Ranger District, Ottawa National Forest
Excellent back country skiing.
No ski trail grooming within the wilderness.
Trail connects with the Watersmeet Trail at two locations (skiing only).
Ski shop and lodging in Watersmeet and Land O' Lakes, Wisconsin.
Many lakes in the area provide for excellent canoeing.
Large area of virgin Northern Hardwoods an Hemlock with some Pine.
Excellent area for winter camping.
Winter wildlife include deer, coyote, fisher, martin, squirrels, birds, etc.

SYLVANIA WILDERNESS

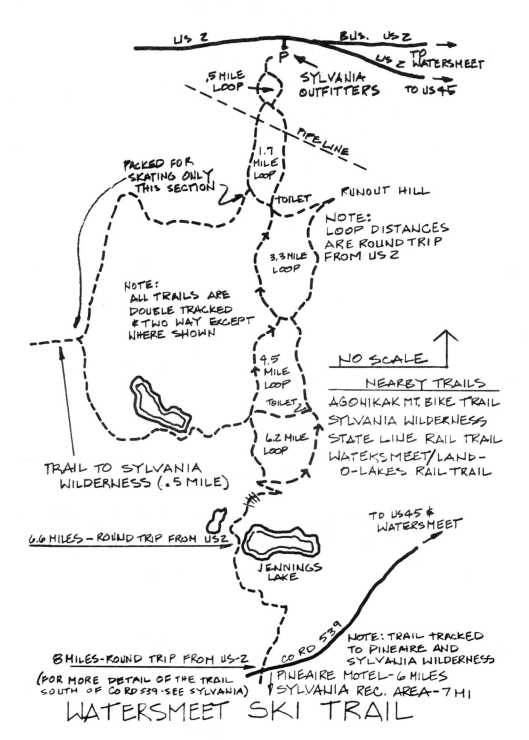

US 2

BUS. US 2

TO WATERSMEET

SYLVANIA OUTFITTERS

TO US 45

.5 MILE LOOP

PIPE LINE

PACKED FOR SKATING ONLY THIS SECTION

1.7 MILE LOOP

TOILET

RUNOUT HILL

NOTE: LOOP DISTANCES ARE ROUND TRIP FROM US 2

3.3 MILE LOOP

NOTE: ALL TRAILS ARE DOUBLE TRACKED & TWO WAY EXCEPT WHERE SHOWN

4.5 MILE LOOP

TOILET

6.2 MILE LOOP

NO SCALE

NEARBY TRAILS
AGONIKAK MT. BIKE TRAIL
SYLVANIA WILDERNESS
STATE LINE RAIL TRAIL
WATERSMEET/LAND-O-LAKES RAIL TRAIL

TRAIL TO SYLVANIA WILDERNESS (.5 MILE)

6.6 MILES - ROUND TRIP FROM US 2

JENNINGS LAKE

TO US 45 & WATERSMEET

CO RD 539

8 MILES - ROUND TRIP FROM US 2

(FOR MORE DETAIL OF THE TRAIL SOUTH OF CO RD 539 - SEE SYLVANIA)

NOTE: TRAIL TRACKED TO PINEAIRE AND SYLVANIA WILDERNESS

PINEAIRE MOTEL - 6 MILES
SYLVANIA REC. AREA - 7 MI

WATERSMEET SKI TRAIL

Watersmeet Ski Trail

Sylvania Outfitters
West US2
Watersmeet , MI 49969   906-358-4766

Watersmeet Ranger District, Ottawa National Forest
PO Box 276   906-358-4551
Watersmeet, MI 49969   906-358-4756

Michigan Atlas & Gazetteer Location: 97BC7

County Location: Gogebic

Directions To Trailhead:
North trailhead - 1 mile west of Watersmeet at Sylvania Outfitters
South trailhead (winter only) - 1 mile north of Land O' Lakes, Wisconsin on US45, then turn west on Co Rd 210, parking on north side near Pineaire Motel.

Trail Type: Hiking/Walking, Cross Country Skiing, Mountain Biking
Trail Distance: 18 mi   Loops: 5   Shortest: 1.7 m i Longest: 6.2 mi
Trail Surface: Natural
Trail Use Fee: Donations accepted
Method Of Ski Trail Grooming: Track set
Skiing Ability Suggested: Novice to advanced
Hiking Trail Difficulty: Easy to difficult
Mountain Biking Ability Suggested: Intermediate to advanced
Terrain: Steep 0%, Hilly 15%, Moderate 85%, Flat 0%
Camping: Campground available nearby and wilderness camping permitted

Maintained by Sylavnia Outfitters in cooperation with the Ottawa National Forest
Ski shop, warming area, rentals, lessons available at Sylavnia Outfitters.
Two trails connect to the Sylvania Wilderness trail system.
Accomodations and food available in Watersmeet, contact the Chamber of Commerce or Sylvania Outfitters for information.
Generally the southbound travel is uphill with northbound travel being downhill. However, because of the trail layout, the uphill climbs are not difficult and are interrupted with downhill sections.
Danger Hill is 160 feet in elveation above the ski shop.
Trails are marked for skiing only.
Mountain biking is limited to the north 12 miles.
The south 6 miles are very wet during the summer.

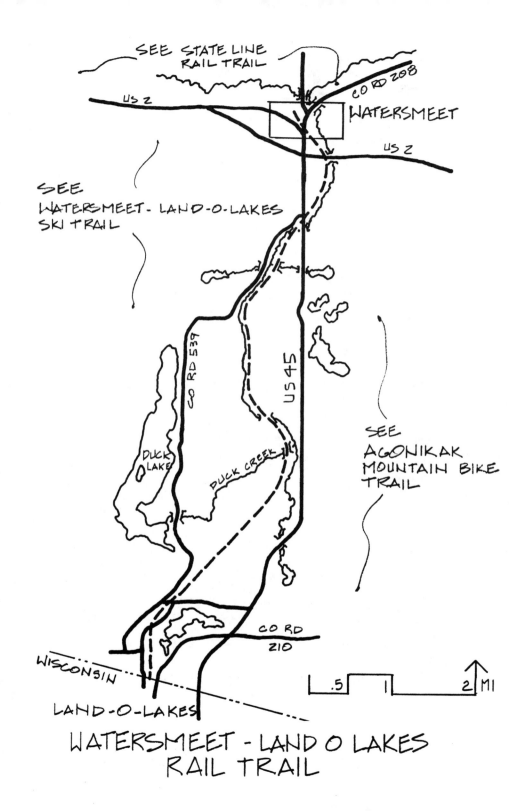

SEE STATE LINE RAIL TRAIL

CO RD 208

US 2

WATERSMEET

US 2

SEE WATERSMEET - LAND-O-LAKES SKI TRAIL

CO RD 539

US 45

SEE AGONIKAK MOUNTAIN BIKE TRAIL

DUCK LAKE

DUCK CREEK

CO RD 210

WISCONSIN

LAND-O-LAKES

.5 1 2 MI

WATERSMEET - LAND O LAKES RAIL TRAIL

Watersmeet Ranger District, Ottawa National Forest
PO Box 276
Watersmeet, MI 49969

906-358-4551

Recreation Staff Officer, Ottawa National Forest
2100 E. Cloverland Drive
Ironwood, MI 49969

906-932-1330

Michigan Atlas & Gazetteer Location: 97BC7

County Location: Gogebic

Directions To Trailhead:
From Land O' Lakes Wisconsin to Watersmeet Michigan on the west side of US45

Trail Type: Hiking/Walking, Mountain Biking
Trail Distance: 8 mi   Loops: NA   Shortest: NA   Longest: NA
Trail Surface: Ballast and natural
Trail Use Fee: None
Method Of Ski Trail Grooming: None
Skiing Ability Suggested: Novice
Hiking Trail Difficulty: Easy
Mountain Biking Ability Suggested: novice
Terrain: 100% Flat
Camping: None along the trail, but neaby

Maintained by the Watersmeet Ranger District, Ottawa National Forest
ORV's and snowmobiles shares this trail
Use in conjunction with the Agonikak Trail to make a loop mountain bike trail

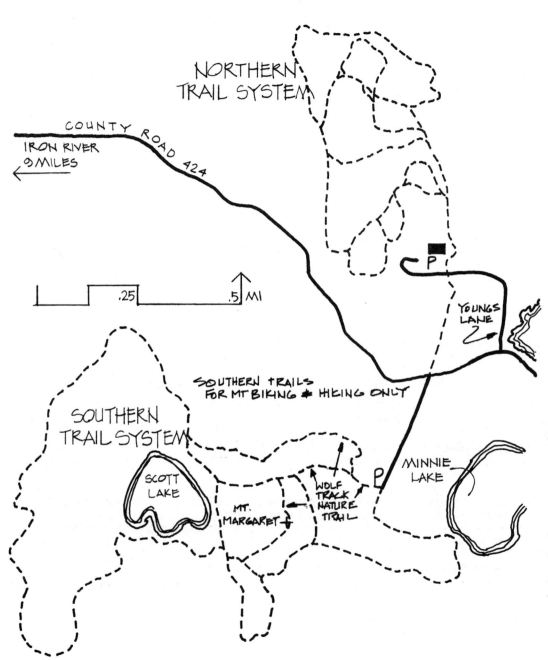

NORTHERN TRAIL SYSTEM

COUNTY ROAD 424

IRON RIVER
9 MILES

.25   .5 MI

YOUNGS LANE

SOUTHERN trails
FOR MT BIKING & HIKING ONLY

SOUTHERN TRAIL SYSTEM

SCOTT LAKE

MT. MARGARET

WOLF TRACK NATURE TRAIL

MINNIE LAKE

P

GEORGE YOUNG
RECREATION COMPLEX

George Young Recreation Complex
PO Box 457   906-265-3401
Iron River, MI 49935

Michigan Atlas & Gazetteer Location: 98D4

County Location: Iron

Directions To Trailhead:
Between Iron River and Crystal Falls on Co Rd 424 on Chicagon Lake

Trail Type: Hiking/Walking, Cross Country Skiing, Mountain Biking, Interpretive
Trail Distance: 30 km   Loops: Many   Shortest: Longest:
Trail Surface: Natural
Trail Use Fee: Yes
Method Of Ski Trail Grooming: Track set
Skiing Ability Suggested: Novice to advanced
Hiking Trail Difficulty: Easy to moderate
Mountain Biking Ability Suggested: Novice to advanced
Terrain: Steep 15%, Hilly 15%, Moderate 40%, Flat 30%
Camping: None

Complete recreational complex including 18 hole golf course, ski and mountain
bike trails, indoor pool, sauna and spa and meeting rooms.
Bike and ski rentals available on site.
The Wolf Track Nature Trail is self guided and 1.5 miles long. It has a 1.3 mile
spur to the top of Mount Margaret.
Mountain biking and hiking is permitted on all trails, while the groomed ski trails
are on the north system only.
A brochure is available.

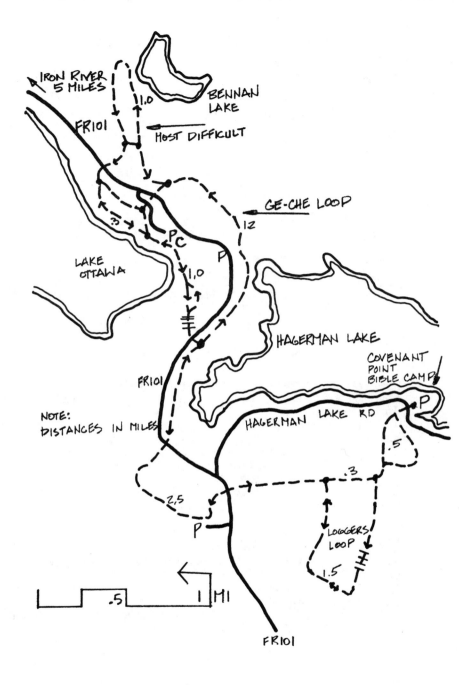

LAKE OTTAWA
RECREATION AREA

Iron River Ranger District, Ottawa National Forest
990 Lalley Rd   906-265-5139
Iron River, MI 49935

Covenant Point Bible Camp
Hagerman Lake   906-265-2117
Iron River, MI 49935

Michigan Atlas & Gazetteer Location: 98D23

County Location: Iron

Directions To Trailhead:
West trailhead - 8 miles SW of Iron River on US2/M73, then north on Hagerman Lake Rd. to Covenant Point Bible Camp
East trailhead - 3 miles SW of Iron River on US2 M73 to Ottawa Lake Rd, then right to Lake Ottawa National Forest campground

Trail Type: Hiking/Walking, Cross Country Skiing
Trail Distance: 10+ mi   Loops: 4   Shortest: Longest:
Trail Surface: Natural
Trail Use Fee: Donations accepted to pay for grooming at trailheads
Method Of Ski Trail Grooming: Track set
Skiing Ability Suggested: Novice to intermediate
Hiking Trail Difficulty: Easy to moderate
Mountain Biking Ability Suggested: NA
Terrain: Steep 5%, Hilly 5%, Moderate 40%, Flat 50%
Camping: Summer camping available at the National Forest campground

Maintained by the Covenant Point Bible Camp in cooperation with the Ottawa National Forest, Iron River Ranger District.
Rentals and group accomodations available from the Covenant Point Bible Camp.
Groomed occasionally but not the entire system all of the time.
Call them if more information is desired.

Ski Brule/Ski Homestead

Ski Brule/Ski Homestead, Att. Bruce Clark
397 Brule Mountain Rd.
Iron River, MI 49935

906-265-4957
800-362-7853

Michigan Atlas & Gazetteer Location: 98D3

County Location: Iron

Directions To Trailhead:
6 miles SW of Iron River between M189 and M73. Follow signs from both M189 and M73 to the ski area. Trailhead is at the Ski Brule Lodge.

Trail Type: Hiking/Walking, Cross Country Skiing
Trail Distance: 23 km   Loops: 5   Shortest: Longest:
Trail Surface: Natural
Trail Use Fee: Yes
Method Of Ski Trail Grooming: Single track set with skating lane
Skiing Ability Suggested: Novice to advance
Hiking Trail Difficulty: Easy to moderate
Mountain Biking Ability Suggested: NA
Terrain: Steep 5%, Hilly 15%, Moderate 30%, Flat 50%
Camping: None

Privately operated alpine and nordic ski resort
Instruction, lodging, restaurant, ski shop and snack bar are available.
A very nice trail system for all levels of skill. Shelters along trails Site of the Brule River Run ski race held in January. Pig roast every Thursday and Saturday nights at the Homestead
Horse back riding, ATB riding and white water rafting trips available in summer months.

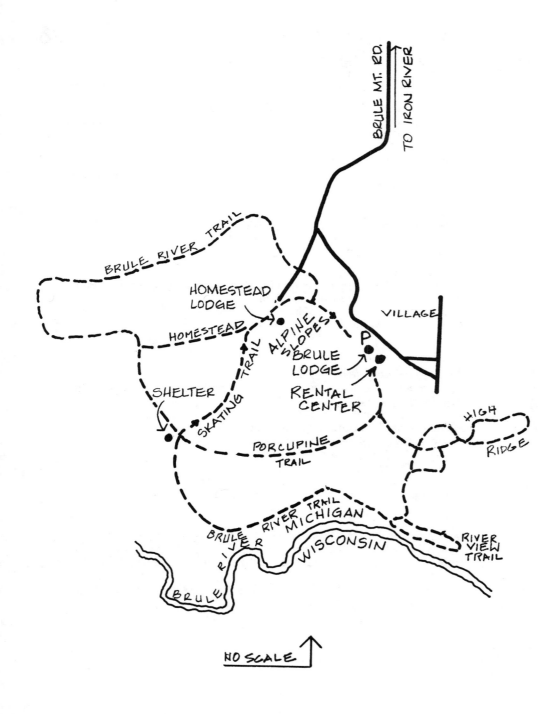

SKI BRULE

NO SCALE

FH 16 ← US 2 → IRON RIVER

10+ MILES

FR 3905

P

.75 MILE

TIMBER LAKE

C   C   C

.5 MI

TIMBER LAKE TRAIL

Timber Lake Trail

Iron River Ranger District, Ottawa National Forest
990 Lalley Rd
Iron River, MI 499350

906-932-5139

Michigan Atlas & Gazetteer Location: 98C2

County Location: Iron

Directions To Trailhead:
West of Iron River about 11 miles on US2. to FR 3905 (south side of US2)

Trail Type: Hiking/Walking
Trail Distance: .75 mi   Loops: NA   Shortest: NA   Longest: .75 mi
Trail Surface: Natural
Trail Use Fee: None
Method Of Ski Trail Grooming: NA
Skiing Ability Suggested: NA
Hiking Trail Difficulty: Easy
Mountain Biking Ability Suggested: NA
Terrain: Steep 0%, Hilly 0%, Moderate 1%, Flat 99%
Camping: Wilderness campsites available on Timber Lake

Maintained by the Iron River Ranger District, Ottawa National Forest
This is an access trail to Timber Lake and the lakeside campsites.

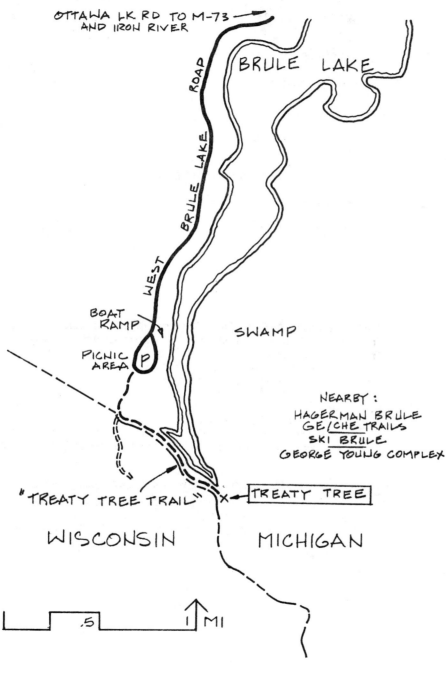

OTTAWA LK RD TO M-73 AND IRON RIVER →

BRULE LAKE

WEST BRULE LAKE ROAD

BOAT RAMP

PICNIC AREA P

SWAMP

NEARBY:
HAGERMAN BRULE
GE/CHE TRAILS
SKI BRULE
GEORGE YOUNG COMPLEX

"TREATY TREE TRAIL" X [TREATY TREE]

WISCONSIN   MICHIGAN

|___|‾‾|___.5___|___↑‾|MI
                    1

TREATY TREE TRAIL

Iron River Ranger District, Ottawa National Forest
990 Lalley Rd
Iron River, MI 49935

906-265-5139

Ottawa National Forest
2100 E. Cloverland Drive
Ironwood, MI 49938

906-932-1330

Michigan Atlas & Gazetteer Location: 98D2

County Location: Iron

Directions To Trailhead:
West of Iron River M73 to Ottawa Lake Rd to West Brule Lake Rd to Stateline Recreation Area

Trail Type: Hiking/Walking
Trail Distance: .2 mi   Loops: NA   Shortest: NA   Longest: NA
Trail Surface: Natrual
Trail Use Fee: None
Method Of Ski Trail Grooming: None
Skiing Ability Suggested: NA
Hiking Trail Difficulty: Easy
Mountain Biking Ability Suggested: NA
Terrain: Steep 0%, Hilly 0%, Moderate 5%, Flat 95%
Camping: At nearby Lake Ottawa Recreation Area

Maintained by the Iron River Ranger District, Ottawa National Forest

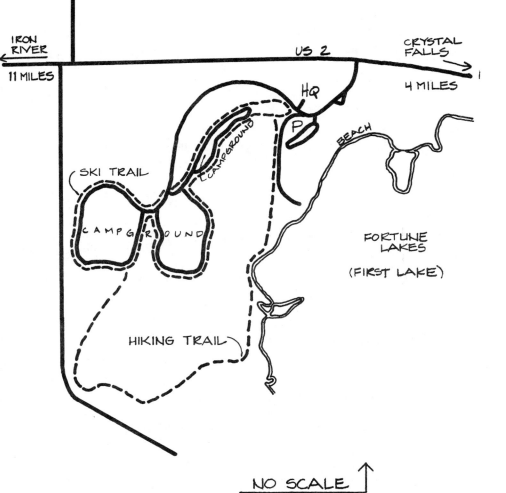

NO SCALE ↑

BEWABIC STATE PARK

Bewabic State Park

Bewabic State Park
1933 US2 West
Crystal Falls, MI 49920

906-875-3324

DNR Parks and Recreation Division

517-373-1270

Michigan Atlas & Gazetteer Location: 99D5

County Location: Iron

Directions To Trailhead:
4 miles west of Crystal Falls on US2

Trail Type: Hiking/Walking, Cross Country Skiing, Interpretive
Trail Distance: 2 mi   Loops: 1   Shortest: Longest: 2 mi
Trail Surface: Natural
Trail Use Fee: None, but vehicle entry fee required
Method Of Ski Trail Grooming: Packed
Skiing Ability Suggested: Novice
Hiking Trail Difficulty: Easy
Mountain Biking Ability Suggested: NA
Terrain: Rolling to hilly
Camping: Campground available in park from May 15th to October 15th

Maintained by the DNR Parks and Recreation Division
Some ski trail sections use unplowed campground roads
Iron Range and StateLine Rail Trails very nearby.
Ski Brule, Lake Ottawa Recreation Area and Lake Mary Plains Pathway in vicinity.

Lake Mary Plains Pathway

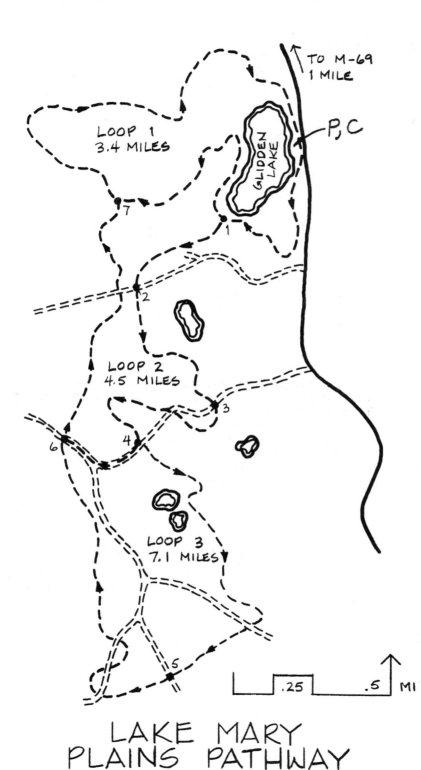

Crystal Falls Forest Area, Copper Country State Forest
1420 US2 West
Crystal Falls, MI 49920

906-875-6622

District Forest Manager, Copper Country State Forest
US41 North, PO Box 440
Baraga, MI 49908

906-353-6651

Michigan Atlas & Gazetteer Location: 99D7

County Location: Iron

Directions To Trailhead:
4 miles west of Crystal Falls on M69, then south on Lake Mary Plains Rd. 1 mile to trailhead at Glidden Lake State Forest Campground

Trail Type: Hiking/Walking, Cross Country Skiing, Mountain Biking
Trail Distance: 7+ mi   Loops: 3   Shortest: 3.4 mi Longest: 6.2 mi
Trail Surface: Natural
Trail Use Fee: None
Method Of Ski Trail Grooming: Track set
Skiing Ability Suggested: Novice & expert trails *
Hiking Trail Difficulty: Moderate
Mountain Biking Ability Suggested: Easy to moderate
Terrain: Steep 0%, Hilly 5%, Moderate 45%, Flat 50%
Camping: Campground at trailhead

Maintained by the DNR Forest Management Division
Forest fire occoured in an area that the trail passes through
Because of the hills, none of the trails area rated intermediate
Other contacts:
      DNR Forest Management Division Office, Lansing, 517-373-1275
      DNR Forest Management Region Office, Marquette, 906-228-6561

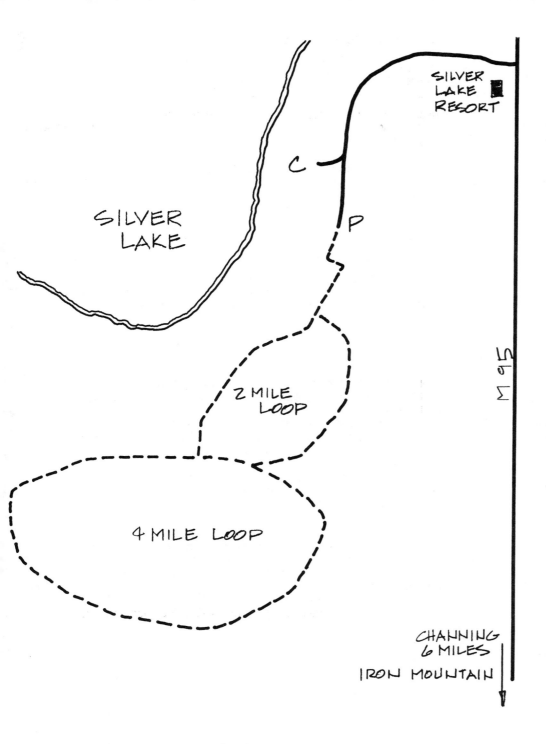

SILVER LAKE

SILVER
LAKE
RESORT

C

P

2 MILE
LOOP

4 MILE LOOP

M 95

CHANNING
6 MILES

IRON MOUNTAIN

SILVER LAKE TRAIL

Silver Lake Trail

Silver Lake Resort, Inc.
N13 195
Channing, MI 49815

906-542-7195

Michigan Atlas & Gazetteer Location: 99C8

County Location: Dickinson

Directions To Trailhead:
On M95, 5 miles north of Channing and north of Iron Mountain

Trail Type: Hiking/Walking, Mountain Biking, Interpretive
Trail Distance: 8 mi   Loops: 2   Shortest: 2 mi   Longest: 6 mi
Trail Surface: Natural
Trail Use Fee: None
Method Of Ski Trail Grooming: Not known
Skiing Ability Suggested: Novice
Hiking Trail Difficulty: Easy
Mountain Biking Ability Suggested: Novice
Terrain: Steep 0%, Hilly 0%, Moderate 20%, Flat 80%
Camping: Campground at the trailhead

Maintained by the Silver Lake Resort, Inc.
30 site campground, 2 cabins, gift shop and gas station on site.

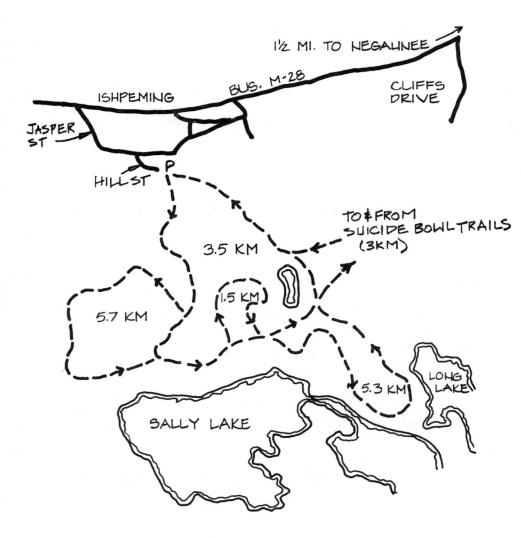

1½ MI. TO NEGAUNEE

BUS. M-28

ISHPEMING

CLIFFS DRIVE

JASPER ST

HILL ST

P

3.5 KM

TO & FROM SUICIDE BOWL TRAILS (3KM)

5.7 KM

1.5 KM

5.3 KM

LONG LAKE

SALLY LAKE

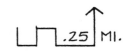

.25 MI.

CLEVELAND CROSS COUNTRY SKI TRAIL

Ishpeming/Negaunee Chamber of Commerce
661 Palms Ave   906-486-4841
Ishpeming, MI 49849

United States Ski Hall of Fame

Ishpeming, MI 49849

Michigan Atlas & Gazetteer Location: 100A3

County Location: Marquette

Directions To Trailhead:
On the south side of Ishpeming via Jasper St south off Bus M28, then right on Hill St. to the parking lot. Trailhead is not signed

Trail Type: Cross Country Skiing
Trail Distance: 12.5 km   Loops: 5   Shortest: 3.5 km Longest: 10.5 km
Trail Surface: Natural
Trail Use Fee: Yes, daily and season passes available
Method Of Ski Trail Grooming: Track set   SKATING NOT PERMITTED
Skiing Ability Suggested: Intermediate to expert
Hiking Trail Difficulty: NA
Mountain Biking Ability Suggested: NA
Terrain: Steep 20%, Hilly 60%, Moderate 20%, Flat 0%
Camping: None

Maintained by the Ishpeming Ski Club on Cleveland Cliffs Co. property
Absolutely one of the finest ski trail systems in the state.
Connected to the Suicide Bowl system with two separate 3 km trails.
Originally developed by Norman Juhola of Ishpeming. Connected to the Suicide Bowl Trails to make a 23 km loop. Groomed regularly.

M 95

CO RD 422

CO RD 581

1.5 MI

GENES POND RD

P C

GENE'S POND

SCENIC OVERLOOK

ABANDON MINE

.5 MI

Norway Forest Area, Copper Country State Forest
PO Box 126
Norway, MI 49870

906-563-9247

District Forest Manager, Copper Country State Forest
PO Box 440
Baraga, MI 49908

906-353-6651

Michigan Atlas & Gazetteer Location: 100D12

County Location: Dickinson

Directions To Trailhead:
At Gene's Pond SFCG. 6.5 miles north of Theodore on Co Rd 581 & 422

Trail Type: Hiking/Walking, Interpretive
Trail Distance: 2.3 mi   Loops: 1   Shortest: NA   Longest: 2.3 mi
Trail Surface: Natural
Trail Use Fee: None
Method Of Ski Trail Grooming: NA
Skiing Ability Suggested: NA
Hiking Trail Difficulty: Easy
Mountain Biking Ability Suggested: NA
Terrain: Steep 0%, Hilly 0%, Moderate 95%, Flat 5%
Camping: Campground at the trailhead

Maintained by the DNR Forest Mangement Divsion
Scenic overlook along the trail

GENES POND PATHWAY

Michigan Biathlon Association
Rte 3, Box 1024
National Mine, MI 49865

906-486-6706
800-544-4321

Ishpeming Chamber of Commerce
661 Palms Ave
Ishpeming, MI 49849

906-486-4841

Michigan Atlas & Gazetteer Location: 100A3

County Location: Marquette

Directions To Trailhead:
At National Mine on Co. Rd. 476 3 miles south of US41. From westbound US41 in Ishpeming, proceed 1 mile west to yellow blinker, turn south on Lakeshore Dr.,, then proceed .4 mile to Washington St, turn right(west) and proceed 2.7 miles to National Mine (unmarked). Trailhead is 200 feet west on road to Tilden Mine (just south of A-frame)

Trail Type: Hiking/Walking, Cross Country Skiing, Mountain Biking
Trail Distance: 10 km   Loops: 10   Shortest: 1.1 km Longest: 5 km
Trail Surface: Natural
Trail Use Fee: Donations accepted to maintain the trail
Method Of Ski Trail Grooming: Groomed for skating
Skiing Ability Suggested: Novice to advanced
Hiking Trail Difficulty: Moderate
Mountain Biking Ability Suggested: Intermediate to advanced
Terrain: Steep 50%, Hilly 44%, Moderate 51%, Flat 1%
Camping: None in the area

Built and maintained by the Michigan Biathlon Association.
The A-frame is the warming house with showers and toilets.
Very significant elevation changes on trail system.
Few signs to trailhead or on trail.
Ask for directions at A-frame.
Most of the trail is groomed for skating.

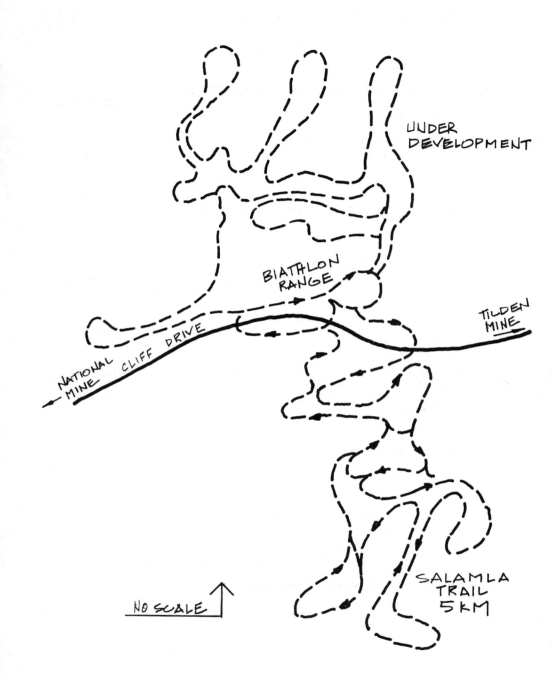

UNDER DEVELOPMENT

BIATHLON RANGE

TILDEN MINE

NATIONAL MINE CLIFF DRIVE

NO SCALE

SALAMLA TRAIL 5 KM

NATIONAL MINE SKI AREA

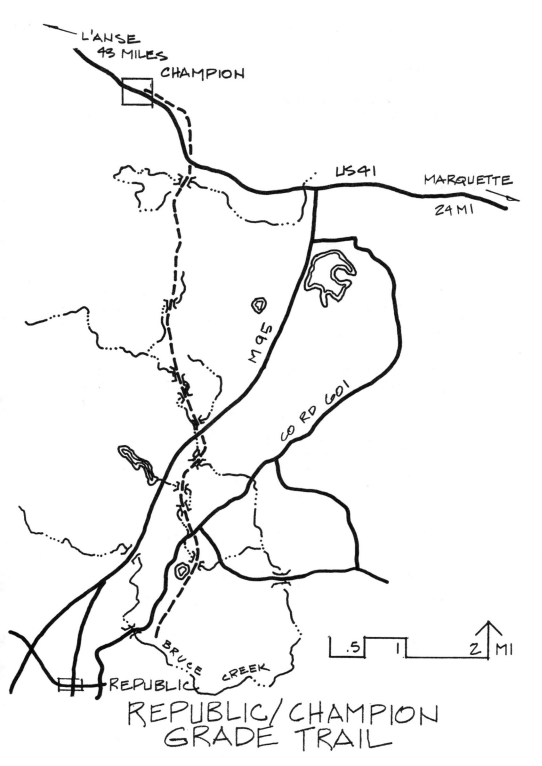

L'ANSE
43 MILES
CHAMPION

US41

MARQUETTE

24 MI

M 95

CO RD 601

BRUCE CREEK

REPUBLIC

REPUBLIC/CHAMPION
GRADE TRAIL

.5 1 2 MI

Ishpeming Forest Area, Escanaba River State Forest
1985 US41 West   906-485-1031
Ishpeming, MI 49849

District Forest Manager, Escanaba River State Forest
6833 US2,41 and M35   906-786-2351
Gladstone, MI 49837

Michigan Atlas & Gazetteer Location: 100A1,112D1

County Location: Marquette

Directions To Trailhead:
North trailhead - Behind Mini-Mart in Champion
South trailhead - Bruce Creek Bridge, 1.6 miles south of Co Rd 601. Take Co
Rd 601 north out of Republic about 2 miles to the trail crossing

Trail Type: Mountain Biking
Trail Distance: 7.5 mi   Loops: NA   Shortest: NA   Longest: NA
Trail Surface: Natural and ballast
Trail Use Fee: None
Method Of Ski Trail Grooming: NA
Skiing Ability Suggested: NA
Hiking Trail Difficulty: NA
Mountain Biking Ability Suggested: Easy
Terrain: 100% Flat
Camping: None

Maintained by the DNR Forest Management Division
This is a rail trail.
Generally wet with eleven bridges.
Ponds, lakes, creeks, rivers beaver ponds, bogs and other wet features along
and on this trail.
Used as a snowmobile trail in the winter.

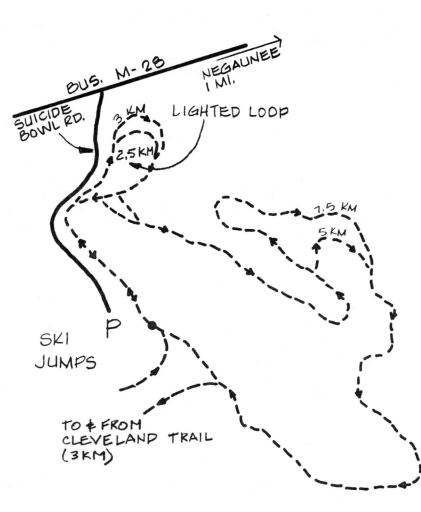

BUS. M-28
NEGAUNEE 1 MI.
SUICIDE BOWL RD.
3 KM
LIGHTED LOOP
2.5 KM
7.5 KM
5 KM
SKI JUMPS
P
TO & FROM CLEVELAND TRAIL (3 KM)

NO SCALE

SUICIDE BOWL

Ishpeming Chamber of Commerce
661 Palms Ave
Ishpeming, MI 49849

906-486-4841

Ski Hall of Fame

906-485-6323

Ishpeming, MI 49849

Michigan Atlas & Gazetteer Location: 100A4

County Location: Marquette

Directions To Trailhead:
Between Ishpeming and Nagaunee on Business M28

Trail Type: Cross Country Skiing
Trail Distance: 12 km   Loops: 4   Shortest: Longest:
Trail Surface: Natural
Trail Use Fee: Yes, available at the Chamber of Commerce
Method Of Ski Trail Grooming: Track set with skating lane
Skiing Ability Suggested: Novice to advanced
Hiking Trail Difficulty: NA
Mountain Biking Ability Suggested: NA
Terrain: Steep 15%, Hilly 25%, Moderate 35%, Flat 25%
Camping: Available in the area

Maintained by the Ishpeming Ski Club, founded in 1887.
Site of many events for both skiing and jumping.
Connected to Cleveland Trail with two separate one way 3 km trails.
One of the finest ski trail systems in the state.
Originally designed by Norman Juhola of Ishpeming.
Connected to the Cleveland Ski Trail to make a 23 km loop.
Groomed weekly as needed. Individual, family and season memberships available.
Site of 5 ski jumps (10, 20, 30, 50 & 70 meters) 2.5 km lighted trail.

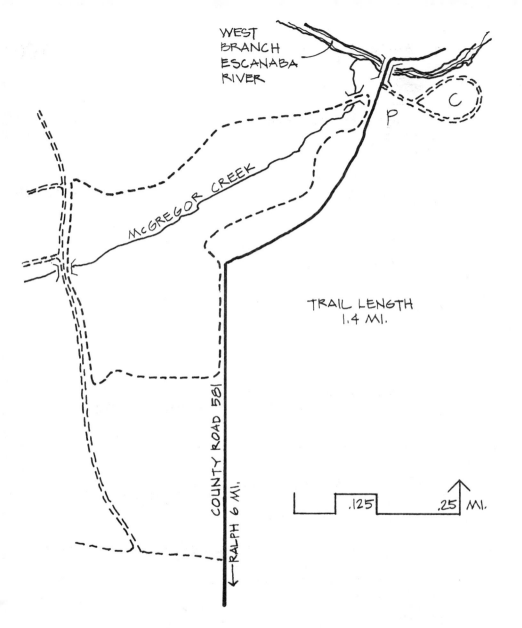

WEST
BRANCH
ESCANABA
RIVER

WEST BRANCH ESCANABA RIVER

McGREGOR CREEK

P

C

TRAIL LENGTH
1.4 MI.

COUNTY ROAD 581

← RALPH 6 MI.

.125   .25 MI.

West Branch Pathway

Norway Forest Area, Copper Country State Forest
US2 West, PO Box 126   906-563-9248
Norway, MI 49870

District Forest Manager, Copper Country State Forest
PO Box 440
Baraga, MI 49908

Michigan Atlas & Gazetteer Location: 100C23

County Location: Dickinson

Directions To Trailhead:
At West Branch SFCG.
7 miles north of Ralph on Co Rd 581

Trail Type: Hiking/Walking, Interpretive
Trail Distance: 1.4 mi   Loops: 1   Shortest: NA   Longest: 1.4 mi
Trail Surface: Natural
Trail Use Fee: None
Method Of Ski Trail Grooming: NA
Skiing Ability Suggested: NA
Hiking Trail Difficulty: Easy
Mountain Biking Ability Suggested: NA
Terrain: Steep 0%, Hilly 0%, Moderate 95%, Flat 5%
Camping: Campground at trailhead.

Maintained by the DNR Forest Mangement Division

WEST BRANCH PATHWAY

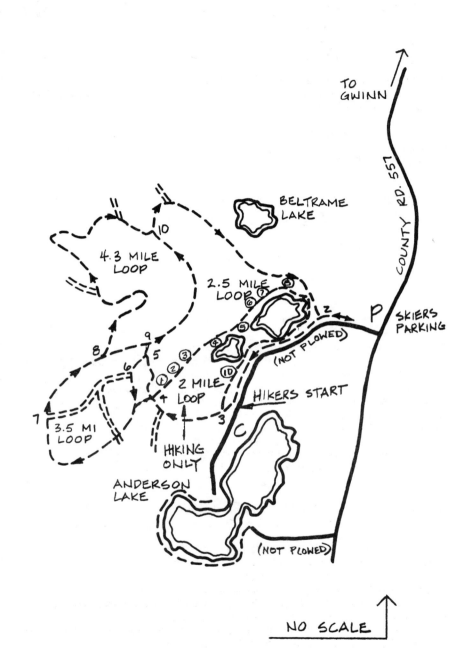

TO
GWINN

COUNTY RD. 551

BELTRAME
LAKE

4.3 MILE
LOOP

10

2.5 MILE
LOOP

8 7 6 5 2 3 4
9

P SKIERS
PARKING

2

(NOT PLOWED)

2 MILE
LOOP

HIKERS START

7 3.5 MI
LOOP

HIKING
ONLY

3

C

ANDERSON
LAKE

(NOT PLOWED)

NO SCALE

ANDERSON LAKE
PATHWAY

Gwinn Forest Area, Escanaba River State Forest
410 West M35   906-346-9201
Gwinn, MI 49841

District Forest Manager, Escanaba River State Forest
US2/41 & M35, PO Box 445   906-786-2351
Gladstone, MI 49837

Michigan Atlas & Gazetteer Location: 101C5

County Location: Marquette

Directions To Trailhead:
5 miles SW of Gwinn on Co Rd 557 at the Anderson Lake Campground. From Gwinn take M35 2.5 miles to CR557, then south for 2.5 miles to the pathway

Trail Type: Hiking/Walking, Cross Country Skiing, Mountain Biking, Interpretive
Trail Distance: 6 mi   Loops: 4   Shortest: 2 mi   Longest: 4.3 mi
Trail Surface: Natural
Trail Use Fee: None, donations accepted for ski trail gooming
Method Of Ski Trail Grooming: None
Skiing Ability Suggested: Novice to intermediate
Hiking Trail Difficulty: Easy
Mountain Biking Ability Suggested: Novice to intermediate
Terrain: Steep 10%, Hilly 15%, Moderate 10%, Flat 65%
Camping: Campground at trailhead

Maintained by the DNR Forest Management Division
Ski trails don't include the 2 mile interpretive trail round the two lakes and do require skiing on the access road to the campground.
The 2 mile interpretive trail around Flack Lakes is not suitable for skiing. This trail has 10 interpreted locations.
Other contacts:
        DNR Forest Management Division Office, Lansing, 517-373-1275
        DNR Forest Management Region Office, Marquette, 906-228-6561

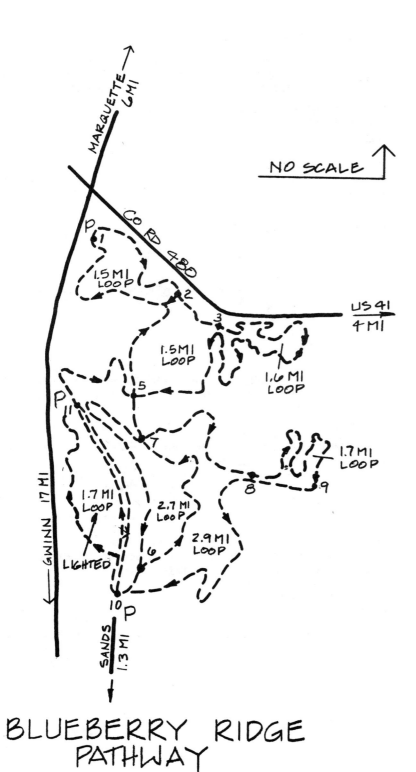

BLUEBERRY RIDGE PATHWAY

Ishpeming Forest Area, Escanaba River State Forest
Box 632, Teal Lake Road
Ishpeming, MI 49849

906-485-1031

Escanaba River State Forest
6833 Hwy 2,41 and M -35
Gladstone, MI 49837

906-786-2351

Michigan Atlas & Gazetteer Location: 101A5

County Location: Marquette

Directions To Trailhead:
6 miles south of Marquette on Co Rd 553 at Co Rd 480

Trail Type: Hiking/Walking, Cross Country Skiing
Trail Distance: 12 mi   Loops: 5   Shortest: 1.5 mi Longest: 2.9 mi
Trail Surface: Natrual
Trail Use Fee: None, but donations accepted for ski trail grooming
Method Of Ski Trail Grooming: Track set with skating lanes
Skiing Ability Suggested: Novice to advanced
Hiking Trail Difficulty: Easy
Mountain Biking Ability Suggested: Novice to intermediate
Terrain: Steep 20%, Hilly 20%, Moderate 40%, Flat 20%
Camping: Campgrounds available nearby in Marquette area

Maintained by the DNR Forest Management Division
Trail originally designed for skiing, but can be used for hiking and mountain biking.
This trail is always groomed exceptionally well.
Very popular and heavily used Marquette area ski trail.
Used by NMU as a nordic training site.
The northern 2 loops are generally flat with some hills.
The southern 3 loops are generally hilly and used by the racers for training.
Donations are needed to fund the grooming operation.
Many other trails in the area including the North Country Trail and Little Presque Isle Tract trails including several more trails for skiing.

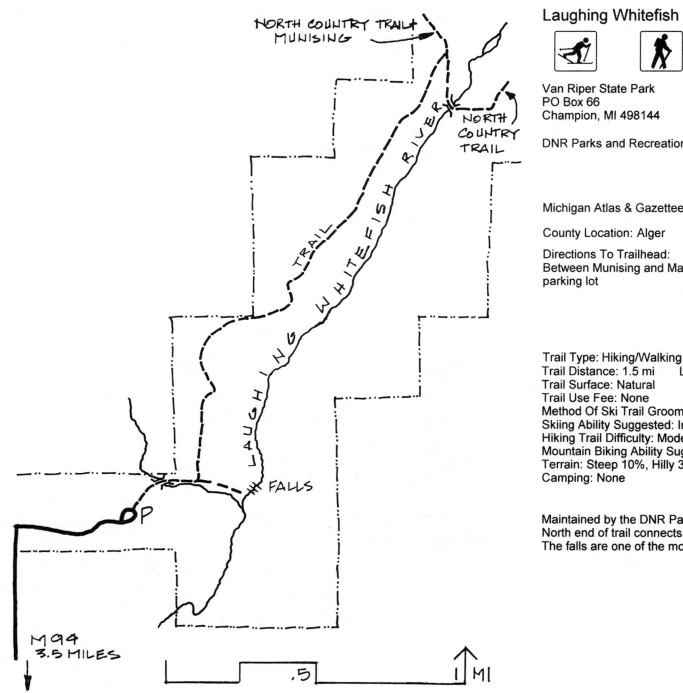

Laughing Whitefish Falls Scenic Site

101

Van Riper State Park
PO Box 66
Champion, MI 498144

906-339-4461

DNR Parks and Recreation Division

517-373-1270

Michigan Atlas & Gazetteer Location: 101A8

County Location: Alger

Directions To Trailhead:
Between Munising and Marquette north of M94 at Sundell about 3.5 miles to parking lot

Trail Type: Hiking/Walking, Cross Country Skiing
Trail Distance: 1.5 mi   Loops: NA   Shortest: NA   Longest: NA
Trail Surface: Natural
Trail Use Fee: None
Method Of Ski Trail Grooming: None
Skiing Ability Suggested: Intermediate to advanced
Hiking Trail Difficulty: Moderate to difficult
Mountain Biking Ability Suggested: NA
Terrain: Steep 10%, Hilly 30%, Moderate 40%, Flat 20%
Camping: None

Maintained by the DNR Parks and Recreation Division
North end of trail connects with the North Country Trail - Munising
The falls are one of the most picturesque in the state.

Maple Lane Touring Center
124 Kreiger Dr.
Skandia, MI 49885

906-942-7662

Ron Stenfors
PO Box 83
Skandia, MI 49885

906-942-7230

Michigan Atlas & Gazetteer Location: 101A67

County Location: Marquette

Directions To Trailhead:
15 miles south of Marquette via US41 to Skandia, then right on Kreiger Dr. for .2 mile to touring center on the right

Trail Type: Cross Country Skiing
Trail Distance: 11 km   Loops: 4   Shortest: 2 km   Longest: 5 km
Trail Surface: Natural
Trail Use Fee: Yes
Method Of Ski Trail Grooming: Track set as needed
Skiing Ability Suggested: Novice to intermediate
Hiking Trail Difficulty: Easy to moderate
Mountain Biking Ability Suggested: NA
Terrain: Steep 2%, Hilly 18%, Moderate 80%, Flat 20%
Camping: None

Privately operated nordic ski area.
Ski shop, rentals, warming area and snack bar is available.
Snowshoe rentals.
Ski repair and maintenance available and waxing area provided.
A small but well designed and groomed trail system that is a lot of fun Mostly forested trails. Within 10 minutes of fine food and lodging.
Ski school on weekends.
Ski season is from December through March

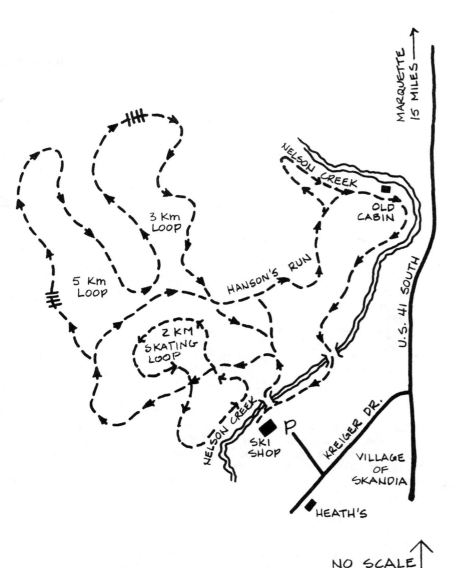

MAPLE LANE
TOURING CENTER

Ishpeming Forest Area, Escanaba River State Forest
1985 US 41 West   906-485-1031
Ishpeming, MI 49849

District Forest Manager, Escanaba River State Forest
6833 US41/2 & M35   906-786-2351
Gladstone, MI 49837

Michigan Atlas & Gazetteer Location: 101A8

County Location: Alger

Directions To Trailhead:
Between Marquette and Munising on M28
Trailhead - North on Deerton Rd from M28 about 2 miles.

Trail Type: Hiking/Walking, Interpretive
Trail Distance: 1.4 mi   Loops: 1   Shortest: NA   Longest: 1.4 mi
Trail Surface: Natural
Trail Use Fee: None
Method Of Ski Trail Grooming: NA
Skiing Ability Suggested: NA
Hiking Trail Difficulty: Moderate
Mountain Biking Ability Suggested: NA
Terrain: Steep 0%, Hilly 25%, Moderate 10%, Flat 55%
Camping: Campground closed at trailhead

Maintained by the DNR Forest Management Division
Developed as a interperative trail with 22 stations explaining the logging days of
the town known as Tyoga and the Tyoga Lumber Company.
Portions of the trail will be wet in the spring and fall.
Another contact is the DNR Forest Management Division Office, Lansing. 517-
373-1275

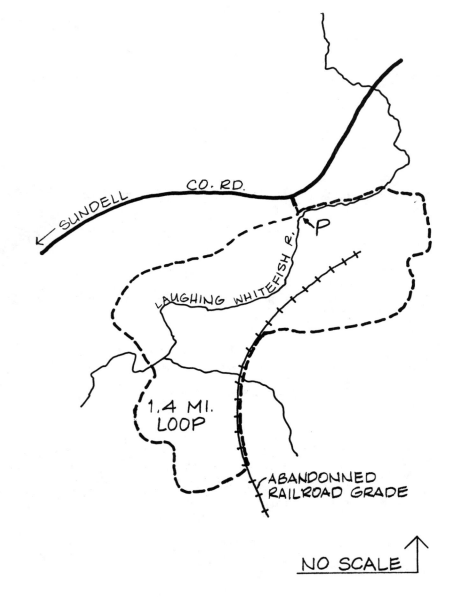

TYOGA HISTORICAL PATHWAY

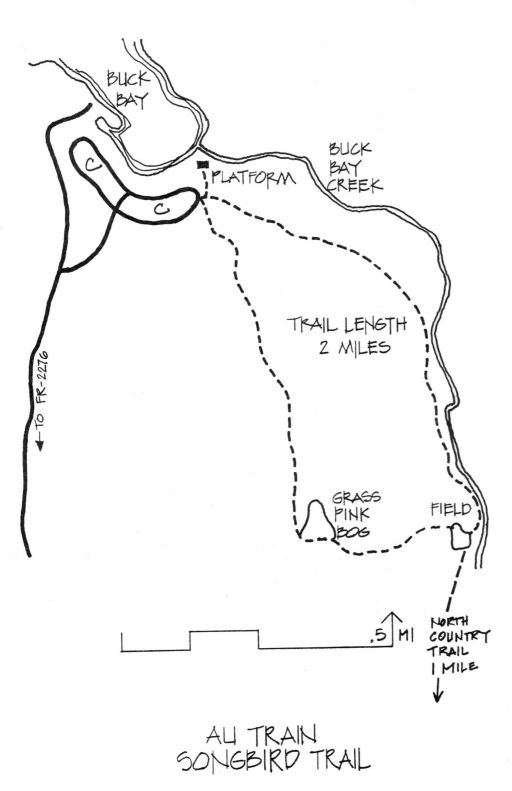

AU TRAIN
SONGBIRD TRAIL

Munising Ranger District, Hiawatha National Forest
RR 2, Box 400   906-387-2512
Munising, MI 49862

Forest Supervisor, Hiawatha National Forest
2727 N. Lincoln Rd   906-786-4062
Escanaba, MI 49829

Michigan Atlas & Gazetteer Location: 102A2

County Location: Alger

Directions To Trailhead:
At the Au Train Lake National Forest Campground located at the south end of
Au Train Lake.
Trailhead - From M28 south 4 miles on H-03 to FR 2276. East on FR 2276 to FR
2596, then north 1 mile to the campground. Trailhead is at the east end of the
campground.

Trail Type: Hiking/Walking
Trail Distance: 2 mi   Loops: 1   Shortest: NA   Longest: 2 mi
Trail Surface: Natural
Trail Use Fee: None
Method Of Ski Trail Grooming: NA
Skiing Ability Suggested: NA
Hiking Trail Difficulty: Easy
Mountain Biking Ability Suggested: NA
Terrain: 100% Flat
Camping: Campground on the site

Maintained by the Hiawatha Nattional Forest
Campground trail along the Buck Bay Creek.
Connector trail to the North Country Trail - Munising
Many other National Forest and National Lakeshore trails in the Munising area.

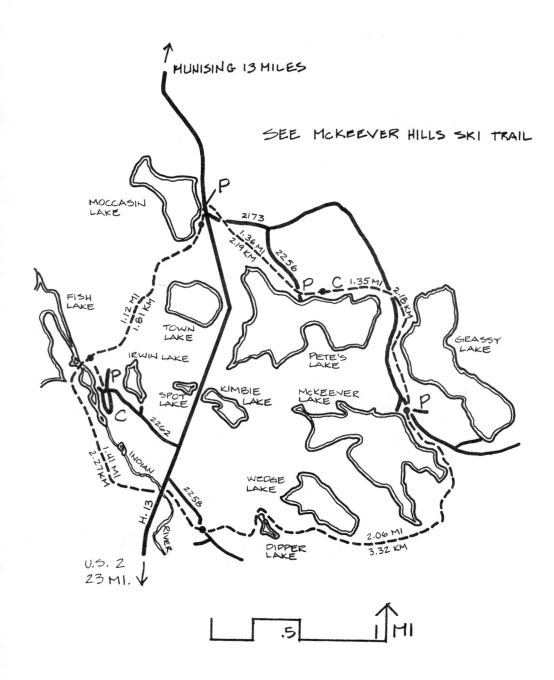

HUNISING 13 MILES

SEE McKEEVER HILLS SKI TRAIL

MOCCASIN LAKE

P

2173

1.36 MI
2.19 KM

2256

P C 1.35 MI

2.18 KM

FISH LAKE

1.12 MI
1.81 KM

TOWN LAKE

IRWIN LAKE

PETE'S LAKE

GRASSY LAKE

P

SPOT LAKE

KIMBIE LAKE

McKEEVER LAKE

P

C

2262

INDIAN

1.41 MI
2.27 KM

WEDGE LAKE

H.13

2258

RIVER

DIPPER LAKE

2.06 MI
3.32 KM

U.S. 2
23 MI.

.5   1 MI

BRUNO'S RUN

Bruno's Run Trail

Munising Ranger District, Hiawatha National Forest
RR 2, Box 400
Munising, MI 49862

906-387-2512

Forest Supervisor, Hiawatha National Forest
2727 N. Lincoln Rd.
Escanaba, MI 49829

906-786-4062

Michigan Atlas & Gazetteer Location: 102C4

County Location: Alger and Schoolcraft

Directions To Trailhead:
Take M28 south from Munising 4 miles to Wetmore, then south 11 miles on H13 (FH13) to the Moccasin Lake Picnic Area where the trailhead is located.

Trail Type: Hiking/Walking, Cross Country Skiing, Mountain Biking
Trail Distance: 11.7 km   Loops: 1   Shortest: NA   Longest: 11.7 km
Trail Surface: Natural
Trail Use Fee: None
Method Of Ski Trail Grooming: Not groomed
Skiing Ability Suggested: Intermediate to advanced
Hiking Trail Difficulty: Easy to moderate
Mountain Biking Ability Suggested: Novice
Terrain: Steep 0%, Hilly 3%, Moderate 40%, Flat 57%
Camping: Pete's Lake and Widewaters NFCG are along the trail

Maintained by the Muising Ranger District, Hiawatha National Forest
Trail is for experienced skiers only since this trail was designed for hiking.
Scenic views, rolling terrain, bridges, lakes and scenic views makes for a very interesting trail. I really enjoyed the trail because of this variety.
This trail is excellent for mountain biking.
See Michigan Cyclist Magazine, winter 1993/94 issue for a review of this trail.
For a nearby trail specially designed for cross country skiing see McKeever Hills Ski Trail which is located adjacent to this trail.

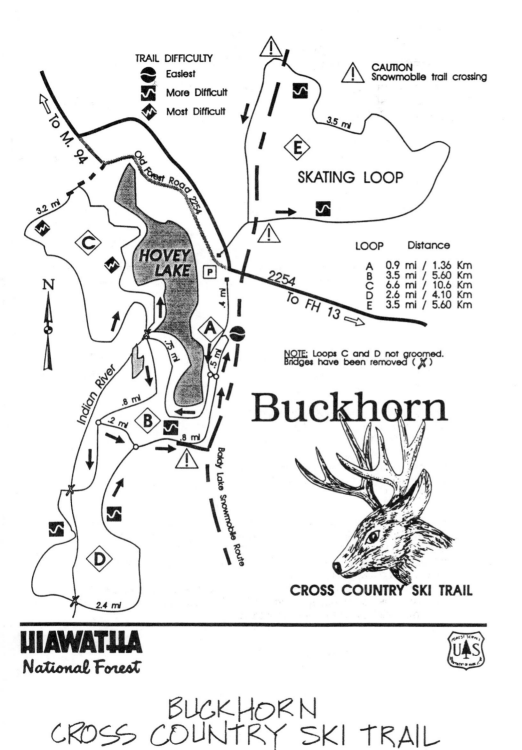

TRAIL DIFFICULTY
⬤ Easiest
◨ More Difficult
◼ Most Difficult

⚠ CAUTION
Snowmobile trail crossing

To M. 94

3.2 ml

Old Forest Road 2254

HOVEY LAKE

N

C

Indian River

A

B

.75 ml
.5 ml
.8 ml
.2 ml
.4 ml
.8 ml

D

2.4 ml

Baby Lake Snowmobile Route

3.5 ml

E

SKATING LOOP

2254
To FH 13 ⇒

LOOP   Distance

A   0.9 mi / 1.36 Km
B   3.5 mi / 5.60 Km
C   6.6 mi / 10.6 Km
D   2.6 mi / 4.10 Km
E   3.5 mi / 5.60 Km

NOTE: Loops C and D not groomed.
Bridges have been removed (✗)

P

Buckhorn

CROSS COUNTRY SKI TRAIL

HIAWATHA National Forest

Munising Ranger District, Hiawatha National Forest
RR 2, Box 400
Munising, MI 49862
906-387-2512

Buckhorn Resort and Otter Lake Campground
Buckhorn Rd
Munising, MI 49862
906-387-3559
906-387-4648

Michigan Atlas & Gazetteer Location: 102B3

County Location: Alger

Directions To Trailhead:
At the Buckhorn Resort on FR2254 (Co Rd H-09) between M94 and FH 13
south of Munising on Hovey Lake.

Trail Type: Cross Country Skiing
Trail Distance: 12.55 mi   Loops: 5   Shortest: .9 mi   Longest: 6.6 mmi
Trail Surface: Natural
Trail Use Fee: None
Method Of Ski Trail Grooming: Track set
Skiing Ability Suggested: Novice to advanced
Hiking Trail Difficulty: NA
Mountain Biking Ability Suggested: NA
Terrain: Steep 0%, Hilly 15%, Moderate 25%, Flat 60%
Camping: Private campground at the trailhead and Hovey Lake NFCG .5 mile
away

Maintained by the Hiawatha National Forest and the Buckhorn Lodge and
Restaurant which is located at the trailhead.
Trail surrounds Hovey Lake and contains loops for all skill levels.

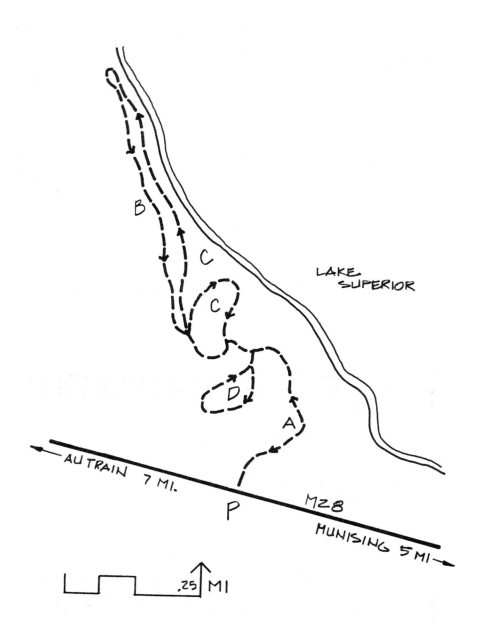

Munising Ranger District, Hiawatha National Forest
RR 2, Box 400
Munising, MI 49862

906-387-2512

Forest Supervisor, Hiawatha National Forest
2727 N. Lincoln Rd
Escanaba, MI 49829

906-786-4062

Michigan Atlas & Gazetteer Location: 102A3

County Location: Alger

Directions To Trailhead:
5 miles west of Munising on M28

Trail Type: Hiking/Walking, Cross Country Skiing
Trail Distance: 3.2 mi   Loops: 3   Shortest: 1.3 mi Longest: 2.3 mi
Trail Surface: Natural in winter
Trail Use Fee: None
Method Of Ski Trail Grooming: None
Skiing Ability Suggested: Novice
Hiking Trail Difficulty: NA
Mountain Biking Ability Suggested: NA
Terrain: Steep 0%, Hilly 0%, Moderate 0%, Flat 100%
Camping: None in winter

Maintained by the Hiawatha Nationa Forest
Trail is the road system of the Bay Furnace National Forest Campground on
Lake Superior.
The campground is not open in the winter.

CHRISTMAS LIGHTED
CROSS COUNTRY SKI TRAIL

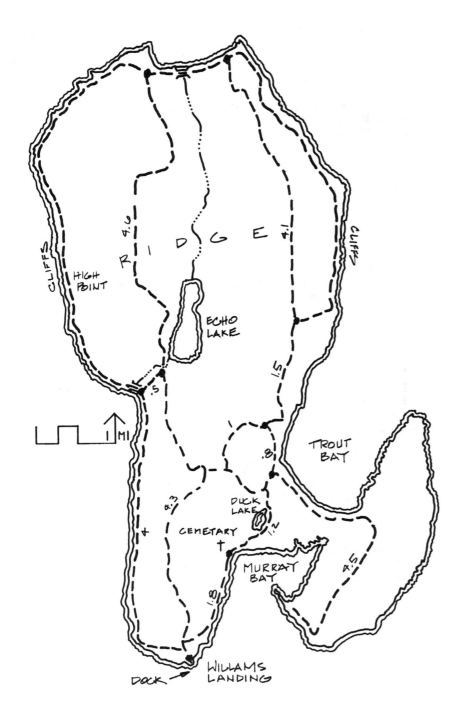

GRAND ISLAND

Munising Ranger District, Hiawatha National Forest
RR 2, Box 400
Munising, MI 49862

906-387-2512

Forest Supervisor, Hiawatha National Forest
2727 N. Lincoln Rd
Escanaba, MI 49829

906-786-4062

Michigan Atlas & Gazetteer Location: 102A34,114D34

County Location: Alger

Directions To Trailhead:
In Lake Superior off shore from Munising. Ferry service from Munising

Trail Type: Hiking/Walking, Cross Country Skiing, Mountain Biking, Interpretive
Trail Distance: 45 km   Loops: Many   Shortest: 2km   Longest: 30 km
Trail Surface: Natural
Trail Use Fee: None
Method Of Ski Trail Grooming: None
Skiing Ability Suggested: Novice to intermediate
Hiking Trail Difficulty: Easy to moderate
Mountain Biking Ability Suggested: Novice
Terrain: Steep 0%, Hilly 0%, Moderate 80%, Flat 20%
Camping: Campgrounds on the island

Maintained by the Munsiing Ranger District, Hiawatha National Forest
A unique island that is well worth the boat ride.
Watch out for bears!
Currently all trails are open to non-motorized trail users. However, the Forest
Service has just completed a development plan for the island. Some trail use
will be restricted. No time table has been established for the implementation of
the plan.

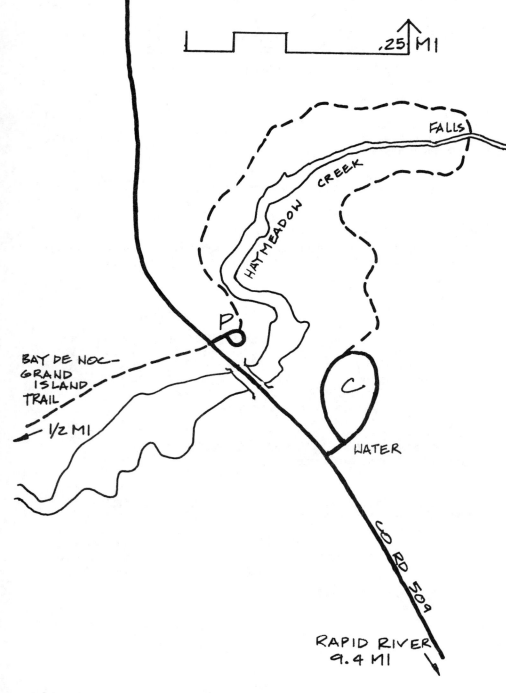

HAYMEADOW CREEK FALLS TRAIL

Rapid River Ranger District, Hiawatha National Forest
8181US 2
Rapid River, MI 49878

906-474-6442

Forest Supervisor, Hiawatha National Forest
2727 N. Lincoln Rd
Escanaba, MI 49829

906-786-4062

Michigan Atlas & Gazetteer Location: 102D2

County Location: Delta

Directions To Trailhead:
At the Haymeadow Falls NFCG. From Rapid River take US2 east to Co Rd 509 about 2 miles, then north 9 miles to the campground which will be on the right.

Trail Type: Hiking/Walking
Trail Distance: 1 mi   Loops: 1   Shortest: NA   Longest: 1 mi
Trail Surface: Natural
Trail Use Fee: None
Method Of Ski Trail Grooming: NA
Skiing Ability Suggested: NA
Hiking Trail Difficulty: Easy
Mountain Biking Ability Suggested: NA
Terrain: Steep 0%, Hilly 0%, Moderate 90%, Flat 10%
Camping: Campground at trailhead

Maintained by the Rapid River Ranger District, Hiawatha National Forest
A North Country Spur (.5 mile long) starts near the north trailhead.

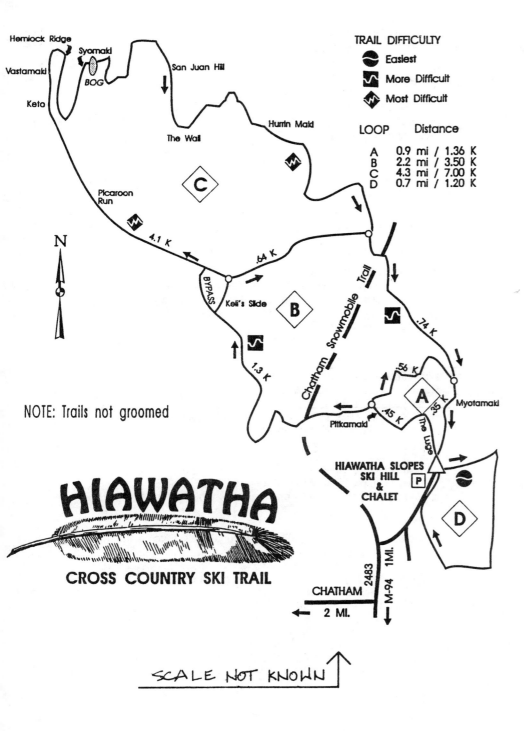

TRAIL DIFFICULTY

⊖ Easiest

♒ More Difficult

◆ Most Difficult

LOOP	Distance
A	0.9 mi / 1.36 K
B	2.2 mi / 3.50 K
C	4.3 mi / 7.00 K
D	0.7 mi / 1.20 K

NOTE: Trails not groomed

N

HIAWATHA

CROSS COUNTRY SKI TRAIL

SCALE NOT KNOWN

HIAWATHA SKI TRAIL

Munising Ranger District, Hiawatha National Forest
RR 2, Box 400
Munising, MI 49862

906-387-3700
906-387-2512

Forest Supervisor, Hiawatha National Forest
2727 N. Lincoln Rd
Escanaba, MI 49829

906-786-4062

Michigan Atlas & Gazetteer Location: 102B1

County Location: Alger

Directions To Trailhead:
Take M28 out of Munising to M94 to FR 2483 (Cemetary Rd), then north 1 mile
to trailhead at small downhill ski area. Trail is 15 miles from Munising.

Trail Type: Hiking/Walking, Cross Country Skiing
Trail Distance: 8.84 mi   Loops: 4   Shortest: .7 mi   Longest: 4.3 mi
Trail Surface: Natural
Trail Use Fee: None
Method Of Ski Trail Grooming: None
Skiing Ability Suggested: Novice to advanced
Hiking Trail Difficulty: Easy to moderate
Mountain Biking Ability Suggested: NA
Terrain: Steep 0%, Hilly 0%, Moderate 50%, Flat 50%
Camping: AuTrain Lake NFCG is 5 miles away

Maintained by the Munising Ranger District, Hiawatha National Forest
Trails may be overgrown in the summer.
At the site of a small local alpine ski area.

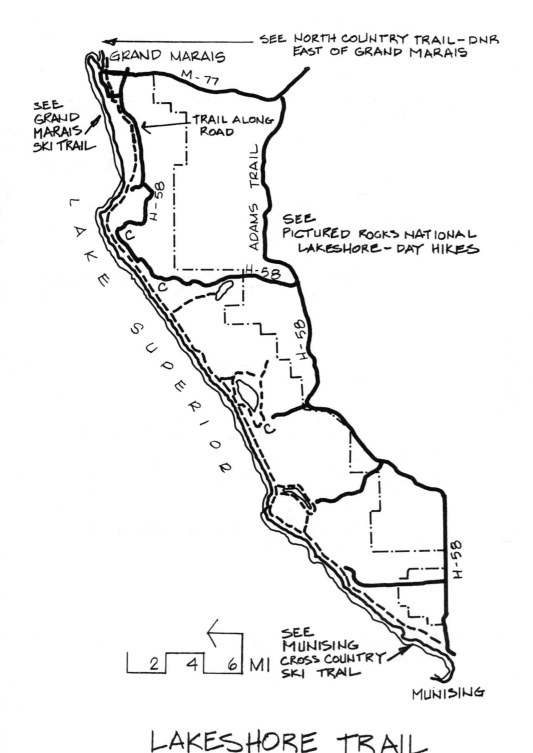

SEE NORTH COUNTRY TRAIL-DNR
EAST OF GRAND MARAIS

GRAND MARAIS

M-77

SEE
GRAND
MARAIS
SKI TRAIL

TRAIL ALONG ROAD

LAKE SUPERIOR

H-58

ADAMS TRAIL

SEE
PICTURED ROCKS NATIONAL
LAKESHORE - DAY HIKES

H-58

H-58

H-58

SEE
MUNISING
CROSS COUNTRY
SKI TRAIL

2 4 6 MI

MUNISING

LAKESHORE TRAIL

Pictured Rocks National Lakeshore
PO Box 40
Munising, MI 49862

906-387-3700

Michigan Atlas & Gazetteer Location: 102A4, 114D4, 115CD5678

County Location: Alger

Directions To Trailhead:
From Munising to Sable Falls west of Grand Marais.
West trailhead - Munising Falls, northeast of Munising.
East trailhead - About 5 miles west of Grand Marais on H58 Other trailheads are all accessible from H58.

Trail Type: Hiking/Walking
Trail Distance: 43 mi   Loops: NA   Shortest: NA   Longest: NA
Trail Surface: Natural
Trail Use Fee: Yes, individual and group permits available
Method Of Ski Trail Grooming: NA
Skiing Ability Suggested: NA
Hiking Trail Difficulty: Easy to moderate
Mountain Biking Ability Suggested: Not permitted
Terrain: Steep 0%, Hilly 0%, Moderate 20%, Flat 80%
Camping: 13 backcountry campgounds are along the trail

Maintained by the Pictured Rocks National Lakeshore.
A segment of the North Country Trail.
Permits are required for the backcountry campsites. Sites are reservable.
Only the following locations have drinking water-Munising Falls, Park HQ, Miner's Castle, Little Beaver CG,Twelvemile Beach CG, Hurricane River CG and Grand Sable Visitor Center.
Most campgrounds have access to untreated Lake Superior water that must be boiled or treated with a filter.
Some campgrounds have no water available.
Parties of 7 to 20 people must use group backcountry campsites only.
Open fires are prohibited at Chapel and Mosquito CG. Pets are not allowed in the backcountry.
Send for additional information and detailed trail booklet.

McKeever Hills Ski Trail

Munising Ranger District, Hiawatha National Forest
RR 2, Box 400   906-387-3700
Munising, MI 49862

Forest Supervisor, Hiawatha National Forest
2727 N. Lincoln Rd   906-786-4062
Escanaba, MI 49829

Michigan Atlas & Gazetteer Location: 102C4

County Location: Alger

Directions To Trailhead:
Take M28 east from Munising, then south on M94 to FH 13, then south again to
the Forest Glen Country Store.
Trail is 13 miles south of Munising.
Park at the country store.

Trail Type: Hiking/Walking, Cross Country Skiing
Trail Distance: 12 km   Loops: 3   Shortest: 1 km   Longest: 7 km
Trail Surface: Natural
Trail Use Fee: None
Method Of Ski Trail Grooming: Track set
Skiing Ability Suggested: Novice to advanced
Hiking Trail Difficulty: Moderate
Mountain Biking Ability Suggested: NA
Terrain: Steep 10%, Hilly 10%, Moderate 50%, Flat 30%
Camping: Neaby at Pete's Lake and Widewaters SFCG

Maintained by the Munising Ranger District, Hiawatha National Forest
Bruno's Run Trail intersects this trail.

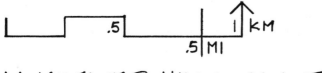

LOOP	DISTANCE
A	.3 mi. / .4 km.
B	3.85 mi. / 6.18 km.
C	2.2 mi. / 3.6 km.
Total	6.35 mi. / 10.18 km.

McKEEVER HILLS SKI TRAIL

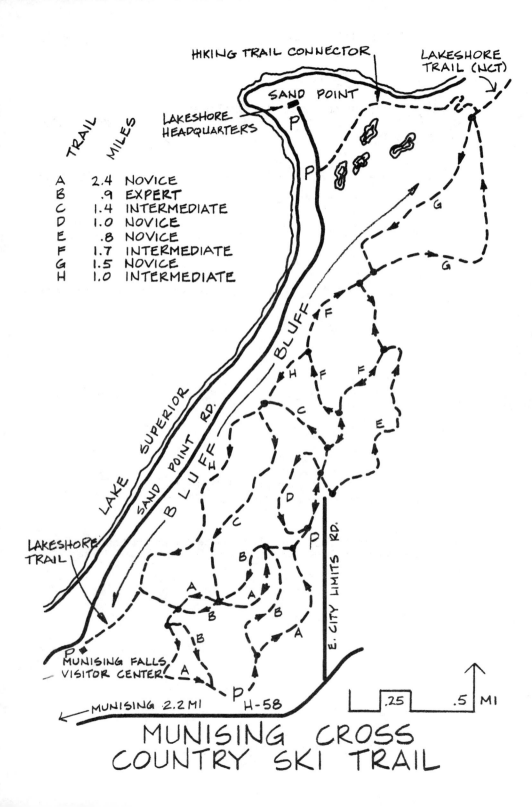

TRAIL MILES

A	2.4	NOVICE
B	.9	EXPERT
C	1.4	INTERMEDIATE
D	1.0	NOVICE
E	.8	NOVICE
F	1.7	INTERMEDIATE
G	1.5	NOVICE
H	1.0	INTERMEDIATE

HIKING TRAIL CONNECTOR

LAKESHORE TRAIL (NCT)

SAND POINT

LAKESHORE HEADQUARTERS

BLUFF

LAKE SUPERIOR

SAND POINT RD.

SAND POINT BLUFF

LAKESHORE TRAIL

P MUNISING FALLS
VISITOR CENTER

E. CITY LIMITS RD.

MUNISING 2.2 MI   H-58

.25   .5 MI

MUNISING CROSS COUNTRY SKI TRAIL

Munising Cross Country Ski Trail

Pictured Rocks National Lakeshore
PO Box 40
Munising, MI 49862

906-387-3700
906-387-2607

Michigan Atlas & Gazetteer Location: 102A4

County Location: Alger

Directions To Trailhead:
NE of Munising on H58
Trailhead - Take H58 east from the blinking traffic light on M28 in Munising about 2.2 miles to the parking lot on the north side of the road. The left fork is Sand Point Rd. to the the Lakeshore Headquarters.

Trail Type: Hiking/Walking, Cross Country Skiing
Trail Distance: 12.3 mi   Loops: 8   Shortest: .9 mi   Longest: 2.5 mi
Trail Surface: Natural
Trail Use Fee: None
Method Of Ski Trail Grooming: Track set twice a week
Skiing Ability Suggested: Novice to advanced
Hiking Trail Difficulty: Easy to moderate
Mountain Biking Ability Suggested: Not permitted
Terrain: Steep 10%, Hilly 30%, Moderate 30%, Flat 30%
Camping: Campgrounds open from May 10 to October 31

Maintained by the Pictured Rocks National Lakeshore
Primarily a ski trail. The trail in the spring has many wet area. Good for hiking in the summer and fall only
Mostly hilly terrain with frozen waterfalls and canyons and some beautiful scenic vistas across Munising Bay to Grand Island.
All trails are well marked and with maps at each intersection Degree of difficulty signs are at the start of each loop.
A well designed and well groomed trail that should not be missed.
A connector trail starts near the Lakeshore Headquarters and ends at the north end of the trail system(not suitable for skiing).
The section of the trail along the cliff is part of the Lakeshore Trail (see separate entry for more detail) which is also part of the North Country Trail.
Pets are not permitted on the trail.
Near the Valley Spur Trail, another great ski trail and many other trails in Alger Co.

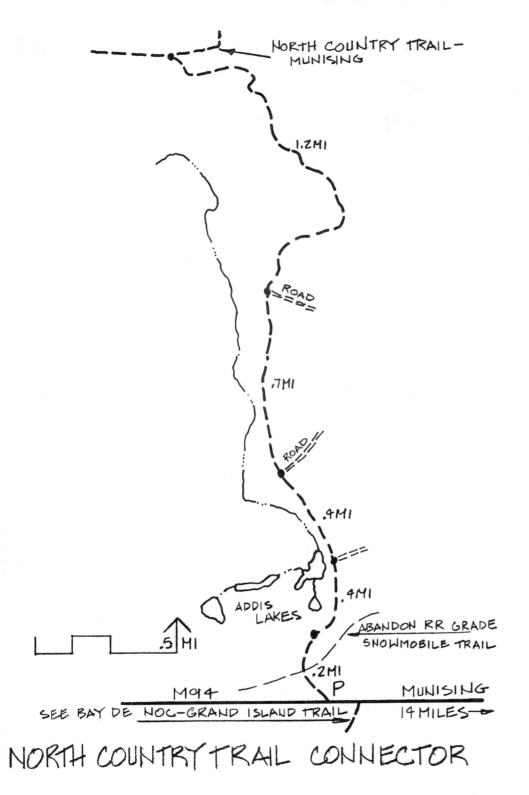

NORTH COUNTRY TRAIL — MUNISING

1.2 MI

ROAD

.7 MI

ROAD

.4 MI

.4 MI

ADDIS LAKES

ABANDON RR GRADE SNOWMOBILE TRAIL

.5 MI

.2 MI

P

M94

MUNISING

SEE BAY DE NOC—GRAND ISLAND TRAIL

14 MILES →

NORTH COUNTRY TRAIL CONNECTOR

Munising Ranger District, Hiawatha National Forest
RR 2, Box 400   906-387-3700
Munising, MI 49862

Forest Supervisor, Hiawatha National Forest
2727 N. Lincoln Rd   906-786-4062
Escanaba, MI 49829

Michigan Atlas & Gazetteer Location: 102B2

County Location: Alger

Directions To Trailhead:
Take M28 east to M94south, then west 9 miles to trailhead at Ackerman Lake

Trail Type: Hiking/Walking
Trail Distance: 5 km   Loops: NA   Shortest: NA   Longest: NA
Trail Surface: Natural
Trail Use Fee: None
Method Of Ski Trail Grooming: NA
Skiing Ability Suggested: NA
Hiking Trail Difficulty: Easy to moderate
Mountain Biking Ability Suggested: NA
Terrain: Steep 0%, Hilly 15%, Moderate 55%, Flat 35%
Camping: Campground at nearby AuTrain Lake NFCG

Maintained by the Munising Ranger District, Hiawatha National Forest
This trail connects the Grand Island -Bay DeNoc Trail to the North Country Trail -
Munising.

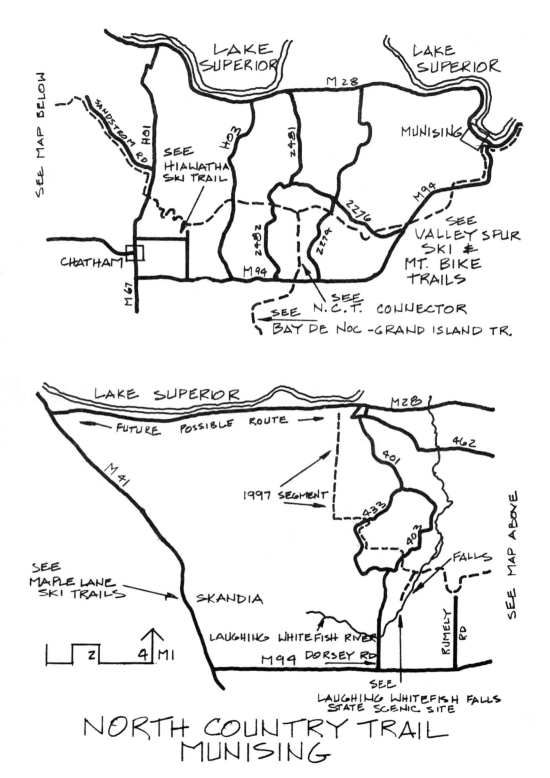

Munising Ranger District, Hiawatha National Forest
RR2, Box 400
Munising, MI 49862

906-387-2512

Forest Supervisor, Hiawatha National Forest
2727 N. Lincoln Rd.
Escanaba, MI 49829

906-786-4062

Michigan Atlas & Gazetteer Location: 102AB123

County Location: Alger

Directions To Trailhead:
East Trailhead - SW of Munising 1.5 miles west of M28 on M94, on south side of the road.
West Trailhead - On Co Rd 433 near Howe Lake, just east of the Marquette Co line and south of Sand River Trailhead - Valley Spur Trail south of Munising (see other listing)
Trailhead - North Country Trail Connector (see other listing)

Trail Type: Hiking/Walking
Trail Distance: 9 mi   Loops: NA   Shortest: NA   Longest: NA
Trail Surface: Natural
Trail Use Fee: None
Method Of Ski Trail Grooming: NA
Skiing Ability Suggested: NA
Hiking Trail Difficulty: Moderate to difficult
Mountain Biking Ability Suggested: NA
Terrain: Steep 0%, Hilly 25%, Moderate 65%, Flat 10%
Camping: Trailside camping is permitted

Maintained by the Munising Ranger District, Hiawatha National Forest
Part of the Valley Spur Ski Trail is included in this section of the NCT.
For further information contact the North Country Trail Association.

NORTH COUNTRY TRAIL
MUNISING

TRAIL NOTES

Pictured Rocks National Lakeshore
PO Box 40
Munising, MI 49862

906-387-3700

Michigan Atlas & Gazetteer Location: 102A4,115CD5678

County Location: Alger

Directions To Trailhead:
Along Lake Superior from Munising on the west end to Grand Marais on the east end

Trail Type: Hiking/Walking, Interpretive
Trail Distance: 30+ mi   Loops: 13   Shortest: .25 mi Longest: 5.4 mi
Trail Surface: Paved and natural
Trail Use Fee: None
Method Of Ski Trail Grooming: NA
Skiing Ability Suggested: NA
Hiking Trail Difficulty: Easy to moderate
Mountain Biking Ability Suggested: Not permitted
Terrain: Varies with trail
Camping: Several campgrounds are located in the national lakeshore

Maintained by the National Park Service
Many different trails scattered throughout the national lakeshore. The maps locate the trails and list their trail distances. The trails are either destination and/or interpretive types.
The two accessible trails are the .25 mile Munising Falls Trail and the .5 mile Sand Point Marsh Trail. A brochure of describing the day hikes and individual brochures of some individual trails are available from the park.
Backcountry camping reservations and fees are now in effect. Contact the HQ for details.
See also the North Country Trail(Lakeshore Trail), Munising Cross Country Ski Trail, Grand Marais Cross Country Ski Trail, Fox River Pathway, School Forest Ski Trail and other trails in the area.

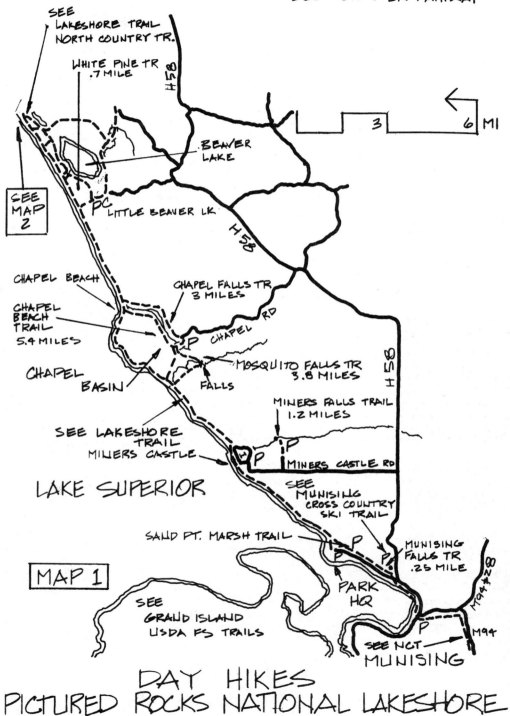

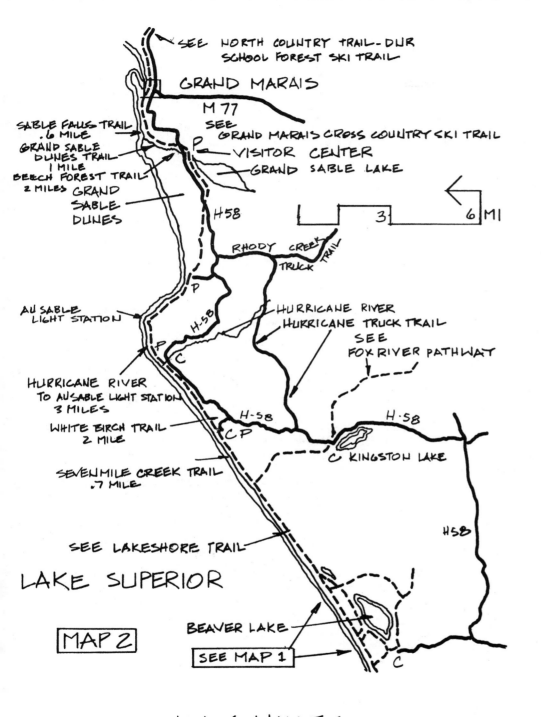

SEE NORTH COUNTRY TRAIL - DUR
SCHOOL FOREST SKI TRAIL

GRAND MARAIS

M 77

SEE
GRAND MARAIS CROSS COUNTRY SKI TRAIL

SABLE FALLS TRAIL
.6 MILE
GRAND SABLE
DUNES TRAIL
1 MILE
BEECH FOREST TRAIL
2 MILES

P

VISITOR CENTER

GRAND SABLE LAKE

GRAND
SABLE
DUNES

H 58

3

6 MI

RHODY CREEK
TRUCK TRAIL

P

AU SABLE
LIGHT STATION

H-58

HURRICANE RIVER
HURRICANE TRUCK TRAIL

SEE
FOX RIVER PATHWAY

P
C

HURRICANE RIVER
TO AUSABLE LIGHT STATION
3 MILES

H-58

H-58

WHITE BIRCH TRAIL
2 MILE

CP

C KINGSTON LAKE

SEVEN MILE CREEK TRAIL
.7 MILE

H58

SEE LAKESHORE TRAIL

LAKE SUPERIOR

MAP 2

BEAVER LAKE

SEE MAP 1

C

DAY HIKES
PICTURED ROCKS NATIONAL LAKESHORE

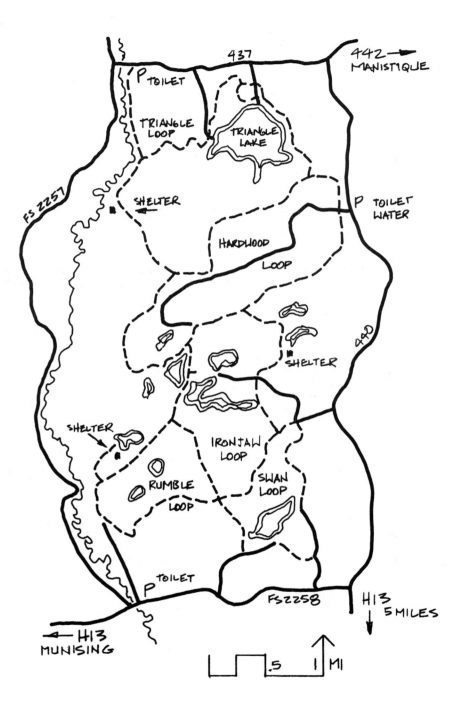

Rapid River/Manistique Ranger Dist. Hiawatha National Forest
8181 US 2   906-474-6442
Rapid River, MI 49878

Forest Supervisor, Hiawatha National Forest
2727 N. Lincoln Rd   906-786-4062
Escanaba, MI 49829

Michigan Atlas & Gazetteer Location: 102C4

County Location: Schoolcraft

Directions To Trailhead:
Located about 30 miles north of Manistique. From Manistique, take US 2 west about 10 miles to Cooks Rd, then north on CR442 to Co. Rd 437, then norht 16 miles to Triangle Lake Loop trailhead

Trail Type: Hiking/Walking, Mountain Biking
Trail Distance: 26 mi   Loops: 6   Shortest: 3.8 mi Longest: 7.2 mi
Trail Surface: Natural
Trail Use Fee: None
Method Of Ski Trail Grooming: NA
Skiing Ability Suggested: NA
Hiking Trail Difficulty: Moderate
Mountain Biking Ability Suggested: Intermediate to advanced
Terrain: Steep 0%, Hilly 20%, Moderate 30%, Flat 50%
Camping: Many national forest campgrounds in the area

Maintained by the Rapid River/Manistique Ranger Districts, Hiawatha National Forest Trail also used by horses but not frequently.
Water and toilets located at the C.R. 440 trailhead.
Toilets only at the Triangle Loop and FS 2258 trailheads.

PINE MARTEN RUN TRAIL

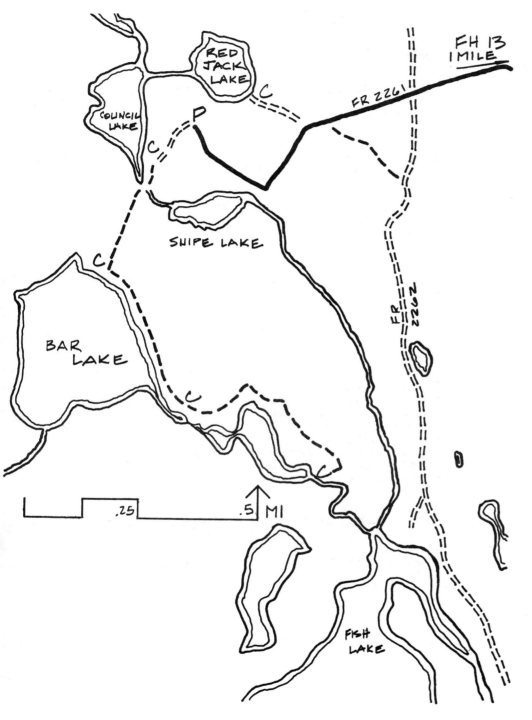

Red Buck Trail

Munising Ranger District, Hiawatha National Forest
RR 2 Box 400
Munising, Mi 49862

906-387-3700
906-387-2512

Forest Supervisor, Hiawatha National Forest
2727 N. Lincoln Rd
Escanaba, Mi 49829

906-786-4062

Michigan Atlas & Gazetteer Location: 102C3

County Location: Alger

Directions To Trailhead:
Take M28 east and FH 13 south 9 miles to Moccasin Lake , then west 1.5 miles west to Council Lake Primitive Campground. Trailhead is in the campground

Trail Type: Hiking/Walking
Trail Distance: 1.7 km   Loops: NA   Shortest: NA   Longest: NA
Trail Surface: Natural
Trail Use Fee: None
Method Of Ski Trail Grooming: NA
Skiing Ability Suggested: NA
Hiking Trail Difficulty: Easy
Mountain Biking Ability Suggested: NA
Terrain: Steep 0%, Hilly 0%, Moderate 20%, Flat 80%
Camping: At trailhead

Maintained by the Munising Ranger District, Hiawatha National Forest
Bruno's Run Trail and McKeever Hills Trail are very nearby.

RED BUCK TRAIL

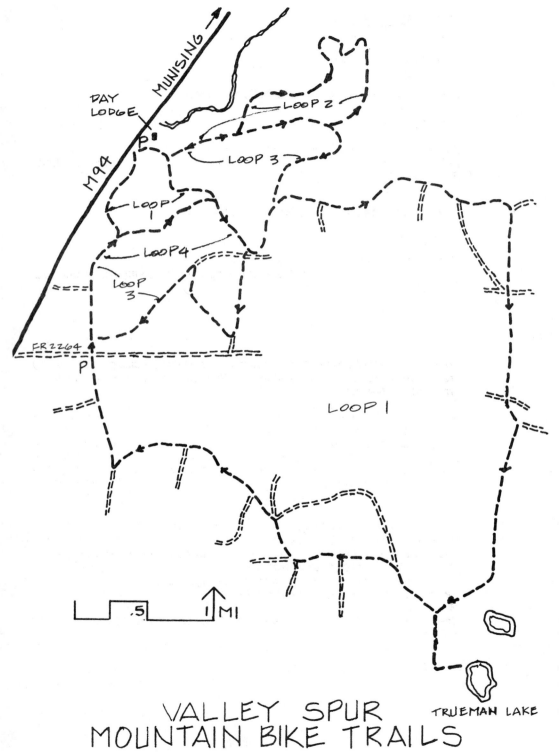

Valley Spur Mountain Bike Trail

Munising Ranger District, Hiawatha National Forest
RR 2, Box 400
Munising, MI 49862

906-387-3700
906-387-2512

Forest Supervisor, Hiawatha National Forest
2727 N. Lincoln Rd
Escanaba, MI 49829

906-786-4062

Michigan Atlas & Gazetteer Location: 102AB3

County Location: Alger

Directions To Trailhead:
From Munising on M28 to M94 south.
Main trailhead - 5 miles to trailhead at the Valley Spur Ski Trail on the east side of the road.
Second trailhead - about 6.5 miles to FR2264(next to Coalwood Rail Trail), east about .5 mile to trailhead parking.

Trail Type: Hiking/Walking, Mountain Biking
Trail Distance: 15+ mi   Loops: 4   Shortest: 3 mi   Longest: 12 mi
Trail Surface: Natural, single track and 2 track
Trail Use Fee: None
Method Of Ski Trail Grooming: NA
Skiing Ability Suggested: NA
Hiking Trail Difficulty: Easy
Mountain Biking Ability Suggested: Novice to advanced
Terrain: Steep 0%, Hilly 10%, Moderate 50%, Flat 30%
Camping: AuTrain Lake NFCG

Maintained by the Munising Ranger District, Hiawatha National Forest
New trail system developed in 1994.

Route 1 - 12 miles, Novice, gentle grades, mostly woods roads, side trip to Truman Lake
Route 2 - 4 miles, Advanced, very challenging route with steep uphills and downhills
Route 3 - 7.5 miles, Novice, generally flat with one steep hill, last .5 mile is all downhill
Route 4 - 3 miles, Novice, flat, access from second trailhead parking area

These trails are not exclusively for use by mountain bikers. Mountain bikers must share the trail with others.

Open May through November.

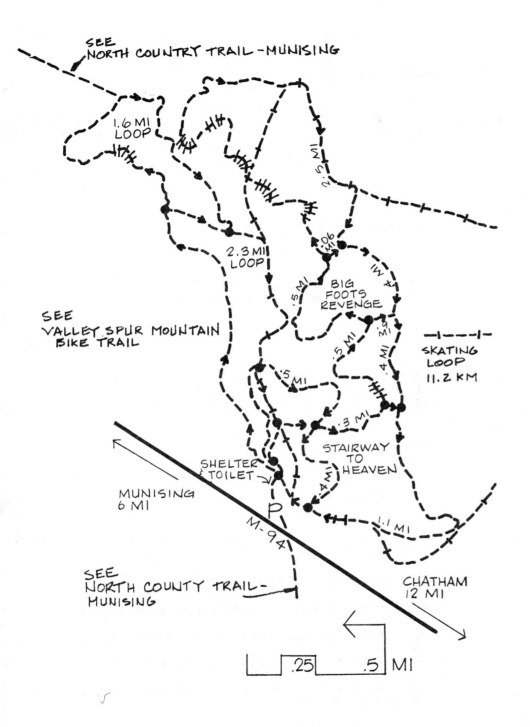

SEE
NORTH COUNTRY TRAIL - MUNISING

1.6 MI
LOOP

2.3 MI
LOOP

SEE
VALLEY SPUR MOUNTAIN
BIKE TRAIL

.06
MI

BIG
FOOTS
REVENGE

.5 MI

.5 MI

SKATING
LOOP
11.2 KM

.4 MI

.5 MI

.3 MI

STAIRWAY
TO
HEAVEN

SHELTER
& TOILET

.4 MI

MUNISING
6 MI

M-94

P

1.1 MI

SEE
NORTH COUNTRY TRAIL -
MUNISING

CHATHAM
12 MI

.25   .5 MI

VALLEY SPUR SKI TRAIL

Valley Spur Ski Trail

Munising Ranger District, Hiawatha National Forest
RR 2, Box 400   906-387-2512
Munising, MI 49862

Forest Supervisor, Hiawatha National Forest
2727 N. Lincoln Rd.   906-786-4062
Escanaba, MI 49829

Michigan Atlas & Gazetteer Location: 102AB3

County Location: Alger

Directions To Trailhead:
6 miles SW of Munising on M94, to the parking lot on the south side of the road.

Trail Type: Hiking/Walking, Cross Country Skiing, Mountain Biking
Trail Distance: 30 km   Loops: Many   Shortest: 1.5 km Longest: 11 km
Trail Surface: Natural
Trail Use Fee: Yes, for skiing only
Method Of Ski Trail Grooming: Track set
Skiing Ability Suggested: Novice to advanced
Hiking Trail Difficulty: Moderate
Mountain Biking Ability Suggested: Novice to advanced
Terrain: Steep 15%, Hilly 35%, Moderate 30%, Flat 20%
Camping: AuTrain Campground, 7 miles west

Maintained by Munising Ranger District, Hiawatha National Forest
A well designed and groomed ski trail for all abilities.
A large trailhead cabin is open on weekends, with food service and ski rentals.
Outdoor toilet is available at the trailhead.
Forest cover includes hardwoods with conifer-ringed valleys.
Part of the North Country Trail - Munising.
Many other nearby trails.
Uses the same trailhead for the Valley Spur Mountain Bike Trail (see other listing)

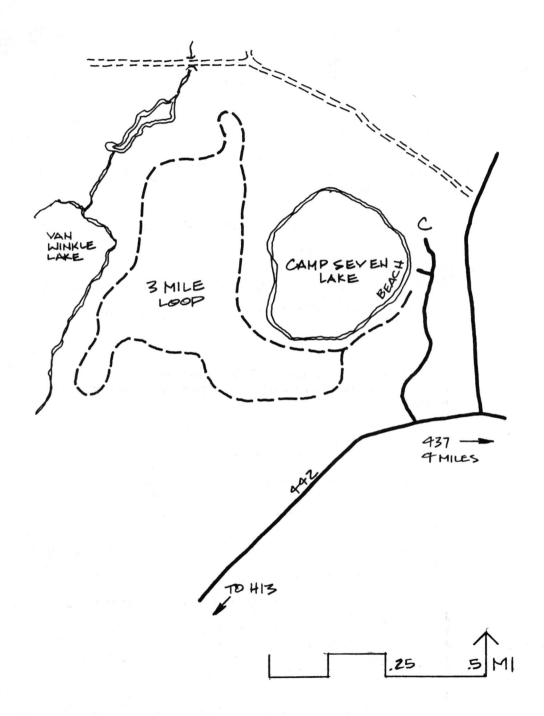

Rapid River/Manistique Ranger Dist., Hiawatha National Forest
8181 US 2   906-474-6442
Rapid River, MI 49878

Michigan Atlas & Gazetteer Location: 102D4

County Location: Delta

Directions To Trailhead:
From Manistique, take US2 west to Co. Rd 437, then north to Co Rd 443, then west to Camp Seven Lake national forest campground

Trail Type: Hiking/Walking, Mountain Biking, Interpretive
Trail Distance: 3 mi   Loops: 1   Shortest: NA   Longest: 3 mi
Trail Surface: Natural
Trail Use Fee: None
Method Of Ski Trail Grooming: NA
Skiing Ability Suggested: NA
Hiking Trail Difficulty: Easy
Mountain Biking Ability Suggested: Novice
Terrain: Steep 0%, Hilly 0%, Moderate 0%, Flat 100%
Camping: Campground at trailhead

Maintained by the Rapid River/Manistique Ranger Districts, Hiawatha National Forest   Trail starts at the boat launch.
Campground has 41 campsites, beach, changing house and picnic area.
Trail provides an explanation of the ecology and history of the area.

VAN WINKLE NATURE TRAIL

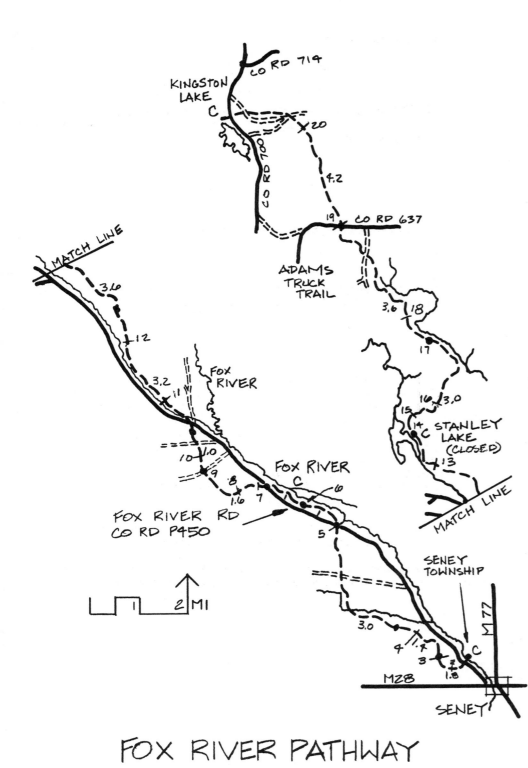

Shingleton Forest Area, Lake Superior State Forest
West M28, PO Box 67
Shingleton, MI 49884

906-452-6236

District Forest Manager, Lake Superior State Forest
South M123, PO Box 77
Newberry, MI 49868

906-239-5131

Michigan Atlas & Gazetteer Location: 103A78,104B1,115D78

County Location: Schoolcraft

Directions To Trailhead:
North trailhead - Kingston Lake Camprgound in Pictured Rocks NLonCo Rd 714
(H58) or Kingston Lake Rd.)
South trailhead - .5 mile north of Seney on Co Rd 450 (Fox River Rd.) at Seney
Township Campground

Trail Type: Hiking/Walking, Mountain Biking, Interpretive
Trail Distance: 27.5 mi   Loops: NA   Shortest: NA   Longest: NA
Trail Surface: NA
Trail Use Fee: None
Method Of Ski Trail Grooming: NA
Skiing Ability Suggested: NA
Hiking Trail Difficulty: Moderate to difficult
Mountain Biking Ability Suggested: Novice to intermediate
Terrain: Steep 0%, Hilly 20%, Moderate 40%, Flat 40%
Camping: Four campgrounds available along the trail

Maintained by the DNR Forest Management Division
Not frequently used trail but does pass through some very beautiful and isolated
land.
Since the trail is rather isolated, prepare well for the trip because emergency
assistance will not be available.
Twenty-one marked locations along the trail provide interesting information
about the history of the area.
Recent (1994) information about the condition of the trail is not favorable. The
first few miles from the south trail are marked. However farther north the
condition is very questionable. Contact the local DNR office listed above
regarding current conditions before planning a trip.

Other contacts:
        DNR Forest Management Division Office, Lansing, 517-373-1275
        DNR Forest Management Region Office, Marquette, 906-228-6561

FOX RIVER PATHWAY

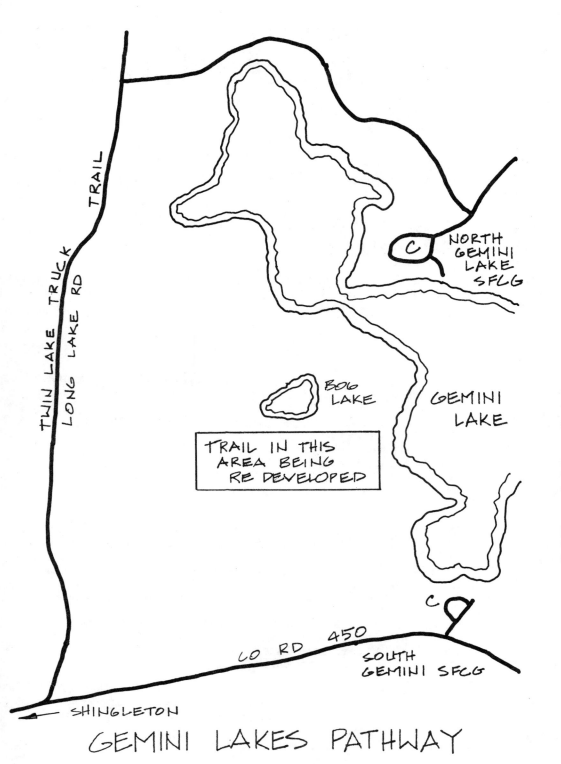

Shingleton Forest Area, Lake Superior State Forest
PO Box 67   906-452-6227
Shingleton, MI 49884

District Forest Manager, Lake Superior State Forest
PO Box 77   906-293-5151
Newberry, MI 49868

Michigan Atlas & Gazetteer Location: 103A6

County Location: Schoolcraft

Directions To Trailhead:
Northeast of Shingleton via north on H15, east on H58, then east on H52, then north on 454, then east on 450

Trail Type: Hiking/Walking

Trail Surface:
Trail Use Fee: None
Method Of Ski Trail Grooming:
Skiing Ability Suggested:
Hiking Trail Difficulty:
Mountain Biking Ability Suggested:
Terrain:
Camping: SFCG at the trailhead

Maintained by the DNR Forest Management Division
Currently under redevelopment (1994)
Contact DNR for current status.

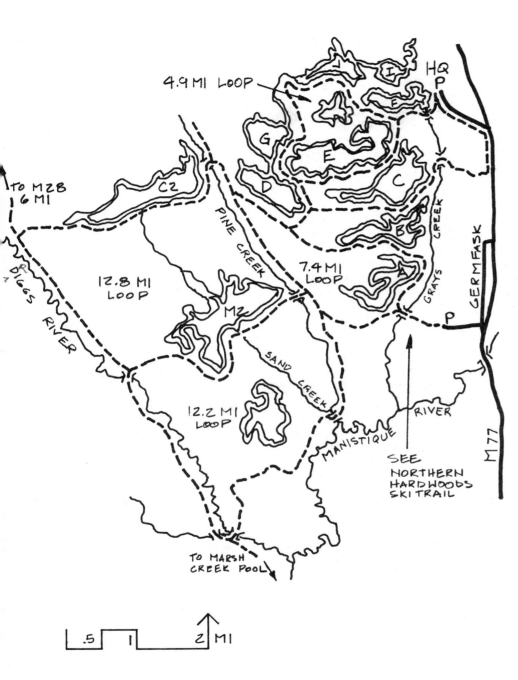

Seney National Wildlife Refuge ✈
HCR2, Box 1
Seney, MI 49883

906-586-9851
906-586-9801

*120 MILES FROM Harbor Springs

Michigan Atlas & Gazetteer Location: 103BC8,104BC1

County Location: Schoolcraft

Directions To Trailhead:
At Germfask on M77, just north of town.

Trail Type: Hiking/Walking, Cross Country Skiing, Mountain Biking, Interpretive
Trail Distance: 50+ mi   Loops: Many   Shortest: .8 mi   Longest: Long
Trail Surface: Gravel and natural
Trail Use Fee: Yes, vehicle entry fee at headquarters parking area only
Method Of Ski Trail Grooming: None
Skiing Ability Suggested: Novice
Hiking Trail Difficulty: Easy
Mountain Biking Ability Suggested: Novice
Terrain: Steep 0%, Hilly 0%, Moderate 30%, Flat 70%
Camping: None

Maintained by the Fish and Wildlife Service
Warming shelter available
Prohibited for use by ORV's and snowmobiles
Over 95,000 acres containing over 250 species of birds
Bike trails: 4.8 to 12.8 mile loops and greater on gravel dike roads
See also Northern Hardwoods Cross Country Ski Trails
Bike, canoe and ski rentals from Gronback-Northern Outfitters in Germfask
906-586-9801

MOUNTAIN BIKE TRAIL
SENEY NATIONAL WILDLIFE REFUGE

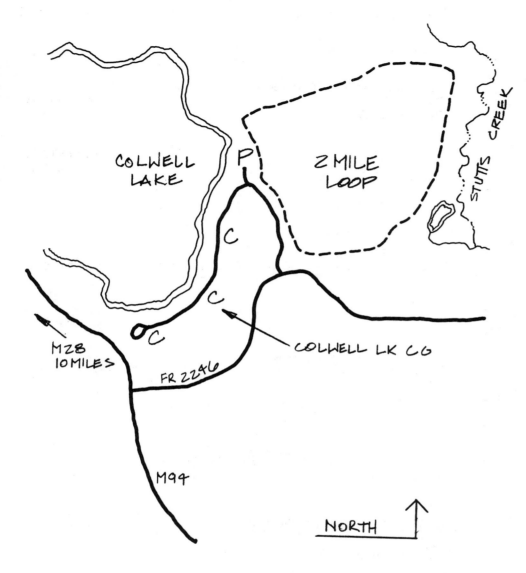

Rapid River/Manistique Ranger Dist., Hiawatha National Forest
8181 US 2
Rapid River, MI 49878   906-474-6442

Michigan Atlas & Gazetteer Location: 103C5

County Location: Schoolcraft

Directions To Trailhead:
 Between Shingleton and Manistique on M 94 about 10 miles south of Shingleton.

Trail Type: Hiking/Walking
Trail Distance: 2 mi   Loops: 1   Shortest: NA   Longest: 2 mi
Trail Surface: Natural
Trail Use Fee: None
Method Of Ski Trail Grooming: NA
Skiing Ability Suggested: NA
Hiking Trail Difficulty: Easy
Mountain Biking Ability Suggested: NA
Terrain: Steep 0%, Hilly 0%, Moderate 0%, Flat 100%
Camping: At trailhead

Maintained by the Rapid River/Manistique Ranger District, Hiawatha National Forest Colwell Lake National Forest campground is at the trailhead.
Trailhead at the boat launch.
Campground has 32 sites.
Trail passes through a variety of forest types and wetlands. Stairs and boardwalks are along the trail.

STUTTS CREEK TRAIL

Curtis Area Chamber of Commerce
PO Box 477   906-586-3700
Curtis, MI 49820

Manilak Resort
RR3, Box 2620   906-586-3285
Curtis, MI 49820   or 6690

Michigan Atlas & Gazetteer Location: 104C2

County Location: Mackinac

Directions To Trailhead:
2 miles west and south of Curtis off Main St, then south on S. Curtis Rd and Sprang Rd, then west on Barrett Rd to the end of the road.

Trail Type: Cross Country Skiing
Trail Distance: 1.1 mi   Loops: 4   Shortest: .2 mi   Longest: .5 mi
Trail Surface: Natural
Trail Use Fee: Donations
Method Of Ski Trail Grooming: Skating
Skiing Ability Suggested: Novice
Hiking Trail Difficulty: NA
Mountain Biking Ability Suggested: NA
Terrain: Steep 0%, Hilly 15%, Moderate 25%, Flat 60%
Camping: None

Community maintained trail system.
Follow blue ribbons.
Another ski trail is in the area.

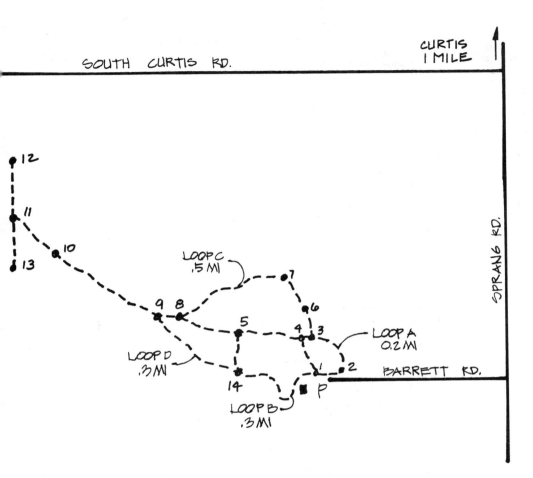

BARRETT ROAD SKI TRAILS.

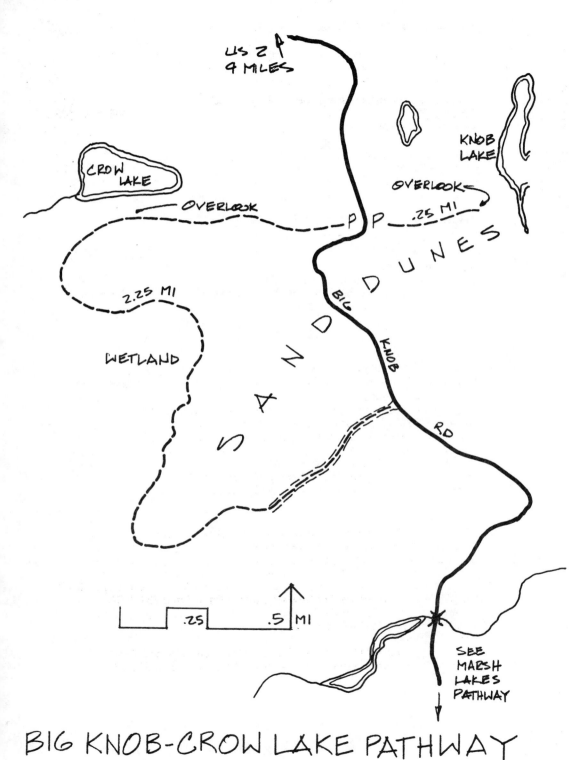

US 2
4 MILES

CROW LAKE

KNOB LAKE

OVERLOOK

OVERLOOK

.25 MI

S A N D   D U N E S

2.25 MI

WETLAND

BIG KNOB RD

.25   .5 MI

SEE MARSH LAKES PATHWAY

BIG KNOB-CROW LAKE PATHWAY

Naubinway Forest Area, Lake Superior State Forest
US2, PO Box 287   906-477-6048
Naubinway, MI 49762

District Forest Manager, Lake Superior State Forest
PO Box 77   906-293-5131
Newberry, MI 49868

Michigan Atlas & Gazetteer Location: 104D4

County Location: Mackinac

Directions To Trailhead:
About 55 miles west of the Mackinac Bridge, then 1.5 miles west of US2 & M123 intersection, then south 4 miles on Big Knob Rd. to the trailhead.

Trail Type: Hiking/Walking
Trail Distance: 2.75 mi   Loops: NA   Shortest: NA   Longest: NA
Trail Surface: Natural
Trail Use Fee: None
Method Of Ski Trail Grooming: NA
Skiing Ability Suggested: NA
Hiking Trail Difficulty: Easy to moderate
Mountain Biking Ability Suggested: NA
Terrain: Steep 20%, Hilly 20%, Moderate 30%, Flat 30%
Camping: On site at the Big Knob SFCG

Maintained by the DNR Forest Management Division
Scenic sand dune trail with 140' high overlook of Knob Lake
A loop route can be taken by using Big Knob Rd for the return trip to the trailhead.
Marsh Lakes Pathway is nearby.
Other contacts:
        DNR Forest Management Division, Lansing 517-373-1270
        DNR Forest Management Division , Marquette 906-228-6561

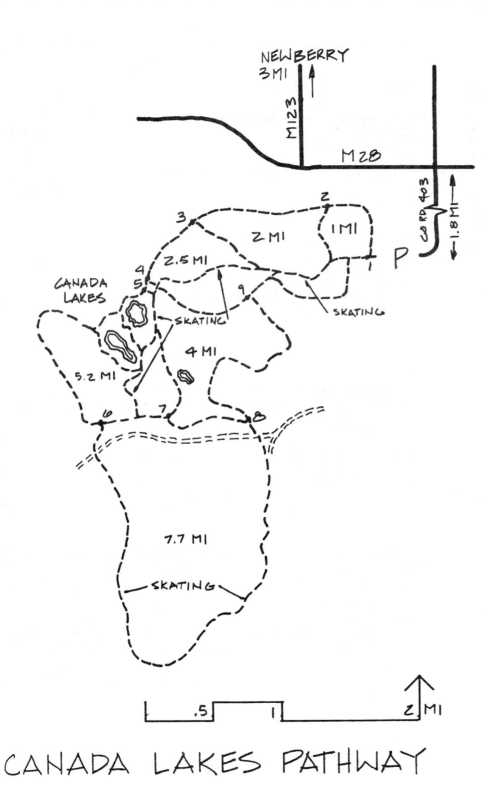

CANADA LAKES PATHWAY

Newberry Forest Area, Lake Superior State Forest
PO Box 428   906-293-3293
Newberry, MI 49868

District Forest Manager, Lake Superior State Forest
PO Box 77   906-293-5131
Newberry, MI 49868

Michigan Atlas & Gazetteer Location: 104B4,105B5

County Location: Luce

Directions To Trailhead:
5.5 miles SE of Newberry.
Trailhead - East 1 mile from the Jct of M123 and M28 to Co Rd 403, then south
1.5 miles to the parking lot trailhead.

Trail Type: Hiking/Walking, Cross Country Skiing, Mountain Biking
Trail Distance: 10+ mi   Loops: 6   Shortest: 1 mi   Longest: 7.7 mi
Trail Surface: Natural with sand
Trail Use Fee: Donation accepted at trailhead for grooming trails
Method Of Ski Trail Grooming: Track set
Skiing Ability Suggested: Novice and intermediate
Hiking Trail Difficulty: Easy
Mountain Biking Ability Suggested: Novice
Terrain: Steep 0%, Hilly 10%, Moderate 60%, Flat 30%
Camping: Public and private campgrounds in area

Maintained by the DNR Forest Management Division
Well groomed and very enjoyable skiing trail.
Some sections groomed for skating.
Site of an annual cross country ski race.
Campgrounds: North Country Campground, 4 miles north of Newberry on M123;
Natalie SFCG, 2 miles west of Newberry off Co Rd 405 and 434; KOA
Campground south of Newberry.
Logging museum in Newberry.
Other contacts:
        DNR Forest Manatement Division Office, Lansing, 517-373-1275
        DNR Forest Management Region Office, Marquette, 906-228-6561

Manilak Resort
RR3, Box 2620
McMillan, MI 49853

906-586-3285
906-586-6690

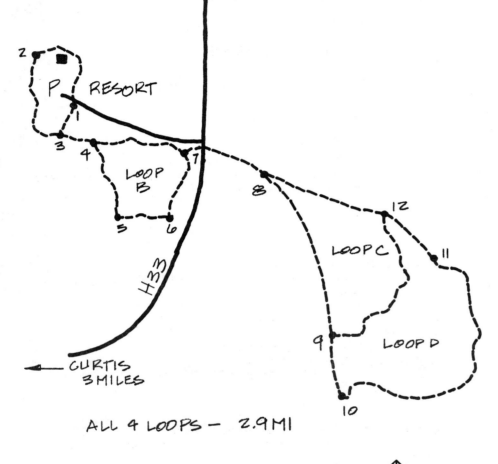

Michigan Atlas & Gazetteer Location: 104C3

County Location: Mackinac

Directions To Trailhead:
2 miles north of Curtis on H-33

Trail Type: Hiking/Walking, Cross Country Skiing
Trail Distance: 2.9 mi   Loops: 4   Shortest: .3 mi   Longest: 1.1 mi
Trail Surface: Natural
Trail Use Fee: None, but donations accepted
Method Of Ski Trail Grooming: Packed
Skiing Ability Suggested: Novice
Hiking Trail Difficulty: NA
Mountain Biking Ability Suggested: NA
Terrain: Steep 0%, Hilly 0%, Moderate 15%, Flat 85%
Camping: None

Privately operated trail system open to the public

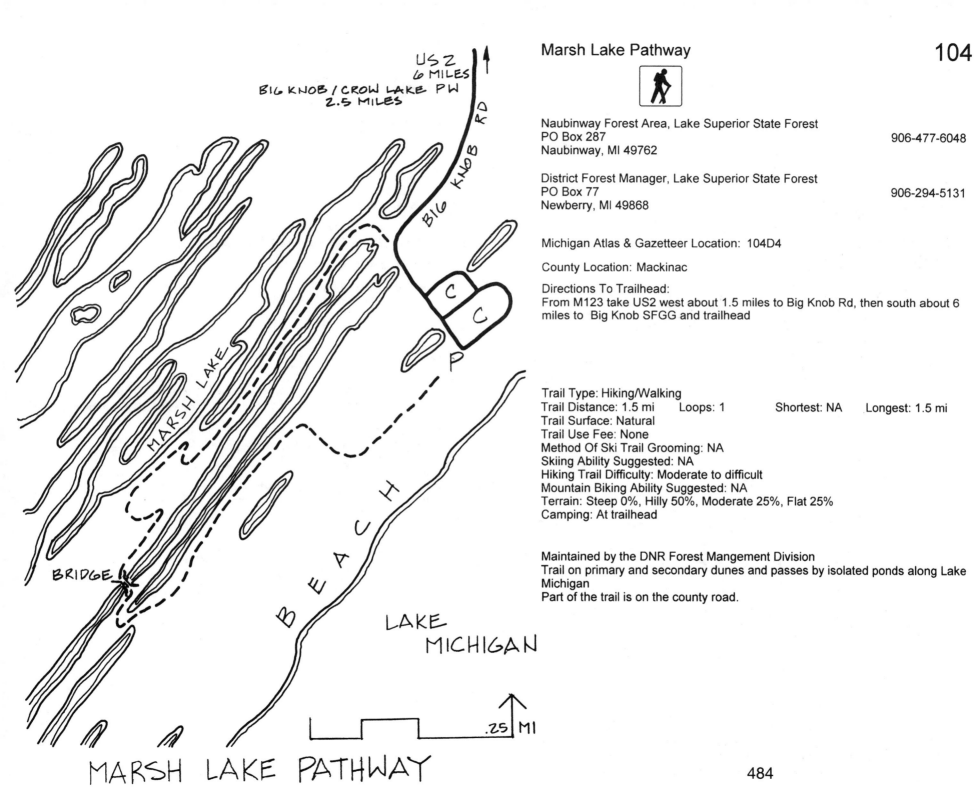

US 2
6 MILES

BIG KNOB / CROW LAKE PW
2.5 MILES

BIG KNOB RD

C
C
P

MARSH LAKE

BRIDGE

BEACH

LAKE
MICHIGAN

.25 MI

MARSH LAKE PATHWAY

Naubinway Forest Area, Lake Superior State Forest
PO Box 287   906-477-6048
Naubinway, MI 49762

District Forest Manager, Lake Superior State Forest
PO Box 77   906-294-5131
Newberry, MI 49868

Michigan Atlas & Gazetteer Location: 104D4

County Location: Mackinac

Directions To Trailhead:
From M123 take US2 west about 1.5 miles to Big Knob Rd, then south about 6 miles to Big Knob SFGG and trailhead

Trail Type: Hiking/Walking
Trail Distance: 1.5 mi   Loops: 1   Shortest: NA   Longest: 1.5 mi
Trail Surface: Natural
Trail Use Fee: None
Method Of Ski Trail Grooming: NA
Skiing Ability Suggested: NA
Hiking Trail Difficulty: Moderate to difficult
Mountain Biking Ability Suggested: NA
Terrain: Steep 0%, Hilly 50%, Moderate 25%, Flat 25%
Camping: At trailhead

Maintained by the DNR Forest Mangement Division
Trail on primary and secondary dunes and passes by isolated ponds along Lake Michigan
Part of the trail is on the county road.

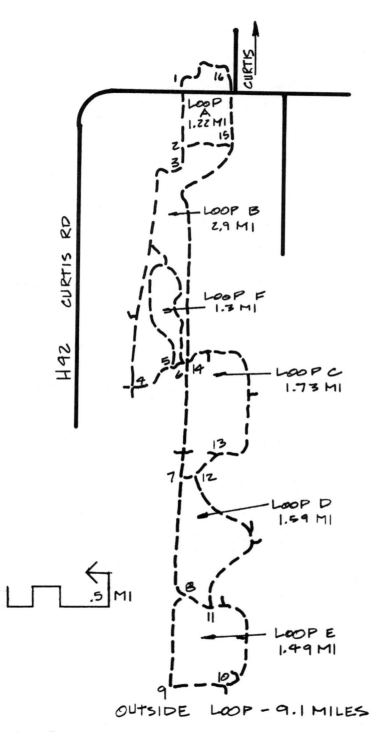

LOOP A
1.22 MI

LOOP B
2.9 MI

LOOP F
1.3 MI

LOOP C
1.73 MI

LOOP D
1.59 MI

LOOP E
1.49 MI

.5 MI

OUTSIDE LOOP - 9.1 MILES

NORTH CURTIS ROAD SKI TRAIL

Curtis Area Chamber of Commerce
Box 447
Curtis, MI 49820

Manilak Resort
RR3 Box 2620
Curtis, MI 49820

906-586-3285
906-586-6690

Michigan Atlas & Gazetteer Location: 104C2

County Location: Mackinac

Directions To Trailhead:
1 mile west of Curtis on Co Rd H-42 (North Curtis Rd) off Main St

Trail Type: Hiking/Walking, Cross Country Skiing, Mountain Biking
Trail Distance: 9.1 mi   Loops: 6   Shortest: 1.22 mi Longest: 2.92 mi
Trail Surface: Natural
Trail Use Fee: None
Method Of Ski Trail Grooming: Skating
Skiing Ability Suggested: Novice
Hiking Trail Difficulty: Easy
Mountain Biking Ability Suggested: Novice
Terrain: Steep 0%, Hilly 10%, Moderate 15%, Flat 75%
Camping: None

Maintained by the Manilak Resort on private property

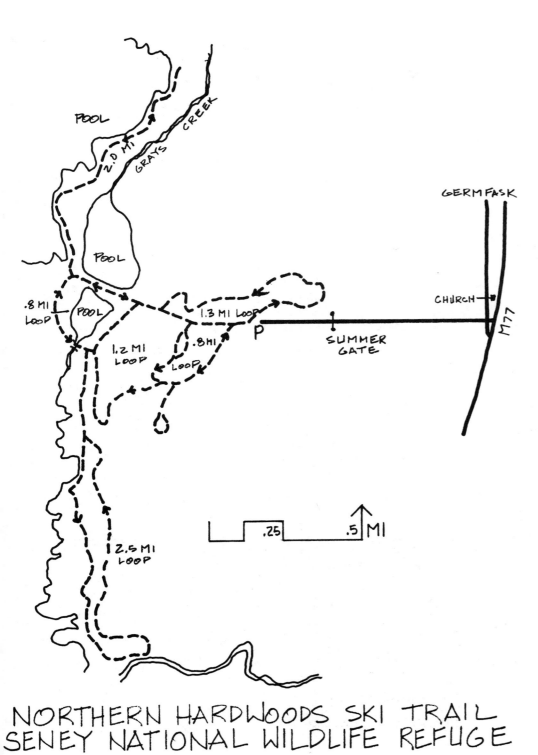

POOL

GRAYS CREEK

2.0 MI

POOL

POOL

.8 MI LOOP

1.2 MI LOOP

.8 MI LOOP

1.3 MI LOOP

P

SUMMER GATE

GERMFASK

CHURCH

M77

2.5 MI LOOP

.25 .5 MI

NORTHERN HARDWOODS SKI TRAIL
SENEY NATIONAL WILDLIFE REFUGE

Northern Hardwoods Cross Country Ski Trail

Seney National Wildlife Refuge
HCR2, Box 1   906-586-9851
Seney, MI 49883

Gronback-Northland Outfitters
PO Box 65   I906-586-9801
Germfask, MI 49836

Michigan Atlas & Gazetteer Location: 104BC1

County Location: Schoolcraft

Directions To Trailhead:
On M77 in Germfask, turn west on street just south of the Grace Lutheran
Church. Take road west to parking lot.
Trailhead is at the parking lot. In summer a gate limits vehicle access. However
actual use is not restricted.

Trail Type: Hiking/Walking, Cross Country Skiing
Trail Distance: 8.5 mi   Loops: 5   Shortest: .8 mi   Longest: 6 mi
Trail Surface: Natural
Trail Use Fee: None
Method Of Ski Trail Grooming: Track set
Skiing Ability Suggested: Novice to intermediate
Hiking Trail Difficulty: Easy
Mountain Biking Ability Suggested: NA
Terrain: Steep 0%, Hilly 0%, Moderate 30%, Flat 70%
Camping: None

Maintained by the Seney Wildlife Refuge and Gronback-Northland Outfitters

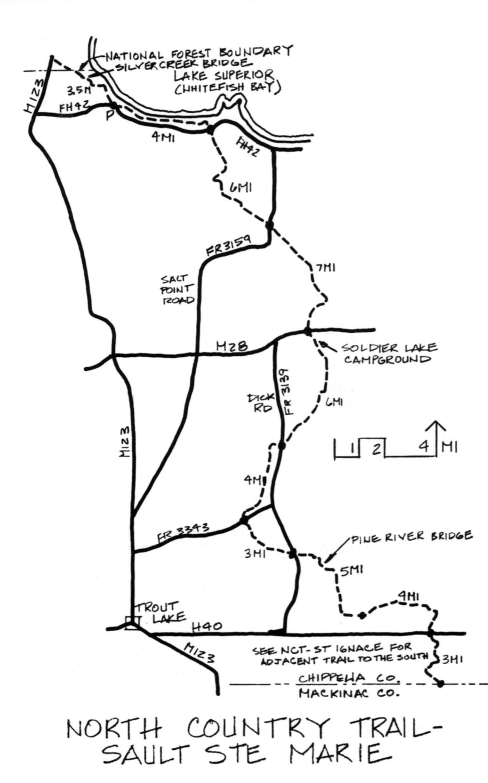

Sault Ste. Marie Ranger District, Hiawatha National Forest
4000 I-75 Business Loop
Sault Ste Marie, MI 49783   906-635-5311

Forest Supervisor, Hiawatha National Forest
2727 N. Lincoln Rd.
Escanaba, MI 49829   906-786-4062

Michigan Atlas & Gazetteer Location: 105A8,106ABC12,117D8

County Location: Chippewa

Directions To Trailhead:
Near East Lake at the Chippewa Co Line to Tahquamenon Falls State Park
South trailhead - Lookout on East Lake Dr. on Chippewa Co Line just south of H40
North trailhead - On FR 42(east of M123) .5 mile west of Lake Superior.

Trail Type: Hiking/Walking
Trail Distance: 42 mi   Loops: NA   Shortest: NA   Longest: NA
Trail Surface: Natural
Trail Use Fee: None
Method Of Ski Trail Grooming: NA
Skiing Ability Suggested: NA
Hiking Trail Difficulty: Moderate to difficult
Mountain Biking Ability Suggested: NA
Terrain: Flat to rolling
Camping: Campground at Soldier Lake and primitive campsites along the trail

Maintained by the Sault Ste. Marie Ranger District, Hiawatha National Forest
Connects to the North Country Trail - St. Ignace, on the south
Write the Sault Ste. Marie Ranger District for a detailed map. The trail continues north of the National Forest boundary for about 2 miles.
The trail can then be picked up at the River Unit campground of the Tahquamenon Falls State Park. See the state park for more detailed information on that section of the trail.
For more information contact the North Country Trail Association,   PO Box 311, White Cloud, MI 49349   616-689-1912
As with all of the North Country Trail in the national forest, wilderness camping is permitted 200' from the trail.

NORTH COUNTRY TRAIL-
SAULT STE MARIE

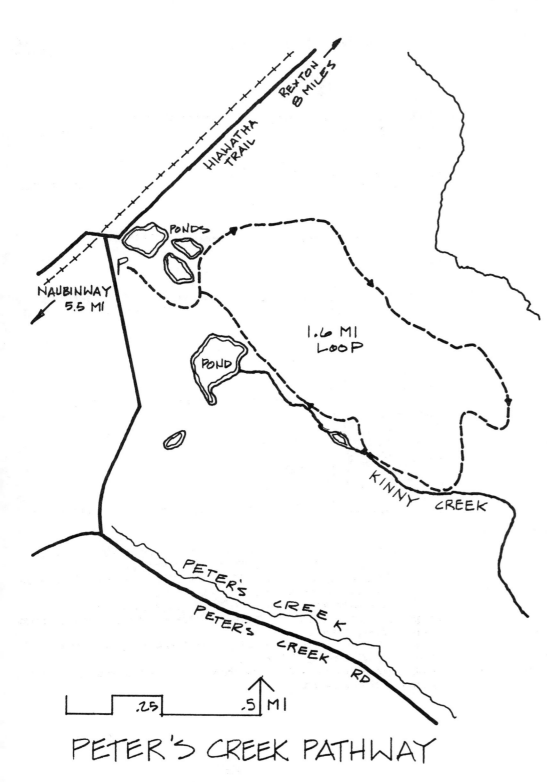

Peters Creek Ski Trail

Naubinway Forest Area, Lake Superior State Forest
PO Box 287   906-477-6048
Naubinway, MI 49762

District Forest Manager, Lake Superior State Forest
South M-123, PO Box 77   906-293-5131
Newberry, MI 49868

Michigan Atlas & Gazetteer Location: 105C5

County Location: Schoolcraft

Directions To Trailhead:
9 miles east of Engadine on Hiawatha Trail (H40) or 8 miles west of Rexton

Trail Type: Cross Country Skiing
Trail Distance: 1.6 mi   Loops: 1   Shortest: NA   Longest: 1.6 mi
Trail Surface: Natural
Trail Use Fee: None
Method Of Ski Trail Grooming: Yes
Skiing Ability Suggested: Novice
Hiking Trail Difficulty: NA
Mountain Biking Ability Suggested: NA
Terrain: 100% Flat
Camping: Black Creek State Forest Campground

Maintained by the DNR Forest Management Division
Trail designed for cross country skiing.
Used mostly by local skiers.

PETER'S CREEK PATHWAY

Naubinway State Forest, Lake Superior State Forest
PO Box 287   906-477-6048
Naubinway, Mi 49762

District Forest Manager, Lake Superior State Forest
PO Box 77   906-477-6048
Newberry, MI 49762

Michigan Atlas & Gazetteer Location: 105D8

County Location: Mackinac

Directions To Trailhead:
East of Brevoort on US2, 2 miles than north .5 mi to Little Brevoort Lake SFCG and trailhead.

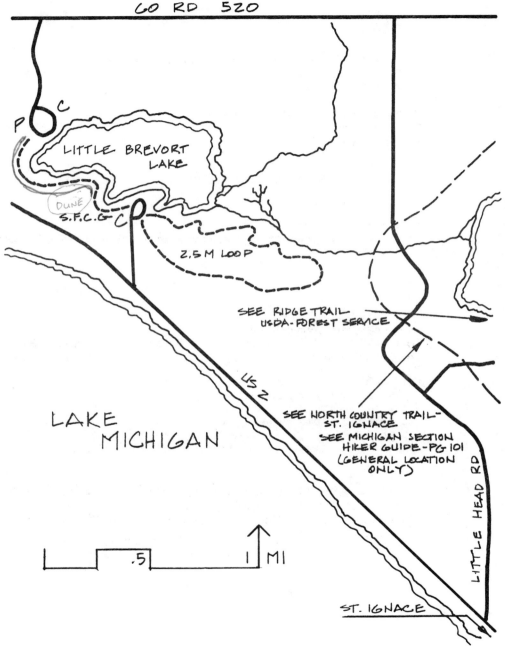

Trail Type: Hiking/Walking
Trail Distance: 2.5 mi   Loops: 1   Shortest: NA   Longest: 2.5 mi
Trail Surface: Natural
Trail Use Fee: None
Method Of Ski Trail Grooming: NA
Skiing Ability Suggested: NA
Hiking Trail Difficulty: Moderate
Mountain Biking Ability Suggested: NA
Terrain: Steep 0%, Hilly 60%, Moderate 40%, Flat 0%
Camping: At trailhead, along trail and neaby SFCG

Maintained by the DNR Forest Management Division
A pleasant short trail along LIttle Brevoort Lake and River.
The North Country Trail - St. Ignace segment is within a mile east of the trail.(see other listing)
The Ridge Trail (see other listing) and Brevoort Lake National Forest Campground is located just to the east on Brevoort Lake.

SWITCHBACK RIDGE PATHWAY

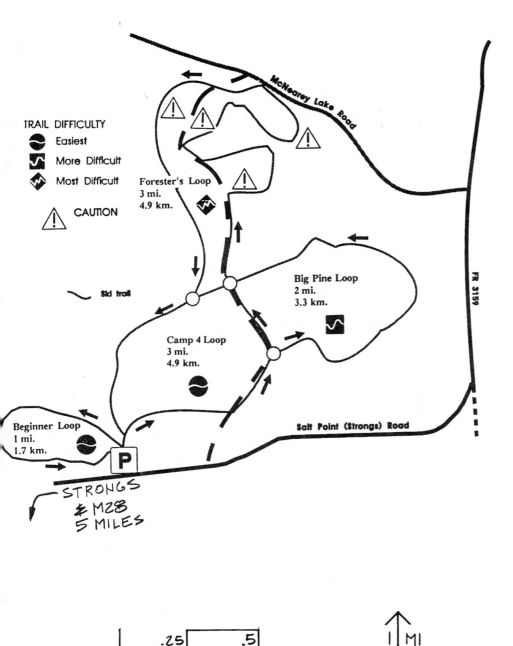

Sault Saint Marie Ranger District, Hiawatha National Forest
4000 I-75 Business Spur   906-635-5311
Sault Ste. Marie, MI 49783

Forest Supervisor, Hiawatha National Forest
2727 N. Lincoln Rd   906-786-4062
Escanaba, MI 49829

Michigan Atlas & Gazetteer Location: 106A1

County Location: Chippewa

Directions To Trailhead:
West of Sault Ste Marie. 4 miles north of M28 on FR 3159 (Salt Point Rd) north of Strongs.

Trail Type: Cross Country Skiing
Trail Distance: 8 mi   Loops: 4   Shortest: 1 mi   Longest: 3 mi
Trail Surface: Natural
Trail Use Fee: None
Method Of Ski Trail Grooming: None
Skiing Ability Suggested: Novice to intermediate
Hiking Trail Difficulty: NA
Mountain Biking Ability Suggested: NA
Terrain: Steep 0%, Hilly 33%, Moderate 23%, Flat 44%
Camping: Nearby at Solder Lake NFCG

Maintained by the Sault Ste Marie Ranger District, Hiawatha National Forest
Four loops with different skill levels requried
North Country Trail - Sault Ste Marie passes this trail about 1.5 miles to the northeast

Map labels

TRAIL DIFFICULTY
- Easiest
- More Difficult
- Most Difficult

⚠ CAUTION

~ Ski trail

McNearey Lake Road

Forester's Loop
3 mi.
4.9 km.

Big Pine Loop
2 mi.
3.3 km.

Camp 4 Loop
3 mi.
4.9 km.

FR 3159

Salt Point (Strongs) Road

Beginner Loop
1 mi.
1.7 km.

P

STRONGS
& M28
5 MILES

.25   .5   1 MI

McNEARNEY SKI TRAIL

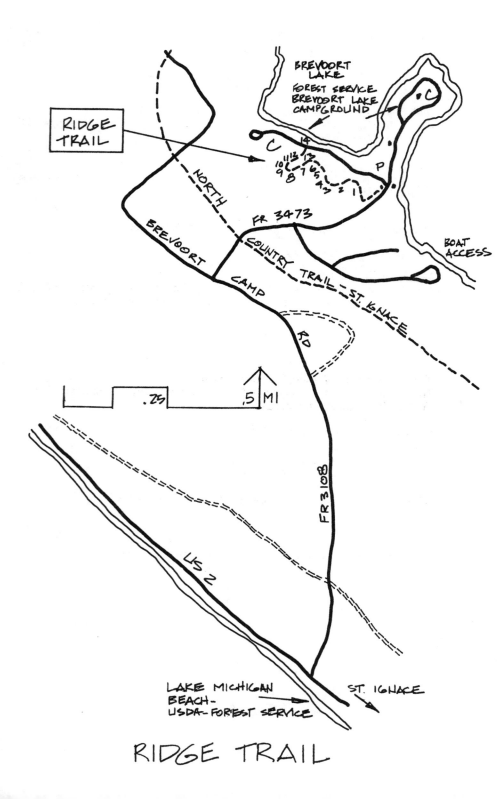

RIDGE TRAIL

St. Ignace Ranger District, Hiawatha National Forest
1498 West US 2
St. Ignace, MI 49781

906-643-7900

Forest Supervisor, Hiawatha National Forest
2727 N. Lincoln Rd
Escanaba, MI 49829

906-786-4062

Michigan Atlas & Gazetteer Location: 106D1

County Location: Mackinac

Directions To Trailhead:
West of St. Ignace at the Brevoort Lake National Forest Campground (not Little Brevoort Lake State Forest Campground) On US 2 , 1/2 mile west of the Lake Michigan National Forest Campground, take the first road north which is the Brevoort Camp Rd (FR 3108), then right on FR 3473 to the campground. Just past the RV trailer dump station, the trailhead is on the left, just before a road to campsites 50 - 71.

Trail Type: Hiking/Walking, Interpretive
Trail Distance: 1 mi   Loops: 1   Shortest: NA   Longest: 1 mi
Trail Surface: Natural
Trail Use Fee: None
Method Of Ski Trail Grooming: NA
Skiing Ability Suggested: NA
Hiking Trail Difficulty: Moderate
Mountain Biking Ability Suggested: NA
Terrain: Steep 10%, Hilly 15%, Moderate 60%, Flat 10%
Camping: National forest campground at the trailhead.

Maintained by the St. Ignace Ranger District, Hiawatha National Forest
The 20 minute nature trail that has 14 stations.
Trail guide available at the campground or district headquarters.
Scenic view from the trail of Lake Michigan 1 1/4 miles from the trail.

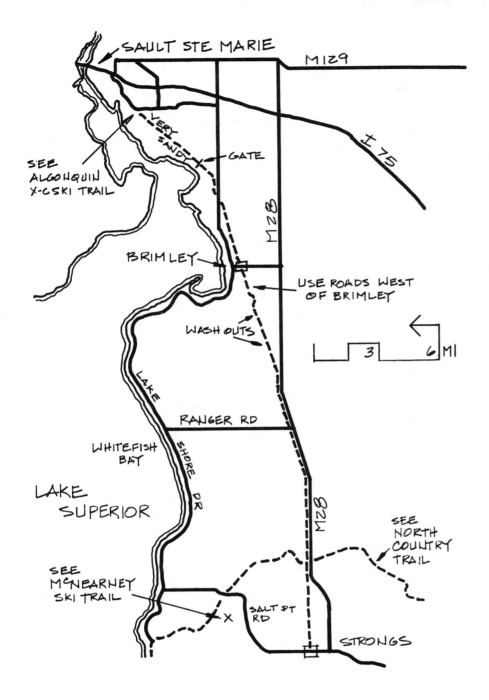

Sault Ste Marie Forest Area, Lake Superior State Forest
2001 Ashman, PO Box 798
Sault Ste Marie, MI 49738

906-635-5281

District Forest Manager, Lake Superior State Forest
PO Box 77
Newberry, MI 49868

906-293-5131

Michigan Atlas & Gazetteer Location: 106AB1234,107A5

County Location: Chippewa

Directions To Trailhead:
East trailhead - Exit I-75 at 3 mile Rd in Sault Ste Marie, then west on 3 Mile Rd for about 1 mile, then right on 20th St for about 1.25 miles to trailhead.

Trail Type: Hiking/Walking, Mountain Biking
Trail Distance: 32 mi   Loops: NA   Shortest: NA   Longest: NA
Trail Surface: Natural and ballast
Trail Use Fee: None
Method Of Ski Trail Grooming: NA
Skiing Ability Suggested: NA
Hiking Trail Difficulty: Easy to moderate
Mountain Biking Ability Suggested: Intermediate
Terrain: 100% Flat
Camping: Campground at nearby Brimley State Park and NFCG

Maintained by the DNR Forest Management Division
The North Country Trail crosses at Soldier Lake NFCG access road.

SOO-STRONGS RAIL-TRAIL

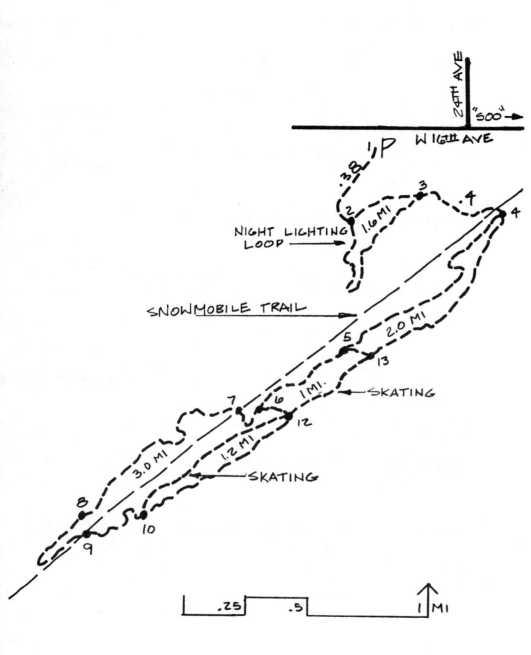

Sault Ste. Marie Forest Area, Lake Superior State Forest
2001 Ashmun St., PO Box 798
Sault Ste. Marie, MI 49783

906-635-5281

District Forest Manager, Lake Superior State Forest
PO Box 77
Newberry, MI 49868

906-293-5131

Michigan Atlas & Gazetteer Location: 107A5

County Location: Chippewa

Directions To Trailhead:
2 miles west of I-75, SW of Sault Ste. Marie, Michigan.
Take 3 Mile Rd. exit off of I-75, then west on 3 Mile Rd about 1 mile to Baker Rd, right on Baker Rd to 16th Ave. Left (west) on 16th Ave to trailhead which is about 1 mile on the left.

Trail Type: Hiking/Walking, Cross Country Skiing
Trail Distance: 8.8 mi   Loops: 5   Shortest: 1 mi   Longest: 3 mi
Trail Surface: Natural
Trail Use Fee: None, but donations are accepted to groom the trail
Method Of Ski Trail Grooming: Track set
Skiing Ability Suggested: Novice to intermediate
Hiking Trail Difficulty: Easy
Mountain Biking Ability Suggested: NA
Terrain: Steep 0%, Hilly 0%, Moderate 10%, Flat 90%
Camping: Campgrounds avaialble locally

Maintained by the DNR Forest Management Division
Although near Sault Ste. Marie, the trail is very secluded in a mixed hardwood and evergreen forest.
A very popular ski trail especially used by the local college students.
The Soo-Strongs Rail Trail passes through trail system, which is used for snowmobiling in the winter months.

ALGONQUIN CROSS COUNTRY SKI TRAIL

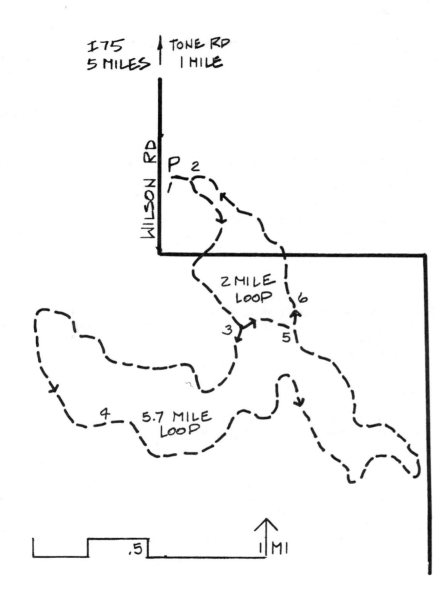

I75
5 MILES

↑ TONE RD
1 MILE

WILSON RD

P 2

2 MILE
LOOP

6

3

5

4   5.7 MILE
LOOP

.5   1 MI

PINE BOWL PATHWAY

Sault Ste. Marie Forest Area, Lake Superior State Forest
2001 Ashmun St., PO Box 798   906-635-5281
Sault Ste Marie, MI 49783

District Forest Manager, Lake Superior State Forest
South M123, PO Box 77   906-293-5131
Newberry, MI 49868

Michigan Atlas & Gazetteer Location: 107C5

County Location: Chippewa

Directions To Trailhead:
16 miles south of Sault Ste. Marie on I-75 at the Kinross exit 378
Trailhead - Exit I-75 east on Tone Rd. 4 miles to Wilson Rd., then south .75 mile
to parking lot

Trail Type: Hiking/Walking, Cross Country Skiing, Mountain Biking
Trail Distance: 7.7 mi   Loops: 2   Shortest: 2 mi   Longest: 5.7 mi
Trail Surface: Track set
Trail Use Fee: Donations accepted at trailhead
Method Of Ski Trail Grooming: Track set weekly or more if needed
Skiing Ability Suggested: Novice
Hiking Trail Difficulty: Easy
Mountain Biking Ability Suggested: Novice to intermediate
Terrain: 100% Flat
Camping: None

Maintained by the DNR Forest Management Division
Wooded trails.
Food and lodging available in Kinross.
Popular trail with local skiers.
Other contacts:
        DNR Forest Management Division Office, Lansing, 517-373-1275
        DNR Forest Management Region Office, Marquette, 906-228-6561

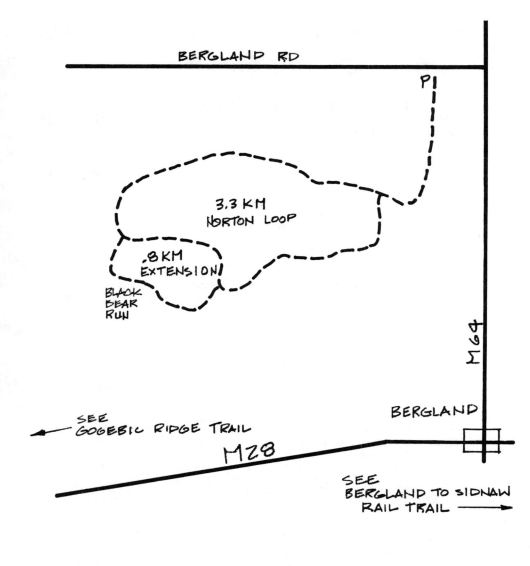

BERGLAND RD

P1

3.3 KM
NORTON LOOP

.8 KM
EXTENSION

BLACK
BEAR
RUN

M64

SEE
GOGEBIC RIDGE TRAIL

M28

BERGLAND

SEE
BERGLAND TO SIDNAW
RAIL TRAIL ➔

.5 KM

BERGLAND SKI TRAIL

Bergland Ski Trail

Bergland Ranger District, Ottawa National Forest
M28, PO Box 126   906-575-3441
Bergland, MI 49910   906-575-3877TTY

Recreation Staff Officer, Ottawa National Forest
2100 E. Cloverland Drive   906-932-1330
Ironwood, MI 49938

Michigan Atlas & Gazetteer Location: 108D4

County Location: Ontonagon

Directions To Trailhead:
Trailhead - 1mile north of the Bergland on M6, then left (west) 100 yds to parking area and trailhead.

Trail Type: Cross Country Skiing
Trail Distance: 2.9 mi   Loops: 2   Shortest: 2.6 mi Longest: 2.9 mi
Trail Surface: Natural
Trail Use Fee: None
Method Of Ski Trail Grooming: Track set occasionally
Skiing Ability Suggested: Novice to intermediate
Hiking Trail Difficulty: NA
Mountain Biking Ability Suggested: NA
Terrain: Steep 0%, Hilly 15%, Moderate 35%, Flat 50%
Camping: Campground available at Lake Gogebic State Park

Maintained by the Bergland Ranger District, Ottawa National Forest
A well marked but not frequently used ski trail.
Food and lodging available in Bergland.
Other trails in the area are the Gogebic Ridge Hiking Trail and the North Country Trail - Bergland.

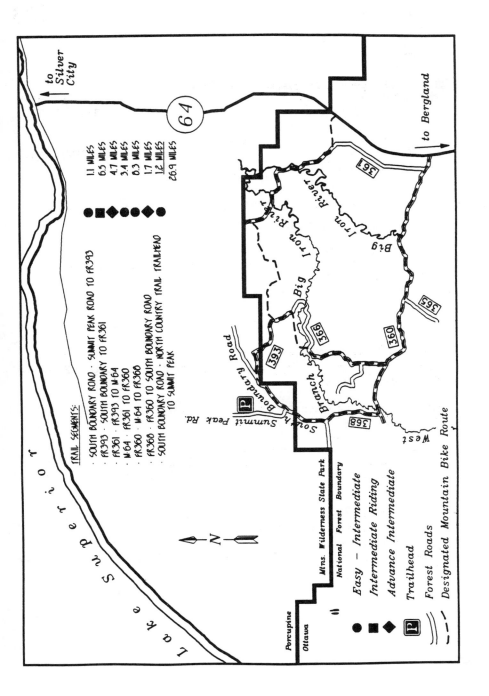

Bergland Ranger District, Ottawa National Forest
M28. PO Box 126
Bergland, MI 49910

906-575-3441

Recreation Staff Officer, Ottawa National Forest
2100 E. Cloverland Drive
Ironwood, MI 49938

906-932-1330

Michigan Atlas & Gazetteer Location: 108BC234

County Location: Ontonagon

Directions To Trailhead:
East Trailhead - West of M64, 5 miles north of Bergland on FR 360

Trail Type: Mountain Biking
Trail Distance: 26.9 mi   Loops: Shortest: Longest:
Trail Surface: Gravel, sand and natural
Trail Use Fee: None
Method Of Ski Trail Grooming: NA
Skiing Ability Suggested: NA
Hiking Trail Difficulty: NA
Mountain Biking Ability Suggested: Novice to advanced
Terrain: Steep 0%, Hilly 30%, Moderate 30%, Flat 40%
Camping: Several Campgrounds in the area

Maintained by the Bergland Ranger District, Ottawa National Forest.
Trails designated in 1994.
From their literature,"Challenging trip through a northern hardwood forest, over
open gravel roads as well as closed, overgrown logging roads. There are many
beaver dams to navigate around....Hazards include beaver ponds, crossing the
West Branch of the Big Iron River (no bridge) and deep ruts in various locations.
Some parts of the trail are open roads used by commercial vehicles; some
closed roads also currently being used as parts of the North Country National
Scenic Hiking Trail. Check conditions of the Big Iron River crossing before
embarking on any trip. Check in at either the State Park or any National Forest
Offices to report any adverse trail conditons and to let the Forest Service know
how you liked the ride."

EHLCO MOUNTAIN BIKE COMLEX

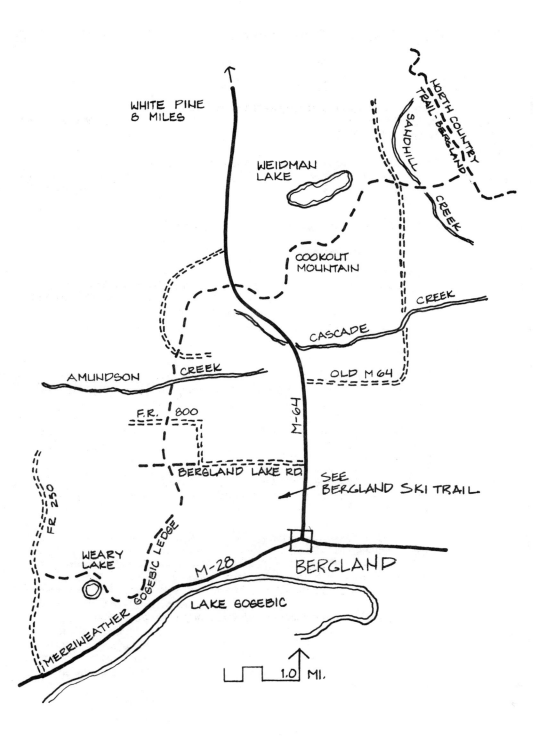

Bergland Ranger District, Ottawa National Forest
M28, PO Box 126
Bergland, MI 49910

906-575-3441

Recreation Staff Officer, Ottawa National Forest
2100 E. Cloverland Drive
Ironwood, MI 49938

906-932-1330

Michigan Atlas & Gazetteer Location: 108CD34

County Location: Ontonagon

Directions To Trailhead:
Bergland Trail trailhead - 3 miles north of Bergland on M64
West trailhead - 1.5 miles north of M28 on FR 250, 3 miles west of Bergland
East trailhead - North Country Trail - Bergland segment near the Sandhill Creek crossing

Trail Type: Hiking/Walking
Trail Distance: 9 mi   Loops: NA   Shortest: NA   Longest: NA
Trail Surface: Natural
Trail Use Fee: None
Method Of Ski Trail Grooming: NA
Skiing Ability Suggested: NA
Hiking Trail Difficulty: Moderate to difficult
Mountain Biking Ability Suggested: NA
Terrain: Rolling with some steep grades not suitable for skiing
Camping: Wilderness camping permitted 200' off trail

Maintained by the Bergland Ranger District, Ottawa National Forest
Connects to the North Country Trail - Bergland Segment

GOGEBIC RIDGE HIKING TRAIL

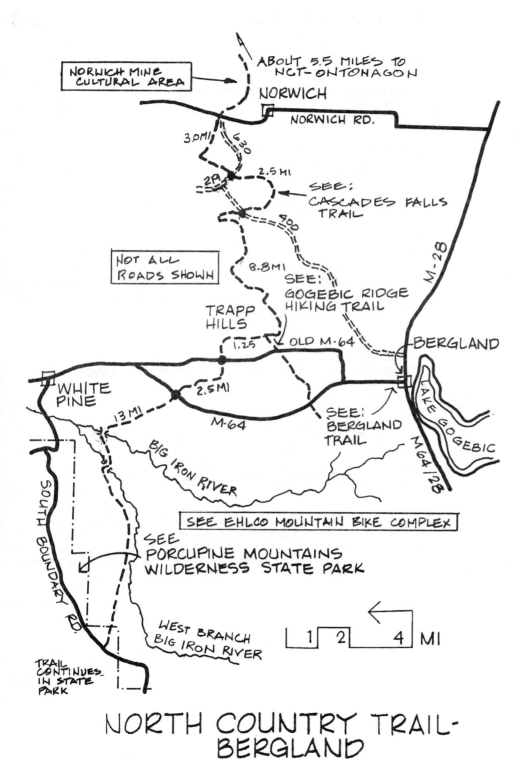

NORTH COUNTRY TRAIL-
BERGLAND

Bergland Ranger District, Ottawa National Forest
M28, PO Box 126   906-575-3441
Bergland, MI 49910

Recreation Staff Officer, Ottawa National Forest
2100 E. Cloverland Drive   906-932-1330
Ironwood, MI 49938   800-562-1201

Michigan Atlas & Gazetteer Location: 108C34,109C56

County Location: Ontonagon

Directions To Trailhead:
West trailhead-Junction of Summit Peak Rd and S. Boundary Rd adjacent to
Procupine Mountains State Park East trailhead-NE of Bergland, 10 miles north
of M28 on Norwich Rd, at the intersection of FR 630
Trailhead -7 miles north of Bergland on M64

Trail Type: Hiking/Walking
Trail Distance: 37 mi   Loops: NA   Shortest: NA   Longest: NA
Trail Surface: Natural
Trail Use Fee: None
Method Of Ski Trail Grooming: NA
Skiing Ability Suggested: NA
Hiking Trail Difficulty: Moderate to difficult
Mountain Biking Ability Suggested: NA
Terrain: Steep 5%, Hilly 14%, Moderate 55%, Flat 26%
Camping: There are no developed campsites but wilderness camping is
permitted.

Maintained by the Bergland Ranger District, Ottawa National Forest
Connected to the east end of the Gogebic Ridge Trail.
A more detailed trail map is available from the Bergland Ranger District.
Wilderness camping is permitted 200' from the trail.
An interpretive trail is planned near Norwich to interpret the Ohio Trap Rock Mine
site.
For more information contact the North Country Trail Association

497

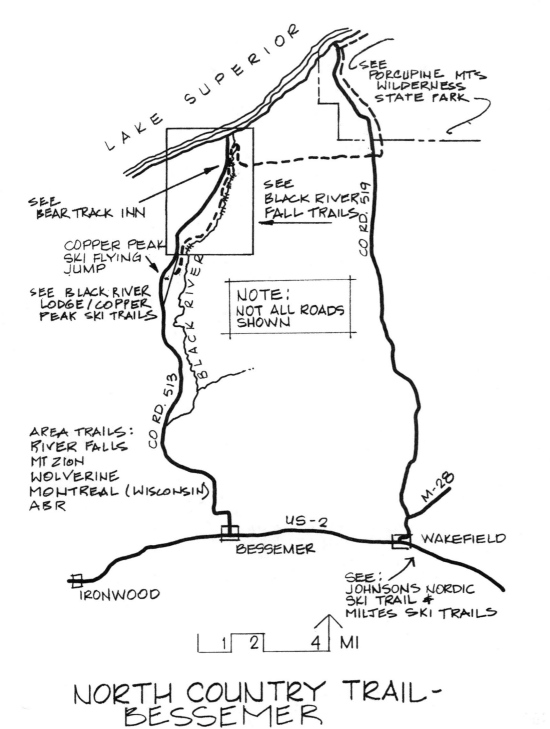

Bessemer Ranger District, Ottawa National Forest
500 N. Moore St.   906-667-0261
Bessemer , MI 49911

Recreation Staff Officer, Ottawa National Forest
2100 E. Cloverland Drive   906-932-1330
Ironwood, MI 49938   800-562-1201

Michigan Atlas & Gazetteer Location: 108C1, 113A8

County Location: Gogebic

Directions To Trailhead:
West Trailhead-Co Rd 513, 11 miles north of Bessemer near Copper Peak
East Trailhead-North of Wakefield on Co Rd 519, .5 mile south of the Porcupine
Mountains Wilderness State Park boundary

Trail Type: Hiking/Walking
Trail Distance: 12 mi   Loops: NA   Shortest: NA   Longest: NA
Trail Surface: Natural
Trail Use Fee: None
Method Of Ski Trail Grooming: NA
Skiing Ability Suggested: NA
Hiking Trail Difficulty: Difficult
Mountain Biking Ability Suggested: NA
Terrain: Steep 10%, Hilly 10%, Moderate 40%, Flat 4%
Camping: Campgound at Black River Harbor on Lake Superior

Maintained by the Bessemer Ranger District, Ottawa National Forest
Several falls are along the trail on the Black River.
Wilderness camping is permitted 200' from the trail.
Drinking water is also available at the Potawatomi and Gorge Falls Picnic Area.
Copper Peak is the largest ski jump in the United States.
Other trails in the area include the Black River Harbor Ski Trails, Black River
Harbor Trails and the Copper Peak Recreation Area.
For more information contact the North Country Trail Association.
A more detailed map is available from the Bessemer Ranger District office.

NORTH COUNTRY TRAIL- BESSEMER

TRAIL NOTES

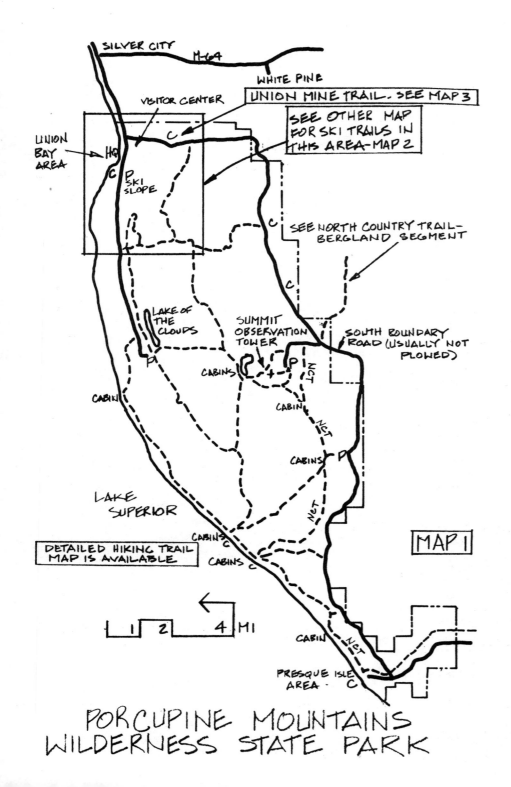

SILVER CITY   M-64

WHITE PINE

VISITOR CENTER

UNION MINE TRAIL. SEE MAP 3

SEE OTHER MAP FOR SKI TRAILS IN THIS AREA - MAP 2

UNION BAY AREA

HQ

P
SKI SLOPE

C

C

SEE NORTH COUNTRY TRAIL - BERGLAND SEGMENT

LAKE OF THE CLOUDS

SUMMIT OBSERVATION TOWER

SOUTH BOUNDARY ROAD (USUALLY NOT PLOWED)

CABINS

CABIN

CABIN

CABINS

NCT

LAKE SUPERIOR

CABINS

DETAILED HIKING TRAIL MAP IS AVAILABLE

CABINS

MAP 1

1 2   4 MI

CABIN

NCT

PRESQUE ISLE AREA

PORCUPINE MOUNTAINS WILDERNESS STATE PARK

Porcupine Mountains Wilderness State Park
412 South Boundary Rd
Ontonagon, MI 49953

906-885-5275

DNR Parks and Recreation Division

517-373-1270

Michigan Atlas & Gazetteer Location: 108B1234

County Location: Ontonagon & Gogebic

Directions To Trailhead:
17 miles west of Ontonagon on the shore of Lake Superior

Trail Type: Hiking/Walking, Cross Country Skiing
Trail Distance: 85+ mi   Loops: Many   Shortest: Longest:
Trail Surface: Natural
Trail Use Fee: None, but vehicle entry fee required
Method Of Ski Trail Grooming: Track set regularly
Skiing Ability Suggested: Novice to intermediate
Hiking Trail Difficulty: Easy to difficult
Mountain Biking Ability Suggested: NA
Terrain: Rolling to very hilly
Camping: Available in park, facilities may be limited during the winter

Maintained by the DNR Parks and Recreation Division
A unique state park at the shore of Lake Superior. Rentals, warming area, snack bar and alpine skiing available. Extensive wilderness hiking trail system has been developed throughout the park complete with shelters and cabins (rental and reservations req.) are available.
About 25 miles of trails are open for skiing and mountain biking (same trail system).
One ski trail leads to the top of the alpine slope for a very spectacular panoramic view of Lake Superior.
Back country cabins are available on a reservation basis for rent throughout the year.
The North Country Trail uses Little Carp River, Lake Superior and LIly Pond Trails
There are three trail maps.

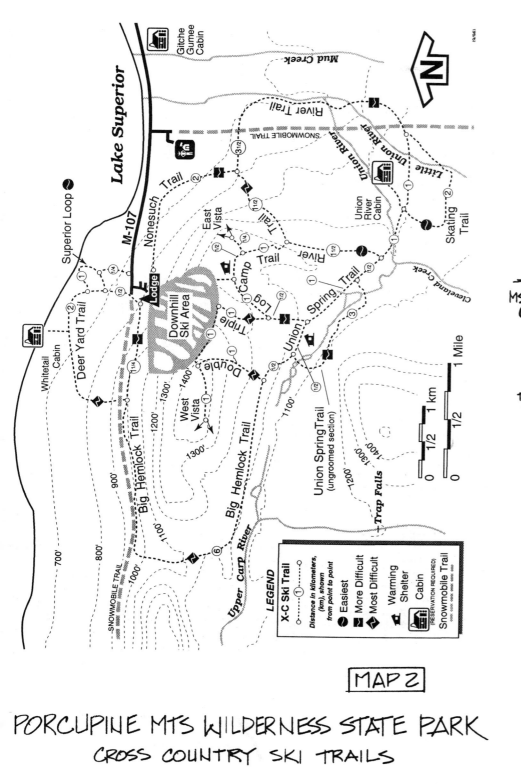

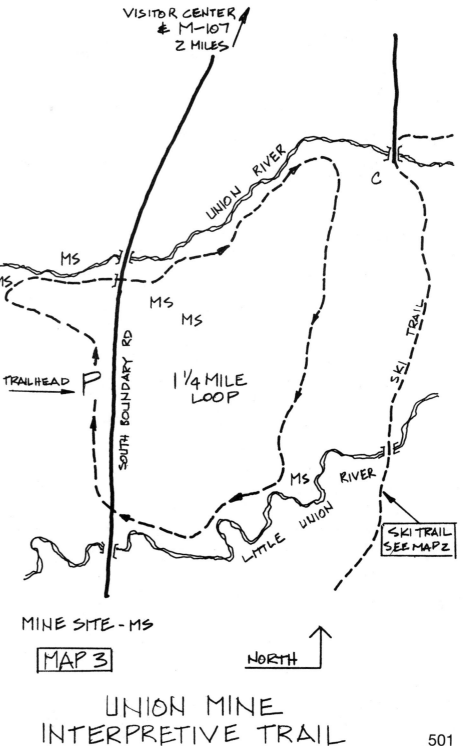

MAP 2

PORCUPINE MTS WILDERNESS STATE PARK
CROSS COUNTRY SKI TRAILS

MAP 3

MINE SITE - MS

UNION MINE
INTERPRETIVE TRAIL

501

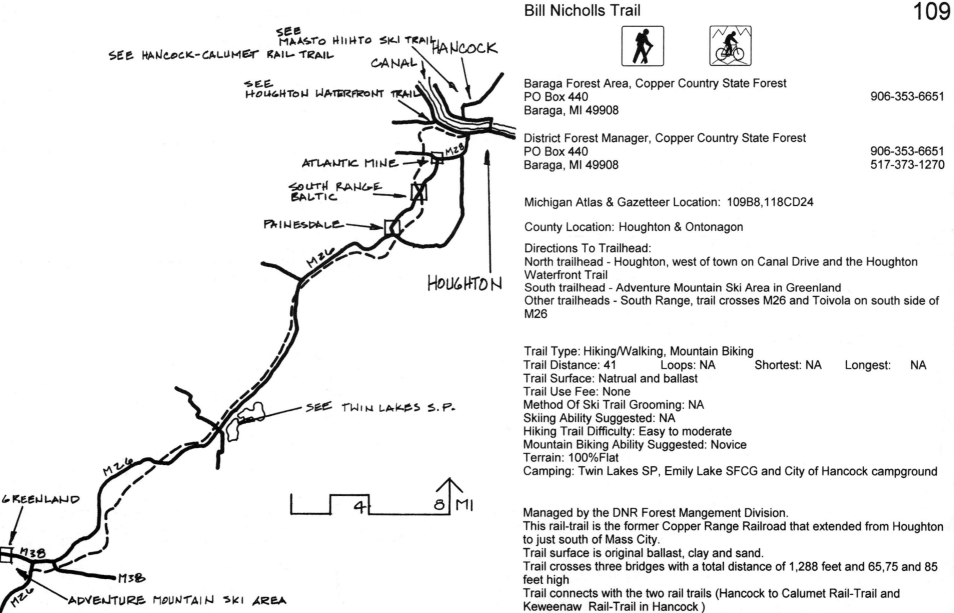

SEE
MAASTO HIIHTO SKI TRAIL
HANCOCK
SEE HANCOCK-CALUMET RAIL TRAIL
CANAL
SEE
HOUGHTON WATERFRONT TRAIL
M28
ATLANTIC MINE
SOUTH RANGE
BALTIC
HOUGHTON
PAINESDALE
M26
SEE TWIN LAKES S.P.
M26
GREENLAND
M38
M38
M26
ADVENTURE MOUNTAIN SKI AREA

4   8 MI

Baraga Forest Area, Copper Country State Forest
PO Box 440   906-353-6651
Baraga, MI 49908

District Forest Manager, Copper Country State Forest
PO Box 440   906-353-6651
Baraga, MI 49908   517-373-1270

Michigan Atlas & Gazetteer Location: 109B8,118CD24

County Location: Houghton & Ontonagon

Directions To Trailhead:
North trailhead - Houghton, west of town on Canal Drive and the Houghton
Waterfront Trail
South trailhead - Adventure Mountain Ski Area in Greenland
Other trailheads - South Range, trail crosses M26 and Toivola on south side of
M26

Trail Type: Hiking/Walking, Mountain Biking
Trail Distance: 41   Loops: NA   Shortest: NA   Longest: NA
Trail Surface: Natrual and ballast
Trail Use Fee: None
Method Of Ski Trail Grooming: NA
Skiing Ability Suggested: NA
Hiking Trail Difficulty: Easy to moderate
Mountain Biking Ability Suggested: Novice
Terrain: 100%Flat
Camping: Twin Lakes SP, Emily Lake SFCG and City of Hancock campground

Managed by the DNR Forest Mangement Division.
This rail-trail is the former Copper Range Railroad that extended from Houghton
to just south of Mass City.
Trail surface is original ballast, clay and sand.
Trail crosses three bridges with a total distance of 1,288 feet and 65,75 and 85
feet high
Trail connects with the two rail trails (Hancock to Calumet Rail-Trail and
Keweenaw Rail-Trail in Hancock)
Used as a snowmobile trail from from December through April.

BILL NICHOLLS RAIL TRAIL

Bergland Ranger District, Ottawa National Forest
M28, PO Box 126   906-575-3441
Bergland, MI 49910

Recreation Staff Officer, Ottawa National Forest
2100 E. Cloverland Drive   906-932-1330
Ironwood, MI 49938

Michigan Atlas & Gazetteer Location: 109C5

County Location: Ontonagon

Directions To Trailhead:
From Bergland, take M28 1 mile east to FR 400, then north 7 miles to sign
leading to parking area and trailhead

Trail Type: Hiking/Walking
Trail Distance: 1.7 mi   Loops: 1   Shortest: NA   Longest: NA
Trail Surface: Natural
Trail Use Fee: None
Method Of Ski Trail Grooming: NA
Skiing Ability Suggested: NA
Hiking Trail Difficulty: Moderate
Mountain Biking Ability Suggested: NA
Terrain: Steep 15%, Hilly 30%, Moderate 25%, Flat 30%
Camping: None

Maintained by the Bergland Ranger District, Ottawa National Forest
Scenic trail to the Cascade Falls.
The North Country National Scenic Trail is nearby

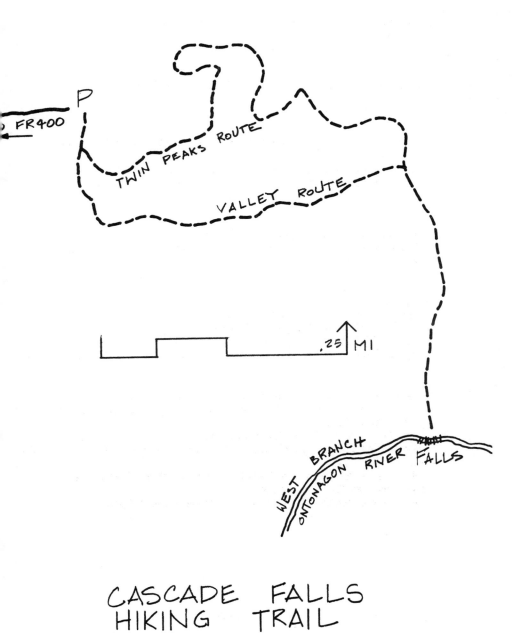

CASCADE FALLS
HIKING TRAIL

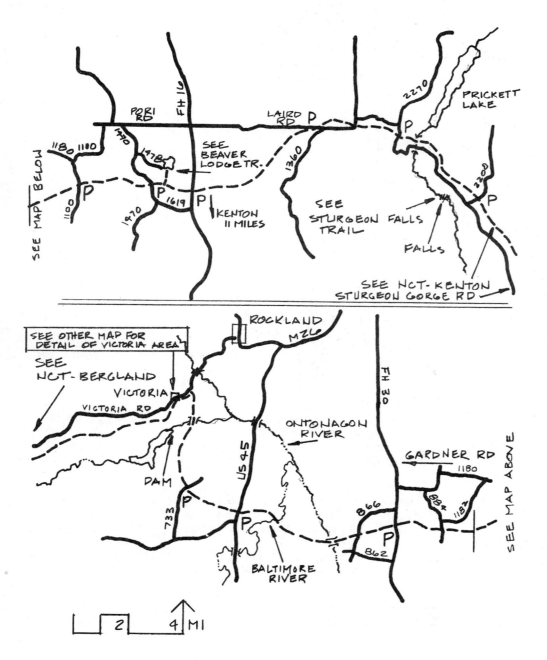

Ontonagon Ranger District - Ottawa National Forest
1209 Rockland Rd   906-884-2085
Ontonagon, MI 49953   906-884-2411

Recreation Staff Officer, Ottawa National Forest
2100 E. Cloverland Drive   906-932-1330
Ironwood, MI 49938   800-562-1201

Michigan Atlas & Gazetteer Location: 109C78,110C123

County Location: Ontonagon, Baraga, Houghton

Directions To Trailhead:
West trailhead - Victoria on Victoria Rd, Trailhead - on US45 about 5 miles
south of M26 and US45 intersection located just east of Rockland.
Trailhead - Bob Lake NFCG.
Trailhead - Sturgeon River Falls.
Trail on east side of Sturgeon Gorge Rd and crosses FR 2200

Trail Type: Hiking/Walking
Trail Distance: 47 mi   Loops: NA   Shortest: NA   Longest: NA
Trail Surface: Natural
Trail Use Fee: None
Method Of Ski Trail Grooming: NA
Skiing Ability Suggested: NA
Hiking Trail Difficulty: Difficult
Mountain Biking Ability Suggested: NA
Terrain: Steep 30%, Hilly 40%, Moderate 20%, Flat 10%
Camping: Bob Lake CG and wilderness camping permitted 200' from trail

Maintained by the Ontonagon Ranger District - Ottawa National Forest
Very rugged, beautiful and isolated segment.
The Sturgeon Falls Gorge near the east end of the segment is worth the short
side trip.
The trail passes through the historic and very interesting Victoria copper mine
area. See separate map. Plan to spend some time in the old historic mining town
of Victoria.
The Bob Lake CG is very nice and water is available.
For further information contact the North Country Trail Association

NORTH COUNTRY TRAIL-
ONTONAGON

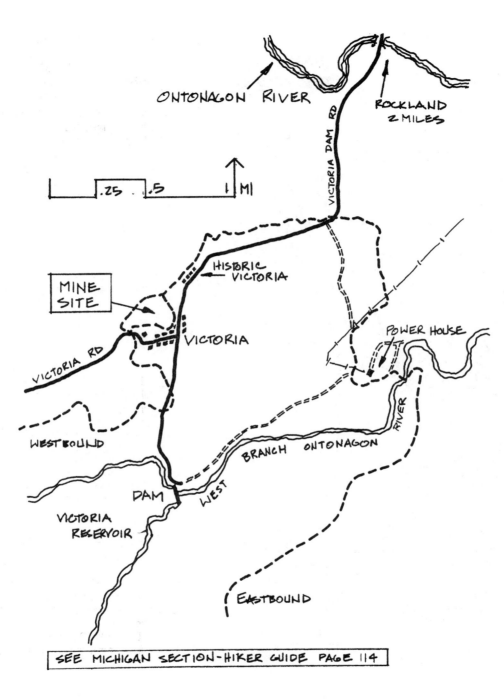

ONTONAGON RIVER

ROCKLAND 2 MILES

VICTORIA DAM RD

.25 .5 1 MI

HISTORIC VICTORIA

MINE SITE

VICTORIA

VICTORIA RD

POWER HOUSE

WESTBOUND

WEST BRANCH ONTONAGON

RIVER

DAM

VICTORIA RESERVOIR

EASTBOUND

SEE MICHIGAN SECTION-HIKER GUIDE PAGE 114

VICTORIA AREA
NORTH COUNTRY TRAIL - ONTONAGON

504.1

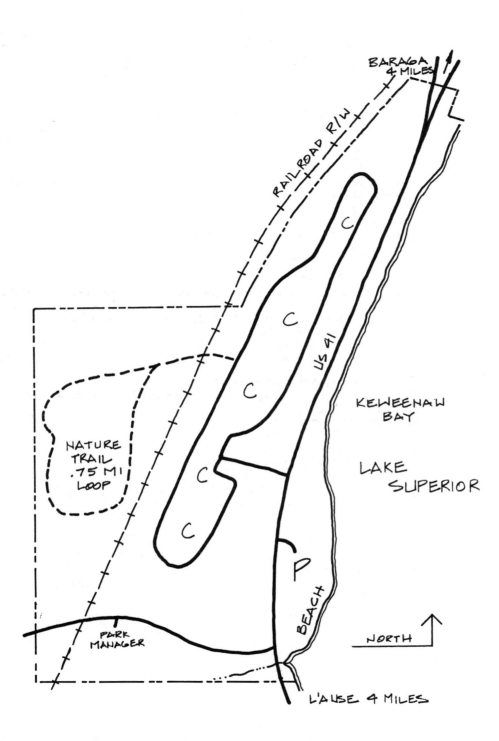

Baraga State Park
Rte 1, Box 566
Baraga, MI 49908-9790

906-353-6558

McLain State Park
Rte 1, Box 82
Hancock, MI 49930

906-482-0278

Michigan Atlas & Gazetteer Location: 110B4, 111B4

County Location: Baraga

Directions To Trailhead:
One mile south of Baraga on US41along the Keweenaw Bay

Trail Type: Hiking/Walking, Interpretive
Trail Distance: .75 mi   Loops: 1   Shortest: NA   Longest: .75 mi
Trail Surface: Natural
Trail Use Fee: None, but vehicle entry permit required
Method Of Ski Trail Grooming: NA
Skiing Ability Suggested: NA
Hiking Trail Difficulty: Easy
Mountain Biking Ability Suggested: NA
Terrain: Steep 5%, Hilly 15%, Moderate 75%, Flat 5%
Camping: Campground on site

Maintained by the DNR Parks and Recreation Division
Compact park on the shore of the Keweenaw Bay, Lake Superior

BARAGA STATE PARK

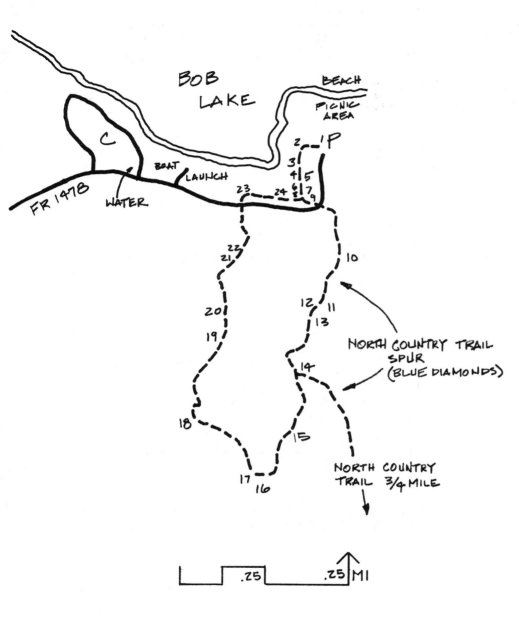

BOB LAKE

BEACH

PICNIC AREA

C

BOAT LAUNCH

FR 1478

WATER

2 1 P
3
4 5
6 7
23 24 8 9

10

22
21

12 11
13

20

19

NORTH COUNTRY TRAIL SPUR (BLUE DIAMONDS)

14

18

15

17 16

NORTH COUNTRY TRAIL ¾ MILE

.25   .25 MI

Ontonagon Ranger District, Ottawa National Forest
1209 Rockland Rd
Ontonagon, MI 49953

906-884-2411

Recreation Staff Officer, Ottawa National Forest
2100 E. Cloverland Drive
Ironwood, MI 49938

906-932-1330

Michigan Atlas & Gazetteer Location: 110C1

County Location: Houghton

Directions To Trailhead:
At the Bob Lake National Forest Campground. From Baraga, take M38 19 miles to FH 16, then south about 7.5 miles to Pori/South Laird Rd, then west 2.5 miles to FR 1470, then south 1.5 miles to campground. Trailhead at picnic area parking lot, beyond campground.

Trail Type: Hiking/Walking, Interpretive
Trail Distance: 1.25   Loops: 1   Shortest: NA   Longest: 1.25 mi
Trail Surface: Natural
Trail Use Fee: None
Method Of Ski Trail Grooming: None
Skiing Ability Suggested: NA
Hiking Trail Difficulty: Easy to moderate
Mountain Biking Ability Suggested: NA
Terrain: Steep 0%, Hilly 5%, Moderate 80%, Flat 10%
Camping: Campground at trailhead

Maintained by the Ottawa National Forest
Trail has 21 stations. A nature trail brochure is available.
Part of the trail was orginally a logging railroad.
At station 14, a spur trail begins to the North Country Trail - Ontonagon

BEAVER LODGE NATURE TRAIL

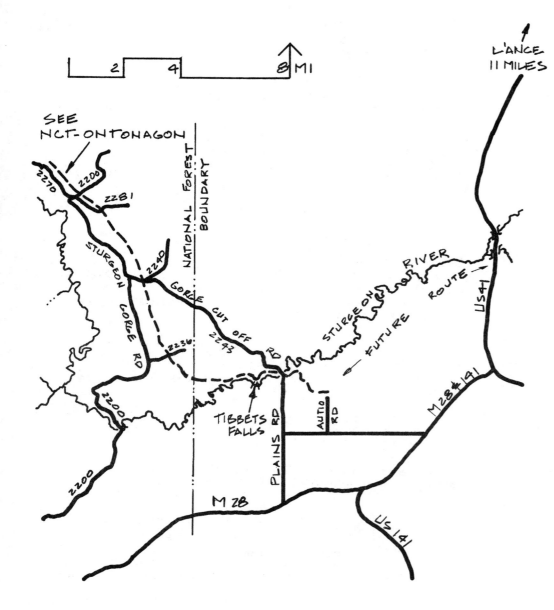

SEE
NCT-ONTONAGON

NATIONAL FOREST BOUNDARY

STURGEON GORGE RD

GORGE CUT OFF RD

2270
2200
2281
2240
2236
2243
2200
2200

TIBBETS FALLS

PLAINS RD

AUTIO RD

STURGEON RIVER

FUTURE ROUTE

US41

M28 & 191

M 28

US 141

L'ANCE
11 MILES

2 4 8 MI

Kenton Ranger District, Ottawa National Forest
M28   906-852-3500
Kenton, MI 49943

Recreation Staff Officer, Ottawa National Forest
2100 E. Cloverland Drive   906-932-1330
Ironwood, MI 49938   800-562-1201

Michigan Atlas & Gazetteer Location: 110CD34

County Location: Ontonagon, Baraga

Directions To Trailhead:
 West trailhead - Take FR2200 north from M28 just east of Sidnaw for about 9 miles to the trail access point on east side of FR2200 near the Surgeon River Falls access trail.
East Tailhead - Two miles west of Covington on M-28, take Plains Rd north about two miles, then west 1 mile on Section 16 Rd to Autio Rd. North on Autio Rd to its end. Trail across Nestor Creek.

Trail Type: Hiking/Walking
Trail Distance: 7.6   Loops: No   Shortest: NA   Longest: NA
Trail Surface: Natural
Trail Use Fee: None
Method Of Ski Trail Grooming: None
Skiing Ability Suggested: NA
Hiking Trail Difficulty: Difficult
Mountain Biking Ability Suggested: NA
Terrain: Steep 0%, Hilly 5%, Moderate 55%, Flat 40%
Camping: There are no developed campsite but wilderness camping permitted

Maintained by the Kenton Ranger District, Ottawa National Forest.
Terrain and remoteness in the nearby Sturgeon River Gorge are exceptional, even for the upper peninsula.
A more detailed map is available from the Kenton Ranger District.
Like all of the North Country Trail, wilderness camping is permitted 200' from the trail
For more information about the North Country Trail, contact the North Country Trail Association, PO Box 311, White Cloud, MI 49349 616-689-1912

NORTH COUNTRY TRAIL
KENTON & TIBBETS FALLS

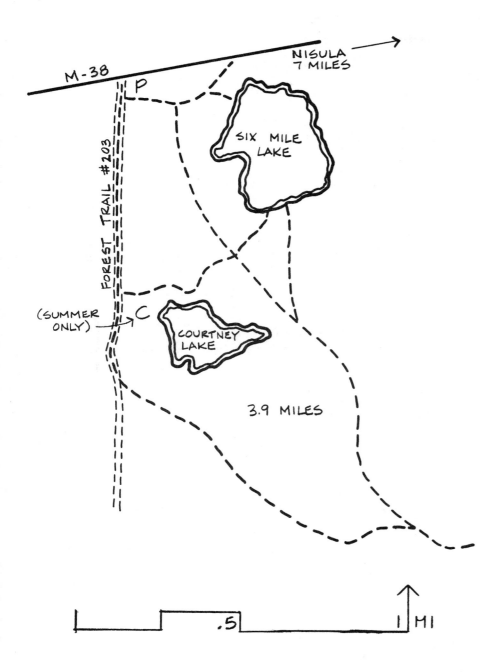

M-38

NISULA
7 MILES

P

FOREST TRAIL #203

SIX MILE LAKE

(SUMMER ONLY) → C

COURTNEY LAKE

3.9 MILES

.5   1 MI

OLD GRADE SKI TRAIL

Ontonagon Ranger District, Ottawa National Forest
PO Box 217   906-884-2411
Ontonagon, MI 49953

Recreation Staff Officer, Ottawa National Forest
2100 Cloverland Drive   906-932-1330
Ironwood, MI 49938   800-562-1201

Michigan Atlas & Gazetteer Location: 110B1

County Location: Ontonagon

Directions To Trailhead:
West of Baraga on M38 7 miles west of Nisula at Courtney Lake Recreation
Area on FH203

Trail Type: Hiking/Walking, Cross Country Skiing
Trail Distance: 4.2 mi   Loops: 2   Shortest: 1.5 mi Longest: 4.2 mi
Trail Surface: Natural
Trail Use Fee: None
Method Of Ski Trail Grooming: None
Skiing Ability Suggested: Novice
Hiking Trail Difficulty: Easy
Mountain Biking Ability Suggested: NA
Terrain: Steep 0%, Hilly 10%, Moderate 40%, Flat 50%
Camping: Campgound at trailhead open in snowless months

Maintained by the Ontonagon Ranger District, Ottawa National Forest
Courtney Lake has a very nice swimming area.
Many other unmarked trails in the area for wilderness skiing.
Trail is not well marked.
FR 203 is plowed to some privately owned cabins near campground.

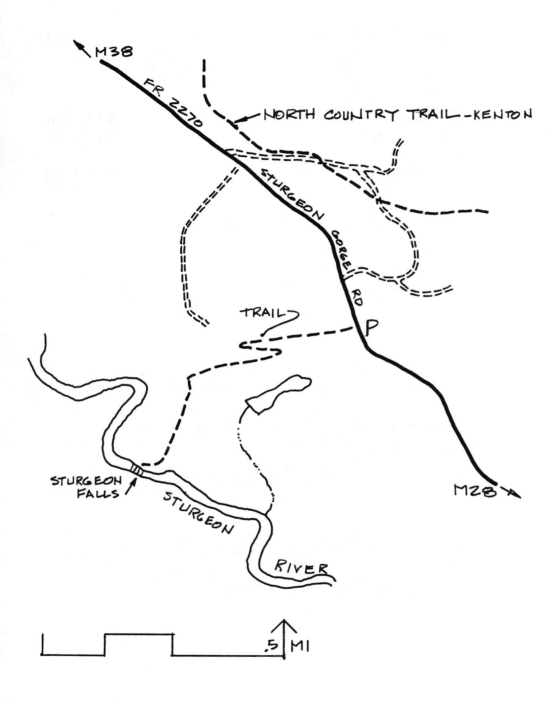

STURGEON FALLS TRAIL

Kenton Ranger District, Ottawa National Forest
M28
Kenton, MI 49943

Recreation Staff Officer, Ottawa National Forest
2100 E. Cloverland Drive   906-932-1330
Ironwood, MI 49938

Michigan Atlas & Gazetteer Location: 110C3

County Location: Houghton

Directions To Trailhead:
14 miles north of Sidnaw via FR 2200 and 2270, or From M38 between Alstion and Baraga, follow Prickett Dam Rd and FR2270 south for 11 miles.

Trail Type: Hiking/Walking
Trail Distance: 1 mi   Loops: NA   Shortest: NA   Longest: NA
Trail Surface: Natural
Trail Use Fee: None
Method Of Ski Trail Grooming: NA
Skiing Ability Suggested: NA
Hiking Trail Difficulty: Moderate
Mountain Biking Ability Suggested: NA
Terrain: Steep 5%, Hilly 20%, Moderate 10%, Flat 65%
Camping: None

Maintained by the Kenton Ranger District, Ottawa National Forest
Spur trail to falls from parking lot and North Country Trail -Ontonagon that is across the road

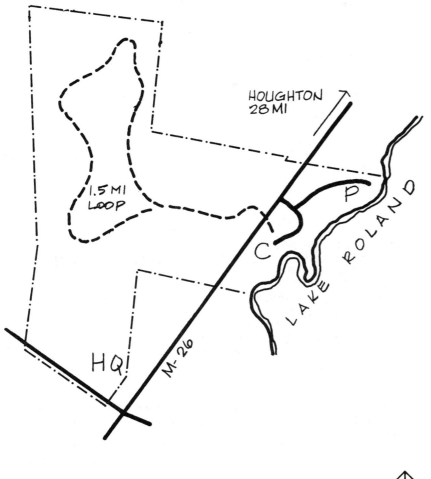

HOUGHTON
28 MI

1.5 MI
LOOP

LAKE ROLAND

P

C

HQ

M-26

.25   .5 MI

TWIN LAKES STATE PARK

McLain State Park
RR!, Box 82 M203
Hancock, MI 49930

906-482-0278
906-288-3321

DNR Parks and Recreation Division

517-373-1270

Michigan Atlas & Gazetteer Location: 110A2

County Location: Houghton

Directions To Trailhead:
28 miles south of Houghton on M-26

Trail Type: Hiking/Walking, Cross Country Skiing, Interpretive
Trail Distance: 1.5 mi   Loops: 1   Shortest: NA   Longest: 1.5 mi
Trail Surface: Natural
Trail Use Fee: None, but vehicle entry fee required
Method Of Ski Trail Grooming: Track set once/week minimum
Skiing Ability Suggested: Novice
Hiking Trail Difficulty: Easy
Mountain Biking Ability Suggested: NA
Terrain: Steep 0%, Hilly 0%, Moderate 50%, Flat 50%
Camping: Seasonal camground on site

Maintained by the DNR Parks and Recreation Division
Two overlooks along the trail, which can permit a view of Lake Superior on a
clear day .
A very popular state park opened only during the summer.
Located on one of the warmest lakes in the UP.

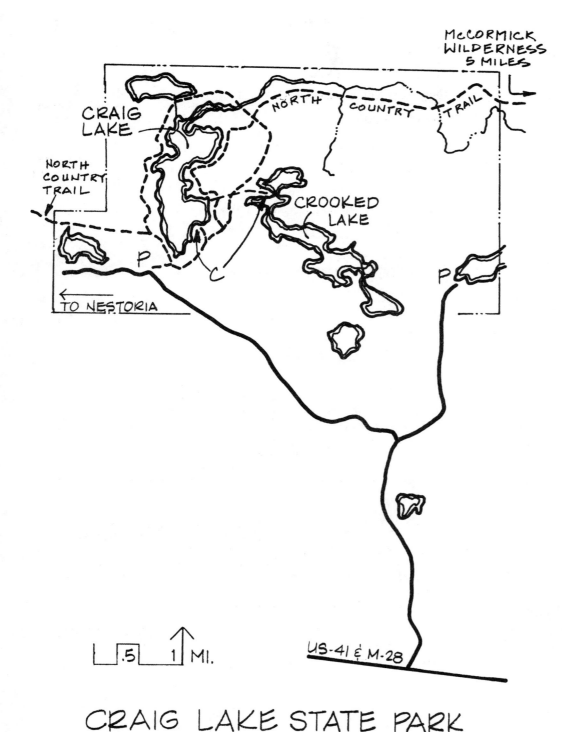

Van Riper State Park
PO Box 66
Champion , MI 49814

906-339-4461

DNR Parks and Recreation Division

517-373-1270

Michigan Atlas & Gazetteer Location: 111CD7

County Location: Marquette

Directions To Trailhead:
West of Marquette and 2 miles west of Michigamme on US41 at Craig Lake Rd.
Axquire detailed road map at Van Riper State Park before going to the park.

Trail Type: Hiking/Walking, Cross Country Skiing, Interpretive
Trail Distance: 6.8 mi   Loops: 1   Shortest: NA   Longest: 6.8 mi
Trail Surface: Natural
Trail Use Fee: None
Method Of Ski Trail Grooming: None - Wilderness area
Skiing Ability Suggested: Advanced
Hiking Trail Difficulty: Difficult
Mountain Biking Ability Suggested: NA
Terrain: Rolling to very hilly with rock outcrops
Camping: Cabin rentals and wilderness camping permitted

Maintained by the DNR Parks and Recreation Division
This is a state park with few facilities.
Suitable for skiing by those with winter survival skills only.
Two primitive campgrounds are located in the park. One is located 1mile from
the trailhead and another is located 1.8 miles from the trailhead.
Contact Van Riper State Park for more detailed information before leaving for
the park.. Wilderness camping permitted off existing trails.
Developed campground available at Van Riper State Park and private
campgrounds nearby.
Craig Lake State Park is managed by Van Riper State Park.

CRAIG LAKE STATE PARK

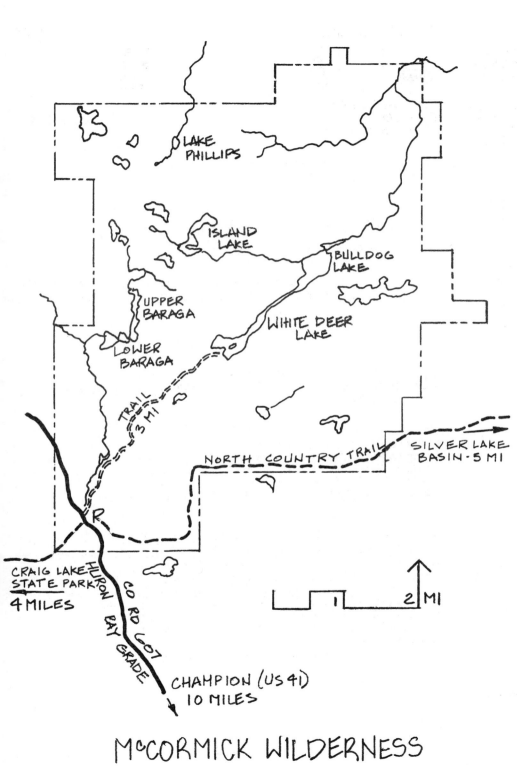

McCormick Wilderness

Kenton Ranger District, Ottawa National Forest
M28   906-852-3500
Kenton, MI 49943

Recreation Staff Officer, Ottawa National Forest
2100 Cloverdale Drive   906-932-1330
Ironwood , MI 49938   800-562-1201

Michigan Atlas & Gazetteer Location: 111C8,112C1

County Location: Marquette

Directions To Trailhead:
12 miles north of US41 from Champion on Co Rd 607 (Huron Bay Grade)

Trail Type: Hiking/Walking, Cross Country Skiing
Trail Distance: 8 mi   Loops: 2   Shortest: Longest:
Trail Surface: Natural
Trail Use Fee: None
Method Of Ski Trail Grooming: None
Skiing Ability Suggested: Advanced
Hiking Trail Difficulty: Moderate to difficult
Mountain Biking Ability Suggested: NA
Terrain: Steep 5%, Hilly 40%, Moderate 45%, Flat 10%
Camping: No developed campground, but wilderness camping is permitted

Maintained by the Kenton Ranger District, Ottawa National Forest
Formerly owned by Cyrus McCormick, son of the inventor of the reaper
harvesting machine. Very rugged, isolated and scenic area.
Nearest developed campground is at Van Riper State Park on US41.
Recommended only for skiers with winter survival skills since the area is very
isolated.
Total forest acreage is over 17,600 acres.

Baraga County Tourist Association
PO Box 556
Baraga, MI 49908

906-524-7444

Baragaland Cross Country Ski Club
c/o Indian Country Sales
L'Anse, MI 49946

906-524-6518

Michigan Atlas & Gazetteer Location: 111B5

County Location: Baraga

Directions To Trailhead:
From downtown L'Anse take Main St. north 1.6 miles to Indian Cemetery Rd., then right 2.5 miles to the trailhead. Park along the road.

Trail Type: Cross Country Skiing
Trail Distance: 8 mi   Loops: 4   Shortest: 1 mi   Longest: 3 mi
Trail Surface:
Trail Use Fee: Donations accepted at trailhead
Method Of Ski Trail Grooming: Track set with skating lane
Skiing Ability Suggested: Novice to advanced
Hiking Trail Difficulty: NA
Mountain Biking Ability Suggested: NA
Terrain: Steep 10%, Hilly 30%, Moderate 40%, Flat 20%
Camping: Available nearby

Maintained by the Baragaland Cross-Country Ski Club
Site of the Baragaland Cross-Country Ski Race held the 2nd Sunday in February

Indian Country Sales is the local ski shop in L'Anse.
Indian cemetary dating back to the 1840's is along the trail.
Well designed and maintained trail system.

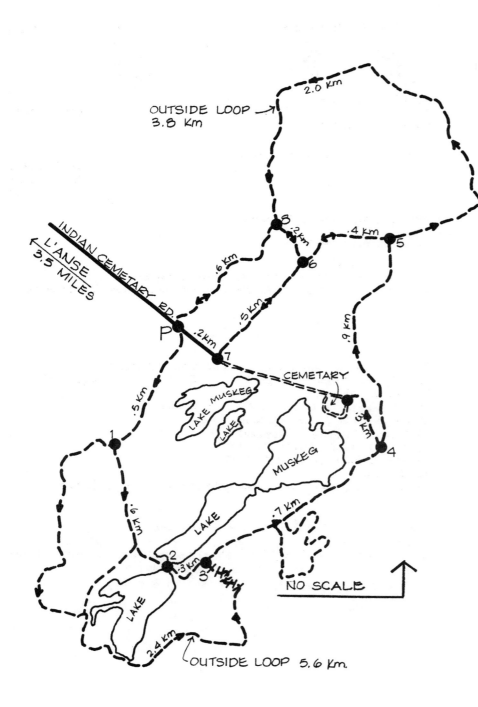

PINERY LAKES TRAIL

Van Riper State Park
Box 66
Champion, MI 49814

906-339-4461

DNR Parks and Recreation Division

517-373-1270
906-228-6561

Michigan Atlas & Gazetteer Location: 111D8,112D1

County Location: Marquette

Directions To Trailhead:
West of Marquette and 5 miles west of M95 on US41/M28
Trailhead is west of main park entrance on north side of US41/M28 at the rustic campground.

Trail Type: Hiking/Walking, Cross Country Skiing, Interpretive
Trail Distance: 4.5 mi   Loops: 4   Shortest: Longest:
Trail Surface: Natural
Trail Use Fee: None, but vehicle entry fee required
Method Of Ski Trail Grooming: None
Skiing Ability Suggested: Advanced
Hiking Trail Difficulty: Moderate to difficult
Mountain Biking Ability Suggested: NA
Terrain: Hilly
Camping: Campground available at trailhead and on Lake Michigamme

Maintained by the DNR Parks and Recreation Divison
Overlooks along the trail
Near the Peshekee to Clowry Rail Trail and the Republic to Champion Rail Trail.

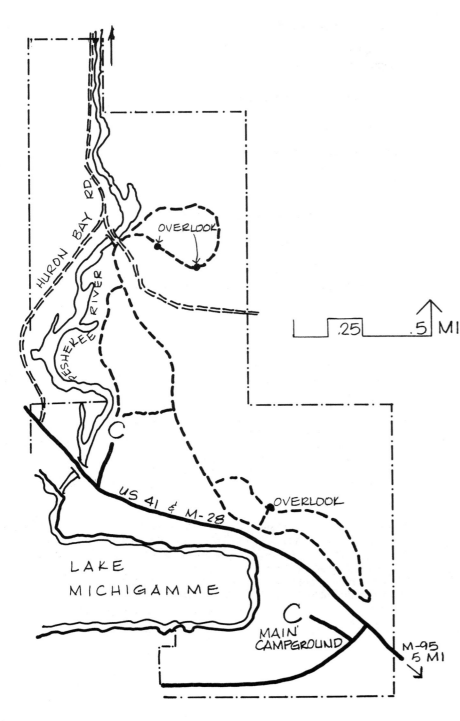

VAN RIPER STATE PARK

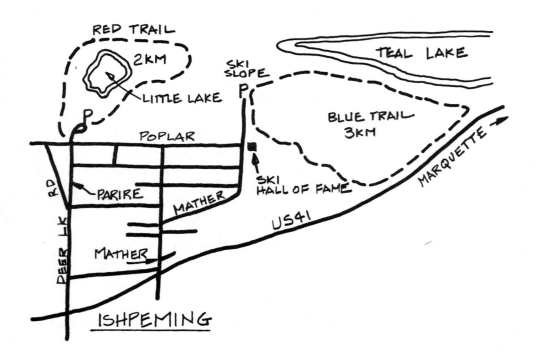

RED TRAIL
2KM
LITTLE LAKE
SKI SLOPE
P
TEAL LAKE
BLUE TRAIL 3KM
POPLAR
PARIRE
MATHER
SKI HALL OF FAME
US41
MARQUETTE
MATHER
DEER LK RD
ISHPEMING

City of Ishpeming
100 Division St.
Ishpeming, MI 49849

906-486-6181
906-486-8301

Michigan Atlas & Gazetteer Location: 112D3

County Location: Marquette

Directions To Trailhead:
Red Trailhead - From M41(stop light) in Ishpeming, turn north on Second St., continue straight onto Prairie St to the park entrance. Trailhead is just inside entrance on left side before "park" sign.
Blue Trailhead - Same as above, but right at park entrance on Poplar St. to the end of the street, then left (north) to the downhill ski area. Trailhead is at the right ski tow.

Trail Type: Cross Country Skiing
Trail Distance: 5 km   Loops: 2   Shortest: 2 km   Longest: 3 km
Trail Surface: Natural
Trail Use Fee: Yes, daily, season and family passes available
Method Of Ski Trail Grooming: Track set
Skiing Ability Suggested: Novice to intermediate
Hiking Trail Difficulty: NA
Mountain Biking Ability Suggested: NA
Terrain: Moderate to hilly
Camping: None

Maintained by the City of Ishpeming.
Trail not suitable for skating.
This trail is typical of the several community cross country ski trails in this area.
They are relatively short but are designed well and well maintained.
Warming hut, restrooms and a small alpine slope are part of the area.
Sledding area and toboggan run that is 1500' long.
The trails were both very well designed and scenic along the shores of Little Lake and Teal Lake.

AL QUAAL RECREATION AREA

GRANITE POINTE

Granite Pointe Nordic Ski Center
101 Snowy Ridge Rd
Negaunee, MI 49866

906-475-8200
800-55X-CSKI

Michigan Atlas & Gazetteer Location: 112D4

County Location: Marquette

Directions To Trailhead:
10 miles Marquette. Take US 41 west 2 miles from the Wal-Mart stop light to Co. Rd 502/Midway Drive, right for about 1/2 mile to Co Rd. 510, then about 4 miles to North Basin Rd, then left 1.7 miles to Snowy Ridge Rd, then right 1/2 mile to Granite Ridge.

Trail Type: Hiking/Walking, Cross Country Skiing, Mountain Biking
Trail Distance: 20 km   Loops: 5   Shortest: 2 km   Longest: 9 km
Trail Surface: Natural
Trail Use Fee: Yes
Method Of Ski Trail Grooming: Track set with a Pisten Bully
Skiing Ability Suggested: Novice to advanced
Hiking Trail Difficulty: Moderate to difficult
Mountain Biking Ability Suggested: Intermediate to advanced
Terrain: Steep 20%, Hilly 40%, Moderate 25%, Flat 15%
Camping: None

Privately operated nordic ski center
Began operation in 1996.
Day Use Cabin overlooks Dead River Basin 300 feet below.
Breathtaking scenery typical of the Huron Mountain range.
Family oriented ski area with day care, free skiing for children and ski playground. Snowshoe and ski rentals available.
Lessons are available.
Dedicated snowshoe trails also on site.
Lodging packages available in Marquette.
They guarantee trail conditions or your money back!

Kivela Road Trail

Negaunee Township
42 M35
Negaunee, MI 49866

906-475-7869

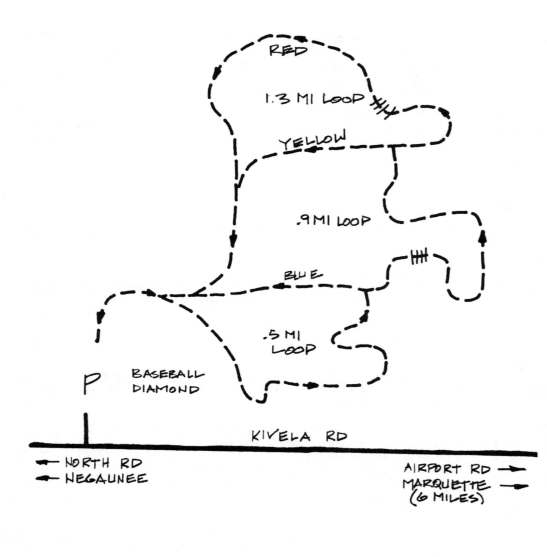

RED

1.3 MI LOOP

YELLOW

.9 MI LOOP

BLUE

.5 MI LOOP

P

BASEBALL DIAMOND

KIVELA RD

NORTH RD
NEGAUNEE

AIRPORT RD →
MARQUETTE →
(6 MILES)

NOT TO SCALE

Michigan Atlas & Gazetteer Location: 112D4

County Location: Marquette

Directions To Trailhead:
North of US41via North Rd.and Kivela Rd. west of the county airport.

Trail Type: Hiking/Walking, Cross Country Skiing, Mountain Biking
Trail Distance: 3 mi   Loops: 3   Shortest: .5 mi   Longest: 1.3 mi
Trail Surface: Natural
Trail Use Fee: None
Method Of Ski Trail Grooming: Track set
Skiing Ability Suggested: Novice to advanced
Hiking Trail Difficulty: Easy to moderate
Mountain Biking Ability Suggested: Easy to moderate
Terrain: Steep 0%, Hilly 20%, Moderate 0%, Flat 80%
Camping: None at the trail

Owned by Negaunee Township
Designed for skiing but available for other uses.
Shortest loop - Novice - Blue trail marking
Middle loop - Intermediate - Yellow trail marking
Longest loop - Advanced - Red trail marking

KIVELA ROAD TRAIL

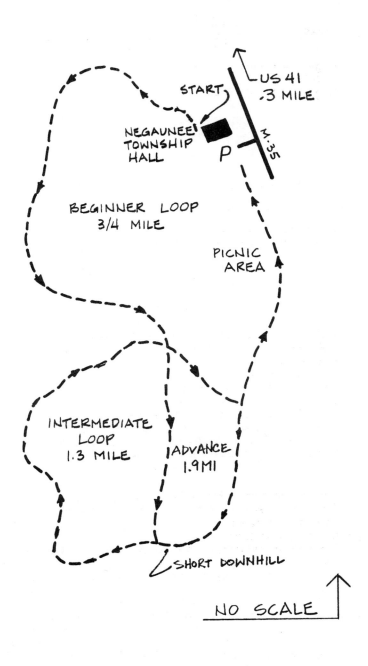

START

US 41
.3 MILE

NEGAUNEE
TOWNSHIP
HALL

P

M.35

BEGINNER LOOP
3/4 MILE

PICNIC
AREA

INTERMEDIATE
LOOP
1.3 MILE

ADVANCE
1.9 MI

SHORT DOWNHILL

NO SCALE

NEGAUNEE TOWNSHIP TOURING TRAIL

Negaunee Township Hall
RR, M35
Negaunee, MI 49866

906-475-7869

Michigan Atlas & Gazetteer Location: 112D4

County Location: Marquette

Directions To Trailhead:
Trailhead - NW corner of the Negaunee Township Offices located .4 mile south of US41 on M35 (intersection is just east of airport)

Trail Type: Hiking/Walking, Cross Country Skiing, Mountain Biking
Trail Distance: Loops: 3   Shortest: Longest: 3
Trail Surface: Natural
Trail Use Fee: None
Method Of Ski Trail Grooming: Track set on occasion
Skiing Ability Suggested: Novice to intermediate
Hiking Trail Difficulty: Easy
Mountain Biking Ability Suggested: Intermediate
Terrain: Steep 0%, Hilly 20%, Moderate 0%, Flat 80%
Camping: None

Maintained by Negaunee Township.
Small but well maintained trail with several long downhill sections

North Country Trail Association
49 Monroe Center, Suite 200B   616-454-5506
Grand Rapids, MI 49503

North Country Trail Association
12 Middle Island   906-225-1704
Marquette, MI 49855

Michigan Atlas & Gazetteer Location: 112C4,113CD56

County Location: Marquette

Directions To Trailhead:
South trailhead - Lakeshore Drive at Hawley at the north end of town on Lake Superior.
Intermediate trailhead - Co Rd 550 between the Mead-Wetmore Pond Interpretive trailhead and the Harlow Lake Pathway trailhead. NCT crosses Co Rd 550. Trail crosses Co Rd 550 again about 2.5 miles north of previous intermediate trailhead. North trailhead - On Co Rd 550 at Garlic River bridge

Trail Type: Hiking/Walking, Cross Country Skiing
Trail Distance: 21 mi   Loops: NA   Shortest: NA   Longest: NA
Trail Surface: Natural
Trail Use Fee: None
Method Of Ski Trail Grooming: NA
Skiing Ability Suggested: Advanced
Hiking Trail Difficulty: Moderate to difficult
Mountain Biking Ability Suggested: NA
Terrain: Steep 10%, Hilly 10%, Moderate 20%, Flat 60%
Camping: Nearby SFCG and in Marquette (see below)

Trail in the Escanaba River State Forest
Trail constructed and maintained by members of the North Country Trail Association.
New members always welcome.
Future develop will extend to the west and southeast from the Garlic Falls section that is already built.
This trail segment passes by several other trail systems including Harllow Lake Pathway, Sugar Loaf Mountain, Little Presque Isle Tract and the Mead-Wetmore Pond Interpretive Trail.
Beautiful segment of the North Country Trail, some of which follows the shore of Lake Superior north of Marquette.

SEE MAPS ON NEXT PAGE

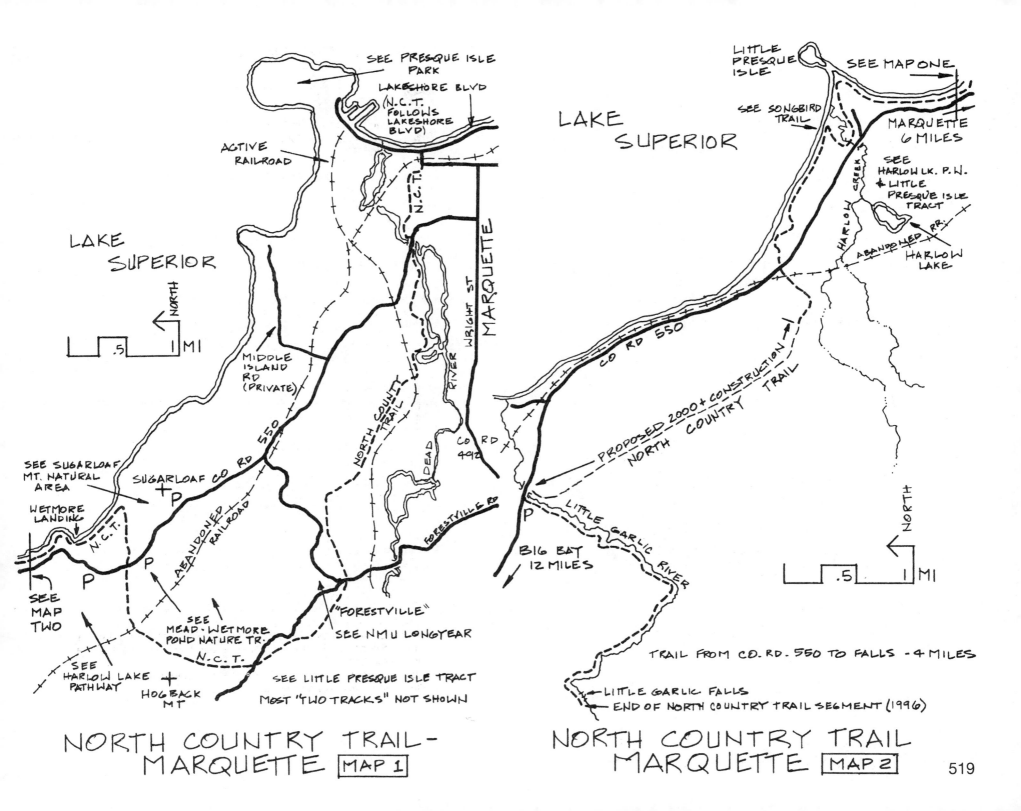

Map 1 labels:

SEE PRESQUE ISLE PARK

LAKESHORE BLVD (N.C.T. FOLLOWS LAKESHORE BLVD)

ACTIVE RAILROAD

LAKE SUPERIOR

NORTH

.5   1 MI

MIDDLE ISLAND RD (PRIVATE)

N.C.T.

WRIGHT ST

MARQUETTE

DEAD RIVER

CO RD 492

NORTH COUNTRY TRAIL

CO RD 550

SEE SUGARLOAF MT. NATURAL AREA

WETMORE LANDING

SUGARLOAF

ABANDONED RAILROAD

FORESTVILLE RD

N.C.T.

SEE MAP TWO

SEE MEAD-WETMORE POND NATURE TR.

"FORESTVILLE"

SEE NMU LONGYEAR

SEE HARLOW LAKE PATHWAY

HOGBACK MT

N.C.T.

SEE LITTLE PRESQUE ISLE TRACT

MOST "TWO TRACKS" NOT SHOWN

NORTH COUNTRY TRAIL- MARQUETTE MAP 1

Map 2 labels:

LITTLE PRESQUE ISLE

SEE MAP ONE

SEE SONGBIRD TRAIL

MARQUETTE 6 MILES

LAKE SUPERIOR

SEE HARLOW LK. P.W. & LITTLE PRESQUE ISLE TRACT

HARLOW CREEK

ABANDONED RR

HARLOW LAKE

CO RD 550

PROPOSED 2000 + CONSTRUCTION NORTH COUNTRY TRAIL

NORTH

.5   1 MI

BIG BAY 12 MILES

LITTLE GARLIC RIVER

TRAIL FROM CO. RD. 550 TO FALLS - 4 MILES

LITTLE GARLIC FALLS

END OF NORTH COUNTRY TRAIL SEGMENT (1996)

NORTH COUNTRY TRAIL MARQUETTE MAP 2

519

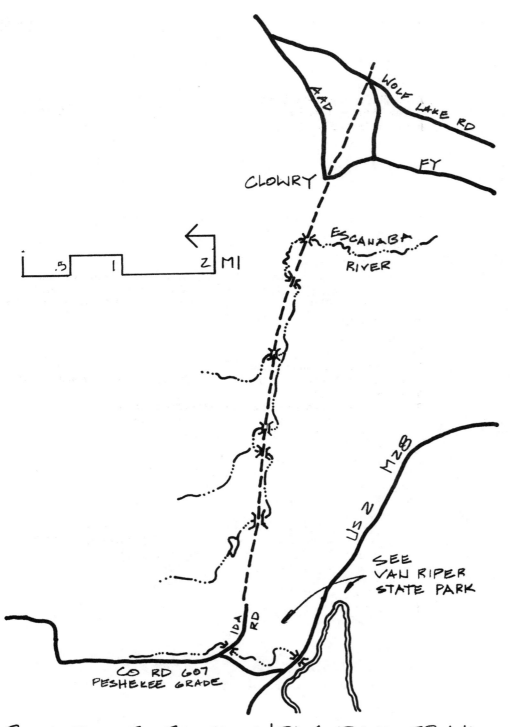

PESHEKEE TO CLOWRY RAILTRAIL

Ishpeming Forest Area, Escanaba River State Forest
1985 US 41 West   906-485-1031
Ishpeming, MI 48949

District Forest Manager, Escanaba River State Forest
6833 US2,41 and M35   906-786-2351
Gladstone, Mi 48937

Michigan Atlas & Gazetteer Location: 112D12

County Location: Marquette

Directions To Trailhead:
West trailhead - West of Champion 2 miles then north on Co Rd 607 1 mile,
theneast .25 mi on Ida Rd to trailhead
East trailhead - Wolf Lake Rd (Ax Rd). 1 mile past Clowry

Trail Type: Hiking/Walking, Mountain Biking
Trail Distance: 6 mi   Loops: NA   Shortest: NA   Longest: NA
Trail Surface: Original ballast and soil
Trail Use Fee: None
Method Of Ski Trail Grooming: NA
Skiing Ability Suggested: NA
Hiking Trail Difficulty: Easy
Mountain Biking Ability Suggested: Novice
Terrain: 100% Flat
Camping: Van Riper State Park at west end of trail.

Maintained by the DNR Forest Management Division
Used also for snowmobiles and ORV's
Outstanding bridges.
Best to park at Van Riper State Park

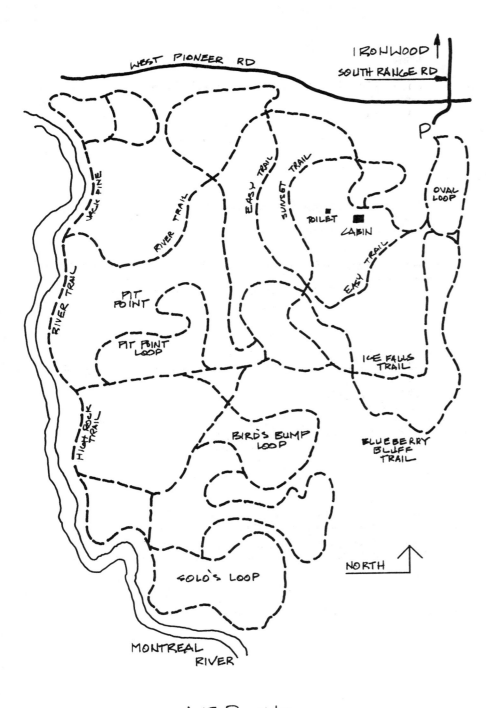

Active Backwoods Retreats Inc.
E-5299 WEst Pioneer Rd
Ironwood, MI 49938

906-932-3502

Michigan Atlas & Gazetteer Location: 113C7

County Location: Gogebic

Directions To Trailhead:
From US2 in Ironwood, take Lake St. south (at the Holiday Inn) past Ayer St, then bear left (southeast) onto Frenchtown Rd. Frenchtown Rd changes to South Range Rd near the Pine St intersection. Continue south on South Range Rd to ABR Ski Trails at the end of the road.

Trail Type: Cross Country Skiing
Trail Distance: 24 km   Loops: 8+   Shortest: 1 km   Longest: 5.6 km
Trail Surface: Natural
Trail Use Fee: Yes - daily, season and discounts available
Method Of Ski Trail Grooming: Groomed and back country
Skiing Ability Suggested: Novice to intermediate
Hiking Trail Difficulty: NA
Mountain Biking Ability Suggested: NA
Terrain: Steep 0%, Hilly 10%, Moderate 60%, Flat 30%
Camping: None

Privately operated nordic ski center.
10 km groomed for skating and classic, 9 km for classic only and 5 km ungroomed for snowshoeing and backcountry skiing.
Warming cabin and sauna is along the trail. Lessons available.
Cabin and Tipi available for rent from 4pm to 9am.
Future plans call for trail expansion.
Ski rentals not available.
Brochure available.

ABR INC
ACTIVE BACKWOODS RETREATS

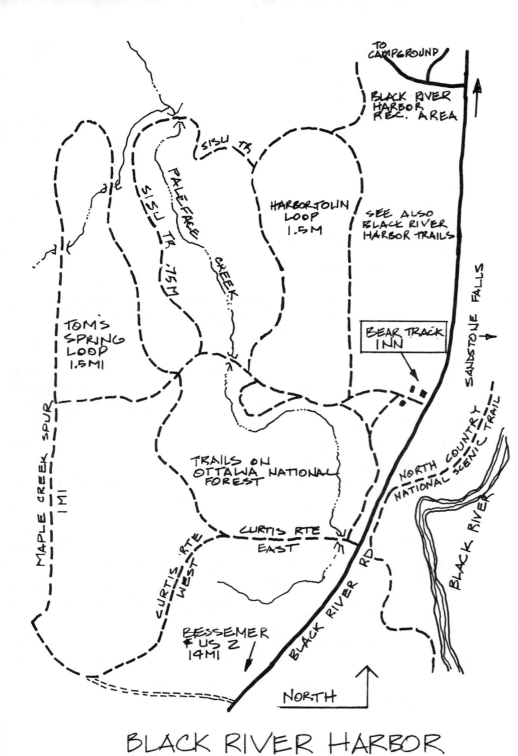

BLACK RIVER HARBOR
CROSS COUNTRY TRAILS

Bear Track Inn
N15325 Black River Rd.
Ironwood, MI 49938

906-932-2144

Michigan Atlas & Gazetteer Location: 113A8

County Location: Gogebic

Directions To Trailhead:
Take Co. Rd 513 (Black River Rd.) nroth from US 2 at Bessemer about 14 miles
to the end of the road at the Black River Harbor Recreation Area

Trail Type: Hiking/Walking, Cross Country Skiing, Mountain Biking
Trail Distance: 8 mi   Loops: 7   Shortest: .5 mi   Longest: 1.5 mi
Trail Surface: Natural and gravel
Trail Use Fee: Donation
Method Of Ski Trail Grooming: Skied in and snowshoe packed
Skiing Ability Suggested: Novice to advanced
Hiking Trail Difficulty: Easy to moderate
Mountain Biking Ability Suggested: Novice to intermediate
Terrain: Steep 10%, Hilly 15%, Moderate 25%, Flat 50%
Camping: Black River Harbor Recreation Area

Maintained by a local non profit group in the Ottawa National Forest.
Backcountry tours also available from the Bear Track Inn.
Cabin accomodations available at the Bear Track Inn.
Inn to Inn mountain bike tours available.
The Inn was featured in "Michigan Off the Beaten Path", Chicago Tribune Travel
Section and "Midwest Living Magazine"

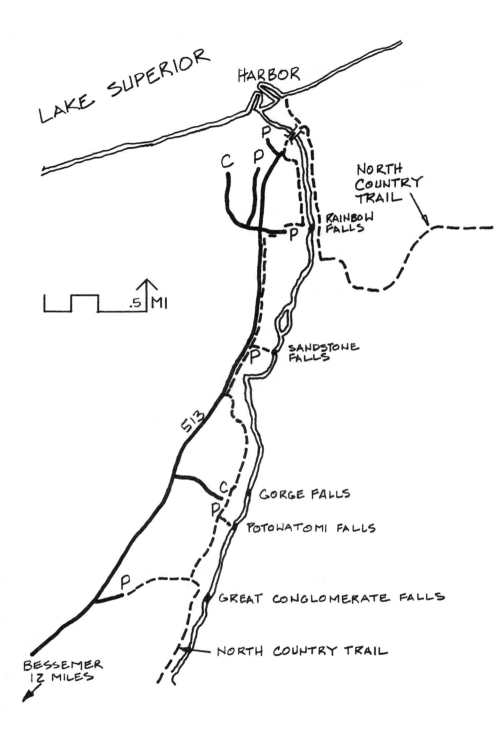

BLACK RIVER HARBOR TRAILS

Black River Harbor Trails

Bessemer Ranger District, Ottawa National Forest
500 N Moore St
Bessemer, MI 49911

906-667-0261

Recreation Staff Officer, Ottawa National Forest
2100 E. Cloverland Drive
Ironwood, MI 49938

906-932-1330

Michigan Atlas & Gazetteer Location: 113A8

County Location: Gogebic

Directions To Trailhead:
Along the Black River north of Bessemer to Lake Superior and Black River Harbor. First trail is 12 miles north of Bessemer and continuing north.

Trail Type: Hiking/Walking
Trail Distance: 5 mi   Loops: 5   Shortest: NA   Longest: NA
Trail Surface: Natural
Trail Use Fee: None
Method Of Ski Trail Grooming: NA
Skiing Ability Suggested: NA
Hiking Trail Difficulty: Moderate to difficult
Mountain Biking Ability Suggested: NA
Terrain: Varies with trail
Camping: Campground at Black River Harbor

Maintained by the Ottawa National Forest
Several individual trails from parking areas off Black River Rd to various falls. These are point to point trails, one way.
Great Conglomerate Falls Trail - .75 mile - 30% steep, 30% moderate, 40% flat
Gorge an Potawatomi Falls National Recreation Trail - .75 mile - 70% steep, 30% flat
Sandstone Falls Trail - .25 mile - 40% steep, 20% moderate, 40% flat
Rainbow Falls Trail, West - .5 mile - 80% steep, 20% moderate - stairs
Rainbow Falls Trail, East - .75 mile - 40% steep, 60% moderate - stairs

Trails are connected togeather by the North Country Trail. Rainbow Falls Trail -East is part of the North Country Trail.

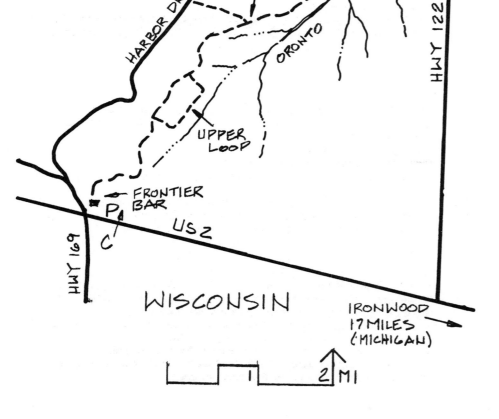

CEDAR TRAIL

Frontier Bar c/o John Innes
HCR Box 484
Saxon, WI 54559

715-893-2461

Michigan Atlas & Gazetteer Location: 113C7

County Location: Wisconsin

Directions To Trailhead:
IN Wisconsin, about 18 miles west of Ironwood on US2 at the intersection of US2 and Hwy 169.
South trailhead - Frontier Bar on US2 at Hwy 169.
North trailhead - Harbor Lights Bar on Co Rd A

Trail Type: Hiking/Walking, Cross Country Skiing, Interpretive
Trail Distance: 15 km   Loops: NA   Shortest: NA   Longest: NA
Trail Surface: Natural
Trail Use Fee: Donations accepted for trail maintenance only
Method Of Ski Trail Grooming: Track set
Skiing Ability Suggested: Intermediate
Hiking Trail Difficulty: Moderate
Mountain Biking Ability Suggested: NA
Terrain: Steep 0%, Hilly 10%, Moderate 20%, Flat 70%
Camping: Campground at south end of the trail

Maintained by volunteers.
The trail is located 18 miles west of the Wisconsin border.
Grooming done by the Frontier Bar. Donations accepted.
The trail has a 600 foot decent to Lake Superior.
Meals available at both trailhead taverns.
Picturesque ravines and mature forest along trail.
Camping: County park, campground and harbor at north trailhead. Private campground with showers and trailer hook-ups available at the south trailhead.

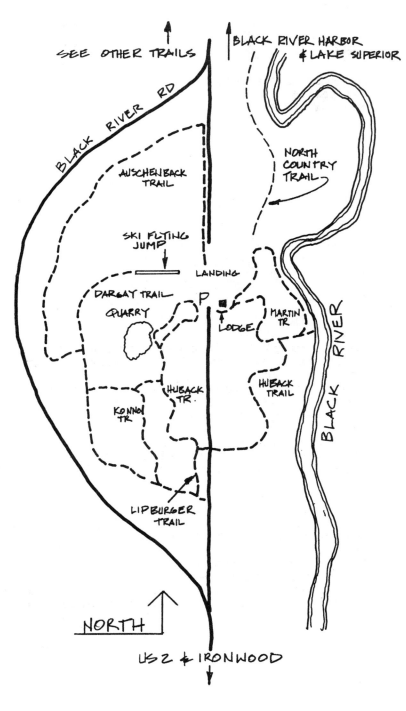

SEE OTHER TRAILS

BLACK RIVER HARBOR & LAKE SUPERIOR

BLACK RIVER RD

AUSCHENBACK TRAIL

NORTH COUNTRY TRAIL

SKI FLYING JUMP

LANDING

DARGAY TRAIL

QUARRY

P

LODGE

MARTIN TR

BLACK RIVER

HUBACK TR.

HUBACK TRAIL

KONNOI TR

LIPBURGER TRAIL

NORTH

US 2 & IRONWOOD

COPPER PEAK RECREATION CENTER

Powderhorn Lodging
Powderhorn Rd
Bessemer, MI 49911

800-222-3131
906-932-3100

Michigan Atlas & Gazetteer Location: 113A8

County Location: Gogebic

Directions To Trailhead:
From Ironwood, take Lake Rd to Airport Rd to Co. Rd. 513 to Copper Peak or from Bessemer take Co. Rd. 513 (Black River Harbor Rd.) north to Copper Peak.

Trail Type: Hiking/Walking, Cross Country Skiing, Mountain Biking
Trail Distance: 6 mi   Loops: 5   Shortest: 1/5 mi Longest: 4 mi
Trail Surface: Paved to natural
Trail Use Fee: None
Method Of Ski Trail Grooming: Not known
Skiing Ability Suggested: Novice to advanced
Hiking Trail Difficulty: Moderate to difficult
Mountain Biking Ability Suggested: Intermediate to advanced
Terrain: Steep 25%, Hilly 50%, Moderate 15%, Flat 10%
Camping: Black River Harbor Recreation Area 6 miles north

Privately maintained trail complex
Located at the only ski flying complex in the western hemisphere and the tallest ski jump in the world. Chalet available with hot drinks, food (limited in the winter) and gift shop. Mountain bike trails are mostly single track.
Chairlift available for transporting bike to the top of the 330 base hill of the ski flying jump. Shuttle available for one way bike trips.
Scenic view of Lake Superior from the top of the base chairlift.
North Country National Scenic Trail continues from Copper Peak north to Lake Superior and then east across the upper peninsula.

Ishpeming Forest Area, Escanaba River State Forest
1985 U.S. 41 West   906-485-1031
Ishpeming, MI 49849

Marquette Field Office, Eacanaba River State Forest
110 Ford Rd   906-249-1497
Marquette, MI 49855

Michigan Atlas & Gazetteer Location: 113D5

County Location: Marquette

Directions To Trailhead:
5 miles north of Marquette on Co Rd 550. Trail is on the west side of the road.
Parking in a former gravel pit.

Trail Type: Hiking/Walking, Cross Country Skiing, Mountain Biking
Trail Distance: 5.6 mi   Loops: 2   Shortest: 3.3 mi Longest: 5.6 mi
Trail Surface: Natrual
Trail Use Fee: None
Method Of Ski Trail Grooming: None
Skiing Ability Suggested: Intermediate
Hiking Trail Difficulty: Easy to moderate
Mountain Biking Ability Suggested: Novice to intermediate
Terrain: Steep 0%, Hilly 0%, Moderate 50%, Flat 50%
Camping: None

Maintained by the DNR Forest Management Divison.
Part of the Little Presque Isle Tract trails.
See map for additional trails that are nearby.
Other contacts:
        DNR Forest Management Division Office, Lansing, 517-373-1275
        DNR Forest Management District Office, Gladstone, 906-786-2351
        DNR Forest Management Region Office, Marquette, 906-228-6561

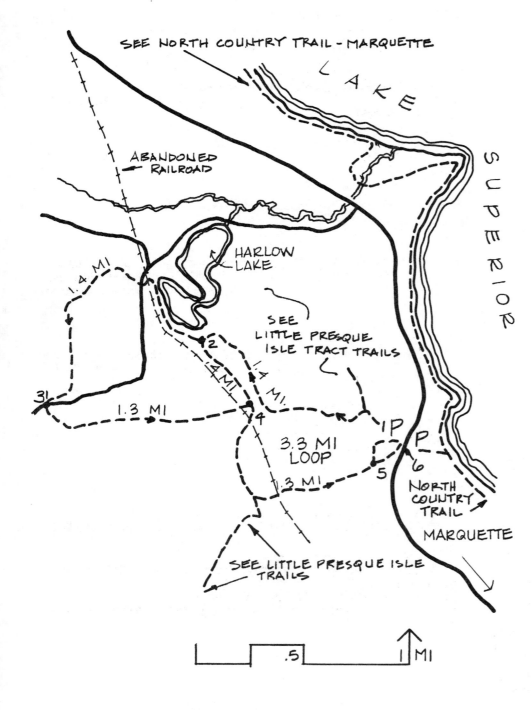

HARLOW LAKE PATHWAY

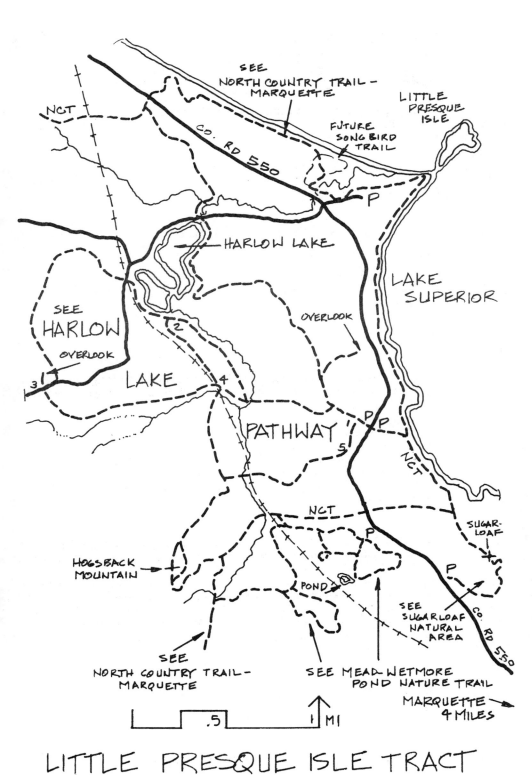

Ishpeming Forest Area, Escanaba River State Forest
1985 US 41 West   906-485-1031
Ishpeming, MI 49849

Escanaba River State Forest
6833 Hwy 2, 41 & M 35   906-786-2351
Gladstone, MI 49837

Michigan Atlas & Gazetteer Location: 113CD5

County Location: Marquette

Directions To Trailhead:
6.5 miles north of Marquette on Co. Rd. 550. Primary parking areas include
Wetmore Landing (4.1 mi north of the city limit and 1.1 mi north of Sugar Loaf
Mt. and Little Presque Isle Point (east of Co. Rd. 550, 1.3 mi north of Wetmore
Landing parking area)

Trail Type: Hiking/Walking, Cross Country Skiing, Mountain Biking, Interpretive
Trail Distance: 18 mi   Loops: 4   Shortest: 3 mi   Longest: 7 mi
Trail Surface: Natural
Trail Use Fee: None
Method Of Ski Trail Grooming: NA
Skiing Ability Suggested: NA
Hiking Trail Difficulty: Easy to difficult
Mountain Biking Ability Suggested: Novice
Terrain: Steep 10%, Hilly 25%, Moderate 40%, Flat 25%
Camping: None

Maintained by the DNR Forest Management Division
Trail system connects the Mead - Wetmore Pond Interpretive Trail, Harlow Lake
Pathway
and Sugar Loaf Mountain Natural Area trail.
Mountain biking and cross country skiing limited to the Harlow Lake Pathway
(see other listing)
Newest trail is the Songbird Trail (see other listing)
For more information contact the Division Headquarters in Lansing 517-373-
1275

LITTLE PRESQUE ISLE TRACT

Mercer MECCA Cross Country Ski Club
PO Box 76
Mercer, WI 54547

715-476-2938

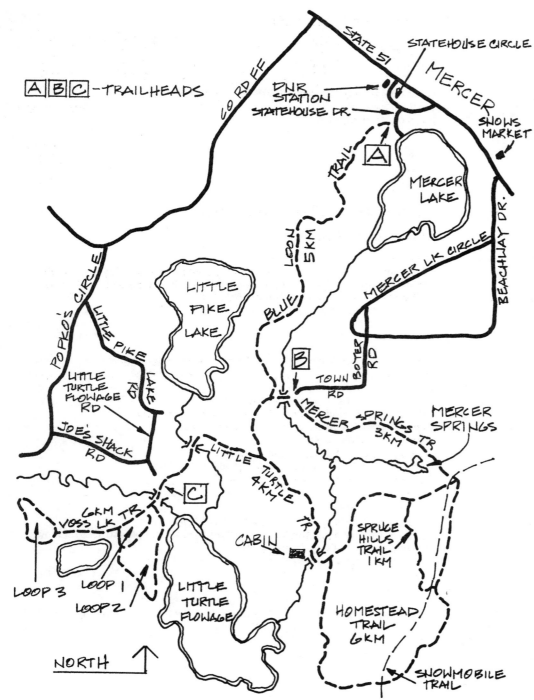

Michigan Atlas & Gazetteer Location: 113 Wisconsin

County Location: Wisconsin

Directions To Trailhead:
23 miles south of Ironwood on US51 at Mercer Wisconsin.
Traihead A - About 1/8 mile north of Mercer on US51 to Statehouse Circle Rd,then follow signs.
Traihead B - .25 south of Mercer on US51 to Beachway Drive, then to Mercer Lake Circle Rd, then to Boyer Rd, then to Town Rd. (follow signs). Trailhead C - From Mercer on US51 north 1 mile to CoRd FF and follow signs.

Trail Type: Cross Country Skiing
Trail Distance: 25 km   Loops: 4   Shortest: 3 km   Longest: 9 km
Trail Surface: Natural
Trail Use Fee: Donations accepted
Method Of Ski Trail Grooming: Track set weekly
Skiing Ability Suggested: Novice to intermediate
Hiking Trail Difficulty: NA
Mountain Biking Ability Suggested: NA
Terrain: Steep 5%, Hilly 20%, Moderate 60%, Flat 15%
Camping: None

Maintained by the MECCA Ski Club. A non-profit organization which maintains, grooms and promotes the trail.
Well designed and interesting ski trail.
This and other Iron County trails were developed through the close cooperation of various local citizen groups and the Iron County Wisconsin Forestry Department.
Strictly a ski trail. Not suitable for mountain biking or hiking because of the many swamps in the area along the trail.
Heated cabin along trail at a scenic wetland vista.
Donations by trail users are an essential part of the fund raising program to maintain these trails.
Several trailheads and a waterfall are along the trail.
Some of the trail is on private land. Please stay on the trail at all times.

MECCA X-C SKI TRAIL

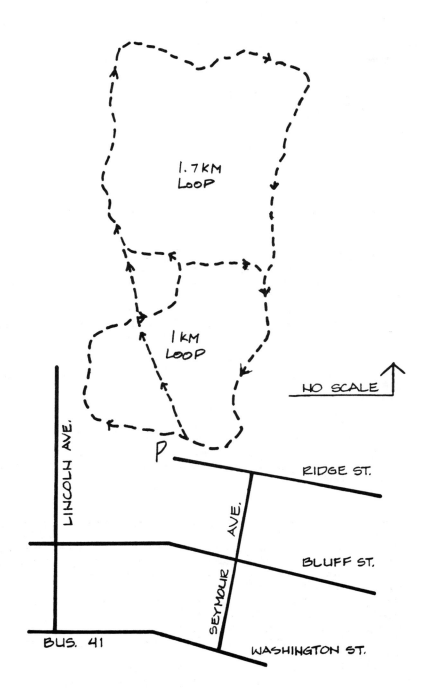

MARQUETTE FITNESS TRAIL

City of Marquette, Department of Parks and Recreation
300 Baraga Ave
Marquette, MI 49855

906-228-0460

Michigan Atlas & Gazetteer Location: 113D5

County Location: Marquette

Directions To Trailhead:
Take Washington St. .5 mile west of the downtown area to Seymour St, then proceed north to Ridge St., then west on Ridge St. to the parking lot. The trailhead is directly north of the parking lot.

Trail Type: Hiking/Walking, Cross Country Skiing, Interpretive
Trail Distance: 4.4 km   Loops: 3   Shortest: 1 km   Longest: 1.7 km
Trail Surface:
Trail Use Fee: Yes, donation for skiing only
Method Of Ski Trail Grooming: Track set with skating trail
Skiing Ability Suggested: Novice to intermediate
Hiking Trail Difficulty: Easy
Mountain Biking Ability Suggested: NA
Terrain: Steep 0%, Hilly 5%, Moderate 95%, Flat 5%
Camping: Available in the Marquette area

Maintained by the Parks Department, City of Marquette
1.7 km lighted loop to 11pm
Trails for traditional and skating styles

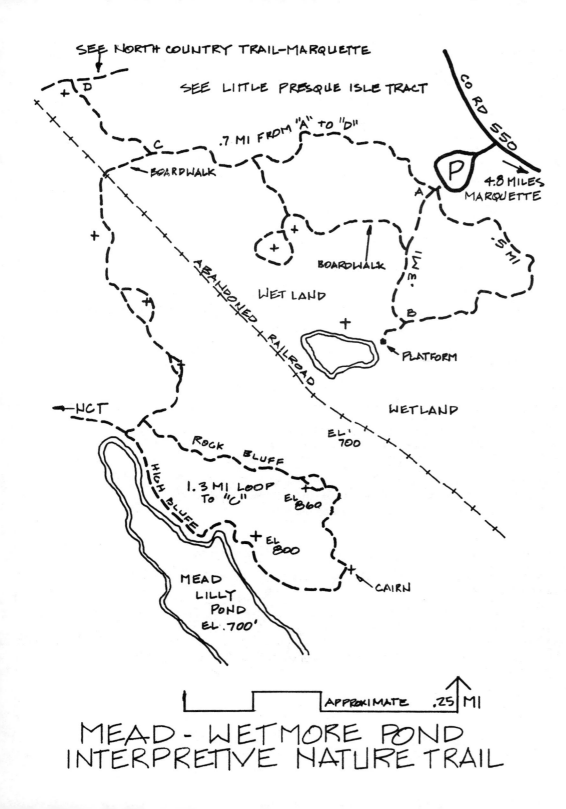

SEE NORTH COUNTRY TRAIL-MARQUETTE

SEE LITTLE PRESQUE ISLE TRACT

CO RD 550

.7 MI FROM "A" TO "D"

P

4.8 MILES MARQUETTE

BOARDWALK

.5 MI

BOARDWALK

WETLAND

M m.

A

B

ABANDONED RAILROAD

WETLAND

PLATFORM

NCT

ROCK BLUFF

EL' 700

HIGH BLUFF

1.3 MI LOOP TO "C"

EL 860

EL 800

CAIRN

MEAD LILLY POND EL .700'

APPROXIMATE .25 MI

MEAD - WETMORE POND INTERPRETIVE NATURE TRAIL

Mead-Wetmore Pond Nature Trail

Mead Paper, Woodlands Department
US41, West
Champion, MI 49814

906-339-2281

Mead Paper, Woodland Communications
PO Box 1008
Escanaba, MI 49829

906-786-1660
Ext. 2194

Michigan Atlas & Gazetteer Location: 113D5

County Location: Marquette

Directions To Trailhead:
4.5 miles north of Marquette on Co. Rd. 550. Between the Sugar Loaf and Harlow Lake trails.

Trail Type: Hiking/Walking, Cross Country Skiing, Interpretive
Trail Distance: 12 mi   Loops: 3   Shortest: Various Longest: Various
Trail Surface: Natural
Trail Use Fee: None
Method Of Ski Trail Grooming: None
Skiing Ability Suggested: Novice to intermediate
Hiking Trail Difficulty: Easy to moderate
Mountain Biking Ability Suggested: NA
Terrain: Steep 2%, Hilly 10%, Moderate 28%, Flat 60%
Camping: None

Owned and developed by Mead Paper.
Trails and facilities built by Mead and and volunteers including members of the North Country Trail Association, Michigan Department of Natural Resources, Northern Michigan University faculty and other volunteers.
Wetmore pond is a floating bog worth the time to view.
North County Trail - Marquette segment passes nearby the area.
Part of a trail system that connects together the North Country Trail, Harlow Lake Pathway and the Sugar Loaf Mountain Interpretive Trail.   All are listed separately in the atlas.

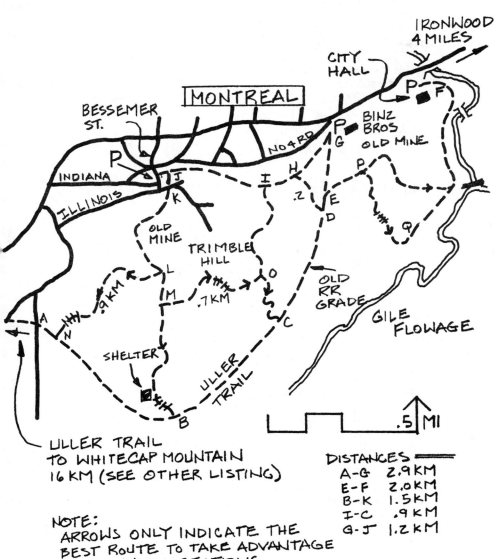

IRONWOOD
4 MILES

CITY HALL

MONTREAL

BESSEMER ST.

NO 4 RD

BINZ BROS
OLD MINE

P

INDIANA

ILLINOIS

J

K

OLD MINE

TRIMBLE HILL

I

H

E

D

Q

.9 KM

L

M

.7 KM

O

C

OLD RR GRADE

GILE FLOWAGE

A

N

SHELTER

B

ULLER TRAIL

.5 MI

ULLER TRAIL
TO WHITECAP MOUNTAIN
16 KM (SEE OTHER LISTING)

NOTE:
ARROWS ONLY INDICATE THE
BEST ROUTE TO TAKE ADVANTAGE
OF DOWNHILL SECTIONS

DISTANCES
A-G   2.9 KM
E-F   2.0 KM
B-K   1.5 KM
I-C   .9 KM
G-J   1.2 KM

Iron County Extension Service
Court House
Hurley, WI 54534

715-561-2695

Penokee Rangers Inc.
301 Birch St.
Pence, WI 54553

715-561-5623

Michigan Atlas & Gazetteer Location: 113C6

County Location: Wisconsin

Directions To Trailhead:
4 miles west of Ironwood via US2 and Wisconsin Hwy 77
Trailhead - In Montreal take Bessemer south to trailheads(2) at the corners of 4
Rd & Bessemer & Illinois & Bessemer.
Trailhead - Montreal City Hall on Hwy 77
Trailhead - West end of Montreal on Spring Camp Rd

Trail Type: Hiking/Walking, Cross Country Skiing, Interpretive
Trail Distance: 15 km   Loops: 6   Shortest: .5 km   Longest: 11 km
Trail Surface: Natural
Trail Use Fee: Donation requested at trailhead
Method Of Ski Trail Grooming: Track set 3 to 4 times per week
Skiing Ability Suggested: Novice to intermediate
Hiking Trail Difficulty: Easy to moderate
Mountain Biking Ability Suggested: Intermediate to advanced
Terrain: Steep 10%, Hilly 40%, Moderate 20%, Flat 30%
Camping: None

Maintained by the Penokee Rangers (a local non-profit ski club)
A delightful trail system in the hills above Montreal.
Shelter cabin is along the trail Trail is well designed with several long downhill
runs and beautiful scenery.
The east end of the 16 km Uller Trail (see other listing) to Weber Lake.
Portion of the trail (Uller Trail) is double track on the old Montreal Iron Mine
railroad grade. Many historic remanents of the Montreal Mine (the deepest iron
mine in the world, almost 1 mile deep) are visible along the trail including tailing
piles, many old structures and the railroad grade cut through bedrock.

MONTREAL PUBLIC TRAIL

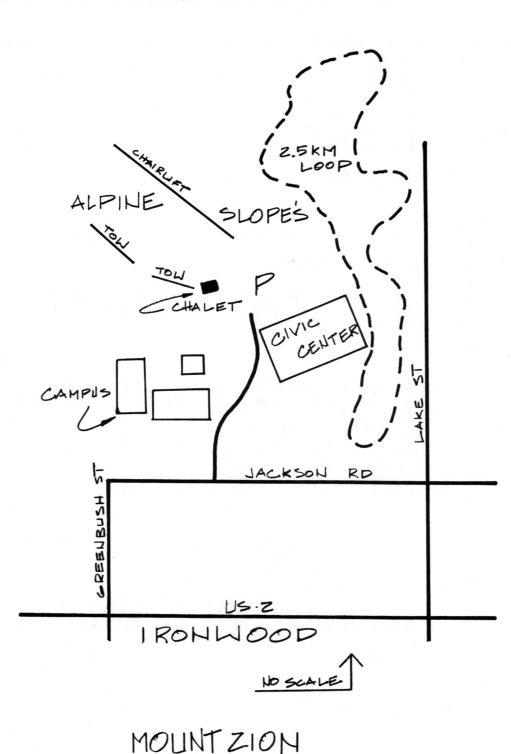

Gogebic Community College
E4946 Jackson Rd
Ironwood, MI 49938

906-932-3718

Michigan Atlas & Gazetteer Location: 113C7

County Location: Gogebic

Directions To Trailhead:
On the campus of Gogebic Community College, .5 mile north of US2

Trail Type: Hiking/Walking, Cross Country Skiing
Trail Distance: 2.5 km   Loops: 1   Shortest: Longest: 2.5 km
Trail Surface: Natural
Trail Use Fee: None
Method Of Ski Trail Grooming: Track set
Skiing Ability Suggested: Novice
Hiking Trail Difficulty: Easy
Mountain Biking Ability Suggested: NA
Terrain: Steep 0%, Hilly 0%, Moderate 10%, Flat 90%
Camping: None

Operated by Gogebic Community College

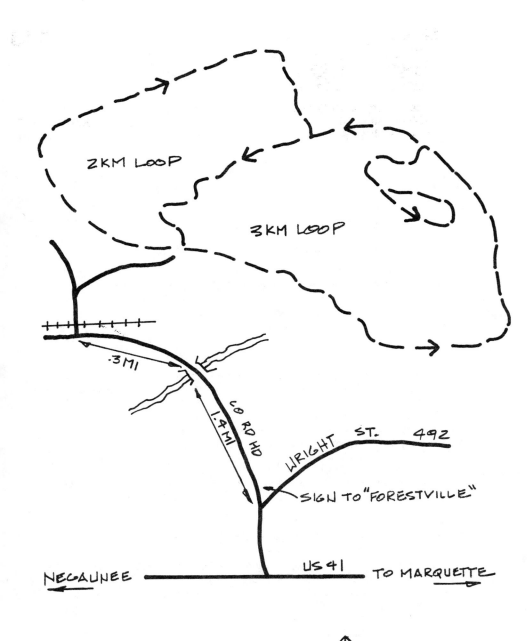

Athletic Department
Northern Michigan Univesity
Marquette, MI 49855

Michigan Atlas & Gazetteer Location: 113D5

County Location: Marquette

Directions To Trailhead:
From US41, take Wright St north to road to Forestville. After crossing Dead River at about 1.7 miles from US23 turn right over railroad tracks, then another right to trail

Trail Type: Cross Country Skiing
Trail Distance: 4.5 km   Loops: 2   Shortest: 2 km   Longest: 3 km
Trail Surface: Natrual
Trail Use Fee: None
Method Of Ski Trail Grooming: None
Skiing Ability Suggested: Intermediate
Hiking Trail Difficulty: NA
Mountain Biking Ability Suggested: NA
Terrain:
Camping: None

Maintained by Northern Michigan University

2KM LOOP

3KM LOOP

.3 MI

1.4 MI

CO RD HD

WRIGHT ST. 492

SIGN TO "FORESTVILLE"

NEGAUNEE   US 41   TO MARQUETTE

NORTH ↑

NMU LONGYEAR

City of Marquette, Parks & Recreation Department
300 Baraga Ave
Marquette, MI 49855

906-228-8200
ext 213

800-544-4321

Michigan Atlas & Gazetteer Location: 113D6

County Location: Marquette

Directions To Trailhead:
2 miles north of Marquette along lakeshore at Presque Isle Park Take
Lakeshore Blvd north to Peter White Dr(2 miles) Trailhead-Adjacent to Peter
White Drive and plowed parking lots.

Trail Type: Hiking/Walking, Cross Country Skiing, Interpretive
Trail Distance: 5 km   Loops: 3   Shortest: 1.5 km Longest: 3.5 km
Trail Surface:
Trail Use Fee: Yes, donation for skiing only
Method Of Ski Trail Grooming: Track set as needed
Skiing Ability Suggested: Novice to intermediate
Hiking Trail Difficulty: Moderate
Mountain Biking Ability Suggested: NA
Terrain: Steep 0%, Hilly 25%, Moderate 35%, Flat 40%
Camping: Very nearby

Maintained by the City of Marquette, Parks and Recreation Department
Both wide (vehicle drive in summer) and narrow (foot paths) trails are available
to the skier A small city zoo is along the return trail Interior trails are through
dense forests.
Beautiful view of Lake Superior and winter ice formations. Also a snow shoe trail
avaialble which is not listed. Traditional and skating style trails. Skating is
goomed on about 70% of the trails.
Because of the warming effect of Lake Superior, this trail looses its snow cover
earlier than the inland trails in the Marquette and Ishpeming area.
Brochure is available for the 14 station interpretive trail.

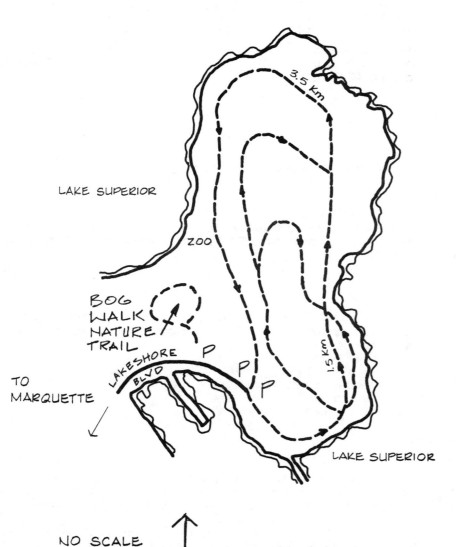

PRESQUE ISLE PARK

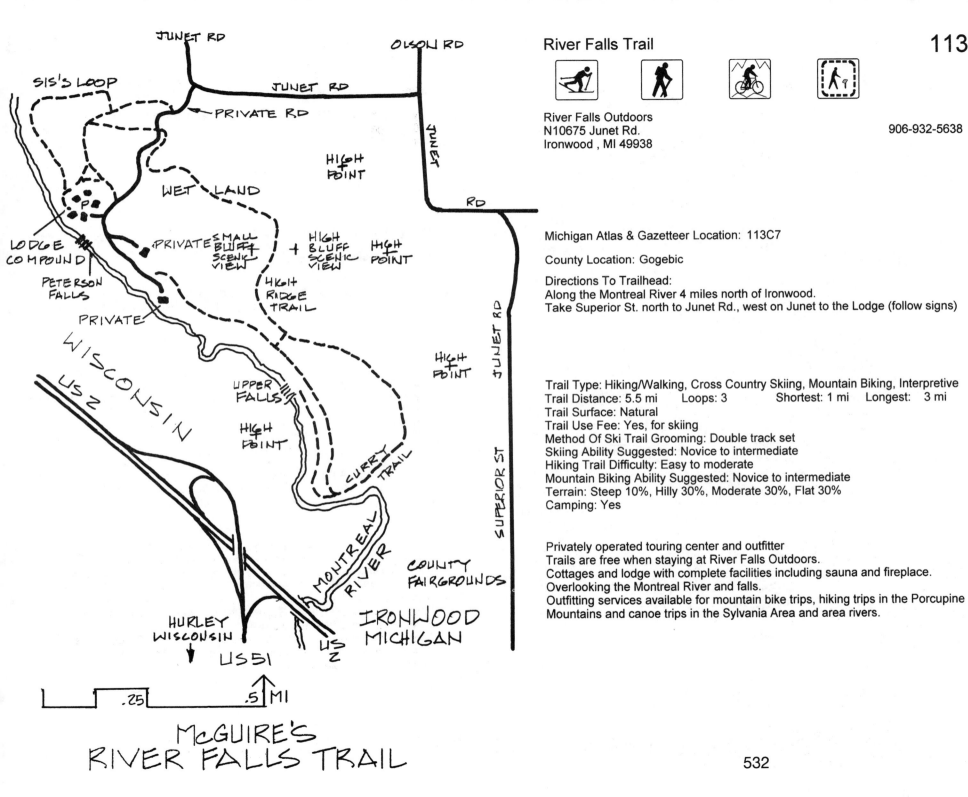

River Falls Outdoors
N10675 Junet Rd.
Ironwood , MI 49938

906-932-5638

Michigan Atlas & Gazetteer Location: 113C7

County Location: Gogebic

Directions To Trailhead:
Along the Montreal River 4 miles north of Ironwood.
Take Superior St. north to Junet Rd., west on Junet to the Lodge (follow signs)

Trail Type: Hiking/Walking, Cross Country Skiing, Mountain Biking, Interpretive
Trail Distance: 5.5 mi   Loops: 3   Shortest: 1 mi   Longest: 3 mi
Trail Surface: Natural
Trail Use Fee: Yes, for skiing
Method Of Ski Trail Grooming: Double track set
Skiing Ability Suggested: Novice to intermediate
Hiking Trail Difficulty: Easy to moderate
Mountain Biking Ability Suggested: Novice to intermediate
Terrain: Steep 10%, Hilly 30%, Moderate 30%, Flat 30%
Camping: Yes

Privately operated touring center and outfitter
Trails are free when staying at River Falls Outdoors.
Cottages and lodge with complete facilities including sauna and fireplace.
Overlooking the Montreal River and falls.
Outfitting services available for mountain bike trips, hiking trips in the Porcupine
Mountains and canoe trips in the Sylvania Area and area rivers.

McGUIRE'S RIVER FALLS TRAIL

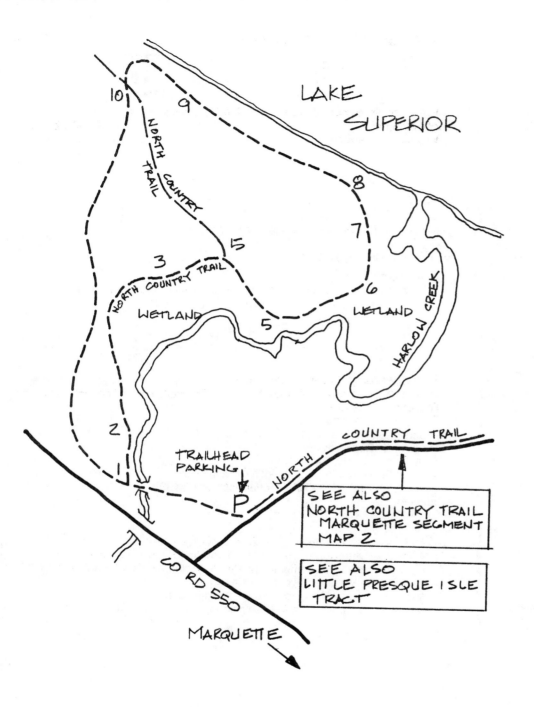

Ishpeming Field Office, Forest Management Division, DNR
1895 US 41
Ishpeming, MI 49849

906-485-1031

Michigan Atlas & Gazetteer Location: 113C5

County Location: Marquette

Directions To Trailhead:
From Marquette, take Co Rd 550 5.4 miles north to trail road (or 2.4 miles north of the Sugar Loaf Mountain parking area). Turn right onto trail road. Parking lot is 100 yds from Co Rd 550.

Trail Type: Hiking/Walking, Interpretive
Trail Distance: 1.1 mi   Loops: 1   Shortest: NA   Longest: 1.1 mi
Trail Surface: Natural
Trail Use Fee: None
Method Of Ski Trail Grooming: NA
Skiing Ability Suggested: NA
Hiking Trail Difficulty: Easy
Mountain Biking Ability Suggested: NA
Terrain: Steep 0%, Hilly 10%, Moderate 30%, Flat 60%
Camping: None, but available in the Marquette area

Maintained by the DNR-Forest Management Division
A 10 station nature trail with audio cassette narative.
Cassettes and walkman players are available from DNR offices in Marquette and Ishpeming and at the 550 store located 2 miles north of Marquette on Co. Rd. 550.
See also the North Country Trail-Marquette, Harlow Lake Pathway and Little Presque Isle Tract that are in the area.
Printed trail guide is also available.

SONGBIRD TRAIL

Marquette Co. Resource Management & Development Dept
234 Baraga   906-228-1535
Marquette, MI 49855

Michigan Atlas & Gazetteer Location: 113D5

County Location: Marquette

Directions To Trailhead:
North from Marquette about 4.4 miles along Lake Superior on Co Rd 550

Trail Type: Hiking/Walking, Interpretive
Trail Distance: .5 mi   Loops: NA   Shortest: NA   Longest: NA
Trail Surface: Natural
Trail Use Fee: None
Method Of Ski Trail Grooming: NA
Skiing Ability Suggested: NA
Hiking Trail Difficulty: Moderate
Mountain Biking Ability Suggested: NA
Terrain: Steep 35%, Hilly 45%, Moderate 15%, Flat 5%
Camping: None

Maintained by the Marquette County Road Commission.
Near Harlow Lake Pathway and the Mead-Wetmore Pond Interpretive Trail.
Very scenic changing panoramic views of the Lake Superior shoreline.

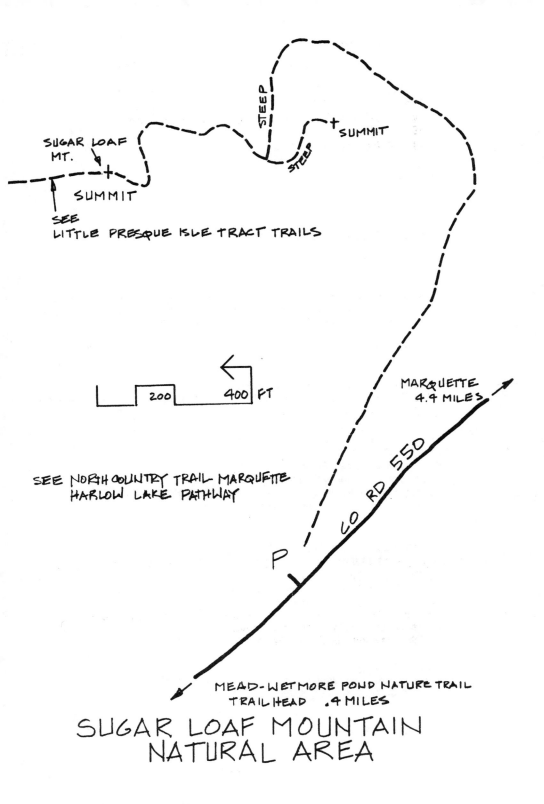

SUGAR LOAF MOUNTAIN
NATURAL AREA

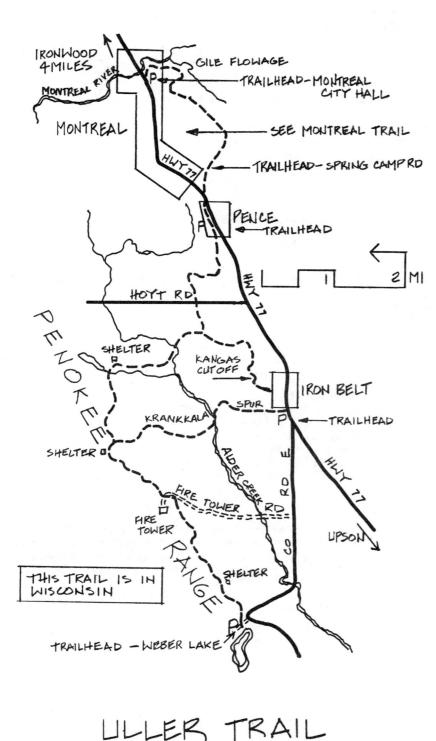

Penokee Rangers Inc.
301 Birch St
Pence, WI 54550

715-561-5623

Michigan Atlas & Gazetteer Location: 113C6

County Location: Wisconsin

Directions To Trailhead:
This trail is in Wisconsin. Gazetteer location is closest location in Michigan
East trailhead - Montreal Public Trail at the Montreal City Hall
Middle trailheads - On Hwy 77 at Pence and north side of Iron Belt (Krankkala Spur and Kangas Cut-off)
West trailhead - Weber Lake next to Whitecap Mountainson Co Hwy E

Trail Type: Cross Country Skiing, Interpretive
Trail Distance: 25 km   Loops: NA   Shortest: NA   Longest: NA
Trail Surface: Natural
Trail Use Fee: Donation accepted
Method Of Ski Trail Grooming: Track set as needed
Skiing Ability Suggested: All levels
Hiking Trail Difficulty: All levels
Mountain Biking Ability Suggested: NA
Terrain: Steep 10%, Hilly 50%, Moderate 30%, Flat 10%
Camping: Along the trail at trailside shelters

Maintained by the Penokee Rangers Inc, a local non-profit cross-country ski club
The trail has 14 interpreted locations coveing geography, wildlife, forestry and history.
A well established ski trail with little interference from snowmobiles, even though there are few signs to prohibit snowmobile use on the trail.
Since this trail is funded solely by the donations of its users, it is essential that you make a donation to fund the grooming .
The Montreal Trail located at the east end of the Uller is also maintained by the Penokee Rangers Inc.
This trail traverses the top of the scenic Penokee Mountains from Montreal to Weber Lake. Two rustic shelters along the trail are available for overnight accomodations.

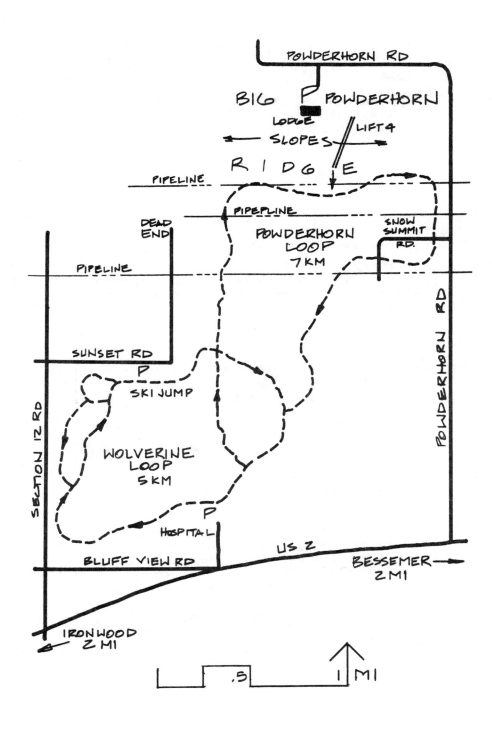

WOLVERINE SKI TRAILS

Wolverine Nordic Ski Club
Sunset Rd
Ironwood, MI

Powderhorn Lodging
Powderhorn Rd
Bessemer, MI 49911

906-932-3100

Michigan Atlas & Gazetteer Location: 113BC78

County Location: Gogebic

Directions To Trailhead:
Wolverine Hill trailhead - East of Ironwood on US2, then north on Section 12 Rd.
1.25 miles, then east 1/2 mile on Sunset Rd to the ski jumps.
Big Powderhorn trailhead - Top of chair lift #4

Trail Type: Cross Country Skiing, Mountain Biking
Trail Distance: 14 km   Loops: 2   Shortest: 5 km   Longest: 7 km
Trail Surface: Natural
Trail Use Fee: Donations accepted
Method Of Ski Trail Grooming: Track set
Skiing Ability Suggested: Novice to intermediate
Hiking Trail Difficulty: NA
Mountain Biking Ability Suggested: Novice to intermediate
Terrain: Steep 0%, Hilly 70%, Moderate 0%, Flat 30%
Camping: None

Maintained by the Wolverine Ski Club and Big Powderhorn Lodging
The trail offers a variety of scenery, maple hardwood forests, old homesteads,
scenic overlooks, streams, a beaver dam, "ice falls", and ski jumps.
Very popular trail, but large enough so you don't get the feeling of being
crowded.
Well designed ski trail for the novice and intermediate skier.
Near many other trails.

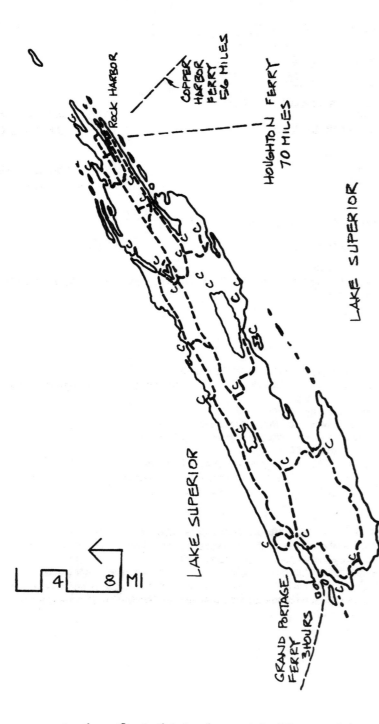

LAKE SUPERIOR

LAKE SUPERIOR

ROCK HARBOR

COPPER HARBOR FERRY 56 MILES

HOUGHTON FERRY 70 MILES

GRAND PORTAGE FERRY 3 HOURS

4 | 8 MI

ISLE ROYALE NATIONAL PARK

Isle Royale National Park
87 N. Ripley St
Houghton, MI 49931-1895

906-482-0984

Michigan Atlas & Gazetteer Location: 114all,115all

County Location: Keweenaw

Directions To Trailhead:
70 miles north of Houghton in Lake Superior Ferry services from Houghton, Copper Harbor and Grand Portage Sea plane service from Houghton

Trail Type: Hiking/Walking, Interpretive
Trail Distance: 165 mi   Loops: Many   Shortest: Longest:
Trail Surface: Paved and mostly natural
Trail Use Fee: Yes
Method Of Ski Trail Grooming: NA
Skiing Ability Suggested: NA
Hiking Trail Difficulty: Easy to extremely difficult
Mountain Biking Ability Suggested: NA
Terrain: Steep 20%, Hilly 30%, Moderate 30%, Flat 20%
Camping: Available throughout the park

Maintained by the National Park Service
The most rugged and remote area in Michigan. The extreme beauty of this island is a delight to the senses. Be completely prepared before attempting to do any extensive hiking on the island. Write to the Park for information on hiking/camping/boating recommendations before planning your trip. Complete lodge facilities are available at Rock Harbor for those not interested in extensive hiking but reservations must be made months in advance to assure accomodation. Likewise, reservations on the two ferry boats should be made a month in advance of departure to assure space on board. Write for information brochures and catalog of publications available. Park season Apr 16th - Oct 31st. Full services are available June-August NOT OPEN IN THE WINTER.

Pictured Rocks National Lakeshore
PO Box 40
Munising, MI 49862-0040

906-387-3700
906-387-2607

906-494-2669

Michigan Atlas & Gazetteer Location: 115C8

County Location: Alger

Directions To Trailhead:
2 mile west of Grand Marais on H 58 or 1.5 miles west of M 77 on Newberg Rd.

Trail Type: Hiking/Walking, Cross Country Skiing
Trail Distance: 10 mi   Loops: 6   Shortest: .8 mi   Longest: 2 mi
Trail Surface: Natural
Trail Use Fee: None
Method Of Ski Trail Grooming: Track set
Skiing Ability Suggested: Novice to intermediate
Hiking Trail Difficulty: Moderate
Mountain Biking Ability Suggested: Not permitted
Terrain: Steep 0%, Hilly 0%, Moderate 20%, Flat 80%
Camping: Campground available May 10 to October 31

Maintained by the Pictured Rocks National Lakeshore
A trail map is in place at each trail intersection.
Pets are not permitted on the ski trails.
The trail crosses H-58 at two locations. Be alert for snowmobile traffic.
The North Country National Scenic Trail follows the Beech Forest hiking trail
along Sable Creek which is located between the ski trail and Sable Creek.

Map labels:

LAKE SUPERIOR

NORTH COUNTRY TRAIL

2 MI LOOP

GRAND MARAIS 1 MI

H-58   P

GRAND SABLE DUNES

2 MI LOOP

2 MI LOOP

CREEK

BEECH FOREST HIKING TRAIL .8M

1.6 MI LOOP

1.1 MILES

NORTH COUNTRY NATIONAL SCENIC TRAIL

SABLE

MIXON RD.

H-58

VISITOR CENTER   P

NEWBERG RD.

P
P

2 MI. LOOP

H-58

TRAIL

NORTH COUNTRY 2 MI LOOP

.5 MI

GRAND MARAIS CROSS COUNTRY SKI TRAIL

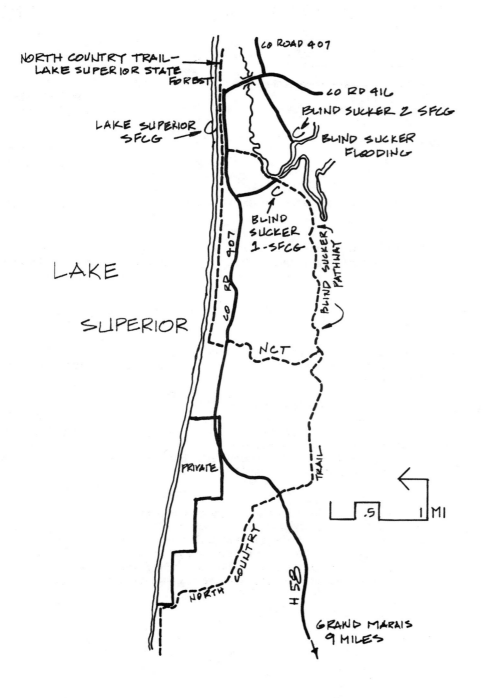

NORTH COUNTRY TRAIL- LAKE SUPERIOR STATE FOREST

CO ROAD 407

CO RD 416
BLIND SUCKER 2 SFCG

BLIND SUCKER FLOODING

LAKE SUPERIOR SFCG

LAKE SUPERIOR

BLIND SUCKER 1-SFCG

C

CO RD 407

BLIND SUCKER PATHWAY

NCT

TRAIL

PRIVATE

.5   1 MI

NORTH COUNTRY

NORTH COUNTRY TRAIL

H 58

GRAND MARAIS 9 MILES

BLIND SUCKER PATHWAY

Newberry Forest Area, Lake Superior State Forest
PO Box 428
Newberry, MI 49868

906-293-3293

District Forest Manager, Lake Superior State Forest
PO Box 77
Newberry, MI 49868

906-293-5132

Michigan Atlas & Gazetteer Location: 116C2

County Location: Luce

Directions To Trailhead:
Along Lake Superior 10 miles east of Grand Marais on H 58 at Blind Sucker 1 State Forest Campground (SFCG)

Trail Type: Hiking/Walking
Trail Distance: 3+ mi   Loops: NA   Shortest: NA   Longest: NA
Trail Surface: Natural
Trail Use Fee: None
Method Of Ski Trail Grooming: NA
Skiing Ability Suggested: NA
Hiking Trail Difficulty: Moderate
Mountain Biking Ability Suggested: NA
Terrain: Steep 0%, Hilly 25%, Moderate 60%, Flat 15%
Camping: Campround along trail and also nearby

Maintained by the DNR Forest Management Division
The trail is a bypass section of the North Country Trail - Lake Superior State Forest
Trail distance is approximate.
By also using the North Country Trail, a 7.6 mile loop can be made.
The trail is in a very scenic and isolated area.

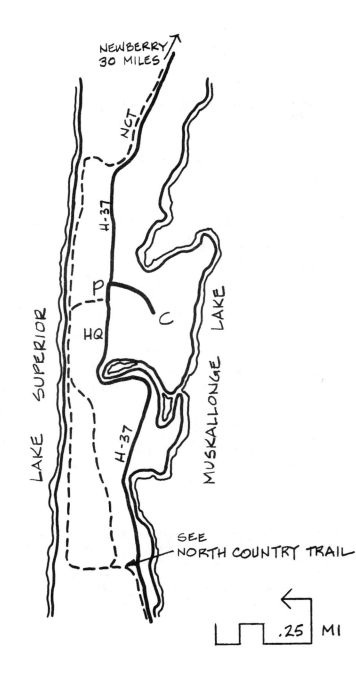

Muskallonge Lake State Park
Rte 1, PO Box 245
Newberry, MI 49868

906-658-3338

DNR Parks and Recreation Division

517-373-1270
906-492-3415

Michigan Atlas & Gazetteer Location: 116C4

County Location: Luce

Directions To Trailhead:
30 miles north of Newberry on Co Rd 407 (H37) 18 miles east of Grand Marais on Co Rd 407

Trail Type: Hiking/Walking, Cross Country Skiing
Trail Distance: .75 mi   Loops: 1   Shortest: Longest: .75 mi
Trail Surface: Natural
Trail Use Fee: None, but vehicle entry fee required
Method Of Ski Trail Grooming: NA
Skiing Ability Suggested: NA
Hiking Trail Difficulty: Easy
Mountain Biking Ability Suggested: NA
Terrain: Steep 0%, Hilly 0%, Moderate 90%, Flat 10%
Camping: Campground in the park

Maintained by the DNR Parks and Recreation Division
Part of the North Country Pathway
Site of a logging town call Deer Park in the 1800's
Good agate hunting along Lake Superior near trail

MUSKALLONGE LAKE STATE PARK

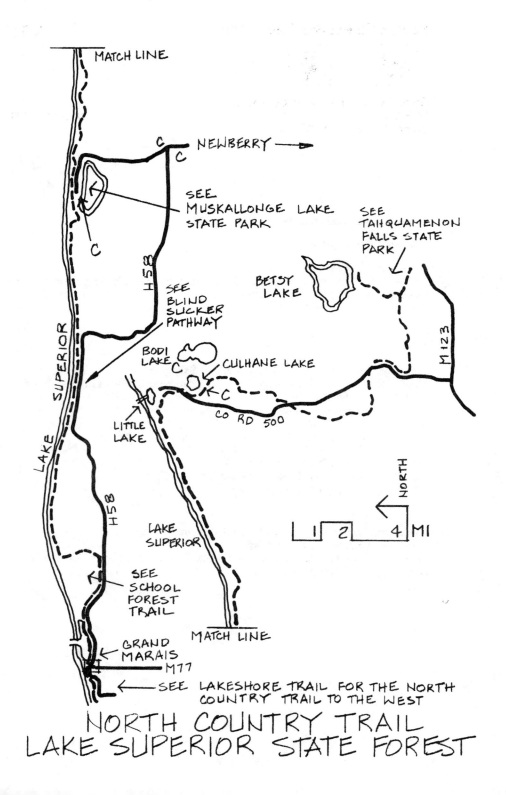

MATCH LINE

C NEWBERRY →
C

SEE
MUSKALLONGE LAKE
STATE PARK

SEE
TAHQUAMENON
FALLS STATE
PARK

C

H58

SEE
BLIND
SUCKER
PATHWAY

BETSY
LAKE

BODI
LAKE
C

CULHANE LAKE

M123

CO RD 500

C

LITTLE
LAKE

LAKE SUPERIOR

H58

LAKE
SUPERIOR

SEE
SCHOOL
FOREST
TRAIL

MATCH LINE

NORTH

1 2 4 MI

GRAND
MARAIS
M77

← SEE LAKESHORE TRAIL FOR THE NORTH
COUNTRY TRAIL TO THE WEST

NORTH COUNTRY TRAIL
LAKE SUPERIOR STATE FOREST

District Forest Manager, Lake Superior State Forest
PO Box 77   906-293-5131
Newberry, MI 49868

Tahquamenon Falls State Park
Rte 48, Box 225   906-492-3415
Paradise, MI 49768   517-373-1270

Michigan Atlas & Gazetteer Location: 116C1234,117CD567

County Location: Luce/Chippewa

Directions To Trailhead:
From Tahquamenon Falls State Park to Pictured Rocks National Lakeshore.
Trailheads - Grand Marais, Tahquamenon Falls SP, Muskallonge Lake SP,
Lake Superior SFCG and Two Hearted River SFCG.

          Additional trailhead-Trail follows Co Rd 500 for a few miles just north of
M123

Trail Type: Hiking/Walking
Trail Distance: 56 mi   Loops: NA   Shortest: NA   Longest: NA
Trail Surface: Natural
Trail Use Fee: None
Method Of Ski Trail Grooming: None
Skiing Ability Suggested: NA
Hiking Trail Difficulty: Moderate to difficult
Mountain Biking Ability Suggested: NA
Terrain: Steep 0%, Hilly 25%, Moderate 50%, Flat 25
Camping: Campgrounds along and near the trail

Maintained by the DNR Forest Management Division.
Some sections have been reported to be not well maintained. Confirm
information before starting out on the trail.
Campgrounds available at Tahquamenon Falls and Muskallonge Lake SP's and
many state forest campgrounds. Water is not available along the trail except at
these campgrounds.
For more information about the North Country Trail contact the North Country
Trail Association

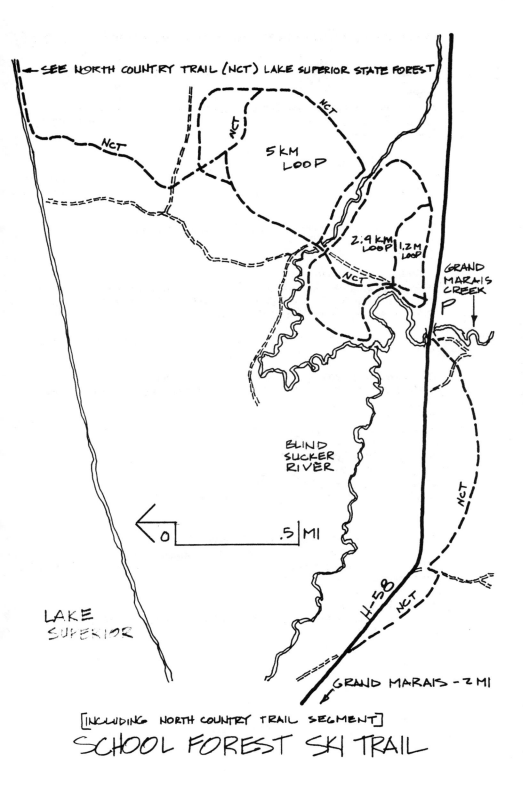

SEE NORTH COUNTRY TRAIL (NCT) LAKE SUPERIOR STATE FOREST

NCT

NCT

NCT

5 KM LOOP

NCT

2.9 KM LOOP

1.2 M LOOP

NCT

GRAND MARAIS CREEK

P

NCT

BLIND SUCKER RIVER

0 .5 MI

NCT

H-58

NCT

LAKE SUPERIOR

GRAND MARAIS - 2 MI

[INCLUDING NORTH COUNTRY TRAIL SEGMENT]
SCHOOL FOREST SKI TRAIL

School Forest Ski Trail

Grand Marais Chamber of Commerce
POB 139
Grand Marais, MI 49839

906-494-2766

Michigan Atlas & Gazetteer Location: 116C1

County Location: Alger

Directions To Trailhead:
4 miles east of Grand Marais on H58 just past the creek. Parking lot on the right side of the road. Trail on the north side of the road. Short distance from the parking lot to the trailhead.

Trail Type: Hiking/Walking, Cross Country Skiing
Trail Distance: 6.8 mi   Loops: 5   Shortest: 1.2 mi Longest: 5 mi
Trail Surface: Natural
Trail Use Fee: None
Method Of Ski Trail Grooming: Track set
Skiing Ability Suggested: Novice to intermediate
Hiking Trail Difficulty: Easy to moderate
Mountain Biking Ability Suggested: NA
Terrain: Steep 10%, Hilly 5%, Moderate 5%, Flat 80%
Camping: Camping not permitted

Maintained by the community of Grand Marais.
Food and lodging in Grand Marais.
The North Country Trail uses part of this trail. See North Country Trail - Lake Superior State Forest

Sault Canal National Historic Site
1 Canal Drive
Sault Ste Marie, Ontario, Canada P6A 6W4

705-942-6262

Michigan Atlas & Gazetteer Location: 117A6

County Location: Ontario, Canada

Directions To Trailhead:
Along the Canadian Soo Locks under the International Bridge. Turn right past customs and right again on Huron Street to Canal Drive, then left on Canal Drive past the power generating station to the Visitor Center.

Trail Type: Hiking/Walking, Cross Country Skiing, Interpretive
Trail Distance: 1.4 mi   Loops: 2   Shortest: Longest:
Trail Surface: Paved and natural
Trail Use Fee: None
Method Of Ski Trail Grooming: None
Skiing Ability Suggested: Novice
Hiking Trail Difficulty: Easy
Mountain Biking Ability Suggested: NA
Terrain: 100% Flat
Camping: None

Maintained by the Canadian Parks Service.
Interesting 13 station interpretive trail of the Canadian Soo locks.
Call or write for trail guide.

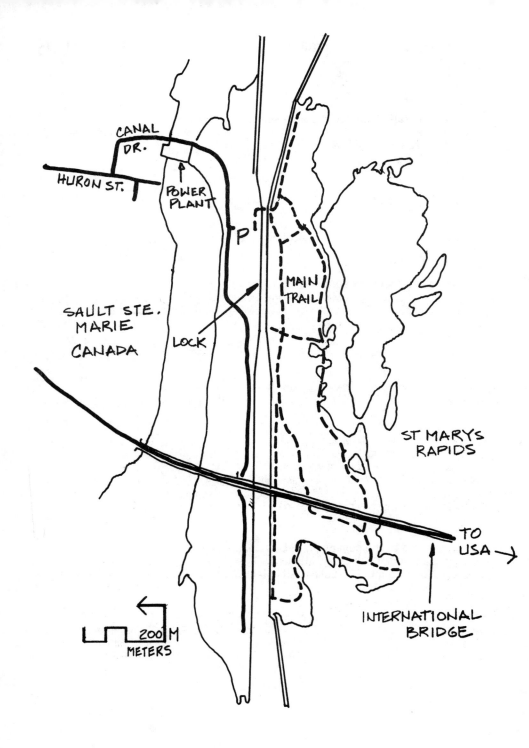

ATTIKAMEK TRAIL

Newberry Forest Area, Lake Superior State Forest
PO Box 428   906-293-3293
Newberry, Mi 49868

District Forest Manger, Lake Superior State Forest
PO Box 77   906-293-5131
Newberry, MI 49868

Michigan Atlas & Gazetteer Location: 117C6

County Location: Luce

Directions To Trailhead:
Near Lake Superior at Bodi Lake SFCG about 35 miles northeast of Newberry

Trail Type: Hiking/Walking
Trail Distance: 1.8 mi   Loops: 1   Shortest: NA   Longest: 1.8 mi
Trail Surface: Natural
Trail Use Fee: None
Method Of Ski Trail Grooming: NA
Skiing Ability Suggested: NA
Hiking Trail Difficulty: Easy
Mountain Biking Ability Suggested: NA
Terrain: Steep 0%, Hilly 0%, Moderate 20%, Flat 80%
Camping: Campground on site

Maintained by the DNR Forest Management Division
Short pathway adjacent to the Bodi Lake SFCG.

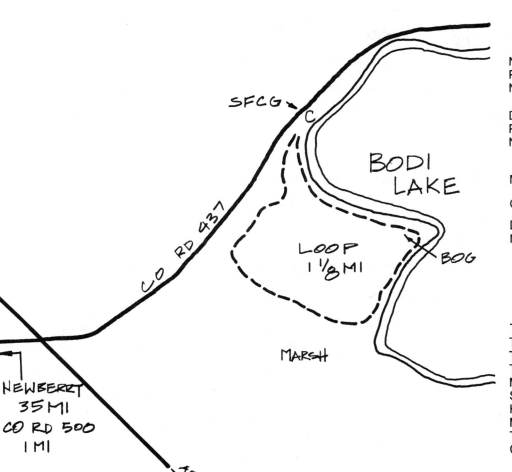

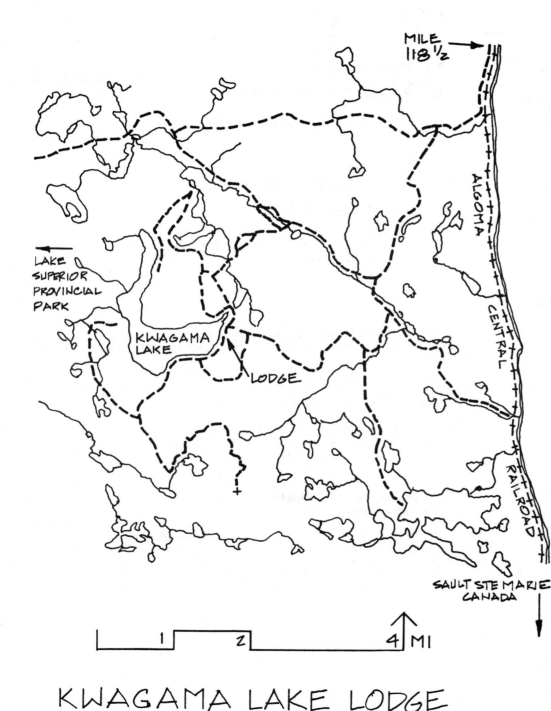

Chadwick's Kwagama Lake Lodge
ACR 118.5
Hawk Junction, Ontario, Canada P0S 1G0

705-856-1104

Michigan Atlas & Gazetteer Location: 117 North

County Location: Canada

Directions To Trailhead:
Take the Algoma Central Railroad 118.5 miles north of Sault Ste Marie, Canada, then 9 miles by bike or skis
Departure location from the railroad is 4 miles north of the famous Agawa Canyon.

Trail Type: Hiking/Walking, Cross Country Skiing, Mountain Biking
Trail Distance: 50+ mi   Loops: 8+   Shortest: 1.5 mi Longest: 8 mi
Trail Surface: Natural
Trail Use Fee: Included in American Plan accomodations
Method Of Ski Trail Grooming: Packed
Skiing Ability Suggested: Intermediate to advanced
Hiking Trail Difficulty: Easy to difficult
Mountain Biking Ability Suggested: Intermediate to advanced
Terrain: Steep 10%, Hilly 50%, Moderate 30%, Flat 10%
Camping: None

Privately operated American Plan wilderness lodge on the Algoma Central Railway
Complete lodge facilities with private cabins.
Extensive trail system is maintained for the exclusive use of the guests.
Trail system is adjacent to the Lake Superior Provincial Park.
Guide service included in the package.
Call or write for more information.
Reservations are absolutely required.

KWAGAMA LAKE LODGE

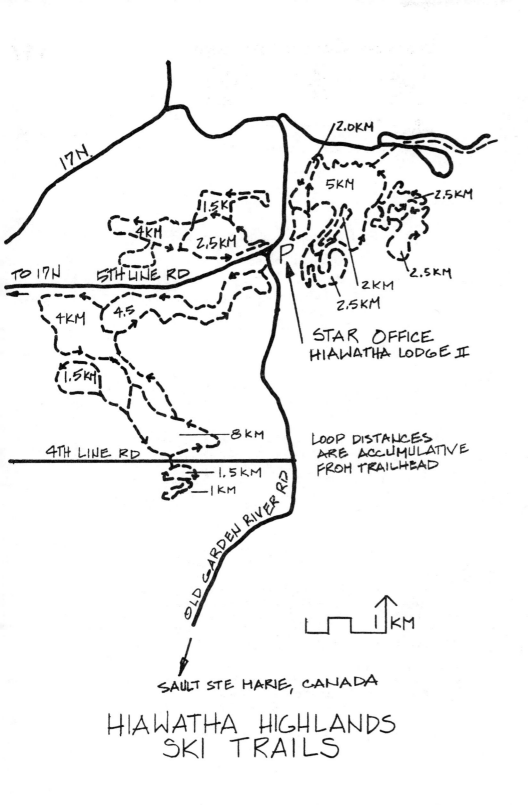

17N.

TO 17N

5TH LINE RD

2.0KM

5KM

1.5KM

4KM

2.5KM

2.5KM

P

2KM

2.5KM

2.5KM

STAR OFFICE
HIAWATHA LODGE II

4KM

4.5

1.5KM

8KM

4TH LINE RD

LOOP DISTANCES
ARE ACCUMULATIVE
FROM TRAILHEAD

1.5KM

1KM

OLD GARDEN RIVER RD

1 KM

SAULT STE MARIE, CANADA

HIAWATHA HIGHLANDS SKI TRAILS

Sault Trails and Recreation Inc.
99 Foster Drive, PO Box 580
Sault Ste Marie, Ontario, Canada P6A 5N1

705-759-3898
705-942-0383

800-361-1522

Michigan Atlas & Gazetteer Location: 117A7

County Location: Ontario, Canada

Directions To Trailhead:
10 miles north of International Bridge, then take Hwy 17N to 5th Line, then right
2 miles to Hiawatha Lodge

Trail Type: Hiking/Walking, Cross Country Skiing
Trail Distance: 35 km   Loops: 12   Shortest: 1 km   Longest: 13+ km
Trail Surface: Natural
Trail Use Fee: Yes, daily, annual and family passes available
Method Of Ski Trail Grooming: Track set with a double track daily
Skiing Ability Suggested: Novice to advanced
Hiking Trail Difficulty: Easy to moderate
Mountain Biking Ability Suggested: NA
Terrain: Steep 5%, Hilly 25%, Moderate 50%, Flat 20%
Camping: None

Outstanding cross country ski area.
Lodge has a restaurant, snack bar, sauna, bar, ski rentals etc.
Expertly groomed trails.
The trail system has a biathlon range, a 150' vertical alpine slope.
Established over 40 years ago as a cross country ski area by Finnish residents
of the Soo. This area is one of the finest trail systems in the Great Lakes area.
2 km lighted trail with 2 tracks and a skating lane, 7 nights a week.
When you're in the Soo to ski Stokely Creek and Searchmont don't pass up this
one.

Searchmont
Box 787
Sault Ste Marie, Ontario, Canada P6A 5N3

705-781-2340
800-663-2546

SEE MAPS ON NEXT PAGE

Michigan Atlas & Gazetteer Location: 117A6

County Location: Ontario, Canada

Directions To Trailhead:
8 miles north of Sault Ste. Marie, Canada on 17N, then east at Heyden on 556
for 17 miles to the town of Searchmont

Trail Type: Hiking/Walking, Cross Country Skiing, Mountain Biking
Trail Distance: See below Loops: Many   Shortest: Longest:
Trail Surface: Natural and gravel
Trail Use Fee: Yes for skiing
Method Of Ski Trail Grooming: Single track set 14' wide with a skating lane
Skiing Ability Suggested: Novice to advanced
Hiking Trail Difficulty: Easy to difficult
Mountain Biking Ability Suggested: Novice to advanced
Terrain: Below
Camping: None

Privately operated 4 season alpine, cross country ski and mountain bike resort.
Lodging, restaurant, rentals, lessons, ski shop and day nursery. Very fine well
designed trail system in the wooded area adjacent to the alpine slopes. Trails
are wide enough for skating with a single track on the right. Over 120 meter
elevation change in the intermediate/advanced trails.
Ski trails:50 km, 8 loops, terrain: 10% Steep, 40% Hilly, 30% Moderate, 10% Flat
Mountain bike trails: 150+ miles, terrain: 15% Steep, 20% Hilly, 35% Moderate,
30% Flat
Mountain bike trails are on public and private land with permission. Most
mountain bike trails are on vehicle roads and "2 tracks"(seldom used) and some
single track. Some tours use the train for part of the trip. Simply spectactular
scenery and challenging trails(if that's your desire)
Near Stokely Creek and Hiawatha Highlands ski trails.

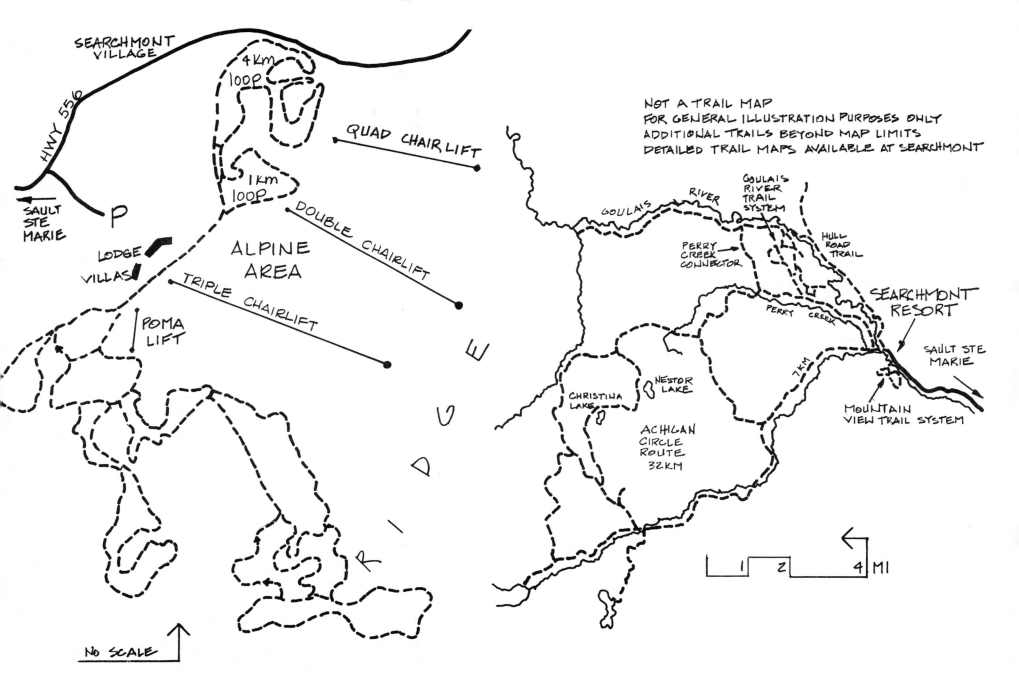

SKI TRAILS
SEARCHMONT RESORT

MOUNTAIN BIKE TRAILS
SEARCHMONT RESORT

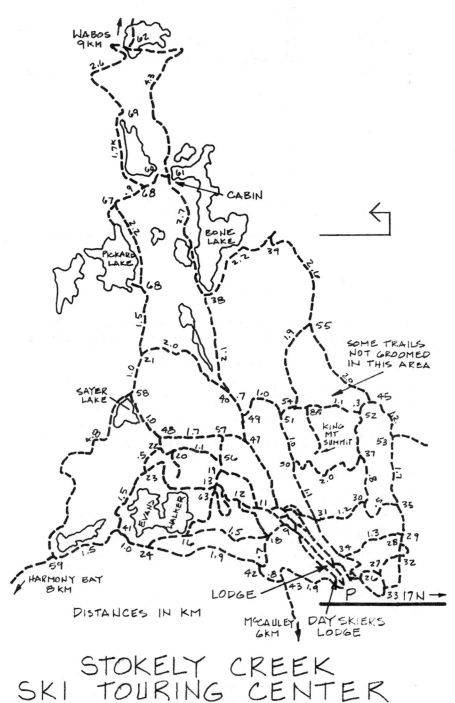

DISTANCES IN KM

STOKELY CREEK
SKI TOURING CENTER

Stokely Creek Ski Touring Center
Karalash Corners
Goulais River, Ontario, Canada P0S 1E0   705-649-3421

HATS
99 Foster Drive, Level 3
Sault Ste Marie, Ontario, Cananda P6A 5X6   800-461-6020

Michigan Atlas & Gazetteer Location: 117 north of map

County Location: Ontario, Canada

Directions To Trailhead:
21 miles north of Sault Ste Marie Canada on 17N. Follow the signs east off Rte 17N just past the Buttermilk alpine ski area

Trail Type: Cross Country Skiing
Trail Distance: 150 km   Loops: Many   Shortest: Longest:
Trail Surface: Natural
Trail Use Fee: Yes
Method Of Ski Trail Grooming: Double track set with skating lane
Skiing Ability Suggested: Novice to advanced
Hiking Trail Difficulty: NA
Mountain Biking Ability Suggested: NA
Terrain: Steep 10%, Hilly 25%, Moderate 50%, Flat 15%
Camping: None

Privately operated ski touring center
One of the premier ski touring centers in the midwest. Named one of the best touring centers in North America by Cross Country Skier magazine.
Site of the annual Wabos Loppet, held in March each year. Good skiing is usually available through the end of March. The terrain and scenery is simply spectacular. One trail loop is 17 km with another trail going past the location of a former hang glider launching platform. Two trails have over 600 feet of vertical change. Day skiers lodge with bunkhouse and lodging is available. Winter lodging reservations should be made by Thanksgiving. You really have not skied the mid west until you have skied STOKELY CREEK. Don't pass up this one.

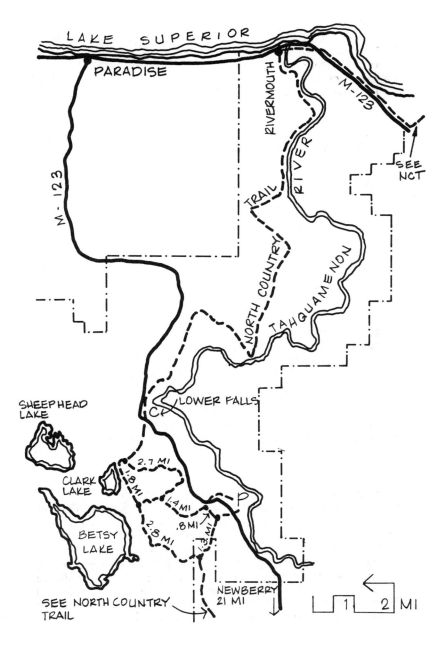

TAHQUAMENON FALLS
STATE PARK

Tahquamenon Falls State Park

Tahquamenon Falls State Park
Rte 48, Box 225
Paradise, MI 49768

906-492-3415

DNR Parks and Recreation Division

517-373-1270

Michigan Atlas & Gazetteer Location: 117CD678

County Location: Chippewa

Directions To Trailhead:
12 miles west of Paradise on M123

Trail Type: Hiking/Walking, Cross Country Skiing, Interpretive
Trail Distance: 25 + mi   Loops: 4+   Shortest: 3.7 mi Longest: 13 mi
Trail Surface: Natural
Trail Use Fee: None, but vehicle entry fee required
Method Of Ski Trail Grooming: Track set
Skiing Ability Suggested: Novice to intermediate
Hiking Trail Difficulty: Easy to moderate
Mountain Biking Ability Suggested: NA
Terrain: Steep 0%, Hilly 0%, Moderate 20%, Flat 80%
Camping: Avaialble in the park in snowless months only

Maintained by the DNR Parks and Recreation Division.
Hiking and skiing trails are not all identical.
Ski trail length is less.
Food and lodging available in Paradise and Newberry .
Wilderness skiing is also possible but deep snow will make that quite difficult.
The North Country Trail passes through this park.

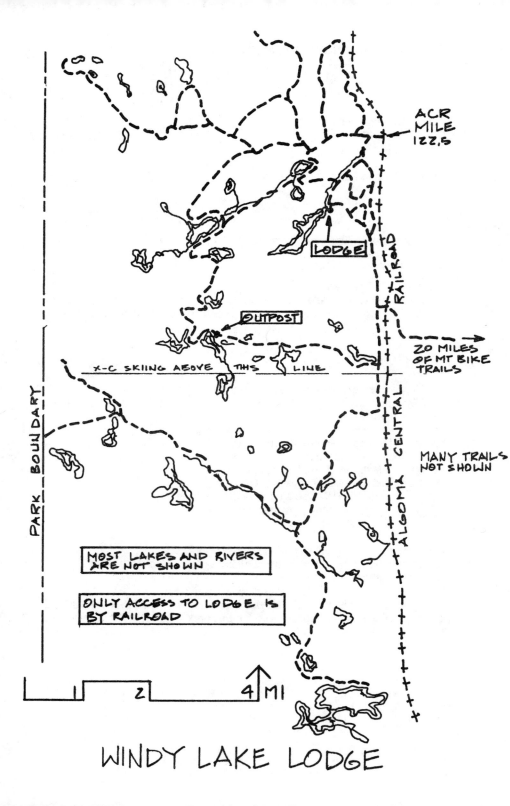

ACR
MILE
122.5

LODGE

OUTPOST

20 MILES
OF MT BIKE
TRAILS

X-C SKIING ABOVE THIS LINE

MANY TRAILS
NOT SHOWN

PARK BOUNDARY

ALGOMA CENTRAL RAILROAD

MOST LAKES AND RIVERS
ARE NOT SHOWN

ONLY ACCESS TO LODGE IS
BY RAILROAD

2   4 MI

WINDY LAKE LODGE

WIndy Lake Lodge
Mile 122.5 A.C.R.
Sault Ste Marie, Ontario, Canada P6A5N9

705-942-0525

Michigan Atlas & Gazetteer Location: 117A6

County Location: Ontario, Canada

Directions To Trailhead:
North of Sault Ste Marie, Canada. at mile post 122.5 Algoma Central Railway
Gazetteer location is not accurate

Trail Type: Hiking/Walking, Cross Country Skiing, Mountain Biking
Trail Distance: 50 + mi   Loops: Many   Shortest: Longest:
Trail Surface: Natural
Trail Use Fee: None, accomodation package includes trail fee
Method Of Ski Trail Grooming: Track set
Skiing Ability Suggested: Novice to advanced
Hiking Trail Difficulty: Easy to difficult
Mountain Biking Ability Suggested: intermediate to advanced
Terrain: Steep 5%, Hilly 15%, Moderate 40%, Flat 40%
Camping: None

A privately owned year around resort in the Canadian wilderness
Ski trail system has 50 km of groomed trails with 6 loops from 22.5 km to 5.2 km long
Accessable only by railroad from Sault Ste Marie, Canada via the Algoma Central Railroad
Extensive trail system of logging roads and 2 tracks.

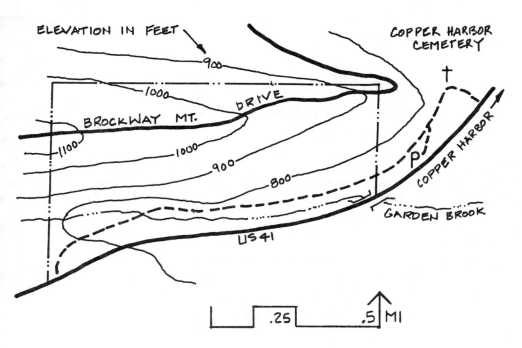

ELEVATION IN FEET

900

1000

BROCKWAY MT. DRIVE

1100

1000

900

800

COPPER HARBOR CEMETERY

COPPER HARBOR

P

GARDEN BROOK

US 41

.25   .5 MI

Michigan Nature Association
PO Box 102
Avoca, MI 48006

810-324-2426

Michigan Atlas & Gazetteer Location: 118A1

County Location: Keweenaw

Directions To Trailhead:
Just south of Copper Harbor on US41 about .5 mile. Park near Garden Brook Bridge. Walk .5 mile on US 41 to a trail on the north(right) side of the road.

Trail Type: Hiking/Walking, Interpretive
Trail Distance: 1.6 mi   Loops: 1   Shortest: NA   Longest: 1.6 mi
Trail Surface: Natural
Trail Use Fee: None
Method Of Ski Trail Grooming: NA
Skiing Ability Suggested: NA
Hiking Trail Difficulty: Moderate
Mountain Biking Ability Suggested: NA
Terrain: Steep 0%, Hilly 50%, Moderate 50%, Flat 0%
Camping: Campground at Ft Wilkins State Park

Owned by the Michigan Nature Association
Sanctuary contains plants only found in the Keweenaw County.
Brockway Mountain is the highest point in the Copper Range.
Write or call for the sanctuary guidebook.

BROCKWAY MOUNTAIN NATURE SANCTUARY

Keweenaw Tourism Council
PO Box 336
Calumet, MI 49913

906-337-4579
800-338-7982

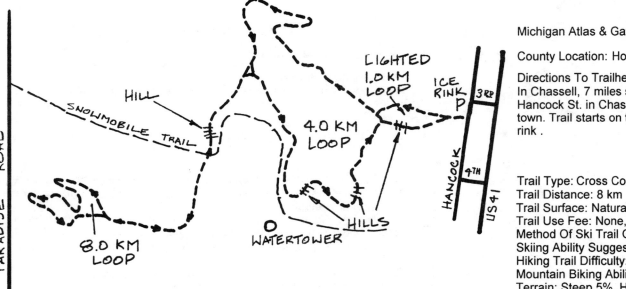

Michigan Atlas & Gazetteer Location: 118D4

County Location: Houghton

Directions To Trailhead:
In Chassell, 7 miles south of Houghton on US41.One block west of US41 on Hancock St. in Chassell next to the ice rink near the school at the north end of town. Trail starts on the left side of the warming building that is next to the ice rink .

Trail Type: Cross Country Skiing
Trail Distance: 8 km   Loops: 2   Shortest: 4 km   Longest: 8 km
Trail Surface: Natural
Trail Use Fee: None, donations accepted
Method Of Ski Trail Grooming: Track set
Skiing Ability Suggested: Novice to intermediate
Hiking Trail Difficulty: NA
Mountain Biking Ability Suggested: NA
Terrain: Steep 5%, Hilly 25%, Moderate 60%, Flat 10%
Camping: None

Maintained by the Villlage of Chassell with volunteers and the Chassell Recreation Club
Most of the trail is on private land so do not wander off the designated trail.
One km lighted trail.
Warming shelter available.
Trail not designed for skating.
A well designed trail that is a delight to ski.
The rolling terrain is used effectively to provide long rolling downhill runs with a minimum of climbing.
The mostly wooded with some open field skiing provides for a very pleasant experience.

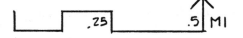

CHASSEL CLASSIC SKI TRAIL

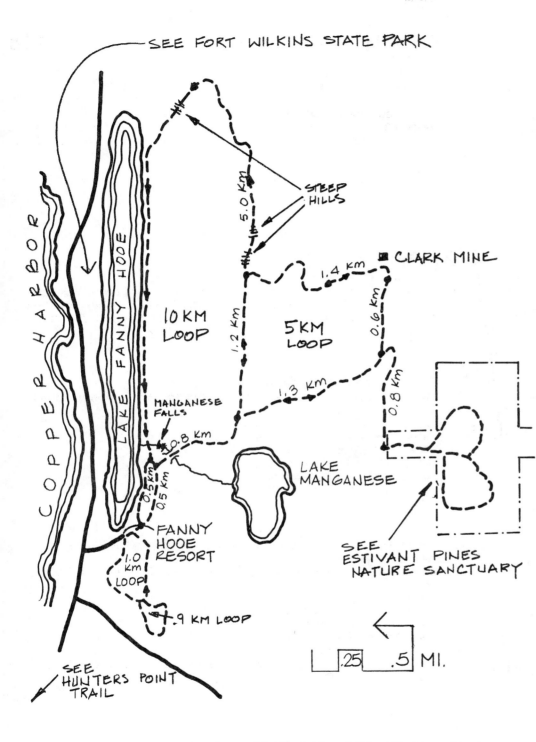

SEE FORT WILKINS STATE PARK

COPPER HARBOR

LAKE FANNY HOOE

10 KM LOOP

5 KM LOOP

5.0 Km

STEEP HILLS

■ CLARK MINE

1.4 Km

0.6 Km

1.2 Km

1.3 Km

0.8 Km

MANGANESE FALLS

0.8 Km

0.5 Km

0.5 Km

LAKE MANGANESE

FANNY HOOE RESORT

1.0 Km LOOP

.9 KM LOOP

SEE HUNTERS POINT TRAIL

SEE ESTIVANT PINES NATURE SANCTUARY

.25   .5 MI.

COPPER HARBOR PATHWAY

Copper Harbor Pathway

Baraga Forest Area, Copper Country State Forest
Box 440
Baraga, MI 49908

906-353-6651

Park Manager
Fort Wilkins State Park
Copper Harbor, MI 49918

906-289-4215

Michigan Atlas & Gazetteer Location: 118A12

County Location: Keweenaw

Directions To Trailhead:
Trailhead - West end of Lake Fanny Hooe near Lake Fanny Hooe Resort

Trail Type: Hiking/Walking, Cross Country Skiing, Mountain Biking, Interpretive
Trail Distance: 18.7 km   Loops: Several   Shortest: 1 km   Longest: 14 km
Trail Surface: Natural
Trail Use Fee: None
Method Of Ski Trail Grooming: Track set (some sections)
Skiing Ability Suggested: Intermediate to advanced
Hiking Trail Difficulty: Moderate
Mountain Biking Ability Suggested: Intermediate to advanced
Terrain: Rolling to hilly
Camping: Available at Fort Wilkins SP and Lake Fanny Hooe Resort

Maintained by the DNR Forest Management and, Parks and Recreation Divisions
Ski rentals and lodging available from Fanny Hooe Resort at the west end of Lake Fanny Hooe 906-289-4451.
Groomed by Fort Wilkins State Park.
Estivant Pines loop is owned by the Michigan Nature Association (see other listing).
Other contacts:
DNR Forest Management Region Office, Marquette, 906-228-6561
DNR Forest Management Division Office, Lansing, 517-373-1275
Keweenaw Tourism Council 906-482-2388 or 800-338-7982

Michigan Nature Association
PO Box 102
Avoca, MI 48006

810-324-2626

Michigan Atlas & Gazetteer Location: 118A12

County Location: Keweenaw

Directions To Trailhead:
From the blinker light at US41 in Copper Harbor, turn right (east) .2 mile, then turn south (right) toward Lake Managanese. Then proceed 1.3 miles past Lake Manganese, then turn left (west) on Burma Rd, then bo .65 mile to the sanctuary.

Trail Type: Hiking/Walking, Cross Country Skiing, Interpretive
Trail Distance: 2.5   Loops: 2   Shortest: 1.4 mi Longest: 2.1 mii
Trail Surface: Natural
Trail Use Fee: None
Method Of Ski Trail Grooming: None
Skiing Ability Suggested: Intermediate
Hiking Trail Difficulty: Easy to moderate
Mountain Biking Ability Suggested: NA
Terrain: Steep 20%, Hilly 20%, Moderate 20%, Flat 40%
Camping: At Copper Harbor State Park

Owned by the Michigan Nature Association
One of the few remaining stands of virgin white pine in the state.
Worth the effort to get to this sanctuary.

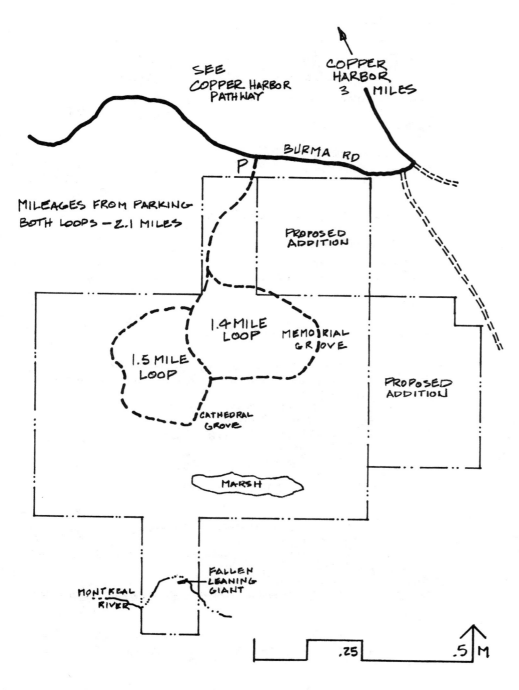

ESTIVANT PINES
NATURE SANCTUARY

Fort Wilkins State Park
US41 East
Copper Harbor, MI 49918

906-289-4215

DNR Parks and Recreation Division

517-373-1270
906-228-6561

Michigan Atlas & Gazetteer Location: 118A2

County Location: Keweenaw

Directions To Trailhead:
Just east of Copper Harbor on US41

Trail Type: Hiking/Walking, Cross Country Skiing, Interpretive
Trail Distance: 5 km   Loops: Several   Shortest: 1 km   Longest: 3.4 km
Trail Surface: Gravel and natural
Trail Use Fee: None, but vehicle entry fee required
Method Of Ski Trail Grooming: Track set
Skiing Ability Suggested: Novice
Hiking Trail Difficulty: Easy
Mountain Biking Ability Suggested: NA
Terrain: Steep 0%, Hilly 10%, Moderate 50%, Flat 40%
Camping: Campground in the park

Maintained by the DNR Parks and Recreation Division
Restored historic Fort built to protect the copper miners in the 1800's
Ski rentals available at the Lake Fanny Hooe Resort at the west end of Lake
Fanny Hooe 906-289-4451
Hiking and ski trailsare not all identical
Copper Harbor Pathway and several other trails are nearby. See other listings.

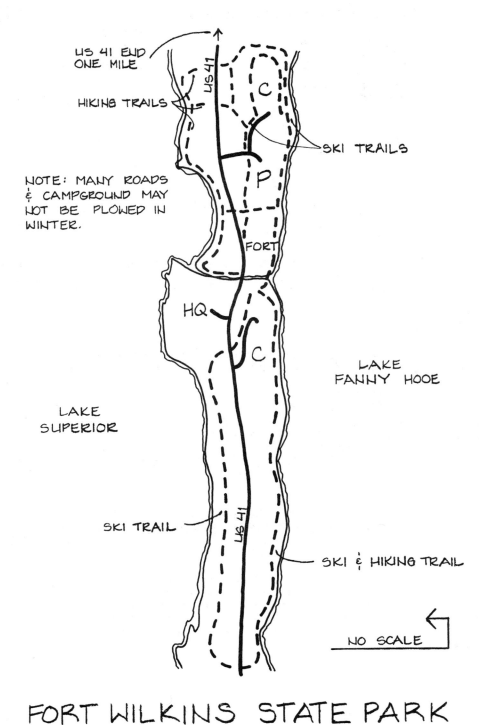

US 41 END ONE MILE

HIKING TRAILS

US 41

C

SKI TRAILS

P

NOTE: MANY ROADS & CAMPGROUND MAY NOT BE PLOWED IN WINTER.

FORT

HQ

C

LAKE FANNY HOOE

LAKE SUPERIOR

SKI TRAIL

US 41

SKI & HIKING TRAIL

NO SCALE

FORT WILKINS STATE PARK

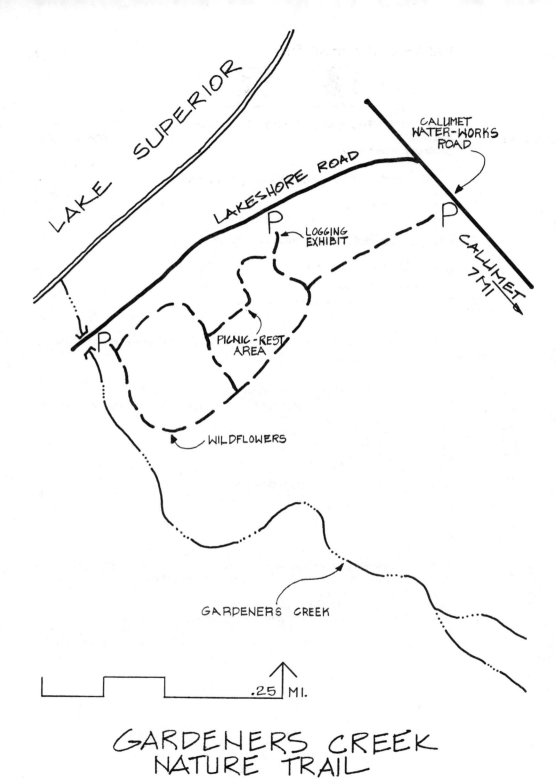

GARDENERS CREEK NATURE TRAIL

Calumet Township
106 Red Jacket Rd
Calumet, MI 49913

906-337-2410

Michigan Atlas & Gazetteer Location: 118B4

County Location: Houghton

Directions To Trailhead:
2 miles northwest of M203 on Waterworks Rd, west of Calumet

Trail Type: Interpretive
Trail Distance: 1 mi   Loops: 1   Shortest: NA   Longest: 1 mi
Trail Surface: Natural with hardwood chips
Trail Use Fee: None
Method Of Ski Trail Grooming: NA
Skiing Ability Suggested: NA
Hiking Trail Difficulty: Easy
Mountain Biking Ability Suggested: NA
Terrain: Steep 0%, Hilly 0%, Moderate 95%, Flat 5%
Camping: Primitive camping for up to 50 people and shelter for 6 people

Owned by the Township of Calumet
Logging exhibit, picnic area along the shore of Lake Superior
Trail includes:
    40 tree and shrubs identified
    mounted maps at intersections
    displays of native pine, cedar and hemlock logs
    3 bridges across Gardeners Creek
Adjacent to Calumet Township Lakeshore park with beach, playgrounds and picnic pavilion

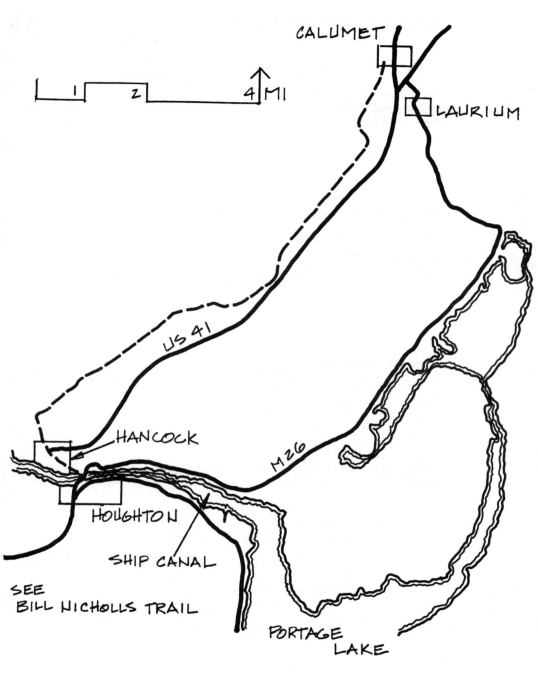

Baraga Forest Area, Copper Country State Forest
Box 440   906-353-6651
Baraga, MI 49908

District Forest Manager, Copper Country State Forest
Box 440   906-353-6651
Baraga, MI 49908

Michigan Atlas & Gazetteer Location: 118BC345

County Location: Houghton

Directions To Trailhead:
Between Hancock to Calumet along US41
South trailhead - Poorvoo Park on the Portage Lake Ship Canal on Tezcuco St
in Hancock
North trailhead - Calumet depot at 9th St. and Oak St on the west edge of town

Trail Type: Hiking/Walking, Mountain Biking
Trail Distance: 13 mi   Loops: NA   Shortest: NA   Longest: NA
Trail Surface: Natural and ballast
Trail Use Fee: None
Method Of Ski Trail Grooming: NA
Skiing Ability Suggested: NA
Hiking Trail Difficulty: Easy
Mountain Biking Ability Suggested: Novice
Terrain: 100% Flat
Camping: None

Managed by the DNR Forest Management Division
A rail trail of the former Mineral Range Railroad built in 1908 to haul copper from
the Red Jacket and other mines in the area and abandon in 1979 by the Soo
Line.

HANCOCK/CALUMENT TRAIL

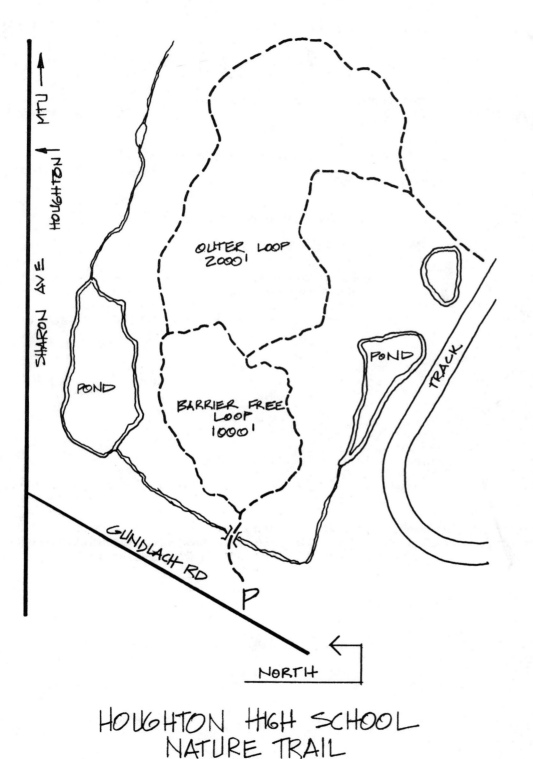

HOUGHTON HIGH SCHOOL
NATURE TRAIL

Houghton High School Nature Trail

Houghton Portage Township Schools
1603 Gundlach Rd
Houghton, MI 49931

906-482-0451

Michigan Atlas & Gazetteer Location: 188D4

County Location: Houghton

Directions To Trailhead:
From M 26, take Sharon Ave. east to th water tower. Turn south (left) on Grundlach Rd. The parking area is immediately on the left (east) side of the road.

Trail Type: Hiking/Walking, Interpretive
Trail Distance: .75 mi   Loops: 1   Shortest: NA   Longest: .75 mi
Trail Surface: Natural and concrete
Trail Use Fee: None
Method Of Ski Trail Grooming: NA
Skiing Ability Suggested: NA
Hiking Trail Difficulty: Easy
Mountain Biking Ability Suggested: NA
Terrain: Steep 0%, Hilly 0%, Moderate 0%, Flat 100%
Camping: None

Owned by the Houghton Portage Township Schools
Short handicapper nature trail on school property

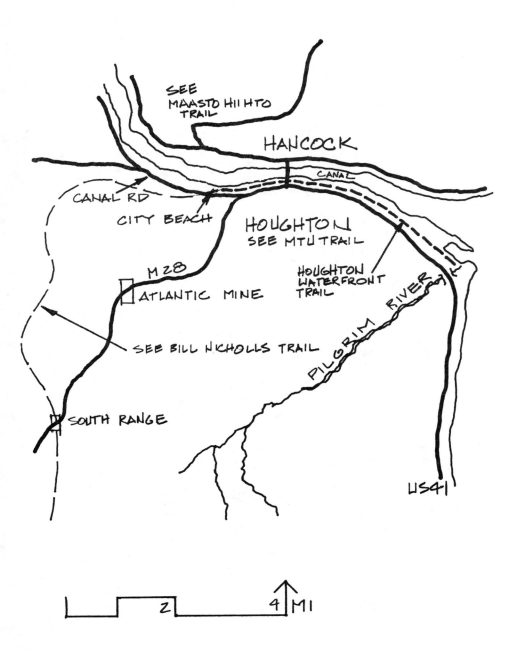

Houghton Waterfront Trail 118

City of Houghton
PO Box 406
Houghton, MI 49931

906-482-1700

Michigan Atlas & Gazetteer Location: 118C4

County Location: Houghton

Directions To Trailhead:
Along the waterfront from the city beach on the west end to Pilgrim River on the east end.

Trail Type: Hiking/Walking
Trail Distance: 4.5 mi   Loops: NA   Shortest: NA   Longest: NA
Trail Surface: Paved
Trail Use Fee: None
Method Of Ski Trail Grooming: NA
Skiing Ability Suggested: NA
Hiking Trail Difficulty: Easy
Mountain Biking Ability Suggested: Novice
Terrain: 100% Flat
Camping: None nearby but state parks and state forest campgrounds in the area

Owned by the City of Houghton.
A paved waterfront trail along the canal that separates Houghton from Hancock.
The west end of the trail connects closely to the Bill Nicholls Rail Trail.
See many other trails in the area.

HOUGHTON WATERFRONT TRAIL

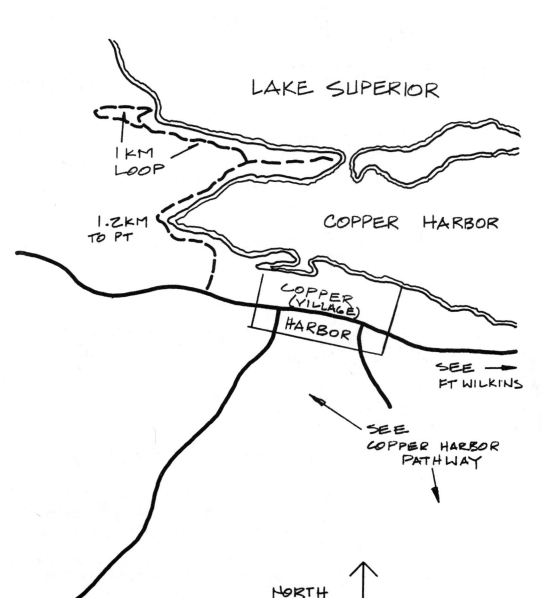

LAKE SUPERIOR

1 KM LOOP

1.2 KM TO PT

COPPER HARBOR

COPPER (VILLAGE)
HARBOR

SEE → FT WILKINS

SEE COPPER HARBOR PATHWAY

NORTH

HUNTERS POINT TRAIL

Copper Harbor Downtown Development Association
Fanny Hooe Resort
Copper Harbor, MI 49918

906-289-4451

Keweenaw Tourism Council

800-338-7982
906-482-2388

Michigan Atlas & Gazetteer Location: 118A1

County Location: Keweenaw

Directions To Trailhead:
Trailhead - West side of the Copper Harbor Marina which is just west of the downtown area.

Trail Type: Hiking/Walking, Cross Country Skiing, Interpretive
Trail Distance: 4 km   Loops: NA   Shortest: NA   Longest: NA
Trail Surface: Natural
Trail Use Fee: None
Method Of Ski Trail Grooming: None
Skiing Ability Suggested: Novice
Hiking Trail Difficulty: Easy
Mountain Biking Ability Suggested: NA
Terrain: Steep 0%, Hilly 0%, Moderate 10%, Flat 90%
Camping: At Fort Wilkins State Park and Fanny Hooe Resort in Copper Harbor

Local trail maintained by the community of Copper Harbor
Easy trail for the entire family along the Lake Superior shoreline

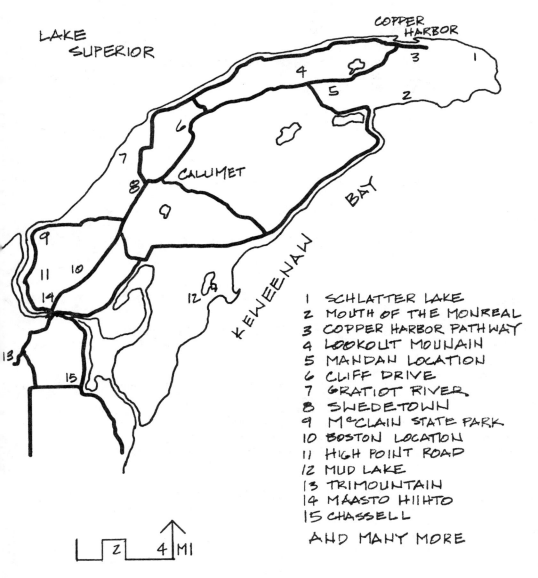

Keweenaw Peninsula

Keweenaw Tourism Council
1197 Calumet Ave., PO Box 336
Calumet, MI 49913

800-338-7982
906-337-4579

Cross Country Sports
507 Oak St
Calumet, MI 49913

906-337-4520

Michigan Atlas & Gazetteer Location: 118all, 119all

County Location: Keweenaw

Directions To Trailhead:
North of Houghton across the Portage Lake ship canal

Trail Type: Hiking/Walking, Cross Country Skiing, Mountain Biking
Trail Distance: 100+ mi   Loops: Shortest: Longest:
Trail Surface: Natural, gravel and rock
Trail Use Fee: None
Method Of Ski Trail Grooming: Varies
Skiing Ability Suggested: Novice to advanced
Hiking Trail Difficulty: Easy to difficult
Mountain Biking Ability Suggested: Novice to advance
Terrain: All types
Camping: Throughout the Keweenaw Peninsula

In addition to those locations shown on the map (some of which are described elsewhere in this atlas) there are many miles of old mining roads and forest trails to explore the beautiful Copper Island.
Because of the isolated location, good compass and map reading skills are essential to explore this area.
For ideas on where to go, see Rick at Cross Country Sports in Calumet (listed above). His complete bike and cross country ski shop will also come in handy if you need repairs or supplies.

LAKE SUPERIOR

COPPER HARBOR

CALUMET

KEWEENAW BAY

1 SCHLATTER LAKE
2 MOUTH OF THE MONREAL
3 COPPER HARBOR PATHWAY
4 LOOKOUT MOUNAIN
5 MANDAN LOCATION
6 CLIFF DRIVE
7 GRATIOT RIVER
8 SWEDETOWN
9 McCLAIN STATE PARK
10 BOSTON LOCATION
11 HIGH POINT ROAD
12 MUD LAKE
13 TRIMOUNTAIN
14 MAASTO HIIHTO
15 CHASSELL

AND MANY MORE

2 4 MI

KEWEENAW PENINSULA

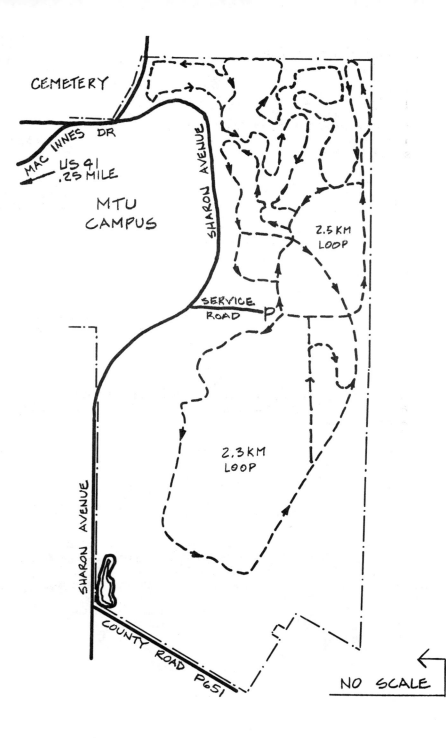

Michigan Technological University-Athletic Department
1400 Townsend Drive   906-487-3070
Houghton, MI 49931-1295

Keweenaw Tourism Council
1197 Calumet   906-337-4579
Calumet, MI 49931   800-338-7982

Michigan Atlas & Gazetteer Location: 118D4

County Location: Houghton

Directions To Trailhead:
On the MTU campus between Sharon Ave and Manninen Rd. Entrance to trail on Sharon Ave.

Trail Type: Hiking/Walking, Cross Country Skiing, Mountain Biking
Trail Distance: 9.2 km   Loops: 7   Shortest: .6 km   Longest: 8.5 km
Trail Surface: Natural
Trail Use Fee: None
Method Of Ski Trail Grooming: Track Set with skating lane
Skiing Ability Suggested: Novice to advanced
Hiking Trail Difficulty: Easy to moderate
Mountain Biking Ability Suggested: Novice to advanced
Terrain: Steep 15%, Hilly 25%, Moderate 25%, Flat 35%
Camping: Camping available in area

Trails maintained on a regular basis by Michigan Technological University. Cut offs from the main loop will bypass the most difficult trail sections which would reduce the required ability from advanced to an intermediate-novice. A beautiful wooded trail system on the edge of the MTU campus. Maintenance of the trail in the summer for mountain biking has not been consistant.

MTU TRAIL

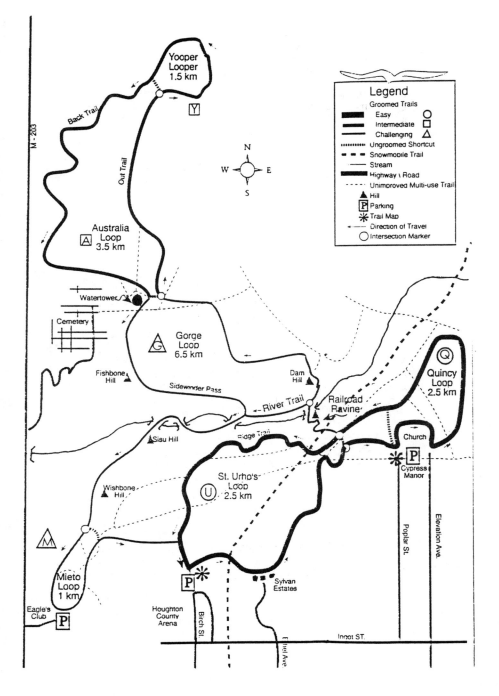

Maasto Hiihto Ski Trail

Houghton-Hancock Ski Club c/o City of Hancock
City Hall   906-483-1770
Hancock, MI 49930

Kewennaw Tourism Council
PO Box 336, 1197 Calumet Ave   800-338-7982
Calumet, MI 49913   906-337-4579

Michigan Atlas & Gazetteer Location: 118C4

County Location: Houghton

Directions To Trailhead:
Northwest edge of Hancock
Trailhead - Behind the Houghton County Arena at Birch and Ingot Streets
Trailhead - North end of Popular St Trailhead - Off M203 behind the Eagles
Club, NW of town

Trail Type: Hiking/Walking, Cross Country Skiing, Mountain Biking
Trail Distance: 17.5+ km Loops: 9+   Shortest: 1 km   Longest: 6.5 km
Trail Surface: Natural
Trail Use Fee: Donations accepted
Method Of Ski Trail Grooming: Track set occasionally
Skiing Ability Suggested: Intermediate to Advanced
Hiking Trail Difficulty: Moderate
Mountain Biking Ability Suggested: Novice to advanced
Terrain: Hilly
Camping: Campground not available nearby

Maintained by the Houghton-Hancock Ski Club and the City of Hancock
Maintained when funds are available - call ahead
Well designed ski trail.

MAASTO HIIHTO SKI TRAIL

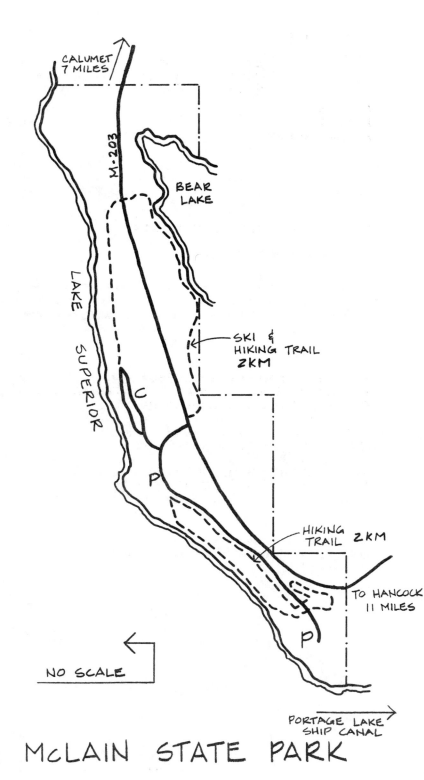

McLAIN STATE PARK

McLain State Park

McLain State Park
M 203
Hancock, MI 49930

906-482-0278

DNR Parks and Recreation Division

517-373-1270

Michigan Atlas & Gazetteer Location: 118BC34

County Location: Houghton

Directions To Trailhead:
7 miles west of Calument on M-203 and 11 miles west of Hancock on M-203

Trail Type: Hiking/Walking, Cross Country Skiing, Interpretive
Trail Distance: 6 km   Loops: 2   Shortest: 2 km   Longest: 4 km
Trail Surface: Natural
Trail Use Fee: None, but vehicle entry fee required
Method Of Ski Trail Grooming: Packed as needed
Skiing Ability Suggested: Novice
Hiking Trail Difficulty: Easy
Mountain Biking Ability Suggested: NA
Terrain: Steep 0%, Hilly 0%, Moderate 4%, Flat 96%
Camping: Campground on site

Maintained by the DNR Parks and Recreation Divsion
Snowmobiles permited in park. Ski carefully

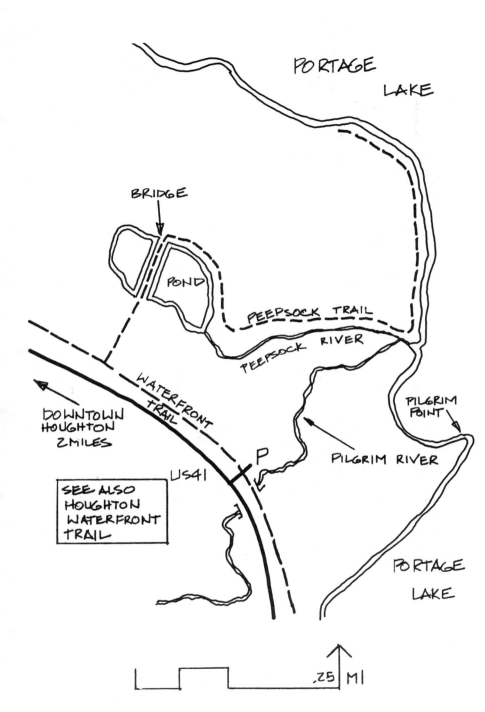

City of Houghton
PO Box 606
Houghton, MI 49931

906-482-1700

Michigan Atlas & Gazetteer Location: 118D4

County Location: Houghton

Directions To Trailhead:
From downtown, take US 41 south about 2 miles to Pilgrim Terrace Industries parking lot

Trail Type: Hiking/Walking, Mountain Biking
Trail Distance: .75 mi   Loops: 1   Shortest: NA   Longest: .75 mi
Trail Surface: Natural and boardwalk/bridge
Trail Use Fee: None
Method Of Ski Trail Grooming: NA
Skiing Ability Suggested: NA
Hiking Trail Difficulty: Easy
Mountain Biking Ability Suggested: Novice
Terrain: Steep 0%, Hilly 0%, Moderate 0%, Flat 100%
Camping: None

Owned by the City of Houghton
Recently developed with no facilities.

PEEPSOCK TRAIL

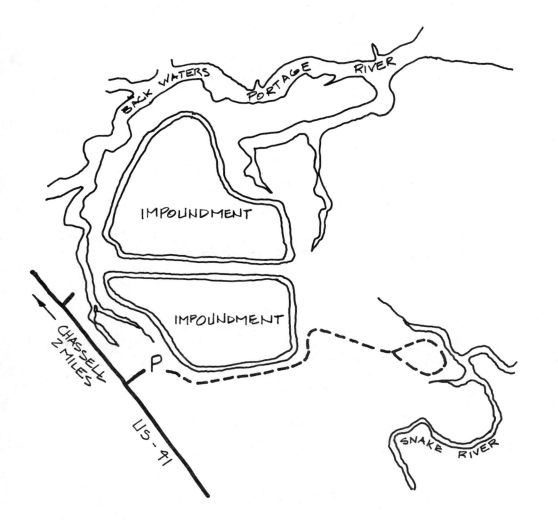

Baraga District Office, DNR Wildlife Division
PO Box 440   906-353-6651
Baraga, MI 49908

DNR Wildlife Division, Region 1 HQ
1990 US41 South
Marquette, MI 49855   517-373-1263

Michigan Atlas & Gazetteer Location: 199D5

County Location:

Directions To Trailhead:
2 miles southwest of Chassell on US41

Trail Type: Hiking/Walking, Interpretive
Trail Distance: .9 mi   Loops: 1   Shortest: Longest: .9 mi
Trail Surface: Natural
Trail Use Fee: None
Method Of Ski Trail Grooming: NA
Skiing Ability Suggested: NA
Hiking Trail Difficulty: Easy
Mountain Biking Ability Suggested: NA
Terrain: 100%Flat
Camping: None but campground at state park in Baraga

Maintained by the DNR Wildlife Divison
Observation platform along trail
Picnic pavilion at the trailhead

BERT DEVRIENDT
NATURE TRAIL

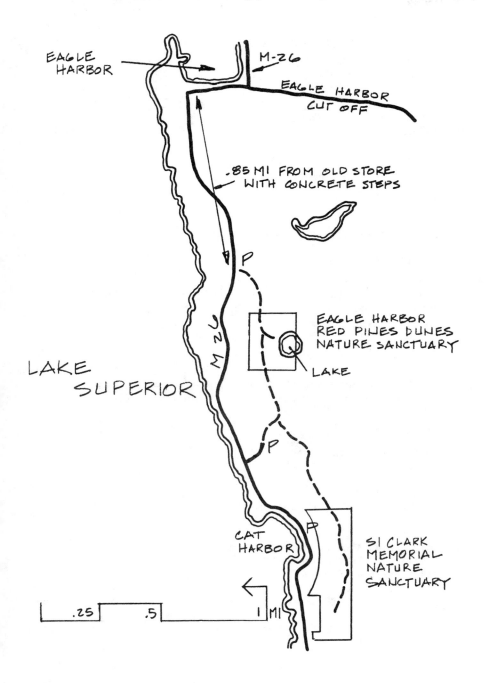

Michigan Nature Association
PO Box 102
Avoca, MI 48006

810-324-2626

Michigan Atlas & Gazetteer Location: 119A7

County Location: Keweenaw

Directions To Trailhead:
From the old store in Eagle Harbor, go .85 mile west on M26 to a 2 track road.
From there, walk on the road as indicated on the map to the two sanctuaries

Trail Type: Hiking/Walking, Cross Country Skiing, Interpretive
Trail Distance: 4.3 mi   Loops: 2   Shortest: 1.8 mi Longest: 4.3 mi
Trail Surface: Natural
Trail Use Fee: None
Method Of Ski Trail Grooming: None
Skiing Ability Suggested: Intermediate to advanced
Hiking Trail Difficulty: Moderate
Mountain Biking Ability Suggested: NA
Terrain: Steep 10%, Hilly 20%, Moderate 20%, Flat 50%
Camping: None

Maintained by the Michigan Nature Association
Complete name is "Eagle Harbor Red Pines Dunes and Si Clark Memorial
Nature Sanctuaries
Red Pines Dunes is 25 acres
Si Clark is 37 acres

EAGLE HARBOR RED PINES DUNES
SI CLARK MEMORIAL NATURE SANCTURIES

LAKE SUPERIOR

M26

ESREY PARK

P

SWAMP

COPPER HARBOR

BROCKWAY MT DRIVE

UPSON CREEK

LAKE UPSON

SWAMP

.25 .5 MI

KEWEENAW SHORE NO. 1
NATURE SANCTUARY

Michigan Nature Association
PO Box 102
Avoca, MI 48006

810-324-2626

Michigan Atlas & Gazetteer Location: 119A8

County Location: Keweenaw

Directions To Trailhead:
East from Eagle Harbor on M26 about 5 miles to the west entrance of Esrey Park. Entrance to the sanctuary is 200 feet west on the south side of M26.

Trail Type: Hiking/Walking, Interpretive
Trail Distance: 2 mi   Loops: 1   Shortest: Longest: 2 mi
Trail Surface: Natural
Trail Use Fee: None
Method Of Ski Trail Grooming: NA
Skiing Ability Suggested: NA
Hiking Trail Difficulty: Difficult
Mountain Biking Ability Suggested: NA
Terrain: Steep 80%, Hilly 0%, Moderate 20%, Flat 0%
Camping: Campground in Copper Harbor

Owned by the Michigan Nature Association
Simply one of the most representative tracts in the Keweenaw.
Boreal forest of spruce, balsam fir, aspen and birch, conglomerate outcrop, sharp ridges, forests of pine, aspen, birch and red maple, swamp grass, alder, sphagnum bog, black spruce, pitcher plants and much more are all along the trail.
"If a person wanted to show some one unfamiliar to the Keweenaw an example of the Peninsula's varied plant communities andrugged ridge valley topography, this trail would be the best place to go." from MNA publication.

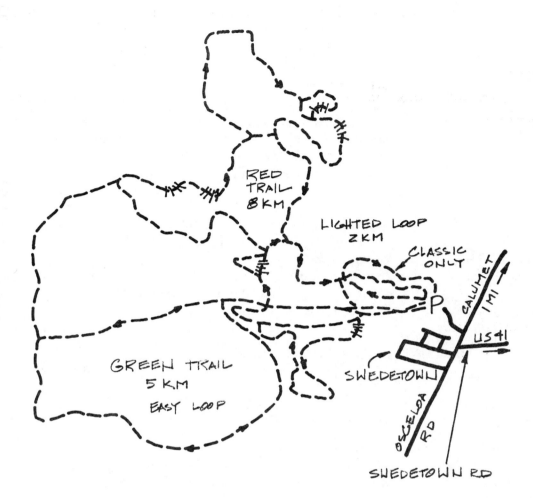

RED TRAIL 8 KM

LIGHTED LOOP 2 KM

CLASSIC ONLY

P

CALUMET 1 MI

US 41

SWEDETOWN

OSCELOA RD

GREEN TRAIL 5 KM EASY LOOP

SWEDETOWN RD

SCALE NOT KNOWN

Copper Island Cross Country Ski Club
PO Box 214
Calumet, MI 49913

906-337-1170

Keweenaw Tourism Council
1197 Calumet Ave., PO Box 336
Calumet, MI 49913

800-338-7982
906-337-4579

Michigan Atlas & Gazetteer Location: 119C5

County Location: Houghton

Directions To Trailhead:
1 mile SW of Calumet on Osceloa Rd
Trailhead - Take Swedetown Rd west from US41 (just before tourist office, sign at intersection), then left on Osceloa Rd to trailhead. Follow signs from US 41 in Calumet.

Trail Type: Cross Country Skiing
Trail Distance: 20 km   Loops: Several   Shortest: 13 km Longest: 2 km
Trail Surface: Natural
Trail Use Fee: Donations accepted
Method Of Ski Trail Grooming: Track set with skating lane, 4 times/week
Skiing Ability Suggested: Novice to intermediate
Hiking Trail Difficulty: NA
Mountain Biking Ability Suggested: NA
Terrain: Steep 2%, Hilly 20%, Moderate 60%, Flat 18%
Camping: None

Maintained by Copper Island Cross-Country Ski Club
Beautifully designed and maintained trail system by local skiers. Site of several events yearly. Normal ski season begins in November and goes through March. Skiing available on the Keweenaw Peninsula through April. Accomodations and food available in Calumet and Houghton/Hancock.
Rentals and ski shop at the Cross-Country Sports, 507 Oak St., Calumet, 337-4520.
Other contact: Keweenaw Peninsula Chamber of Commerce, 326 Shelden Ave., Houghton, MI 49931 906-482-5240

SWEDETOWN SKI TRAIL

Additional Reading Sources

Allen, Pat and DeRuiter, Gerald, *Backpacking In Michigan - 3rd Ed..* Ann Arbor, MI: The University of Michigan Press (1994)

DuFresne, Jim, *Fifty Hikes in Lower Michigan.* Woodstock, VT: The Countryman Press, Inc.(1991)

DuFresne, Jim, *Michigan's Porcupine Mountains Wilderness State Park,* Clarkston, MI: Glovebox Guidebooks (1993), P.O. Box 852, Clarkston, MI 48347

DuFresne, Jim, *Lower Michigan's 75 Best Campgrounds,* Clarkston, MI: Glovebox Guidebooks (1993), P.O. Box 852, Clarkston, MI 48347

DuFresne, Jim, *OutdoorAdventures With Children.* Seattle: The Mountaineers (1990)

Gentry, Karen, *Cycling Michigan.* Clarkston, Ml: Glovebox Guidebooks (1993), PO Box 852, Clarkston, Ml. 48347

Johnson, Arden, *North Country National Scenic Trail - Michigan Section Hiker Guide,* North Country Trail Association Bookstore, PO Box 311, White Cloud, Ml 49349 (under constant revision). The entire guide of 117 maps can be purchased in its entirety, or prepackaged mapsets of various sections of the trail can be purchased separately. Write for an order form. Allow considerable time for a response and/or purchase since the NCTA operates with all volunteers including the bookstore.

Kraut, Ruth, *Footloose in Washtenaw, 2nd Ed.,* Ann Arbor, Ml: Ecology Center of Ann Arbor (1990)

Michigan Nature Association Sanctuary Guidebook (most current edition), Michigan Nature Association, PO Box 102, Avoca, Ml 48006 (810) 324-2626 Other pubications of selected sanctuaries and groups of sanctuaries are available.

Penrose, Laurie, Bill T., Ruth, Bill J., *Michigan Waterfalls.* Davison, MI: Friede Publications, 2339 Venezia, 48423 (1988)

Powers, Tom, *Natural Michigan.* Davison, MI: Friede Publications, 2339 Venezia, 48423 (1987)

Powers, Tom, *More Natural Michigan.* Davison, MI: Friede Publications, 2339 Venezia, 48423 (1992)

Powers, Tom, *Michigan State Parks,* Davison, MI: Friede Publications, 2339 Venezia, 48423 (1994)

Ruchhoft, Robert H., *Exploring North Manitou, South Manitou, High and Garden Islands, Of the Lake Michigan Archipelago.* Cincinnati, OH: The Pucelle Press, P.O. Box 19161, Cincinnati, 45219 (1991)

Storm, Roger; Wedzel, Susan; Ryan, Karen-Lee and Ulm, Mike, 40 *Great Rail-Trails.* Washington, D.C.:Rails to Trails Conservancy (1994)

Phone Numbers for Chamber of Commerce/Tourist Bureau/Visitors Bureau

ADA BUSINESS ASSOCIATION	(616)676-6482	BESSEMER CHAMBER OF COMMERCE	(906)663-4542
ANCHOR BAY CHAMBER OF COMMERCE	(810)949-4120	BEULAH CHAMBER OF COMMERCE	(616)882-5802
ALBION CHAMBER OF COMMERCE	(517)629-5533	BIG RAPIDS CHAMBER OF COMMERCE	(616)796-7649
ALGER COUNTY CHAMBER OF COMMERCE	(906)387-2138	BIRCH RUN CHAMBER OF COMMERCE-TOURISM DEPT	(517)624-9193
ALGONAC CHAMBER OF COMMERCE	(810)794-5511	BIRMINGHAM/BLOOMFIELD CHAMBER OF COMMERCE	(810)644-1700
ALLEGAN COUNTY TOURISM AND RECREATION COUNCIL	(616)673-2479	BLISSFIELD CHAMBER OF COMMERCE	(517)486-3642
ALLEGAN AREA CHAMBER OF COMMERCE	(616)673-2479		(517)486-2236
ALLEGAN COUNTY	(616)673-8471	BLUE WATER AREA TOURIST BUREAU	(810)987-8687
ALLEN CHAMBER OF COMMERCE	(517)439-4341		(800)852-4242
ALLEN PARK CHAMBER OF COMMERCE	(313)382-7303	BOYNE COUNTRY CONVENTION AND VISITORS BUREAU	(616)348-2755
	(313)388-5207		(800)845-2828
ALMA CHAMBER OF COMMERCE	(517)463-5525	BOYNE CITY CHAMBER OF COMMERCE	(616)582-6222
	(517)463-8979	BOYNE COUNTRY CONVENTION AND VISITORS BUREAU	(800)456-0197
ALPENA AREA CHAMBER OF COMMERCE	(800)582-1906	BERRIEN CHAMBER OF COMMERCE	(616)723-2575
	(517)354-4181	BRIDGEPORT AREA CHAMBER OF COMMERCE	(517)777-9180
AMERICAN-ISREAL CHAMBER OF COMMERCE OF MICHIGAN	(810)661-1948	BRONSON CHAMBER OF COMMERCE	(517)369-5085
ANN ARBOR AREA CHAMBER OF COMMERCE	(313)665-4433	BROOKLYN CHAMBER OF COMMERCE	(517)592-8907
ANN ARBOR CVB	(313)995-7281	BUCHANAN AREA CHAMBER OF COMMERCE	(616)695-3291
ARCADIA CHAMBER OF COMMERCE	(616)723-2575	BURR OAK CHAMBER OF COMMERCE	(616)489-5075
ASSOCIATION OF COMMERCE & INDUSTRY OF OTTAWA CO	(616)842-4910	CADILLAC AREA CHAMBER OF COMMERCE	(616)775-9776
ATLANTA CHAMBER OF COMMERCE	(517)785-3400	CADILLAC AREA VISITORS BUREAU	(800)22-LAKES
AU GRES CHAMBER OF COMMERCE	(517)876-6688	CANTON CHAMBER OF COMMERCE	(313)453-4040
AUBURN AREA CHAMBER OF COMMERCE	(517)662-4001	CAPAC AREA CHAMBER OF COMMERCE	(810)395-2243
AUBURN HILLS CHAMBER OF COMMERCE	(810)853-7862		(810)395-4321
BAD AXE CHAMBER OF COMMERCE	(517)269-7411	CARO CHAMBER OF COMMERCE	(517)673-5211
BALDWIN CHAMBER OF COMMERCE	(616)745-4331	CARSON CITY AREA CHAMBER OF COMMERCE	(517)584-6543
BARAGA COUNTY TOURIST & RECREATION ASSOCIATION	(906)524-7444	CASEVILLE CHAMBER OF COMMERCE	(517)856-3818
BATTLE CREEK AREA CHAMBER OF COMMERCE	(616)962-4076	CASPIAN CHAMBER OF COMMERCE	(906)265-3822
BATTLE CREEK/CALHOUN CO VIS & CONVENTION BUREAU	(616)962-2240	CASS CITY CHAMBER OF COMMERCE	(517)872-3434
BAY AREA CHAMBER OF COMMERCE	(517)893-4567	CASSOPOLIS AREA CHAMBER OF COMMERCE	(616)445-2703
BAY AREA CVB	(800)424-5114	CEDAR SPRINGS CHAMBER OF COMMERCE	(616)696-3260
	(517)893-1222	CEDAR/MAPLE CITY CHAMBER OF COMMERCE	(616)228-6077
BEAR LAKE CHAMBER OF COMMERCE	(616)723-2575	CEDARVILLE CHAMBER OF COMMERCE	(906)484-3935
BEAVER ISLAND CHAMBER OF COMMERCE	(616)448-2505	CENTRAL LAKE AREA CHAMBER OF COMMERCE	(616)544-3322
BELDING CHAMBER OF COMMERCE	(616)794-2210		(616)544-5015
BELLAIRE CHAMBER OF COMMERCE	(616)533-6023		(616)533-6114
	(616)533-6473	CENTRAL MACOMB COUNTY CHAMBER OF COMMERCE	(810)463-1528
BELLEVILLE CHAMBER OF COMMERCE	(313)697-7151	CHARLEVOIX AREA CONVENTION AND VISITORS BUREAU	(800)367-8557
BELLEVUE CHAMBER OF COMMERCE	(616)763-9571	CHARLEVOIX CHAMBER OF COMMERCE	(616)547-2101
BENZIE COUNTY CHAMBER OF COMMERCE	(616)882-5802	CHARLOTTE CHAMBER OF COMMERCE	(517)543-0400
BERRIEN SPRINGS/EAU CLAIRE CHAMBER OF COMMERCE	(616)471-9680	CHEBOYGAN AREA CHAMBER OF COMMERCE	(800)968-3302

CHEBOYGAN AREA TOURIST BUREAU	(616)627-7183
CHELSEA CHAMBER OF COMMERCE	(313)475-1145
CHESANING CHAMBER OF COMMERCE	(517)845-3055
CIRCLE MICHIGAN, INC	(800)513-MICH
	(616)941-4994
CLARE CHAMBER OF COMMERCE	(517)386-2442
CLARKSTON CHAMBER OF COMMERCE	(810)625-8055
CLAWSON CHAMBER OF COMMERCE	(810)435-2450
COLDWATER CHAMBER OF COMMERCE	(517)278-5985
COLOMA CHAMBER OF COMMERCE	(616)468-3377
COLON CHAMBER OF COMMERCE	(517)278-5985
	(616)432-2403
	(616)432-2532
COOPERSVILLE AREA CHAMBER OF COMMERCE	(616)837-9731
COPPER HARBOR IMPROVEMENT ASSOCIATION	(906)289-4287
CORNERSTONE ALLIANCE	(616)925-6100
CRYSTAL FALLS CHAMBER OF COMMERCE	(906)265-3822
CRYSTAL FALLS INFORMATION CENTER	(906)875-4454
CURTIS AREA CHAMBER OF COMMERCE	(906)586-3700
DAVISON AREA CHAMBER OF COMMERCE	(810)658-5355
DAVISON CHAMBER OF COMMERCE	(810)653-6266
DE TOUR VILLAGE CHAMBER OF COMMERCE	(906)297-5987
DEARBORN CHAMBER OF COMMERCE	(313)584-6100
DEARBORN HEIGHTS CHAMBER OF COMMERCE	(313)274-7480
DELTA COUNTY TOURIST & CONVENTION BUREAU	(800)437-7496
DELTA COUNTY CHAMBER OF COMMERCE	(906)786-2192
DICKINSON COUNTY TOURISM ASSOCIATION	(906)774-2002
DICKINSON COUNTY CHAMBER OF COMMERCE	(800)236-2447
DISCOVER GOLF ON MICHIGAN'S SUNRISE SIDE	(517)742-4350
	(800)729-9373
DOUGLAS	(616)857-1701
DOWAGIAC CHAMBER OF COMMERCE	(616)782-8212
DRUMMOND ISLAND CHAMBER OF COMMERCE	(906)493-5245
DURAND CHAMBER OF COMMERCE	(517)288-3715
EAST JORDAN CHAMBER OF COMMERCE	(616)536-7351
EASTPOINTE (DETROIT) CHAMBER OF COMMERCE	(810)776-5520
EDMORE AREA CHAMBER OF COMMERCE	(517)427-5821
EDWARDSBURG CHAMBER OF COMMERCE	(616)663-2023
ELBERTA CHAMBER OF COMMERCE	(616)352-7251
ELK COUNTRY VISITORS BUREAU	(517)742-4350
ELK RAPIDS CHAMBER OF COMMERCE	(616)264-8202
EMPIRE BUSINESS ASSOCIATION	(616)326-5287
	(616)326-5157
ESCANABA CHAMBER OF COMMERCE	(906)786-2192
EVART CHAMBER OF COMMERCE	(616)734-5554
FARMINGTON CHAMBER OF COMMERCE	(810)474-3440
FENNVILLE CHAMBER OF COMMERCE	(616)561-5013
	(616)561-6311
FENTON CHAMBER OF COMMERCE	(810)629-5447

FERNDALE CHAMBER OF COMMERCE	(810)542-2160
FIFE LAKE CHAMBER OF COMMERCE	(616)879-4471
FIFE LAKE AREA CHAMBER OF COMMERCE	(616)879-4287
FLINT AREA CHAMBER OF COMMERCE	(810)232-7101
FLINT AREA CHAMBER OF COMMERCE	(810)233-7437
FLINT AREA CVB	(800)288-8040
	(810)232-8900
FLUSHING AREA CHAMBER OF COMMERCE	(810)659-4141
FOUR FLAGS AREA COUNCIL ON TOURISM	(616)683-3720
FRANKENMUTH CHAMBER OF COMMERCE	(517)652-6106
FRANKENMUTH CVB	(800)FUN TOWN
	(517)652-6106
FRANKFORT/ELBERTA CHAMBER OF COMMERCE	(616)352-7251
FRANKFORT VISITORS BUREAU	(616)352-7251
FREELAND AREA CHAMBER OF COMMERCE	(517)695-6620
FREMONT CHAMBER OF COMMERCE	(616)924-0770
GARDEN CHAMBER OF COMMERCE	(906)786-2192
GARDEN CITY CHAMBER OF COMMERCE	(313)422-4448
GAYLORD GOLF MECCA	(517)732-6333
	(800)345-8621
GAYLORD/OTSEGO CHAMBER OF COMMERCE	(517)732-4000
GAYLORD AREA CONVENTION & TOURISM BUREAU	(517)732-6333
	(800)345-8621
GLADSTONE CHAMBER OF COMMERCE	(906)786-2192
GLADWIN CHAMBER OF COMMERCE	(517)426-5451
GLEN LAKE/SLEEPING BEAR CHAMBER OF COMMERCE	(616)334-3238
GOGEBIC AREA CVB	(800)272-7000
	(906)932-4850
GRAND RAPIDS AREA CVB	(800)678-9859
	(616)459-8187
GRAND LEDGE AREA CHAMBER OF COMMERCE	(517)627-2383
GRAND BEACH CHAMBER OF COMMERCE	(616)469-5409
GRAND BLANC CHAMBER OF COMMERCE	(810)695-4222
GRAND RAPIDS AREA CHAMBER OF COMMERCE	(616)771-0300
GRAND RAPIDS AREA CVB	(800)678-9859
	(616)459-8287
GRAND HAVEN/SPRING LAKE VISITORS BUREAU	(616)842-4499
GRAND MARAIS CHAMBER OF COMMERCE	(906)494-2766
GRANDVILLE CHAMBER OF COMMERCE	(616)531-8890
GRAYLING AREA VISITORS COUNCIL	(517)348-2921
	(800)937-8837
GRAYLING REGIONAL CHAMBER OF COMMERCE	(517)348-2921
GREATER BATTLE CREEK/CALHOUN CO VISITORS & CONVENTION BUREAU	(800)397-2240
GREATER BERKLEY CHAMBER OF COMMERCE	(810)544-9464
GREATER BRIGHTON AREA CHAMBER OF COMMERCE	(810)227-5086
GREATER CROSWELL/LEXINGTON CHAMBER OF COMMERCE	(810)359-2262
GREATER DETROIT CHAMBER OF COMMERCE	(313)964-4000
GREATER JACKSON CHAMBER OF COMMERCE	(517)782-8221

GREATER KALKASKA AREA CHAMBER OF COMMERCE	(616)258-4906	IDLEWILD CHAMBER OF COMMERCE	(616)745-4331
GREATER LANSING CVB	(517)487-6800	IMLAY CITY AREA CHAMBER OF COMMERCE	(313)724-1361
	(800)648-6630	INDIAN RIVER TOURIST BUREAU	(616)238-9325
GREATER ORTONVILLE CHAMBER OF COMMERCE	(810)627-2811	INTERLOCHEN CHAMBER OF COMMERCE	(616)276-7141
GREATER ROMULUS CHAMBER OF COMMERCE	(313)326-4290	IONIA CHAMBER OF COMMERCE	(616)527-2560
GREENBUSH CHAMBER OF COMMERCE	(517)739-7635	IRON COUNTY TOURISM COUNCIL	(906)265-3822
GREENBUSH-OSCODA-AU SABLE LODGING ASSOCIATION	(517)739-5156		(800)255-3620
	(800)235-GOAL	IRON RIVER CHAMBER OF COMMERCE	(906)265-3822
GREENVILLE CHAMBER OF COMMERCE	(616)754-4697	IRONS AREA TOURIST ASSN	(616)266-8101
GROSSE POINTE SHORES CHAMBER OF COMMERCE	(810)777-2741	IRONS AREA TOURIST ASSN	(616)266-5317
GUN LAKE AREA CHAMBER OF COMMERCE	(616)672-7822	IRONWOOD TOURISM COUNCIL	(906)932-1000
HALE AREA CHAMBER OF COMMERCE	(517)728-2051	IRONWOOD AREA CHAMBER OF COMMERCE	(906)932-1122
	(800)722-8229	ISABELLA COUNTY CVB	(800)77-CHIEF
HAMTRAMCK CHAMBER OF COMMERCE	(313)875-7877		(517)772-4433
HARBERT CHAMBER OF COMMERCE	(616)469-5409	ISHPEMING-NEGAUNEE AREA CHAMBER OF COMMERCE	(906)486-4841
HARBOR BEACH CHAMBER OF COMMERCE	(517)479-6450	ITHACA CHAMBER OF COMMERCE	(517)875-3640
HARBOR COUNTRY CHAMBER OF COMMERCE	(616)469-5409		(517)875-3456
HARBOR COUNTRY LODGING ASSOCIATION	(800)362-7251	JACKSON CONVENTION & TOURIST BUREAU	(800)245-5282
HARBOR SPRINGS CHAMBER OF COMMERCE	(616)347-4150		(517)764-4440
HARRISON CHAMBER OF COMMERCE	(517)539-6011	JENISON CHAMBER OF COMMERCE	(616)457-5610
HARRISVILLE CHAMBER OF COMMERCE	(517)724-5107	JONESVILLE CHAMBER OF COMMERCE	(517)439-4341
HART/SILVER LAKE CHAMBER OF COMMERCE	(616)873-2247	KALAMAZOO COUNTY CVB	(616)381-4003
HARTLAND TOURIST ASSN	(616)754-5697		(800)945-KALA
HASTINGS CHAMBER OF COMMERCE	(616)945-2454	KALEVA CHAMBER OF COMMERCE	(616)723-2575
HAZEL PARK CHAMBER OF COMMERCE	(810)543-8556	KALKASKA COUNTY CHAMBER OF COMMERCE	(616)258-9103
HESPERIA AREA CHAMBER OF COMMERCE	(616)854-3695	KEWEENAW TOURISM COUNCIL	(906)337-4579
HIGHLAND PARK CHAMBER OF COMMERCE	(313)868-6420		(800)338-7982
HILLMAN AREA CHAMBER OF COMMERCE	(517)742-3739		(906)482-2388
HILLSDALE CHAMBER OF COMMERCE	(517)439-4341	KEWEENAW PENINSULA CHAMBER OF COMMERCE	(906)482-5240
HOLLAND AREA CVB	(616)396-4221	LAKE CITY AREA CHAMBER OF COMMERCE	(616)839-4969
	(800)822-2770	LAKE COUNTY CHAMBER OF COMMERCE	(616)745-4331
HOLLAND CHAMBER OF COMMERCE	(616)392-2389	LAKE GOGEBIC AREA CHAMBER OF COMMERCE	(906)575-3265
HOLLY AREA CHAMBER OF COMMERCE	(810)634-1900	LAKE MICHIGAN CVB	(616)925-0044
HONOR CHAMBER OF COMMERCE	(616)882-5802		(616)925-6100
HOUGHTON LAKE CHAMBER OF COMMERCE	(517)366-5644	LAKE ODESSA AREA CHAMBER OF COMMERCE	(616)374-0766
HOUGHTON LAKE CHAMBER OF COMMERCE	(800)248-LAKE	LAKES AREA CHAMBER OF COMMERCE	(810)624-2826
	(800)292-9071	LAKESHORE CHAMBER OF COMMERCE	(616)429-1170
HOWELL CHAMBER OF COMMERCE	(517)546-3920	LAKESHORE CVB	(616)637-5252
HUBBARD LAKE CHAMBER OF COMMERCE	(517)736-8111	LAKESIDE CHAMBER OF COMMERCE	(616)469-5409
	(517)727-9919	LANSING REGIONAL CHAMBER OF COMMERCE	(517)487-6340
HUDSON AREA CHAMBER OF COMMERCE	(517)448-8983	LAPEER AREA CHAMBER OF COMMERCE	(810)664-6641
HUDSONVILLE CHAMBER OF COMMERCE	(616)896-9020	LEELANAU PENINSULA CHAMBER OF COMMERCE	(616)256-9895
HURON COUNTY VISITORS BUREAU	(800)35-THUMB	LELAND BUSINESS ASSOCIATION	(616)256-9382
HURON COUNTY VISITORS BUREAU	(517)269-6413	LENAWEE COUNTY CHAMBER OF COMMERCE	(517)265-5141
HURON SHORES CHAMBER OF COMMERCE	(800)423-2823	LENAWEE COUNTY CONFERENCE & VISITORS BUREAU	(800)682-6580
	(517)724-5107		(517)263-7000
HURON TOWNSHIP CHAMBER OF COMMERCE	(313)753-4220		(800)536-2933
HURON VALLEY AREA CHAMBER OF COMMERCE	(313)685-7129	LEROY CHAMBER OF COMMERCE	(616)768-4443

LES CHENEAUX CHAMBER OF COMMERCE	(906)484-3935	METRO EAST CHAMBER OF COMMERCE	(810)777-2741
LEWISTON CHAMBER OF COMMERCE	(517)786-2293	METROPOLITAN DETROIT CVB	(800)DE-TROIT
	(800)428-2293		(313)259-4333
	(517)786-2112	MICHIANA CHAMBER OF COMMERCE	(616)469-5409
LEXINGTON CHAMBER OF COMMERCE	(810)359-2262	MICHIGAN DEPARTMENT OF NATURAL RESOURCES	(517)373-1204
LINCOLN PARK CHAMBER OF COMMERCE	(313)386-0140	MICHIGAN STATE CHAMBER OF COMMERCE	(517)371-2100
LINDEN/ARGENTINE CHAMBER OF COMMERCE	(810)750-8794	MICHIGAN TRAVEL & TOURISM ASSOCIATION	(517)485-8000
LITCHFIELD CHAMBER OF COMMERCE	(313)542-2351	MICHIGAN CHARTER BOAT ASSOCIATION	(517)886-3999
LIVINGSTON COUNTY VISITORS BUREAU	(800)686-8474	MICHIGAN BICYCLE TOURING GUIDE	(616)263-5885
	(517)548-1795	MICHIGAN RIVER GUIDES ASSOCIATION	(616)848-4597
LIVONIA CHAMBER OF COMMERCE	(313)427-2122	MICHIGAN TRAVEL BUREAU	(800)5432-YES
LOWELL AREA CHAMBER OF COMMERCE	(616)897-9161	MICHIGAN BED & BREAKFAST DIRECTORY	(800)832-6657
LUCE COUNTY ECONOMIC DEVELOPMENT CORP	(906)293-3307	MICHIGAN UNDERWATER PRESERVES COUNCIL	(906)643-8717
	(906)293-5982	MICHIGAN'S SUNRISE SIDE, INC	(800)424-3022
LUDINGTON AREA CHAMBER OF COMMERCE	(800)542-4600		(517)469-4544
LUDINGTON AREA CVB	(616)845-0324	MIDLAND COUNTY CVB	(517)839-9901
MACKINAC ISLAND CHAMBER OF COMMERCE	(906)847-3783	MILAN CHAMBER OF COMMERCE	(313)439-7932
	(906)847-6418	MILFORD CHAMBER OF COMMERCE	(810)685-7129
MACKINAW CITY CHAMBER OF COMMERCE	(616)436-5574	MIO CHAMBER OF COMMERCE	(517)826-3331
MACKINAW AREA TOURIST BUREAU	(616)436-5664	MONROE COUNTY CHAMBER OF COMMERCE	(313)242-3366
	(800)666-0160	MONROE COUNTY CONVENTION & TOURISM BUREAU	(800)252-3011
MADISON HEIGHTS CHAMBER OF COMMERCE	(810)542-5010		(313)457-1030
MANCHESTER CHAMBER OF COMMERCE	(313)428-7722		
	(313)747-1294	MONTAGUE CHAMBER OF COMMERCE	(616)893-4585
MANISTEE AREA CHAMBER OF COMMERCE	(616)723-2575	MONTMORENCY COUNTY TOURISM BUREAU	(517)742-4347
MANISTEE FILER AREA TOURIST ASSOCIATION	(616)723-8385	MONTMORENCY COUNTY TOURISM BUREAU	(517)742-3739
MANISTIQUE AREA TOURIST COUNCIL	(906)341-5838		(517)742-4350
	(800)342-4282	MONTROSE AREA CHAMBER OF COMMERCE	(810)639-3475
MANISTIQUE CHAMBER OF COMMERCE	(906)341-5010	MOUNT CLEMENS CHAMBER OF COMMERCE	(810)463-1528
MANISTIQUE LAKES AREA TOURISM BUREAU	(906)586-9732	MOUNT PLEASANT AREA CHAMBER OF COMMERCE	(517)772-2396
MANTON AREA CHAMBER OF COMMERCE	(616)824-4158	MUNISING VISITORS BUREAU	(906)387-2138
MARINE CITY CHAMBER OF COMMERCE	(810)765-4501	MUSKEGON COUNTY CVB	(800)235-FUNN
MARION CHAMBER OF COMMERCE	(616)743-2461		(616)722-3751
MARLETTE AREA CHAMBER OF COMMERCE	(517)635-2429		(616)893-4585
MARQUETTE AREA CHAMBER OF COMMERCE	(906)226-6591	MUSKEGON ECONOMIC GROWTH ALLIANCE	(616)722-3751
MARQUETTE COUNTRY CVB	(800)544-4321		(616)728-7251
	(906)228-7749	NASHVILLE CHAMBER OF COMMERCE	(517)852-0845
MARSHALL CHAMBER OF COMMERCE	(616)781-5163	NAUBINWAY/ENGADINE MERCHANTS ASSOCIATION	(906)477-6271
MARYSVILLE CHAMBER OF COMMERCE	(810)364-6180	NEGAUNEE CHAMBER OF COMMERCE	(906)226-6591
MASON AREA CHAMBER OF COMMERCE	(517)676-1016	NEGAUNEE/ISHPEMING AREA CHAMBER OF COMMERCE	(906)486-4841
MASON COUNTY CVB	(616)845-0324	NEW BUFFALO CHAMBER OF COMMERCE	(616)469-5409
MASON COUNTY CVB	(800)542-4600	NEW ERA CHAMBER OF COMMERCE	(616)861-4303
MCBAIN AREA CHAMBER OF COMMERCE	(616)825-2387	NEWAGO CHAMBER OF COMMERCE	(616)652-3068
MCBAIN CHAMBER OF COMMERCE	(616)825-2416	NEWAGO COUNTY TOURIST COUNCIL	(616)652-9298
MECOSTA COUNTY CHAMBER OF COMMERCE	(616)796-7649	NEWBERRY AREA TOURISM ASSOCIATION	(800)831-7292
MECOSTA COUNTY CVB	(800)833-6697	NEWBERRY MERCHANTS ASSOCIATION	(906)293-3931
MECOSTA COUNTY CVB	(616)796-7640	NEWBERRY AREA CHAMBER OF COMMERCE & TOURIST ASSN	(906)293-5562
MENOMINEE AREA CHAMBER OF COMMERCE	(906)863-2679	NILES FOUR FLAGS AREA	(616)683-3720
MESICK CHAMBER OF COMMERCE	(616)885-1280	HORTHPORT CHAMBER OF COMMERCE	(616)386-5806
		HORTHVILLE CHAMBER OF COMMERCE	(810)349-7640

NORTHWEST MICHIGAN GOLF COUNCIL	(800)937-7272	ROCHESTER CHAMBER OF COMMERCE	(810)651-6700
NOVI CHAMBER OF COMMERCE	(810)349-3743	ROCKFORD CHAMBER OF COMMERCE	(616)866-2000
OAKLAND COUNTY CHAMBER OF COMMERCE	(810)456-8600	ROGERS CITY CHAMBER OF COMMERCE	(517)734-2535
OCEANA COUNTY TRAVEL BUREAU	(616)873-7141		(800)622-4148
ONAWAY CHAMBER OF COMMERCE	(517)733-2874	ROMEO CHAMBER OF COMMERCE	(810)752-4436
ONEKAMA CHAMBER OF COMMERCE	(616)723-2575	ROTHBURY CHAMBER OF COMMERCE	(616)894-2385
ONTONAGON TOURISM COUNCIL	(906)884-4735	ROYAL OAK CHAMBER OF COMMERCE	(810)547-4000
ORION AREA CHAMBER OF COMMERCE	(810)693-6300	RV & CAMPSITE DIRECTORY	(800)422-6478
OSCODA CHAMBER OF COMMERCE	(616)694-6880		(517)349-8881
	(517)739-7322	SAGINAW COUNTY CHAMBER OF COMMERCE	(517)752-7161
OSCODA COUNTY (MIO) CHAMBER OF COMMERCE	(517)826-3606	SAGINAW COUNTY CVB	(800)444-9979
	(517)826-3331		(517)752-7164
	(800)800-6133	SAINT CHARLES AREA CHAMBER OF COMMERCE	(517)865-8287
OSCODA/AUSABLE CHAMBER OF COMMERCE	(800)235-GOAL	SAINT LOUIS AREA CHAMBER OF COMMERCE	(517)681-3825
OSSINEKE CHAMBER OF COMMERCE	(517)471-2493	SALINE CHAMBER OF COMMERCE	(313)429-4494
OTSEGO CHAMBER OF COMMERCE	(616)694-6880	SANDUSKY CHAMBER OF COMMERCE	(810)648-4445
OWOSSO CHAMBER OF COMMERCE	(517)723-5149	SANFORD AREA CHAMBER OF COMMERCE	(517)687-2800
OXFORD CHAMBER OF COMMERCE	(810)628-0410	SANILAC TOURISM COUNCIL	(313)679-2300
PARADISE AREA TOURISM COUNCIL	(906)492-3310	SAUGATUCK/DOUGLAS CVB	(616)857-1701
PAW PAW CHAMBER OF COMMERCE	(616)657-5395	SAULT AREA CHAMBER OF COMMERCE	(906)632-3301
PENTWATER CHAMBER OF COMMERCE	(616)869-4150	SAULT STE MARIE TOURIST BUREAU	(800)MI-SAULT
PETOSKEY REGIONAL CHAMBER OF COMMERCE	(616)347-4150		(906)632-3301
PETOSKEY BOYNE COUNTRY CVB	(800)845-2828	SAWYER CHAMBER OF COMMERCE	(616)469-5409
	(800)456-0197	SCHOOLCRAFT COUNTY CHAMBER OF COMMERCE	(906)341-5010
PIGEON CHAMBER OF COMMERCE	(517)453-3441	SCHOOLCRAFT COUNTY ECONOMIC DEVELOPMENT CORP	(906)341-5126
	(517)453-2733	SCOTTVILLE CHAMBER OF COMMERCE	(616)757-4729
PINCONNING CHAMBER OF COMMERCE	(800)44-PINNY		(616)757-4304
	(517)879-2816		(616)757-3673
PLAINWELL CHAMBER OF COMMERCE	(616)685-8877	SEBEWAING CHAMBER OF COMMERCE	(517)883-2150
PLYMOUTH CHAMBER OF COMMERCE	(313)453-1540	SHELBY CHAMBER OF COMMERCE	(616)861-4054
PONTIAC CHAMBER OF COMMERCE	(810)335-9600	SHEPHERD AREA CHAMBER OF COMMERCE	(517)828-6683
	(810)683-4747	SILVER LAKE AREA CHAMBER OF COMMERCE	(616)873-2247
	(313)335-9190	SKIDWAY LAKE AREA CHAMBER OF COMMERCE	(517)873-4150
PORCUPINE MT PROMOTIONAL CHAMBER	(906)885-5885	SOUTH HAVEN CHAMBER OF COMMERCE	(616)637-5171
PORT HURON CHAMBER OF COMMERCE	(810)985-7101	SOUTH LYON CHAMBER OF COMMERCE	(810)437-3257
PORTLAND AREA CHAMBER OF COMMERCE	(517)647-2100	SOUTHERN WAYNE COUNTY CHAMBER OF COMMERCE	(313)284-6000
POSEN CHAMBER OF COMMERCE	(517)766-8128	SOUTHFIELD CHAMBER OF COMMERCE	(810)557-6400
PRESQUE ISLE AREA COMMERCE COMMITTEE	(517)595-5095	SOUTHWEST MICHIGAN TOURIST COUNCIL	(616)925-6301
	(517)595-6970	SPARTA CHAMBER OF COMMERCE	(616)887-2454
QUINCY CHAMBER OF COMMERCE	(517)639-3745	SPRING LAKE VISITORS BUREAU	(616)842-4499
RAPID RIVER CHAMBER OF COMMERCE	(906)786-2192	ST. CLAIR SHORES CHAMBER OF COMMERCE	(810)777-2741
RAVENNA CHAMBER OF COMMERCE	(616)853-2241	ST. HELEN CHAMBER OF COMMERCE	(517)389-3725
RECREATIONAL CANOEING ASSOCIATION	(906)238-7868	ST. IGNACE AREA TOURIST ASSOCIATION	(800)338-6660
REDFORD TOWNSHIP CHAMBER OF COMMERCE	(313)535-0960	ST. IGNACE CHAMBER OF COMMERCE	(906)463-8717
REED CITY CHAMBER OF COMMERCE	(616)832-5431	ST. JAMES CHAMBER OF COMMERCE	(616)448-2505
REESE CHAMBER OF COMMERCE	(517)776-7525	ST. JOHNS CHAMBER OF COMMERCE	(517)224-7248
RICHMOND AREA CHAMBER OF COMMERCE	(810)727-3975	ST. JOSEPH LAKE MICHIGAN CVB	(616)925-0044
	(810)727-7513	ST. JOSEPH TODAY	(616)982-6739
RIVER COUNTRY TOURISM COUNCIL	(616)467-4505	STANDISH CHAMBER OF COMMERCE	(517)846-7867

STERLING HEIGHTS AREA CHAMBER OF COMMERCE	(810)731-5400	VASSAR CHAMBER OF COMMERCE	(517)823-2601
STEVENSVILLE CHAMBER OF COMMERCE	(616)429-1170	WAKEFIELD CHAMBER OF COMMERCE	(906)224-2222
STURGIS CHAMBER OF COMMERCE	(616)651-5758		(906)229-5122
SUTTONS BAY CHAMBER OF COMMERCE	(616)271-4444	WARREN, CENTER LINE, STERLING HTS	
SWARTZ CREEK CHAMBER OF COMMERCE	(810)635-9643	CHAMBER OF COMMERCE	(313)751-3939
TAWAS BAY TOURIST & CONVENTION BUREAU	(517)362-8643	WATERSMEET CHAMBER OF COMMERCE	(906)358-4569
TAWAS CITY (INC. TAWAS BAY) CHAMBER OF COMMERCE	(800)55-TAWAS		(906)358-4766
	(517)362-8643	WAYLAND CHAMBER OF COMMERCE	(616)792-2265
TECUMSEH CHAMBER OF COMMERCE	(517)423-3740	WAYNE CHAMBER OF COMMERCE	(313)721-0100
THOMPSONVILLE CHAMBER OF COMMERCE	(616)882-5802	WELLSTON AREA TOURIST ASSOCIATION	(616)848-4896
THREE RIVERS CHAMBER OF COMMERCE	(616)278-8193	WELLSTON CHAMBER OF COMMERCE	(616)723-2575
THREE OAKS CHAMBER OF COMMERCE	(616)469-5409	WEST BRANCH - OGEMAW TRAVEL & VISITORS BUREAU	(517)345-2821
THUNDER BAY REGION	(800)582-1906	WEST MICHICAN TOURIST ASSOCIATION	(616)456-8557
	(517)354-4181	WEST BRANCH-OGEMAW TRAVEL & VISITORS BUREAU	(800)755-9091
TIPTON CHAMBER OF COMMERCE	(517)592-8907	WEST BLOOMFIELD CHAMBER OF COMMERCE	(810)626-3636
TRAVERSE CITY CVB	(800)TRAVERS	WESTLAND CHAMBER OF COMMERCE	(313)326-7222
	(616)947-1120	WHITE LAKE AREA CHAMBER OF COMMERCE	(616)893-4585
TRAVERSE CITY AREA CHAMBER OF COMMERCE	(616)947-5075	WHITE CLOUD CHAMBER OF COMMERCE	(616)689-6607
TROY CHAMBER OF COMMERCE	(810)641-8151	WHITE LAKE AREA CHAMBER OF COMMERCE	(800)497-4580
TRUFANT CHAMBER OF COMMERCE	(616)984-2555	WHITEHALL CHAMBER OF COMMERCE	(616)893-4585
TWIN CITIES AREA CHAMBER OF COMMERCE	(616)925-0044	WHITMORE LAKE CHAMBER OF COMMERCE	(313)449-8540
UNION CITY CHAMBER OF COMMERCE	(517)278-5985	WILLIAMSTON CHAMBER OF COMMERCE	(517)655-1549
UNION CITY BETTERMENT ASSOCIATION	(517)741-5861	WYOMING CHAMBER OF COMMERCE	(616)531-5990
UNION PIER CHAMBER OF COMMERCE	(616)469-5409	YPSILANTI CHAMBER OF COMMERCE	(313)482-5920
UPPER PENINSULA TRAVEL & RECREATION ASSOCIATION	(800)562-7134	YPSILANTI CVB	(313)483-4444
	(906)774-5480	ZEELAND CHAMBER OF COMMERCE	(616)772-2494
UTICA CHAMBER OF COMMERCE	(810)731-5400		

Land Preservation Organizations

Grand Traverse Regional Land Conservancy The Grand Traverse Regional Land Conservancy was incorporated in 1991 with the mission to protect significant natural, agricultural, scenic areas and advance land stewardship in Antrim, Benzie, Grand Traverse and Kalkaska Counties now and for future generations. For more information call or write them at 624 Third St., Traverse City, Ml 49684 (616) 9297911

The Nature Conservancy The Nature Conservancy is an international nonprofit organization with one mission: *To Protect Rare Plants, Animals, and Natural Communities by Preserving the Critical Lands and Waters They Need to Survive.* In Michigan, the Nature Conservancy has helped protect over 43,000 acres of our states finest wetlands, forests, shorelines and prairies. Please treat all nature preserves with the respect they deserve for being the original nature of Michigan. For more information call or write, the Michigan Chapter, 2840 E. Grand River, Suite 5, East Lansing, Ml 48823 (517) 332-1741.

Michigan Nature Association The Michigan Nature Association (MNA) is a private, non-profit citizens' organization which is not affiliated with any other conservation group. Beginning in 1960, it pioneered a program of *acquiring natural areas in Michigan without the use of government funds.* Most of the work is done by volunteers. The MNA now has 140 preservation projects in fifty counties. Many are easy to visit while others require a guide. To obtain a MNA sanctuary guidebook or for more information, write or call, the MNA, PO Box 102, Avoca, Ml 48006 (810) 324-2626.

Little Traverse Conservancy The Little Traverse Conservancy is a non-profit conservation organization working to protect the natural diversity and beauty of northern Michigan by preserving significant land and scenic areas and fostering appreciation and understanding of the environment. Since 1972, over 3,000 acres of land have been acquired which are open to the public. Also the Conservancy uses conservation easements to protect significant natural and scenic features of northern Michigan. Hiking, bird watching, nature study, photography are encouraged. Hunting and overnight use is allowed only with permission. For more information, call or write the Little Traverse Conservancy, 3264 Powell Rd., Harbor Springs, Ml 49740 (616) 347-0991.

Trail Advocacy Organizations

Rails to Trails Conservancy The mission of the Rails-to-Trails Conservancy is to *enhance America's communities and countrysides by converting thousands of miles of abandoned rail corridors, and connecting open space, into a nationwide network of public trails*. The goal of the Michigan Chapter is the creation of the Discover Michigan Trail, an interconnecting statewide trail system largely on abandoned railroads rights-of-way. Toward that end, the Michigan Chapter works to: educate the public and officials about rail-trails; help organize local groups to promote specific trail segments; provide technical assistance to local groups and governmental agencies; support appropriate state and local legislation, policy, and planning regarding rail-trails. For more information call or write the Rails-to-Trails Conservancy, Michigan Chapter, 913 W. Holmes, Suite 145, Lansing, MI 48910-0411 (517) 393-6022, fax 393-1960.

North Country Trail Association The North Country Trail Association is a non-profit organization, with local chapters, whose purpose is to promote and develop the North Country National Scenic Trail. For more information and addresses of local chapters, write the NCTA, 49 Monroe Center, Suite 200B, Grand Rapids, MI 49503. (616) 454-5506 voice, (616) 454-7139 fax. Email NCTAssoc@aol.com Web Site http://people.delhi.com/wesboyd.ncnst.htm

Michigan Mountain Biking Association The Michigan Mountain Biking Association (MMBA) is a non-profit organization, with regional chapters. It was established in 1990 for the purpose of providing riding opportunities by promoting responsible riding and sharing the responsibility for developing and maintaining trails. With over 1,000 members statewide, the MMBA is active in keeping the existing trails open to mountain bikes and developing new trails throughout the state. For more information call or write the MMBA, 4217 Highland Rd. #268, Waterford, MI 48328-2165. (616) 785-0120, voice and fax. Email Go_MMBA@aol.com Web Site http://www.mmba.org

Pigeon River Country Association The Pigeon River Country Association was established in 1971 to be a citizen advocacy group for the Pigeon River Country State Forest. Part of that charge includes the development and promotion of the High Country Pathway. The association sells a detailed trail guidebook, forest map and book titled *Pigeon River Country, A Michigan Forest*. For more information or to purchase the publications write the Pigeon River Country Association, P.O. Box 122, Gaylord, MI 49735. The publications can also be purchased through the DNR Gaylord office.

League of Michigan Cyclists The League of Michigan Bicyclists, a statewide organization of bicyclists, was formed in 1982. With a membership of over 1500 (1994) individuals and 18 affiliated clubs, LMB is responsive to the interests of those members and the bicycling conditions of Michigan. LMB sponsors various weekend conferences about transportation issues, bicycle safety education and in club leadership. They have compiled the Bicycle Michigan Poster-Calendar of events for several years, which is distributed at MDOT Welcome Centers. Since 1993, the League has produced PSAs on bicycling for TV, a video for law enforcement officers "the Law's for All," and a bicycle safety literature program. The League promotes the Shoreline Bicycle Tours - West, East and North routes. These tours effectively promote "proper" bicycling on the roads for both the riders and the public, as well as provide the funding for their programs. For more information write or call PO Box 16201, Lansing, MI 48901, (313) 379-2453.

Sierra Club The Sierra Club is an international environmental organization involved in both advocacy and outdoor activities. In Michigan, the Mackinac Chapter and its 15 regional groups are active in hiking, canoeing and cross country skiing, as well as lobbying for protection of public lands and clean and healthy environment. For more information contact the Mackinaw Chapter, 300 North Washington Square, Suite 411, Lansing, MI 48933 (517) 484-2372.

Outdoors Forever Outdoors Forever is a non-profit organization established in 1968 dedicated to promoting life-long "inclusive" outdoor recreation. The organization philosophy is that everyone should be able to hunt, fish, camp, hike, picnic, bird watch or enjoy any other outdoor recreational activity for as long as they WANT to, regardless of age or physical abilities. For more information, contact them at PO Box 4832, East Lansing, MI 48823 (517) 337-0018.

INDEX

TRAIL NOTES

1999

① Sunday, June 27th — Fisherman's Island State Pk. South of Charlevoix (p. 342)
Single file trail / rustic. We took this hike beginning @ 10 a.m.; ended
at 1:30 p.m. Pretty level walk overall. Spotted incredible black and iridescent
blue/green-bodied dragonfly-type creature @ McGeach creek. Also walked
great portion of the way along beach on the leg back to the trail head. Many petoskey
stones for the taking along beach; I've never seen them in such supply!
Paul found the perfect walking stick along the trail. Next
time = wear super-strength bug repellant!!!

② Saturday, July 3 — Pine Haven & Mud Trails, Midland Mi., 2.5 miles (p 218)

TRAIL NOTES

TRAIL NOTES

TRAIL NOTES

TRAIL NOTES

TRAIL NOTES

TRAIL NOTES